T0214967

# Communications
# in Computer and Information Science 546

*Commenced Publication in 2007*
Founding and Former Series Editors:
Alfredo Cuzzocrea, Dominik Ślęzak, and Xiaokang Yang

More information about this series at http://www.springer.com/series/7899

Hongbin Zha · Xilin Chen
Liang Wang · Qiguang Miao (Eds.)

# Computer Vision

CCF Chinese Conference, CCCV 2015
Xi'an, China, September 18–20, 2015
Proceedings, Part I

 Springer

*Editors*
Hongbin Zha
Peking University
Beijing
China

Liang Wang
Chinese Academy of Sciences
Beijing
China

Xilin Chen
Chinese Academy of Sciences
Institute of Computing Technology
Beijing
China

Qiguang Miao
Xidian University
Shaanxi
China

ISSN 1865-0929          ISSN 1865-0937  (electronic)
Communications in Computer and Information Science
ISBN 978-3-662-48557-6          ISBN 978-3-662-48558-3  (eBook)
DOI 10.1007/978-3-662-48558-3

Library of Congress Control Number: 2015951339

Springer Heidelberg New York Dordrecht London

Printed on acid-free paper

Springer-Verlag GmbH Berlin Heidelberg is part of Springer Science+Business Media (www.springer.com)

# Preface

Welcome to the proceedings of the First Chinese Conference on Computer Vision (CCCV 2015) held in Xi'an!

The CCCV conference is organized by the Computer Vision Task Forces of China Computer Federation (CCF), and is an important event for the computer vision community in China. In recent years, computer vision has increasingly become an enabling technology for many important and often mission-critical applications such as video surveillance and human–machine interface. The aim of CCCV is to provide a forum for scientific exchanges between computer vision researchers in China, and will be held every two years from 2015.

CCCV 2015 invited regular submissions for presentations and as well internationally renowned researchers to give keynote speeches. We received 176 full submissions, each of which was reviewed by at least two reviewers selected from the Program Committee and by other qualified researchers. Based on the reviewers' reports, 89 papers were finally accepted for presentation at the conference, yielding an acceptance rate of 51 %.

We are grateful to the keynote speakers, Prof. Fatih Porikli from the Australian National University, Prof. Maja Pantic from Imperial College London, Prof. Xiaoou Tang from the Chinese University of Hong Kong, and Prof. Demetri Terzopoulos from UCLA, USA.

Thanks go to the authors of all submitted papers, the Program Committee members and the reviewers, and the members of the Organizing Committee. Without their contributions, this conference would not have been a success. Special thanks go to all of the sponsors and the organizers of the five special forums. Their support made the conference successful. We are also grateful to Springer for publishing the proceedings and especially to Celine (Lanlan) Chang of Springer Asia for her efforts in coordinating the publication.

We hope you find the proceedings of CCCV 2015 enjoyable.

September 2015

Tieniu Tan
Xinbo Gao
Hongbin Zha
Xilin Chen
Liang Wang
Qiguang Miao

# Organization

CCCV 2015 (CCF Chinese Conference on Computer Vision 2015) was sponsored by CCF, co-sponsored by the CCF Task Force on Computer Vision, and hosted by the School of Computer Science and Technology, the School of Electronic Engineering and the State Key Laboratory of Integrated Service Networks of Xidian University.

## General Chairs

| | |
|---|---|
| Tieniu Tan | Institute of Automation, Chinese Academy of Sciences |
| Xinbo Gao | Xidian University |

## Program Chairs

| | |
|---|---|
| Hongbin Zha | Peking University |
| Xilin Chen | Institute of Computing Technology, Chinese Academy of Science |
| Liang Wang | Institute of Automation, Chinese Academy of Sciences |
| Qiguang Miao | Xidian University |

## Organizing Chairs

| | |
|---|---|
| Quan Wang | Xidian University |
| Jianhuang Lai | Sun Yat-sen University |
| Tao Wang | IQIYI Inc. |
| Wen Lu | Xidian University |

## Finance Chair

| | |
|---|---|
| Yining Quan | Xidian University |

## Publicity Chairs

| | |
|---|---|
| Deyu Meng | Xi'an Jiaotong University |
| Peiyi Shen | Xidian University |

## Publications Chair

| | |
|---|---|
| Cheng Deng | Xidian University |

## Program Committee

| | |
|---|---|
| Haizhou Ai | Tsinghua University |
| Xiang Bai | Huazhong University of Science and Technology |

Xiaochun Cao          Chinese Academy of Sciences
Shengyong Chen        Zhejiang University of Technology
Songcan Chen          Nanjing University of Aeronautics and Astronautics
Xilin Chen            Chinese Academy of Science
Xiaowu Chen           Beihang University
Xiaoming Deng         Chinese Academy of Science
Jing Dong             Chinese Academy of Science
Fuqing Duan           Beijing Normal University
Lichun Fang           Shanghai University
Jufu Feng             Peking University
Xin Geng              Southeast University
Ping Guo              Beijing Normal University
Huiguang He           Chinese Academy of Science
Ran He                Chinese Academy of Science
Zhiqiang Hou          Air Force Engineering University
Baiming Huang         University of Wisconsin-Madison
Hua Huang             Beijing Institute of Technology
Kaiqi Huang           Chinese Academy of Science
Qingming Huang        University of Chinese Academy of Sciences
Yongzhen Huang        Chinese Academy of Science
Rongrong Ji           Xiamen University
Yunde Jia             Beijing Institute of Technology
Xiaoyuan Jing         Wuhan University
Xiangwei Kong         Dalian University of Technology
Jianhuang Lai         Sun Yat-sen University
Chunming Li           University of Electronic Science and Technology of China
Hua Li                Chinese Academy of Science
Jian Li               National University of Defense Technology
Lingling Li           Zhengzhou Institute of Aeronautical Industry Management
Peihua Li             Dalian University of Technology
Shiying Li            Hunan University
Yongjie Li            University of Electronic Science and Technology of China
Zongmin Li            China University of Petroleum
Liang Lin             Sun Yat-sen University
Zhouchen Lin          Peking University
Hong Liu              Peking University
Huafeng Liu           Zhejiang University
Huaping Liu           Tsinghua University
Li Liu                National University of Defense Technology
Qingshan Liu          Nanjing University of Information Science and Technology
Yiguang Liu           Sichuan University
Guoliang Lu           Shandong University
Huchuan Lu            Dalian University of Technology
Bin Luo               Anhui University
Ke Lv                 University of Chinese Academy of Sciences
Qiguang Miao          Xidian University

| Pinle Qin | North University of China |
| Qiuqi Ruan | Beijing Jiaotong University |
| Nong Sang | Huazhong University of Science and Technology |
| Shiguang Shan | Chinese Academy of Science |
| Linlin Shen | Shenzhen University |
| Peiyi Shen | Xidian University |
| Wei Shen | Shanghai University |
| Fei Su | Beijing University of Posts and Telecommunications |
| Dongmei Sun | Beijing Jiaotong University |
| Zhengxing Sun | Nanjing University |
| Taizhe Tan | Guangdong University of Technology |
| Tieniu Tan | Chinese Academy of Science |
| Xiaoyang Tan | Nanjing University of Aeronautics and Astronautics |
| Jianliang Tang | Shenzhen University |
| Jinhui Tang | Nanjing University of Science and Technology |
| Yandong Tang | Chinese Academy of Science |
| Zengfu Wang | Chinese Academy of Science |
| Hanzi Wang | Xiamen University |
| Hao Wang | Philips Research Institute of China |
| Liang Wang | Chinese Academy of Science |
| Qing Wang | Northwestern Polytechnical University |
| Ruiping Wang | Chinese Academy of Science |
| Shiquan Wang | Philips Research Institute of China |
| Tao Wang | IQIYI Inc. |
| Qian Wang | Shanghai Jiaotong University |
| Wei Wang | Chinese Academy of Science |
| Yuanquan Wang | Tianjin University of Technology |
| Yunhong Wang | Beijing University of Aeronautics and Astronautics |
| Shikui Wei | Beijing Jiaotong University |
| Wei Wei | Xi'an University of Technology |
| Gongjian Wen | National University of Defense Technology |
| Jianxin Wu | Nanjing University |
| Guisong Xia | Wuhan University |
| Shiming Xiang | Chinese Academy of Science |
| Jinbiao Xu | Agilent Technologies(America) |
| Zenglin Xu | University of Electronic Science and Technology of China |
| Chenhui Yang | Xiamen University |
| Guosheng Yang | Minzu University of China |
| Jie Yang | Shanghai Jiaotong University |
| Jinfeng Yang | Civil Aviation University of China |
| Jingyu Yang | Nanjing University of Science and Technology |
| Jufeng Yang | Nankai University |
| Xianghua Ying | Peking University |
| Xingang You | Beijing Institute of Electronics Technology and Application |
| Xinge You | Huazhong University of Science and Technology |
| Jian Yu | Beijing Jiaotong University |

# Organizers

**Organized by**

China Computer Federation, China

CCF Task Force on Computer Vision

**Hosted by**

Xidian University

**Sponsoring Institutions**

![NVIDIA logo]

NVIDIA Corporation.

IQIYI Inc.

公安部第三研究所
The Third Research Institute of Ministry of Public Security

The Third Research Institute of Ministry of Public Security

Hangzhou Hikvision Digital Technology Co., Ltd.

Vion Technology Inc.

HUAWEI

Huawei Technologies Co., Ltd.

PARATERA 并行

# Contents – Part I

# Contents – Part II

# Fusion Technique for Infrared and Visible Images Based on Improved Quantum Theory Model

Weiwei Kong[✉], Yang Lei, and Minmin Ren

Engineering University of Armed Police Force, Xi'an 710086, Shaanxi, China
{kwwking,surina526,violet_212}@163.com

**Abstract.** Quantum theory model (QTM) owns a superior characteristic to turn a complex problem into the form of the linear combination of several much simpler components. Therefore, a novel fusion technique based on improved quantum theory model (IQTM) is proposed in this paper, aiming at dealing with the fusion problem of infrared and visible images. Firstly, the traditional QTM is modified to be a better version called IQTM. Compared with the traditional QTM, IQTM has three qubit states responsible for reflecting much more information of the represented pixel in the image. Then, the pixels of the source images are transformed into the qubit state representation, and the corresponding quantum results can be obtained according to the basic principle of quantum theory. Finally, the quantum results are transformed into the final fused image. Experimental results show that the proposed technique has remarked superiorities over other current typical ones in terms of both fusion performance and computational efficiency.

**Keywords:** Quantum theory · Qubit state · Image fusion · Infrared and visible images

## 1 Introduction

As known to us, there is considerable complementary and redundant information in the images from different imaging sensors with the same scene. For example, the visible image places great emphasis on the reflection of the entire background information. However, the information amount of the visible image relies on the lighting condition to a great extent. Thus, we may scarcely see anything from it under poor light conditions. Unlike visible images, infrared ones are greatly sensitive to thermal sources, so the information of thermal objects can still be captured regardless of the lighting conditions. It is a useful property which is beneficial for noticing the objects such as humans and idled motors hiding in the shelters. Due to the facts mentioned above, it is necessary to extract their respective advantages and fuse them into a single one to enhance the amount of the useful information. So far, the fusion of infrared and visible images has increasingly become a hot topic in the field of image processing, and the corresponding research results has also been widely utilized in the civilian and military applications.

© Springer-Verlag Berlin Heidelberg 2015
H. Zha et al. (Eds.): CCCV 2015, Part I, CCIS 546, pp. 1–11, 2015.
DOI: 10.1007/978-3-662-48558-3_1

Recently, a great many of fusion techniques [1-10] for infrared and visible images have been proposed. According to the processing modes towards the source image, the main approaches can be categorized into two categories including transform domain (TD) ones and non-transform domain (NTD) ones. The core idea of TD is to capture and extract the information of the edge and details of the source images as much as possible via geometric analysis. Commonly, the whole process of TD methods consists of three steps. Firstly, the source images are decomposed into several sub-images with different scales and directions. Then, certain fusion rules are adopted to complete the fusion course of the corresponding sub-images. Finally, the final fused image can be restored by using inverse TD models. During the early stage of the image processing research, TD methods indeed enhanced the fusion performance. However, along with the advancement of research and technique, several of its inherent drawbacks begin to appear. For example, the problem with discrete wavelet transform (DWT) is that it is merely adept at capturing point-wise singularities, but cannot be sensitive to other types of features such as lines. Therefore, DWT often causes artifacts in the final fused image. In order to overcome the drawbacks of DWT, the contourlet transform (CT) theory [2] is proposed, but CT does not have the property of shift-invariance, so the final result based on CT has the Gibbs phenomena. Compared with DWT and CT, non-subsampled contourlet transform (NSCT) [4,10] and non-subsampled shearlet transform (NSST) [9] are characterized by much better fusion performance, but the higher requirements of the computational resources prove to be their major limitations to the real-time applications.

The current NTD methods mainly involve the theories of pulse coupled neural networks (PCNN) [11-13], non-negative matrix factorization (NMF) and quantum theory model (QTM). As a third generation of artificial neural networks, PCNN has been already widely used in the field of image fusion. However, the inherent complex mechanism and too many existing parameters requiring setting in PCNN always restrict its performance. NMF must meet the requirement that the original non-negative matrix can be rewritten as the product of two non-negative matrixes. Unlike PCNN, NMF [6] is a purely mathematical model which is able to eliminate the subject influences on the final result as much as possible. Unfortunately, the parameters in NMF are commonly initialized at random so that the performances of NMF-based methods often vary a lot. QTM [14-16] is a recently developed theory in the area of information processing. A remarked distinction between QTM and other methods lies in that QTM is able to turn a complex problem into several simpler components which can be comprehended or done easily. However, QTM has been rarely involved in the field of image fusion. Under the above background, it is necessary and meaningful to investigate the potential of QTM on the image fusion issue especially the fusion of infrared and visible images which is with increasing importance. Meanwhile, a novel fusion technique for infrared and visible images based on improved quantum theory model (IQTM) is proposed. During this paper, the traditional QTM is modified to be IQTM with three qubit states responsible for reflecting much more information of the represented pixel in the image. Then, the pixels of the source images are transformed into the qubit state representation, and the corresponding quantum results can be obtained according to the basic principle of quantum theory. Finally, the quantum results are transformed into the final fused image. To evaluate the proposed technique with several current popular fusion methods, simulation experiments are conducted in terms of both fusion performance and computational efficiency.

The rest of this paper is organized as follows. In section 2, a brief introduction to the QTM is presented. Section 3 concretely describes the structure of IQTM and the proposed fusion algorithm for infrared and visible images in detail. Experimental results and performance analysis are presented and discussed in section 4. Concluding remarks and future work are given in section 5.

## 2    Traditional Quantum Theory Model

Unlike the traditional concept of bit, qubit is the abbreviation of the dual-state quantum system which includes two distinct states denoted by 0 and 1, respectively. Commonly, a qubit is used to represent the two different probabilities of one quantum system, and the corresponding mathematical expression can be written as

$$|\varphi> = c_0 |0> + c_1 |1> \tag{1}$$

Obviously, the quantum system $\varphi$ can be expressed as the linear combination of two basic states namely zero and one. The probability amplitude of state 0 and state 1 are denoted as $c_0$ and $c_1$ whose values must be satisfy the following requirement.

$$c_0^2 + c_1^2 = 1 \tag{2}$$

Therefore, the quantum system $\varphi$ will converge to the state 0 with the probability $c_0^2$. Similarly, the state 1 will be achieved at the probability $c_1^2$.

According to Eq. (1) and (2), for the quantum system $\varphi$ with $m$ qubits, the $p^{th}$ qubit can be expressed as follows.

$$|\varphi^p> = c_0^p |0> + c_1^p |1> \tag{3}$$

As a result, the quantum system $\varphi$ can be written as the tensor product of the $m$ qubits, whose mathematical expression is given as follows.

$$
\begin{aligned}
|\varphi> &= |\varphi^1> \otimes |\varphi^2> \otimes...\otimes |\varphi^p>...\otimes |\varphi^m> \\
&= (c_0^1 |0> + c_1^1 |1>) \otimes (c_0^2 |0> + c_1^2 |1>) \otimes... \\
&\quad \otimes (c_0^p |0> + c_1^p |1>)...\otimes (c_0^m |0> + c_1^m |1>) \\
&= (c_0^1 c_0^2 ... c_0^m) |00...0> + (c_0^1 c_0^2 ... c_1^m) |00...1> +... \\
&\quad + (c_1^1 c_1^2 ... c_1^m) |11...1>
\end{aligned}
\tag{4}
$$

It is noteworthy that the quadratic sum of the coefficients mentioned in Eq. (4) still equals to one. Moreover, the number of the basic vectors in the quantum system $\varphi$ is $2^m$.

In the quantum theory, each pixel in the image is necessarily in the form of the qubit state, so its original gray value have to be normalized into the range [0, 1]. Let a gray image denoted by $A$ with the size of $m \times n$, the qubit state of the pixel $p$ in $A$ can be represented as follows.

$$| p(x, y) >= \sin \alpha | 0 > + \cos \alpha | 1 > \qquad 0 \leq x \leq m, 0 \leq y \leq n \qquad (5)$$

Where $p(x, y)$ denotes the pixel $p$ located at coordinates $(x, y)$. $\sin \alpha$ and $\cos \alpha$ are the probabilities of 0 and 1, respectively.

## 3    Proposed Fusion Technique

### 3.1    Improved Quantum Theory Model

As mentioned above, we can find that only the extreme points namely 0 and 1 have been concerned when the traditional quantum theory are used to deal with the issue of image processing. As a result, on the one hand, the interval analyzed is somewhat coarse and much information may be omitted in the reassigning process of the gray value of the pixel. On the other hand, the absolute probability distribution on the value 0 or 1 is actually not large towards a common gray image. On the contrary, the gray values of most pixels commonly range from 0 to 1, so it is neither scientific nor objective to consider the extreme points alone.

In this paper, another qubit state 0.5 is added to the traditional quantum theory model to form an improved one called improved quantum theory model (IQTM) whose mathematical expression is given as follows.

$$| p(x, y) >= a | 0 > + b | 1 > + c | 0.5 > \qquad 0 \leq x \leq m, 0 \leq y \leq n \qquad (6)$$

Where $a$, $b$ and $c$ denotes the probability amplitude of states 0, 1 and 0.5. They have to meet the following requirement.

$$a^2 + b^2 + c^2 = 1 \qquad (7)$$

Compared with the traditional model, IQTM has remarked superiorities as follows.

- IQTM is able to describe and reflect the realistic gray distribution of pixels in the image. The adding of state 0.5 is helpful to represent the gray information of pixels much more accurately.
- In spite of the variation of the number of parameters, the fundamental principle of quantum theory is still satisfied in IQTM. In other words, the inherent advantages of quantum theory are also expected to be inherited and developed in the new model. According to Eq. (7), the correlation of the three parameters is shown in Fig. 1.

The variables $a$, $b$ and $c$ construct a three-dimensional coordinate system where the pixel $p(x, y)$ normalized into the range [0, 1] can be regarded as the point. Obviously, the original pixel is transformed into a new point $P(a, b, c)$ with three-dimensional characteristics. In addition, point $P$ can be projected into three mutually perpendicular planes respectively, so that a tetrahedron can be obtained as depicted in the right area in Fig. 1.

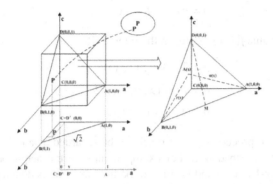

**Fig. 1.** Correlation of the parameters $a$, $b$ and $c$

During the interval [0, 1], the two extremes 0 and 1 precisely indicate the most stable state in nature. Moreover, the value 0.5 is the most uncertain state, based on which the qubit state 0.5 in IQTM is utilized to play a role in buffering the interval. As a result, there are three typical parameter selection regarding $a$, $b$ and $c$ as follows.

- When the gray value of the pixel $p(x, y)$ equals to 1, the values of $a$, $b$ and $c$ should be 0, 1 and 0 respectively.
- When the gray value of the pixel $p(x, y)$ equals to 0, the values of $a$, $b$ and $c$ should be 1, 0 and 0 respectively.
- When the gray value of the pixel $p(x, y)$ equals to 0.5, the values of $a$, $b$ and $c$ should be 0, 0 and 1 respectively.

Obviously, except for the above three cases, the gray values of most pixels widely distribute in other points in the interval [0, 1]. In QTM, the gray value $f(x, y)$ is supposed to be the probability of 1, whereas the gray value $(1-f(x, y))$ is supposed to be the probability of 0. In IQTM, the description of the probability of 1 and 0 can be conducted by the concept of real-value denoted by $R$.

The mathematical expression of the probability of 1 and 0 are given respectively as follows.

$$P_1 = R = a*0+b*1+c*0.5 \tag{8}$$

$$P_0 = 1-P_1 = 1-(a*0+b*1+c*0.5) \tag{9}$$

Based on the three typical cases, the values of the parameters $a$, $b$ and $c$ can be decided as follows.

(a) If the gray value $f(x, y)$ locates in the interval $[0, 0.5]$,

$$
\begin{aligned}
c &= 2 * f(x, y) \\
a &= 1 - f(x, y) - c/2 \\
b &= c/2 - f(x, y)
\end{aligned}
\tag{10}
$$

(b) If the gray value $f(x, y)$ locates in the interval $[0.5, 1]$,

$$
\begin{aligned}
c &= 2 * (1 - f(x, y)) \\
a &= 1 - f(x, y) - c/2 \\
b &= f(x, y) - c/2
\end{aligned}
\tag{11}
$$

In the field of image processing, each pixel can be regarded as a qubit with which the gray value can be described well. For example, suppose the neighboring three pixels in the location $(x, y\text{-}1)$, $(x, y)$ and $(x, y+1)$ to be the three qubits denoted by $|p(x, y\text{-}1)\rangle$, $|p(x, y)\rangle$ and $|p(x, y+1)\rangle$. The tensor product of the three qubits can be written as follows.

$$
\begin{aligned}
&| f(x, y-1) f(x, y) f(x, y+1) > \\
&=| f(x, y-1) > \otimes | f(x, y) > \otimes | f(x, y+1) > \\
&= \sqrt{P_0(x, y-1)}\sqrt{P_0(x, y)}\sqrt{P_0(x, y+1)}\,|000> \\
&+ \sqrt{P_0(x, y-1)}\sqrt{P_0(x, y)}\sqrt{P_1(x, y+1)}\,|001> \\
&+ \sqrt{P_0(x, y-1)}\sqrt{P_1(x, y)}\sqrt{P_0(x, y+1)}\,|010> \\
&+ \sqrt{P_0(x, y-1)}\sqrt{P_1(x, y)}\sqrt{P_1(x, y+1)}\,|011> \\
&+ \sqrt{P_1(x, y-1)}\sqrt{P_0(x, y)}\sqrt{P_0(x, y+1)}\,|100> \\
&+ \sqrt{P_1(x, y-1)}\sqrt{P_0(x, y)}\sqrt{P_1(x, y+1)}\,|101> \\
&+ \sqrt{P_1(x, y-1)}\sqrt{P_1(x, y)}\sqrt{P_0(x, y+1)}\,|110> \\
&+ \sqrt{P_1(x, y-1)}\sqrt{P_1(x, y)}\sqrt{P_1(x, y+1)}\,|111>
\end{aligned}
\tag{12}
$$

In Eq. (12), the correlation system is composed of eight different base states, and the coefficients denote the probabilities of corresponding state. According to the collapse theory of wave function, the eight base states would be collapsed to two different systems including $|\varphi_0\rangle$ and $|\varphi_1\rangle$ whose mathematical expressions are given as follows.

$$
\begin{aligned}
&| \varphi_0(x, y) > \\
&= \sqrt{P_0(x, y-1)}\sqrt{P_0(x, y+1)}\,|000> + \sqrt{P_0(x, y-1)}\sqrt{P_1(x, y+1)}\,|001> \\
&+ \sqrt{P_1(x, y-1)}\sqrt{P_0(x, y+1)}\,|100> + \sqrt{P_1(x, y-1)}\sqrt{P_1(x, y+1)}\,|101>
\end{aligned}
\tag{13}
$$

$$|\varphi_1(x,y)>$$
$$= \sqrt{P_0(x,y-1)}\sqrt{P_0(x,y+1)}\,|010> + \sqrt{P_0(x,y-1)}\sqrt{P_1(x,y+1)}\,|011> \quad (14)$$
$$+ \sqrt{P_1(x,y-1)}\sqrt{P_0(x,y+1)}\,|110> + \sqrt{P_1(x,y-1)}\sqrt{P_1(x,y+1)}\,|111>$$

Obviously, the real and direct effect of the collapse theory is to eliminate the influence of the gray value of the central pixel. What is more, multi-level analysis based on the gray value has also been reflected.

## 3.2 Concrete Fusion Algorithm

In this section, we present the overall framework of the fusion algorithm for infrared and visible images in detail. For a simple case, we suppose that a gray-scale visible light image and an infrared image respectively denoted by $V$ and $IR$ have been already accurately registered. $F$ is the final fused image. The concrete steps of the proposed fusion algorithm are given as follows.

**Inputs:** A gray-scale visible light image $V$ and an infrared image $IR$.
**Outputs:** Fused image $F$.
**Steps:**

1. The gray values of the source images $V$ and $IR$ are normalized into the interval $[0, 1]$.
2. Each pixel in the source images is transformed into the qubit state representation via IQTM theory.
3. Compute the real-value of each pixel by using Eq. (8), (10) and (11).
4. The final fused image $F$ can be reconstructed via the collapse theory.

As for a single image, the constructed gray value of the central pixel based on Eq. (12) and Eq. (14), we can obtain whose mathematical can be written like this.

$$f(x,y) = \frac{P_1(x,y-1)P_1(x,y)P_1(x,y+1)|111>}{P_1(x,y-1)P_1(x,y+1)|111>} \quad (15)$$

Similarly, we can achieve the reconstruct equation in the case of two source images as follows.

$$f(x,y)$$
$$= \frac{P_1^V(x,y-1)P_1^V(x,y)P_1^V(x,y+1)|111> + P_1^{IR}(x,y-1)P_1^{IR}(x,y)P_1^{IR}(x,y+1)|111>}{P_1^V(x,y-1)P_1^V(x,y+1)|111> + P_1^{IR}(x,y-1)P_1^{IR}(x,y+1)|111>} \quad (16)$$

Eq. (16) can be further rewritten as

$$f(x, y)$$

$$= \frac{P_1^V(x, y-1)P_1^V(x, y)P_1^V(x, y+1) + P_1^{IR}(x, y-1)P_1^{IR}(x, y)P_1^{IR}(x, y+1)}{P_1^V(x, y-1)P_1^V(x, y+1) + P_1^{IR}(x, y-1)P_1^{IR}(x, y+1)}$$

$$= \frac{P_1^V(x, y-1)P_1^V(x, y+1)}{P_1^V(x, y-1)P_1^V(x, y+1) + P_1^{IR}(x, y-1)P_1^{IR}(x, y+1)} \cdot P_1^V(x, y)$$

$$+ \frac{P_1^{IR}(x, y-1)P_1^{IR}(x, y+1)}{P_1^V(x, y-1)P_1^V(x, y+1) + P_1^{IR}(x, y-1)P_1^{IR}(x, y+1)} \cdot P_1^{IR}(x, y)$$

$$(17)$$

Obviously, the sum of the coefficients of $P_1^V(x, y)$ and $P_1^{IR}(x, y)$ equals to 1, which is consistent with the basic nature of quantum theory model. Furthermore, the gray value of the pixel $p(x, y)$ in the fused image $F$ depends largely on the real-values of neighboring pixels. Under special circumstances, for example, the denominator of the coefficient in Eq. (17) is zero, the pixel with larger real-value in the location $(x, y)$ from the source images would be regarded as the one in the fused image.

## 4      Experimental Results and Discussion

In order to verify the superiorities of the proposed fusion technique, one pair of gray-scale visible light and infrared images with 256 gray levels have been chosen as the source images in this section. The experimental platform here is based on a PC with 32-bit windows 7 OS, 4G memory and matlab 2010a. Apart from the proposed technique (T4), three other different typical ones named T1-T3 are used for comparison, which are NSST-improved-PCNN based technique [13] (T1), SCM based technique [17] (T2), and NSCT based technique [18] (T3). The objective quality metrics including space frequency (SF) [19], mutual information (MI) [19], and information entropy (IE) have been used for evaluating the fused images based on different methods from the perspective of the quantity. The fused results based on four techniques are shown in Fig. 2.

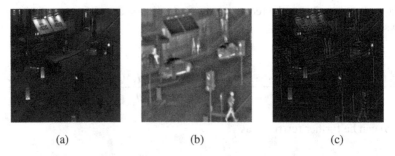

(a)                              (b)                              (c)

**Fig. 2.** Fused results of 'quad'. (a) Gray-scale visible light image. (b) Infrared image. (c) Result based on T1. (d) Result based on T2. (e) Result based on T3. (f) Result based on T4.

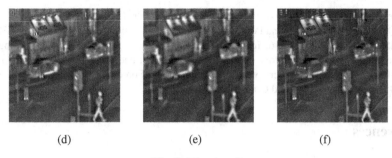

(d)                        (e)                        (f)

**Fig. 2.** (*Continued*)

As shown in Fig. 2, the fused image based on T1 has not effectively extracted the important information from the infrared image and fused it in the result, so the infrared information is missing in Fig. 2(c). Compared with T1, the fused images based on T2 and T3 have much better visual performance, and the main features in both the gray-scale visible light and infrared images have been reflected in the corresponding results to a great extent. However, T4 is superior to T2 and T3 in both preserving important details information and inheriting the characteristics of source images.

Table 1 report the objective evaluation results from the objective perspective of point. Bold values indicate the best result in the same index among the four techniques. Obviously, the statistics results in Table 1 are also consistent with the above subjective visual effects.

**Table 1.** Objective Evaluation Results Based on T1-T4 about 'quad'

|      | SF     | MI    | IE    |
|------|--------|-------|-------|
| T1   | 10.186 | 1.377 | 4.396 |
| T2   | 10.753 | 3.694 | 6.816 |
| T3   | 5.971  | 3.395 | 6.769 |
| T4   | **12.014** | **3.957** | **6.840** |

## 5    Conclusions

In this paper, a novel fusion technique for infrared and visible images based on IQTM is proposed. The original pixels of the source images are transformed into the three qubit state representation. Compared with the traditional QTM, the adding of the new qubit state 0.5 in IQTM is helpful to represent the gray information of pixels much more accurately. Finally, the quantum results are transformed into the final fused image. The superiorities of the proposed technique in terms of both subjective visual performance and objective quantitative criteria are verified in simulation experiments. How to further enhance the performance of the proposed technique is the focus in our future work.

**Acknowledgments.** The authors would like to thank the anonymous reviewers and editors for their invaluable suggestions. This work was supported in part by the National Natural Science Foundations of China under Grant 61309008 and Grant 61309022, in part by the Natural

Science Foundation of Shannxi Province of China under Grant 2013JQ8031 and Grant 2014JQ8049, in part by the China Postdoctoral Science Foundation under Grant 2013M532133, 2014M552718 and 2014T71016, in part by the Foundation of Science and Technology on Information Assurance Laboratory under Grant KJ-13-108, and the Natural Science Foundations of the Engineering University of the Armed Police Force of China under Grant WJY-201214, Grant WJY-201414 and Grant WJY-201312.

## References

1. Li, X., Qin, S.Y.: Efficient fusion for infrared and visible images based on compressive sensing principle. IET Image Processing **5**(2), 141–147 (2011)
2. Chang, X., Jiao, L.C., Liu, F., et al.: Multicontourlet-based adaptive fusion of infrared and visible remote sensing images. IEEE Geoscience and Remote Sensing Letters **7**(3), 549–553 (2010)
3. Ulusoy, I., Yuruk, H.: New method for the fusion of complementary information from infrared and visual images for object detection. IET Image Processing **5**(1), 36–48 (2011)
4. Kong, W.W., Lei, Y., Ni, X.L.: Fusion technique for grey-scale visible light and infrared images based on non-subsampled contourlet transform and intensity-hue-saturation transform. IET Signal Processing **5**(1), 75–80 (2011)
5. Eisler, K., Homma, C., Goldammer, M., et al.: Fusion of visual and infrared thermography images for advanced assessment in non-destructive testing. Review of Scientific Instruments **84**(6), 064902-1–064902-5 (2013)
6. Wang, J., Peng, J.Y., Feng, X.Y., et al.: Fusion method for infrared and visible images by using non-negative sparse representation. Infrared Physics & Technology **67**, 477–489 (2014)
7. Liu, Z.D., Yin, H.P., Fang, B., et al.: A novel fusion scheme for visible and infrared images based on compressive sensing. Optics Communications **335**, 168–177 (2015)
8. Lu, X.Q., Zhang, B.H., Zhao, Y., et al.: The infrared and visible image fusion algorithm based on target separation and sparse representation. Infrared Physics & Technology **67**, 397–407 (2014)
9. Kong, W.W., Lei, Y., Zhao, H.X.: Adaptive fusion method of visible light and infrared images based on non-subsampled shearlet transform and fast non-negative matrix factorization. Infrared Physics & Technology **67**(11), 161–172 (2014)
10. Chen, Y., Xiong, J., Liu, H.L., et al.: Fusion method of infrared and visible images based on neighborhood characteristic and regionalization in NSCT domain. Optik **125**(17), 4980–4984 (2014)
11. Subashini, M.M., Sahoo, S.K.: Pulse coupled neural networks and its applications. Expert System and Applications **41**(8), 3965–3974 (2014)
12. Shi, C., Miao, Q.G., Xu, P.F.: A novel algorithm of image fusion based on shearlets and PCNN. Neurocomputing **117**(10), 47–53 (2013)
13. Kong, W.W., Liu, J.P.: Technique for image fusion based on nonsubsampled shearlet transform and improved pulse-coupled neural network. Optical Engineering **52**(1), 017001-1–017001-12 (2013)
14. Tseng, C.C., Hwang, T.M.: Quantum digital image processing algorithms. In: 16th IPPR Conference on Computer Vision, Graphics and Image Processing. ROC, Kinmen, pp. 827–834 (2003)
15. Xie, K.F., Zhou, X.Y., Xu, G.P.: Morphology filtering inspired by quantum collapsing. Journal of Image Graphics **14**(5), 967–972 (2009)

16. Fu, X.W.: Research on image processing methods based on quantum mechanics. Huazhong University of Science and Technology (2010)
17. Wang, N.Y., Ma, Y.D., Zhan, K.: Spiking cortical model for multifocus image fusion. Neurocomputing **130**(4), 44–51 (2014)
18. Adu, J.H., Gan, J.H., Wang, Y., et al.: Image fusion based on nonsubsampled contourlet transform for infrared and visible light image. Infrared Physics & Technology **61**(1), 94–100 (2013)
19. Liu, Z., Blasch, E., Xue, Z.Y., et al.: Fusion algorithms for context enhancement in night vision: a comparative study. IEEE Transactions on Pattern Analysis and Machine Intelligence **34**(1), 94–109 (2012)

# Skeleton-Based Human Action Recognition with Profile Hidden Markov Models

Wenwen Ding[1,2], Kai Liu[1]([✉]), Fei Cheng[1], Huan Shi[1], and Baijian Zhang[1]

[1] School of Computer Science and Technology, Xidian University, Xi'an, China
[2] School of Mathematical Sciences, Huaibei Normal University, Anhui, China
{dww2048,chengfei8582}@163.com, kailiu@mail.xidian.edu.cn,
shihuan.xidian@gmail.com, zhangbaijian0307@126.com

**Abstract.** Recognizing human actions from image sequences is an active area of research in computer vision. In this paper, a novel HMM-based approach is proposed for human action recognition using 3D positions of body joints. First, actions are segmented into meaningful action units called dynamic instants and intervals by using motion velocities, the direction of motion, and the curvatures of 3D trajectories. Then action unit with its spatio-temporal feature sets are clustered using unsupervised learning, like SOM, to generate a sequence of discrete symbols. To overcome an abrupt change or an abnormal in its gesticulation between different performances of the same action, Profile Hidden Markov Models (Profile HMMs) are applied with these symbol sequences using Viterbi and Baum-Welch algorithms for human activity recognition. The experimental evaluations show that the proposed approach achieves promising results compared to other state of the art algorithms.

**Keywords:** View-invariant representation · Skeleton joints · Human activity recognition · Profile HMM · Self-organizing map

## 1 Introduction

Recognizing human activity is a key component in many applications, such as Video Surveillance, Ambient Intelligence, Human-Computer Interaction systems, and even Health-Care. Despite remarkable research efforts and many encouraging advances in the past decade, accurate recognition of the human actions is still a quite challenging task.

Many recent state-of-the-art techniques for human action recognition rely on: Bag-of-Word (BoW) [1] representations extracted from Spatio-Temporal Interest Points (STIP) [2], Dynamic Time Warping (DTW)[3] algorithm derived from exemplar-based approaches, Eigenjoints [4] stem from skeleton-based approaches, etc. Despite these good results were achieved by state of the art activity recognition approaches, these still have some limitations.

To address these issues and enhance human action recognition performance, time-sequential representation is more appropriate for these problem. Frame by

© Springer-Verlag Berlin Heidelberg 2015
H. Zha et al. (Eds.): CCCV 2015, Part I, CCIS 546, pp. 12–21, 2015.
DOI: 10.1007/978-3-662-48558-3_2

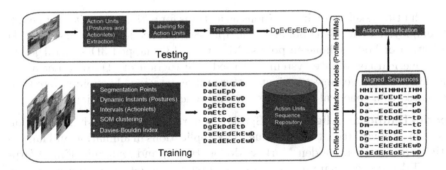

**Fig. 1.** The general framework of the proposed approach.

frame representations suffer from redundancy. Therefore segmenting video into states and handling unaligned video sequences are two main problems. In this paper, we use action-units and novel probabilistic methods (Profile HMM [5]) to handle unaligned video sequences. The principle is illustrated in Fig. 1. First, trajectories of action, also referred to as discrete curves, can be drawn by several 3D joint points. The segmentation points $S$, splitting actions into meaningful action-units, can be captured by the direction of motion and curvature of the trajectory having maximum velocity. Then, the features of action units, consisting of dynamic instants (postures) $\xi_p$ and intervals (actionlets [6]) $\xi_a$, are extracted from these segmented trajectories and then are mapped into two Self Organizing Mappings (SOMs) [7] recorded as $T_{\xi_p}$ and $T_{\xi_a}$, respectively. Unlike actions that have labels showing on, postures and actionlets do not have such labels. Therefore, $T_{\xi_p}$ and $T_{\xi_a}$ can be scattered in plots according to the Davies-Bouldin Index (DBI) value [8] which decide the number of labels of postures and actionlets. These plots in SOM can be named with upper-case letters and lower-case letters respectively referred as the labels of postures and actionlets. Finally, capturing the sptio-temporal relationships between action-units of a given action, Profile HMMs are generated by sequences of discrete symbols of each action. With these profile HMMs, each action represented by time-series is trained and aligned, thus elevating classification performance.

The rest of the paper is organized as follows: Section 2 presents the related work; Section 3 elaborates our method of features extraction, clustering and classification of action units consisting of postures and actionlets; Section 4 and discusses the parameters setting presents our experimental results; and Section5 concludes this paper.

## 2   Related Work

**Action Recognition.** In the past decade, video-based action recognition and detection has tremendous amount of background literature [9,10]. Recently, with the development of the commodity depth sensors like Microsoft Kinect [11],there has been a lot of interests in human action recognition from depth data. Several research utilize skeleton joint positions as features for action recognition. Li et al. [12] employed a bag-of-3D-points graph approach to encode actions based on 3D projection of body silhouette points. Xia et al. [13] mapped 3D skeletal joints to a spherical coordinate system and used a histogram of 3D Joint Locations (HOJ3D) to achieve view-invariant posture representation. The joints were then translated to a spherical coordinate system to achieve view-invariance.

**Spatio-Temporal Alignment.** Spatio-temporal alignment of human action has been a topic of recent interest due to its applications in animation and human activity recognition. Hidden Markov Model (HMM) and Dynamic Time Warping (DTW) are two main approaches based on sequential representation of the activity for this problem. In [14], each action is modeled as a series of synthetic 2D human poses matched by using the Viterbi algorithm. Mapping poses or frames into symbols is the main challenge of HMM approaches. But these frame by frame representations suffer from redundancy. Furthermore, HMM structure must be adaptively designed for specific application domains. DTW is a method for temporally aligning multi-modal sequences from multiple subjects performing similar activities. DTW deals with sequence aligning by operations of deleting and inserting compression expansion, and substitution, of subsequences. Zhou and Torre [15] extended DTW to propose Canonical Time Warping (CTW) for finding the temporal alignment that maximizes the spatial correlation between two behavioral samples coming from two subjects.

## 3   Proposed Method

### 3.1   Representation of Meaningful Action Units

Action is represented as a sequence of dynamic instants and intervals, which are computed using the direction of motion and the spatio-temporal curvature of a 3D trajectory. It use depth cameras to track 3D trajectories that

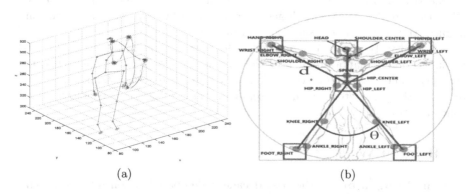

(a)                                          (b)

**Fig. 2.** (a) The trajectory of an action of *high hand wave* is segmented by *red stars*. (b) Illustration of human posture representation based on relative distance and angles of star skeleton.

each trajectory represents the evolution of one coordinate $x$, $y$, or $z$ over time, and indicates the position of a specific joint of human. Motion trajectories provide rich spatio-temporal information about an object's behavior. To obtain meaningful action units, we must learn superior segmentation points $S = \{s_1, ...s_i, ..., s_j, ..., s_m\}(1 < i < j < m)$ to segment 3D trajectory of an action, as shown in Fig. 2a. The problems of under-segmented and over-segmented trajectories will always lead to insignificant action units. Based on [6], superior segmentation points $S$ for a trajectory can be obtained.

For dynamic instants of action, we can utilize human postures to represent in this moment. Human postures can be represented by relative distances $d$ and angles $\theta$ from 3D star skeleton,as shown in Fig. 2b. For intervals of action, we can utilize actionlets to represent these intervals from paper [6].

### 3.2   Clustering Feature Using Unsupervised Learning

Action labels are easily labeled in real life, such as walk, sit down, stand up, throw, etc. Unlike actions with labels that are shown on a map grid, an actionlet or a posture is hardly labeled or highly generalized using our human language. Therefore, Self Organizing Map (SOM) [7] and the Davies-Bouldin Index (DBI) [8] value are used to cluster postures and actionlets.

**Self Organized Mapping.** A self-organizing map(SOM) is a type of artificial neural network for the visualization of high-dimensional data using unsupervised learning. It can project complex, nonlinear statistical relationships between high-dimensional patterns into simple geometric relationships on a low-dimensional topology map. The training process of SOM is an incremental learning algorithm. The weight vectors $m$ of nodes are initialized either to small random values or sampled evenly from the subspace spanned by the two largest principal component eigenvectors, which is a good initial approximation.

**Davies Bouldin Index.** The feature of postures $\xi_p$ and actionlet $\xi_a$ map to SOM forming similar neural units in $T_{\xi_p}$ and $T_{\xi_a}$ need to be grouped and labeled later. To find initial partitioning, we use the Davies-Bouldin index value to scattered the $T_{\xi_p}$ and $T_{\xi_a}$ in plots. By definition, the lower the $DBI$, the better the separation of the clusters and the tightness inside the clusters.

The number of plots of the $T_{\xi_p}$ and $T_{\xi_a}$ can be decided by the definiton of $DBI$. Each plot was symbolized by capital or lower-case letters according to the posture of actionlet. Therefore, The feature of postures $\xi_p$ and actionlet $\xi_a$ were transformed into symbols from a discrete alphabet so that an action can be represented by upper-case and low-case letters generated alternately in a individual sequence, for example, $DaEvEvEwD$. Similar actions will correspond a sequence family $F$ for generating a Profile HMM or say a motif.

### 3.3   Profile HMMs for Temporal Alignment of Human Motion

In this section, we describe the design of general Profile HMMs and our Profile HMMs in greater detail. The classifiers we build for human action recognition are based on our Profile HMMs. Using the Forward-Backward algorithm [16], we can compute the total probability of a sequence being generated by Profile HMMs, i.e. can be used to classify unknown sequences as belonging to which model. Using the Viterbi algorithm [17], we can compute the most likely path through Profile HMMs that generates a sequence, i.e. the most likely alignment of the sequence against the model. Using initial parameters that assign uniform probabilities over all action units in each time step, we apply the well known Baum-Welch algorithm [18] to iteratively find new Profile HMM parameters which maximize the likelihood of the model for the sequences of action units in the training videos.

**Profile Hidden Markov Models.** Profile HMMs consist of several types of states: match states $M_i$, insert states $I_i$, and delete states $D_i$. For each position $i$ in a Profile HMM, there is one match state, one insert state, and one delete state. A Profile HMM can thus be visualized as a series of columns, where each column represents a position $i$ in the sequence as shown in Figure 3a. Any arbitrary sequence can then be represented as a traversal of states from column to column. Each state emits symbols with a probability distribution specific to its position in the chain.

Given a Profile HMM, how to align multiple sequences based on the model is the first problem to solve. Viterbi algorithm is used for seeking the most likely path of each sequence generated by the model. Multiple sequence alignment is mean to find Viterbi path of each sequence. Fig. 3b shows a small example of a set of human posture sequences. Profile HMM (Fig. 3a) can be constructed from the set of sequences by using the Baum-Welch algorithm. The result of aligned sequences can be showed in Fig. 3c.

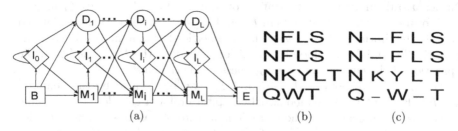

(a)          (b)          (c)

**Fig. 3.** (a) A general Profile HMM of length L. $M_i$ is the $i$th match state, $I_i$ is the $i$th insert state, $Di$ is the $i$th delete state. $B$ is the begin state, and $E$ is the end state. (b) Illustration of human posture representation based on relative distance and angles of star skeleton.

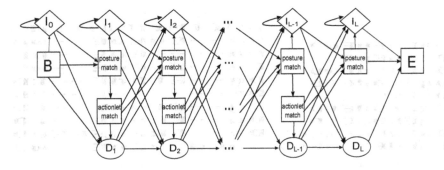

**Fig. 4.** The Profile HMM for human action recognition.

**Adapting Profile HMMs for Human Action Recognition.** In this section we describe the structure of our profile HMMs as shown in Fig. 4. The main difference between our profile HMM and others is that the Profile HMMs used in biology have only a single chain of Match states. In our case, the addition of a second match state per position was intended to allow the model to represent the correlation between action units in videos. In the context of human action recognition, actions are segmented into meaningful action-units called dynamic instants and intervals being incarnated in human postures and action-lets, which labels of postures and actionlets are upper-case and lower-case letters respectively. Therefore, an action can be represented by a string, for example, *DaEvEvEwD*. Pay attention to the first and the end symbol which is upper-case letters meaning that an action begin or end with a posture in our observation. This change is necessary as postures and actionlets obviously alternated in an action. To allow for variations between the observed action-units in the same action sequences, the model has two additional states for each position in the chain. One is insert states $I_i$ representing one or more extra abrupt or abnormal action-units inserted in a sequence between two normal parts of the chain. The other is Delete states $D_i$ allowing period action-units to be omitted from the action sequences.

We now explain the design and use of profile HMMs $\Lambda$ of $k$ classes with models $\Lambda_1, \Lambda_2, ..., \Lambda_k$ which employ to capture characteristics exhibited by every kind of actions. If we already have a set of action-unit sequences (Fig. 5a) belonging to a family, a profile HMM $\Lambda_c(1 < c < k)$ as shown in Fig. 4 can be constructed from the set of unaligned sequences after using the Baum-Welch algorithm. The length $L$ of the $\Lambda_c(1 < c < k)$ must be chosen, and is usually equal to the average length of the unaligned action unit sequences in the training set. The transition and emission probabilities are initialized from Dirichlet distributions.

Once Profile HMMs $\Lambda$ have been constructed, we then construct a classifier $\mathcal{C}_1$ for the task of choosing the best model $\Lambda_c(1 < c < k)$ for new test sequence $q$ of action-units

$$c = \mathcal{C}_1(q) = \underset{c}{\operatorname{argmax}} P(q|\Lambda_c). \tag{1}$$

(a)                                    (b)

**Fig. 5.** (a) A set of action-unit sequences of action *high arm wave*. (b)The alignment generated via the Profile HMM method for the set of action-unit sequences of action *high arm wave*. The match and insert columns are marked with the letters $M$ and $I$ respectively in the first line.

This is done via a straightforward application of the forward-backward algorithm, i.e. to get the full probability of the given sequence $q$.

The second classifier $C_2$ makes use of the well-known Viterbi algorithm for finding the most likely alignment of the sequence to the family, i.e. Viterbi path $V$. For a given output sequence $q$ and the associated probability of the most likely Viterbi path $V_c$ to each Profile HMM, the viterbi classifier $C_2$ finds Viterbi paths for the sequence in each Profile HMM $\Lambda_1, \Lambda_2, ..., \Lambda_k$ and chooses the class $c$ whose model produces the best Viterbi path $V_c$.

$$c = C_2(q) = \operatorname*{argmax}_c P_{viterbi}(q, \Lambda) = \max_{V_c} P(q, V|\Lambda). \tag{2}$$

In practical terms, the Viterbi classifier $C_2$ finds each model's best explanation for how the action-units in the sequence were generated. We choice the Viterbi classifier $C_2$ that provides the best explanation for the observed action-units.

## 4    Experimental Evaluation

The performance of the activity recognition was primarily evaluated based on its accuracy. In this section, we evaluate the proposed skeletal representation using three different datasets: MSR-Action3D [12], UTKinect-Action [13], and UCF Kinect Dataset [19].

### 4.1    Evaluation Settings

For MSR Action3D Dataset, in order to allow a fair comparison with the state of the art methods, we followed the test setting of [12], dividing the 20 actions into three subsets $AS_1$, $AS_2$ and $AS_3$ and using two experimental settings: one is non-cross-subject test setting and another is cross-subject test setting.

For UTKinect-Action Dataset, to allow for comparison with [13], we followed the same experimental set up using Leave One Sequence Out Cross Validation (LOOCV) on the 200 sequences. For UCF Kinect Dataset, we followed the same experimental set up using the Latency Aware Learning in [19].

## 4.2 Experimental Results

We first evaluate the performance of the proposed approach on the three challenging 3D action datasets. The proposed method's primary advantage is robustness temporal misalignment. The experiment results on the three datasets are shown in Table 1. We can see that the proposed approach gives the best results on all datasets. In our experiments, the cross-subjects action recognition is conducted, which is more difficult than using the same subjects for both training and testing. From the results of MSR Action3D dataset on cross-subjects test, the recognition accuracy of our method on test three was 88.6% significantly outperforming the other joint-based action recognition methods, including Bag-of-3D-Points[12], Histogram of 3D joints[13], and EigenJoints [4], which achieved accuracies of 74.4%, 78.97%, and 82.3%, respectively. Specifically, it outperforms the state-of-the-art on UTKinect-Action dataset and UCT Kinect dataset. On the UTKinect-Action dataset, our approach has an accuracy of 91.7% which outperforms the HOJ3D feature in [13] (90.9%). Finally, we compare our result with all others on the UCF Kinect dataset. The results are shown in Table 1.

Fig. 6 shows the confusion matrices for MSRAction3D AS1, MSR-Action3D AS2 and MSR-Action3D AS3. We can see that most of the confusions are between highly similar actions like *forward punch* and *high throw* in the case of

Table 1. Human recognition accuracies on three datasets.

| MSR Action3D(Test Three) | Accuracy |
|---|---|
| Bag of 3D Points[12] | 74.7 |
| Histogram of 3D Joints[13] | 78.9 |
| Eigenjoints[4] | 82.3 |
| Spatio-temporal Feature Chain [6] | 84.4 |
| Random Occupancy Patterns[? ] | 86.2 |
| Proposed Method | 88.6 |
| **UTKinect-Action** | **Accuracy** |
| HO3DJ[13] | 90.9 |
| Spatio-temporal Feature Chain [6] | 91.5 |
| Proposed Method | 91.7 |
| **UCF Kinect** | **Accuracy** |
| LAL[19] | 95.9 |
| Eigenjoint[4] | 97.1 |
| Spatio-temporal Feature Chain [6] | 98.04 |
| Proposed Method | 97.6 |

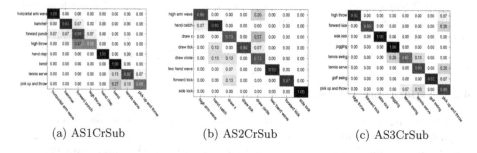

(a) AS1CrSub          (b) AS2CrSub          (c) AS3CrSub

**Fig. 6.** Confusion matrix in AS1, AS2 and AS3 under Cross Subject Test using STFC.

MSR-Action3D AS1, *draw X*, *draw tick*, and *draw circle* in the case of MSRAc-tion3D AS2, and *tennis swing*, *tennis serve*, and *pick up and throw* in the case of MSR-Action3D AS3.

## 5    Conclusions and Future Work

In this paper, we obtain meaningful action-units through take advantage of seg-mentation points. With labeling these action-units, an action can be represented by discrete symbol sequences. To overcome an abrupt change or an abnormal in its gesticulation between different performances of the same action, Profile Hidden Markov Models (Prifile HMMs) are applied with these symbol sequences using Viterbi and Baum-Welch algorithms for human activity recognition. These methods eliminate the noise and the periodic motion problems experienced by methodologies that either solve it only by hand setup or else ignore it. Apply-ing action sequences to Profile HMMs resulted in our approach to significantly outperform other state of the art methods. The next step is to understand and predict human activities and object affordances combining more contextual infor-mation, and more importantly, of human interactions with the objects in the form of associated affordances.

**Acknowledgments.** This work was supported in part by the National Natural Sci-ence Foundation of China under Grant No. 61350110239, the Fundamental Research Funds for the Central Universities under Grant No. K5051203005, the Open Research Funds of State Key Lab. for novel software technology under Grant No.KFKT2012B16, and the Natural Science Foundation of the AnHui Higher Education Institutions of China under Grant No. KJ2014B14.

## References

1. Niebles, J.C., Wang, H., Fei-Fei, L.: Unsupervised learning of human action cat-egories using spatial-temporal words. International Journal of Computer Vision **79**(3), 299–318 (2008)

2. Laptev, I.: On space-time interest points. International Journal of Computer Vision. **64**(2–3), 107–123 (2005)
3. Rabiner, L.R., Juang, B.-H.: Fundamentals of speech recognition, vol. 14. PTR Prentice Hall Englewood Cliffs (1993)
4. Yang, X., Tian, T.: Effective 3d action recognition using eigenjoints. Journal of Visual Communication and Image Representation **25**(1), 2–11 (2014)
5. Krogh, A., Brown, M., Mian, I.S., Sjolander, K., Haussler, D.: Hidden Markov models in computational biology: Applications to protein modeling. Journal of Molecular Biology **235**(5), 1501–1531 (1994)
6. Ding, W., Liu, K., Cheng, F., et al.: STFC: Spatio-temporal feature chain for skeleton-based human action recognition. Journal of Visual Communication and Image Representation **26**, 329–337 (2015)
7. Kohonen, T.: The self-organizing map. Proceedings of the IEEE **78**(9), 1464–1480 (1990)
8. Davies, D.L., Bouldin, D.W.: A cluster separation measure. IEEE Transactions on Pattern Analysis and Machine Intelligence PAMI **1**(2), 224–227 (1979)
9. Poppe, R.: A survey on vision-based human action recognition. Image and Vision Computing **28**(6), 976–990 (2010)
10. Weinland, D., Ronfard, R., Boyer, E.: A survey of vision-based methods for action representation, segmentation and recognition. Computer Vision and Image Understanding **115**(2), 224–241 (2011)
11. Zhang, Z.: Microsoft kinect sensor and its effect. IEEE MultiMedia **19**(2), 4–10 (2012)
12. Li, W., Zhang, Z., Liu, Z.: Action recognition based on a bag of 3d points. In: 2010 IEEE Computer Society Conference on Computer Vision and Pattern Recognition Workshops (CVPRW), pp. 9–14.IEEE (2010)
13. Xia, L., Chen, C.-C., Aggarwal, J.: View invariant human action recognition using histograms of 3d joints. In: 2012 IEEE Computer Society Conference on Computer Vision and Pattern Recognition Workshops (CVPRW), pp. 20–27. IEEE (2012)
14. Lv, F., Nevatia, R.: Single view human action recognition using key pose matching and viterbi path searching. In: 2007 IEEE Conference on Computer Vision and Pattern Recognition, CVPR 2007, pp. 1–8. IEEE (2007)
15. Zhou, F., Torre, F.: Canonical time warping for alignment of human behavior. In: Advances in Neural Information Processing Systems, pp. 2286–2294 (2009)
16. Ferguson, J.D.: Variable duration models for speech. In: Proceedings of the Symposium on the Application of HMMs to Text and Speech, pp. 143–179 (1980)
17. Viterbi, A.J.: Error bounds for convolutional codes and an asymptotically optimum decoding algorithm. IEEE Transactions on Information Theory **13**(2), 260–269 (1967)
18. Baum, L.E., Petrie, T., Soules, G., Weiss, N.: A maximization technique occurring in the statistical analysis of probabilistic functions of Markov chains. The Annals of Mathematical Statistics 164–171 (1970)
19. Ellis, C., Masood, S.Z., Tappen, M.F., Laviola Jr, J.J., Sukthankar, R.: Exploring the trade-off between accuracy and observational latency in action recognition. International Journal of Computer Vision **101**(3), 420–436 (2013)

# Single Image Super-Resolution via Blind Blurring Estimation and Dictionary Learning

Xiaole Zhao[1], Yadong Wu[1(✉)], Jinsha Tian[1], and Hongying Zhang[2]

[1] School of Computer Science and Technology,
Southwest University of Science and Technology, Mianyang, China
wyd028@163.com
[2] School of Information Engineering,
Southwest University of Science and Technology, Mianyang, China

**Abstract.** Learning-based methods have been becoming the mainstream of single image super resolution (SR) technologies. It is effective to generate a high-resolution image from a single low resolution input. However, the quality of training data and the computational demand are two main problems. We propose a novel process framework for single image SR tasks aiming at these two problems, which consists of blur kernel estimation (BKE) and dictionary learning. BKE is utilized for improving the quality of training samples and compatibility between training samples and test samples, which is realized by minimizing the dissimilarity between cross-scale patches iteratively (intuitively be equivalent to maximizing the similarity of cross-scale patches). A selective patch processing (SPP) strategy is adopted in BKE and sparse recovery to reduce the number of patches needed to be processed. The fact that nature images usually contain continuity and discontinuity simultaneously ensures the feasibility of SPP. The experimental results show that our method produces more precise estimation for blurring kernel and better SR effect than several state-of-the-art SR algorithms on equal conditions, but needs much less computation time.

**Keywords:** Super resolution · Non-Local Self-Similarity (NLSS) · Blind Blurring Estimation (BBE) · Dictionary learning

## 1 Introduction

Image super-resolution (SR) is a family of technologies recovering a super-resolved image from a single image or a sequence of images of the same scene. However, it is not easy to obtain an adequate number of LR observations in many practical applications. Therefore, single image super-resolution has attracted great attentions in recent years.

Machine learning based methods are promising technologies for SR problem, and it has become the most popular topic in single image SR field. Freeman et al. [1] proposed example-based learning method firstly. The algorithm predicted HR patches from LR patches by solving Markov Random Field (MRF) model via belief-propagation algorithm. Then, Sun et al. enhanced discontinuous features such as edges and corners etc.

© Springer-Verlag Berlin Heidelberg 2015
H. Zha et al. (Eds.): CCCV 2015, Part I, CCIS 546, pp. 22–33, 2015.
DOI: 10.1007/978-3-662-48558-3_3

by primal sketch priors, which extended example-based method further [2]. To improve execution efficiency, Chang et al. [3] proposed nearest neighbor embedding (NNE) method motivated by the philosophy of locally linear embedding (LLE) [4]. They assumed LR patches and HR patches have similar space structure. The coefficients of LR patch can be solved through least square problem, which are then applied to HR patches directly. NNE utilizes a few of training data to represent a test sample and reduces the computation time dramatically. However, fixed number of NNs may cause over-fitting and/or under-fitting phenomenon [5]. Aiming at this problem, Yang et al. [6] proposed an effective method based on sparse representation, which selects the number of NNs adaptively. However, there exist two main issues about original sparse representation methods: the compatibility between training samples and test samples, and the mapping relation between LR patch space and HR patch space. More recently, Glasner et al. [7] exploited image patch non-local self-similarity within image scale and cross-scale for single image SR tasks, which makes an effective solution for the compatibility problem between training samples and test samples. As for the mapping relation, LR patch space and HR patch space are tied by some mapping function, which could be unknown and not necessarily linear [8]. The direct mapping [6] actually could not reflect this unknown relation correctly. Yang et al. [9] proposed another joint dictionary training approach to learn the duality relation between LR/HR patch spaces. The method essentially concatenated the two patch spaces and converts the problem to the standard sparse representation in a single feature space. Further, they explicitly learned the sparse coding problem across different feature spaces. The learning problem was modeled as a bilevel optimization problem, where the optimization included an $L_1$ norm minimization problem in its constraints. This is the so-called coupled dictionary learning (CDL) [8] algorithm.

The precision of the training data and the computational time demanding are two main challenges of current single image SR algorithms. The performance of SR methods significantly deteriorates when the blur kernel we used deviates from the true one [10]. To ensure the precision of the training data, it is necessary to estimate the true blue kernel from the input image itself. But abundant samples and iterations make it very time-consuming. In addition, solving a $L_0/L_1$ norm constrained optimization problem for test samples is also computationally demanding. In this paper, we present a novel single image SR method considering both SR effect and the acceleration for the algorithm. The proposed approach estimated the true blur kernel based on minimizing the dissimilarity between cross-scale patches firstly. Then, LR/HR coupled dictionaries were trained through input image downsampled by estimated blur kernel, which improved the quality of training samples and compatibility between training set and test set. A SPP strategy is employed both in blur estimation and SR recovery stage, which is based on the observation that nature images usually consist of continuity and discontinuity concurrently, and traditional interpolation methods (such as bicubic and cubic convolution interpolation) have a higher efficiency but perform on par with learning based methods in smooth area.

# 2      Related Work

## 2.1      Internal Statistics and Blur Kernel Estimation

One of the most useful internal statistical attributes of natural image patches is the patch recurrence within and cross scale, which is exploited by Glasner et al. in 2009 [7]. NLSS can be exploited as useful prior knowledge for various image restoration tasks, such as super resolution [7, 12-15], image denoising [16], deblurring [17] and inpainting [18] etc. However, it is not necessary to consider the redundancy of all patches most of the time. Maria et al. [12] quantified the property by relating it to the spatial distance from the patch and the mean gradient magnitude |grad| of the patch. Tomer Michaeli et al. [10] utilizes the non-local self-similarity to estimate the optimal blur kernel, which maximizes the cross-scale patch redundancy iteratively. For each small patch in input image, they find a few NNs in down-sampled version of input image and each NN for the small patch corresponds to a large patch in input image. All the patch pairs construct a set of linear equations which is solved using weighted least-squares to obtain an updated kernel. Fig.1 (a) shows the cross-scale blur kernel estimation process.

Actually, the method of [10] is designed to solve a convolution kernel, which makes cross-scale patch as redundant as possible. It could be interpreted as maximum a posteriori (MAP) estimation process. However, as we can see in Fig.1 (b) and Fig.1 (c), the effect of blurring in smooth area is unconspicuous. Therefore, smooth patch almost contributes nothing in blur kernel estimation with respect to structured patch.

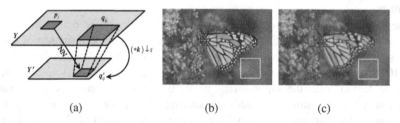

$$\text{(a)} \qquad\qquad\qquad \text{(b)} \qquad\qquad\qquad \text{(c)}$$

**Fig. 1.** Descriptions of cross-scale patch redundancy and blurring effect on different patches in natural images. (a) Cross-scale patch redundancy (see context), where $k$ is blurring kernel. (b) Structured patch and smooth patch in clean "Monarch". (c) Structured patch and smooth patch in blurred "Monarch". (c) The result of convolving (b) with a $11 \times 11$ Gaussian kernel with $\sigma = 1.5$. Obviously, Red structured patch is very different after blurring with Gaussian kernel, whereas yellow smooth patch almost do not changes visually.

## 2.2      Coupled Dictionary Learning

In SR tasks, HR feature space $\mathcal{F}_H$ and LR feature space $\mathcal{F}_L$ constitute the coupled feature space together. There exists a certain unknown relation $\mathcal{M}: \mathcal{F}_L \to \mathcal{F}_H$ between two feature spaces. For some specific feature $x \in \mathcal{F}_H$ and $y \in \mathcal{F}_L$, we have $x = \mathcal{M}(y)$. The goal for coupled dictionary learning is to find a coupled dictionary pair $D_H$ and $D_L$ for feature space $\mathcal{F}_H$ and $\mathcal{F}_L$ respectively, so that we can use the sparse representation of any test signal $y \in \mathcal{F}_L$ in terms of $D_L$ to recover the corresponding latent HR signal $x \in \mathcal{F}_H$ in terms of $D_H$ directly. Under the condition of $L_1$ norm, it can be expressed as following equations for any coupled signal pair formally:

$$\boldsymbol{\pi}_i = \arg\min_{\alpha_i} \left\| y_i - D_L\alpha_i \right\|_2^2 + \lambda \left\| \alpha_i \right\|_1, \quad \forall i = 1,\ldots,N_L \tag{1}$$

$$\boldsymbol{\pi}_i = \arg\min_{\alpha_i} \left\| x_i - D_H\alpha_i \right\|_2^2, \qquad \forall i = 1,\ldots,N_H \tag{2}$$

where $\boldsymbol{\pi} = \{\boldsymbol{\pi}_i \mid i = 1,2,\ldots,N_H\}$ is the set of sparse representation on coupled feature spaces. $N_L$ and $N_H$ are the numbers of atom in $D_L$ and $D_H$ respectively. $\alpha_i$ is the sparse representation coefficient vector for the $i$th signal pair, and $\lambda$ is the regularization parameter as tradeoff between the reconstruction error and the $L_1$ norm regularization terms. To balance the reconstruction error on observation feature space and latent feature space, CDL algorithm changes the objective function of [8]:

$$\arg\min_{D_H,D_L,\pi} \sum_{i=1}^{N_H} \left( \left\| D_H\alpha_i - x_i \right\|_2^2 + \left\| D_L\alpha_i - y_i \right\|_2^2 + \lambda \left\| \alpha_i \right\|_1 \right) \quad \text{s.t.} \ \left\| D_H(:,i) \right\|_2 \le 1, \ \left\| D_L(:,i) \right\|_2 \le 1 \tag{3}$$

to the following form:

$$\arg\min_{D_H,D_L,\pi} \sum_{i=1}^{N_H} \frac{1}{2} \left( \gamma \left\| D_H\alpha_i - x_i \right\|_2^2 + (1-\gamma) \left\| D_L\alpha_i - y_i \right\|_2^2 \right) \quad \text{s.t.} \ \left\| D_H(:,i) \right\|_2 \le 1, \ \left\| D_L(:,i) \right\|_2 \le 1 \tag{4}$$

where $\gamma$ is the parameter balancing the reconstruction error terms on both feature spaces. Eqn. (4) is solved by alternatively optimizing over $D_L$ and $D_H$ while keeping the other fixed. Stochastic gradient descent using implicit differentiation is employed to solve $D_L$ during the iterative process.

## 3    Proposed Approach

### 3.1    Blind Kernel Estimation with SPP

We use $Y$ to represent input LR image, and $X$ to be latent HR image. For each small patch $p_i$ in the input image $Y$, we can find a few NNs $q_{ij}^s$ for it in down-sampled version $y^s$. The "parent" patches $q_{ij}$ right above $q_{ij}^s$ are viewed as the candidate parent patches of $p_i$. The patch pairs $\{p_i, q_{ij}\}$ are used to construct a set of linear equations, which is solved by weighted least square method. According to [10], the weight of each "parent" patch is calculated by the following formula, so that good NNs contribute more than their poor counterparts:

$$w_{ij} = \frac{\exp\left(-\left\|p_i - q_{ij}^s\right\|^2 / \sigma^2\right)}{\sum_{j=1}^{M_i} \exp\left(-\left\|p_i - q_{ij}^s\right\|^2 / \sigma^2\right)} \tag{5}$$

where $M_i$ is the number of NNs of each small patch $p_i$ in $Y$. $\sigma$ is the standard deviation of noise added on $p_i$, and $s$ is scale factor. Note that we apply the same symbol to express column vector corresponding to the patch. Maximizing the cross-scale NLSS of $Y$ with respect to scale factor s is equivalent to minimizing the dissimilarity between cross-scale patches. Therefore, we solve the following L$_2$ norm optimization problem for BKE:

$$\arg\min_k \sum_{i=1}^{N} \left\| p_i - \sum_{j=1}^{M_i} w_{ij} R_{ij} \, k \right\|_2^2 + \lambda \|Ck\|_2^2 \tag{6}$$

where $N$ is the number of small patches in $Y$. Matrix $R_{ij}$ corresponds to the operation of convolving with $q_{ij}$ and down sampling by $s$. $C$ is a matrix used as the penalty of non-smooth kernel. The second term of Eqn. (6) is kernel prior and $\lambda$ is the balance parameter as the tradeoff between the error term and kernel prior. By setting the gradient of the objective function in Eqn. (6) to zero, we can get the update formula of $k$:

$$\hat{k} = \left( \sum_{i=1}^{N} \sum_{j=1}^{M_i} w_{ij} R_{ij}^T R_{ij} + \lambda C^T C \right)^{-1} \cdot \sum_{i=1}^{N} \sum_{j=1}^{M_i} w_{ij} R_{ij}^T p_i \tag{7}$$

This is similar to the result of [10], which can be interpreted as maximum a posteriori (MAP) estimation on $k$. However, our blur kernel estimation has two essential differentials with respect to [10]. Firstly, our method is driven by the idea of minimizing the dissimilarity between cross-scale patches while [10] tends to maximize the similarity directly. Secondly, the number of NNs of each small patch is not fixed which provides more flexibility during solving least square problem. Therefore, the terminal criterion cannot be the totality of NNs. We use the average patch dissimilarity (APD) as terminal condition of iteration:

$$\text{APD} = \left( \sum_{i=1}^{N} \sum_{j=1}^{M_i} \left\| p_i - q_{ij}^s \right\|_2^2 \right) \cdot \left( \sum_{i=1}^{N} M_i \right)^{-1} \tag{8}$$

To eliminate the effect on BKE caused by smooth patches, we selectively employ structured patches to calculate blur kernel (see Fig.1) according to the average gradient magnitude |grad| of a small patch. Specifically, with removing DC component, if the average gradient magnitude |grad| of each query patch is smaller than a threshold, then we abandon it. Otherwise, we use it to estimate blur kernel according to Eqn. (7). According to the research of [12], finding NNs for structured patches requires larger search region. We need to perform search in entire image here.

## 3.2    SR Recovery

We assume $y_p$ is a LR patch which contains original image data, $y$ is LR patch feature extracting from $y_p$. We solve $L_1$ norm constrained optimization problem:

$$\arg\min_{\alpha} \|y - D_L\alpha\|_2^2 + \mu\|\alpha\|_1 \tag{9}$$

where $\mu$ allows alleviating the ill-posed problems and stabilizes the solution. $y$ corresponds to a test LR patch extracted from enhanced interpolation version of input image. $D_L$ is the LR dictionary trained by CDL. The solution of Eqn. (9) is found by solving a $L_1$-regularized Lasso problem. This can be done by Sparse Learning with Efficient Projections (SLEP) [20]. After we get the coefficient vector $\alpha$ of LR patch feature vector $y$, HR patch feature then can be computed directly by:

$$x = \frac{D_H\alpha}{\|D_H\alpha\|_2} \tag{10}$$

where $D_H$ is the HR dictionary trained by CDL. Then, Recovery HR image patch $x_p$ can be obtained by:

$$x_p = (c\times u)\cdot x + v \tag{11}$$

where

$$u = \text{Mean}(y_p), \text{ and } v = \|y_p - u\|_2$$

Here $c$ is a constant. Generally, there are two directions to accelerate the SR process: reducing the number of patches to process and finding a fast solver for $L_1$ norm minimization problem Eqn. (1). A selective patch process strategy is adopted in our method as [8]. However, the criterion of selecting patches is the gradient magnitude |grad| instead of the variance of a patch for the spatial gradient magnitude of a patch is more expressive than variance when removing mean according to [12]. Thus, if the spatial gradient magnitude of a patch is smaller than a threshold, we simply apply bicubic interpolation for SR recovery. Otherwise, we employ sparse representation method to estimate HR image patch.

## 4    Experimental Results

In this section, we give some experimental results about blur kernel estimation and SR recovery. All the experiments are performed on a Philips PC with 8.0 GB memory and running a single core of Intel Xeon 2.53 GHz CPU. We mainly compare our blur kernel estimation method with [10] in terms of kernel accuracy and efficiency, while SR performance is compared with several state-of-the-art SR algorithms.

## 4.1    Comparisons for BKE

We performed $\times 2$ and $\times 3$ SR in our experiments on BKE. When scale factor $s = 2$, we set the size of small query patches $p_i$ and candidate patches $q_{ij}^s$ of NNs to $5 \times 5$, while the size of "parent" patches $q_{ij}$ are set to $9 \times 9$. Both $p_i$ and $q_{ij}^s$ do not change size, but "parent" patches are set to be $13 \times 13$ patches when perform $\times 3$ SR. Noise standard deviation $\sigma$ is assumed to be 5. Parameter $\lambda$ in equation (6) is set to 0.25, and matrix $C$ is chosen to be the derivative matrix corresponding to $x$ and $y$ directions of "parent" patches. The threshold of |grad| for selecting query patches is set to 10. Fig. 2 shows the structured parts used to perform BKE, and the blur kernels of "Monarch" and "Flower". It can be cleanly seen that input data are seriously blurred and inaccurate. Besides, there is only a few part of original image data that can used for BKE due to selective patch processing.

Firstly, we present the BKE results estimated from "Monarch" and "Flower" in Fig. 3 to illustrate the accuracy of the recovered kernel qualitatively. As shown, both algorithms can estimate the rough shape of the ground-truth kernel, but our approach gives more accurate results on both kernel size and shape. This is true especially when the ground-truth one is motion kernel. On the one hand, our blurring kernel estimation does not take fixed number of NNs for each query patch in LR images. This makes

(a)                                                    (b)

**Fig. 2.** Blurring on original images and selective patch process in BKE. (a) The first one is gray "Monarch" image blurred by a $9 \times 9$ Gaussian kernel with standard deviation $\sigma = 1.5$, the second one is structured content selected to estimate blur kernel. (b) The first image is gray "Flower" image blurred by a $9 \times 9$ "motion" kernel with len = 5 and theta = 45, the second one is same as top row.

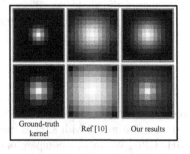 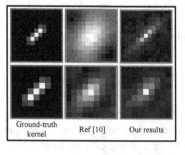

(a) Gaussian estimation                    (b) Motion estimation

**Fig. 3.** BKE Comparisons with [10]. (a) Gaussian kernel estimation with "Monarch" image showed in Fig.2. (b) Motion kernel estimation with "Flower" image showed in Fig.2. The size of kernel in first row is $13 \times 13$, the second row is $9 \times 9$.

BKE more flexible, and reduces the adverse impact caused by over-fitting or/and under-fitting. On the other hand, Selective patch processing strategy measured by the average gradient amplitude |grad| abandoned useless smooth patches and kept more structured non-smooth patches, which relieved the computational demanding for CPUs significantly.

We collect the average MSE of each NN during iterations as shown in Fig4 (a). Though we selectively use structured patches to estimate blur kernels, the average MSE of our algorithm still smaller than [10]. This is mainly attributed to that we employ unfixed number of NNs to construct the set of linear equations. As we can see in Fig. 4 (a), our BKE method converges about 8th iteration, whereas the algorithm of [10] converges at almost 15th iteration. After the convergence of algorithms, the average MSE between cross-scale patches of our algorithm is also smaller than Michaeli's algorithm. Therefore, the selective patch process and adaptive number of NNs produce more accurate BKE results, but need less iteration times.

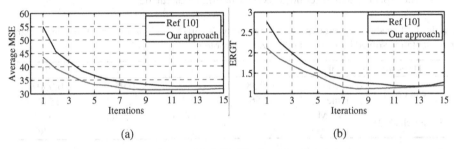

(a)                                                            (b)

**Fig. 4.** BKE efficiency Comparisons with [10]. SR algorithm is original sparse representation proposed by Yang et al. [6]. (a) The attenuation of average MSE. (b) The change of ERGT as presented in [10].

We apply the same measures with [10] to compare the effect of estimated kernels on SR algorithms: The Error Ratio to Ground Truth (ERGT), which measures the ratio between the SR reconstruction error with estimated kernels and the SR reconstruction error with the ground-truth one

$$\text{ERGT} = \frac{\| X - \overline{X}_{\hat{k}} \|_2}{\| X - \overline{X}_k \|_2} \tag{12}$$

where $\overline{X}_{\hat{k}}$ and $\overline{X}_k$ are the recovered HR images with estimated kernel $\hat{k}$ and ground-truth kernel $k$ respectively. If ERGT is close to 1, it indicates that the estimated kernel is nearly as good as the ground-truth kernel. Fig. 4 (b) shows the results of applying both estimated kernels in the SR algorithm proposed by Yang et al. [6]. Here, we super resolve all the five test images with scale factor $s = 2$, and collect the average ERGT at each iteration. In the whole iterative process, the ERGT of our algorithm is always closer to 1 than [10].

Table 1 presents the effects of thresholding on SR recovery accuracy and processing time with sparse representation solved by $L_1$ norm minimization problem. Instead of simply using the variance of a small patch as the criterion of patch selection, we adopted average gradient magnitude |grad| presented in [12] to filter smooth patches. As showed in table 1, with the increase of the threshold of |grad|, the consumed time decreases rapidly whereas SSIM reduces slightly. Table 2 shows the time statistics of several methods consumed in reconstruction. We use bicubic interpolation as reference and assume its time consumption is 0 for each case. Because of selective patch processing, our method provides the least amount of time consumption.

Table 3 shows PSNR and SSIM comparisons between the proposed method and several state-of-the-art SR algorithms on equal conditions. The most important equivalent condition is all input images for each algorithm are obtained by clean images blurred with default blur kernels, which is also very different from current general experimental methodologies. Our approach brings big improvement over PSNR and SSIM. Actually, this is mainly due to that our BKE process aimed directly at counteracting the blurring effect during degeneration of natural images. Moreover, the coupled dictionary learning [8] gives us accurate mapping relation between LR and HR feature spaces, which reduces reconstruction error further.

**Table 1.** Thresholding effects on SR recovery accuracy and processing time with sparse representation solved by $L_1$ norm optimization problem

| Thresholds on |grad| | | 0 | 10 | 20 | 30 |
|---|---|---|---|---|---|
| Lena (× 2) | SSIM | 0.9538 | 0.9527 | 0.9514 | 0.9507 |
| | Time (s) | 53.56 | 44.25 | 27.74 | 15.67 |
| Monarch (× 2) | SSIM | 0.9428 | 0.9415 | 0.9405 | 0.9386 |
| | Time (s) | 63.78 | 41.13 | 22.87 | 11.86 |

**Table 2.** Computation comparisons between several typical methods and proposed algorithm (threshold on |grad| is 15)

| Test images | Bicubic (s) | Yang et al. [6] (s) | Zeyde et al. [19] (s) | Ours (s) |
|---|---|---|---|---|
| Baboon | 0 | 86.49 | 56.81 | 36.54 |
| Flower | 0 | 34.60 | 38.62 | 23.03 |
| Lena | 0 | 79.04 | 53.72 | 32.82 |
| Monarch | 0 | 38.91 | 57.82 | 24.71 |
| Tower | 0 | 41.19 | 24.46 | 17.05 |

**Table 3.** SR comparisons between several state-of-the-art methods and proposed algorithm (threshold on |grad| is 15)

| No. | scale | Yang et al. [6] | | Zeyde et al. [19] | | Timofte et al. [11] | | Our results | |
|---|---|---|---|---|---|---|---|---|---|
| | | PSNR | SSIM | PSNR | SSIM | PSNR | SSIM | PSNR | SSIM |
| 1 | × 2 | 30.2146 | 0.9083 | 30.3194 | 0.9152 | 30.3491 | 0.9127 | **30.5430** | **0.9335** |
| 2 | × 2 | 32.7452 | 0.9361 | 32.7342 | 0.9368 | 32.7703 | 0.9376 | **33.1741** | **0.9496** |
| 3 | × 3 | 28.9768 | 0.8935 | 29.3156 | 0.8994 | 29.3036 | 0.8967 | **29.8251** | **0.9163** |
| 4 | × 3 | 28.3827 | 0.8921 | 28.3294 | 0.8954 | 28.3278 | 0.8917 | **29.0495** | **0.9083** |
| 5 | × 3 | 27.1774 | 0.8618 | 27.3329 | 0.8574 | 27.3863 | 0.8613 | **28.6172** | **0.8853** |

The number of test images: 1. Baboon; 2. Flower; 3. Lena; 4. Monarch; 5. Tower

Fig.5 shows some visual comparisons of SR reconstruction between our algorithm and several state-of-the-art SR algorithms proposed recently. For layout purpose, all images are diminished when inserted in the paper. Note that the input images of all algorithms are obtained through reference images blurring with several blur kernel. Namely, input image data is set to be of low quality via some blur kernels in our experiments for the sake of simulating many actual application scenarios. When down-sampling blurred input images with kernels before SR reconstruction, all of the algorithms adopted bicubic kernel to simulate the degradation of input images, whereas our method employed the results of BKE. Though it is well known that the three SR algorithms presented in Fig.5 are efficient for many SR tasks, they fail to reconstruct distinct details when test images are degenerated severely. This is mainly because of the great deviation between the blurring kernel used by these algorithms and the ground-truth one.

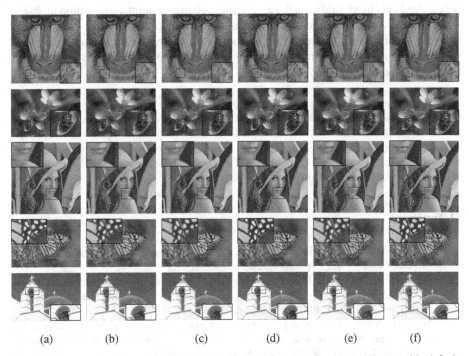

(a)    (b)    (c)    (d)    (e)    (f)

**Fig. 5.** SR reconstruction comparisons. (a). reference images. (b). blurred input with default kernels. (c). Yang et al. [6]. (d). Zeyde et al. [19]. (e). Timofte et al. [11]. (f). our results. Note that input images are obtained by blurring original clean images with different blur kernels for test purpose. (c), (d) and (e) adopted bicubic kernel to down-sample input images while our method employed estimated kernel. Ground-truth kernels: top row ($\times 2$) is $9 \times 9$ Gaussian kernel with $\sigma = 1.5$; the second row ($\times 2$) is $9 \times 9$ motion kernel with len = 5 and theta = 45; the third row ($\times 3$) is $13 \times 13$ Gaussian kernel with $\sigma = 1.5$; the fourth row ($\times 3$) is $11 \times 11$ Gaussian kernel with $\sigma = 1.5$ and the last row ($\times 3$) is $13 \times 13$ motion kernel with len = 5 and theta = 45.

## 5    Conclusion

We proposed a novel single image SR framework aiming at improving the SR effect and time performance in this paper. The algorithm framework mainly contains blur kernel estimation and SR recovery based on CDL. The former is realized by minimizing dissimilarity of cross-scale image patches, which is slightly similar to the $MAP_k$ estimation approach proposed by Michaeli et al. [10]. The latter relies on a coupled dictionary learning process [8]. The selective patch processing utilized in these two stages is dependent on the criterion of average gradient amplitude. The SR effect of our method is guaranteed by improving the quality of training samples. The SPP strategy has ensured the improvement of time performance via reducing the number of query patches. All above-mentioned processes make our SR algorithm could achieve the better level of performance than several typical SR approaches. However, we can find out, from Table 1 and Table 2, that solving $L_1$ norm optimization problem when reconstructing is extraordinarily time-consuming. SPP should not be the single and final solution for efficiency improvement. Therefore, our further research work will be finding out other better methods for improving the SR effect and reducing the time consumption of the algorithm further.

**Acknowledgment.** This work is partially supported by National Natural Science Foundation of China (Grant No. 61303127), Western Light Talent Culture Project of Chinese Academy of Sciences (Grant No.13ZS0106), Project of Science and Technology Department of Sichuan Province (Grant Nos.2014SZ0223, 2015GZ0212), Key Program of Education Department of Sichuan Province (Grant Nos.11ZA130, 13ZA0169), and the innovation funds of Southwest University of Science and Technology (Grant No. 15ycx053).

## References

1. Freeman, W.T., Jones, T.R., Pasztor, E.C.: Example-Based Super-Resolution. J. IEEE Computer Graphics and Applications **22**(2), 56–65 (2002)
2. Sun, J., Zheng, N.N., Tao, H., Shum, H.Y.: Image hallucination with primal sketch priors. In: 2003 IEEE Computer Society Conference on Computer Vision and Pattern Recognition (CVPR), pp. 729–736. IEEE Press, Monona (2003)
3. Chang, H., Yeung, D.Y., Xiong, Y.: Super-resolution through neighbor embedding. In: IEEE Computer Society Conference on Computer Vision and Pattern Recognition (CVPR), pp. 275–282. IEEE Press, Washington DC (2004)
4. Roweis, S., Saul, L.: Nonlinear Dimensionality Reduction by Locally Linear Embedding. J. Science **290**(5500), 2323–2326 (2000)
5. Bevilacqua, M., Roumy, A., Guillemot, C., Alberi-Morel, M.: Low-complexity single-image super-resolution based on nonnegative neighbor embedding. In: 23rd British Machine Vision Conference (BMVC), Guildford, pp. 1–10 (2012)
6. Yang, J.C., Wright, J., Huang, T., Ma, Y.: Image super-resolution as sparse representation of raw image patches. In: IEEE Conference on Computer Vision and Pattern Recognition (CVPR), pp. 1–8. IEEE Press, Anchorage (2008)
7. Glasner, D., Bagon, S., Irani, M.: Super-resolution from a single image. In: IEEE Conference on Computer Vision, pp. 349–356. IEEE Press, Kyoto (2009)

8. Yang, J.C., Wang, Z.W., Lin, Z., Cohen, S., Huang, T.: Coupled Dictionary Training for Image Super-Resolution. J. IEEE Transaction on Image Processing **21**(8), 3467–3478 (2012)

9. Yang, J.C., Wright, J., Huang, T.S., Ma, Y.: Image Super-Resolution via Sparse Representation. J. IEEE Transactions on Image Processing **19**(11), 2861–2873 (2010)

10. Michaeli, T., Irani, M.: Nonparametric blind super-resolution. In: 2013 IEEE International Conference on Computer Vision (ICCV), pp. 945–952. IEEE Press, Sydney (2013)

11. Timofte, R., Smet, V.D., Gool, L.V.: Anchored neighborhood regression for fast example-based super-resolution. In: 2013 IEEE International Conference on Computer Vision (ICCV), pp. 1920–1927. IEEE Press, Sydney (2013)

12. Zontak, M., Irani, M.: Internal statistics of a single natural image. In: IEEE Conference on Computer Vision and Pattern Recognition (CVPR), pp. 977–984. IEEE Press, Providence (2011)

13. Yang, C.Y., Huang, J.B., Yang, M.H.: Exploiting self-similarities for single frame super-resolution. In: The 10th Asian Conference on Computer Vision, pp. 497–510. IEEE Press, Queenstown (2010)

14. Zoran, D., Weiss, Y.: from learning models of natural image patches to whole image restoration. In: 2011 IEEE International Conference on Computer Vision (ICCV), pp. 479–486. IEEE Press, Barcelona (2011)

15. Hu, J., Luo, Y.P.: Single-Image Super-Resolution Based on Local Regression and Non-Local Self-Similarity. Journal of Electronic Imaging **23**(3), 033014 (2014)

16. Zhang, Y.Q., Liu, J.Y., Yang, S., Guo, Z.M.: Joint image denoising using self-similarity based low-rank approximations. In: Visual Communications and Image Processing (VCIP), pp. 1–6. IEEE Press, Kuhing (2013)

17. Michaeli, T., Irani, M.: Blind deblurring using Internal patch recurrence. In: Fleet, D., Pajdla, T., Schiele, B., Tuytelaars, T. (eds.) ECCV 2014, Part III. LNCS, vol. 8691, pp. 783–798. Springer, Heidelberg (2014)

18. Guillemot, C., Meur, O.L.: Image Inpainting: Overview and Recent Advances. J. Signal Processing Magazine **31**(1), 127–144 (2014)

19. Zeyde, R., Elad, M., Protter, M.: On single image scale-up using sparse-representations. In: Boissonnat, J.-D., Chenin, P., Cohen, A., Gout, C., Lyche, T., Mazure, M.-L., Schumaker, L. (eds.) Curves and Surfaces 2011. LNCS, vol. 6920, pp. 711–730. Springer, Heidelberg (2012)

20. Liu, J., Ji, S., Ye, J.: SLEP: Sparse Learning with Efficient Projections. http://www.yelab.net/software/SLEP/

# Two-Layers Local Coordinate Coding

Wei Xiao[1]([✉]), Hong Liu[1], Hao Tang[1], and Huaping Liu[2]

[1] Engineering Lab on Intelligent Perception for Internet of Things (ELIP),
Key Laboratory for Machine Perception, Shenzhen Graduate School,
Peking University, Beijing, China
`xiaoweithu@163.com`
[2] State Key Laboratory of Intelligent Technology and Systems,
Department of Computer Science and Technology,
Tsinghua University, Beijing, China

**Abstract.** Extracting informative regularized representations of input signals plays a key role in the field of artificial intelligence, such as machine learning and robotics. Traditional approaches feature $\ell_2$ norm and sparse inducing $\ell_p$ norm ($0 \leq p \leq 1$) based optimization methods, imposing strict regularization on the representations. However, these approaches overlook the fact that signals and atoms in the overcomplete dictionaries usually contain such wealth of structural information that could improves representations. This paper systematically exploits data manifold geometric structure where signals and atoms reside in, and thus presents a principled extension of sparse coding, i.e. two-layers local coordinate coding, which demonstrates a high dimensional nonlinear function could be locally approximated by a global linear function with quadratic approximation power. Moreover, to learn each latent layer, corresponding patterned optimization approaches are developed, encoding distance information between signals and atoms into the representations. Experimental results demonstrate the significance of this extension on improving the image classification performance and its potential applications for object recognition in robot system are also exploited.

**Keywords:** Local coordinate coding · Machine learning · Sparse coding · Robotics

## 1 Introduction

Recent years have witnessed a fast growing interest in the research on sparse representations of signals with overcomplete dictionaries. Scholars from various research fields promote the progress, such as, Donoho from the statistics community [1], Elad from the machine learning community[2], and Kouskouridas from the robotics community[3], etc. Recent theoretical analyses observed that sparse

This work is supported by National Natural Science Foundation of China (NSFC, No. 61340046), National High Technology Research and Development Program of China (863 Program, No. 2006AA04Z247), Scientific and Technical Innovation Commission of Shenzhen Municipality (No. JCYJ20130331144631730).

H. Zha et al. (Eds.): CCCV 2015, Part I, CCIS 546, pp. 34–45, 2015.
DOI: 10.1007/978-3-662-48558-3_4

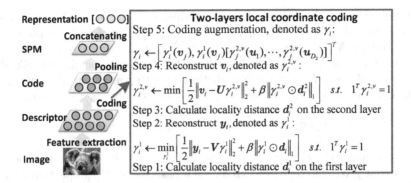

**Fig. 1.** Left: The traditional image representation pipeline. Right: the proposed two-layers local coordinate coding.

representation could be extended to "local" representation: nonzero coefficients are often assigned to atoms nearby to the encoded point [4–6]. An extension to sparse representation, called Local Coordinate Coding (LCC) is thus proposed, which learns a nonliear function in high dimension by forming a set of local bases on the data manifold. The nonlinear function approximation view of sparse representation not only brings about in-depth understanding of its fundamental connotation and success, but also provides opportunities to get a deeper insight into its parentage ties with the essence – locality.

This paper follows these lines of research, and scratches the surface of its utilization potential in computer vision and robotics, where we try to make a principled extension of the traditional single-layer coding to a more generalized two-layers local representation problem, called Two-layers Local Coordinate Coding (Two-layers LCC). This coding strategy takes advantage of the underlying data manifold geometric structure to locally embed points on the manifold into a lower dimensional two-layers structure, see Figure 1. Therefore, Two-layers LCC turns a very difficult high dimensional nonlinear learning problem into a simpler linear learning problem, which could be effectively solved using for instance, $\ell_1$ optimization. More important, it could achieve higher approximation power than its single-layer counterpart, especially in the situation of fewer or noise-polluted training samples, see theoretical analysis in Section 3.

The remainder of this paper is organized as follows: Section 2 surveys the evolution of related coding strategies. And Section 3 makes a theoretical introduction into the Two-layers LCC. Accordingly, specific coding formulations to each layer are proposed in Section 4. Experimental evaluations on popular benchmarks and a practical application in robotics are presented in Section 5 and conclusions are drawn in Section 6.

## 2   Prior Art

This section provides a brief review to help comprehend the underlying relationship between sparsity and locality.

One of popular extensions of sparse coding is LLC [5,7], which supposes that although signals $Y = [y_1, y_2, \cdots, y_N] = \{y_i\}_{i=1}^N$, $y_i \in \mathbb{R}^m$ are physically represented by $X = [x_1, x_2, \cdots, x_N] = \{x_i\}_{i=1}^N$, $x_i \in \mathbb{R}^p$, where $p \gg m$, they often lie on a manifold with a much smaller intrinsic dimensionality. Specifically, let $D = [d_1, d_2, \cdots, d_p] \in \mathbb{R}^{m \times p}$ be a dictionary with $p$ atoms in $\mathbb{R}^m$, for signals $Y$, the corresponding LLC representations $X$, can be obtained by solving:

$$\min_x [\sum_{i=1}^N \|y_i - Dx_i\|_2^2 + \lambda \|b_i \odot x_i\|_2^2] \quad s.t. \quad \mathbf{1}^\mathsf{T} x_i = 1, \tag{1}$$

where $\odot$ denotes the element-wise multiplication, and $b_i \in \mathbb{R}^p$ is the locality adaptor that gives different freedom for each basis vector $d_j$ proportional to its similarity of the input descriptor $y_i$. Specifically,

$$b_i = \exp(\frac{dist(y_i, D)}{\sigma}), \tag{2}$$

where $dist(y_i, D) = [dist(y_i, d_1), \cdots, dist(y_i, d_p)]^\mathsf{T}$, and $dist(.,.)$ is the Euclidean distance, and $\sigma$ is used for adjusting weight decay speed for locality.

Diverse representation strategies mentioned above can essentially be interpreted as taking fully advantages of infinitely many possible solutions $x$ to the underdetermined systems of equation $y = Dx$ with different regularization terms to finally find a solo solution with desired suitable form. Compared with sparse coding, local coding can achieve: (i) more accurate correlations capturing and (ii) local smooth sparsity. For instance, the LLC can catch atoms structure of manifold where the signals reside in, and further use these atoms for coding; while sparse coding only pursues the solo goal, as sparse as possible in the final representation, as in the extreme case of sparse coding, i.e. vector quantization, only a few of atoms without structure would be selected. Similar to sparse coding, the LLC has achieve less reconstruction error by using multiple atoms [7], overcoming the shortcoming that sparse-inducing regularization terms are not smooth, thus provide incoherent atoms for similar signals to favor sparsity, losing correlations between codes.

However, LLC has a major disadvantage. In order to achieve higher approximation, one has to use a large number of so-called "anchor points", i.e. atoms close to the signal, to describe these signals. Finding enough powerful anchor points plays a key role in the representation pipeline. Unfortunately these anchor points are vulnerable to noise and inadequate training samples, and some of them are not necessarily have powerful descriptive ability. Therefore, it is eager to equip them with more descriptive power for better approximating $y_i$ in order to guarantee accurate inferences from it. Shall we fix it or frankly speaking, fully explore the potential of the manifold to empower the anchors to better describe $y_i$? The following section will give the answer.

## 3   Two-Layers Local Coordinate Coding

Let's first consider the problem of learning a nonlinear function $f(y)$ defined on a high dimensional space: $\mathbb{R}^m$, with large $m$. We have sampled this underlying distribution and obtained a set of labeled data: $(\boldsymbol{y}_1, l_1), \cdots, (\boldsymbol{y}_n, l_n)$. There are a lot of approaches to learn such a function in low dimension, while many of them are more or less suffer from the so-called "curse of dimensionality". One of intuitive explanation is since we do not have enough expressive data, i.e., $m \gg n$, it is hard to fully describe how this nonlinear function would appear in $\mathbb{R}^m$. One would argue, if we obtain more data points than $n$? While it is still hard due to the redundancy of the data. However, the good news is, in many real applications with high dimensionality, we do not observe this so-called curse of dimensionality, this is because although data are physically represented in a high dimensional space, they often lie on a manifold which has a much smaller intrinsic dimensionality [4,6]. That is, many areas of this space are empty, or viewed empty.

The recent coding approach called LCC in [4] addresses this issue, which turns a difficult high dimensional nonlinear learning problem into a linear learning problem. While, its approximation accuracy is vulnerable to the limited anchor points, where this paper systematically makes effort to equip them with more descriptive power.

### 3.1  Lipschitz Smoothness

This section reviews the Lipschitz smoothness for further analysis of two-layers representation.

**Definition 1 (Lipschitz Smoothness).** *A function $f(\boldsymbol{y})$ on $\mathbb{R}^m$ is $(\alpha, \beta, \upsilon)$ Lipschitz smoothness with respect to a norm $\|\cdot\|$, if*

$$\begin{cases} |f(\boldsymbol{y}') - f(\boldsymbol{y})| \le \alpha \|\boldsymbol{y}' - \boldsymbol{y}\|, & (3) \\ |f(\boldsymbol{y}') - f(\boldsymbol{y}) - \nabla f(\boldsymbol{y})^T (\boldsymbol{y}' - \boldsymbol{y})| \le \beta \|\boldsymbol{y}' - \boldsymbol{y}\|^2, & (4) \\ |f(\boldsymbol{y}') - f(\boldsymbol{y}) - 0.5(\nabla f(\boldsymbol{y})^T + \nabla f(\boldsymbol{y}')^T)(\boldsymbol{y}' - \boldsymbol{y})| \le \upsilon \|\boldsymbol{y}' - \boldsymbol{y}\|^3, & (5) \end{cases}$$

where we assume $\alpha, \beta, \upsilon \ge 0$, and the norm always refers to the Euclidean norm ($\ell_2$ norm). These three types of smoothness would be used in the following derivations.

Lipschitz smoothness characterizes different levels of smoothness of function $f(\boldsymbol{y})$. Intuitively, Lipschitz smoothness offers an opportunity to zoom in on the function $f(\boldsymbol{y})$ at different levels, that is at $0th$ order level (constant approximation level), $f(\boldsymbol{y})$ could be roughly approximated by $f(\boldsymbol{y}')$, corresponding approximation quality could be measured by $\alpha \|\boldsymbol{y}' - \boldsymbol{y}\|$; at $1st$ order level (linear approximation level), $f(\boldsymbol{y})$ could be roughly approximated by $f(\boldsymbol{y}')$ and its gradient $\nabla f(\boldsymbol{y})^T$, corresponding approximation quality could be measured by $\beta \|\boldsymbol{y}' - \boldsymbol{y}\|^2$; at $2nd$ order level (quadratic approximation level), $f(\boldsymbol{y})$ can be roughly approximated by $f(\boldsymbol{y}')$ and its gradient $\nabla f(\boldsymbol{y})^T$ and $\nabla f(\boldsymbol{y}')^T$, corresponding approximation quality can be measured by $\upsilon \|\boldsymbol{y}' - \boldsymbol{y}\|^3$. It is also observed that, if we want to approximate to $f(\boldsymbol{y})$ more accurately (e.g., at the level of $\upsilon \|\boldsymbol{y}' - \boldsymbol{y}\|^3$ in $\|\boldsymbol{y}' - \boldsymbol{y}\|$), higher order approximation item should be adopted (e.g., $\nabla f(\boldsymbol{y})^T$ and $\nabla f(\boldsymbol{y}')^T$), namely, the more information of $f(\boldsymbol{y})$ are explored, the more approximation we would achieve.

## 3.2   Two-Layers Coordinate Coding

Before defining two-layers coordinate coding, let's review the single-layer coordinate coding defined in [4] for its close relationship with Two-layers LCC.

**Definition 2 (Single-layer Coordinate Coding).** *A single-layer coordinate coding is a pair* $(\gamma^1, C^1)$, *where* $C^1 \subset \mathbb{R}^m$ *is a set of anchor points to* $y$ *(aka basis functions in* $C^1$), *and* $\gamma^1$ *is a map of* $y \in \mathbb{R}^m$ *to* $\gamma^1(y) \in \mathbb{R}^{|C^1|}$ *such that* $[\gamma_v^1(y)]_{v \in C^1} \in \mathbb{R}^1$ *and* $\sum_{v \in C^1} \gamma_v^1(y) = 1$. *It induces the following physical approximation of* $y$ *in* $\mathbb{R}^m$:

$$h_{\gamma^1, C^1}(y) \triangleq y' = \sum_{v \in C^1} \gamma_v^1(y)v, \tag{6}$$

where, for conciseness, let's align all $\gamma_v^1(y)$ into a column vector: $\gamma^1(y) = [\gamma_{v_1}^1, \gamma_{v_2}^1, \cdots, \gamma_{v_{|C^1|}}^1]^\mathsf{T} \in \mathbb{R}^{|C^1|}$. In fact, the pre-image $y$ is mapped into the image $y'$ by the mapping $\gamma^1$. Following the line of research, here we introduce two-layers coordinate coding form, accordingly:

**Definition 3 (Two-layers Coordinate Coding).** *A two-layers coordinate coding is two pairs with close relationship* $(\gamma^1, C^1)$ *and* $(\gamma^{2,v}, C^{2,v})$, *where* $C^{2,v} \subset \mathbb{R}^m$ *is a set of anchor points to* $v$ *rather than* $y$, *and* $\gamma^{2,v}$ *is a map of* $v \in \mathbb{R}^m$ *to* $\gamma^{2,v}(v) \in \mathbb{R}^{|C^{2,v}|}$ *such that* $[\gamma_u^{2,v}(v)]_{u \in C^{2,v}} \in \mathbb{R}^1$ *and* $\sum_{u \in C^{2,v}} \gamma_u^{2,v}(v) = 1$. *It induces the following physical approximation of* $v$ *in* $\mathbb{R}^m$: $v' = \sum_{u \in C^{2,v}} \gamma_u^{2,v}(v)u$, *and corresponding two-layers approximation of* $y$ *in* $\mathbb{R}^m$:

$$h_{\gamma^{2,v}, C^{2,v}}(y) \triangleq y'' = \sum_{v \in C^1} [\gamma_v^1(y) \sum_{u \in C^{2,v}} \gamma_u^{2,v}(v)u]. \tag{7}$$

For conciseness, let's rearrange all $\gamma_u^{2,v}(v)$ into a column vector: $\gamma^{2,v}(v) = [\gamma_{u_1}^{2,v}(v), \gamma_{u_2}^{2,v}(v), \cdots, \gamma_{u_{|C^{2,v}|}}^{2,v}(v)]^\mathsf{T} \in \mathbb{R}^{|C^{2,v}|}$. The condition $\sum_{u \in C^{2,v}} \gamma_u^{2,v}(v) = 1$ is shift-invariance requirement, which means the coding $v'$ should remain the same if we use a different origin of the $\mathbb{R}^m$ coordinate system for representing $v$.

**Lemma 1 (Single-layer Linearization).** *Let* $f$ *be a* $(\alpha, \beta, v)$ *Lipschitz smooth function and* $(\gamma^1, C^1)$ *an arbitrary single-layer coordinate coding on* $\mathbb{R}^m$. *For all* $y \in \mathbb{R}^m$:

$$\left| f(y) - \sum_{v \in C^1} \gamma_v^1(y)f(v) \right| \leq \alpha \left\| y - h_{\gamma^1, C^1}(y) \right\| + \beta \sum_{v \in C^1} \left[ |\gamma_v^1(y)| \left\| v - h_{\gamma^1, C^1}(y) \right\|^2 \right]$$

$$= \alpha \left\| y - y' \right\| + \beta \sum_{v \in C^1} \left[ |\gamma_v^1(y)| \left\| v - y' \right\|^2 \right]. \tag{8}$$

A nonliear function $f(y)$ in $\mathbb{R}^m$ could be approximated by a linear function $\sum_{v \in C^1} \gamma_v^1(y)f(v)$ with respect to $h_{\gamma^1, C^1}$, i.e. the linear representation of $y$, where $[f(v)]_{v \in C^1}$ is the set of coefficients viewed as unknown vectors and estimated from data using a standard learning method such as SVM.

The quality of this approximation is bounded by the right side of the inequation, which has two terms: the first term $\left\| y - h_{\gamma^1, C^1}(y) \right\|$ indicates the residual should be as small as possible; the second term suggests that $\sum_{v \in C^1} \gamma_v^1(y) v$ should be localized, that is the sum of weighted distance between $y'$ and each anchor point $v \in C^1$ should be as small as possible. The first term encourages the best approximation $y'$ of $y$, in particular, as illustrated in [4], for a smooth manifold, one can choose appropriate anchor points $C \in \mathbb{R}^{|C^1|}$ so that the first layer linearization could achieve local linear approximation power. While please note that, this approximation power is guaranteed under the precondition that we have to find enough descriptive anchor points to minimize the first term $\left\| y - h_{\gamma^1, C^1}(y) \right\|$, however, these anchor points are usually insufficient and noise-polluted in practical. The motivation of this paper is just to find this approximation at the second-layer level that provides an opportunity for zooming into each single basis $v \in \mathbb{R}^{|C^1|}$ of the first layer for finer local details, in order to finally incorporate more details about $f$ extracting from the second layer and improve the approximation quality. Along the lines of researches, we principled generalize it to the two-layers structure, which is illustrated in the following lemma:

**Lemma 2 (Two-layers Linearization).** *Let $f$ be a $(\alpha, \beta, \upsilon)$ Lipschitz smooth function and $(\gamma^2, C^2) = \{(\gamma^1, C^1)\} \cup \{(\gamma^{2,v}, C^{2,v}) : v \in C^1\}$ be an arbitrary two-layer coordinate coding on $\mathbb{R}^m$. For all $y \in \mathbb{R}^m$:*

$$|f(y) - \sum_{v \in C^1} [\gamma_v^1(y) \sum_{u \in C^{2,v}} \gamma_u^{2,v}(v) f(u)]|$$

$$\leq \alpha_1 \left\| y - h_{\gamma^1, C^1}(y) \right\| + \beta_1 \sum_{v \in C^1} [|\gamma_v^1(y)| \left\| v - h_{\gamma^1, C^1}(y) \right\|^2]$$

$$+ \alpha_2 \sum_{v \in C^1} [|\gamma_v^1(y)| \left\| v - \sum_{u \in C^{2,v}} \gamma_u^{2,v}(v) u \right\|]$$

$$+ \beta_2 \sum_{v \in C^1} [|\gamma_v^1(y)| \sum_{u \in C^{2,v}} |\gamma_u^{2,v}| \left\| u - \sum_{u \in C^{2,v}} \gamma_u^{2,v}(v) u \right\|^2] \tag{9}$$

$$= \alpha_1 \left\| y - y' \right\| + \beta_1 \sum_{v \in C^1} [|\gamma_v^1(y)| \left\| v - y' \right\|^2]$$

$$+ \alpha_2 \sum_{v \in C^1} [|\gamma_v^1(y)| \left\| v - v' \right\|] + \beta_2 \sum_{v \in C^1} [|\gamma_v^1(y)| \sum_{u \in C^{2,v}} |\gamma_u^{2,v}| \left\| u - v' \right\|^2].$$

On the left side of the inequation, a nonlinear function $f(y)$ in $\mathbb{R}^m$ is approximated by a linear function: $\sum_{v \in C^1} [\gamma_v^1(y) \sum_{u \in C^{2,v}} \gamma_u^{2,v}(v) f(u)]$ with respect to $h_{\gamma^{2,v}, C^{2,v}}$, where $[f(u)]_{u \in C^{2,v}}$ is the set of coefficients, which could also be estimated using the same approach as in the single-layer linearization. The quality of this approximation is bounded by the right side of the equation: the first two terms have the same meaning as the ones introduced in the Lemma 1. The third term indicates the weighted residual should be as small as possible, i.e., $v' \in \mathbb{R}^{|C^{2,v}|}$ should be close to its preimage $v \in C^1$; while the forth term encourages localization in the coding $v'$ of $v$.

In addition, we also make a critical observation that a nonlinear function $f(y)$ in $\mathbb{R}^m$ could be approximated by a linear function with two-layers structure: at first layer, the original $f(\boldsymbol{y})$ is divided into $|\boldsymbol{C}^1|$ components: $f(\boldsymbol{v}_1), \cdots, f(\boldsymbol{v}_{|\boldsymbol{C}^1|})$, which are then linearly combined to compose $f(\boldsymbol{y}')$, and if some preconditions are guaranteed (i.e., the first two terms of the bound in Lemma 2), the $1st$ order approximation $f(\boldsymbol{y}')$ could achieve a satisfactory result; while in second layer, each $f(\boldsymbol{v})$ is further divided into $|\boldsymbol{C}^{2,\boldsymbol{v}}|$ sub-components $f(\boldsymbol{u}_1), \cdots, f(\boldsymbol{u}_{|\boldsymbol{C}^{2,\boldsymbol{v}}|})$, which are then linearly combined to compose corresponding $f(\boldsymbol{v}')$. Then, all these various $f(\boldsymbol{v}'_1), \cdots, f(\boldsymbol{v}'_{|\boldsymbol{C}^1|})$ are delivered up to the first layer for finally composing $f(\boldsymbol{y}'')$ linearly, and if some preconditions are guaranteed (i.e., the remainders of the bound in Lemma 2), the $2nd$ order approximation $f(\boldsymbol{y}'')$ could achieve a more satisfactory result than its single-layer counterpart.

Moreover, the two-layer structure also incarnates the quality of computation saving, namely, each set of sub-bases $\boldsymbol{u} \in \boldsymbol{C}^{2,\boldsymbol{v}}$ corresponding to $\boldsymbol{v}$ with nonzero coefficients at the first layer could be calculated simultaneously, for instance, instead of fitting a single model with many atoms in the dictionary $\boldsymbol{C} \in \mathbb{R}^m$, two-layer hierarchical structure need only fit a dozens of small local system with grouped atoms in parallel, which dramatically improves the computational complexity. So in the next section, we will pay more attention to practical computational procedure.

## 4 Two-Layers Coding Formulation

This section will discuss practical computational procedure. In the spirit of reducing the error and encouraging the locality at different levels, a hierarchical method accommodating the underlying intuition is designed.

### 4.1 First-Layer Formulation

Let $\boldsymbol{Y}$ be a set of $m$-dimensional local descriptors extracted from a sampled data, i.e., $\boldsymbol{Y} = [\boldsymbol{y}_1, \cdots, \boldsymbol{y}_N] \in \mathbb{R}^{m \times N}$. Given a first-layer codebook with $D_1$ entries, $\boldsymbol{V} = [\boldsymbol{v}_1, \boldsymbol{v}_2, \cdots, \boldsymbol{v}_{D_1}] \in \mathbb{R}^{m \times D_1}$, first-layer coding schemes will convert each local descriptor $\boldsymbol{y}_i$ into a $D_1$-dimensional code $\boldsymbol{\gamma}_i^1 = \left[ \gamma_i^1(\boldsymbol{v}_1), \gamma_i^1(\boldsymbol{v}_2), \cdots, \gamma_i^1(\boldsymbol{v}_{D_1}) \right]^{\mathsf{T}} \in \mathbb{R}^{D_1}$, hence, arrange all codes into a matrix: $\boldsymbol{\gamma}^1 = [\boldsymbol{\gamma}_1^1, \boldsymbol{\gamma}_2^1, \cdots, \boldsymbol{\gamma}_N^1] \in \mathbb{R}^{D_1 \times N}$. Specifically, each code could be obtained using the following optimization form:

$$\min_{\boldsymbol{\gamma}_i^1} \left[ \tfrac{1}{2} \left\| \boldsymbol{y}_i - \boldsymbol{V}\boldsymbol{\gamma}_i^1 \right\|_2^2 + \beta \left\| \boldsymbol{\gamma}_i^1 \odot \boldsymbol{d}_i^1 \right\|_1 \right] \quad s.t. \quad \mathbf{1}^{\mathsf{T}}\boldsymbol{\gamma}_i^1 = 1 \tag{10}$$

where $\boldsymbol{d}_i^1 \in \mathbb{R}^{D_1}$ is a distance vector, each item of which measures the distance between $\boldsymbol{y}_i$ and $\boldsymbol{v}_i$, and $\odot$ denotes the element-wise multiplication, which enables corresponding items of both vectors ($\boldsymbol{\gamma}_i^1$ and $\boldsymbol{d}_i^1$) to multiply. Typically, $\boldsymbol{d}_i^1$ can be obtained using $\ell_2$ norm, that is $\boldsymbol{d}_i^1 = [\|\boldsymbol{y}_i - \boldsymbol{v}_1\|_2, \|\boldsymbol{y}_i - \boldsymbol{v}_2\|_2, \cdots, \|\boldsymbol{y}_i - \boldsymbol{v}_{D_1}\|_2]^{\mathsf{T}}$. The constraint $\mathbf{1}^{\mathsf{T}}\boldsymbol{\gamma}_i^1 = 1$ follows the shift-invariant requirements of the two-layer code.

## 4.2   Second-Layer Formulation

At the second layer, we would further refine each basis $v$ belonging to the first layer. Concretely, the third and fourth terms of the bound in Lemma 2 specify how we refine each basis vector $v$ at the second layer, during which, more information about the gradient of $f$: $\nabla f(v')^\mathsf{T}$ are then be incorporated. Before optimizing the third and fourth terms, both of them are further transformed into the following form:

$$\min[\sum_{v \in C^1} [|\gamma_v^1(y)| (\|v - v'\| + \sum_{u \in C^{2,v}} |\gamma_u^{2,v}| \|u - v'\|^2))]]$$
$$\leq \sum_{v \in C^1} \min[|\gamma_v^1(y)| (\|v-v'\| + \sum_{u \in C^{2,v}} |\gamma_u^{2,v}| \|u-v'\|^2)], \tag{11}$$

which indicates the problem could be further divided into a set of small models at the second layer, and thus be tackled individually. In addition, fitting the small models can be done in parallel, from which two-layer coding is benefited.

Therefore, this leads to the following formulation for each small model:

$$\min \left[ \tfrac{1}{2} \|v_i - U\gamma_i^{2,v}\|_2^2 + \beta\|\gamma_i^{2,v} \odot d_i^2\|_1 \right] \quad s.t. \quad \mathbf{1}^\mathsf{T}\gamma_i^{2,v} = 1, \tag{12}$$

where $d_i^2 \in \mathbb{R}^{D_2}$ is also a distance vector recording the distance between $v_i$ and each atom in the dictionary matrix $U = [u_1, u_2, \cdots, u_{D_2}]$; $v_i \in V$ is one of basis vectors adopted in the representation of $y_i$ at the first layer, which could then be augmented into a $D_2$-dimensional code $\gamma_i^{2,v} = \left[\gamma_i^{2,v}(u_1), \gamma_i^{2,v}(u_2), \cdots, \gamma_i^{2,v}(u_{D_2})\right]^\mathsf{T} \in \mathbb{R}^{D_2}$, hence after rearranging each code corresponding to each basis vector $v$ into a matrix, we obtain the coding matrix for all $v$ adopted in the representation of $y_i$: $\gamma^{2,v} = \left[\gamma_1^{2,v}, \gamma_2^{2,v}, \cdots, \gamma_{|C_{y_i}^1|}^{2,v}\right] \in \mathbb{R}^{D_2 \times |C_{y_i}^1|}$. This matrix comprises the second layer coding for each local descriptor $y_i$ indirectly. Furthermore, the final form of two-layers coding for each $y_i$ could be obtained by integrating each single-layer coding organically. Specifically, each item (e.g., the $j$th item) in the first layer coding $\gamma_i^1$ is augmented into a vector, $\gamma_i = \left[\gamma_i^1(v_j), \ \gamma_i^1(v_j)[\gamma_j^{2,v}(u_1), \gamma_j^{2,v}(u_2), \cdots, \gamma_j^{2,v}(u_{D_2})]\right]^\mathsf{T} \in \mathbb{R}^{1+D_2}$, which constitutes the final form of two-layer coding in $\mathbb{R}^{D_1 \times (1+D_2)}$.

# 5   Experiment Verification

We present experiments on: the Extended YaleB [8], Caltech101 [9], the MNIST [4], and a realistic robot system to evaluate the every aspect of the proposed strategy.

## 5.1   Quantitative Results

Due to the space limitation, we omit brief introduction of these popular databases, for more details, one can refer to the references marked behind them.

**Table 1.** Description of experimental settings.

| Database | Training samples | V | U | Train\Test |
|---|---|---|---|---|
| eYaleB | 32 | 570 | 64 | 2000\ 600 |
| Caltech101 | 5,10,20,30 | 510,1020,2040,3060 | 64 | 8230\ 914 |
| MNIST | 3000 | 500 | 64 | 60000\ 10000 |

**Table 2.** Recognition results and computation time comparisons on the extended YaleB database.

| Method | LLC [7] | SRC [10] | LC-KSVD1 [11] | LC-KSVD2 [11] | ITDL [12] | Ours (15 per person) |
|---|---|---|---|---|---|---|
| Included | 0.9070 | 0.8050 | 0.9450 | 0.9500 | 0.9539 | **0.9813** |
| Excluded[1] | 0.9670 | 0.8670 | 0.9830 | 0.9880 | 0.9886 | **0.9903** |
| Average Time (ms) | - | 11.22 | 0.52 | 0.49 | - | **55.90** |

1: This column is the result when 10 poor-quality images excluded for each class.

**Table 3.** Recognition results on the MNIST database.

| Method | Laplacian Eigenmap [13] | Deep Belief Network [14] | LLE [15] | LCC [4] | DCN [6] | RGF [16] | Ours |
|---|---|---|---|---|---|---|---|
| Accuracy(%) | 0.9727 | 0.9810 | 0.9762 | 0.9810 | 0.9815 | 0.9809 | **0.9857** |

**Table 4.** Recognition results on Caltech101 database.

| Training samples | LLC [7] | SRC [10] | K-SVD [2] | LC-KSVD2 [11] | SSC [17] | Ours |
|---|---|---|---|---|---|---|
| 5 | 0.5115 | 0.4880 | 0.4980 | 0.5400 | 0.5560 | **0.5783** |
| 10 | 0.5977 | 0.6010 | 0.5980 | 0.6310 | 0.6550 | **0.6572** |
| 20 | 0.6774 | 0.6770 | 0.6870 | 0.7050 | 0.7620 | **0.7535** |
| 30 | 0.7344 | 0.7070 | 0.7320 | 0.7360 | 0.7760 | **0.7989** |

**Table 5.** Recognition results (computation time (ms) for classifying a test image) on the Caltech101 dataset (varying dictionary size).

| Dictionary size | 510 | 1020 | 2040 | 3060 |
|---|---|---|---|---|
| SRC [10] | 0.48 (173.44) | 0.60 (343.12) | 0.67 (662.40) | 0.71 (987.55) |
| LC-KSVD1 [11] | 0.71 (0.59) | 0.72 (1.09) | 0.72 (2.21) | 0.74 (3.50) |
| LC-KSVD2 [11] | 0.72 (0.54) | 0.73 (0.98) | 0.73 (1.94) | 0.74 (3.17) |
| Ours | **0.72** (99.85) | **0.75** (196.52) | **0.79** (384.23) | **0.80** (595.93) |

For fair comparison, we adopt the same experiment setups suggested by the homepages of the databases and related literatures [7,10–12,17], etc. We summarize the key details of experimental settings in Table 1. From Table 2 to Table 5, it is consistently observed that our method exhibits a prominent recognition accuracy in all databases, even with fewer training samples and smaller dictionary size. The main reason lies in, two-layers strategy fully exploits the intrinsic structure of the manifold where datapoints reside in, and incorporates more information about the nonlinear function $f$ in anchor points of each layers, which could greatly benefit their approximation power, especially in the situation of fewer training samples.

## 5.2  Applications in Robotics

Since the proposed coding strategy exhibits outstanding performance on popular databases, how it works in practical use, especially in noise polluted conditions? This section reveals applications of our theoretical results on a real robot system. For better understanding, we briefly present the experimental settings and tasks as follows: we have employed Barrett$^{TM}$robot hand fixed on a 7-DOF Schunk$^{TM}$modular robot to perform a task of multi-objects grasping and classification, see Figure 2(a). One of features of this robotic system lies in its large amount of informative tactile data provided by the tactile sensor matrix mounted on the fingers and palm, see Figure 2(b), illustrating distributions of tactile sensors mounted on each fingertip (F1, F2 and F3) and the palm of Barrett$^{TM}$hand, and each part samples the force variation in the contact area. Distributions and magnitude of tactile time-series have the ability to reflect meticulous state of fingertips and objects, therefore we could infer target class from it. While this type of data has a major disadvantage: it is vulnerable to noise, which greatly challenges signal processing, see the bottom of Figure 2(b).

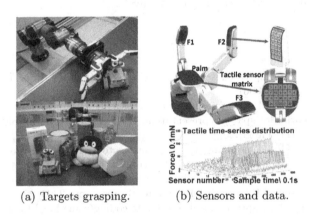

(a) Targets grasping.    (b) Sensors and data.

**Fig. 2.** Targets grasping and distributions of tactile data.

How to fully exploit this informative data for an accurate inference is a challenging problem, which provides just an nice opportunity for our proposed representation approach. To verify the proposed strategy, we repeat grasping dozens of targets with various shape and material, and record the tactile time-series; then various coding strategies are further employed to describe these signals and finally classified by linear SVM. Classification accuracy comparison is presented in Table 6. It is observed that our two-layers coding strategy outperforms sparse coding and LLC methods at every signal-to-noise (SNR) level, except at 5dB SNR, showing that it is capable of resisting the noise even in some extreme case of noise level 10dB or 15dB SNR.

**Table 6.** Recognition results on robotic testbed with varying noise levels.

| Noise level | 5dB | 10dB | 15dB | 20dB | 30dB | 40dB |
|---|---|---|---|---|---|---|
| LLC[7] | 0.70 | 0.74 | 0.78 | 0.81 | 0.83 | 0.85 |
| SRC[10] | **0.71** | 0.74 | 0.83 | 0.84 | 0.88 | 0.89 |
| Ours | **0.71** | **0.76** | **0.85** | **0.87** | **0.89** | **0.91** |

# 6    Conclusions

This paper systematically proposes a principled extension of the traditional single-layer sparse coding scheme for high dimensional nonlinear learning. The proposed method is viewed as generalized local linear function approximation, but can achieve higher approximation power due to additional gradient information about the nonlinear function included. The main advantages of two-layers coding is that it can potentially achieve better performance due to the introduction of the second layer, which incorporates abundant information about nonlinear function. Experiment evaluations on both popular benchmarks and robotic application further confirm our analysis.

# References

1. Donoho, D.L.: Compressed sensing. IEEE Transactions on Information Theory **52**(4), 1289–1306 (2006)
2. Aharon, M., Elad, M., Bruckstein, A.: K-svd: An algorithm for designing overcomplete dictionaries for sparse representation. IEEE Transactions on Signal Processing **54**(11), 4311–4322 (2006)
3. Kouskouridas, R., Charalampous, K., Gasteratos, A.: Sparse pose manifolds. Autonomous Robots **37**(2), 191–207 (2014)
4. Yu, K., Zhang, T., Gong, Y.: Nonlinear learning using local coordinate coding. In: Advances in Neural Information Processing Systems, pp. 2223–2231 (2009)
5. Yu, K., Zhang, T.: Improved local coordinate coding using local tangents. In: Proceedings of the 27th International Conference on Machine Learning, pp. 1215–1222 (2010)
6. Lin, Y., Tong, Z., Zhu, S., Yu, K.: Deep coding network. In: Advances in Neural Information Processing Systems, pp. 1405–1413 (2010)
7. Wang, J., Yang, J., Yu, K., Lv, F., Huang, T., Gong, Y.: Locality-constrained linear coding for image classification. In: IEEE Conference on Computer Vision and Pattern Recognition, pp. 3360–3367 (2010)
8. Georghiades, A.S., Belhumeur, P.N., Kriegman, D.J.: From few to many: Illumination cone models for face recognition under variable lighting and pose. IEEE Transactions on Pattern Analysis and Machine Intelligence **23**(6), 643–660 (2001)
9. Fei-Fei, L., Fergus, R., Perona, P.: Learning generative visual models from few training examples: An incremental bayesian approach tested on 101 object categories. Computer Vision and Image Understanding **106**(1), 59–70 (2007)
10. Wright, J., Yang, A.Y., Ganesh, A., Sastry, S.S., Ma, Y.: Robust face recognition via sparse representation. IEEE Transactions on Pattern Analysis and Machine Intelligence **31**(2), 210–227 (2009)

11. Jiang, Z., Lin, Z., Davis, L.S.: Learning a discriminative dictionary for sparse coding via label consistent k-svd. In: IEEE Conference on Computer Vision and Pattern Recognition, pp. 1697–1704 (2011)
12. Qiu, Q., Patel, V.M., Chellappa, R.: Information-theoretic dictionary learning for image classification. IEEE Transactions on Pattern Analysis and Machine Intelligence **36**(11), 2173–2184 (2014)
13. Belkin, M., Niyogi, P.: Laplacian eigenmaps for dimensionality reduction and data representation. Neural computation **15**(6), 1373–1396 (2003)
14. Hinton, G.E., Salakhutdinov, R.R.: Reducing the dimensionality of data with neural networks. Science **313**(5786), 504–507 (2006)
15. Roweis, S.T., Saul, L.K.: Nonlinear dimensionality reduction by locally linear embedding. Science **290**(5500), 2323–2326 (2000)
16. Fan, M., Zhang, X., Lin, Z., Zhang, Z., Bao, H.: A regularized approach for geodesic-based semisupervised multimanifold learning. IEEE Transactions on Image Processing **23**(5), 2133–2147 (2014)
17. Oliveira, G.L., Nascimento, E.R., Vieira, A.W.: Montenegro Campos, M.F.: Sparse spatial coding: A novel approach to visual recognition. IEEE Transactions on Image Processing **23**(6), 2719–2731 (2014)

# A Graph Matching and Energy Minimization Based Algorithm for Lunar Surface Image Mosaic

Chuan Li, Zhi-Yong Liu[✉], Xu Yang, Hong Qiao, and Chuan-Kai Liu

The State Key Laboratory of Management and Control of Complex Systems,
Institute of Automation, Chinese Academy of Sciences, Beijing, China
zhiyong.liu@ia.ac.cn

**Abstract.** This paper concerns the problem of lunar surface image mosaic, including both image registration and image stitching procedures. A wide viewing composite obtained by mosaic technique plays an important role in many lunar rover's operations. Considering particular characters in lunar surface images, such as large geometrical deformations, significant illumination differences and repeated patterns, previous image mosaic techniques often fail to create a qualified composite. In this paper, a novel algorithm is introduced to tackle the lunar surface image mosaic problem. Specifically, in the image registration procedure, to deal with the misregistration problem caused by large geometrical deformation and repeated patterns, structural information is introduced to solve the feature correspondence by formulating it as a graph matching problem. In the image stitching procedure, an energy minimization method is proposed based on the graduated nonconvexity and concavity procedure (GNCCP), to handle the visible seams caused by illumination differences and ghosting problem caused by large parallax in the overlapped area. Comparative experiments on real lunar surface images acquired by Yutu rover and Apollo image gallery validate the effectiveness of the proposed method.

**Keywords:** Lunar image mosaic · Graph matching · Energy Minimization · GNCCP

## 1 Introduction

Image mosaic is the technique to combine two or more images into a high resolution and wide viewing composite. It lays the foundation for many lunar rover operations. For instance, a wide viewing composite can benefit the lunar rover's self location, which further helps its navigation operations. The special environment of lunar surface leads to certain particular image characters. For instance, the lunar surface images taken by the moving lunar rover often have large geometrical deformations, and suffer from large illumination changes caused by different sunlight angles. Besides, the barren lunar surface, mainly composed of

© Springer-Verlag Berlin Heidelberg 2015
H. Zha et al. (Eds.): CCCV 2015, Part I, CCIS 546, pp. 46–55, 2015.
DOI: 10.1007/978-3-662-48558-3_5

rocks and dust, makes the acquired images contain lots of repeated patterns, and often lack salient features. Thus performing image mosaic on lunar surface images remains a challenging task, and there are few techniques dedicated to the lunar surface image mosaic problem.

Image mosaic mainly includes two procedures, i.e., image registration and image stitching. Image registration is the process that transforms images from different views into one coordinate system. A comprehensive survey on image registration methods is in [1], in which the image registration techniques are classified into area-based methods and feature-based methods. In the last two decades, together with the emergence of a bunch of splendid local feature descriptors, e.g. SIFT [2] and SURF [3], the feature-based methods become more popular in image registration. The success of feature-based methods can be attributed to the rotation and scale invariance of the features, thus they can be used to register images with significant deformations, while the area-based methods are only applicable on images with translational and rotational transformations. However, the feature-based methods still fail in dealing with lunar surface image registration, mainly due to less distinctive local features and repeated patterns in the lunar surface images. That is because they only utilized the appearance similarity, without considering other useful information, such as the structure information.

Image stitching takes the registered images as input to create a wide viewing composite. It can be very difficult for lunar surface images because perfect image registration can hardly be obtained and real lunar surface images are rarely under constant light exposure. Therefore, blurring caused by misregistration, visible seams caused by light exposure difference and ghosting caused by possible moving objects often occur in lunar surface images. Traditional mosaic algorithms also aimed at the above problems or part of them. For instance, early in the image mosaic research, researchers [4,5] tried to eliminate the blurring and visible seams by a weighted average method, which is called feathering. However, when the misregistration is significant and moving objects exist, the feathering usually results in visual artefacts and ghosting in the composite. Some other researchers used the optimal seam method [6,7] to deal with the moving objects. By introducing the Dijkstra's algorithm [9], the method can find a path avoiding cutting through the moving objects, which, therefore, makes the moving objects all in or all out of the composite. Unfortunately, this method may fail when the light exposure difference is significant, because it may treat the areas with different light exposures as areas with moving objects. In [8] they used the region of difference (ROD) to find the regions where the moving objects lie and then choose the right region to keep, which to some extent improved the the optimal seam method. But it is not robust against significant light exposure in lunar surface images. Generally, rare approaches can well tackle the image stitching problem under all the above specific difficulties in lunar surface images.

In this paper, we propose an novel algorithm for lunar surface image mosaic. Specifically, in the image registration procedure, to deal with the repeated patterns in the lunar surface images, the structural information of the feature points is introduced to solve the feature correspondence problem by formulating it as a graph matching problem, which is approximately solved by a probabilistic spectral graph matching algorithm. In the image stitching procedure, exposure compensation is firstly conducted to correct the illumination difference between lunar surface images. Then an energy minimization method based on the recently proposed graduated nonconvexity and concavity procedure (GNCCP) [11] is used to handle the ghosting problem caused by large parallax in the overlapped area.

## 2   The Proposed Lunar Surface Image Mosaic Algorithm

There are mainly two procedures in the proposed algorithm: image registration and image stitching. The detailed discission is given below.

### 2.1   Graph Matching Based Image Registration

To automatically utilize the information from the input images to create a high resolution and wide viewing composite, the very beginning step is geometrically aligning the images, i.e. to overlapping the input images of the same scene.

Given two images, the reference image $I_1$ and the sensed image $I_2$, taken from different viewpoints with overlapping area, the image registration procedure is to find a geometric transformation matrix $T$. Matrix $T$ can project the sensed image $I_2$ to the reference image $I_1$, so that two images can share the same coordinate system and the overlapping scene of two images should have the same coordinates. The projective matrix $T$ is estimated by a modified feature based algorithm. This is done in the following steps.

**Feature Extraction.** Salient and distinctive objects of the input images $I_1, I_2$ are automatically detected by the Speeded Up Robust Features(SURF). For each feature point, it has a 64-dimensional descriptor gathering the information of the surrounding area. In this paper, we denote the descriptors of image $I_1$ and $I_2$ as $D_1, D_2$, where $D_1 \in \Re^{M \times 64}, D_2 \in \Re^{N \times 64}$. $M, N$ is the number of feature points of $I_1, I_2$ respectively.

**Feature Correspondence.** In this step, the correspondence between the features detected in the sensed image and reference image is established. Different from some conventional methods [19] which only use the descriptor similarity, in the proposed algorithm we take the structural information into account and apply a graph matching method to tackle the feature correspondence problem. We use the our newly published probabilistic spectral graph matching algorithm [23] to tackle this combinational optimization problem. This algorithm approximately solve the optimization problem(4) by spectral decomposition. After the spectral matching procedure, a probabilistic assignment is obtained. We can also set an probabilistic threshold to control the numbers of the final correspondence feature points.

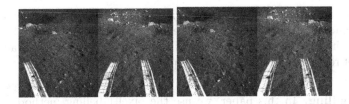

**Fig. 1.** Feature correspondence results. The correct correspondence points are connected by blue lines and The wrong correspondence points are connected by red lines. **a** Without combining the structural information. **b** Combining the structural information

(a)                    (b)                    (c)

**Fig. 2.** Image Registration results. **a** The reference image after registration; **b** The sensed image after registration; **c** The two input images in the same coordinate system

The example feature correspondence experiment is conducted on real lunar surface images acquired by Yutu lunar rover. The results are illustrated in Fig.1. As we can see, the proposed algorithm which combines the structural information gets a more accurate correspondence sets.

**Image Transformation and Interpolation.** After the feature correspondence has been established, we use RANSAC [13]to robustly get an estimation of the projective matrix $T$ by utilizing the correspondence points. Next we apply the matrix $T$. The registration result of two lunar surface images is illustrated in Fig.2. As we can see, after the registration procedure, two input images have the same size and the overlapping area has the same coordinates in two images.

### 2.2   Energy Minimization Based Image Stitching

In the image stitching stage, we still have to decide how to blend the images to create a clean composite. In this paper, we use an energy minimization method to choose the right image for the composite at every pixel. The pre-processing and post-processing are also given to enhance composite quality.

**Exposure Compensation.** To adjust the exposure, we assume the reflective properties of the scene remain unchanged. This allows us to use a linear approximation to make the adjustment in intensity. Given two images $I_1, I_2$, the intensity of the images is denoted as $e_1, e_2$. Then the exposure compensation is done by a linear approximation as in

$$e_2 = \alpha e_1 + \beta. \tag{1}$$

The gain $\alpha$ and bias $\beta$ are found by utilizing the intensity of the correspondence feature points. We apply the linear regression to acquire the optimal $\alpha$ and $\beta$, which has the least mean square error. Next $\alpha$ and $\beta$ are used to adjust the intensity of registered image $I_2$ at every pixel.

**Pixel Labelling.** In this paper, we use the pixel labelling method to choose the right image for the composite to achieve a smooth transition between the images.

Given a registered source image sets $I = \{I_1, I_2, ..., I_k\}$, indexed by a label sets $L = \{l_1, l_2, ..., l_k\}$, where k is the number of source images. The image stitching problem is assigning every pixel $p$ in composite a label in the label set $P = \{p_1, p_2, ..., p_n\}$, where n is the number of pixels in the composite. Then the image stitching problem is converted to a pixel labelling task, i.e. finding a mapping function $F$ between sets $P$ and $L$.

$$F : P \rightarrow L; \quad F = \{f_1, f_2, ..., f_n\}, \tag{2}$$

where $f_i$ denotes the label of pixel $p_i$.

In the proposed algorithm, we use an energy minimization method to solve the pixel labelling problem. We build the energy function based on the assumption that the natural images can be formulated as Markov Random Field(MRF) [10], i.e. the images are local smoothing. The smooth prior makes the label of each pixel affect by both the information of current pixel and the neighbouring pixels. Therefore when moving objects and misregistration area exist in the overlapping scene, the label tend to totally keep or remove the moving objects and put a seam at the misregistration area.

In this paper, the energy function $E(F)$ is defined by

$$E(F) = \sum_p S(p, f_p) + \sum_p \sum_{\{p,q\} \in \mathcal{N}} V_{pq}(f_p, f_q), \tag{3}$$

where $S(p, f_p)$ is called data energy, it penalizes assigning the label $f_p$ to pixel $p$. $V_{pq}(f_p, f_q)$ denotes the smooth energy built based on the smooth prior. It penalizes the inconsistency between neighbouring pixels. $\mathcal{N}$ is the neighbouring system of the image. Then to find an optimal label set is equivalent to find a mapping function $f$, which makes the energy function has the global minimum as $F^* = \arg\min_F E(F)$. Particularly in this paper, the data energy $S(p, f_p)$ for selecting image $f_p$ as the label at pixel $p$ is given as

$$S(p, f_p) = \begin{cases} 0, & if \ I_{f_p}(p) \ isvalid \\ +\infty, & otherwise \end{cases}, \tag{4}$$

where a valid pixel is a pixel in the original image but not a padding from the image transformation. If all the registered images is valid at pixel $p$, the data energy is all set to zero, which is reasonable when no prior is given about which image is better.

The smooth energy penalizes the inconsistency between neighbouring pixels,i.e. assigning different labels to adjacent pixels. The smooth energy in this paper is a modified function derived from [12]. The energy is defined by the inconsistency in color and gradient space between neighbours as follow.

$$V_{pq}(f_p, f_q) = \begin{cases} Y + \lambda Z, & if \ \{p, q\} \in \mathcal{N} \\ 0, & otherwise \end{cases},$$
(5)

where $Y$ evaluates the inconsistency in color space. It is the euclidean distance in RGB space defined by $Y = \left\| I_{f_p}(p) - I_{f_q}(p) \right\| + \left\| I_{f_p}(q) - I_{f_q}(q) \right\|$. $Z$ evaluates the inconsistency in gradient space, it can protect the edges in images. It is given by $Z = \left\| \nabla_{pq} I_{f_p} \right\| + \left\| \nabla_{pq} I_{f_q} \right\|$, where $\nabla_{pq} I$ is the gradient of image $I$ in RGB space. $\lambda$ is used to balance the color and gradient inconsistency.

Minimizing the energy function(9) is a typical combinational optimization problem, which is an NP-hard problem with factorial complexity. In this paper we use our recently published GNCCP algorithm to tackle (9). GNCCP was originally proposed to approximately solve the assignment problem under one-to-one constraint [11]. Recently GNCCP was generalized to solve the Maximum A Posteriori(MAP) estimation in MRF, called GNCCP MAP algorithm [22]. Here in this paper we modify GNCCP to solve the energy minimization problem in MRF. The GNCCP energy minimization algorithm is given in Algorithm 1.

---

**Algorithm 1** Energy minimization algorithm

---

**Input:** Energy matrix $Q$ corresponding to the pairwise smooth energy and $A$ corresponding to the data energy
**Initialization:** $x = \frac{1}{nk}$, $\varsigma = 1$
**repeat**
  **repeat**
    $y = \arg\min_y \nabla E_\varsigma(x)^T y, s.t. y \in \Omega$
    $\alpha = \arg\min_\alpha E_\varsigma(x + \alpha(y - x))^T, s.t. 0 \leq \alpha \leq 1$
    $x \leftarrow x + \alpha(y - x)$
  **until** converged
  $\varsigma = \varsigma - d\varsigma$
**until** $\varsigma < -1 \vee x \in \Pi$
**Output:** An assignment vector x

---

In the algorithm, by relaxing the integer constrain $\Pi$ to its convex hull $\Omega$, GNCCP is proved to realize the Convex-Concave Relaxation Procedure(CCRP) [14], which has an ideal convergence to the global minimum, detailed proof of GNCCP is given in [11]. The final label set$F$ is finally obtained by utilizing assignment vector $x$. The labelling result conducted on two registered lunar surface images is given in Fig.3(c).

**Gradient Reconstruction.** Once the label of each pixel has been computed, we can directly copy the information of the input images according to the label

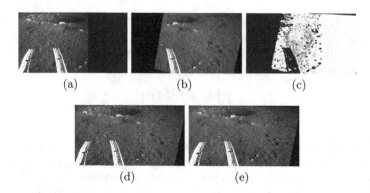

(a)                (b)                (c)

(d)                (e)

**Fig. 3.** An illustration of the image stitching procedure.**a b** are the registered input images. **c** is the labelling result of the proposed method. **d** is composite directly copying the values of the input images according to the labelling result. **e** is the composite reconstructed from the gradient domain

to form the final composite. But the pixels will still exist some degree of inconsistency. We use the gradient domain reconstruction technique [15] as the post-process to minimize the inconsistency. Rather than copying pixel values, the gradient domain reconstruction copies the gradients of the registered images according to the labelling result. The actual pixel values of the composite image $C$ are then computed by solving a Poisson equation that best matches the gradients and satisfies the boundary condition$\Omega$ given by the labelling result above.

$$\min_{C(p)} ||\nabla C(p) - \nabla I_{f_p}(p)||s.t.C(p) = I_{f_p}(p), for \quad p \in \Omega \tag{6}$$

In Eq(19), $\nabla X$ denotes the gradient of X and $\Omega$ is the boundary of the composite.

After the stitching procedure above, we can get the final composite. The image stitching result of the two example lunar surface images are shown in Fig.3. As we can see after an energy minimization procedure, the proposed algorithm make the composite smoothly transit from one image to another as shown in Fig.3(d), which is the result of directly copying the color information according to the labelling result. The gradient domain reconstruction result is given in Fig.3(e), which further eliminating the inconsistency in Fig.3(d).

## 3    Experiment

In this paper, the proposed algorithm is implemented in Matlab 2013(a) and tested on real lunar images acquired by Yutu rover and Apollo image gallery. The size of the lunar surface images used in the experiments is $460 \times 460$. To sufficiently verify the effectiveness of our proposed algorithm, we compare it with four popular mosaic softwares, including Autostitch[1], panorama maker[2],

---

[1] www.cs.bath.ac.uk/brown/autostitch/autostitch.html
[2] www.arcsoft.com/panorama-maker/

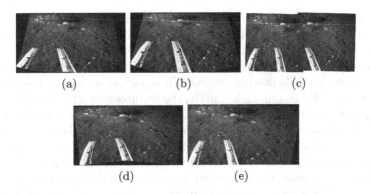

**Fig. 4.** Mosaic results on lunar images acquired by Yutu rover 1.**a** Autostitch. **b** Panorama maker. **c** Panorama factory. **d** Microsoft ICE. **e** Proposed algorithm

panorama factory[3] and Microsoft ICE[4]. All these mosaic softwares apply the traditional feature based method which utilizes the feature descriptor similarity only to automatically register the images. After registration, Autostitch uses a multi-band blending technique [21] to stitch the registered images together directly, while panorama maker, panorama factory and Microsoft ICE have an optimal seam searching procedure to deal with the moving objects and misregistration area and then use a blending technique to improve the quality of the composite. The mosaic results of these softwares and our algorithm tested on real lunar images acquired by Yutu rover and Apollo image gallery are given in Fig.4 and Fig.5 respectively.

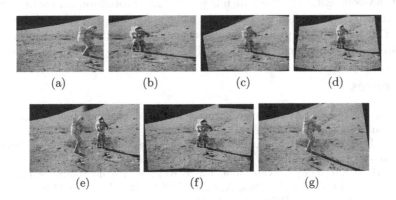

**Fig. 5.** Mosaic results on Apollo image gallery 1.**a, b** Images for mosaic.**c** Autostitch. **d** Panorama maker. **e** Panorama factory. **f** Microsoft ICE. **g** Proposed algorithm

---

[3] www.panoramafactory.com/

[4] research.microsoft.com/en-us/projects/ice/

From the mosaic experiments above, we can see that the special environment of lunar surface adds particular character to the images. The acquired lunar images always lack significant features due to the barren lunar surface and usually suffer from different illumination conditions. In some special cases, there also exists possible moving objects. These factors makes the lunar surface images mosaic a challenging task. Firstly, the features extracted from lunar surface images are not distinctive, which increases the difficulty of feature matching and further increases the probability of misregistration. As in the Fig.4 and Fig.5, some mosaic softwares, like panorama maker and panorama factory, can hardly get a satisfactory registration of the input images. Secondly, since the perfect registration of the lunar images are hard to obtain and some possible moving objects exist in the overlapping area, simple blending of the registered images, as Autostitch does, may lead to ghost and visual artefacts. Thirdly, the exposure difference between the input images, if not properly handled, will cause visible seam in the final composite.

As shown in the experiments, traditional mosaic softwares are not capable of lunar surface images mosaic. Overall our algorithm are robust against various situations in the lunar images and all get pleasing composite.

## 4    Conclusion

In this paper, a general framework of lunar surface image mosaic is proposed. Considering the speciality of lunar surface images, like large exposure difference, structural deformation and repeating patterns, we improve the traditional feature based image registration method by incorporating the structural information of features. The experiments shows the robustness of the proposed method against environmental changes. In image stitching procedure, an energy minimization method is applied to choose the right image at every pixel of the composite. Our method get pleasing results when dealing with different situations as illustrated in experiments.

## References

1. Zitova, B., Flusser, J.: Image registration methods: a survey. Image and Vision Computing **21**(11), 977–1000 (2003)
2. Lowe, D.G.: Distinctive image features from scale-invariant keypoints. International Journal of Computer Vision **60**(2), 91–110 (2004)
3. Bay, H., Tuytelaars, T., Van Gool, L.: SURF: speeded up robust features. In: Bischof, H., Leonardis, A., Pinz, A. (eds.) ECCV 2006, Part I. LNCS, vol. 3951, pp. 404–417. Springer, Heidelberg (2006)
4. Shum, H.-Y., Szeliski, R.: Panoramic image mosaics. Technical Report MSR-TR-97-23, Microsoft Research (1997)
5. Szeliski, R.: Image alignment and stitching: a tutorial. Foundations and Trends? in Computer Graphics and Vision 2(1), 1–104 (2006)
6. Davis, J.: Mosaics of scenes with moving objects. In: 1998 IEEE Computer Society Conference on Computer Vision and Pattern Recognition, Proceedings 1998, pp. 354–360 (1998)

7. Mills, A., Dudek, G.: Image stitching with dynamic elements. Image and Vision Computing **27**(10), 1593–1602 (2009)
8. Uyttendaele, M., Eden, A., Skeliski, R.: Eliminating ghosting and exposure artifacts in image mosaics. In: Proceedings of the 2001 IEEE Computer Society Conference on Computer Vision and Pattern Recognition. CVPR 2001, vol. 502, pp. II-509-II-516 (2001)
9. Dijkstra, E.W.: A note on two problems in connexion with graphs. Numerische mathematik **1**(1), 269–271 (1959)
10. Besag, J.: On the statistical analysis of dirty pictures. Journal of the Royal Statistical Society. Series B (Methodological), 259–302 (1986)
11. Liu, Z.Y., Qiao, H.: GNCCP-Graduated NonConvexityand Concavity Procedure. IEEE Transactions on Pattern Analysis and Machine Intelligence **36**(6), 1258–1267 (2014)
12. Agarwala, A., Dontcheva, M., Agrawala, M., Drucker, S., Colburn, A., Curless, B., Salesin, D., Cohen, M.: Interactive digital photomontage. In: ACM Transactions on Graphics (TOG) 2004, vol. 3, pp. 294–302 (2004)
13. Fischler, M.A., Bolles, R.C.: Random sample consensus: a paradigm for model fitting with applications to image analysis and automated cartography. Communications of the ACM **24**(6), 381–395 (1981)
14. Liu, Z.Y., Qiao, H., Xu, L.: An extended path following algorithm for graph-matching problem. IEEE Transactions on Pattern Analysis and Machine Intelligence **34**(7), 1451–1456 (2012)
15. Prez, P., Gangnet, M., Blake, A.: Poisson image editing. ACM Transactions on Graphics (TOG) **3**, 313–318 (2003)
16. Liu, Z.Y., Qiao, H., Yang, X., Hoi, S.C.: Graph Matching by Simplified Convex-Concave Relaxation Procedure. International Journal of Computer Vision, 1–18 (2014)
17. Frank, M., Wolfe, P.: An algorithm for quadratic programming. Naval research logistics quarterly, 95–110 (1956)
18. Brown, M., Lowe, D.G.: Automatic panoramic image stitching using invariant features. International Journal of Computer Vision **74**(1), 59–73 (2007)
19. Torresani, L., Kolmogorov, V., Rother, C.: Feature correspondence via graph matching: Models and global optimization. In: Computer Vision. CECCV 2008, pp. 596–609. Springer (2008)
20. Zaslavskiy, M., Bach, F., Vert, J.-P.: A path following algorithm for the graph matching problem. IEEE Transactions on Pattern Analysis and Machine Intelligence **31**(12), 2227–2242 (2009)
21. Burt, P.J., Adelson, E.H.: A multiresolution spline with application to image mosaics. ACM Transactions on Graphics **2**(4), 217–236 (1983)
22. Liu, Z.Y., Qiao, H., and Su, H.: MAP inference with MRF by graduated non-convexity and concavity procedure. In: Neural Information Processing, pp. 404–412. Springer International Publishing (2014)
23. Yang, X., Liu, C.K., Liu, Z.Y., Qiao, H., Wang, Z.D.: A Probabilistic Spectral Graph Matching Algorithm for Robust Correspondence between Lunar Surface Images. World Congress on Intelligent Control and Automation (2014)

# A Real Time Robust Hand Tracking Method with Normal Cameras

Yang Liu[1]([✉]), Man Yau Chiu[1], Hailiang Li[1], Kangheng Wu[1],
Zhibin Lei[1], and Qiang Ding[2]

[1] Hong Kong Applied Science and Technology Research Institute Company Limited HK,
and Huawei Technologies Co., Ltd., Hong Kong, China
yangliu@astri.org
[2] Huawei Technologies Co., Ltd., Shenzhen, China

**Abstract.** Driven by the wide usage of smart devices today, gesture control with normal cameras is in great need to be studied further, especially in healthcare sector, for example, patient monitoring and rehabilitation. This paper proposes a practical hand tracking method to tackle the related challenges including efficiency and robustness. Based on an efficient framework which integrates segmentation and tracking, several enhancements are proposed for a robust hand chasing. Experiments on both PC and android smartphones prove the proposed method is efficient and robust.

**Keywords:** Tracking · Hand · Robust · Real time · Normal camera

## 1 Introduction

Recent solutions to hand tracking have been using cameras with depth sensor which can produce a 3D point presentation of the hand [1] [2] [9]. Although these methods appeared attractive in some applications, for example, healthcare and character animation, the imaging hardware required is not often available for normal cameras on various devices, especially on the smart devices. On the other hand, gestures controls are already important to the devices with normal cameras. For example, gestures may be used in the smart phone navigation while the user is moving, or for a demo in a smart TV in an exhibition, or to simply control a PC with a normal camera in a presentation, or for a patient to tell a nurse that he or she has a special need. There is still a huge market for a real time (in PC over 30fps, in smart phone over 15fps) and robust hand tracking methods to support all the scenarios.

Unfortunately, a normal camera system for hand tracking is often suffered from various challenges such as hand appearance changes, camera limitations, and the disturbing environments. In the related previous work, TLD proposed by Kalal [10] is a solid integration of detection and tracking but do not handle articulated objects well. Liu and his team proposed to combine skin color information to trace the hand in TLD but the tracking rate is hard to meet the real time requirements [3]. Zhang's work for structure-preserving object tracker revealed improvements in multi-object

© Springer-Verlag Berlin Heidelberg 2015
H. Zha et al. (Eds.): CCCV 2015, Part I, CCIS 546, pp. 56–65, 2015.
DOI: 10.1007/978-3-662-48558-3_6

tracking while the articulated objects still remained an issue. In addition, seldom previous work took the tracking failure into consideration to make the tracking as continuous as possible [1]-[3].

In our practice, we realized a single method may not tackle the challenges well and therefore multiple cues should be used to extract the hand in each frame. Accordingly, we tried to integrate segmentation and tracking first to have an efficient hand tracking scheme. After that, we enhanced tracking and segmentation separately with several measurement including tracking failure compensation, adaptive threshold segmentation and skin color interference detection/mitigation. Accordingly, the proposed tracking method is efficient and robust in a practical scenario.

The rest of the paper is divided into four parts. Section 2 introduces the efficient tracking framework where we start to build the system. Section 3 illustrate the enhancement details to tackle the robustness issues. Accordingly, some experiments are presented in section 4 to prove the tracking performance. Finally, Section 5 concludes our work.

## 2    Efficient Tracking Framework

As shown in Figure 1 (a), the efficient tracking framework tries to get the current segmentation result (as complete as possible) for the next frame tracking object. Therefore, the tracking is expected to reach the real time requirement.

In details, as in Figure 1(b), before the tracking starts, a hand with five fingers open is stored as the default initial gesture. When the system finds the default gesture, the hand detected will be defined as the object to be tracked in the next frame. In addition, the detected hand determines the initial segmentation skin color threshold. Therefore our proposal is expected to be useful for people with different skin colors.

In the next frame and the latter frames where tracking is continuously successful, the hand is segmented. In details, the exact hand contour will be found based on the segmentation result and the segmentation is done based on the tracking box area.

For example, assuming the hand is detected at frame n, in the latter frames (n+1, n+2,..., n+k), a tracker can be used to track the given hand. The segmentation result in n+m is defined as the tracking object for n+m +1 (1<m<k).

Finally, if the tracking fails, the initial hand detection has to restart.

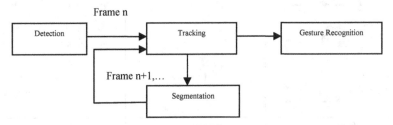

**Fig. 1.** (a) An Efficient Tracking Framework: Diagram

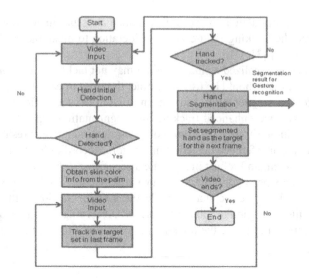

**Fig. 1.** (b) An Efficient Tracking Framework: Detailed Flowchart

## 2.1    Initial Hand Detection

Adaboost detector with histogram of gradient (HOG) feature is used for our initial hand detection. HOG characterize the hand appearance and shape well by the distribution of local intensity gradients or edge directions. Therefore, the detector with HOG feature can capture the hand no matter what skin color it is. As shown in figure 2, various hand images are collected/generated to present the diversity of hands and backgrounds. Through this way, a robust hand detector can be trained.

In details, the off-line training stage can be divided into two phases. Phase one is to collect hand samples and crop them to normalized size (64 × 64) as shown in above figures. And phase two is to train an Adaboost detector with HOG feature including 20 stages. For example, we trained with 10,000 positive samples (hands) and got the converged detector after more than 7 days.

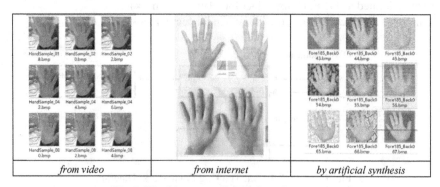

**Fig. 2.** Hand images collected from three ways

After the hand is detected in an initial frame (white box in Figure 3), the palm area will be easily defined (red box in Figure 3.2). For example, assuming the initial hand area box has a width $W_{initial}$, a height $H_{initial}$, and a center with coordinates ($X_{initial}$, $Y_{initial}$), the palm area box can be defined to have a width $W_{palm} = 0.2 W_{initial}$, and a height $H_{palm} = 0.4 H_{initial}$, and a center ($X_{palm}$, $Y_{palm}$) where $X_{palm} = X_{initial}$, and $Y_{palm} = Y_{initial}$. The skin color information found in the palm can be used further for segmentation.

**Fig. 3.** Palm area defined by the hand detection result

## 2.2    Segmentation Module

For segmentation, a segmentation area is defined based on the tracking box. For example, the segmentation area can be defined twice of tracking box size with the same area center. Therefore, if the tracking is robust, the skin color based segmentation result will always be the hand.

In details, the color space $YCrCb$ is used. Color is represented by luma component $Y$ (computed from nonlinear RGB, constructed as a weighted sum of the RGB values), and two color difference values $Cr$ and $Cb$ that are formed by subtracting luma from RGB red and blue components. The mean value of Cr, Cb component ($M_{Cr}$, $M_{Cb}$) can be determined by the palm pixels obtained in the initial hand detection. Accordingly, we have an initial threshold:

$$Th_{initial} = \frac{|M_{Cr} - M_{Cb}|}{\sqrt{2}} \tag{1}$$

Any pixel with (Cr, Cb) values lies in the circle with center ($M_{Cr}$, $M_{Cb}$) and radius ($K * Th_{initial}$) will be considered as a skin pixel, otherwise, it is non-skin pixel. The parameter K is flexible. In our practice, K = 0.15-0.2 works fine.

## 2.3    Tracking Module

In our framework, optical flow is used for the tracking module. In details, optical flow generates dense flow fields by computing the flow vector of each tracking pixel under the brightness constraint. Since the tracking object is limited by the segmentation every frame, most of the tracking pixels will be distributed on the hand.

# 3    Enhancements for Robust Tracking

Several enhancement are implemented to ensure the tracker works as continuous as possible. For instance, when the tracking box shrinks too much, generally the tracking will be considered failed. We propose tracking failure compensation to handle the failure case while the hand is still in the camera. In addition, adaptive threshold segmentation is proposed as well to define a better tracking object for the next frame. Finally, we design an interference alert mechanism to let the user mitigate the interference from face in the camera.

Figure 4 shows how some of the enhancements helped in the tracking flow. Besides the functions mentioned above, a small but useful step is that the tracking box may be refined with removing the border false hand pixel. The assumption here is that the hand is always moving so the static pixels with skin color at the tracking box border will probably not belong to the hand.

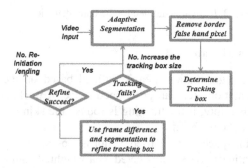

**Fig. 4.** Robust Tracking Enhancement Flowchart

## 3.1    Failure Compensation

Due to the tracking box size shrink caused by illumination change/gesture change, sometimes the tracking fails even when the hand is still in the frame (Fig.5 (a)). To compensate the "wrong lost", the frame difference result is used. In our practice, a threshold from 10 to 20 for frame difference calculation works fine.

In details, there are three steps to compensate the tracking failure. Firstly, the small tracking box is determined (less than $30 \times 30$ for one $640 \times 480$ image) as the red box in figure 5 (b). Secondly, the frame difference region around the small tracking box is determined as the black box in figure 5(b). Finally, if the frame difference region defined by the search results is large enough, the segmentation result based on the region is set as a new target for continuous tracking without restarting the tracker. The steps can be summarized in equation (2).

$$\text{Tracking Box}_{n+1} = \begin{cases} Seg(\text{Tracking Box}_n) & tracking\ success \\ Seg(Diff(\text{Tracking Box}_n)) & tracking\ fails \end{cases} \quad (2)$$

where Seg(A) means to segment the given area A to find skin color pixels and Diff(B) means to find the frame difference area around the given box B.

**Fig. 5.** (a) Tracking Failure Example (b) Failure Compensation Steps

## 3.2    Adaptive Threshold Segmentation

After the initial threshold is available, the segmentation result may be impacted by gestures. For example, when an open hand changes to a fist, the palm's color/luma may be a little different from that of the thumb and therefore the contours will be discrete.

Therefore, we propose to segment with adaptive skin color thresholds if needed. The term adaptive means we use multiple thresholds when necessary and the new threshold is generated based on the tracking result instantly. For example, one threshold is the initial skin color threshold (mandatory), and the others are updated from different hand sectors. The conditions to use the adaptive skin color threshold may be when the some part of the hand is dark or the light on the hand is not uniform.

In details, the tracking box can be divided into $s$ sectors ($i =1,2,...s$). The mean values of $Cr$ and $Cb$ in sector $i$ ($M_{Cri}$, $M_{Cbi}$) can be updated in a given period. Therefore, the updated threshold in sector $i$ is

$$Th_i = \frac{|M_{Cri} - M_{Cbi}|}{\sqrt{2}} \tag{3}$$

Any pixel with ($Cr$, $Cb$) values lies in the circle with center ($M_{Cri}$, $M_{Cbi}$) and radius ($K_i \times Th_i$) will be considered as a skin pixel, otherwise, it is non-skin pixel. The parameter $K_i$ is flexible. In our practice, $K_i = 0.15$- $0.25$ works fine.

Taking YCrCb color space and two sectors (upper and lower) as an example. The initial threshold is always used to segment the hand. In addition, in some cases, the updated skin color threshold will be also used. The case include: when the luma value in one sector is smaller than a threshold (e.g. 130); the luma difference between various sectors is larger than a threshold (e.g. $0.3 \times$ *initial luma*). The method can be written as follows.

```
If (lower sector luma < threshold 1
|two sectors luma difference/initial luma > threshold 2)
   {Th_initial in(1) and Th_i in (3) shall be used}
else
   {only Th_initial in(1) shall be used}
```

### 3.3    Interference Alert/Mitigation

Since the skin color space is used in our tracking and segmentation scheme, skin-color like background (such as the face of the user) may interfere the segmentation as well as the tracking.

A simple "black hole" method is used in our practice to alert such interference.

In a sentence, the "black hole" method means all the pixels in the skin color threshold but outside the current tracking box in the same frame are set black(RGB values are set as (0,0,0)).

In details, there are three steps for "black hole" method.

Firstly, when one hand is detected in one frame, a black hole picture will be available with all the skin color pixels outside the detection box are set black.

Secondly, the black hole picture is updated with a given period. In our practice, the period can be set tens of frames, such as 50 frames.

Finally, when the hand is moving, the ratio of black pixels to all the pixels in the tracking box is calculated every frame. If the ratio is higher than one certain number (e.g. 10%), interference will be alerted.

In addition, it is noticeable that the "black hole" method itself already mitigate some interference. For instance, without the "black holes", the tracking box may drift when the hand is very close to a face. After the interference alert is implemented, the tracking box is more stable on the hand when it is closed to a face.

## 4    Tracking Performance

### 4.1    Evaluation Setup

Our algorithm is implemented in both PC and android smart phones. Accordingly, three scenarios are set up for the evaluation. Two of them are evaluated on PC with Intel i7 core, and the rest is on an android phone with Quad-core.

We invite five colleagues to demo various groups of gestures in front of the normal cameras of the PC and the android phone in various offices. All the rooms we test are of normal bright light. For each gesture group, users repeat one gesture 40 times in their normal paces unless they are told to rapid move hands as in 4.3. When the user is sitting near to the camera, only one hand is used to control the device. Otherwise, two hands are used. Details of the environment can be seen in the table below.

**Table 1.** Details of the evaluation environment

|  | User's distance to the camera | Single hand/Two hands | Device running the camera | Input frame rate | Input image resolution |
|---|---|---|---|---|---|
| Scenario 1 | 0.3m-1m | Single | PC | 60fps | 640 × 480 |
| Scenario 2 | 1m-2m | Two | PC | 60fps | 640 × 480 |
| Scenario 3 | 0.3m-1m | Single | Smart Phone | 30fps | 640 × 480 |

The gesture groups for scenario 1 and 3 are the same:

Index finger up and down (click) 40 times
Thumb open and close (click) 40 times
Palm moving forward 40 times
Palm moving backward 40 times

The gesture groups for scenario 2 are:

Move 2 hands with opening palms towards the right 40 times
Move 2 hands with opening palms towards the left 40 times
Move 2 hands with opening palms upwards 40 times
Move 2 hands with opening palms downwards 40 times
Move 2 hands with opening palms near to each other 40 times
Move 2 hands with opening palms away from each other 40 times
Move 2 hands with opening palms along a circle
Open and close 2 hands 40 times

## 4.2    Tracking Efficiency

The experiment results reveal that the proposed tracking scheme runs over 30fps in average for the PC and over 15fps in average for the smart phone. As a contrast, the average tracking rate for hands is around 10 fps for original TLD algorithm in our local PC test.

**Fig. 6.** Screen shot for demos on (a) the PC (scenario 2) (b) the smart phone (scenario 3)

**Table 2.** Tracking rate results (fps)

|          | Scenario 1 | Scenario 2 | Scenario 3 |
|----------|-----------|-----------|-----------|
| USER 1   | 35.1      | 31.0      | 15.9      |
| USER 2   | 34.3      | 31.4      | 15.8      |
| USER 3   | 33.4      | 30.3      | 16.0      |
| USER 4   | 32.8      | 31.4      | 15.7      |
| USER 5   | 35.8      | 31.5      | 15.9      |
| Average  | 34.3      | 31.1      | 15.9      |

## 4.3    Tracking Robustness

Tracking accuracy is defined as the ratio of success hand tracked time to the whole tracking period in the test video. For all the three scenarios we tested in a normal office room with sufficient light, the tracking accuracy is over 98%.

In order to prove the robust tracking enhancements, two extra evaluations are further executed. One is to test the failure compensation mechanism in a rapid gesture change case, and the other is to test the adaptive segmentation in an uneven light room.

In the rapid gesture change scenario, the tracking fails when the hand is move fast (figure 6 (a)). Since the hand is still in the camera, with the proposed tracking failure compensation mechanism, the enhanced tracking successfully defines a new object for further tracking (figure 6 (b)).

**Fig. 7.** Failure compensation experiment (a) without compensation (b) with compensation

In the uneven light scenario, the contour is not completed when only the initial threshold is used to segment the hand (figure 8 (a)). As a contrast, when the proposed adaptive threshold is used, a more completed gesture contour is available (figure 8 (b)). As a consequence, the tracking box in this frame is also larger so the tracking object for the next frame is better defined.

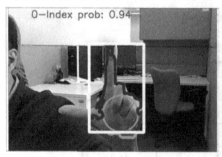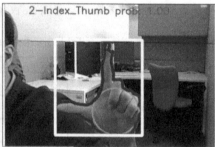

**Fig. 8.** (a) Initial threshold segmentation (b) adaptive threshold segmentation

In a summary, the experiment results reveal our proposal is robust in various indoor scenarios.

# 5    Conclusions

Our work for a real-time robust hand tracking with normal single camera input is presented in this paper. When users raise their hand(s) with an open hand facing the camera, the proposed running algorithm will detect the hand(s) and trace the detected object continuously. The experiments prove the proposed method is efficient to meet the real time requirements for the cameras on PC and smart phones, and robust in various indoor scenarios. With the automatically hand detection, tracking and segmentation, the tracking will be useful for people with various skin colors.

The future work may include two directions. One is the enhancement for outdoor scenarios. The other is the enhancement for the cameras on wearable devices.

# References

1. Yilmaz, A., Javed, O., Shah, M.: Object Tracking: A Survey. ACM Computing Surveys (CSUR) Surveys Homepage archive, 38(4), Article No. 13 (2006)
2. Mohr, D., Zachmann, G.: A survey of vision-based markerless hand tracking approaches. Preprint submitted to Computer Vision and Image Understanding (2013)
3. Liu, H., Liu, X.: Robust hand tracking based on online learning and multi-cue flocks of features. In: 2013 20th IEEE International Conference on Image Processing (ICIP) (2013)
4. Shimada, K., Muto, R., Endo, T.: A Combined Method Based on SVM and Online Learning with HOG for Hand Shape Recognition. Journal of Advanced Computational Intelligence and Intelligent Informatics (JACIII) **16**, 687–695 (2012)
5. Draiss, K.F.: Advanced Man-Machine Interaction, Fundamentals and Implementation. Signals and Communication Technology. Springer, Heidelberg (2006). Chapter 2
6. Zhang, L., van der Maaten, L.: Structure preserving object tracking. In: Proceedings of the IEEE Conference on Computer Vision and Pattern Recognition (CVPR) (2013)
7. Ibraheem, N.A., Khan, R.Z., Hasan, M.M.: Comparative Study of Skin Color based Segmentation Techniques. International Journal of Applied Information Systems (IJAIS), 5(10), Foundation of Computer Science FCS, New York, USA, August 2013. ISSN: 2249-0868
8. Vezhnevets, V., Sazonov, V., Andreeva, A.: A survey on pixel-based skin color detection techniques. In: Proceedings of the GraphiCon 2003 (2003), pp. 85–92, Key: citeulike:4847952
9. Wu, Y., Zhao, L., Ding, H.: Robust Hand Gesture Recognition with Feature Selection and Hierarchical Temporal Self-Similarities. International Journal of Information and Electronics Engineering 3(5), 510–515 (2013)
10. Kalal, Z., Mikolajczyk, K., Matas, J.: Tracking-Learning-Detection. Pattern Analysis and Machine Intelligence (2011)

# Hypergraph Regularized Autoencoder for 3D Human Pose Recovery

Chaoqun Hong, Jun Yu$^{(\boxtimes)}$, You Jane, and Xuhui Chen

School of Computer and Information Engineering,
Xiamen University of Technology, 361024 Xiamen, China
yujun@hdu.edu.cn

**Abstract.** Image-based human pose recovery is usually conducted by retrieving relevant poses with image features. However, semantic gap exists for current feature extractors, which limits recovery performance. In this paper, we propose a novel feature extractor with deep learning. It is based on denoising autoencoder and improves traditional methods by adopting locality preserved restriction. To impose this restriction, we introduce manifold regularization with hypergraph Laplacian. Hypergraph Laplacian matrix is constructed with patch alignment framework. In this way, an automatic feature extractor for silhouettes is achieved. Experimental results on two datasets show that the recovery error has been reduced by 10% to 20%, which demonstrates the effectiveness of the proposed method.

**Keywords:** Human pose recovery · Deep learning · Manifold regularization · Hypergraph · Patch alignment framework

## 1 Introduction

3D human pose recovery tries to generate a visually pleasing and semantically correct human skeleton with sensor data. Traditionally, it is usually achieved by motion capture system. These systems are expensive and require attached markers. Markerless solutions currently draw plenty of attention. The most successful of them is Microsoft Kinect. It makes use of RGBD data. However, RGBD cameras are still not commonly used. In this way, researchers devote themselves into image-based 3D human pose recovery over recent years as the demand for high-quality and accurate poses in vision systems has increased [9][7].

Typical routine of image-based pose recovery rely on the same three-step procedure: 1) extracting the visual features from the 2D images (usually silhouettes); 2) mapping the 2D visual features to the 3D poses using a specified learning algorithm; 3) reconstructing the 3D poses based on the mapping function obtained. Well-designed feature should be discriminative with respect to 2D images and 3D poses. Until now, quite a lot of features have been proposed for human pose analysis, such as shape context[2], histograms of oriented gradients[4], Hierarchical centroid[12] and so on. However, feature descriptors are still ambiguous due

© Springer-Verlag Berlin Heidelberg 2015
H. Zha et al. (Eds.): CCCV 2015, Part I, CCIS 546, pp. 66–75, 2015.
DOI: 10.1007/978-3-662-48558-3_7

to the so-called semantic gap between images and features, since they cannot completely represent the semantic content and information of images.

Deep learning architectures [11] have been useful for exploring hidden representations in natural images and have proven success in a variety of vision tasks. In the current big data era, the extensive availability of training images enables deep models to be generic and flexible. Inspired by the learning capability and capacity of the deep learning model, we hypothesized that deep architectures would be perfectly suited to seeking the proper representations for 2D images and 3D poses and modelling their relationship. Current solutions generally learn multilevel representations by deep learning [5]. For instance, autoencoder [13] is an unsupervised feature-learning scheme in which the internal layer acts as a generic extractor of inner image representations. A double-layer structure, which can efficiently map the input data onto appropriate outputs, is obtained by using a multilayer perceptron. However, in these methods, the locality of features is lost. This makes similar pose silhouettes being described by totally different hidden vectors, and unstable performance in pose reconstruction. In order to solve this problem, one possible solution is to add an additional locality-preserving term to the formulation of deep learning [14].

In this paper, a novel approach is proposed to recover 3D human poses from silhouettes with hypergraph regularized autoencoder (HRA). It is based on marginalized denoising autoencoders (MDA) [3]. Different from previous works, it makes use of locality information of samples. The main contribution of this work is two-fold:

- The state-of-the-art work in pose recovery with autoencoders is improved by imposing locality preserved restriction. To impose this restriction, an Laplacian matrix is constructed to describe the internal relationship of samples.
- The construction of Laplacian matrix is further improved by using hypergraph. This process is based on a real-valued form of combinatorial optimization problem. The weights of hyperedges for the whole alignment are computed by statistics of distances between neighboring pairs.

The remainder of this paper is organized as follows. The proposed hypergraph regularized autoencoder is presented in Section 2. Then, experimental results on human pose recovery and comparisons with other state-of-the-art methods are presented in Section 3. Finally, we conclude the paper in Section 4.

## 2   Hypergraph Regularized Autoencoder

### 2.1   Marginalized Denoising Autoencoders

In denoising autoencoders, inputs $x_1, ..., x_n$ are corrupted by random feature removal. $\hat{x}_i$ is denoted as the corrupted version of $x_i$ and $W : \mathbb{R}^d \to \mathbb{R}^d$ is denoted as the mapping of reconstructing the corrupted inputs. In this way, we can defined the squared reconstruction loss as:

$$\frac{1}{2n} \sum_{i=1}^{n} \| x_i - W\hat{x}_i \|^2 . \tag{1}$$

The solution to (1) depends on which features of each input are randomly corrupted. To lower the variance, MDA [3] perform multiple passes over the training set, each time with different corruption. In this way, the overall squared loss is defined as:

$$\frac{1}{2mn} \sum_{j=1}^{m} \sum_{i=1}^{n} \| x_i - W\hat{x}_{i,j} \|^2,$$

(2)

where $\hat{x}_{i,j}$ represents the $j$th corrupted version of the original input $x_i$ and $m$ is the number of layers.

For the matrix form, $X = [x_1, ..., x_n] \in \mathbb{R}^{d \times n}$ is denoted as the data matrix, $\overline{X} = [X, .., , X]$ is denoted as the $m$-times repeated version and $\hat{X}$ is defined as the corrupted version of $\overline{X}$. Then, the loss in (2) is reduced to:

$$\frac{1}{2mn} tr[(\overline{X} - W\hat{X})^T (\overline{X} - W\hat{X})].$$

(3)

The minimization to (3) can be expressed as the well-known closed-form solution for ordinary least squares:

$$W = PQ^{-1} \text{ with } Q = \hat{X}\hat{X}^T \text{ and } P = \overline{X}\hat{X}.$$

(4)

In our implementation, we further reduce the stacked form of MDA to a overlapped form. Instead of concatenating the output of each layer, we simply use the output of each layer as the input of the next layer. In this way, (2) can be rewritten as:

$$\frac{1}{2n} \sum_{i=1}^{n} \| x_i - W\hat{x}_{i,m} \|^2 .$$

(5)

(3) can be also rewritten as:

$$\frac{1}{2n} tr[(\overline{X}_m - W\hat{X})^T (\overline{X}_m - W\hat{X})].$$

(6)

## 2.2 Manifold Regularization

As mentioned before, due to the loss of locality information, similar features can be encoded as totally different hidden representation, which may bring about the loss of the locality information of the features to be encoded. To preserve such locality information, we introduce manifold regularization to (5). Then, the reconstruction loss can be defined by:

$$\frac{1}{2n} (\sum_{i=1}^{n} \| x_i - W\hat{x}_{i,m} \|^2 + \alpha \sum_{i,k}^{n} \| x_i - x_k \|^2 \omega_{i,k}),$$

(7)

where $\alpha$ indicates the weights of locality reservation term and $\omega_{i,k}$ represents the similarity between sample $i$ and sample $k$. With the introduction of locality reservation term, the matrix form can be defined as:

$$\frac{1}{2n}tr[(\overline{X}_m - W\hat{X})^T(\overline{X}_m - W\hat{X}) + \alpha\overline{X}_m^T L\overline{X}_m],    \tag{8}$$

where $L$ is known as Laplacian matrix.

## 2.3   Hypergraph Optimization

The key to solve (8) is to construct Laplacian matrix $L$. Traditional methods assumed that the relationships among images are pairwise. However, this assumption is over-simplified and a lot of information is lost. To avoid this problem, hypergraph representation is proposed [15]. Different from traditional graph-based representation, one edge is able to connect more than two vertices in hypergraph representation. In other words, vertices connected by an edge are thought as a subset of vertices in the graph. Therefore, hypergraph representation is much more descriptive and powerful. The definitions are shown in Table 1.

**Table 1.** Definition of symbols in the hypergraph.

| Symbol | Definition |
|--------|------------|
| $u, v$ | Vertices in the hypergraph |
| $e$ | Edges in the hypergraph |
| $\omega(e)$ | The weight of an edge $e$ |
| $\delta(e)$ | The degree of an edge, $e$. It illustrates how many vertices are connected by $e$. In traditional graph representation, $\delta(e) = 2$. |
| $d(v)$ | The degree of a vertex, $v$. It is calculated by summing the weighting values of edges connected to this vertex. |
| $D_v$ | The diagonal matrix containing the vertex degrees |
| $D_e$ | The diagonal matrix containing the edge degrees |
| $H$ | In this matrix, $H(v, e) = 1$ if $v \in e$ |
| $\Omega$ | The diagonal matrix containing the weights of hyperedges |
| $V$ | The set of vertices |
| $E$ | The set of edges |

In our method, we construct hypergraph Laplacian matrix inspired by patch alignment framework [6], which consists of two steps.

1. Part Optimization: We define one patch to be the vertices connected by one hyperedge. Thus, the patch in the proposed learning process is defined by:

$$\arg\min_{f\in R^{|V|}} \sum_{m,n\subset e} \frac{w(e)}{\delta(e)}\left(\frac{y_m}{\sqrt{d_m}} - \frac{y_n}{\sqrt{d_n}}\right)^2    \tag{9}$$

For one patch, we should compute:

$$\sum_{m,n\subset e} \frac{w(e)}{\delta(e)}\left(\frac{y_m}{\sqrt{d_m}} - \frac{y_n}{\sqrt{d_n}}\right)^2,    \tag{10}$$

which means that we randomly choose two vertices in the subset of vertices contained by a hyperedge, $e$, and sum the value of

$$\frac{w(e)}{\delta(e)}\Big(\frac{y_m}{\sqrt{d_m}} - \frac{y_n}{\sqrt{d_n}}\Big)^2. \tag{11}$$

Expanding (9) and combining items, we can get the patch optimization for each hyperedge:

$$\frac{1}{2}\sum_{v \subset e}\frac{F}{DV_v^{\frac{1}{2}}}EH'_e\frac{\Omega}{DE}H_eE'\frac{F}{DV_v^{\frac{1}{2}}}. \tag{12}$$

Matrix $E$ is

$$\begin{bmatrix} -e^T \\ I \end{bmatrix} \tag{13}$$

where $e = [1, ..., 1]^T$, $I$ is an $n \times n$ identity matrix.

2. Whole alignment: In the hypergraph, the weight of a hyperedge is computed by summing the similarity scores of all the pairs of vertices contained in this hyperedge. The similarity score of any pair of vertices is defined as the distance of image features:

$$S(u, v) = exp(-\frac{1}{\sigma}dist(feat(u), feat(v))), \tag{14}$$

where $feat(u)$ represents the image feature vector of vertex $u$, $dist(x, y)$ is usually set to be the L2 distance and $\sigma$ is the standard deviation of all distances. With the hyper edge weighting matrix, the multi-view hypergraph Laplacian can be computed by summing the patch optimization defined in (11) of all the hyperedges:

$$\frac{1}{2}\sum_{e \in E}\sum_{v \in e}\frac{F}{DV_v^{\frac{1}{2}}}EH'_e\frac{\Omega}{DE}H_eE'\frac{F}{DV_v^{\frac{1}{2}}}. \tag{15}$$

One hyperedge is defined to contain one sample and its $k$ nearest neighbors. In this way, the computational complexity of hypergraph-based manifold regularization can be divided into two parts. The first part is finding nearest neighbors with Euclidean distances, which is $O(k \times n \times d^2)$. The second part is computing Laplacian matrix, which is $n^2$. The introduction of manifold regularization may reduce the speed of extracting features.

## 3    Experimental Evaluation

### 3.1    Datasets and Settings

In our experiments, we use two datasets to evaluate the performance and emphasize the advantage of the proposed HRA.

The first dataset is that used in [1]. In this dataset, a person is walking in a spiral pattern, and we name this dataset Walking. The training data consists of all the pose vectors taken from sequences 01-07. All sequences are concatenated to give 1691 training pose vectors. Sequence 08 is used for testing, and contains 418 testing poses. Mocap data are retrieved for a 54 degrees of freedom body model, with three angles for each of 18 joints, including body orientation with respect to the camera. For evaluation, the mean RMS absolute difference errors between the true and estimated joint angle vectors are reported in degrees:

$$d_{degree}(y, y^r) = \frac{1}{M} \sum_{i=1}^{M} |(y - y_i^r) \bmod \pm 180°)|, \tag{16}$$

where $y$ is the ground truth, $y^r$ is the recovered degree, $M = 54$ is the number of degrees and $(\bullet) \bmod \pm 180°)(\bullet + 180°) \bmod 360° - 180°$ reduces angles to the interval $[-180°, +180°]$. The training silhouettes are created by using POSER to render the Mocap poses.

The second dataset is the HumanEva-I dataset, which is widely used in evaluating the performance of pose recovery [10]. This dataset contains five motion types performed by four subjects. A 3D pose is encoded as a collection of joint coordinates in 3D space and there are 14 joints in the HumanEva data set, therefore each 3D action data is represented by a $14 \times 3 = 42$-dimensional feature vector. For evaluation, Trial 1 of Subjects 1 and 2 is used. Since there are many invalid motions in Mocap data, we collect all the valid frames. The frames in Trial 1 of Subject 1 are used as the training set. The number of frames is 701. The frames in Trial 1 of Subject 1 are used as the testing set. The number of frames is 604. For evaluation, the retrieval error is computed. The distance between two poses is then calculated as the average Euclidean distance between corresponding joint markers:

$$d_{pose}(y, y^r) = \frac{1}{M} \sum_{i=1}^{M} \| m_i(y) - m_i(y^r) \|, \tag{17}$$

where $\| \bullet \|$ computes the 3D distance between two markers which are represented by 3D coordinates:

$$\| m_i(y) - m_i(y^r) \| = \sum_{j=1}^{3} \| m_i(y_j) - m_i(y_j^r) \| . \tag{18}$$

All the images are resized to be $128 \times 128 = 16384$ for fairness of comparison. With silhouettes features, we get recovered poses by relevance vector machine [1].

## 3.2 Optimization of Autoencoders

When we adopt manifold regularization in (7), parameter $\alpha$ is introduced to balance reconstruction loss and locality loss. We show the performance with different settings of $\alpha$ to look into its influence. The curve is shown in Fig. 1.

We can figure out that the proposed method performs the best when $\alpha = 0.4$ for Walking dataset while it performs the best when $\alpha = 0.2$ for HumanEva-I dataset.

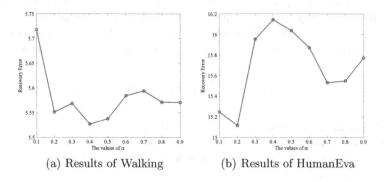

(a) Results of Walking                  (b) Results of HumanEva

**Fig. 1.** The influence of $\alpha$

### 3.3   Comparison with State-of-the-Arts

In this subsection, we compare the proposed HRA with the following existing features.

- Hierarchical centroid (HC) [12]: The number of dimensions is $n \times \sum_{i=1}^{n} (2 \times 2^{2 \times (i-1)})$ in which $n$ is the level of the computed centroids. In the experiments, $n = 3$.
- Histograms of oriented gradients (HOG) [4]. The number of HOG windows per bound box is $3 \times 3$ and the number of histogram bins is 9. Each image is thus represented by a feature vector with 81 dimensions.
- Shape context (SC) [2]: 200 points are sampled for each silhouette image. In each image, the histogram of shape contexts is constructed from 12 angular bins and 5 radial bins. To match the shape context features efficiently, the shape signature histograms known as shapemes, proposed by Mori et al. [8] are applied. Theoretically speaking, a shapeme is the bag-of-feature form of shape contexts. A codebook containing 200 codes is trained, giving the shapeme a dimensionality of 200.
- Marginalized Denoising Autoencoder (MDA) [3]: MDA approximates the expected loss function of traditional denoising autoencoders with its Taylor expansion. The dimensionality of hidden representation is the same as the size of original images.

To compare the performance of these methods, we show the average recovery error of each pose component. The Walking poses consist of a body model with 54 degrees of freedom, so the average recovery error for each degree is shown.

**Table 2.** The performance on each marker of Walking.

| index | HC | HOG | SC | MDA | HRA | index | HC | HOG | SC | MDA | HRA |
|---|---|---|---|---|---|---|---|---|---|---|---|
| 1 | 4.20 | 3.74 | 4.05 | 3.91 | 3.66 | 28 | 4.69 | 3.57 | 4.52 | 4.37 | 3.93 |
| 2 | 3.78 | 2.84 | 2.79 | 1.89 | 1.49 | 29 | 12.20 | 12.76 | 10.29 | 10.90 | 10.07 |
| 3 | 31.38 | 23.37 | 22.51 | 11.83 | 12.02 | 30 | 7.87 | 8.15 | 7.74 | 7.24 | 6.46 |
| 4 | 3.48 | 2.83 | 3.19 | 3.60 | 3.09 | 31 | 9.06 | 10.10 | 9.77 | 8.91 | 8.26 |
| 5 | 2.72 | 2.86 | 2.75 | 2.90 | 2.71 | 32 | 4.97 | 4.08 | 4.71 | 4.83 | 4.38 |
| 6 | 3.31 | 3.69 | 3.67 | 3.24 | 2.84 | 33 | 13.18 | 12.16 | 11.06 | 10.94 | 10.04 |
| 7 | 3.42 | 3.17 | 3.53 | 3.76 | 3.45 | 34 | 4.61 | 4.23 | 4.03 | 4.52 | 3.83 |
| 8 | 2.24 | 1.92 | 2.68 | 2.67 | 2.23 | 35 | 3.00 | 3.44 | 3.01 | 3.11 | 2.77 |
| 9 | 4.72 | 3.81 | 5.06 | 5.03 | 4.58 | 36 | 0.84 | 1.14 | 1.23 | 1.12 | 0.73 |
| 10 | 9.20 | 8.80 | 9.44 | 9.30 | 8.99 | 37 | 13.62 | 13.56 | 10.74 | 11.08 | 10.68 |
| 11 | 4.46 | 4.03 | 4.23 | 3.92 | 3.35 | 38 | 4.44 | 4.14 | 4.10 | 4.35 | 3.85 |
| 12 | 4.19 | 3.38 | 4.30 | 4.67 | 4.40 | 39 | 4.69 | 4.03 | 3.80 | 4.11 | 3.89 |
| 13 | 2.01 | 1.61 | 2.06 | 2.36 | 1.95 | 40 | 16.39 | 14.95 | 13.49 | 13.35 | 12.80 |
| 14 | 0.03 | 0.33 | 0.59 | 0.45 | 0.05 | 41 | 5.92 | 5.65 | 5.28 | 5.41 | 4.88 |
| 15 | 0.53 | 0.68 | 0.91 | 0.85 | 0.44 | 42 | 8.07 | 8.14 | 8.04 | 7.71 | 7.67 |
| 16 | 3.93 | 4.04 | 4.37 | 3.79 | 3.38 | 43 | 10.44 | 10.53 | 8.93 | 9.60 | 9.54 |
| 17 | 11.45 | 11.07 | 10.14 | 9.53 | 9.72 | 44 | 12.42 | 12.63 | 12.40 | 12.51 | 11.44 |
| 18 | 9.43 | 8.23 | 8.09 | 6.75 | 6.64 | 45 | 10.06 | 9.80 | 9.50 | 10.10 | 9.05 |
| 19 | 8.91 | 8.41 | 7.85 | 8.12 | 7.51 | 46 | 11.22 | 10.88 | 9.74 | 8.94 | 8.34 |
| 20 | 1.76 | 1.64 | 1.96 | 1.85 | 1.40 | 47 | 4.71 | 4.54 | 4.19 | 3.84 | 3.64 |
| 21 | 11.96 | 10.57 | 10.77 | 12.19 | 11.34 | 48 | 7.29 | 6.46 | 6.44 | 6.88 | 6.65 |
| 22 | 3.08 | 2.71 | 2.92 | 3.14 | 2.69 | 49 | 16.34 | 16.68 | 15.77 | 15.44 | 14.80 |
| 23 | 2.06 | 2.29 | 2.31 | 2.29 | 1.90 | 50 | 3.87 | 3.77 | 3.92 | 3.65 | 3.23 |
| 24 | 0.26 | 0.54 | 0.72 | 0.64 | 0.25 | 51 | 18.83 | 17.07 | 17.31 | 17.40 | 15.51 |
| 25 | 1.06 | 1.21 | 1.44 | 1.43 | 0.98 | 52 | 10.56 | 9.94 | 9.24 | 10.67 | 10.05 |
| 26 | 2.32 | 2.14 | 2.32 | 2.08 | 1.57 | 53 | 1.57 | 1.76 | 2.03 | 1.95 | 1.52 |
| 27 | 0.34 | 0.58 | 0.77 | 0.66 | 0.24 | 54 | 8.81 | 8.97 | 8.85 | 8.04 | 7.50 |
| AVG | 6.78 | 6.36 | 6.21 | 6.00 | 5.53 | | | | | | |

The HumanEva-I poses consist of 14 3D joint coordinates, so the average recovery error for each joint position is shown. The results are shown in Table 2 and Table 3. Average recovery errors for all the items are also shown at the end of tables. In each row, the smallest error is highlighted. Of the 52 items in Table 2, HRA performs the best in 37 items (68.52%). Of the 14 items in Table 3, HRA performs the best in 12 items (85.71%). This illustrates that HRA outperforms the other methods in most cases. Its average performance is also the best. Thanks to the descriptive power of autoencoders, HRA works well for joints that are easily occluded such as hands. Further more, HRA usually outperforms MDA due to the introduction of manifold regularization.

**Table 3.** The performance on each marker of HumanEva-I.

| index | HC | HOG | SC | MDA | HRA | index | HC | HOG | SC | MDA | HRA |
|-------|-------|-------|-------|-------|-------|-------|-------|-------|-------|-------|-------|
| 1 | 18.68 | 24.65 | 19.32 | 17.76 | 17.62 | 8 | 26.43 | 24.35 | 19.08 | 18.97 | 17.73 |
| 2 | 14.20 | 23.75 | 18.60 | 22.18 | 20.93 | 9 | 18.22 | 25.78 | 20.22 | 12.40 | 9.57 |
| 3 | 14.89 | 25.23 | 19.79 | 9.73 | 9.21 | 10 | 25.87 | 23.03 | 18.02 | 18.52 | 15.99 |
| 4 | 25.33 | 24.17 | 18.93 | 18.09 | 16.55 | 11 | 26.43 | 24.38 | 19.11 | 18.96 | 18.77 |
| 5 | 26.03 | 23.33 | 18.26 | 22.64 | 21.05 | 12 | 18.18 | 21.06 | 16.45 | 12.36 | 7.09 |
| 6 | 27.12 | 17.55 | 13.64 | 19.51 | 5.79 | 13 | 18.62 | 23.03 | 18.02 | 16.71 | 15.99 |
| 7 | 25.71 | 24.19 | 18.95 | 18.39 | 16.51 | 14 | 26.29 | 24.38 | 19.11 | 18.85 | 18.78 |
| AVG | 22.29 | 23.49 | 18.39 | 17.51 | 15.11 | | | | | | |

Some recovery results are shown in Fig 2. Due to the limitation of paper space, we only show the results of Walking. We can see that the proposed HRA gives recovered poses more close to the original images.

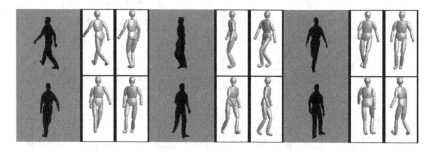

**Fig. 2.** Recovery results of Walking. For each set of images, the first image is the original image, the second image is the result of HRA and the third image is the result of MDA

## 4    Conclusion

In this paper, a novel approach of 3D pose recovery with 2D silhouettes is proposed. It improves the previous approach of image feature extractors with denoising autoencoders by introducing locality sensitive constriction. Locality reservation is able to keep the mutual dependency in the encoding procedure and makes similar silhouettes from the same pose grouped together. Hypergraph regularization with patch alignment framework is adopted to impose locality reservation, which improves the descriptive power of autoencoders and reduces ambiguity of extracted features. Experimental results on both Walking and HumanEva-I datasets show that the proposed method outperforms previous method on recovery performance.

# References

1. Agarwal, A., Triggs, B.: Recovering 3D human pose from monocular images. IEEE Trans. Pattern Anal. Mach. Intell. **28**(1), 44–58 (2006)
2. Belongie, S., Malik, J., Puzicha, J.: Shape matching and object recognition using shape contexts. IEEE Trans. Pattern Anal. Mach. Intell. **24**(4), 509–522 (2002)
3. Chen, M., Weinberger, K.Q., Sha, F., Bengio, Y.: Marginalized denoising autoencoders for nonlinear representations. In: IEEE International Conference on Machine Learning, pp. 1476–1484. IEEE (2014)
4. Dalal, N., Triggs, B.: Histograms of oriented gradients for human detection. In: Proceedings of the IEEE International Conference on Computer Vision and Pattern Recognition, pp. 886–893. IEEE Press (2005)
5. Hinton, G.E., Osindero, S., Teh, Y.W.: A fast learning algorithm for deep belief nets. Neural Computing **18**(7), 1527–1554 (2006)
6. Hong, C., Yu, J., Li, J., Chen, X.: Multi-view hypergraph learning by patch alignment framework. Neurocomputing **118**(22), 79–86 (2013)
7. Hong, C., Yu, J., Tao, D., Wang, M.: Image-based three-dimensional human pose recovery by multiview locality-sensitive sparse retrieval. IEEE Transactions on Industrial Electronics **62**(6), 3742–3751 (2015)
8. Mori, G., Belongie, S., Malik, J.: Efficient shape matching using shape contexts. IEEE Trans. Pattern Anal. Mach. Intell. **27**(11), 1832–1837 (2005)
9. Shen, J., Liu, G., Chen, J., Fang, Y., Xie, J., Yu, Y., Yan, S.: Unified structured learning for simultaneous human pose estimation and garment attribute classification. IEEE Transactions on Image Processing **23**(11), 4786–4798 (2014)
10. Sigal, L., Balan, A.O., Black, M.J.: Humaneva: Synchronized video and motion capture dataset and baseline algorithm for evaluation of articulated human motion. International Journal of Computer Vision **87**(1–2), 4–27 (2010)
11. Srivastava, N., Hinton, G., Krizhevsky, A., Sutskever, I., Salakhutdinov, R.: Dropout: A simple way to prevent neural networks from overfitting. Journal of Machine Learning Research **15**, 1929–1958 (2014)
12. Yang, M., Qiu, G., Huang, J., Elliman, D.: Near-duplicate image recognition and content-based image retrieval using adaptive hierarchical geometric centroids. In: Proceedings of the IEEE International Conference on Pattern Recognition, pp. 958–961. IEEE Press (2006)
13. Yoshua, B.: Learning deep architectures for AI. Foundations and Trends in Machine Learning **2**(1), 1–127 (2009)
14. Yuan, Y., Mou, L., Lu, X.: Scene recognition by manifold regularized deep learning architecture. IEEE Transactions on Neural Networks and Learning Systems (2015)
15. Zhou, D., Huang, J., Scholkopf, B.: Learning with hypergraphs: clustering, classification, and embedding. In: Advances in Neural Information Processing Systems. vol. 19, pp. 1601–1608. MIT Press (September 2007)

# Target Recognition Based on Feature Weighted Intuitionistic FCM

Yang Lei[1(✉)], Shuguang Liu[1], and Weiwei Kong[2]

[1] Key Laboratory of CAPF for Cryptology and Information Security, Electronics Department, Engineering University of Armed Police Force, Xi'an 710086, People's Republic of China
surina526@163.com
[2] Department of Information Engineering, Engineering University of Armed Police Force, Xi'an 710086, People's Republic of China

**Abstract.** To the issue of categorical attributes data of target recognition tending to false well-proportioned weight, a renewed technique for feature weighted intuitionistic fuzzy $c$ means (FWIFCM) is presented, whose validity are checked by utilizing a practical experiment for categorical attributes data. Finally, classifying function of additional feature weighted is analyzed and compared by providing an explicit experiment on 20 typical targets, and FWIFCM algorithm is well applied to typical target recognition on air. Simulation experiments prove that the technique proposed is promising and effective, while satisfactory results verify their applicability greatly.

**Keywords:** Intuitionistic fuzzy sets · Fuzzy $c$-means clustering · Feature weighted · Target recognition

## 1 Introduction

Clustering analysis [1-3] is a general technique for diversified statistical analysis, which is also a significant branch of non-surveillance pattern classification in statistic pattern recognition. In nature, clustering can be used to diversified statistical analysis according to a natural rule "Like attracts like" classify data. There is a focus on the reasonable classification on the basis of data objections' characteristic in clustering. In particular, the same class of data must have more similarity, and conversely the different classes of data must have more diversity. Clustering analysis originates in the many fields, commonly including mathematics, computer science, statistic, biology, economics and so forth. Furtherly, more and more clustering analysis algorithms[4,5] emerging currently have been made full use of in various application fields, such as voice recognition[6,7], image segmentation[8-10], data compression[11-13], network information security[14,15] and so on. In addition, it is such an important role on research about other fields such as biology [16], psychology, archeology, geology, social intercourse network [17] and marketing management.

In the application of target recognition, target characteristic information getting from various kinds of sensors can effectively be fused and reasoning so that we can

© Springer-Verlag Berlin Heidelberg 2015
H. Zha et al. (Eds.): CCCV 2015, Part I, CCIS 546, pp. 76–85, 2015.
DOI: 10.1007/978-3-662-48558-3_8

catch the accurate description of target attributes. In general, as for every dimension characteristic of the samples' vectors in the traditional or classical algorithms, their construction degree to classification is well-proportioned. In contrast, owing to every dimension' attributions consisting of vectors of samples' features coming from different sensors, dimension, preciseness and reliability are greatly different and the construction degree to classification is confirmedly not well-proportioned. Whereas the cases of actualities above, we have presented a novel technique for target recognition based on feature weighted intuitionistic fuzzy $c$-means clustering. In this paper, we have made full use of feature selection technology Relief algorithm[18], namely, every features' attribution in the feature set can be add to different weighted values, as demonstrated theoretically and empirically study, and it has been concluded that the structure and significance of samples' characteristic values must to be more and more complete and truthful.

## 2   Algorithm for Feature Weighted Intuitionistic Fuzzy $c$-means Clustering

In the practical application of clustering analysis, generally, feature data extracting from the samples' attributions are not complete and precise. Besides, vectors' features obtained from the formed pattern are also not independent, and that inevitably possesses a performance of redundancy. Owing to every dimension' attributions consisting of vectors of samples' features coming from different sensors, dimension, preciseness and reliability are greatly different and the construction degree to classification is confirmedly not well-proportioned. Furthermore, we have made full use of feature selection technology——Relief algorithm, namely, every features' attribution in the feature set can be add to different weighted value. Therefore, as for the issue of clustering about categorical attributes data, the novel algorithm for feature weighted intuitionistic fuzzy $c$-means clustering has been introduced.

The data samples $X=\{x_1, x_2, \ldots, x_n\} \subset R^S$ is given firstly, denoted as a group of limited measured samples in $n$ pattern spaces. And the feature vector of the measured sample $x_j$ is also given, denoted as $x_i= (<x\mu_{i1}, x\gamma_{i1}, x\pi_{i1}>, <x\mu_{i2}, x\gamma_{i2}, x\pi_{i2}>, <x\mu_{is}, x\gamma_{is}, x\pi_{is}>)$, whose weighted values $<x\mu_{ik}, x\gamma_{ik}, x\pi_{ik}>$ in every dimension are all intuitionistic fuzzy values. Besides, $P= \{p_1, p_2, \ldots, p_c\}$ is represented as containing $c$ clustering prototypes and $c$ denote as the clustering classification quantity. Among the above clustering prototype, $p_i$ denotes as the vectors of the sort $i$ of clustering prototype. $p_i$ is represented as $p_i=(<p\mu_{i1}, p\gamma_{i1}, p\pi_{i1}>, <p\mu_{i2}, p\gamma_{i2}, p\pi_{i2}>, <p\mu_{is}, p\gamma_{is}, p\pi_{is}>)$, similarly, whose value given in $k$ dimension is constantly an intuitionistic fuzzy value, represented as $p_{ik}=<p\mu_{ik}, p\gamma_{ik}, p\pi_{ik}>$.

The descriptive formula of feature weighted intuitionistic fuzzy $c$-means clustering is as follows.

$$J_m(U_\mu, U_\gamma, P) = \sum_{j=1}^{n} \sum_{i=1}^{c} \left( (\mu_{ij})^m / 2 + (1 - \gamma_{ik})^m / 2 \right) \tag{1}$$

$$\omega_i \delta(x_j, p_k), m \in [1, \infty), U_\mu, U_\gamma \in M_{IFC}$$

In the formula (1), $\delta(x_j, p_k)$ denotes as the dissimilar matching measure of categorical feature. And $\delta(\cdot)$ is definite to be as follows.

$$\delta(a, b) = \begin{cases} 0, & a = b \\ 1, & a \neq b \end{cases} \tag{2}$$

Also in the expression (1), $\omega_i$ and $m$ denotes respectively feature weighted values and smooth parameter. Besides, $U_\mu$ and $U_\gamma$ denotes intuitionistic fuzzy partition membership matrix and intuitionistic fuzzy partition nonmembership matrix, so we can acquire the expression $M_{IFC} = \{U_\mu \in R^{cn}, U_\gamma \in R^{cn} \mid \mu_{ik} \in [0,1], \gamma_{ik} \in [0,1], 0 < \sum \mu_{ik} < n, 0 < \sum \gamma_{ik} < n\}$, where $\mu_{ij}, \gamma_{ij}, \pi_{ij} = 1, \sum \mu_{ik} = 1$.

The expression of target function getting from Lagrange theorem is as follows.

$$F = \sum_{i=1}^{c} \left( (\mu_{ij})^m / 2 + (1 - \gamma_{ik})^m / 2 \right) \omega_i \delta(x_j, p_k)$$

$$- \lambda \left( \sum_{i=1}^{c} \mu_{ij} - 1 \right) - \beta \left( \mu_{ij} + \gamma_{ij} + \pi_{ij} - 1 \right) \tag{3}$$

**Algorithm 1.** Algorithm for feature weighted intuitionistic fuzzy $c$-means clustering

**Input:** Sample datasets $X$, Smooth parameter $m$, weighted coefficient matrix $W$, clustering classification quantity $c(2 \leq c \leq n)$.
**Output:** Partition membership matrix $U_\mu$, partition nonmembership matrix $U_\gamma$, clustering prototype $P$, iteration times $b$, target function' value $E$.
**Step 1:** Initialization. Calculate the quantity of samples $n$, set the iteration ceasing threshold $\varepsilon$ and iteration counter $b=0$, initialize the clustering prototype $P^{(0)}$.
**Step 2:** Calculate and update categorical features' weighted values based on Relief algorithm.

$$\omega_i = \omega_i - diff\_hit / R + diff\_miss / R$$

$$= \omega_i - \sum_{j=1}^{R} \delta(h_j, x_i) + \sum_{l \neq class(x_i)} \frac{p(l)}{1 - p(class(x_i))} \sum_{j=1}^{R} \delta(m_l, x_i) \tag{4}$$

In Eq.(4), $h_j (j=1,2,\ldots,R)$ is represented as similar kind to $x_i$ nearest samples with the quantity $R$, yet $m_{lj}(l \neq class(x_i), j=1,2,\ldots,R)$ represented as different kind to $x_i$ nearest samples. $diff\_hit$ denotes the discriminate features between $h_j$ and $x_i$. And $diff\_miss$ denotes the discriminate features between $m_{lj}$ and $x_i$.

**Step 3:** Calculate and update partition membership matrix $U_\mu$ and partition nonmembership matrix $U_\gamma$. As for $\forall i, j$, if $\delta(x_j, p_k)^{(b)} > 0$,

$$
\begin{cases}
\mu_{ij}^{(b)} = \left\{ \sum_{k=1}^{c} \left( \dfrac{\delta(x_j, p_i)^{(b)}}{\delta(x_j, p_k)^{(b)}} \right)^{\frac{1}{m-1}} \right\}^{-1} \\[4mm]
\gamma_{ij} = 1 - \pi_{ij} - \left\{ \sum_{k=1}^{c} \left( \dfrac{\delta(x_j, p_i)^{(b)}}{\delta(x_j, p_k)^{(b)}} \right)^{\frac{1}{m-1}} \right\}^{-1}
\end{cases}
\tag{5}
$$

If $\exists k$, and satisfy $\delta(x_j, p_k)^{(b)} = 0$,

$$
\begin{cases}
\mu_{ij} = 1, \quad \gamma_{ij} = 0 \quad & i = k \\
\mu_{ij} = 0, \quad \gamma_{ij} = 1 \quad & i \neq k
\end{cases}
\tag{6}
$$

**Step 4:** Compute and update the clustering prototype matrix $p_i^{(b+1)}$, then calculate and ascertain $p\mu_i^{(b+1)}$, $p\gamma_i^{(b+1)}$ and $p\pi_i^{(b+1)}$;

**Step 5:** If $\| p^{(b)} - p^{(b+1)} \| > \varepsilon$, $b = b+1$, then convert to Step2; If else, output partition membership matrix $U_\mu$, partition nonmembership matrix $U_\gamma$ and clustering prototype $P$. $\| \cdot \|$ is the certained appropriate matrix norm. That's the ending of the algorithm.

Attentively, Relief algorithm is focus on the application of classification technology with the definite classification mark on samples. However, it is uncertained that the classifications mark on every sample in clustering analysis. Above all, first the all samples are carried on a process of clustering. Then we have selected the bigger value of membership of the sample $x_i$, serving to find the nearest $x_i$ samples of similar and different sort with the quantity $R$. Next we calculate feature weighted values according to step2, that are effectively given to every dimension features. Finally, the clustering analysis is synthetically carried on.

## 3    Experimental Results and Analysis

In this experiment, first a group of practical categorical attributes data has been selected and carried out based on the other clustering algorithm namely Fuzzy $c$-means clustering (FCM) and FWIFCM algorithms. Comparing to FCM algorithm, the classification results and error rate of the two algorithms have been obtained and analyzed, results of that verified the improved classification performance and valid of FWIFCM algorithm. Then the next applied experiment has been carried out, that is a recognition experiment against 20 group of classical target on air. In detail, we have been adopted FWIFCM algorithm to carry out a clustering testation, also that is against target attributive data. By the analysis on the clustering results, we can find that the feature weighted values have a significant effect on target recognition, additionally, the applicability of the presented algorithm has been verified.

## 3.1    FWIFCM Algorithm's Clustering Experiment

In the experiment, we have selected a group of practical categorical attributes data Breast Cancer Wisconsin(as be "Wisc" for short ) from UCI international standard database (http://www.ics.uci.edu/~mlearn/MLRepository.html) to carry on the emulative experiment based on algorithm 1, aiming to test its classification performance and valid. Furthermore, it is greatly general to select Wisc samples for checking the performance and valid of the kind of clustering and classification algorithms. Wisc samples consist of 569 samples and distribute in 32 dimension space. Wisc samples' the interior continuous variables number is 30, and the samples contain 32 characteristic attributes, 10 important characteristic attributes including radius, texture, perimeter, area, smoothness, compactness, concavity, concave points, symmetry, fractal dimension. Besides, every Wisc sample can be distinguished to be Benign or Malign. Generally, the whole Wisc samples contain 357 benign samples and 212 malign samples.

We have respectively made use of FCM algorithm and algorithm 1 to carry on the classification experiment with the Wisc categorical attributes samples. In this experiment, we have predefined the appointed parameters both in the algorithms: smooth parameter $m=2$, clustering classification quantity $c=2$, samples quantity $n=569$, iteration ceasing threshold $\varepsilon=10^{-5}$, $\eta_i=0.2$, iteration counter $b=0$. Then the classification results based on both comparing algorithms have been illustrated respectively in Figure1 and Figure 2. In Figure1, "$\triangle$"is represented as benign samples, and "$\circ$"is conversely represented malign samples. Besides, "$\blacktriangle$"and "$\bullet$"are represented as benign error samples and malign error samples. So we can easily and explicitly obtain 10 error samples in Figure1. In Figure 1, "$\triangle$"and "$\circ$"are explicitly represented as benign samples and malign samples, differently, "$\blacktriangle$"and "$\bullet$"are also appeared in Figure 2, respectively represented as the clustering center points of benign and malign samples. Obviously, it is favorable that the experiment carried on with algorithm 1 has no error classification as for all experimental samples. Moreover, the exhaustive classification results are explicit showed in Table 1, which are effectively displayed that the error rate of FCM is evidently bigger than FWIFCM, with having no error classification. Therefore the proposed algorithm has a superior classification performance on clustering. Wisc samples is composed of 32 dimension space's samples, namely that has 32 characteristic attributions. We have obtained the weighted values in all dimension as follows {0.6, 0.3, 0.7, 0.1, 0, 0.3, 0.3, 0.3, 0.1, 0.1, 0.2, 0.3, 0, 0, 0, 0, 0.5, 0.5, 0.4, 0.6, 0.1, 0.2, 0.3, 0.8, 0, 0, 0, 0, 0, 0.7, 0.5, 0.4}, among that, the weighted values of 5, 13~16, 25~29 dimension attributions are all equal to 0, demonstrating that the characteristic attributions in the above 10 dimension have no effect on the renewed algorithm. Consequently, the novel algorithm's improvement on its using the attributions' weighted values, not only has been effectively improved the clustering performance but also ascertained every dimension in attributions' construction degree to classification.

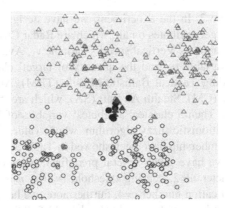

**Fig. 1.** Wisc samples' classification results based on FCM

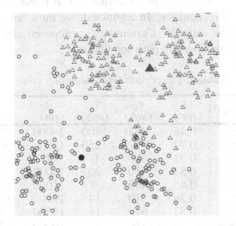

**Fig. 2.** Wisc samples' classification results based on FWIFCM

**Table 1.** The clustering results of FCM and FWIFCM algorithm

| Clustering Algorithm | Benign | Malign | Error quantity | Error rate |
|---|---|---|---|---|
| FCM | 352 | 207 | 10 | 0.018 |
| FWIFCM | 357 | 212 | 0 | 0 |

## 3.2 Target Recognition Simulation Instance Based on the Algorithm of FWIFCM

In the simulation instance of target recognition on air, we have been carried on simulation experiment on target recognition using algorithm 1, whose testing samples' data obtained via the different kind of senor yet every feature the affection of classification unbalanced. We select 20 group attributes parameter values of 20 typical targets, showed in Table 2. In the experiment, we have designed several significant variables of classical target attributes on air, which are Radar Cross Section's variable $s$, Cruising speed's variable $v_H$, Vertical speed's variable $v_V$, Aviating altitude's variable $h$, Acceleration's variable $a$. And the quantity of target' classification has been predefined as 4, including Tactical Ballistic Missile (TBM), Air to Ground Missile (AGM), Cruise Missile (CM), Stealth Aircraft (SA), which are the main focus of this experiment to research. Then 5 classical attributes' variables of 20 group target have been calculated by intuitionistic fuzzy algorithm, whose values of the corresponding membership and nonmembership have been showed in Table 3.

In the experiment, we have given several predefined parameters, specifically including smooth parameter $m=2$, ceasing threshold $\varepsilon=10^{-5}$, $\eta_i=0.2$, samples quantity $n=20$, clustering classification number $c=4$. Furthermore, we have made use of Relief algorithm to ascertain and renew the weighted values $\{1.5, 0.8, 1.6, 1.2, 0.7\}$. Thus, it is obvious that targets' different type of attributes can make different effect for targets' classification and recognition. In additional, we must have randomly chosen 4 clustering centers in the samples. Currently, the proposed algorithm has been run normally to obtain the membership partition matrix $U_\mu$.

**Table 2.** Target's attributes measuring values

| Target | $s$ $(m^2)$ | $v_H$ $(m/s)$ | $v_v$ $(m/s)$ | $h$ $(m)$ | $a$ $(m/s^2)$ |
|:---:|:---:|:---:|:---:|:---:|:---:|
| $x_1$ | 0.48 | 1900 | 1800 | 28000 | 420 |
| $x_2$ | 0.72 | 1650 | 1250 | 12000 | 300 |
| $x_3$ | 0.31 | 360 | 0 | 60 | 0.3 |
| $x_4$ | 0.53 | 410 | 20 | 11000 | 0.6 |
| $x_5$ | 0.45 | 440 | 9 | 21000 | 0.1 |
| $x_6$ | 0.28 | 310 | 14 | 17000 | 0.5 |
| $x_7$ | 0.37 | 510 | 18 | 14500 | 0 |
| $x_8$ | 0.51 | 470 | 12 | 10000 | 0 |
| $x_9$ | 0.70 | 460 | 8 | 17500 | 0.2 |
| $x_{10}$ | 0.77 | 2100 | 2000 | 30000 | 470 |
| $x_{11}$ | 0.73 | 1400 | 1550 | 8000 | 380 |
| $x_{12}$ | 0.65 | 1500 | 1300 | 15000 | 350 |
| $x_{13}$ | 0.81 | 1450 | 1450 | 8500 | 320 |
| $x_{14}$ | 0.60 | 300 | 0 | 95 | 0.1 |
| $x_{15}$ | 0.63 | 350 | 0 | 110 | 0 |
| $x_{16}$ | 0.35 | 340 | 0 | 75 | 0.2 |
| $x_{17}$ | 0.69 | 320 | 4 | 13000 | 0 |
| $x_{18}$ | 0.59 | 530 | 6 | 14000 | 0 |
| $x_{19}$ | 0.50 | 430 | 10 | 22000 | 0.4 |
| $x_{20}$ | 0.49 | 410 | 9 | 19000 | 0.3 |

**Table 3.** Targets' feature values

| $x_i$ | $s$ | $v_H$ | $v_V$ | $h$ | $a$ |
|---|---|---|---|---|---|
| $x_1$ | <0.868,0.111> | <0.475,0.355> | <0.250,0.528> | <0.833,0.166> | <0.157,0.812> |
| $x_2$ | <0.802,0.099> | <0.250,0.671> | <0.479,0.510> | <0.589,0.410> | <0.112,0.833> |
| $x_3$ | <0.915,0.035> | <0.860,0.120> | <0.000,0.999> | <0.025,0.965> | <0.999,0.000> |
| $x_4$ | <0.854,0.103> | <0.510,0.450> | <0.095,0.900> | <0.576,0.421> | <0.998,0.002> |
| $x_5$ | <0.876,0.102> | <0.540,0.441> | <0.043,0.933> | <0.750,0.210> | <0.999,0.001> |
| $x_6$ | <0.923,0.035> | <0.810,0.177> | <0.067,0.899> | <0.667,0.300> | <0.998,0.000> |
| $x_7$ | <0.898,0.101> | <0.610,0.333> | <0.086,0.911> | <0.619,0.322> | <1.000,0.000> |
| $x_8$ | <0.860,0.121> | <0.570,0.420> | <0.057,0.900> | <0.564,0.421> | <1.000,0.000> |
| $x_9$ | <0.807,0.177> | <0.560,0.422> | <0.038,0.940> | <0.677,0.100> | <0.999,0.000> |
| $x_{10}$ | <0.788,0.200> | <0.525,0.399> | <0.167,0.810> | <1.000,0.000> | <0.176,0.532> |
| $x_{11}$ | <0.799,0.198> | <0.167,0.810> | <0.354,0.644> | <0.540,0.460> | <0.142,0.842> |
| $x_{12}$ | <0.821,0.160> | <0.200,0.785> | <0.459,0.500> | <0.625,0.365> | <0.131,0.855> |
| $x_{13}$ | <0.777,0.200> | <0.183,0.766> | <0.396,0.601> | <0.546,0.444> | <0.120,0.870> |
| $x_{14}$ | <0.835,0.126> | <0.800,0.200> | <0.000,1.000> | <0.040,0.900> | <0.999,0.001> |
| $x_{15}$ | <0.827,0.122> | <0.850,0.147> | <0.000,1.000> | <0.046,0.911> | <1.000,0.000> |
| $x_{16}$ | <0.904,0.006> | <0.840,0.154> | <0.000,0.955> | <0.031,0.933> | <0.999,0.001> |
| $x_{17}$ | <0.810,0.180> | <0.820,0.160> | <0.019,0.922> | <0.601,0.388> | <1.000,0.000> |
| $x_{18}$ | <0.838,0.120> | <0.630,0.360> | <0.029,0.897> | <0.613,0.377> | <1.000,0.000> |
| $x_{19}$ | <0.862,0.111> | <0.530,0.455> | <0.048,0.917> | <0.771,0.222> | <0.998,0.002> |
| $x_{20}$ | <0.865,0.120> | <0.510,0.465> | <0.043,0.935> | <0.708,0.222> | <0.999,0.000> |

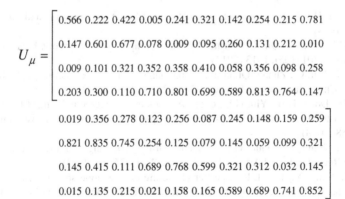

$$U_\mu = \begin{bmatrix} 0.566 & 0.222 & 0.422 & 0.005 & 0.241 & 0.321 & 0.142 & 0.254 & 0.215 & 0.781 \\ 0.147 & 0.601 & 0.677 & 0.078 & 0.009 & 0.095 & 0.260 & 0.131 & 0.212 & 0.010 \\ 0.009 & 0.101 & 0.321 & 0.352 & 0.358 & 0.410 & 0.058 & 0.356 & 0.098 & 0.258 \\ 0.203 & 0.300 & 0.110 & 0.710 & 0.801 & 0.699 & 0.589 & 0.813 & 0.764 & 0.147 \end{bmatrix}$$

$$\begin{bmatrix} 0.019 & 0.356 & 0.278 & 0.123 & 0.256 & 0.087 & 0.245 & 0.148 & 0.159 & 0.259 \\ 0.821 & 0.835 & 0.745 & 0.254 & 0.125 & 0.079 & 0.145 & 0.059 & 0.099 & 0.321 \\ 0.145 & 0.415 & 0.111 & 0.689 & 0.768 & 0.599 & 0.321 & 0.312 & 0.032 & 0.145 \\ 0.015 & 0.135 & 0.215 & 0.021 & 0.158 & 0.165 & 0.589 & 0.689 & 0.741 & 0.852 \end{bmatrix}$$

# 4    Conclusions

The problem of clustering about categorical attributes data of targets has been deeply analyzed and researched. Therefore the novel thought has been proposed, which is the technique for target recognition based on feature weighted intuitionistic fuzzy c-means clustering. The contributions of the novel technique for solving the above problem are respectively as follows.

First, to the issue of categorical attributes data of target recognition tending to false well-proportioned weight, a renewed technique for feature weighted intuitionistic fuzzy c means has fatherly proposed, which has been improved using Relief algorithm to according different weight values to every feature attributes. Additionally, the simulation testing experiments on both algorithms of FWIFCM and FCM have been carried on. Comparing to FCM algorithm, FWIFCM algorithm's valid and superiority can be obviously verified by the testing results. Finally, the proposed algorithms FWIFCM has been applied in the field of classical target recognition on air. Furthermore, the affection of classification with adding to weight values has been shown by analysis on experiment results, whose valid and widespread application have been also shown.

**Acknowledgments.** The authors would like to thank the anonymous reviewers and editors for their invaluable suggestions. This work was supported in part by the National Natural Science Foundations of China under Grant 61309022 and Grant 61309008, in part by the Natural Science Foundation of Shannxi Province of China under Grant 2013JQ8031 and Grant 2014JQ8049, in part by the China Postdoctoral Science Foundation under Grant 2014M552718, in part by the Foundation of Science and Technology on Information Assurance Laboratory under Grant KJ-13-108, and the Natural Science Foundations of the Engineering University of the Armed Police Force of China under Grant WJY-201312 and Grant WJY-201414.

# References

1. Ruspini, E.H.: A new approach to clustering. Elsevier Information and Control **15**(1), 22–32 (1969)
2. Lu, Z.M., Zhang, Qi: Clustering by data competition. Science China (Information Sciences) **56**(012105), 1–13 (2013)
3. Lu, Z.M., Liu, C., Zhang, Qi, et al.: Visual analytics for the clustering capability of data. Science China (Information Sciences) **56**(052110), 1–14 (2013)
4. Hou, W., Dong, H.B., Yin, G.S., et al.: A membership degree refinement-based evolutionary clustering algorithm. Journal of Computer Research and Development **50**(3), 548–558 (2013)
5. Li, X.Y., Wang, K.J., Guo, G.D.: Selection of clustering algorithms based on Grid-MST. Pattern Recognition and Artificial Intelligence **26**(1), 34–41 (2013)
6. Wu, K., Song, Y., Dai, L.R.: Speaker clustering of telephone speech based on front-end factor analysis. Pattern Recognition and Artificial Intelligence **26**(1), 1–5 (2013)
7. Hemakumar, G., Punitha, P.: Speaker dependent continuous Kannada speech recognition using HMM. In: International Conference on Intelligent Computing Applications, pp. 402–405 (2014)
8. Song, C.X., Ma, K., Qin, C., et al.: Infrared image segmentation based on clustering combined with sparse coding and spatial constraints. Acta Physica Sinica **62**(4), 040702/1–040702/10 (2013)
9. Xu, H.X., Wen, H.B., Zou, Y.L., et al.: Segmentation of multispectral remote sensing image based on clustering and multiscale Markov model in contourlet domain. Journal of Optoelectronics Laser **24**(5), 999–1005 (2013)

10. Gou, S.P., Zhuang, X., Zhu, H.M., et al.: Parallel sparse spectral clustering for SAR image segmentation. IEEE Journal of Selected Topics in Applied Earth Observations and Remote Sensing **6**(4), 1949–1963 (2013)
11. Deng, H.T., Deng, J.X., Deng, X.M.: Joint compression and tree structure encryption algorithm based on EZW. Acta Physica Sinica **62**(11), 110701/1–110701/8 (2013)
12. Pan, S.M., Li, H., Tang, G.: Point cloud clustering compression algorithm for spatial statistical data based on cloud computing. Huazhong University of Science and Technology (Natural Science Edition) **42**(4), 64–67 (2014)
13. Tu, J., Wang, Z.L., Li, L.J.: Clustering Compression of Test Pattern for BIST. Journal of Computer-Aided Design & Computer Graphics **26**(6), 983–990 (2014)
14. Wu, Y.J., Tang, Q.M., Ni, W.W., et al.: A clustering hybrid based algorithm for privacy preserving trajectory data publishing. Journal of Computer Research and Development **50**(3), 578–593 (2013)
15. Huang, J.B., Sun, H.L., Song, Q.B.: Revealing density-based clustering structure from the core-connected tree of a network. IEEE Transactions on Knowledge and Data Engineering **25**(8), 1876–1889 (2013)
16. Yu, Z.W., Li, L., Youe, J., et al.: Triple spectral clustering-based consensus clustering framework for class discovery from cancer gene expression profiles. IEEE/ACM Transactions on Computational Biology and Bioinformatics **9**(6), 1751–1765 (2012)
17. Chen, K.H., Han, P.P., Wu, J.: User clustering based social network recommendation. Chinese Journal of Computers **36**(2), 349–359 (2013)
18. Zhang, X., Deng, Z.H., Wang, S.T., et al.: Maximum entropy relief feature weighting. Journal of Computer Research and Development **48**(6), 1038–1048 (2011)

# The Modified Mumford-Shah Model Based on Nonlocal Means Method for Textures Segmentation

Jingge Lu, Guodong Wang$^{(\boxtimes)}$, and Zhenkuan Pan

College of Information Engineering, Qingdao University, Qingdao, China
`cgjingge730@163.com, doctorwgd@gmail.com`

**Abstract.** Textures segmentation is a very important subject in the fields of computer vision. In order to segment the textures, a new method is achieved. The traditional Mumford-Shah model is modified. In detail, a smoothness term is added which used the nonlocal means method. The traditional Mumford-Shah model can be used to segment the conventional images. The modified Mumford-Shah model can dispose the textures well. What's more, in order to improve the computation efficiency, this paper designs the Split-Bregman algorithm. At last, our performance is demonstrated by segmenting many real texture images.

**Keywords:** Textures segmentation · Nonlocal means method · Modified Mumford-Shah model · Split-Bregman algorithm

## 1 Introduction

Texture is an aspect so easy to be visually recognized but hard enough to be mathematically characterized. Various methods of extracting textural features from images have been designed. The filters, geometric, statistical models have shown promising results. But these methods have different shortcomings more or less.

The classical filter forms are Gabor and Wavelet [1]. The summation of the filter responses can synthesize a new image without texture which is the basic idea of the texture segmentation using filter theory. Such active contour models need to search for help from the edge detecting methods .And these methods are time consuming.

In recent years, local binary pattern method achieves good result in texture segmentation [2]. The LBP characteristic achieve better result than Gabor and Wavelet features. It needs lower computational burden [3].

The segmentation methods mentioned above rely on the choice of the initial condition. And all these methods can achieve good results especially for easy images. But the results are sometimes not good for complicated images. Because the texture on an object is very similar to its boundary, it always leads to the wrong segmentation result. But we can get good results to use our method.

The outline of the paper is as follows. The next section introduces the conventional Mumford-Shah model for image segmentation. Then the modified Mumford-Shah model based on the nonlocal means method is proposed. What's more, we design the

© Springer-Verlag Berlin Heidelberg 2015
H. Zha et al. (Eds.): CCCV 2015, Part I, CCIS 546, pp. 86–93, 2015.
DOI: 10.1007/978-3-662-48558-3_9

Split-Bregman algorithm. At last, we make some numerical experiments and   obtain
the final conclusion.

## 2    The Mumford-Shah Model

The model of piecewise smooth is the basis of variational image segmentation re-
search. For the gray image f(x) of defining on the rectangular open area $\Omega:\Omega \rightarrow R, x \in \Omega$, Mumford-shah model [4] is

$$\underset{u,K}{Min}\left\{E(u,K)=\int_{\Omega/K}(u-f)^2 dx+\lambda\int_{\Omega/K}|\nabla u|^2 dx+\gamma H^{N-1}(K)\right\} \tag{1}$$

The original image will be segmented into the area of smooth image $u(x)$ by the edge
point set K. The first item means the proximity between the original image with the
approximate image of the smooth regions. The second item is the penalty item of
piecewise smooth image. The third item $H^{N-1}(K)$ is the length of segmentation-line.
$\lambda, \gamma$ are the penalty parameters. The larger the $\lambda$ is, the more smooth the piecewise
image becomes. The larger the $\gamma$ is, the shorter the segmentation-line made by the
edge point set becomes. For avoiding the optimization problem because of the co-
existence of the different dimensions space variable, u is defined as the function of the
special function space of bounded variation in the document [5], the formula(1) is
rewritten

$$\underset{u}{Min}\left\{E(u)=\int_{\Omega}\left((u-f)^2+\lambda|\nabla u|^2\right)dx+\gamma H^{N-1}(S_u)\right\} \tag{2}$$

$S_u$ is the set of the discrete points.
Vese et al [6] use sign distance function $\phi(x)$ zero level set to express the continuous
contour line of divisiory area, they use variational level set method to make formu-
la(2) being similar with the formula(3).

$$\underset{u}{Min}\left\{E(u)=\alpha_1\int_{\Omega}\left((u_1-f)^2+\lambda_1|\nabla u_1|^2\right)H(\phi)dx+\alpha_2\int_{\Omega}\left((u_2-f)^2+\lambda_2|\nabla u_2|^2\right)(1-H(\phi))dx+\gamma\int_{\Omega}|\nabla H(\phi)|dx\right\} \tag{3}$$

If $\Omega_1$ means the prospect of the image, $\Omega_2 = \Omega \setminus \Omega_1$ means the background of the
image, $\Gamma$ means the contour line. When $u_1, u_2$ means the piecewise smooth image of
prospect and background, the first two items are the estimated data of the piecewise
smooth images, the third item is similar with the third item of the formula(2).
$\alpha_1, \alpha_2, \lambda_1, \lambda_2, \gamma$ are the penalty parameters. The level set function $\phi(x)$   which be
defined by the sign distance function is

$$\phi(x)=\begin{cases} d(x,\Gamma), & x \in \Omega_1 \\ 0, & x \in \Gamma \\ -d(x,\Gamma), & x \in \Omega_2 \end{cases} \tag{4}$$

$d(x,\Gamma)$ is the minimum distance between arbitrary point with contour line in the image space. $H(\phi)=\begin{cases} 1, & \phi \geq 0 \\ 0, & otherwise \end{cases}$ is Heaviside function.

The document [7] use binary tag function $\phi(x) = \begin{cases} 1, & x \in \Omega_1 \\ 0, & x \in \Omega_2 \end{cases}$ , $\Omega = \Omega_1 \cup \Omega_2$ ,

$\Omega_1 \cap \Omega_2 = \phi$, the formula(3) is rewritten the constrained optimization problem:

$$\underset{u_1,u_2,\phi \in \{0,1\}}{Min} \left\{ E(u_1,u_2,\phi) = \alpha_1 \int_{\Omega} \left( (u_1 - f)^2 + \lambda_1 |\nabla u_1|^2 \right) \phi dx + \alpha_2 \int_{\Omega} \left( (u_2 - f)^2 + \lambda_2 |\nabla u_2|^2 \right)(1 - \phi) dx + \gamma \int_{\Omega} |\nabla \phi| dx \right\} \quad (5)$$

# 3    The Modified Mumford-Shah Model Based on Nonlocal Means Method

## 3.1    Nonlocal Operators

Gillboa and Osher defined in [8] the variational formulation of nonlocal means, with a non-local partial differential equation (PDE).The nonlocal means algorithm can be seen as the generalization of the Yaroslavsky filter [9] and bilateral filters [10] to intensity patch feature instead of single pixel feature. See also the paper on Texture Synthesis [11]. The nonlocal means can be used the image denoising and other aspects [12].

The traditional local operator means the relationship between the current pixels with the consecutive pixels. The nonlocal method is based on the image slice similarity. It defines as follows:

$$w(x, y) = \exp \left\{ -\frac{G_\sigma * (\|f(x + \bullet) - f(y + \bullet)\|)^2}{h^2} \right\} \quad (6)$$

$x \in \Omega$, $y \in \Omega$, in which $G_\sigma$ is the Gaussian kennel function. $\sigma$ is the width parameter of the gaussian kernel function,h is the threshold value for similarities between two patch windows. So the nonlocal gradient for two points x and y in the image is defined as

$$\nabla_{NL} u(x, y) = (u(y) - u(x)) \sqrt{w(x, y)} \quad (7)$$

$x, y \in \Omega$ .The nonlocal gradient is not the general vector but the map of $\Omega \times \Omega \to R$.The nonlocal vector is v(x,y): $\Omega \times \Omega \to R$,the inner product is defined

$$\langle v_1 \bullet v_2 \rangle(x) = \int_{\Omega} v_1(x, y) v_2(x, y) dx \quad : \Omega \to R \quad (8)$$

The module is

$$|v|(x) = \sqrt{\int_{\Omega} (v(x, y))^2 dy} \quad : \Omega \to R \quad (9)$$

With the inner product , The nonlocal divergence is defined as

$$(\nabla_{NL} \bullet v)(x) = \int_{\Omega} (v(x, y) - v(y, x)) \sqrt{w(x, y)} dy \quad (10)$$

Then the nonlocal laplacian can be defined as

$$\Delta_{NL} u(x) = \frac{1}{2} (\nabla_{NL} \bullet (\nabla_{NL} u))(x) = \int_{\Omega} (u(y) - u(x)) w(x, y) dy \quad (11)$$

With the above mentioned definitions ,we can write the norm of the nonlocal gradient for a function u as follows.

$$|\nabla_{NL}u|(x)=\sqrt{\int_{\Omega}(u(y)-u(x))^2 w(x,y)dy} : \Omega \to R \qquad (12)$$

## 3.2    The Proposed Model

Based on the above definitions, the modified Mumford-Shah model can be defined as

$$\underset{u,\phi \in \{0,1\}}{Min}\left\{E(u,\phi)=\sum_{i=1}^{2}\alpha_i\int_{\Omega}\left((u_i-f)^2+\beta_i|\nabla u_i|^2+\lambda_i|\nabla_{NL}u_i|^2\right)\chi_i(\phi)dx+\sum_{i=1}^{1}\gamma\int_{\Omega}|\nabla \phi_i|dx\right\} \qquad (13)$$

$\chi_i(\phi)$ can be defined as follows.

$$\chi_i(\phi)=\phi_i\prod_{j=0}^{i-1}(1-\phi_j)(\phi_0\equiv 0,\phi_{n+1}\equiv 1) \qquad (14)$$

When $\lambda_i$ is zero, the formula (13) is the conventional Mumford-Shah model. When $\beta_i$ is zero, the formula (12) is the Mumford-Shah model with nonlocal means method. But when $\lambda_i$ and $\beta_i$ are not equal to the zero, this model can segment not only the conventional images but also the texture images. The answer in detail of the formula (12) is defined as follows.

The energy function about u is

$$\underset{u_i}{Min}\left\{E(u_i)=\sum_{i=1}^{2}\alpha_i\int_{\Omega}\left((u_i-f)^2+\beta_i|\nabla u_i|^2+\lambda_i|\nabla_{NL}u_i|^2\right)\chi_i(\phi)dx\right\} \qquad (15)$$

The Euler-Lagrange equation solved by the variational method about u is

$$(u_i-f)\chi_i(\phi)-\beta_i\Delta u_i-\lambda_i\nabla_{NL}\bullet\left(\chi_i(\phi)|\nabla_{NL}u_i|\right)=0 \qquad (16)$$

Considering the equation (15), we can obtain $u_i(x)$ as follows

$$u_i(x)=\frac{f(x)\chi_i(\phi)+\beta_i*C+\lambda_i\int_{\Omega}(\chi_i(\phi(y))+\chi_i(\phi(x)))u_i(y)w(x,y)dy}{\chi_i(\phi)+4*\beta_i+\lambda_i\int_{\Omega}(\chi_i(\phi(y))+\chi_i(\phi(x)))w(x,y)dy} \qquad (17)$$

Without the loss of generality, we represent a gray image as an $N\times N$ matrix. Where m, n=1,...,N, C is defined as follows.

$$C=u_{m+1,n}+u_{m-1,n}+u_{m,n+1}+u_{m,n-1} \qquad (18)$$

The energy function about $\phi$ is

$$\underset{\phi_i}{Min}\left\{E(\phi_i)=\sum_{i=1}^{2}\int_{\Omega}\left((u_i-f)^2+\beta_i|\nabla u_i|^2+\lambda_i|\nabla_{NL}u_i|^2\right)\chi_i(\phi)dx+\sum_{i=1}^{1}\gamma|\nabla \phi_i|dx\right\} \qquad (19)$$

This paper designs to use the split Bregman iteration method, the instrumental variable $v_i$ and Bregman iteration parameter $b_i$ are introduced, then the formula(16) is transformed into the iterative optimization format.

$$\min_{\phi_i \in \{0,1\}} \left\{ (\phi, v) = \sum_{i=1}^{2} \alpha_i \int_{\Omega} Q_i(u) \chi_i(\phi) dx + \sum_{i=1}^{1} \gamma \int_{\Omega} |v_i| dx + \sum_{i=1}^{1} \frac{\theta}{2} \int_{\Omega} (v_i - \nabla \phi - b_i^{k+1})^2 dx \right\} \tag{20}$$

And the constrains is defined by

$$b_i^{k+1} = b_i^k + \nabla_{NL} u_i^k - v_i^k, b_i^0 = v_i^0 = 0 \tag{21}$$

The form of $Q_i(u)$ is

$$Q_i(u) = (u_i - f)^2 + \beta_i |\nabla u_i|^2 + \lambda_i |\nabla_{NL} u_i|^2 \tag{22}$$

The Euler-Lagrange equation about $\phi$ and the approximate generalized soft threshold formula about $v_i$ based on the alternating iterative optimization strategy and variational method can be obtained.

$$\begin{cases} \nabla \bullet (v_i - \nabla \phi - b_i^{k+1}) + \sum_{i=1}^{2} Q_i(u) \dfrac{\partial \chi_i(\phi)}{\partial \phi} = 0 & in \Omega \\ (v_i^k - \nabla \phi_i - b_i^{k+1}) \bullet \vec{n} = 0 & on \partial \Omega \end{cases} \tag{23}$$

In the equation (20), the form of $\dfrac{\partial \chi_i(\phi)}{\partial \phi_k}$ is

$$\frac{\partial \chi_i(\phi)}{\partial \phi_k} = \begin{cases} \displaystyle\prod_{j=0}^{i-1} [1 - \phi_j] & k = i \\ -\displaystyle\prod_{j=0, k \neq i}^{i-1} [1 - \phi_j] \phi_i & k \neq i \end{cases} \tag{24}$$

With the equation (21), we can obtain $v_i^{k+1}$ as follows.

$$v_i^{k+1} = Max \left( |\nabla \phi_i^{k+1} + b_i^{k+1}| - \frac{\gamma}{\theta}, 0 \right) \frac{\nabla \phi_i^{k+1} + b_i^{k+1}}{|\nabla \phi_i^{k+1} + b_i^{k+1}|} \tag{25}$$

Where

$$\phi_i = Max (Min(\phi_i, 1), 0) \tag{26}$$

## 4      Experiment and Analysis

In the section, several numerical experiments is presented to show the performance of the model proposed in the paper for texture image segmentation. And we make comparison with the method which is referenced from literature [13]. This method combines image decomposition model and active contour model.

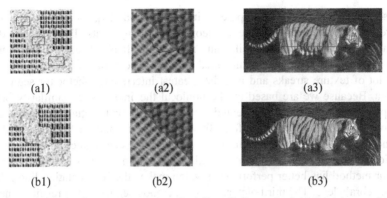

**Fig. 1.** Texture images for segmentation: (a1), (a2) and(a3) are the initialized images.(b1) ,(b2) and (b3) are the segmentation results.

We first present the initialized contour line, the second line is the segmentation result in Fig. 1. For the first picture(a1), there are two cut-off rules between the two opposite angles texture areas with the middle area. And the cut-off rule is very long. But the cut-off rule is close to the edge good. The second picture (a2) is similar. The third picture (a3) is a tiger. We know the body of the tiger has some texture streaks. We can segment the tiger from the whole picture very well. No matter the simple complex texture images or the real texture image, we can obtain very good results. The segmentation line can be fully fit with the edge of the segmentation area.

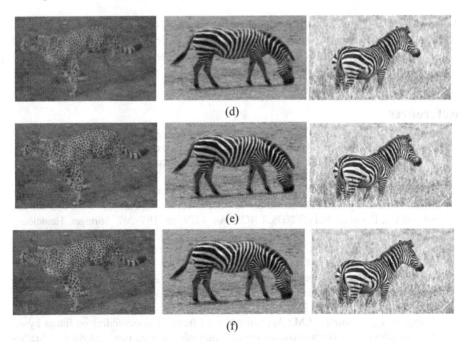

**Fig. 2.** Comparison results between our method and the method in [13]: (d) original image,(e)shows the results using the method in [13], (f) shows the results of our method.

These images are typical. Compared with the method [13], the results of our method are exact. For the first picture, the leopard has many spots. The foreground leopard and the background has similar hue meanwhile. It is difficult to segment this picture which used the conventional method well. The following two zebras have quite a lot of texture streaks and it is the greatest interference factor for segmenting the zebra. Because we are based on the nonlocal the image slice similarity but the image pixel. So the zebra is segmented well. From the first picture, we can see that the whole body of the leopard is fully fit with the segmentation line, especially the head and the legs. The second picture shows the great performance of the legs' segmentation. The segmentation line of the old method has a certain gap with the zebra's legs. Our method has better performance which makes the segmentation line fully fit with the zebra's legs. The third picture shows the good segmentation result of the legs and the head. Meanwhile the segmentation effect of the zebra's ears is good too.

## 5    Conclusions

In this paper, by using the relevant concepts of nonlocal operators and the modified Mumford-shah model, we proposed this model for texture image segmentation. In this model, we design a Split Bregman algorithm and provide the implementations. Numerical experiments confirm the performance of the proposed model for texture image segmentation.

**Acknowledgments.** This work was supported by National Natural Science Foundation of China (No.61305045 and No.61170106), National "Twelfth Five-Year" development plan of science and technology (No.2013BAI01B03), Qingdao science and technology development project (No. 13-1-4-190-jch).

## References

1. Paragios, N., Deriche, R.: Geodesic active contours for supervised texture segmentation. In: Proceedings of the IEEE Computer Society Conference on Computer Vision and Pattern Recognition (CVPR 1999), pp. 699–706, June 1999
2. Savelonas, M.A., Iakovidis, D.K., Maroulis, D.E., Karkanis, S.A.: An Active Contour Model Guided by LBP Distributions. In: Blanc-Talon, J., Philips, W., Popescu, D., Scheunders, P. (eds.) ACIVS 2006. LNCS, vol. 4179, pp. 197–207. Springer, Heidelberg (2006)
3. Savelonas, M.A., Iakovidis, D.K., Maroulis, D.: LBP-guided active contours. Pattern Recognition Letters **29**(9), 1404–1415 (2008)
4. Mumford, D., Shah, J.: Optimal approximation by piecewise smooth functions and associated variational problems. Communications on Pure and Applied Mathematics **42**, 577–685 (1989)
5. Ambrosio, L., Tortorelli, V.M.: Approximation of functionals depending on jumps by elliptic functionals via Gamma-convergence. Communications on Pure and Applied Mathematics **43**, 999–1036 (1990)

6. Chan, T.F., Vese, L.A.: Active contours without edges. IEEE Trans. Image Processing **10**(2), 266–277 (2001)
7. Bresson, X., Esedoglu, S., Vandergheynst, P., Thiran, J.P., Osher, S.: Fast global minimization of the active contour/snake model. Journal of Mathematical Imaging and Vision **28**(2), 151–167 (2007)
8. Gilboa, G., Osher, S.: Nonlocal Linear Image Regularization and Supervised Segmentation. SIAM Multiscale Modeling and Simulation (MMS) **6**(2), 595630 (2007)
9. Yaroslavsky, L.P.: Digital Picture Processing, an Introduction. Springer-Verlag (1985)
10. Tomasi, C., Manduchi, R.: Bilateral Filtering for Gray and Color Images. In: International Conference on Computer Vision (ICCV), pp. 839–846 (1998)
11. Efros, A., Leung, T.: Texture Synthesis by Non-Parametric Sampling. In: International Conference on Computer Vision, pp. 1033–1038 (1999)
12. Bresson, X., Chan, T.F.: Non-local unsupervised variational image segmentation models. CAM-report No.08-67 (2008)
13. Wang, G., Pan, Z., Dong, Q., Zhao, X., Zhang, Z., Duan, J.: Unsupervised Texture Segmentation Using Active Contour Model and Oscillating Information. Journal of Applied Mathematics **2014** (2014). Article ID614613, 11 pages

# Segmentation-Based Salient Object Detection

Kai-Fu Yang, Xin Gao, Ju-Rong Zhao, and Yong-Jie Li[✉]

Key Laboratory for Neuroinformation of Ministry of Education,
University of Electronic Science and Technology of China, Chengdu 610054, China
yang_kf@163.com, liyj@uestc.edu.cn

**Abstract.** Salient object detection is an important task for both the human perception and computer vision applications. Contrary to the popular pixel- or superpixel-based salient object detection methods, we employ high quality segmentation to facilitate salient object detection in this paper. After segmenting the input image using a recent method of gPb-owt-ucm, we easily extract the salient objects from candidate segments only with some very simple intrinsic features of the segments. In addition, for more reasonable performance evaluation, we build a perception based dataset, which contains 499 complex natural images and the corresponding hierarchical salient object ground-truth defined with the assistance of eye-tracker recorded fixations. Experiments on the public ASD dataset and our new dataset show that our segmentation-based salient object detection method (SBSO) achieves competitive performance comparing to some state-of-the-art algorithms.

**Keywords:** Segmentation · Salient object · Fixation · Saliency map

## 1 Introduction

Saliency computation is an important step which accelerates the computer vision system to efficiently understand natural scenes. There are mainly two categories methods involving in saliency-related visual tasks: (1) fixation prediction methods [1-3], which are usually used to cover the most interesting information of visual scenes; (2) salient object detection methods [4, 5], which are developed mainly to detect the dominant objects from the given images. These two saliency-related tasks are meaningful for various computer vision applications such as image compression [6], image retargeting [7], object recognition [8], etc.

Fixation prediction is aimed at predicting where people look when observing a natural scene. This selective attention is considered as a key step for coding and compressing visual information for visual perception [9] (see [10] for a review). Methods for fixation prediction try to obtain a saliency map which indicates the regions of interest in the given images, but usually missing the accurate shape information of salient objects or regions. In contrast, salient object detection usually requires to label pixel-accurate object silhouettes and is used to detect dominant objects in simple scenes [5, 11]. Recent years, a lot of salient object detection methods are developed,

© Springer-Verlag Berlin Heidelberg 2015
H. Zha et al. (Eds.): CCCV 2015, Part I, CCIS 546, pp. 94–102, 2015.
DOI: 10.1007/978-3-662-48558-3_10

and most of which detect salient objects based on region contrast. They usually segment the image into lots of small regions with over-segmentation or super-pixel methods, and subsequently, local or global contrast is computed to indicate the saliency level of each region [12-14] (see [4] for a recent review).

Recent years, great advance is made in the area of image segmentation, and some methods have achieved excellent performance even for complex images [15, 16]. In this paper, we attempt to clarify how segmentation contributes to salient object detection. Although some authors have proposed the segmentation-based methods [4, 17], they need extra learning process to detect salient objects. In contrast, in this work we first segment the image into several regions with gPb-owt-ucm method [15]. Then, without the need of machine learning, salient objects are detected in our method by directly selecting the object segments from all candidate regions with several simple features and simple computation. This means that we can easily obtain salient objects under the help of high quality segmentation.

In addition, most existing benchmark datasets provide binary object mask as the ground-truth. Because multiple salient objects are usually present in natural scenes, binary object mask is not enough for comprehensive evaluation of the performance. In this study, we also build a dataset based on the fixations recorded by eye-tracker and human segmentations by hand. Our dataset provides hierarchical object benchmark for each image. Finally, experimental results demonstrate that our method performs well on both ASD  dataset [5] and our hierarchical dataset.

## 2    Method

### 2.1    Salient Object Detection with Segmentation

In this work, we first employ the segmentation method of gPb-owt-ucm [15] for image segmentation. The gPb-owt-ucm algorithm transforms the output of any contour detector into hierarchical regions, and thus reduce the problem of image segmentation to that of contour detection[15]. With the segmented patches, we define three simple properties of each segment for the computation of its saliency: (a) *Centricity*, (b) *Border Ratio*, and   (c) *Boundary Ratio*.

Firstly, centricity is related to the distance between the center of a segment and the center of the whole image. With centricity, the segments (or patches) closer to the center of the image usually is assigned with a higher saliency level, which is normally referred to as *Center Prior* [1]. We denote the center of segment $i$ as $\left(x_c^i, y_c^i\right)$, and the normalized center can be computed as $R_c^i = \left(x_c^i / H, \ y_c^i / W\right)$, where $H$ and $W$ are respectively the height and width (in pixel) of the image. In addition, the center of the image is denoted as $M_c = (0.5, 0.5)$. Therefore, the centricity-based saliency value of segment $i$ is defined as

$$S_c^i = 1 - \left\| R_c^i - M_c \right\| \tag{1}$$

Secondly, with $NB_r^i$ denoting the number of intersection (shown in Fig. 1 with the red lines) between the boundary pixel set of segment $i$ and border pixel set of the image, we define *Border Ratio* as the percentage of $NB_r^i$ in all border pixels of the image. A region with a higher border ratio is more likely to be background and hence should have less possibility of a salient object. With $NB_m = 2(H+W)$ denoting the number of the border pixels of the whole image, the border ratio based saliency of segment $i$ is defined as

$$S_{b1}^i = 1 - \frac{NB_r^i}{NB_m} \tag{2}$$

Thirdly, we use $NR_m^i$ to denote the number of all boundary pixels of segment $i$, and *Boundary Ratio* indicates the percentage of $NB_r^i$ in all boundary pixels of the segment $i$. Similarly, a region with a higher boundary ratio has less possibility of a salient object. The boundary ratio based saliency of segment $i$ is defined as

$$S_{b2}^i = 1 - \frac{NB_r^i}{NR_m^i} \tag{3}$$

Finally, the three properties of a segment defined above are combined to compute the saliency level of each candidate segment. Fig. 1 shows an example of salient object detection from the result of image segmentation. The final saliency level of segment $i$ is given by

$$S_m^i = \prod_{k \in \{c,b1,b2\}} S_k^i \tag{4}$$

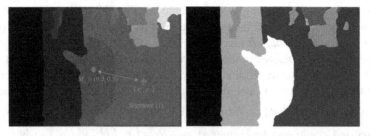

**Fig. 1.** An illustration of salient object detection from candidate regions. **Left:** the result of image segmentation. The green arrow indicates the distance between the center of segment $i$ and the center of the image; red line is the intersection between the boundary pixels of segment $i$ and border pixels of the image. **Right:** hierarchical salient objects are labeled, where brighter pixels correspond to higher saliency levels.

## 2.2 A New Dataset Labeled with Hierarchical Salient Objects

There are a lot of datasets for benchmarking the salient object detection algorithms. However, almost all the existing datasets provide a binary mask of objects as the ground-truth of each image. The object mask usually covers the most salient object, but ignoring those smaller objects or regions. We believe that labeling all objects with different saliency levels is important for real scene analysis.

In this paper, aiming to evaluate salient object detection models from the perceptual point of view, we built a new dataset based on the human fixations recorded by eye-tracker (Eyelink-2000 at 1000Hz) and human segmentations. In the experiment, ten subjects (6 males and 4 females) were asked to explore the given images displayed on the screen with a free-viewing manner. Each image was presented for 5 seconds after a visual cue of cross ("+") in the center of screen. In addition, eye-tracking re-calibration was performed on every 30 images. Finally, we obtain the fixations of 10 subjects on 499 natural images that are from the BSDS500 dataset [15]. Note that one image was failed to get reasonable fixation data because the sizes of the objects in that image is too small.

BSDS500 dataset provides 500 images and the corresponding multiple ground-truth segmentations for each image [15]. Therefore, we use the eye fixations recorded in our experiment and the provided human segmentations of BSDS500 to build a new hierarchical salient object dataset. For each segmented patch, we compute the density of the fixation points weighted by fixation duration as its saliency level. Note that the results on multiple segmentations are added together. Fig. 2 shows the steps to generate the ground-truth of hierarchical salient objects from the eye fixations and human segmentations.

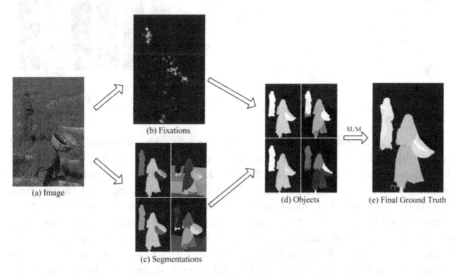

**Fig. 2.** The framework of building the dataset of hierarchical salient object ground-truth with eye-tracker recorded fixations and human segmentations.

## 3    Experimental Results

We first tested our model (SBSO) on a public salient object dataset (i.e., ASD dataset [5]), which contains 1000 natural images and the corresponding binary object mask for each image. For quantitative evaluation, the commonly used general P-R curve is employed. In addition, considering that some authors suggest that P-R curve (or F-measure) might be not always quite appropriate for performance evaluation of saliency detection [5], we also employ the new *weighted F-measure* proposed in [18] for comprehensive performance evaluation in this work.

Figure 3 shows the performance comparison of various methods on ASD dataset. The existing methods considered here include AC [19], LC [20], FT [5], HC [14], RC [14], and HS [12]. It is clear from Fig. 3 that the proposed SBSO obtains higher score than most of the considered methods except HS [12]. However, our SBSO method usually obtains the hierarchical salient objects by labeling different saliency values to different candidate regions. This will result in that SBSO has the potential to achieve higher recall but lower precision (Fig. 3(left)), since fewer salient objects are regarded as false alarm.

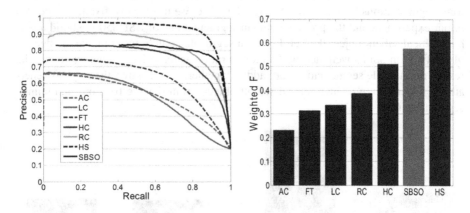

**Fig. 3.** The performance on ASD dataset. **Left**: P-R curves. **Right**: weighted F-measure.

Based on the drawbacks of binary salient object datasets mentioned in Section 2.2 (i.e., all the detected objects in a scene have equal saliency), the hierarchical salient object dataset built in this paper can be considered as a more reasonable benchmark for salient object detection algorithms. Fig. 4 lists several examples of images from the proposed dataset. For each image, the dataset provides a hierarchical object ground-truth, i.e., each object (or patch) is assigned with a perceptually determined saliency value. For example, it is generally accepted that human face is usually more salient than the body (the second column in Fig. 4), and closer objects have higher saliency values than distant objects (the fifth column in Fig. 4). From Fig. 4, we believe that the hierarchical object ground-truth built in this work is more reasonable referring to our daily experience of visual perception.

**Fig. 4.** Several examples of images (Top row) and their ground-truth (Bottom row) selected from the proposed dataset.

Considering that the P-R curve and weighted F-measure are unavailable for non-binary ground-truth, we employ correlation coefficient as a quantitative measure when evaluating on our dataset. The *Correlation Coefficient* is defined as [21]

$$\rho = \frac{\sum\limits_{x,y} ((S_m(x,y) - \mu_m) \cdot (S_h(x,y) - \mu_h))}{\sqrt{\sigma_m^2 \cdot \sigma_h^2}} \qquad (5)$$

where $S_m(x,y)$ and $S_h(x,y)$ are the salient object maps of the model and ground-truth, respectively. $\mu_m$ and $\mu_h$ are respectively the mean of $S_m(x,y)$ and $S_h(x,y)$, $\sigma_m$ and $\sigma_h$ are the variance of $S_m(x,y)$ and $S_h(x,y)$, respectively. $\rho$ is the correlation coefficient, which indicates the correlation between the two maps.

Figure 5 shows the mean correlation coefficient over the whole hierarchical salient object dataset comparing to other methods. The performance of the proposed SBSO model with individual feature of segmented patches (i.e., Centricity, Border Ratio, and Boundary Ratio described in Section 2.1) is shown in Fig. 5 (left). By combining all prosperities of the segments, our SBSO model achieves better performance than that using individual prosperity. In addition, different from the observation of the results on ASD dataset, our SBSO obtains the best performance in terms of correlation coefficient when comparing to other salient object methods (Fig. 5 (right)).

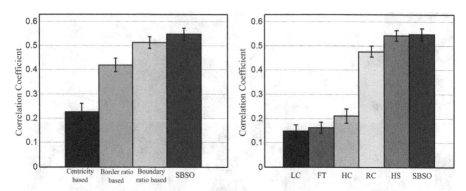

**Fig. 5.** The performance (Correlation Coefficient) on our hierarchical salient object dataset. The error bars represent the 95% confidence intervals.

Figure 6 lists several examples of salient object detection on ASD and our dataset. Based on the segmentations with weighted saliency values, SBSO obtains good salient object detection that is mainly seen in two aspects: (a) each object has uniform saliency level, and (b) the boundaries of objects are very accurate. These merits are mainly inherited from the high quality of image segmentation. Each segment will be given uniform salient values after saliency computation. This is beneficial for obtaining high performance when evaluating on benchmark datasets, especially on the datasets with binary object mask ground truth. This is the main superiority of the proposed method when comparing to other super-pixel or over-segmentation based methods, such as HS[12], RC[14].

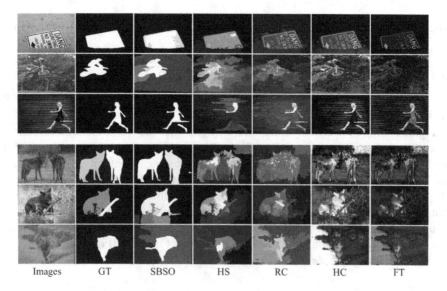

**Fig. 6.** Several examples of salient object detection. The images in the first to third rows are from ASD dataset and the images in the forth to sixth rows are from the proposed dataset.

# 4     Conclusion and Discussion

In this paper, we proposed a new salient object detection method based on image segmentation. Salient object detection is easily achieved based on three simple features defined for each patches when employing a high quality image segmentation algorithm as a pre-phase processing. In addition, for benchmarking saliency related methods, a new hierarchical object dataset was built based on the eye-tracker recorded fixations. Experimental results show that image segmentation can remarkably promote salient object detection. However, there is no doubt that the performance of the proposed SBSO is strongly dependent on the efficiency of the image segmentation method. To our knowledge, the proposed method is the first framework to use gPb-owt-ucm for segmentation before saliency computation. In addition, there are other segmentation methods which can obtain good boundaries can also be used as the first step in our framework. However, most existing segmentation methods are too complex to be as pre-phase processing of salient object detection. Thus, a simpler yet efficient image segmentation algorithm is expected to further facilitate salient object detection. In addition, besides the three measures of segmented patches (i.e., Centricity, Border Ratio, and Boundary Ratio) for saliency computation, more measures for defining patch saliency can be easily introduced into the proposed framework.

**Acknowledgments.** This work was supported in part by the Major State Basic Research Program under Grant 2013CB329401, in part by the National Natural Science Foundation of China under Grant 61375115, and Grant 91420105, and in part by the 111 Project of China under Grant B12027.

# References

1. Judd, T., Ehinger, K., Durand, F., Torralba, A.: Learning to predict where humans look. In: IEEE International Conference on Computer Vision, pp. 2106–2113 (2009)
2. Harel, J., Koch, C., Perona, P.: Graph-based visual saliency. In: Advances in Neural Information Processing Systems, pp. 545–552 (2006)
3. Itti, L., Koch, C., Niebur, E.: A model of saliency-based visual attention for rapid scene analysis. IEEE Transactions on Pattern Analysis and Machine Intelligence **20**(11), 1254–1259 (1998)
4. Borji, A., Cheng, M.-M., Jiang, H., Li, J.: Salient object detection: A survey (2014). arXiv preprint arXiv:1411.5878
5. Achanta, R., Hemami, S., Estrada, F., Susstrunk, S.: Frequency-tuned salient region detection. In: IEEE Conference on Computer Vision and Pattern Recognition, pp. 1597–1604 (2009)
6. Christopoulos, C., Skodras, A., Ebrahimi, T.: The JPEG2000 still image coding system: an overview. IEEE Transactions on Consumer Electronics **46**(4), 1103–1127 (2000)
7. Goferman, S., Zelnik-Manor, L., Tal, A.: Context-aware saliency detection. IEEE Transactions on Pattern Analysis and Machine Intelligence **34**(10), 1915–1926 (2012)
8. Rutishauser, U., Walther, D., Koch, C., Perona, P.: Is bottom-up attention useful for object recognition? In: IEEE Conference on Computer Vision and Pattern Recognition, pp. II-37–II-44 (2004)

9. Itti, L., Koch, C.: Computational modeling of visual attention. Nature Reviews Neuroscience **2**(3), 194–203 (2001)

10. Borji, A., Itti, L.: State-of-the-art in visual attention modeling. IEEE Transactions on Pattern Analysis and Machine Intelligence **35**(1), 185–207 (2013)

11. Liu, T., Sun, J., Zheng, N.-N., Tang, X., Shum, H.-y.: Learning to detect a salient object. In: IEEE Conference on Computer and Vision Pattern Recognition, pp. 1–8 (2007)

12. Yan, Q., Xu, L., Shi, J., Jia, J.: Hierarchical saliency detection. In: IEEE Conference on Computer Vision and Pattern Recognition, pp. 1155–1162 (2013)

13. Perazzi, F., Krahenbuhl, P., Pritch, Y., Hornung, A.: Saliency filters: Contrast based filtering for salient region detection. In: IEEE Conference on Computer Vision and Pattern Recognition (CVPR), pp. 733–740. (2012)

14. Cheng, M.-M., Zhang, G.-X., Mitra, N.J., Huang, X., Hu, S.-M.: Global contrast based salient region detection. IEEE Conference on Computer Vision and Pattern Recognition (CVPR), pp. 409–416 (2011)

15. Arbelaez, P., Maire, M., Fowlkes, C., Malik, J.: Contour detection and hierarchical image segmentation. IEEE Transactions on Pattern Analysis and Machine Intelligence **33**(5), 898–916 (2011)

16. Alpert, S., Galun, M., Basri, R., Brandt, A.: Image segmentation by probabilistic bottom-up aggregation and cue integration. IEEE Conference on Computer Vision and Pattern Recognition, pp. 1–8 (2007)

17. Li, Y., Hou, X., Koch, C., Rehg, J., Yuille, A.: The secrets of salient object segmentation. IEEE Conference on Computer Vision and Pattern Recognition (2014)

18. Margolin, R., Zelnik-Manor, L., Tal, A.: How to Evaluate Foreground Maps. IEEE Conference on Computer Vision and Pattern Recognition, pp. 248–255 (2014)

19. Achanta, R., Estrada, F.J., Wils, P., Süsstrunk, S.: Salient Region Detection and Segmentation. In: Gasteratos, A., Vincze, M., Tsotsos, J.K. (eds.) ICVS 2008. LNCS, vol. 5008, pp. 66–75. Springer, Heidelberg (2008)

20. Zhai, Y., Shah, M.: Visual attention detection in video sequences using spatiotemporal cues. In: Proceedings of the 14th Annual ACM International Conference on Multimedia, pp. 815–824 (2006)

21. Kootstra, G., Nederveen, A., De Boer, B.: Paying attention to symmetry. In: Proceedings of the British Machine Vision Conference, pp. 1115–1125 (2008)

# Non-uniform Motion Deblurring
# Using Normalized Hyper Laplacian Prior

Guodong Wang[1(✉)], Bin Wei[2], Zhenkuan Pan[1], Jingge Lu[1], and Zhaojing Diao[1]

[1] College of Information Engineering, Qingdao University, Qingdao 266071, China
doctorwgd@gmail.com
[2] The Affiliated Hospital of Qingdao University, Qingdao 266003, China

**Abstract.** Non-uniform motion deblurring is a hard topic for image processing. Non-uniform blur is often caused by camera motion in 3D while taking photos. Existing non-uniform deblurring methods formulate the blur as a linear combination of homographic transforms of a clear image. But they are computationally expensive and require large memory because the amount of the unknown variables are large. In this paper we use patch-wise method for the deblurring process. The patch-wise method are proved to be an effective method for non-uniform motion deblurring. The key issues are the accuracy of kernel estimation and the substitution of the erroneous kernels. In this paper, we use normalized smoothing term for the blur kernel estimation because it is effective and stable. When the erroneous kernels are conformed, we use a minimization method using neighborhood information for estimating the kernels. Experiments demonstrate the validity of the proposed method.

**Keywords:** Non-uniform motion deblur · Normalized hyper laplacian prior · Variational method · Patch -wise method

## 1 Introduction

The image is often blurred with the camera shake while taking photos. Deblurring from a single image is an ill posed question because the blur kernel and the clear image are not known.

In the last decade, significant progress has been made for removing uniform blur from a single image. There are many successful deblurring algorithms for uniform blur. When camera motions only contain translations, these algorithm can achieve good results. However, in real case, camera shake includes translation and camera rotations. So this procedure is also called non-uniform blur. That is to say, the blur kernels are not the same at different points. This is a hard work for the researchers. Several non-uniform deblurring algorithms have been proposed, which model the blur as an integration of the clear scene under a sequence of planar projective transforms. The drawbacks of these algorithm are that they require a large memory and are computational expensive.

For reducing the memory and computation requirement, patch-wise deblurring algorithms are proposed. The idea is that in a small neighborhood the blur kernels are

© Springer-Verlag Berlin Heidelberg 2015
H. Zha et al. (Eds.): CCCV 2015, Part I, CCIS 546, pp. 103–113, 2015.
DOI: 10.1007/978-3-662-48558-3_11

similar. In these methods, images are divided into patches and the blur kernels are estimated from each patch using a uniform deblurring algorithm. Then using estimated blur kernels the clear image can be recovered. There are two main steps: The first step is dividing the image into overlapped patches and obtaining the blur kernels using uniform motion deblurring algorithm. The second step is to verify erroneous kernels and estimate the kernels again.

To obtain accurate blur kernels efficiently, we use normalized smoothing term in the energy function. We select normalized hyper laplacian prior as the normalized smoothing term. The hyper laplacian prior can model the heavy-tailed distribution of the natural image gradient which is an important prior for clear image processing. The normalized hyper laplacian prior can lead the energy decreasing while solving the equation. So using normalized hyper laplacian prior , we needn't use additional steps for kernel estimation.

To detect the erroneous kernels, we use the error residue to measure the accuracy. We calculate all the error between the blurred image and the image convolve with the calculated kernel. After detecting the poorly estimated blur kernels, previous works replace the rejected kernels with the average of their neighboring kernels. However, simply averaging the kernels causes the substituted kernel inaccurate and may lead to artifacts in the deblurred images. For the erroneous kernels, we use the neighborhood information to recaluate the kernels. We build a new energy function by incorporating neighborhood information with an stable kernel. Then the estimated kernel is stable.

The organization of this paper goes as follows. In Section 2, we will introduce the related work for motion deblurring. The new proposed method and the solving procedure is introduced in section 3. Then some numerical examples are shown in Section 4. Section 5 makes some concluding remarks.

## 2    Related Work

We briefly introduce the uniform and non-uniform motion deblurring algorithms. We deblur an image without any additional information. The uniform blur means that the kernels are the same in the image. The non-uniform blur means the kernels varies according to the location. The uniform deblurring algorithms were extensively studied in the past few years and achieved great success.

By convention, the invariant motion blurred image can be expressed as follows :

$$f = k * u + n \tag{1}$$

where $k$ , $u$ and $n$ denote the blur kernel, the original unblurred image and the noise respectively, $f$ denote the blurred image. $*$ is the convolution operation. The uniform motion deblurring is well studied. Chan [1] firstly proposed using variational method for solving the question of blind deconvolution by using total variation method. He used total variation terms for restricting both the blur kernel and image gradients. The method laid the foundation of deblurring by variation method. After Chan's method, Fergus [2] using the heavy tailed probabilistic distribution for image gradients because he observed that natural image's gradient obeys this rule but the blurred image doesn't fit the law. His method is the first successful one for real case deblurring using variational method. Shan [3] presented an analysis of the reasons of common artifacts found in current deblurring methods. Then he computed deblurred image using a unified probabilistic model of both blur kernel estimation and clear image restoration. He incorporated first and second derivatives into his proposed model and make the deblurring image clear from ring artifact. Levin [4] points out that some deblurring methods can fail because the detail sections have negative effects on the process by comparing the methods in [2] and [3]. After this discovery, many researchers used additional method such as shock filter for reducing the effort of little details. Hui [5] proposed a method for identifying motion blurs form image gradients. Using the gradients, he will estimate the blur kernels. Cho [6] proposes a fast deblurring method by accelerating both latent image and kernel estimation by introducing a novel prediction step and working with image derivatives rather than pixel values. In the auxiliary step, he use bilateral filter for enhancing  strong edges and eliminating tiny edges. For further accelerating the implementation, GPU is used for speed-up the method which makes the method fast enough for practical usage. Xu [7] use large gradients selection for reducing the negative effect of the tiny gradient. Then, kernel refinement procedure is used by the fact that motion caused blur kernel is spatially continuous. His method is a stable one for estimating blur kernels. Hong [8] used nonlinear diffusion method for motion deblurring. Then, the blur kernel correction is done by the consumption that blur path should be curve with single point width. Xu [9] proposed using L0 sparse prior [12] for gradient restriction. The L0 term has the ability of enhancing large gradient and eliminating small edges. This feature can make the method doesn't need additional steps for kernel estimation.

When the blur kernels are spatial variant, the blur image can be written into a matrix form:

$$f = Ku + n \tag{2}$$

K represents the matrix form of k. Gupta et al. model the blur matrix as a motion density function and the blur image f as the summation over images taken from different poses.

$$f = \sum_i a_i K_i u + n \tag{3}$$

where $a_i$ is the weighting coefficient. There are little work on the non-uniform motion deblurring.

There has been relatively little work on spatially varying blind motion blurring. Levin et al. [14] proposed a spatially varying motion deblurring method by segmenting the image into different areas through the depth information and then deblurred each region. Whyte et al. [16] proposed a new model for non-uniform motion deblurring. In his method, he model the spatially varying motion blur by 3D rotational camera motion model. Gupta et al. [17] proposed model the spatially variant motion blur by the motion density function which can represent a different set of 3D camera motions. Then the calculated motion density function can model the spatially varying kernel function. Harmeling et al. [18] built on a framework for space-variant filtering by Hirsch et al. [20] and a fast algorithm for single image blind deconvolution for space-invariant filters by Cho and Lee [6] to construct a method for blind deconvolution in the case of space-variant blur. Hirsch et al. [19] proposed a framework of the efficient filter flow for deblurring images with spatially varying motion blurring effects. In his method, he assume that in every small area the motion blur can be deemed as an uniform blur. Ji [20] proposed two-stage approach for blind spatially-varying motion deblurring. First, he calculated the blur kernels by patch based method. Then he recovered the clear image by using a robust non-blind deblurring method.

## 3     Proposed Method

In this paper, we also use patch-wise deblurring method for spatially varying blur image. To obtain accurate blur kernels efficiently, we use patch wise normalized hyper laplacian prior in the energy function. After detecting the erroneous kernels, we use the neighborhood information to re-estimate the erroneous kernels. Because the patch based method is first proposed by Hirsch so we will introduce the efficient filter flow first.

### 3.1     Framework of Efficient Filter Flow

Hirsch *et al.* [19] proposed a framework of the EFF (Efficient Filter Flow) for handling smoothly space-variant convolutions. He found that a spatially variant filtering can be implemented by chunking a signal into overlapping patches, then he filtered each patch with a spatially invariant PSF, finally assembling the filtered image from the filtered patches using the overlap-add method. The framework of the EFF aims to extend a uniform moton deblurring to a non-uniform motion deblurring and is defined as:

$$f_i = \sum_{r=1}^{p} \sum_{j=1}^{s} k_j^{(r)} w_{i-j}^{(r)} u_{i-j}^{(r)}, \text{ for } 1 \le i \le m \tag{4}$$

where $p$ is the number of the overlapping patches, $k_j^{(r)}$ is the blur kernel of the $r$-th patch ($1 \le r \le p$), and is a window function to fade the $r$-th patch in and masking the others out. The sum of the weights at each pixel should be equal to one, i.e., $\sum_{r=1}^{p} w_i^{(r)} = 1$, for $1 \le r \le m$ .Without the normalization, there will be artifacts in the overlapping areas.

As indicated in Eqn. (3), the EFF is linear in $u$ and in $k$ , where $k$ is a vector stacked by $p$ PSFs $k^{(1)}, \ldots, k^{(p)}$ . It implies there are matrices $K$ and $U$ such that $B = Ku = Uk$ . According to [19], the matrices are expressed as

$$K = Z_b \sum_{r=1}^{p} C_r^T F^{-1} Diag(FZ_k k^{(r)}) FC_r Diag(w^{(r)}) \tag{5}$$

$$U = Z_b \sum_{r=1}^{p} C_r^T F^{-1} Diag(FC_r Diag(w^{(r)})l) FZ_k B_r \tag{6}$$

where $Z_b$ is a matrix that appends zeros to the valid part of the space-variant convolution such that its size matches the full size of an input image u, $C_r$ is a matrix that crops the $r$-th patch from the input image, is the Discrete Fourier Transform matrix, Diag(v) is a diagonal matrix with along its diagonal, is a matrix that appends zeros to such that its size matches the patch size, and is a matrix that crops the r-th PSF from the vector k.

Eqn. (6) implies that the patches are firstly recovered locally and then assembled into a latent image. Eqn. (7) implies that each PSF can be estimated from the corresponding patch locally. It indicates that space-variant convolutions can be implemented in the EFF as efficiently as space-invariant ones. In the next section, we will introduce our method under the framework of EFF.

## 3.2    Normalized Hyper Laplacian Prior in EFF

In the deblurring process, the image gradient's amplitude will became bigger while the image get more clearer. This phenomenon makes the traditional methods failed. So additional steps such as shock filter and bilateral filter should be added for the kernel estimation. Krishnan [11] proposed using normalized total variation term [10] for the motion deblurring. The energy is decreasing in the deblurring processing by using the normalized total variation term. So he needn't use additional filters for the deblurring. In this paper, we use hyper laplacian prior for motion deblurring. The hyper laplacian prior is a good model for reflecting the clear image's gradient distribution which is expressed as heavy tailed distribution. The energy function incorporating normalized hyper laplacian prior can be expressed as:

$$E(\nabla u, k) = \sum_{r=1}^{p} \left( \frac{1}{2} \int_{\Omega} \left( k^{(r)} * \nabla u^{(r)} - \nabla f^{(r)} \right)^2 dx + \lambda_1 \frac{\int_{\Omega} |\nabla u^{(r)}|^p dx}{\int_{\Omega} |\nabla u^{(r)}|^2 dx} + \lambda_2 \int_{\Omega} |k^{(r)}| dx \right), (0.5 \leq p \leq 0.8) \tag{7}$$

The first term in the energy equation is the data fidelity term where $k$, $u$ and $f$ denote the blur kernel, the recovered image and the blurred image respectively, $*$ is the convolution operation. In this paper, we use the residual error of the deblurred image's gradient and the kernel convolved with the gradient of the image for the data fidelity. This term is easy for energy resolving because the smoothing term also containing the gradient operation. $r$ denotes the $r$ th patch. The second term is the normalized hyper laplacian item. This term can make the energy decreasing while in the deblurring process. The third term is the restriction term of the blur kernel. The absolution operator make the kernel sparse. For convenience, we let $x = \nabla u$, $y = \nabla f$.

The energy function can be rewritten as:

$$E(x,k) = \sum_{r=1}^{p} \left( \frac{1}{2} \int_{\Omega} \left( k^{(r)} * x^{(r)} - y^{(r)} \right)^2 dx + \lambda_1 \frac{\int_{\Omega} \left| x^{(r)} \right|^p dx}{\int_{\Omega} \left| x^{(r)} \right|^2 dx} + \lambda_2 \int_{\Omega} \left| k^{(r)} \right| dx \right) (0.5 \le p \le 0.8) \quad (8)$$

After dividing the image into overlaped patches, we use the following energy equation for solving the blur kernels.

$$E(x^{(r)}, k^{(r)}) = \frac{1}{2} \int_{\Omega} \left( k^{(r)} * x^{(r)} - y^{(r)} \right)^2 dx + \lambda_1 \frac{\int_{\Omega} \left| x^{(r)} \right|^p dx}{\int_{\Omega} \left| x^{(r)} \right|^2 dx} + \lambda_2 \int_{\Omega} \left| k^{(r)} \right| dx \quad (9)$$

We use iterative minimization method for solving the above equation.

Fixing $k^{(r)}$ for solving $x^{(r)}$, the relative energy function is:

$$E(x^{(r)}) = \frac{1}{2} \int_{\Omega} \left( k^{(r)} * x^{(r)} - y^{(r)} \right)^2 dx + \lambda_1 \frac{\int_{\Omega} \left| x^{(r)} \right|^p dx}{\int_{\Omega} \left| x^{(r)} \right|^2 dx} \quad (10)$$

In above equation, because the denominator containing x, so the energy is not convex and the energy solving is a hard work. In the iteration of energy solving, because the item of $\int_{\Omega} |x|^2 dx$ doesn't change dramatically, we can use the value of the last step. So the Euler-Lagrange equation can be written as:

$$k^{\prime(r)} * \left( k^{(r)} * x^{(r)} - y^{(r)} \right) + \lambda_1 \frac{p \left| x^{(r)} \right|^{p-1}}{\int_{\Omega} \left| x^{(r)} \right|^2 dx} \frac{x^{(r)}}{\left| x^{(r)} \right|} = 0 \quad (11)$$

where $k^{\prime(r)}(x, y) = k^{(r)}(-x, -y)$, in other word $k'$ is the centrosymmetric matrix of k.

$x^{(r)}$ is not easy to be solved, so we rewrite the equation in the following form.

$$x^{(r)} - x^{(r)} + k^{\prime(r)} * \left( k^{(r)} * x^{(r)} - y^{(r)} \right) + \lambda_1 \frac{p \left| x^{(r)} \right|^{p-1}}{\int_{\Omega} \left| x^{(r)} \right|^2 dx} \frac{x^{(r)}}{\left| x^{(r)} \right|} = 0 \quad (12)$$

$$x^{(r)k+1} = x^{(r)k} - k'^{(r)}*(k^{(r)}*x^{(r)k} - y^{(r)}) - \frac{\lambda_1 p |x^{(r)k}|^{p-1}}{\int_\Omega |x^{(r)k}|^2 dx} \frac{x^{(r)k+1}}{|x^{(r)k+1}|} \tag{13}$$

The $x^{(r)}$ can be got by using soft shrinkage-thresholding [13]:

$$x^{(r)k+1} = \max\left( abs\left(x^{(r)k} - k'^{(r)}*(k^{(r)}*x^{(r)k} - y^{(r)})\right) - \frac{\lambda_1 p |x^{(r)k}|^{p-1}}{\theta \int_\Omega |x^{(r)k}|^2 dx}, 0 \right) \cdot sign\left(x^{(r)k} - k'^{(r)}*(k^{(r)}*x^{(r)k} - y^{(r)})\right) \tag{14}$$

For calculate k, the energy function is:

$$E(k^{(r)}) = \frac{1}{2} \int_\Omega \left(k^{(r)}*x^{(r)} - y^{(r)}\right)^2 dx + \lambda_2 \int_\Omega |k^{(r)}| dx \tag{15}$$

The Euler-Lagrange equation is:

$$x'^{(r)}*\left(x^{(r)}*k^{(r)} - y^{(r)}\right) + \lambda_2 \frac{k^{(r)}}{|k^{(r)}|} = 0 \tag{16}$$

Because the dimension of x is much larger than k, we use unconstrained iterative re-weighted least squares (IRLS) [14] for solving k for the calculation precision. Then a projection is followed by the contraints which is setting negative elements to 0 and renormalizing the elements to [0,1].

Although the proposed method can make the energy decreasing while in the deblurring processing, we will use multiscale method which is a common approach for motion deblurring for avoiding the kernels falling into local minimization.

After the blur kernels are estimated, we choose to use the TV[15] model as non-blind deconvolution method, since it is fast and robust to small kernel errors.

$$E(u^{(r)}) = \frac{1}{2} \int_\Omega (k^{(r)}*u^{(r)} - f^{(r)})^2 dx + \lambda \int_\Omega |\nabla u^{(r)}| dx \tag{17}$$

### 3.3    Removing Poorly Estimated Blur Kernels

In the patch based non-nuniform deblurring procedure, there are always erroneous initial estimation of local kernels because the edges are not efficient for kernel estimation. So after the initial kernel estimation, we will detect erroneous kernels. We use the method proposed by Ji [20] for the reason of simplicity and efficient. For each patch $P_i$, let $k_i$ denote the kernel obtained from the previous step. We use the residual $r_i = (k_i * u_i - f_i)^2$ to measure its accuracy and set the accuracy threshold by $\varepsilon = \frac{3}{2} \times median\{r_1, r_2, ..., r_n\}$. Then any local kernel whose residual $r_i$ larger than the accuracy threshold  is considered as wrongly estimated kernel and discarded.

## 3.4    Re-estimating Erroneous Local Kernels

Several method for re-estimating erroneous kernels only use the estimated kernels in the neighborhood. To re-estimate the discarded local blur kernels, we need some additional information outside these regions to help the estimation of blur kernels as these regions by themselves do not have sufficient image content for a reliable kernel estimation.

We use a minimization method using neighborhood information for estimating the kernels. It is observed that the blur kernels of neighboring regions changes not dramatically. This motivates us to combine the local image information and the correlation among the kernel to estimate and the available kernels in its neighborhood. We incorporating the neighborhood information into the energy equation and the equation can be written as:

$$E(k^{(r)}) = \sum_{\substack{i=1 \\ i \neq r}}^{m} \left( \frac{1}{2} \int_{\Omega} \left( k^{(r)} * u^{(i)} - f^{(i)} \right)^2 dx + \lambda \int_{\Omega} \left| k^{(r)} \right| dx \right) \tag{18}$$

In the above equation, $m$ is the number of the patches used for re-estimating kernels. In our experiment, we set m as 4. That is to say, we use the north, south, east and west neighbors of re-estimating erroneous kernels.

The Euler-Lagrange equation is:

$$\sum_{\substack{i=1 \\ i \neq r}}^{m} u'^{(i)} * \left( u^{(i)} * k^{(r)} - f^{(i)} \right) + \lambda \frac{k^{(r)}}{\left| k^{(r)} \right|} = 0 \tag{19}$$

Because the dimension of u is larger than k, we also use unconstrained iterative reweighted least squares (IRLS) [14] for solving k. Using the estimated kernels, we will get the patch-based clear images.

## 4    Numerical Experiments

To validate the effect of our proposed method, we use several images selected from several papers as experiments. The deblurred images and the calculated kernels are also shown in the experiments. Figure 1 shows an elephant and several people standing before a church. We divide the image into 7*5 patches. From the deblurred kernel, we can see that the image is blurred with camera rotation. The deblurred image is clear and has no ringing artifacts. In the following two experiments, using the same procedure, we also get the clear image and the corresponding kernels.

To prove the effect of our method, we also compare our method with the method of Jia [7]. Figure 2 shows the results using the proposed non-uniform method. From the results, we can find that our method can reasonable results. The estimated blur kernel is reasonable for motion camera's trajectory. The blur kernel is sparse because only on the motion path, the elements are not zero. This finding conforms the sparse prior of the kernel. The divided patches have different blur kernels and the neighborhood kernels are changing smoothly. These phenomena also proved that patch-based non-uniform deblurring method is useful.

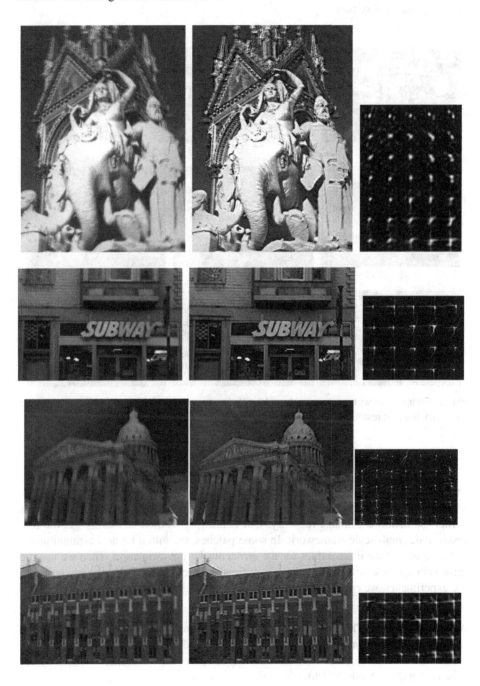

**Fig. 1.** Non-uniform motion deblur using the proposed method. (From left to right: the blurry images; our results; and our refined PSFs after using the strategy of identifying and replacing the poorly estimated kernels.)

**Fig. 2.** Comparison with the approach of Jia [7]. For every experiments, from left to right are the blurry images; results of Jia; our results.

## 5    Conclusion

In this paper, we have presented a novel patch-wise motion deblurring method for non-uniform deblurring. In every patches, we use normalized hyper laplacian prior for kernel estimation and image recovery. Our deblurring method can easily get the real result under multiscale framework. In some patches, the initial kernels estimation are not accurate, so we use residues for the erroneous kernel estimation. Then we use the information of the neighborhood for re-estimating the erroneous local kernels. From the experiments, we can see that our method get proper results.

**Acknowledgements.** This work was supported by National Natural Science Foundation of China (No.61305045 and No.61170106), National "Twelfth Five-Year" development plan of science and technology (No.2013BAI01B03) and Qingdao science and technology development project (No. 13-1-4-190-jch).

# References

1. Chan, T., Wong, C.: Total variation blind deconvolution. IEEE Tran. Image Processing 7(3), 370–375 (1998)
2. Fergus, R., Singh, B., Hertzmann, A., et al.: Removing camera shake from a single photograph. ACM Transaction on Graphics 25(3), 787–794 (2006)
3. Shan, Q., Jia, J., Agarwala, A.: High-quality motion deblurring from a single image. ACM Transaction on Graphics 27(3), 731–740 (2008)
4. Levin, A., Weiss, Y., Durand, E., et al.: Understanding and evaluating blind deconvolution algorithms. CVPR:1964-1971 (2009)
5. Hui, J., Liu, C.: Motion blur identification from image gradients. CVPR (2008)
6. Cho, S., Lee, S.: Fast motion deblurring. ACM Transaction on Graphics 28(5), 1450–1451 (2009)
7. Xu, L., Jia, J.: Two-Phase Kernel Estimation for Robust Motion Deblurring. In: Daniilidis, K., Maragos, P., Paragios, N. (eds.) ECCV 2010, Part I. LNCS, vol. 6311, pp. 157–170. Springer, Heidelberg (2010)
8. Hong, H., Park, K.: Single-image motion deblurring using adaptive anisotropic regularization. Optical Engineering 49(9), 097008-1–097008-13 (2010)
9. Xu, L., Zheng, Sh., Jia, J.: Unnatural L0 Sparse Representation for Natural Image Deblurring. CVPR (2013)
10. Hurley, N., Rickard, S.: Comparing measures of sparsity. IEEE Trans. Inf. Theory pp. 4723–4741 (2009)
11. Krishnan, D., Tay, T., Fergus, R.: Blind deconvolution using a normalized sparsity measure. In: CVPR, pp. 233–240 (2011)
12. Xu, L., Lu, C., Xu, Y., Jia, J.: Image Smoothing via L0 Gradient Minimization. ACM Transactions on Graphics 30(6), 1741–1752 (2011)
13. Osher, S., Mao, Y., Dong, B., et al.: Fast linearized bregman iteration for compressive sensing and sparse denoising. Commun. Math. Sci. 8(1), 93–111 (2010)
14. Levin, A., Fergus, R., Durand, F., et al.: Image and depth from a conventional camera with a coded aperture. ACM Transaction on Graphics 26(3), 701–709 (2007)
15. Rudin, L., Osher, S., Fatemi, E.: Nonlinear total variation based noise removal algorithms. Physica D 60, 259–268 (1992)
16. Whyte, O., Sivic, J., Zisserman, A., Ponce, J.: Non-uniform Deblurring for Shaken Images. In: CVPR (2010)
17. Gupta, A., Joshi, N., Lawrence Zitnick, C., Cohen, M., Curless, B.: Single Image Deblurring Using Motion Density Functions. In: Daniilidis, K., Maragos, P., Paragios, N. (eds.) ECCV 2010, Part I. LNCS, vol. 6311, pp. 171–184. Springer, Heidelberg (2010)
18. Harmeling, S., Hirsch, M., Schölkopf, B.: Space-Variant Single-Image Blind Deconvolution for Removing Camera Shake. NIPS 2010
19. Hirsch, M., Schuler, C., Harmeling, S., Schölkopf, B.: Fast Removal of Non-uniform Camera Shake. In: ICCV (2011)
20. Ji, H., Wang, K.: A two-stage approach to blind spatially-varying motion deblurring. In: 2012 IEEE Conference on Computer Vision and Pattern Recognition (CVPR), pp. 73–80. IEEE (2012)

# Robust Mean Shift Tracking Based on Refined Appearance Model and Online Update

Wangsheng Yu$^{(\boxtimes)}$, Zhiqiang Hou, Xiaohua Tian, and Dan Hu

Information and Navigation College, Air Force Engineering University, Xi'an, China
xing_fu_yu@sina.com

**Abstract.** In this paper, a robust mean shift tracking algorithm based on refined appearance model and online update strategy is proposed. The main idea of the proposed algorithm is to construct a more accurate appearance model and design an online update strategy. At the beginning of the tracking, the simple mean shift tracking algorithm is applied on the first few frames to collect a set of target templates, which contains both foreground and background of the target. During the model construction, simple linear iterative clustering (SLIC) algorithm is exploited to obtain the superpixels of the target templates, and the superpixels are further clustered to classify the background from foreground. A weighted vector is then obtained based on the classified background and foreground, which is utilized to modify the kernel histogram appearance model. The following frames are processed based on the mean shift tracking algorithm with the modified appearance model, and the stable tracking results with no occlusion will be selected to update the appearance model. The concrete operation of model update is the same as model construction. Experiment results on challenging test sequences indicate that the proposed algorithm can well cope with both appearance variation and background change to obtain a robust tracking performance.

## 1 Introduction

With the development of computer vision and multimedia technology, visual tracking has been widely applied in many civil and military fields. It plays more and more important roles in improving the efficiency of industrial and agricultural production, as well as the performances of weapons and equipment. In the past decade, visual tracking technology made much progress [1]. However, there exists limitation in most of the tracking methods because they are designed for the specific or relatively simple situations [2].

As one of the famous tracking methods, mean shift tracking attracts many attentions for the well-developed theory, simple course, outperformed performance and easy to implement. The mean shift algorithm was firstly proposed by Fukunaga *et al.* [3] to cope with the data analysis. Cheng [4] introduced it into the fields of image processing and computer vision. Bradski [5]

This research was supported by National Natural Science Foundation of China (No. 61175029 and No. 61473309).

H. Zha et al. (Eds.): CCCV 2015, Part I, CCIS 546, pp. 114–123, 2015.
DOI: 10.1007/978-3-662-48558-3_12

developed its application in face tracking and proposed a continuously adaptive mean shift (CAMSHIFT) algorithm. Comaniciu $et$ $al.$ summarized the mean shift as a robust approach to feature space analysis [6] and successfully applied it to visual tracking [7]. Collins [8] discussed the limitation of the scale adaptation in original mean shift tracking algorithm, and proposed a modified one in scale space. Zivkovic $et$ $al.$ [9] and Ning $et$ $al.$ [10] also discussed the scale and orientation estimation for mean shift tracking. Comaniciu $et$ $al.$ [7] proposed a background weighted kernel to increase the discriminative of foreground, which is widely applied in mean shift tracking [11]. Some other fruitful works have also promoted the development of mean shift tracking, such as online selection a discriminative feature [12], novel histogram for model representation [13], and cross-bin based similarity measure [14].

In this paper, we centralize on how to improve the robustness of the mean shift tracking algorithm. Wang $et$ $al.$ [15] proposed a superpixel method ro refine the appearance model, which improves the model precision. Zhuang $et$ $al.$ [16] proposed a discriminative sparse appearance model for visual tracking, which improves the tracking success rate in most cases. We based on our tracking algorithm partially on these two methods. Firstly, a clustering analysis method is introduced into classifying the background from foreground, which may distinctively improve the precision of the appearance model. Secondly, a simple but effective rule is proposed to select the stable results to update the appearance model. Finally, a set of challenging test sequences is exploited to verify the robustness of the proposed tracking algorithm.

## 2    Mean Shift Tracking Algorithm

In mean shift tracking algorithm, the target is usually defined as a rectangular or ellipsoidal region, and represented by a color histogram model. Given a target model, the main procedure of mean shift tracking is to iteratively search the best similar target candidate along the gradient ascent direction in feature space. Denote by $q = \{q_u | u = 1, 2, ..., B\}$ the target model, and $p(\mathbf{y}) = \{p_u(\mathbf{y}) | u = 1, 2, ..., B\}$ the target candidate. The similarity between them is defined by Bhattacharyya coefficient

$$\rho(\mathbf{y}) = \rho(p(\mathbf{y}), q) = \sum_{u=1}^{B} \sqrt{p_u(\mathbf{y})q_u} \tag{1}$$

A Taylor series expansion around the target candidate $p_u(\mathbf{y}_0)$ yields a linear approximation to the coefficient

$$\rho(\mathbf{y}) \approx \frac{1}{2} \sum_{u=1}^{B} \sqrt{p_u(\mathbf{y}_0)q_u} + \frac{1}{2} \sum_{u=1}^{B} \sqrt{p_u(\mathbf{y})} \sqrt{\frac{q_u}{p_u(\mathbf{y}_0)}} \tag{2}$$

Searching the best target candidate is namely to find the $\mathbf{y} = \mathbf{y}_{opt}$ that maximizes the formula (2). By substituting $p_u(\mathbf{y})$ with the kernel-based histogram representation, formula (2) is then translated into

$$\rho(\mathbf{y}) \approx \frac{1}{2} \sum_{u=1}^{B} \sqrt{p_u(\mathbf{y}_0)q_u} + \frac{C_h}{2} \sum_{i=1}^{N_h} \omega_i K(\|\frac{\mathbf{y} - \mathbf{x}_i}{h}\|^2) \tag{3}$$

where $C_h$ is the normalization constant, $B$ is the total number of the histogram bins, $N_h$ is the total pixels in target candidate region, and $K(x)$ is the kernel profile with a bandwidth of $h$.

Denote by $\omega_i$ the weight of pixel $\mathbf{x}_i$. This weight is calculated by

$$\omega_i = \sum_{u=1}^{B} \sqrt{\frac{q_u}{p_u(\mathbf{y}_0)}} \delta[b(\mathbf{x}_i - u)] \tag{4}$$

where $\delta(x)$ is the Kronecker delta function, $b(\mathbf{x}_i)$ associates the pixel to the histogram bin.

Taking the derivation of Equation (3) with respect to $\mathbf{y}$ and setting $\frac{\partial \rho}{\partial \mathbf{y}} = 0$ yields

$$\mathbf{y}_1 = \frac{\sum_{i=1}^{N_h} \omega_i g(\|\frac{\mathbf{y}_0 - \mathbf{x}_i}{h}\|^2)\mathbf{x}_i}{\sum_{i=1}^{N_h} \omega_i g(\|\frac{\mathbf{y}_0 - \mathbf{x}_i}{h}\|^2)} \tag{5}$$

where $g(x) = -K'(x)$ is the negative derivative of the kernel profile. Equation (5) is the final iteration formula for standard mean shift tracking.

## 3     The Proposed Tracking Algorithm

The main idea of this proposed algorithm is to improve the robustness of mean shift tracking by refining the appearance model. The whole algorithm consists of (1) simple tracking, (2) model construction, (3) tracking with refined model, and (4) model update. Fig. 1 gives the tracking flowchart of the proposed algorithm. The following contents of this section will introduce these four parts.

### 3.1     Simple Tracking

Most of the traditional tracking algorithms construct the appearance model relying only on the target template of the initial frame. However, it is known that more prior knowledge of the target may produce a more accurate appearance model, which is very important to improve the tracking robustness. In this paper, we exploit the simple mean shift tracking algorithm to process the first few frames. During this course, a set of target templates are collected to construct target model. In order to ensure the templates contain both background and foreground, we set the target template four times as large as the predefined target area.

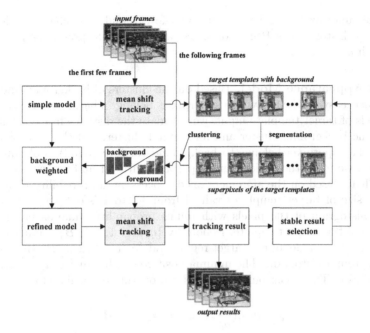

**Fig. 1.** The flowchart of the proposed tracking algorithm.

## 3.2    Model Construction

Based on the collected target templates, some image processing algorithms are introduced to construct the appearance model. Firstly, the simple linear iterative clustering (SLIC) [17] algorithm is exploited to obtain the superpixels of the target templates. Then, the mean shift clustering algorithm is applied to cluster the superpixels based on HSI space to classify the background from foreground. Finally, a background weighted vector is calculated from the background and foreground.

**SLIC Segmentation.** SLIC is a very efficient superpixel algorithm. It groups pixels into perceptually meaningful atomic regions which can be used to replace the rigid structure of the pixel grid. SLIC is very simple to use and understand. By default, the only parameter of this algorithm is $N$, the desired number of approximately equally sized superpixels. We refer to literature [17] for more details about SLIC segmentation.

**Mean Shift Clustering.** During the segmentation, the templates are grouped into lots of superpixels. In most cases, the superpixel contains only background or foreground. However, it is hard to classify the superpixels into background and foreground. So, we introduce the mean shift clustering algorithm to further group the superpixels into background and foreground. The clustering feature is $8 \times 8 \times 8$ histogram in HSI color space, and we should preset the clustering bandwidth $h$.

**Refined Appearance Model.** Based on the clusters of background and foreground, it is easy to identify which superpixels belong to background. When the superpixels of target template input, we calculate the distance from each superpixel to the background cluster and foreground cluster, and then a probability whether the superpixel belongs to background (or foreground) is obtained. In this paper, we mark the background superpixel with $-1$ and foreground superpixel with 1. Based on the aforementioned processing, a probability map (with the same size of target template) valued from $-1$ to 1 is obtained. We calculate the histogram of the pixels with minus probability value as background histogram of the target template. Denote by $\{q_u | u = 1, 2, ..., B\}$ the normalized kernel histogram model of the target region and $\{o_u | u = 1, 2, ..., B\}$ the normalized background histogram. The minima positive number in $\{o_u | u = 1, 2, ..., B\}$ is marked as $\hat{o}$. The background weighted vector can be calculated by

$$v_u = min(\frac{\hat{o}}{o_u}, 1) \ , \quad u = 1, 2, ...B \tag{6}$$

and the final refined appearance model is $\{q'_u = C \cdot v_u q_u | u = 1, 2, ..., B\}$, where $C$ is the normalization constant.

### 3.3  Tracking with Refined Model

With the refined model, the mean shift search will obtain a more accurate target location. So, we exploit the mean shift tracking algorithm with the refined appearance model to process the following frames to improve the tracking performance. More details about the tracking course please refer to subsection 3.1.

### 3.4  Model Update

During the tracking course, the target may undergo appearance variation and background change. In order to cope with these interfering to improve the robustness of long term tracking, we design an online strategy to update the appearance model. We set a rule to estimate whether the tracking result of the current frame is suitable for model update. The rule is as follows. We draw out a tracking result every $U_1$ frames to calculate the sum value of the weighted map $W$, if the value is not less than a preset ratio $r$ to that of the last frame, we select it as a sample which will be exploited to update the target model.

The selected target template according to the tracking result is then grouped into superpixels using SLIC algorithm. When the number of the collected target templates equals the preset threshold $U_2$, the mean shift clustering algorithm is then exploited to renew the background cluster and foreground cluster. So, a new background weighted vector is obtained to refine the kernel histogram model, and the final appearance model is updated.

## 3.5    Summary of the Whole Algorithm

Based on the aforementioned introduction, we summarize the proposed tracking algorithm as follows.

---

**Algorithm 1** Mean shift tracking based on refined appearance model and online update.

---

| | |
|---|---|
| 01 | **Input**: frames with the ground truth of the initial frame. |
| 02 | **For** $i = 1$ to $k$ ($k$ is a preset parameter not greater than 5); |
| 03 |     Do the tracking using the basic mean shift tracking algorithm; |
| 04 |     Do the segmentation of the target template using SLIC algorithm; |
| 05 | **End For.** |
| 06 | Cluster the collected superpixels using mean shift clustering algorithm. |
| 07 | Refine the appearance model using the obtained background weighted vector. |
| 08 | **For** $i = k + 1$ to the last frame; |
| 09 |     Do the tracking using the mean shift algorithm with refined model; |
| 10 |     Pick out the tracking result if it is suitable for model update; |
| 11 |     Update the model if the number of the collected templates equals $U_2$; |
| 12 | **End For.** |
| 13 | **Output**: frames with tracking results marked by bounding boxes. |

---

# 4    Experiments

To give an objective evaluation of the proposed tracking algorithm, we tested it on the dataset OTB2013 and compared the tracking results with standard mean shift tracking algorithm and its amelioration. The test dataset contains 50 challenging sequences with all kinds of variation from the target and background. Considering the paper length, we only selected 8 representative ones to give a qualitative comparison and quantitative analysis.

During the experiments, the target deformation (sequence *skiing* and *bolt*), occlusion (sequence *subway* and *crossing*), illumination variation (sequence *coke* and *tiger2*), and complicated background (*basketball* and *football1*) bring challenging to the tracking test. The referenced tracking algorithms consist of standard mean shift tracking (MS) [7], scale space mean shift tracking (SMS) [8], E-M shift tracking (EMS) [9], background weighted mean shift tracking (BWMS) [11], and two recent trackers, SPT [15] and DSST [16].

To be mentioned is that there are several parameters should be initialized before tracking. (1) The number of simple tracking frames, $k = 5$. (2) The maximum of superpixels in one target template, $N = 200$. (3) The bandwidth of mean shift clustering, $h = 0.1 \sim 0.3$. (4) The frequency of tracking result selection, $U_1 = 3$. (5) The threshold to select stable tracking result, $r = 0.7 \sim 0.9$. (6) The number of target templates to update model, $U_2 = 5$. The only two parameters need to adjust are h and r. In this paper, we run the tracker many times to obtain relatively better values, and finally give an experimental evaluation as $h = 0.21$ and $r = 0.82$.

Fig. 2 shows some of the tracking results of the test tracking algorithms. We marked the results of different algorithms with different colored bounding boxes. For the sequences with target deformation, the proposed algorithm obtains relative better results by the refined appearance model. We refer to the frame # 40 in sequence *skiing* and frame # 150 sequence *bolt* for examples. When the target undergoes partial occlusion or fully occlusion, the model stops updating to prevent wrongly update. See the frame # 58 in sequence *subway* and the frame # 40 in sequence *crossing*. As the frame # 610 in sequence *basketball* and the frame # 68 in sequence *football1* show, the refined appearance model relies much more on the foreground of the target and suppresses the background. So, the background change during the tracking affects little to the tracking results. The online model update improves the tracking robustness when the target undergoes illumination change. We refer to the frame # 240 in sequence *coke* and frame # 310 sequence *tiger2* for more details.

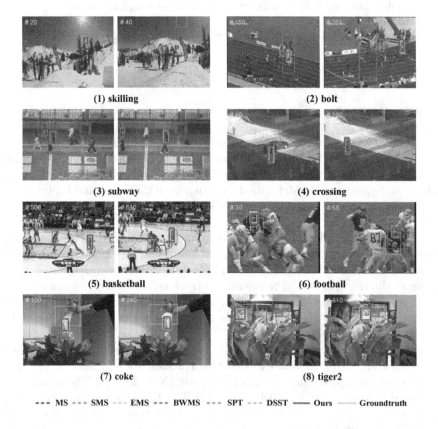

Fig. 2. Tracking results comparison of different algorithms.

We quantitative compared the proposed algorithm with the referenced algorithms using a popular metric, Center Location Error (CLE for short). It measures the error between the center location of tracking window and the ground truth. Certainly small errors in this metric are expected for an optimal tracker. We write down the test results for each algorithm and plot the error comparisons in Fig. 3. More statistic comparisons are detailed in Tab. 1.

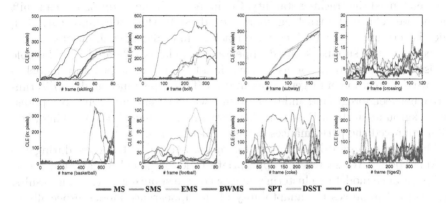

**Fig. 3.** The Center Location Error (CLE) comparison of different algorithms.

As shown in Tab. 1, the proposed algorithm obtains the smallest Mean Center Location Errors except for the sequence *skiing*, which indicates that the proposed algorithm improves the tracking performance in most cases. To be mentioned is that all the algorithms behave disappointed when tracking the sequence *skiing*.

**Table 1.** The *Mean Center Location Errors* (in pixels) of different algorithms. Bold red font indicates the best performance, green font indicates the second best.

| sequences | MS | SMS | EMS | BWMS | SPT | DSST | Ours |
|---|---|---|---|---|---|---|---|
| *skiing* | 254.8 | 195.6 | 185.0 | 82.0 | 81.1 | 54.2 | 96.4 |
| *bolt* | 109.9 | 115.9 | 112.1 | 349.5 | 6.9 | 8.8 | 7.3 |
| *subway* | 116.7 | 140.9 | 132.4 | 133.6 | 10.8 | 3.9 | 4.1 |
| *crossing* | 8.4 | 8.3 | 4.6 | 5.6 | 5.5 | 7.1 | 3.2 |
| *basketball* | 76.3 | 85.2 | 59.7 | 6.7 | 10.4 | 19.2 | 11.2 |
| *football1* | 17.1 | 6.8 | 38.5 | 35.8 | 8.2 | 5.9 | 5.5 |
| *coke* | 55.9 | 81.6 | 80.7 | 149.9 | 15.6 | 15.1 | 12.1 |
| *tiger2* | 71.4 | 53.6 | 52.4 | 40.6 | 26.3 | 24.0 | 21.6 |

## 5    Discussion

We introduced the proposed tracking algorithm in the former content. A set of tracking experiments on challenging sequences demonstrate that the proposed tracker obtains better performances than traditional trackers in most cases. We conclude the success of the proposed algorithm as three reasons.

Firstly, we exploited the mean shift algorithm as the tracking framework, which enhanced the tracking stability. Compared with the traditional mean shift tracker, we refined the tracking course to adjust to the appearance variation, which is very important for long term tracking in challenging situations.

Secondly, the suppixels based appearance model is validated as a feasible for visual tracking. We introduce this method to construct appearance model to improve the precision of target representation. This appearance model is discriminative between foreground and background, which is very important to suppress the background clutters. Based on this discriminative model, the tracking algorithm improved the performances in target localization.

Thirdly, we designed a strategy for appearance model update during the tracking course. We search the appropriate time for model update and renew the appearance model by clustering analysis of the suppixels of tracking results. This method improves the adaptability of the appearance model, especially in long term tracking tasks.

We keep the parameters unchanged as the former section described during the whole experiments, which indicates that the proposed tracking algorithm is effective in most cases with out parameters tuning. Further tuning of parameters may produce a slightly better performance in some given situations. However, the adopted parameters of the proposed algorithm are relatively better in most cases. The proposed tracker is an integration of mean shift tracking algorithm, suppixels appearance model and model update strategy. It improves the tracking performances at the cost of decreasing the tracking efficiency. The tracking experiments indicate that the proposed tracker runs at an average speed of 3.2 fps. Note that the clustering algorithm is time-consuming and an amelioration of clustering algorithm may improve the tracking speed.

## 6    Conclusion

We proposed a modified mean shift tracking algorithm with refined appearance model and online update. A background distribution is learned from the clustering analysis of the superpixels of the first few target templates. A background weighted vector is then calculated to refine the initial target model. During the tracking course, the stable tracking results are selected to online update the appearance model. The proposed algorithm improves the tracking performance in most of the cases. However, One of the main drawbacks is that the processing of model refining and updating increases the run time of the whole algorithm.

# References

1. Wu, Y., Lim, J., Yang, M.H.: Online object tracking: a benchmark. In: Proceedings of the IEEE Computer Society Conference on Computer Vision and Pattern Recognition, pp. 2411–2418. IEEE Press, Portland (2013)
2. Smeulders, A., Chu, D., Cucchiara, R., Calderara, S., Dehghan, A., Shah, M.: Visual tracking: an experimental survey. IEEE Transactions on Pattern Analysis and Machine Intelligence **36**(7), 1442–1468 (2014)
3. Fukunaga, F., Hostetler, L.: The estimation of the gradient of a density function, with applications in pattern recognition. IEEE Transactions on Information Theory **21**(1), 32–40 (1975)
4. Cheng, Y.: Mean shift, mode seeking and clustering. IEEE Transactions on Pattern Analysis and Machine Intelligence **17**(8), 790–799 (1995)
5. Bradski, G.: Real time face and object tracking as a component of a perceptual user interface. In: Proceedings of the Fourth IEEE Workshop on Applications of Computer Vision, pp. 214–219. IEEE Press, Princeton (1998)
6. Comaniciu, D., Meer, P.: Mean shift: A robust approach toward feature space analysis. IEEE Transactions on Pattern Analysis and Machine Intelligence **24**(5), 603–619 (2002)
7. Comaniciu, D., Ramesh, V., Meer, P.: Kernel-based object tracking. IEEE Transactions on Pattern Analysis and Machine Intelligence **25**(2), 564–577 (2003)
8. Collins, R.: Mean-shift blob tracking through scale space. In: Proceedings of the IEEE Computer Society Conference on Computer Vision and Pattern Recognition, pp. 234–240. IEEE Press, Wisconsin (2003)
9. Zivkovic, Z., Kröse, B.: An EM-like algorithm for color-histogram based object tracking. In: Proceedings of the IEEE Computer Society Conference on Computer Vision and Pattern Recognition, pp. 798–803. IEEE Press, Washington (2004)
10. Ning, J., Zhang, L., Zhang, D., Wu, C.: Scale and orientation adaptive mean shift tracking. IET Computer Vision **6**(1), 52–61 (2012)
11. Ning, J., Zhang, L., Zhang, D., Wu, C.: Robust mean-shift tracking with corrected background-weighted histogram. IET Computer Vision **6**(1), 62–69 (2012)
12. Collins, R., Liu, Y., Leordeanu, M.: Online selection of discriminative tracking features. IEEE Transactions on Pattern Analysis and Machine Intelligence **27**(10), 1631–1643 (2005)
13. Birchfield, S., Rangarajan, S.: Spatiograms versus histograms for region-based tracking. In: Proceedings of the IEEE Computer Society Conference on Computer Vision and Pattern Recognition, pp. 1158–1163. IEEE Press, San Diego (2005)
14. Leichter, I.: Mean shift trackers with cross-bin metrics. IEEE Transactions on Pattern Analysis and Machine Intelligence **34**(4), 695–706 (2012)
15. Wang, S., Lu, H., Yang, F., Yang, M.: Superpixel tracking. In: Proceedings of the International Conference on Computer Vision, pp. 1323–1330. IEEE Press, Barcelona (2011)
16. Zhuang, B., Lu, H., Xiao, Z., Wang, D.: Visual tracking via discriminative sparse similarity map. IEEE Transactions on Image Processing **23**(4), 1872–1881 (2014)
17. Achanta, R., Shaji, A., Smith, K., Pascal, F., Sabine, S.: SLIC Superpixels compared to state-of-the-art superpixel methods. IEEE Transactions on Pattern Analysis and Machine Intelligence **34**(11), 2274–2281 (2012)

# An Effective Multiview Stereo Method for Uncalibrated Images

Peng Cui, Yiguang Liu$^{(\boxtimes)}$, Pengfei Wu, Jie Li, and Shoulin Yi

Vision and Image Processing Lab(VIPL), College of Computer Science,
SiChuan University, Chengdu 610065, People's Republic of China
liuyg@scu.edu.cn, lygpapers@aliyun.com

**Abstract.** For most dense multi-view stereo methods, the process of finding correspondences is the basis and is independent of acquiring 3D information, and this often brings about erroneous correspondences followed by erroneous 3D information. To tackle this problem, by expanding matched points and by expanding 3D patches, this paper proposes an effective approach to acquire dense and accurate point clouds from multi-view uncalibrated images. In the approach, two novel algorithms are newly designed and are placed before and after the Bundler: 1) the *match expansion* algorithm, which generates evenly distributed correspondences with geometric consistency; after using Bundler to produce geometry estimation and quasi-dense point clouds which are not dense and accurate, 2) the *point-cloud expansion* algorithm, which is proposed to improve the density and accuracy of point clouds by optimizing the geometry of each 3D patch and expanding each good patch to its neighborhood. A large number of experimental results demonstrate the proposed approach get more accurate and denser point clouds than the state-of-the-art methods. A quantitative evaluation shows the accuracy of the proposed method favorable to PMVS.

**Keywords:** Multiview stereo · Match expansion · Point-cloud expansion

## 1 Introduction

Mutli-view stereo (MVS) reconstruction from a set of images, which have been collected from Internet, has achieved great development in the last decade. The construction of realistic object models can be applied to the film, television, and video game industries, etc. According to [10], the state-of-the-art MVS algorithms can be categorized into four classes: The *Voxel* based approaches [11,18] compute a cost function on a three-dimensional (3D) volume by first, and then reconstruct a surface from this volume, they are suitable for small compact objects. The *surface evolution* based methods [2,3] work by iteratively evolving a surface to decrease or minimize a cost function, the algorithms rely on a reliable initial guess which limits their applicability. The *depth maps* based methods [12,16] compute a set of depth maps by first, and then merge the set of depth maps into a 3D scene. However more computations and memory are required.

© Springer-Verlag Berlin Heidelberg 2015
H. Zha et al. (Eds.): CCCV 2015, Part I, CCIS 546, pp. 124–133, 2015.
DOI: 10.1007/978-3-662-48558-3_13

**Fig. 1.** The pipeline of the proposed approach.

The *feature point* based methods [4] extract and match a set of feature points firstly, and then fit a surface to the reconstructed scenes. They are simple and effective, but rely on the accuracy of the correspondences.

This paper addresses the problem of acquiring dense and accurate point clouds from multiple uncalibrated images. For uncalibrated images, the common methods are based on sparse feature points which are tracked across sequences, and then automate acquisition of a sparse point cloud together with the camera motion, such as [7,8,14]. Although this approach can estimate the camera parameters, it's not always sufficient as limited by the correspondences without geometric constraint, meanwhile it cannot acquire dense point clouds. So we propose *match expansion* technique in this paper, which is similar to [6] but our method replaces ZNCC by DASIY [16] as DASIY is more robust and efficient for wide-baseline stereo, to process initial correspondences and make them more suitable for Bundler.

For calibrated images, many dense stereo methods have been proposed [4,5, 17]. Our *point-cloud expansion* algorithm is similar with the expansion step of PMVS [4], but our algotithm takes these 3D points reconstructed by Bundler as seeds rather than re-extracting feature points, and we only expand once instead of three times, as PMVS does, that can efficiently improve the process. The following point-cloud expansion technique is mainly used to refine and expand 3D patches, and produces accurate and dense point clouds. Fig. 1 shows the pipeline of the proposed approach.

The rest of this paper is organized as follows: Section 2 introduces the overview of the proposed approach. Section 3 presents the detail of the proposed match expansion algorithm. Section 4 describes the point-cloud expansion algorithm. Experimental results and discussion are given in Section 5, and Section 6 concludes this paper.

## 2   Overview

Our MVS method attempts to reconstruct dense and accurate point clouds from uncalibrated images, and it can be divided into four steps (Fig. 1): 1) *Extract Feature & Match*: Features extracted by *VLFeat* [1] operator, which is a fast dense version of SIFT, are firstly matched across multiple images by *kd-tree*, then that will yield a sparse set of correspondences associated with salient image regions; 2) *Match Expansion*: Based on *best-first* strategy, this step expands the initial matches to their neighborhoods, and generates further dense correspondences which are suitable for geometric computation. The detail will describe in Section 3; 3) *Bundler*: The Bundler [13,14] procedure can estimate the camera postures and simultaneously construct a sparse scene structure by taking these correspondences as input; and 4) *Point-Cloud Expansion*: This step optimizes and expands these reconstructed 3D points, and then filters erroneous points. The detail will describe in Section 4.

## 3    Match Expansion

Since the performance of Bundler depends on the correspondences, we propose the *match expansion* algorithm to produce enough good correspondences suitable for geometric estimation. Before discussing the match expansion algorithm, we define the correlation score between two points from different images as:

$$C_{ij}(\mathbf{x}, \mathbf{x}') = ||\mathcal{D}_i(\mathbf{x}) - \mathcal{D}_j(\mathbf{x}')||. \tag{1}$$

Where $\mathcal{D}_i(\mathbf{x})$ denotes a DAISY descriptor in the $\mathbf{x}$ coordinate of the $i$th image. The reason why is DAISY used for correlation is that DAISY is rarely affected by perspective distortion and occlusion in wide-baseline situation, and it can be computed much fast.

After the feature extraction and matching, we obtain initial matches of image salient regions, but which contain inevitable errors. In order to effectively avoid these errors, we estimate a fundamental matrix for each pair of images using the Random Sample And Consensus (RANSAC) framework, and remove the outliers to the recovered F-matrix. Then we expand these remaining matches which meet the epipolar constraint.

We divide each image into regular grids of $\beta_1 \times \beta_1$ pixels as in Fig. 2 ($\beta_1 = 2$ in all our experiments), that effectively guarantees the uniqueness of correspondence. Then, we sort the remaining matches for each pair of images by increasing correlation score as seeds. At each step, the match $(\mathbf{x}, \mathbf{x}')$ with the best correlation score is used for current expansion, and simultaneously removed from the list of seeds. Next we collect the neighboring image points $\mathcal{N}(\mathbf{x})$ defined as:

$$\mathcal{N}(\mathbf{x}) = \{\mathbf{q} | \mathbf{q} - \mathbf{x} \in \{(\beta_1, 0), (-\beta_1, 0), (0, \beta_1), (0, -\beta_1)\}\}. \tag{2}$$

For each collected point $\mathbf{q}$ in $\mathcal{N}(\mathbf{x})$, the following expansion procedure is performed to generate new match $(\mathbf{q}, \mathbf{q}')$: We calculate the epipolar line $\mathbf{l}' = F\hat{\mathbf{q}}$, where $F$ is the fundamental matrix between the pair of images, and $\hat{\mathbf{q}}$ denotes the homogeneous coordinate of the point $\mathbf{q}$ [9]. Next we search for the candidate points along the epipolar line $\mathbf{l}'$, and also within the neighborhood of location $\mathbf{x}'$, that can be formalized as:

$$\mathcal{N}'(\mathbf{x}') = \{\mathbf{q}' | \mathbf{l}'^T \hat{\mathbf{q}}' = 0, ||\mathbf{q}' - \mathbf{x}'|| < r\} \tag{3}$$

($r = 6.0$ in all our experiments). We also add a *random perturbation* for each $\mathbf{q}'$ in our experiments, that sufficiently improves the robustness of correspondences. Then the candidate matches problem, which satisfied the epipolar constraint and limited by the neighbor region, can be formalized as:

$$\mathcal{N}(\mathbf{x}, \mathbf{x}') = \{(\mathbf{q}, \mathbf{q}') | \mathbf{q} \in \mathcal{N}(\mathbf{x}), \mathbf{q}' \in \mathcal{N}'(\mathbf{x}')\}. \tag{4}$$

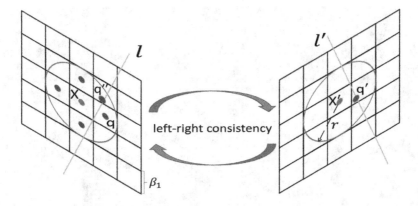

**Fig. 2.** Possible match $(\mathbf{q}, \mathbf{q}')$ indicated by the red dots around a seed match $(\mathbf{x}, \mathbf{x}')$ indicated by green dots. The point $\mathbf{q}'$ satisfies the epipolar constraint and within the neighborhood of $\mathbf{x}'$. if the match $(\mathbf{q}, \mathbf{q}')$ has the best correlation score and satisfies the *left-right consistency*, we add it to the list of seed matches. See text for more details.

Candidate matches are sorted by increasing correlation score using (1), then we select the best correlation for each $\mathbf{q}$ in $\mathcal{N}(\mathbf{x})$ by *left-right consistency* testing. The left-right consistency testing is just used to find the best correspondence $\mathbf{q}''$ in the first image of $\mathbf{q}'$ by the above procedure conversely. If the formula $\|\mathbf{q} - \mathbf{q}''\| < \alpha$ is satisfied and the correspondence has the best correlation score related to the current grid, we add the match $(\mathbf{q}, \mathbf{q}')$ to the current list of seeds($\alpha = 4.0$ in all our experiments). Fig. 2 illustrates the entire procedure. In the match expansion procedure, we choose only the best match that has not been selected, and expands only the reliable matches whose correlation score below a certain threshold $\gamma$ ($\gamma = 0.4$ in all our experiments). This drastically limits the bad matches for expansion and guarantees the ending of the process.

The expansion procedure produces dense but irregular distribution correspondences. Since these correspondences are not suitable for geometric computation, resampling procedure is proposed to refine these correspondences. We regularize these correspondences by locally selecting the best correspondence. Concretely, we redivide the first image into new regular square grids of $\beta_2 \times \beta_2$ pixels ($\beta_2 = 8$ in all our experiments). For each new grid, we select the correspondence with best correlation score and only accept it when its score below the threshold $\lambda$ ($\lambda = 0.08$ in all our experiments).

The resampling procedure can effectively filter the erroneous correspondences and generate evenly distributed correspondences with geometric consistency, which are suitable for Bundler. In practice, we keep the original correspondences of feature points as they have better property of tracking than other points obtained by expansion. One example for a real pair of images is illustrated in Fig. 3. Next, we estimate the camera postures by Bundler procedure taking these correspondences as input and simultaneously acquire quasi-dense scene point clouds. One real example is illustrated in Fig. 4a.

a          b          c

**Fig. 3.** The examples of *match expansion* algorithm. (a) The initial sparse matches from feature points. (b) The dense correspondences after expansion procedure. (c) The resampled correspondences.

## 4    Point-Cloud Expansion

As the quasi-dense scene point clouds reconstructed by Bundler are not dense and accurate, we propose the *point-cloud expansion* algorithm to further generate dense and accurate point clouds, which includes optimization and expansion of two steps. The optimization step aims to improve accuracy of point clouds under geometric constraint, and the other expansion step is used to produce dense point clouds combined with the optimization.

### 4.1    Optimization

Since the quasi-dense point clouds are not accurate, the optimization procedure is proposed to improve the accuracy of the point clouds. In order to achieve the goal and improve the robustness of experiments, we add orientation to each 3D point and draw a local tangent plane at that point, called *patch*. The patch's geometry is fully determined by its center $c(p)$ and unit normal vector $n(p)$. Then we define the photometric discrepancy function $\mathcal{G}(p)$ for patch $p$ as:

$$\mathcal{G}(p) = \frac{1}{|V(p) \setminus R(p)|} \sum_{i=V(p) \setminus R(p)} \mathcal{C}_{ri}(q_r, q_i), \tag{5}$$

where $V(p)$ is a set of images in which $p$ is visible and $R(p)$ denotes the reference image. The symbol backslash represents removing $R(p)$ from $V(p)$. The symbol $q_r$ indicates the intersection of projecting the $c(p)$ into the reference view $R(p)$. The formula $\mathcal{C}_{rj}(q_r, q_i)$ indicates the correlation score between $q_r$ and $q_i$ by using (1). The map from $q_r$ to $q_i$ is the homography induced by the plane where the

**Fig. 4.** (a) The quasi-dense point cloud reconstructed by Bundler. (b) The point cloud after optimization. (c) The final point cloud after expansion.

patch $p$ is located. For a pair of images, the camera parameters can be represented by $\{K_i, R_i, C_i\}$ and $\{K_j, R_j, C_j\}$, thus the projection matrixes can denoted as: $P_i = K_i[R_i|-R_iC_i] = [M_i|-M_iC_i]$, $P_j = K_j[R_j|-R_jC_j] = [M_j|-M_jC_j]$, where $M_i = K_iR_i$, $M_j = K_jR_j$. The homography induced by the plane $f = \{c(p), n(p)\}$ for the cameras $P_i$ and $P_j$ is:

$$H_{ij} = M_j M_i^{-1} + \frac{M_j(C_i - C_j)n^T(p)M_i^{-1}}{n^T(p)(c(p) - C_i)}. \tag{6}$$

Then, the map can be represented by the formula, $q_i = H_{ri}q_r$.

Having defined the photometric discrepancy function $\mathcal{G}(p)$, our optimization strategy is to minimize discrepancy score of the patch. The corresponding parameters of the patch $p$ can be simplified as:

$$c(p) = C_r + \lambda R_{ay}(p), \tag{7}$$

$$n(p) = [sin\theta cos\phi, sin\phi, -cos\theta cos\phi]^T. \tag{8}$$

We constrain $c(p)$ to lie on the viewing ray of $p$, $R_{ay}(p)$, from the reference camera, such that its image projection in the reference image does not change, reducing its three degrees of freedom to one and solving only for a depth $\lambda$. And the normal $n(p)$ can be parameterized by two angles $\theta$ and $\phi$ in spherical coordinate ($|\theta|, |\phi| < \pi/2$ in our experiments). So the optimization problem is reduced to three degrees of freedom and is solved by a conjugate gradient method. After the optimization procedure, we accept $p$ only when its photometric discrepancy satisfies $\mathcal{G}(p') < \eta$ ($\eta = 0.2$ in all our experiments), this drastically limits erroneous patches and effectively improves accuracy of point clouds.

### 4.2 Expansion

To obtain dense point clouds, we further expand these patches under geometric constraint. For each patch $p$, the following expansion step is performed to generate new patches: We first find the candidate patches in the neighborhood of patch $p$, and these candidate patches also on the plane containing $p$ (see an example in Fig. 5). For a candidate patch $p'$, $c(p')$ is initialized as the 3D point

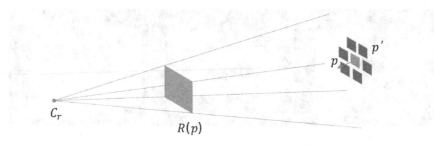

**Fig. 5.** Expansion three-dimensional(3D) patch $p$. We find the neighboring patches $p'$ and refine them by the optimization procedure. See the text for more details.

near $c(p)$, and $n(p')$ is initialized by the formula $\frac{C_r - c(p')}{||C_r - c(p')||}$, where $C_r$ is the camera center of the reference image of the patch $p$. And then, we refine $c(p')$ and $n(p')$ by the optimization procedure described above. After the optimization, we add the patch $p'$ to the queue of expansion, when its photometric discrepancy is small enough.

After the point-cloud expansion procedure, we acquire dense point clouds, but still exist errors. We use some heuristic rules to remove these erroneous patches. Finally, the reconstructed point clouds of scenes or objects are dense and accurate, one real example shows in Fig. 4.

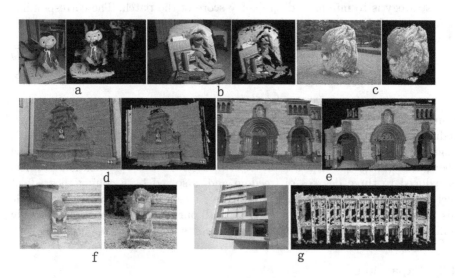

**Fig. 6.** Sample input images of data sets used in our experiments and corresponding results reconstructed by our method. From left ro right and top to bottom: (a) *ET*, (b) *kermit*, (c) *stone*, (d) *fountain*, (e) *herz-Jesu*, (f) *lion*, (g) *hall*. In each case, one of the images is shown, along with the reconstructed point clouds.

# 5    Experimental Results and Comparisons

We show our experimental results on some different data sets in Fig. 6. The *stone* and *lion* data sets have been acquired in our lab, while other data sets have been provided by S.Seitz (*ET, kermit* [14]), Y.Furukawa (*hall* [4]), C.Strecha (*fountain, herz-Jesu* [15]). Fig. 6 shows sample input images of all of the data sets used in our experiments and corresponding results reconstructed by our method. Table 1 lists the number of input images, their approximate size, and the number of 3D points reconstructed. All the experiments are implemented on an Intel 4GHz CPU with 32GB RAM. As illustrated by the figure, the object and scene point clouds reconstructed by our method are quite dense and accurate.

**Table 1.** Characteristics of the Data Sets

| Data set | ET | kermit | stone | lion | fountain | herz-Jesu | hall |
|---|---|---|---|---|---|---|---|
| Num of Images | 9 | 11 | 9 | 145 | 11 | 8 | 61 |
| Size of Image | 480 × 640 | 640 × 480 | 2848×2136 | 640×480 | 3072×2048 | 3072×2048 | 1200×797 |
| Num of points finally | 162650 | 132110 | 2182491 | 1506239 | 6752176 | 6087278 | 1918973 |

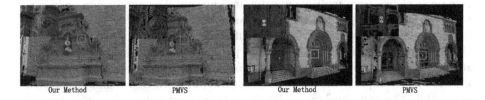

Our Method          PMVS          Our Method          PMVS

**Fig. 7.** Compared with PMVS using the benchmark data sets, *fountain-P11* and *herz-Jesu-P8*. The regions framed by the green squares have been enlarged, and displayed in the top left corner.

Before comparing with PMVS [4], we set parameters for the proposed approach and PMVS, and all parameters for the proposed approach have been discussed above. For PMVS, we set its parameters as: *level = 0, csize = 1, threshold = 0.7, wsize = 7*. Fig. 6d, e respectively show sample images of the two benchmark *fountain* and *herz-Jesu* data sets and results reconstructed by the proposed approach. In order to further demonstrate the accuracy and density of our results, we compare our method with PMVS, see Fig. 7. Our method can get denser results than PMVS visually, as the regions denoted by green squares. To quantitatively evaluate the proposed approach, together with PMVS, the quantitatively measure provided by [10] is used in the evaluation. Fig. 8 shows the *accuracy* of PMVS and the proposed approach, and the results demonstrate that our method is more accurate than PMVS.

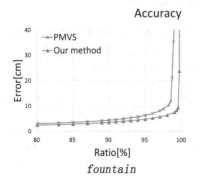
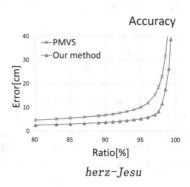

*fountain*                    *herz–Jesu*

**Fig. 8.** The quantitative evaluation between the two benchmark data set *fountain* and *herz-Jesu*. For each data set, we evaluate the *accuracy* between ground truth and the reconstructed results by PMVS and the proposed approach.

## 6    Conclusion

An effective multi-view stereo approach is developed that obtains dense and accurate point clouds from multiple uncalibrated images. The approach mainly contains two algorithms: 1) the *match expansion* algorithm, which is used to expand initial matches to the geometric consistent correspondences, based on which the Bundler procedure can estimate camera parameters and simultaneously reconstruct quasi-dense point clouds; 2) the *point-cloud expansion* algorithm, which is used to further improve the density and accuracy of point clouds under geometric constraint. The experimental results demonstrate our approach is effective and can reconstruct quite dense and accurate point clouds from uncalibrated images. Quantitative evaluation shows that the proposed approach is favorable to the state-of-the-art method PMVS in terms of *accuracy* for the two benchmark data sets.

**Acknowledgments.** The authors thank the editors and anonymous reviewers for their insights. This work is supported by NSFC under grants 61173182 and 613111154, funding from Sichuan Province (2014HH0048, 2014HH0025) and the Science and Technology Innovation seedling project of Sichuan (2014-033, 2014-034).

## References

1. Bosch, A., Zisserman, A., Muoz, X.: Image classification using random forests and ferns. In: IEEE 11th International Conference on Computer Vision (ICCV 2007), pp. 1–8 (2007)
2. Cremers, D., Kolev, K.: Multiview stereo and silhouette consistency via convex functionals over convex domains. IEEE Transactions on Pattern Analysis and Machine Intelligence **33**(6), 1161–1174 (2011)

3. Furukawa, Y., Ponce, J.: Carved visual hulls for image-based modeling. International Journal of Computer Vision **81**(1), 53–67 (2009)
4. Furukawa, Y., Ponce, J.: Accurate, dense, and robust multiview stereopsis. IEEE Transactions on Pattern Analysis and Machine Intelligence **32**(8), 1362–1376 (2010)
5. Goesele, M., Snavely, N., Curless, B., Hoppe, H., Seitz, S.M.: Multi-view stereo for community photo collections. In: IEEE 11th International Conference on Computer Vision (ICCV 2007), pp. 1–8 (2007)
6. Lhuillier, M., Quan, L.: A quasi-dense approach to surface reconstruction from uncalibrated images. IEEE Transactions on Pattern Analysis and Machine Intelligence **27**(3), 418–433 (2005)
7. Liu, Y., Cao, L., Liu, C., Pu, Y., Cheng, H.: Recovering shape and motion by a dynamic system for low-rank matrix approximation in l1 norm. The Visual Computer **29**(5), 421–431 (2013)
8. Liu, Y., Liu, B., Pu, Y., Chen, X., Cheng, H.: Low-rank matrix decomposition in L1-norm by dynamic systems. Image and Vision Computing **30**(11), 915–921 (2012)
9. Liu, Y., Sun, B., Shi, Y., Huang, Z., Zhao, C.: Stereo Image Rectification Suitable for 3D Reconstruction 用于3维重建的图像校正. Journal of Sichuan University (Engineering Science Edition) **45**(03), 79–84 (2013)
10. Seitz, S.M., Curless, B., Diebel, J., Scharstein, D., Szeliski, R.: A comparison and evaluation of multi-view stereo reconstruction algorithms. In: 2006 IEEE Computer Society Conference on Computer Vision and Pattern Recognition, vol. 1, pp. 519–528. IEEE (2006)
11. Seitz, S.M., Dyer, C.R.: Photorealistic scene reconstruction by voxel coloring. International Journal of Computer Vision **35**(2), 151–173 (1999)
12. Shen, S.: Accurate multiple view 3D reconstruction using patch-based stereo for large-scale scenes. IEEE Transactions on Image Processing **22**(5), 1901–1914 (2013)
13. Snavely, N., Seitz, S.M., Szeliski, R.: Photo tourism: Exploring photo collections in 3D. ACM Trans. Graph. **25**(3), 835–846 (2006)
14. Snavely, N., Seitz, S.M., Szeliski, R.: Modeling the World from Internet Photo Collections. International Journal of Computer Vision **80**(2), 189–210 (2007)
15. Strecha, C., von Hansen, W., Van Gool, L., Fua, P., Thoennessen, U.: On benchmarking camera calibration and multi-view stereo for high resolution imagery. In: IEEE Conference on Computer Vision and Pattern Recognition (CVPR 2008), pp. 1–8, June 2008
16. Tola, E., Strecha, C., Fua, P.: Efficient large-scale multi-view stereo for ultra high-resolution image sets. Machine Vision and Applications **23**(5), 903–920 (2012)
17. Uh, Y., Matsushita, Y., Byun, H.: Efficient multiview stereo by random-search and propagation. In: 2014 2nd International Conference on 3D Vision (3DV), vol. 1, pp. 393–400, December 2014
18. Vogiatzis, G., Torr, P.H.S., Cipolla, R.: Multi-view stereo via volumetric graph-cuts. In: IEEE Computer Society Conference on Computer Vision and Pattern Recognition (CVPR 2005), vol. 2, pp. 391–398, June 2005

# The Human Image Segmentation Algorithm Based on Face Detection and Biased Normalized Cuts

Shaojun Qu$^{(\boxtimes)}$ and Qiaoliang Li

College of Mathematics and Computer Science, Hunan Normal University,
Changsha 410081, China
{powerhope,lqlbox}@163.com

**Abstract.** Attributed to pose variation (frontal, profile, et.), the color and texture difference of clothes, the presence of noise, low contrast, uneven illumination and complex background. There are enormous difficultly in human image segmentation. In this paper, we propose an automatic human image segmentation method based on the face detection and biased normalized cuts. First, we use face detection algorithm to detect human faces, and get facial contours. Then we establish object seeds estimation model based on the position of the detected face, and get the object seeds. Using these seeds, we use biased normalized cuts algorithm to segment the image. Finally, we perform region merging based on the previous seeds and segmentation results, and the image is divided into two parts (object and background). We implement a large amount of experiments over a public segmentation database of Berkeley etc. Experiments show that our method can segment different types of human image and obtain satisfactory results. Compared with Grabcut method, our propose method can be obtained more accurate results in many images. Qualitative and quantitative experimental results demonstrate our method produces high quality segmentations and effectively improve the segmentation efficiency.

**Keywords:** Face detection · Human image segmentation · Biased normalized cuts · Seeds estimation model

## 1 Introduction

Human body segmentation in human images is a very important step in many computer vision tasks, such as image processing, video tracking, pose estimation, content-based image retrieval, pedestrian detection, action understanding, etc. However, to segment a human body in a human image is still a very challenging task because of segmentation is inherently ill-posed, the appearance and pose variation, the presence of noise, low contrast, and intensity inhomogeneity.

In the last decade the most popular approach to interacitve image segmentaiton in computer vision was graph cut. To avoid the minimum cut criteria favors cutting small sets of isolated nodes in the graph. Using the volume for

© Springer-Verlag Berlin Heidelberg 2015
H. Zha et al. (Eds.): CCCV 2015, Part I, CCIS 546, pp. 134–143, 2015.
DOI: 10.1007/978-3-662-48558-3_14

the normalized weights. It aims at extracting the global impression of an image. The normalized cuts [1] criterion measures both the total dissimilarity between the different groups as well as the total similarity within the groups. Subhransu Maji [2] present a modification of "Normalized cuts" to incorporate priors which can be used for constrained image segmentation.

In this paper, we employ face detection and biaed normalized cuts to segment human body in static image. Different from the previous methods, our approach requires much less training data for face detection, and seeds estimation model is simple and effective. Moreover, our method is different from biased normalized cuts which we have better constraints and need to do a region merging after biaed normalized cuts segmentation. Also, our method does not require human interaction, and it is a fully automated segmentation method. Our segmentation results are more accurate and effective.

The rest of this paper is organized as follows. Section 2 discusses the most related work with ours. Section 3 describes the details of our proposed method. Analysis and experimental results in Section 4. Finally, Section 5 concludes the paper and propose some future work..

## 2   Related Work

### 2.1   Face Detection

Face detection is dominated by discriminatively-trained scanning window classifiers [3], most ubiquitous of which is the Viola Jones detector [4]. Zhu [5] model was based on a mixtures of trees with a shared pool of parts. They modeled every facial landmark as a part and used global mixtures to capture topological changes due to viewpoint. Their system was also trained discriminatively, but with much less training data, particularly when compared to commercial systems.

### 2.2   Human Image Segmentation

Ashwini T. Magar et. [6] divided human segmentation techniques to exemplar based, part based and other based. In exemplar based approach [7–9], an exemplar pool should be constructed first, and then, the test images was matched with the exemplars. Agarwal and Triggs [10] modeled the image window with a dense grid of local gradient orientation histograms to select similar human features, which made them capable of handling complex backgrounds. But the problem with these approaches were that in exemplar based approaches cannot always accurately segment the human body, because human poses are arbitrary and an exemplar pool cannot cover all the situations of poses and appearance variation.

In part based approaches, one can recover human body configurations by assembling set of candidate parts [11–13]. Drawback of these methods were that their performance depends on individual part detector and they were very hard to design a robust part detector.

In order to overcome drawback of both exemplar and part based approach.
Some different techniques were developed. Mori [14] proposed a body model
to estimate the human pose from static images based on superpixels. Shifeng Li
et. [15] proposed a method to segment human body in static images by graph cuts
based on two deformable models at two-scale superpixel. This method needed
prior knowledge of the face. [16] presented a fully-automatic Spatio-Temporal
GrabCut human segmentation methodology that combined tracking and segmentation. But the limitations of the method is that it depends on the initialization of the ST-GrabCut algorithm. However, these approaches typically have
a large number of parameters, which leads to difficulty in calculating problem in
high-dimensional space.

## 3    Our Algorithm Based on Face Detection and Biased Normalized Cuts

An overview of our method is show in Fig. 1. The whole segmentation methodology is detailed in algorithm 1. We combined face detection and biased normalized
cuts. First, we performed face detection for input image(line 1-2).

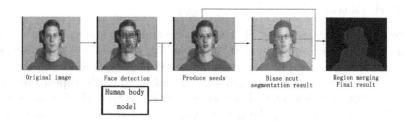

**Fig. 1.** Overview of our method.

Step 2(line 3). Compute seeds based on face detection results and human
body model. The detailed in algorithm 2. Through statistical analysis propo-
tional relationship of various parts of the body and the relationship between
the size of human after we have carried out a lot of experiments. We established a human body model to choose seeds automatically in Fig. 2. According to recognized human faces, we deduce the coordinate of the rest of seeds.
The rectangle(red) represents the recognized face region. It's width is $w$, height
is $h$, Vertex coordinates of the upper left corner is $(minx, miny)$ and lower
right corner of the vertex coordinates is $(maxx, maxy)$. We calculate the 23
seeds coordinates of other body parts based on the model. The seeds coordi-
nates are $[(minx + w/2, miny - 15), (minx, maxy + h/2), (minx + w/2, maxy + h/2), (maxx, maxy + h/2), (minx, maxy + h), (minx + w/4, maxy + h), (minx + w/2, maxy+h), (maxx-w/4, maxy+h), (maxx, maxy+h), (minx-w/4, maxy+ 3*h/2), (maxx+w/4, maxy+3*h/2), (minx, maxy+2*h), (minx+w/4, maxy+$

---

**Algorithm 1** Our algorithm based on face detection and biased normalized cuts($G, w, S_T, \gamma$)

---

1: $im$ =read input image.
2: Face detection for $im$.
3: Compute seeds $S_T$ based on face detection results and human body model(Algorithm 2).
4: Construction graph $G = (V, E)$, compute edge weight, the similarity matrix $w$ based on intervening contours, a correlation parameter $\gamma \in (-\infty, \lambda_2(G))$
5: $A_G(i,j) \leftarrow w(i,j), D_G(i,j) \leftarrow \sum_j w(i,j)$
6: $L_G \leftarrow D_G - A_G, \mathbb{L}_G \leftarrow D_G^{-1/2} L_G D_G^{-1/2}$
7: Compute $u_1, u_2, \cdots, u_K$ the eigenvectors of $\mathbb{L}_G$ corresponding to the $K$ smallest eigenvalues $\lambda_1, \lambda_2, \cdots, \lambda_k$
8: $w_i \leftarrow \frac{u_i^T D_G S_T}{\lambda_i - \gamma}$, for $i = 2, \cdots K$
9: Obtain the biased normalized cuts, $x* \propto \sum_{i=2}^{K} w_i u_i$
10: Region merging.
11: Output results.

---

$2 * h), (minx + w/2, maxy + 2 * h), (maxx - w/4, maxy + 2 * h), (maxx, maxy + 2 * h), (minx, maxy + 3 * h), (minx + w/2, maxy + 3 * h), (maxx, maxy + 3 * h), (minx, maxy + 4 * h), (maxx, maxy + 4 * h), (minx, maxy + 5 * h), (maxx, maxy + 5 * h), ]$. Finally, we detect seeds that falls outside the human body and the image, and then correcting the seeds. Green dots represent inferred seeds by algorithm 2.

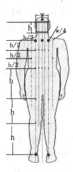

**Fig. 2.** Human body model.

Step 3(line 4-9). Step2's seeds as biased normalized cuts constraints condition. We use biased normalized cuts algorithm to segment the image, and obtain the initial segmentation result.

Step 4(line 10). Region merging. First, we merge the region where have a seed as the object. Then from top to down, from left to right continue scan image, if there are more than two object regions around the undetermined regions, we merged this region into object. Finally, we considered the undetermined regions

---

**Algorithm 2** Automatic produce seeds

---
1: **if**  the number of identify the face detection  == 1 **then**
2:    According to face detection results and human body model to compute seeds.
3:    Detect seeds that falls outside the image, and correcting the seeds.
4: **else**
5:    **for** each $i \in$ the number of identify the face region **do**
6:      Compute seeds for region $i$ based on face detection results and human body model.
7:      Detect seeds that falls outside the image, and correcting the seeds.
8:    **end for**
9: **end if**

---

as a background region, we can obtain segmentation results that include two parts(object and background).

# 4    Analysis and Experiments

On the basis of normalized cuts, biased normalized cuts introduced the constraint condition, and convert image segmentation problem became a constrained problem. Our approach strengthen and optimize the constraints. Moreover, different from biased normalized cuts which we need to do a region merging after segmentation, we can obtain segmentation results that include two parts(object and background). Our segmentation results are more accurate and effective.

We evaluate the proposed method on three datasets. The first one is the Berkeley segmentation dataset [17] which contains 78 images of only one person. The second one is the Grabcut dataset [18] which contains 16 images. The last one is Ramanan's annotated dataset [5]. In order to quantitatively evaluate our method, we chose 31 representative of images from which these datasets. These images cover front, side, half-length, whole body, complex background, all kinds of clothes, light conditions, as shown in Fig. 3.

The evaluation setup is as follows. Manually segmentations are used to construct ground-truth segmentation, this produces a binary segmentation that will be used as ground truth, as shown in Fig. 4.

First, we assess quality of seed selection by our human body model. In addition to the two images in Fig. 7 , there are some error seeds, other pictures can get right seeds. Image 189011.jpg identified two face, which one is wrong. We found that the accuracy of automatically obtained seeds is closely related to the accuracy of face recognition. Results indicates that our human body model is a good seed selection method for image segmentation.

*Select parameter.* It is necessary to set the number of segment block(*nbSegments*) since our method based on biased normalized cuts, In our method, we chose the *nbSegments* to be 12 or 15 or 20 or 30 or 50. We then choose a relatively desirable results, as shown in Table 1. Our method can accurately segment human body on the dataset. As shown in Fig. 5.

**Fig. 3.** Original image.

**Fig. 4.** Ground truth by human segmentations.

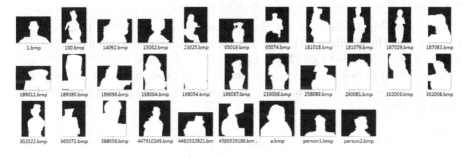

**Fig. 5.** Our method segmentation results.

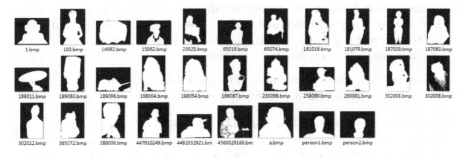

**Fig. 6.** Grabcut segmentation results.

**Fig. 7.** Exist error seeds in images.

**Table 1.** Select the number of segmentation blocks

| nbSegments | The optimal number of results | nbSegments | The optimal number of results |
|---|---|---|---|
| 12 | 5 | 15 | 10 |
| 20 | 10 | 30 | 5 |
| 50 | 1 | | |

*Comparison with Other Methods.* We apply the proposed method to gether with the existing Grabcut method. GrabCut is a way to perform 2D segmentation in an image that is very user friendly. The user only need to input the a very rough segmentation between foreground and background. The initial information given about the foreground and the background are given by the user as a rectangular selection around the object of interest. Pixels outside this selection are treated as known background and the pixels inside are marked as unknown.

In experiment, we selected the object use polygon, instead of rectangle, and the object bounding box is comparatively precise. Parameters $k = 6$ or $9$, $\beta = 0.3$. The Grabcut optimum results as show in Fig. 6.

*Accuracy of Our Method.* To test the accuracy of our method and Grabcut, we use Fig. 4 as the ground truth, and use Jaccard similarity coefficient [19] and a Modified Hausdorff distance [20] to evaluate the accuracy.

The Jaccard coefficient measures similarity between finite sample sets, and is defined as the size of the intersection divided by the size of the union of the sample sets:

$$J(A, B) = \frac{|A \cap B|}{|A \cup B|}. \tag{1}$$

If A and B are both empty, we define $J(A, B) = 1$. Clearly, $0 \leq J(A, B) \leq 1$. The more similar A and B, the more the value is larger.

Fig. 8 reports our approach and grabcut compared with the ground truth. The dots represent our methods and the asterisks represent grabcut. In most of images, our method obtain satisfactory results.

*The Hausdorff Distance.* Given two finite point sets $A = \{a_1, \cdots, a_p\}$, $B = \{b_1, \cdots, b_p\}$, the Hausdorff distance [21] is defined as

$$H(A, B) = max(h(A, B), h(B, A)). \tag{2}$$

where $h(A, B) = \max_{a \in A} \min_{b \in B} ||a - b||$. and $||.||$ is some underlying norm on the points of A and B(e.g., the $L_2$ or Euclidean norm). A Modified Hausdorff

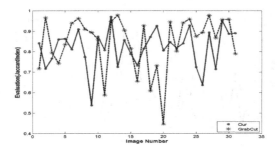

**Fig. 8.** Comparison between grabcut and our method with jaccardIndex.

distance [20] introduces 24 possible distance measures based on the Hausdorff distance between two point sets. Our method and Grabcut compared with the ground truth, with the results as show in Fig. 9.

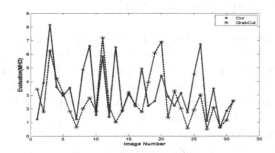

**Fig. 9.** Comparison between grabcut and our method with MHD.

Finally, Given two finite point sets $A$ and $B$ , the mean error rtate(ME) is defined as

$$ME = \frac{1 - p_1 - p_4}{r \times c}. \tag{3}$$

$p_1$ represents the number of A and B correspond to the position of the pixel label are background. $p_4$ represents the number of A and B correspond to the position of the pixel label are object. Results is shown in Fig. 10. The results show that our method is superior to grabcut in a lot of images.

Comparison shows that more than a third of the results are better than GrabCut. There are several results are the same. The grabcut is better than our method in other results. Experiments shows that Grabcut is sensitive to body pose. If the pose varies drastically, the results of Grabcut are imprecise. So, in our experiment, we selected the object use polygon, instead of rectangle, and the object bounding box is comparatively precise. From these examples, we can

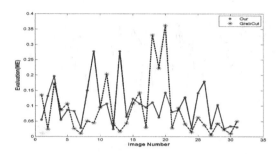

**Fig. 10.** Comparison between grabcut and our method with Mean error.

see that in most cases, our method can segment the human body accurately. Moreover, our method automatic select seeds and automated segmentation can reduce human interaction time, greatly improving the efficiency of segmentation.

## 5    Conclusions and Future Work

We proposed a framework for human body segmentation using face detection and biased normalized cuts, and present a simple and effective method for computing seeds for biased normalized cuts. First, we used face detection technology to identify face of the human, and used a human body model to estimate the lower body by recognized human face, then using a part of face and body as seeds, we use biased normalized cuts algorithm to segment the image. Finally, we conducted region merging, and the image is divided into two parts(object and background). Our algorithm could segment the whole human from the image. Experiment demonstrated that our method could reduce the time of human interaction and the efficiency of segmentation. The main limitation of our approach is that it depends on a correct detection of the person and his/her face.

As a future work, the algorithm could be extended in order to segment more than one person present in the images, since our current method only segments one subject in the images.

**Acknowledgments.** The work was supported by the National Natural Science Foundation of China(NSFC), NO. 11471002 and Hunan Provincial Science and Technology Plan, NO. 2013FJ4052.

## References

1. Shi, J., Malik, J.: Normalized cuts and image segmentation. IEEE Transactions on Pattern Analysis and Machine Intelligence **22**, 888–905 (1997)
2. Maji, S., Vishnoi, N.K., Malik, J.: Biased normalized cuts. In: CVPR, pp. 2057–2064. IEEE Computer Society, Colorado Springs (2011)

3. Heisele, B., Serre, T., Poggio, T.: A component-based framework for face detection and identification. International Journal of Computer Vision **74**, 167–181 (2007)
4. Viola, P., Jones, M.: Robust real-time face detection. International Journal of Computer Vision **57**, 137–154 (2004)
5. Zhu, X., Ramanan, D.: Face detection, pose estimation, and landmark localization in the wild. In: CVPR, pp. 2879–2886. IEEE Computer Society, Providence (2012)
6. Magar, A.T., Shinde, J.V.: A survey of techniques for human segmentation from static images. In: International Association of Scientific Innovation and Research, pp. 66–75. United State (2014)
7. Kohli, P., Rihan, J., Bray, M., Torr, P.H.: Simultaneous segmentation and pose estimation of humans using dynamic graph cuts. International Journal of Computer Vision **79**, 285C–298 (2008)
8. Lin, Z., Davis, L., Doermann, D., DeMenthon, D.: Hierarchical part-template matching for human detection and segmentation. In: ICCV, pp. 1–8. IEEE Press, Brazil (2007)
9. Kumar, M.P., Torr, P., Zisserman, A.: Objcut: Efficient segmentation using top-down and bottom-up cues. IEEE Transactions on Pattern Analysis and Machine Intelligence **32**, 530–545 (2010)
10. Agarwal, A., Triggs, B.: A local basis representation for estimating human pose from cluttered images. In: Narayanan, P.J., Nayar, S.K., Shum, H.-Y. (eds.) ACCV 2006. LNCS, vol. 3851, pp. 50–59. Springer, Heidelberg (2006)
11. Mori, G., Ren, X., Efros, A., Malik, J.: Recovering human body configurations: combining segmentation and recognition. In: CVPR, pp. 326–333. IEEE Computer Society, Washington (2004)
12. Ren, X., Berg, A., Malik, J.: Recovering human body configurations using pairwise constraints between parts. In: ICCV, pp. 824–831. IEEE Computer Society, Beijing (2005)
13. Hua, G., Yang, M.H., Wu, Y.: Learning to estimate human pose with data driven belief propagation. In: CVPR, pp. 747–754. IEEE Computer Society, San Diego (2005)
14. Mori, G.: Guiding model search using segmentation. In: ICCV, pp. 1417–1423. IEEE Computer Society, Beijing (2005)
15. Li, S., Lu, H.C., Ruan, X., Chen, Y.W.: Human body segmentation based on deformable models and two-scale superpixel. Pattern Analysis and Applications **15**, 399–413 (2012)
16. Hernndez-Vela, A., Reyes, M., Ponce, V., Escalera, S.: Grabcut-based human segmentation in video sequences. Sensors **12**, 15376–15393 (2012)
17. Martin, D., Fowlkes, C., Tal, D., Malik, J.: A database of human segmented natural images and its application to evaluating segmentation algorithms and measuring ecological statistics. In: ICCV, pp. 416–423. IEEE Computer Society, Vancouver (2001)
18. Rother, C., Kolmogorov, V., Blake, A.: Grabcut - interactive foreground extraction using iterated graph cuts. ACM Trans. Graph. **23**, 309–314 (2004)
19. Jain, A.K., Dubes, R.C.: Algorithms for Clustering Data. Prentice-Hall, Upper Saddle River (1988)
20. Dubuisson, M.P., Jain, A.K.: A modified Hausdorff distance for object matching. In: CVPR. IEEE Computer Society, Seattle (1994)
21. Huttenlocher, D.P., Klanderman, G.A., Rucklidge, W.J.: Comparing Images Using the Hausdorff Distance. IEEE Transactions on Pattern Analysis and Machine Intelligence **15**, 850–863 (1993)

# Survey on Eye Movement Based Authentication Systems

Yun Zhang and Xuanqin Mou[✉]

Institute of Image Processing and Pattern Recognition,
Xi'an Jiaotong University, No. 28 West Xianning Road, Xi'an, China
{zhangyun2011,xqmou}@mail.xjtu.edu.cn

**Abstract.** No matter how sophisticated an authentication system has been de-vised, human is often considered as the weakest link in the security chain. Secu-rity problems can stem from bad interactions between humans and systems. Eye movement is a natural interaction modality. The application of eye tracking technology in authentication offers a promising and feasible solution to the trad-ing-off between the usability and the security of an authentication system. This paper conducts a comprehensive survey on existing Eye Movement Based Au-thentication (EMBA) methodologies and systems, and briefly outlines the tech-nical and methodological aspects of EMBA systems. We decompose the EMBA technique into three fundamental aspects: (1) eye movement input modality, (2) eye movement interaction mechanism, and (3) eye movement data recognition. The features and functions of the EMBA modules are further analyzed. An emphasis is put on the interrelationship among the modules and their general impacts on the formation and function of the EMBA framework. The paper at-tempts to provide a systemic treatment on the state of the art technology and al-so to outline some potential future development directions in eye movement based interaction or security systems.

**Keywords:** Eye tracking · Authentication · Access control · Human computer interaction · Fixations · Saccades · Graphical password

## 1 Introduction

Eye tracking technology is very promising as an alternation or an auxiliary channel to human-computer interaction (HCI). Applications of eye movements to real time user interfaces can be divided into two categories: (1) using eye movements as an directly control tool, such as a non-touchable mouse pointer for the disable [1], and (2) ana-lyzing eye movements to obtain the user's intention and then to facilitate the interac-tion environment, such as interactive graphical displays [2] and interface usability measurements [3-4]. The two areas utilized the eyes' behavioral features and atten-tional features, respectively.

The authentication system, as a specific application of eye movement based inte-raction, happens to be an ideal combination between the two features. First of all, from the perspective of interaction modality, eye tracking device is highly resistance to shoulder surfing which is done either by simply looking over a victims shoulder, or using technical devices like binoculars or miniature cameras to get the personal

H. Zha et al. (Eds.): CCCV 2015, Part I, CCIS 546, pp. 144–159, 2015.
DOI: 10.1007/978-3-662-48558-3_15

identification number (PIN) [5].Secondly, from the perspective of system usability, eye tracking based interaction is so different from the traditional alpha-number schemes that a new authentication mechanism such as a graphical based password system is more fitting for the human innate memory capability [6-9]. Last but not least, from the perspective of system security, eye movement is also a unique biometric trait which is determined by both conscious and sub-conscious viewing behaviors. Such information can be combined with other channels to enhance the validity of identification. This paper is structured as follows. Section 2 describes the three main aspects/modules of a general EMBA system and outlines the techniques and methodologies of each module. Section 3 reviews eight present EMBA systems by thoroughly discussing how the different modules are assembled together and how they affect the system performance. In Section 4, we further analyze the strengths and weaknesses of each module and reveal their coherent relationship in the EMBA framework. Section 5 concludes the paper with a summary of achievements and future research directions in this area.

## 2    Eye Movement Based Authentication Framework and Technical Modules

The general structure of an eye movement based authentication system is different from a conventional authentication system [10]. In spite of different applications, an EMBA system in general consists of the following three main modules:

1. Eye movement input modality
2. Eye movement interaction mechanism
3. Eye movement data recognition/identification

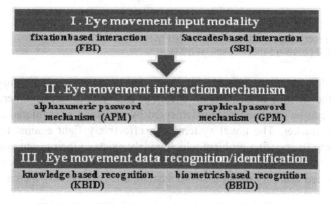

**Fig. 1.** The *EMBA framework and technical modules.*

As shown in Figure 1, the three modules are three main steps and elements to construct an EMBA system, which are all driven by the characteristics of eye movements and eye tracking device. In each module, we present the possible techniques and methodologies which can be assembled together to form different functional EMBA systems.

## Module 1

- Fixation-based interaction   (FBI)
- Saccades-based interaction   (SBI)

As previously mentioned, an authentication system is a special case of eye movement based HCI. Therefore, Module 1 is the first step and the most principal component to be considered. In other words, what kind of features from eye movements you choose will decide the whole design of the system.

Fixation shows the static characteristics of the human vision system, which is the eye movement to stabilize the retina over a stationary object of Area of Interest (AOI). Sometimes, it can also be defined as the total duration and the average location of a series of fixations within an AOI [11]. Fixation-based interaction, or sometimes called "gaze-based interaction" [12], has long been the predominant techniques in eye movement based HCI as a real time input medium. The user's fixations are extracted and utilized as a pointing device, like a mouse. By fixating his eye for a certain period of time (dwell time), the user can activate the particular command (or input).

Saccades are kind of dynamic characteristics, which are the discrete movements that quickly change the orientation of the eyes, thereby translating the image of the object of interest from an eccentric retinal location to the fovea. Saccades-based interaction is a recently emerged technique [13]. Unlike the fixation-based interaction, the saccades-based interaction utilizes the dynamic features of eye movements to transmit the user's personal information or command. A typical example of such dynamic features is scanpath, which is an eye movement pattern consisted of series of saccades. Different patterns can be assigned to different input commands for HCI.

## Module 2

- Alphanumeric password mechanism   (APM)
- Graphical password mechanism   (GPM)

As a novel element, eye tracking technology provides a new interaction mechanism to strengthen the existing authentication ones. For example, the alphanumeric password mechanism can be conveniently implemented by replacing a traditional input device with an eye tracker. The novel systems can effectively fight against the prevalent eavesdropping or spoofing problem which widely exists in the present system. Moreover, such "tradition mechanism + novel input (eye tracker)" not only reserves the well-established usability on a password system, but considerably increases the security as well.

Alternatively, a graphical password mechanism equipped with eye tracking technology could be a feasible solution not only to security problems, but also usability problems as well. Graphical password is first proposed by Greg Blonder [6] to replace the precise recall of a PIN by image recognition, a skill at which humans are proficient [14]. Whereas, the tradeoff is that graphical password seems more vulnerable to shoulder surfing attack. For instance, the larger image interface can be more exposed to those malicious attacks, despite the potential bigger password space [15]. When combined with eye tracker, such mechanism can easily bypass the disadvantage of graphical password and make best use of their advantages.

**Module 3**

- Knowledge-based identification  (KBID)
- Biometrics-based identification  (BBID)

After the first two steps to select and collect the eye movement data, the other aspect of authentication system design is to process the data to authenticate the user.

Knowledge-based mechanisms [16] are the most widely used identification method today. The user needs to remember the PIN or password and the system verifies an encrypted version of the user input to a stored encrypted copy. Biometrics-based authentication is another option which uses physical /or behavioral (learned) characteristics to replace the PIN/password [17]. Eye movement characterizes human's physiological and perceptual behaviors in the same time, which constitutes a rich source of personal characteristics and features. Exploration of such a source may lead to a new approach for foolproof or multivariate dynamic identification systems.

# 3     Cases Study

In this section, a comprehensive analysis of EMBA systems is given by analyzing eight cases in five types module combination (in fact, there are 2x2x2, eight combinations of two approaches in each of three modules. Heretofore, the present's cases have only covered 5 of them). The survey emphases (1) how the three modules of the EMBA system are working together and (2) what are the detailed techniques and methodologies within each module.

## 3.1     FBI + APM + KBID

Kumar and their group proposed a fixation-based authentication prototype *EyePassword* mainly to reduce shoulder surfing [18]. Their system retains the traditional alphanumeric password mechanism, as illustrated in Figure 2. *EyePassword* uses the on-screen keyboard and tracks the users' fixations as the password entry. In doing so, their EMBA system retains the simplicity of a traditional password scheme. The only difference to the user is to enter the passwords by "looking at them" instead of "clicking them".

To enhance the fixation-based interaction, the authors developed a series of designs of different target sizes, keyboard layouts, trigger mechanisms and feedbacks. The first two parameters need to be optimized to overcome the eye tracker's limitation to resolution and accuracy. The second two approaches are proposed to solve the problems in active vision control. The purpose is to disambiguating tracking data for an eye tracking system.

As a typical knowledge-based identification, *EyePassword* is a most straightforward application of eye tracking techniques in the authentication system. It retains the established user's habits while makes the stealing virtually impractical in the fixation-based interaction. The authors also conducted usability studies to compare the fixation-based control and a normal keyboard. The result shows that an eye tracking method needs a longer time than using a keyboard. However, the error rate is quite similar and most of the subjects tested prefer the fixation-based interaction over the traditional ones. According to a recent report, the concept of *EyePassword* has already been converted into real products.

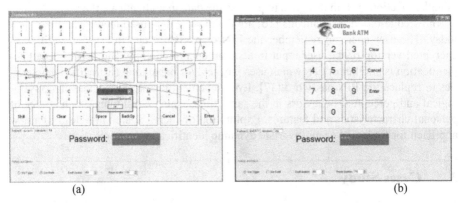

(a)                                                                                    (b)

**Fig. 2.** On-screen keyboard of *EyePassword*   (a) The alphabetic layout with gaze points superimposed; (b) Keypad layout for a practical ATM application.

## 3.2     FBI + GPM + KBID

Maeder et al.[19] and Hoanca et al.[20] also proposed fixation-based password systems which are different from Kumar's system although two were all motivated by the graphical password mechanism. Maeder et al's work uses a nature image instead of an on-screen keyboard. The visual features or objects of the image serve as the symbol set. The user just fixates in a specified sequence on those features or objects to input the PIN. In order to distinguish possible image objects from the other regions, the image is superimposed with 3x3 non-uniform grids (Figure 3(a)) to help identify the distinctive fixations and gazes.

Hoanca's work is based on a well known graphical password *Passfaces*[1]. Instead of a nature image, the *Passfaces* interface is composed of human faces pictures, usually 3x3 tiles (Figure 3(b)). The user is asked to fixate on the prescribed faces among the decoy ones for authentication. Such technique is based on the assumption that people can recall human faces better than any other pictures. Hoanca's contribution is to use eye tracking in *Passfaces* and to refine the authentication algorithm. Furthermore, such kind of interface provides a predictable object's location and the error area, which may increase the certainty of the user's attentive fixations.

---

[1] http://www.realuser.com/

(a)                                                         (b)

**Fig. 3.** (a) Prague image used in the experiments with a non-uniform 3x3 grid superimposed on the image. (b) On tiled face images, the user selects a face out of a series of faces for their password

(a)                                                         (b)

**Fig. 4.** Dunphy et al.'s gaze-contingent passwords at ATM. (a) The password interface; (b) The simulated ATM scenario in the lab.

Another case in this category is work from Dunphy et al.[21] whose contribution is to implement the (FBI + GPM + KBID) system to a real ATM password system (Figure 4). Based on the *Passfaces* design, they created a naturalistic ATM setting with similar sight, sounds and operation experience by using the video technique in the lab. A study on twenty users showed that the participants felt ease with the eye tracker. Another conclusion drawn is that the public environment does not cause undue distraction of user's fixations, which demonstrates the feasibility and practicability of an EMBA system.

### 3.3    FBI + GPM + BBID

Using eyes to perform human identification in biometric methods has a long tradition such as iris pattern recognition and retina scanning. However, the ideal forms of biometrics would be based on non-visible and non-physiological information hidden within the person, such as the behavior or cognitive processes of a human being. Different from their previous model discussed in Section 3.2, Maeder and Fookes [22] presented a visual attention based biometric identification. As shown in Figure 5, the fixation permits a subject to view an AOI near the center of the field with a high resolution, which is known as foveal. In this respect, visual attention acts as a "spotlight", and by analyzing the spatial and temporal patterns of fixation sequences, the traits of overt or cover viewing behaviors can be disclosed. The authors undertook a set of conscious and sub-conscious viewing experiments and the eye movement patterns are processed to find the individual features. In a conscious/overt viewing test, the fixation locations are prescribed (the yellow circles in Figure 5), while in a sub-conscious /covert test, the user just view the picture naturally without a clear task. They estimated the number of fixations, the order of fixations, the first five fixations and their numbers of revisits. The preliminary statistics of fixations show greater intra variances than inner variances. However, further work is expected to be carried out to solve the problems with identification and validation, which are the two basic issues of a biometric system.

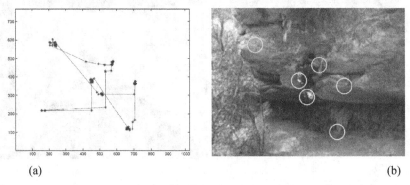

(a)                                                                                  (b)

**Fig. 5.** Maeder et al.'s visual attention approach for biometric identification. (a) and (b) are the examples of a participant's gazes data and the corresponding viewing points which are used for personal authentication.

### 3.4    SBI + APM + KBID

De Luca et al.[23-24] proposed a saccade-based password system *EyePass*, which use "gaze gesture" to reduce the likelihood of shoulder surfing in public terminals. Gaze gesture, first proposed by Drewes and Schmidt [25], is a series of eye movement patterns each of which is formed by consecutive saccades. The concept was originated from the mouse gesture2 in the Firefox web browser.

As shown in Figure 6, EyePass uses alphanumeric password mechanism which is based on EdgeWrite [26]. The user should follow the prescriptive eye movement pattern of the corresponding digit to encrypt the entry just like mouse or pen strokes on a tablet PC. For the system, decryption is done by using a two-step recognition

---

2 http://optimoz.mozdev.org/gestures/

algorithm. Firstly, it needs to extract each sub-gesture or stroke from the input gaze points; secondly, it needs to assemble those recognized strokes together and map them to the given gesture pattern. In EyePass, a "press button" motion is added to help the recognition of eye strokes, which require the user to hold the button during the performing to indicate they are trying to enter an authentication token. The preliminary user study shows that the gaze gesture is a suitable method for PIN entry and such a method potentially has a better memorability than the gestures used by the tablet PC.

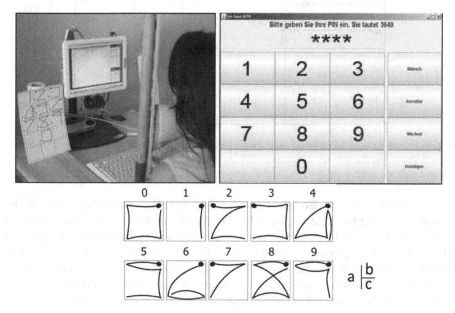

**Fig. 6.** The EyePass system. (a) The lab setting; (b) The screenshot of the prototype; (c) The numeric gaze gestures used for the prototype.

## 3.5   SBI + GPM + BBID

Saccades can also be used in a biometric-based authentication system. Kasprowski and Ober [27] provided a scheme based on the "dynamic" physiological properties of eye movements. As the saying goes, the eye is "the window to our mind". Eye movements may encode muscle activities and brain information simultaneously. The fixation-based biometric approach discussed in Section 3.3 (FBI + GPM + BBID) recognizes individuals by their cognitive processes, which is paid more attention to "where" the persons are looking at. By contrast, the saccades-based biometric approach recognizes individuals by their viewing behavioral traits, which focuses on "how" they are viewing the pictures. In this regard, it is closely comparable to biometric traits such as signature, keystroke and gait.

As shown in Figure 7, to avoid the 'learning effects', a 3x3 'jumping point' design is chosen as a visual stimulus to generate a series of saccades. Reaction times and drifts during the eye calibrations are recorded to extract the distinctive and permanent features which have exactly the same values for the same person in every experiment.

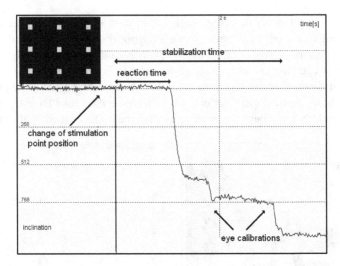

**Fig. 7.** Explanation of Kasprowski and Ober's work . The 3x3 matrix with the "jumping point" stimuli shown on the top left. The rest of display depicts the definition of the reaction time and the stabilization time.

The similar work was also done by Bednarik et al. [28], in which they extracted the features including pupil sizes, gaze velocities and the distances of infrared reflections of the eyes. Figure 8 shows eight vision stimuli proposed by Bednarik et al. Although these two pieces of pioneering research work furnished the possibility of such a new authentication mechanism, there is still a long way to go from a good idea to a reliable methodology. The issues such as how to acquire the most informative features and how to establish the recognition model need to be addressed in the future.

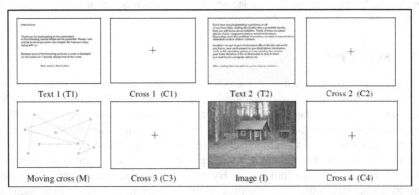

**Fig. 8.** Explanation of Bednarik et al.'s  work. The eight vision stimulus including texts, image, static and dynamic crosses are used to extract biometric information of personal eye movements.

# 4 Discussion

Although the classifications here are artificial, the aim is to bring out those significant modules or factors of the EMBA system design, and to give a systemic perspective on the state of the art technology and possible future development. Table 1 summarizes the current situations of all possible eight combinations of three modules.

**Table 1.** Systemic perspective on the EMBA system

|  | Fixation-based interaction | Saccades-based interaction | Row Sum |
|---|---|---|---|
| **APM + KBID** | √ (1 case) | √ (1 case) | 25% |
| **APM + BBID** | × | × |  |
| **GPM + KBID** | √ (3 cases) | × | 75% |
| **GPM + BBID** | √ (1 case) | √ (2 cases) |  |
| **Colum Sum** | **62.5%** | **37.5%** |  |

(APM: alphanumeric password mechanism; GPM: graphical password mechanism; KBID: knowledge-based identification; BBID: biometrics-based identification; "√": application cases reported "×": no application case reported).

## 4.1 Fixation vs. Saccade

Column-wisely, the EMBA system is firstly highlighted by two different types of eye movements: fixation and saccades. Just as languages are important to human communication, so are such medium to eye movement based interaction. Fixation is the most utilized feature in both HCI and EMBA systems (67.5%) to date. However, saccades-based interaction has some unique features. Take "gaze gesture" as a typical example, the advantages and disadvantages are given as follows:

**Advantages**

- It is free from the calibration shift; sometimes it even does not need a calibration. For example, gaze gesture is based on relative eye movement patterns but not absolute gaze positions.
- It does not demand high spatial and temporal resolutions for an eye tracker because the recognition of the user eye movement can be assisted by the HCI design. For example, in Drewes and Schmidt's case, eye gestures can be as large as 10°visual angle and the sampling interval can be a few hundred milliseconds.

**Disadvantages**

- It needs the user to practice and perform those gestures correctly, which is not natural but a technical eye movement. By contrast, the fixation-based interaction is more intuitive and direct.
- It may need some efforts for a user to remember the "gaze gesture table" which maps gestures to the computer commands (Figure 6(c)). However, the application

to a password system benefits from a relatively small gesture table. According to De Luca et al.'s online survey, the user may feel ease to perform gaze gesture.

## 4.2    APM vs. GPM and KBID vs. BBID

Once the input modality is set, the corresponding interaction mechanism and data processing methodology can be developed based on it. From Table 1, we can see that 75% of EMBA systems use the graphical password mechanism instead of the alphanumeric password mechanism. Because, on the one hand, eye tracking can fight well against the shoulder surfing problem which is an intrinsic one in graphical password. On the other hand, the increasingly mature graphical password help to develop a platform to introduce eye controlled input devices, whose schemes is to replace the precise recall of alphanumeric password entry with the imprecise recognition of the images .A comprehensive survey with detailed analysis on graphical password can be found in [29].

Eye tracking technology can be combined with either knowledge-based identification or biometrics-based identification. While KBID is the most straightforward and convenient authentication method, its weaknesses are apparent, such as difficulty to memorize, being vulnerable to social engineering which refers to trick someone into disclose a password than to spend the effort to hack into the system. Combined with eye tracking technology, some pragmatic solutions can be developed. For example, (GPM + KBID) has a feature of being easy to memorize passwords but being difficult to be divulged. This is because the validation operations can be conducted by eyes and graphical password is difficult to write down or to describe to somebody else. Although no (SBI+ GPM + KBID) has been reported to date, such direction is worth exploiting, which may result in a perfect combination of dynamic eye movement' characteristics in an authentication system.

BBID is based on something you are or something you do, which cannot be lost or forgotten, be written down or stolen by social engineering. An important issue in BBID is clonability. Obtaining a copy of an individual's fingerprint can be trivial, even the trick of iris images is not difficult. Another problem is the measurement of physical features may be intrusive to users. Eye movements are sorts of dynamic and living-body biometric traits, which are non-intrusive and very difficult to be forged. Such good properties have already been demonstrated in the (GPM+BBID) cases reported. However, BBID with eye tracking technology is still at a very primary stage. There are a few questions needed to be answered: (1) What kinds of eye movement modalities should be enrolled? (2) What templates should be formed from the enrollee's data? and (3) How a live eye movement data is matched against one or many templates in the system database? More research and studies along this direction are expected to come in the future.

## 4.3    Summary and Comparison of State-of-the-Art    EMBA Systems Technical Details

Though still in its infancy, the field of eye movement based authentication is growing rapidly. To facilitate the others who are interested in the study and application on such field, we gather all the experiment conditions and technical details of latest eye movement based authentication systems cases in the survey into Table 2. The main purpose of the table is to provide a substantial and extensive reference for other peers to conveniently setup a EMBA system based on the prior's empirical data.

The first row of the table divides the EMBA into two categories: fixation-based and saccades-based password system. Then all the eight cases discussed in section 3 are classified in the two categories with their five types of features, which are abbreviated as follows:

- **T1:** FBI + APM + KBID = fixation-based interaction + alphanumeric password mechanism + knowledge-based identification
- **T2:** FBI + GPM + KBID = fixation-based interaction + graphical password mechanism + knowledge-based identification
- **T3:** FBI + GPM + BBID = fixation-based interaction + graphical password mechanism + biometrics-based identification
- **T4:** SBI + APM + KBID = saccades-based interaction + alphanumeric password mechanism + knowledge-based identification
- **T5:** SBI + GPM + BBID = saccades-based interaction + graphical password mechanism + biometrics-based identification

The second row is the eight specific EMBA systems which belong to five type and two categories. For example, case "Kumar et al." belongs to T1, type "fixation-based interaction + alphanumeric password mechanism + knowledge-based identification", and category "Fixation-based password". Column-wisely, each column is the collection of the technical features of one case .The first column represents nice types of the technical features of EMBA system, which are explained as follows

1. **Eye Tracker:** The cases' use what kind of state-of-the-art eye tracker models. While most of them are commercial ones, there is still self-developed eye tracker, such as OBER2, used in the prototype system.
2. **Accuracy:** The maximum precision of view angle the eye tracker models can reach .
3. **Frame rate**: The sampling rate of the eye tracker models. Usually it covers from 10Hz ~3000Hz. The rate around 30Hz~120Hz are mostly used in HCI system.
4. **Interface** : Here means the size of interaction screen and its resolution. It is an important factor, because it directly affects the interaction precision and interface design. Generally speaking, the larger the better the user experience is, and the higher input precision the system can get.
5. **Viewing distance:** means the distance between the user and the eye tracker. Such item is also an important factor to be considered, because there are objective distance measurement limitations in all eye trackers. They cannot be too closer or too far. The empirical distance value is between 40cm~70cm.
6. **Visual angle ranges for viewing (WxH) :** It means the how wide and large the user's visual field is in the current case. WxH represent Width x Height. It is another measuring unit by means of feature "interface" and "viewing distance".
7. **Target size/area:** It means the size of the button or the graphical pattern to be triggered by the eye movement. It is a feature to reflect the design and interaction friendliness. The general attribute of the target size is similar to those of the feature "interface".

**Table 2.** Experimental conditions and technical details of EMBA systems

| Techniques | Fixation-based password | | | | Saccades-based password | | |
|---|---|---|---|---|---|---|---|
| | T1 | T2 | | | T4 | T5 | |
| Cases | Kumar et al. | Maeder et al.[1] (T2 & T3) | Hoanca et al. | Dunphy et al. | De Luca et al. | Kasprowski and Ober | Bednarik et al. |
| Eye Tracker | Tobii 1750 | Eye Tech | Eye Response Technologies ERICA | Tobii X50 | Eye Response Technologies ERICA | OBER2 [2] | Tobii 1750 |
| Accuracy | 0.5 deg | 1.0 deg | ±0.5 deg | 0.5 ~ 0.7 deg | ±0.5 deg | ±0.5 deg | 0.5 deg |
| Frame rate | 50 Hz | 15 Hz | 60 Hz | 50 Hz | 60 Hz | 250 Hz | 50 Hz |
| Interface | 1280x1024 pixels at 96 dpi | 1024 x768 pixels at 96 dpi | 1024 x768 pixels at 106dpi | ≤1280x1024 pixels at 96 dpi | 730 x 450 pixels at 106dpi | Targets are 3x3 dynamic jumping ball | 1280x1024 pixels at 96 dpi |
| Viewing distance | 50 cm | 60 cm | 48 cm±2 cm | 30 cm-50 cm away | 48 cm±2 cm | | 80 cm with chinrest |
| Visual angle ranges for viewing (WxH) | ±18.7 deg x 15.2 deg | ±15 deg x10 deg | ±14 deg x 11 deg | ≤±18 deg x15deg | ±11 deg x 6.25 deg | 2048 gaze points positions of both eye are sampled in 8128 ms | Multi-targets including: text, images, static and dynamic cross marks |
| Target size/area | 84 pix/each with 12 pix interval | average-ly 341x 256 pixels | 96 X 96 pixels | 196 pix/each with 196 pix interval | 180 x 90 pixels | | |
| Target visual angle | ±1.275 deg | uneven | ±1.375 deg | ±1.5 deg | ± 2.5 x 1.5 deg | | |

[1] Maeder et al.'s cases of T2 [Maeder et al. 2004] and T3 [Maeder and Fookes.2003] use the same experimental setups. The difference is in the use of "targets". T3 used the natural objects of the image whose visual angles are not fixed.

[2] The OBER2 system is an infrared oculography (IROG) based system, more details can be find in [Ober et al. 1997].

**8. Target visual angle:** It means the how wide and large the user's visual field is on each interactive target. It is another measuring unit by means of "interface" and "viewing distance".

All these features are main components of an EMBA system. When we analyze an existing EMBA system or build a new one, these features are essential factors should be taken into account. The function of table 2 is to list all those features of current cases together to facilitate future reference and experiment comparison.

# 5    Conclusion

The past decade has seen a wide variety of applications on eye movement based HCI. In the application for authentication, the strengths of eye tracking technology are substantial. The most immediate benefit is that the eye movement based interaction is immune from shoulder surfing or other trickery for the purpose of password stealing at public terminals.

Generally speaking, the current Eye Movement Based Authentication (EMBA) techniques are still immature. One of future developments can come from the direction of eye movement interaction mechanism. Normally, eye behaviors include both voluntary (conscious) and involuntary (sub-conscious) movements. Voluntary eye movements are more often used on the computer user interface, although involuntary eye movements can also be used. In both interface designs, the PIN is encrypted by the eye movements. The difference is that, in the voluntary case, the PIN is consciously inputted by the eye, whereas in the involuntary case, the PIN is interpreted from the natural eye movement data. Among the eight cases reviewed in this paper, there is only one case which is based on involuntary eye movements: (FBI + GPM + BBID) discussed in Section 3.3. In fact, eye movements convey physiological and perceptual information concurrently, which are good sources of physiological biometrics as well as behavioral biometrics. For example, the traits of extra-ocular muscle movements are different from one person to another. On the other hand, the cognition process expressed by the eye movements is qualitatively distinct from each other. Such a complex biometric traits have not been well developed yet, which may bring a new direction to the next generation of biometric identification.

The other direction is to develop multichannel or multimodal authentication systems. One possible combination is "iris/face + eye movement". In such a multichannel system, high-quality digital cameras may collect iris, human face, and eye movement data simultaneously. Another possible combination is (KBID + BBID). For example, in the case of *EyePassword* discussed in Section 3.1, the eye movements can not only be used to input the password, but also be used as a biometric pattern. Both the knowledge-based and biometric-based identifications can be performed at the same time. Such a new multimode *EyePassword* can fill the blank "FBI+APM + BBID" in Table 1. In the same manner, a multimode *Eyepass* discussed in Section 3.4 can fill the blank of "SBI+APM + BBID".

In summary, eye movement based authentication techniques are very promising but more research and user studies are required in order to achieve a higher level of maturity and usefulness.

# References

1. Duchowski, A.T.: Eye Tracking Methodology: Theory and Practice. Springer-Verlag New York Inc., Secaucus (2003)
2. O'sullivan, C., Dingliana, J., Howlett, S.: Eye-movements and Interactive Graphics (2003)
3. Parkhurst, D., Culurciello, E., Niebur, E.: Evaluating variable resolution displays with visual search: task performance and eye movements. In: ETRA 2000: Proceedings of the 2000 Symposium on Eye Tracking Research & Applications, Palm Beach Gardens, Florida, United States, pp. 105–109. ACM, New York (2000)
4. Loschky, L.C., Mcconkie, G.W.: User performance with gaze contingent multiresolutional displays. In: ETRA 2000: Proceedings of the 2000 Symposium on Eye tracking Research & Applications, Palm Beach Gardens, Florida, United States, pp. 97–103. ACM, New York (2000)
5. Li, Z., Sun, Q., Lian, Y., Giusto, D.D.: An association-based graphical password design resistant to shoulder-surfing attack. In: IEEE International Conference on Multimedia and Expo., ICME 2005, pp. 245–8 (2005)
6. Blonder, G.E.: Graphical Password, United State Patent, 5559961 (1996)
7. Jermyn, I., Mayer, A., Monrose, F., Reiter, M.K., Rubin, A.D.: The design and analysis of graphical passwords. In: SSYM 1999: Proceedings of the 8th Conference on USENIX Security Symposium, Washington, D.C., pp.1–1. USENIX Association, Berkeley (1999)
8. Dhamija, R., Perrig, A.: Déjà Vu: a user study using images for authentication. In: SSYM 2000: Proceedings of the 9th Conference on USENIX Security Symposium, Denver, Colorado, pp. 4–4. USENIX Association, Berkeley (2000)
9. Sabzevar, A.P., Stavrou, A.: Universal multi-factor authentication using graphical passwords. In: SITIS 2008: Proceedings of the 2008 IEEE International Conference on Signal Image Technology and Internet Based Systems, pp. 625–632. IEEE Computer Society, Washington, DC (2008)
10. Jobusch, D.L., Oldenhoeft, A.E.: A survey of password mechanisms: weaknesses and potential improvement, part 1 & 2. Comput. Secur. **8**, 587–601 (1989)
11. Poole, A., Ball, L.: Eye tracking in human-computer interaction and usability research: current status and future prospects. In: Ghaoui, C. (ed.) Encyclopedia of Human Computer Interaction. IGI Global (2005)
12. Jacob, R., Karn, K.: Eye tracking in human-computer interaction and usability research: ready to deliver the promises. In: Hyona, J., Radach, R., Deubel, H. (eds.) The Mind's Eye: Cognitive and Applied Aspects of Eye Movement Research. Elsevier Science, Oxford (2003)
13. Qvarfordt, P., Zhai, S.: Conversing with the user based on eye-gaze patterns. In: CHI 2005: Proceedings of the SIGCHI Conference on Human Factors In Computing Systems, Portland, Oregon, USA, pp. 221–230. ACM, New York (2005)
14. Weinshall, D., Kirkpatrick, S.: Passwords you'll never forget, but can't recall. In: CHI 2004 Extended Abstracts on Human Factors in Computing Systems, Vienna, Austria, pp. 1399–1402. ACM, New York (2004)
15. Wiedenbeck, S., Waters, J., Sobrado, L., Birget, J.: Design and evaluation of a shoulder-surfing resistant graphical password scheme. In: AVI 2006: Proceedings of the Working Conference On Advanced Visual Interfaces, Venezia, Italy, pp. 177–184. ACM, New York (2006)
16. Patrick, A.S., Long, A.C., Flinn, S.: HCI and security systems. In: CHI 2003 Extended Abstracts On Human Factors In Computing Systems, Ft. Lauderdale, Florida, USA, pp. 1056–1057. ACM, New York (2003)

17. Faundez Zanuy, M.: Biometric security technology. IEEE Aerospace and Electronic Systems Magazine **21**, 15–26 (2006)
18. Kumar, M., Garfinkel, T., Boneh, D., Winograd, T.: Reducing shoulder-surfing by using gaze-based password entry. In: SOUPS 2007: Proceedings of the 3rd Symposium on Usable Privacy And Security, Pittsburgh, Pennsylvania, pp 13–19. ACM, New York (2007)
19. Maeder, A.J., Fookes, C.B., Sridharan, S.: Gaze based user authentication for personal computer applications (2004)
20. Hoanca, B., Mock, K.: Secure graphical password system for high traffic public areas. In: ETRA 2006: Proceedings of the 2006 symposium on Eye Tracking Research \& Applications, San Diego, California, pp. 35–35. ACM, New York (2006)
21. Dunphy, P., Fitch, A., Olivier, P.: Gaze-Contingent Passwords at the ATM. Czech Republic, Prague, pp. 50–62, September 2–3, 2008
22. Maeder, A.J., Fookes, C.B.: A visual attention approach to personal identification. In: Eighth Australian and New Zealand Intelligent Information Systems Conference, December 10–12, 2003
23. De Luca, A., Weiss, R., Drewes, H.: Evaluation of eye-gaze interaction methods for security enhanced PIN-entry. In: OZCHI 2007: Proceedings of the 19th Australasian Conference on Computer-Human Interaction, Adelaide, Australia, pp. 199–202. ACM, New York (2007)
24. De Luca, A., Weiss, R., Hußmann, H., An, X.: Eyepass - eye-stroke authentication for public terminals. In: CHI 2008 Extended Abstracts on Human Factors in Computing Systems, Florence, Italy, pp. 3003–3008. ACM, New York (2008)
25. Drewes, H., Schmidt, A.: Interacting with the computer using gaze gestures. In: Baranauskas, C., Abascal, J., Barbosa, S.D.J. (eds.) INTERACT 2007. LNCS, vol. 4663, pp. 475–488. Springer, Heidelberg (2007)
26. Wobbrock, J.O., Myers, B.A., Kembel, J.A.: Edgewrite: a stylus-based text entry method designed for high accuracy and stability of motion. In: UIST 2003: Proceedings of the 16th annual ACM symposium on User Interface Software and Technology, Vancouver, Canada, pp. 61–70. ACM, New York (2003)
27. Ober, J., Hajda, J., Loska, J., Jamicki, M.: Application of eye movement measuring system OBER 2 to medicine and technology. In: Andresen, B.F., Scholl, M.S. (eds.) Society of Photo-Optical Instrumentation Engineers (SPIE) Conference Series; Society of Photo-Optical Instrumentation Engineers (SPIE) Conference Series, pp. 327–336, August 1997
28. Bednarik, R., Kinnunen, T., Mihaila, A., Fränti, P.: Eye-movements as a biometric. In: Kalviainen, H., Parkkinen, J., Kaarna, A. (eds.) SCIA 2005. LNCS, vol. 3540, pp. 780–789. Springer, Heidelberg (2005)
29. Suo, X., Zhu, Y., Owen, G.: Graphical passwords: a survey, 10 pp. (2005)
30. Kasprowski, P., Ober, J.: Eye movements in biometrics. In: Maltoni, D., Jain, A.K. (eds.) BioAW 2004. LNCS, vol. 3087, pp. 248–258. Springer, Heidelberg (2004)
31. Surakka, V., Illi, M., Isokoski, P., Hyönä, J., Radach, R., Deubel, H.: Voluntary eye movements in human-computer interaction. Elsevier Science, Oxford (2003)
32. Zhu, Z., Ji, Q.: Eye and gaze tracking for interactive graphic display. Machine Vision and Applications **15**, 139–148 (2004)

# A Discriminant Sparse Representation Graph-Based Semi-Supervised Learning for Hyperspectral Image Classification

Yuanjie Shao, Changxin Gao, and Nong Sang$^{(\boxtimes)}$

Science and Technology on Multi-spectral Information Processing Laboratory,
School of Automation, Huazhong University of Science and Technology,
Wuhan 430074, China
nsang@hust.edu.cn

**Abstract.** The classification of hyperspectral image with a paucity of labeled samples is a challenging task. In this paper, we present a discriminant sparse representation (DSR) graph for semi-supervised learning (SSL) to address this problem. For graph-based methods, how to construct a graph among the pixels is the key to a successful classification. Our graph construction method contains two steps. Sparse representation (SR) method is first employed to estimate the probability matrix of the pairwise pixels belonging to the same class, and then this probability matrix is integrated into the SR graph, which can be obtained by solving an $\ell_1$ optimization problem, to form a DSR graph. Experiments on Hyperion and AVIRIS hyperspectral data show that our proposed method outperforms state of the art.

**Keywords:** Hyperspectral image classification · Graph · Semi-Supervised Learning (SSl) · Sparse Representation (SR)

## 1 Introduction

Hyperspectral image data contains high-resolution spectral information on land covers, which is attractive for discriminating the subtle differences between classes with similar spectral signatures. However, hyperspectral image classification often faces the issue of limited number of labeled samples, as it is labor intensive and time-consuming to collect large number of training samples [1–3]. Semi-supervised learning (SSL) , which can utilize both small amount of labeled samples and abundant yet unlabeled samples, has recently been proposed to tackle the challenge [4,5]. Due to its practical success and its computational efficiency, graph-based SSL is pretty appealing among the semi-supervised methods.

Graph-based SSL is dependent on a graph to represent the data structures, where each vertex corresponding to one sample and the edge weight denotes the similarity between the pairwise samples. Label information of labeled instances can then be efficiently propagated to the unlabeled samples through the graph. In order to expect desired result, it is critical to construct a good graph for all

© Springer-Verlag Berlin Heidelberg 2015
H. Zha et al. (Eds.): CCCV 2015, Part I, CCIS 546, pp. 160–167, 2015.
DOI: 10.1007/978-3-662-48558-3_16

graph-based SSL methods. Nevertheless, it is still an open problem about how to construct such a good graph [6–8].

Recently, Cheng and Yan [9,10] proposed an $\ell_1$-graph structure based on sparse representation(SR).The latent philosophy is that each sample can be encoded as a sparse linear superposition of the remaining samples via solving an $\ell_1$ optimization problem. In this way, the adjacency relationship and the weights of graph are derived automatically and simultaneously. Comparing with the traditional methods, e.g., $k$-nearest neighbors ($k$NN) graph and local linear embedding (LLE) graph [8,11], $\ell_1$-graph (SR graph) explores higher order relationships among data points, and hence has the natural discriminating powerful. However, it finds the sparse representation of each sample in an unsupervised manner, encoding the similarity between samples ineffectively.

Inspired by above insights, we propose to combine both $\ell_1$-graph and partial labeled information to construct a discriminant sparse representation (DSR) graph. It could reduce the weight of two samples if they belong to the different clusters. On top of DSR graph, SSL is then conducted to obtain the final classification results. The experimental results on Hyperion and AVIRIS hyperspectral data clearly show it outperforms the state of the art.

## 2    Related Works

In the following, we will introduce the graph-based SSL methods. They are all dependent on a graph to represent the data structures, where each vertex corresponding to one sample and the edge weight denotes the similarity between the pairwise samples. Popular methods include Gaussian Harmonic Function (GHF) [6], local and global consistency (LGC) [7], linear neighborhoods propagation (LNP) [8]. These methods usually relay on the assumption label smoothness over the graph. They can be viewed as estimating a function $f$ on the graph, one wants $f$ to satisfy both the label consistency on the labeled samples and label smoothness over the graph, where smoothness can be measured by a graph Laplacian regularization term.

Given the labeled samples $\mathbf{X}_l = [\mathbf{x}_1, \mathbf{x}_2, ..., \mathbf{x}_l]$ and the unlabeled samples $\mathbf{X}_u = [\mathbf{x}_{l+1}, \mathbf{x}_{l+2}, ..., \mathbf{x}_{l+u}]$, there are $c$ classes denoted as $\mathbf{C} = [1, 2, ..., c]$. Both the labeled and unlabeled samples $\mathbf{X} = [\mathbf{X}_l, \mathbf{X}_u]$ produce a connected graph $G = (V, E)$, where the nodes $V$ corresponding to the $n = l + u$ samples, and the edges $E$ are represented by a weight matrix $\mathbf{W} \in R^{n \times n}$. Then we can obtain the graph Laplacian matrix $\mathbf{L_W} = \mathbf{D} - \mathbf{W}$, where $\mathbf{D}$ is the diagonal degree matrix with $\mathbf{D}_{ii} = \sum_j \mathbf{W}_{ij}$. Let $\mathbf{Y} = [\mathbf{Y}_l, \mathbf{Y}_u]^T \in R^{n \times c}$ be a label matrix, where $\mathbf{Y}_{ij} = 1$ if the label of sample $\mathbf{X}_i$ belongs to class $j$ for $j \in [1, 2, ..., c]$ and $\mathbf{Y}_{ij} = 0$ otherwise. The objective of SSL is to obtain the labels of unlabeled samples based on the label matrix $\mathbf{Y}_l$ and the whole data set $\mathbf{X}$.

The graph Laplacian regularization term is denoted as

$$Tr(\mathbf{F}^T \mathbf{L_W} \mathbf{F}) = \frac{1}{2} \sum_{i,j=1}^{n} \mathbf{W}_{ij} \|\mathbf{f}_i - \mathbf{f}_j\|^2 \qquad (1)$$

where $\mathbf{F}= [\mathbf{F}_l,\mathbf{F}_u]^T \in R^{n \times c}$ indicates the prediction matrix of data $\mathbf{X}$, and $\mathbf{f}_i \in R^{1 \times c}$ and $\mathbf{f}_j \in R^{1 \times c}$ are the predictions of samples $x_i$ and $x_j$.

Since the graph-based SSL methods are similar to each other, we only apply DSR graph to GHF, although it can also be used in other methods. GHF learns a prediction function $\mathbf{F} \in R^{n \times c}$ to realize the label propagation. It constrains the predictions of labeled data to be equal to true label information, and solves the following optimization problem:

$$\min_{\mathbf{F} \in R^{n \times c}} \ Tr(\mathbf{F}^T \mathbf{L_W} \mathbf{F})$$
$$s.t \quad \mathbf{F}_l = \mathbf{Y}_l \tag{2}$$

We can partition the matrix $\mathbf{L_W}$ into four blocks based on labeled and unlabeled nodes,

$$\begin{pmatrix} \mathbf{L_W}_{ll} & \mathbf{L_W}_{lu} \\ \mathbf{L_W}_{ul} & \mathbf{L_W}_{uu} \end{pmatrix} \tag{3}$$

and we obtain the solution:

$$\mathbf{F}_u = -\mathbf{L_W}_{uu}^{-1} \mathbf{L_W}_{ul} \mathbf{Y}_l \tag{4}$$

The predicted label of unlabeled samples is given by:

$$y_i = \arg \max_{j=1,2,...,c} \mathbf{F}_u(i,j) \quad i = 1, 2, ..., u \tag{5}$$

## 3   Discriminant Sparse Representation Graph Construction

In this section we propose a new approach to construct an SR graph with non-uniform class-probability called discriminant sparse representation (DSR) graph. In such a graph structure, each pairwise nodes are treated differently according to the probability that they belong to the same class. Different from SR graph, DSR graph explores class relationships among data samples, hence is more discriminative. Firstly, we provide a method on how to estimate the class-probability of unlabeled samples, and then present our DSR graph definition.

### 3.1   Estimation of Class-Probability

For labeled samples, they have a certain membership with one class. However, those unlabeled samples have an uncertain class relationship. Fortunately, we can estimate the class-probability of unlabeled samples via partial label information. According to the sparse representation based classification (SRC) [13], a test sample in the unlabeled samples can be encoded as a sparse linear superposition of the training samples, two samples that have non-zero coefficients in the decomposition will be in the same class and the coefficient denotes the similarity of the two samples. For its merit, SRC is applied to estimate the class-probability.

Given the initial label matrix $\mathbf{Y}_l \in R^{l \times c}$, where $\mathbf{Y}_{ij} = 1$ if the label of data $\mathbf{x}_i$ belongs to class $j$ for $j \in [1, 2, ..., c]$ and $\mathbf{Y}_{ij} = 0$ otherwise. Let $\mathbf{D}$ be the training samples, $\mathbf{x}_i \in \mathbf{X}_u$ be a test sample, we can acquire a sparse vector $\mathbf{A} \in R^{l \times 1}$, which denotes the similarity between test sample $\mathbf{x}_i$ and $l$ training samples, via solving following $\ell_1$ minimization:

$$\min \|\mathbf{A}\|_1$$
$$s.t. \quad \mathbf{DA} = \mathbf{x}_i \tag{6}$$

where $\|\mathbf{A}\|_1$ denotes the $\ell_1$ norm, i.e., the sum of the absolute value of all components in $\mathbf{A}$.

The class-probability vector of $\mathbf{x}_i$ then can be calculated by

$$\mathbf{P}_i = \mathbf{A}^T \mathbf{Y}_l \tag{7}$$

where $\mathbf{P}_i = (\mathbf{P}_{i1}, \mathbf{P}_{i2}, ..., \mathbf{P}_{ic}) \in R^{1 \times c}$, the entry $\mathbf{P}_{ic}$ of the vector represents the probability of data $\mathbf{x}_i$ belonging to class $c$. Then we can obtain a class-probability matrix $\mathbf{P}_U \in R^{u \times c}$ of unlabeled samples. For labeled samples, we denote class-probability matrix $\mathbf{P}_L \in R^{l \times c}$ as $\mathbf{Y}_L$.

Therefore, the probability of $\mathbf{x}_i$ and $\mathbf{x}_j$ belonging to the same class can be given by

$$\mathbf{P}_{ij} = \begin{cases} 1 & i = j \\ \mathbf{P}_i \mathbf{P}_i^T & i \neq j \end{cases} \tag{8}$$

### 3.2 Discriminant Sparse Representation Graph

Compared with the $k$NN graph and LLE graph, SR graph can discover the local relationship and obtain the edge weights simultaneously, and has discriminating power. For each sample $\mathbf{x}_i$, SR can encode it as a sparse linear superposition of the remaining samples by solving following problem:

$$\min \|\alpha_i\|_1$$
$$s.t. \quad \mathbf{B}\alpha_i = \mathbf{x}_i, \quad \alpha \geq 0 \tag{9}$$

where $\mathbf{B} = \{\mathbf{x} | \mathbf{x} \in \mathbf{X}, \mathbf{x} \neq \mathbf{x}_i\}$ denotes all the data points except $\mathbf{x}_i$. We can construct an SR graph with a norm that an edge connects $\mathbf{x}_i$ and $\mathbf{x}_j$ if the coefficient $\alpha_{ij} \neq 0$, and the edge wight $\mathbf{W}_{(sr)_{ij}} = \alpha_{ij}$.

However, SR graph did not take prior knowledge into account. Sometimes we may know a prior the existence of certain edges and we would like to include those edges in the final graph. Therefore, we construct a DSR graph by considering partial label information, the weight of two samples $\mathbf{x}_j$ and $\mathbf{x}_i$ in which is given by

$$\mathbf{W}_{(dsr)_{ij}} = \mathbf{W}_{(sr)_{ij}} \mathbf{P}_{ij} \tag{10}$$

Different from SR graph, the DSR graph explores the classified information among the samples, and therefore is more powerful and discriminative.

# 4    Experiments and Analysis

## 4.1    Experimental Datasets

In our experiments, two hyperspectral images were employed to evaluate the performance of the DSR graph. The first one was collected by the Hyperion instrument on the NASA EO-1 satelite, and the other by the NASA Airborne Visible/Infrared Imaging Spectrometer (AVIRIS). Hyperion acquires 242-band data at 30-m spatial resolution, covering the 357-2576-nm portion of the spectrum in 10-nm bands. Removal of uncalibrated and noisy bands resulted in 145. The Hyperion images utilized in the experiments were acquired over the Okavango Delta, Botswana (BOT) in May 2001. There are 9 classes in BOT images. The 224-band AVIRIS data was collected over Indiana Pine (IND PINE) in 1992, with a 20-m spatial resolution and 10-nm spectral resolution over the range of 400-2500 nm. 220 available bands remained after removal of noisy and water absorption bands. The RGB images and ground reference information are shown in Fig. 1.

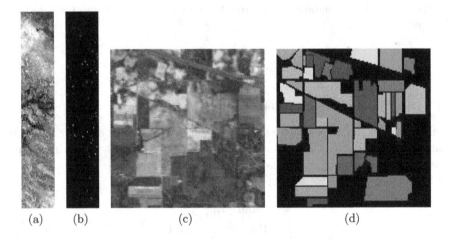

(a)    (b)         (c)              (d)

**Fig. 1.** (a) The BOT scence (band 29, 23, 16 for red, green, and blue, resp.). (b) Ground reference of BOT image. (c) The IND PINE scence (band 57, 27, 17 for red, green, and blue, resp.). (d) Ground reference of IND PINE image.

For IND PINE data set, we selected a sub data set from 16 classes with a modest number of labeled samples. The class names and number of data ponits in the BOT and IND PINESUB data are shown in Table 1.

## 4.2    Results of Classification Experiments

Four graph construction methods, e.g., ($k$NN) graph, LLE graph, SR graph, DSR graph, were applied to GHF for comparison. We randomly selected 3, 5, 10, 15,

**Table 1.** Class names and numbers of samples

| BOT | | IND PINESUB | |
| --- | --- | --- | --- |
| ID | Class Name | ID | Class Name |
| 1 | Water (158) | 1 | Alfalfa (54) |
| 2 | Floodplain (228) | 2 | Corn - No till (100) |
| 3 | Riparian (237) | 3 | Corn C Min till (270) |
| 4 | Firescar (178) | 4 | Corn (234) |
| 5 | Island Interior (183) | 5 | Grass/pasture (63) |
| 6 | Woodlands (199) | 6 | Grass/trees (101) |
| 7 | Savanna (162) | 7 | Grass/pasture-mowed (26) |
| 8 | Short Mopane (124) | 8 | Hay- windrowed (489) |
| 9 | Exposed Soils (111) | 9 | Oats (20) |
| | | 10 | Soy C No till (66) |
| | | 11 | Soy C Min till (122) |
| | | 12 | Soy C clean (261) |
| | | 13 | Wheat (212) |
| | | 14 | Woods (117) |
| | | 15 | Bldg-grass-trees-drives (291) |
| | | 16 | Stone-steel towers (95) |

20 data points per class as training samples, and the remainder as test samples. We run the algorithms twenty times with the randomly selected samples, and the mean of overall accuracy (OA) were applied to evaluate the classification results. The optimal parameter was obtained by leave-one-out (LOO) [14] methods. For $k$NN graph, the number of nearest neighbors are each set to 7 and 5, and the gaussian kernel parameter $\sigma$ are both set to 0.1 in BOT and IND PINESUB data. For LLE graph, the number of nearest neighbors are both set to 7 in BOT and IND PINESUB data.

Fig. 2 shows the the classification results of our algorithm with optimal parameters on two data sets, where the $x$-axis denotes the number of labeled samples per class, and the $y$-axis represents the mean of OA, we can observe that:

1) The performance of DSR graph is the best on the two data sets with different proportions of labeled samples, which denotes that the DSR graph can describe the true local linear relationship of the data points, and thus is more discriminative than other three graphs.

2) The DSR graph construction method obtain higher OA than SR graph on both two data sets with different numbers of labeled points, since the latter only considers similarity between data points, whereas the former method calculates the weights by exploiting partial labeled information, which means the lower probability that the pairwise points belong to the same class, the smaller weights are given to them, thus resulting in more discriminative ability for classification.

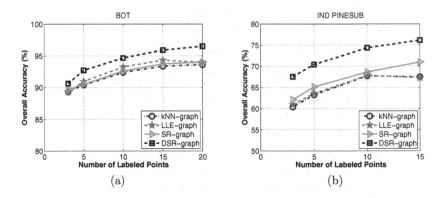

**Fig. 2.** Overall accuracy of four graphs combined with GHF under different proportions of labeled samples. (a) BOT data with 9 classes, (b)IND PINESUB data with 16 classes.

## 5    Conclusion

This paper has developed a novel discriminative graph, called discriminative sparse representation (DSR) graph, for graph-based SSL. DSR graph has not only the merits of the SR graph, but also exploits partial labeled information. It obtains a more discriminant graph construction by combining above two aspects. The experimental results on Hyperion and AVIRIS hyperspectral data show that, DSR graph is better at reveal the true local linear relationships of the data points, and thus is more discriminative than other graphs for graph-based SSL.

**Acknowledgments.** This work is supported by the Project of the National Natural Science Foundation of China No.61433007 and No.61401170.

## References

1. Kim, W., Crawford, M.: Adaptive classification for hyperspectral image data using manifold regularization kernel machines. IEEE Transactions on Geoscience and Remote Sensing **48**(11), 4110–4121 (2010)
2. Lunga, D., Prasad, S., Crawford, M., Ersoy, O.: Manifold-learning-based feature extraction for classification of hyperspectral data: a review of advances in manifold learning. IEEE Signal Process **31**(1), 55–66 (2014)
3. Gao, Y., Ji, R., Cui, P., Dai, Q., Hua, G.: Hyperspectral image classification through bilayer graph-based learning. IEEE Transactions on Image Processing **23**(7), 2769–2778 (2014)
4. Zhu, X.: Semi-supervised learning literature survey. Computer Sciences. University of Wisconsin-Madison (2009)
5. Camps-Valls, G., Bandos, T., Zhou, D.: Semi-supervised graph-based hyperspectral image classification. IEEE Transactions on Geoscience and Remote Sensing **45**(10), 3044–3054 (2007)

6. Zhu, X., Lafferty, J., Ghahramani, Z.: Semi-supervised learning using gaussian fields and harmonic functions. In: Proceedings of the 20th International Conference on Machine Learning, pp. 912–919. AAAI Press, California (2003)
7. Zhou, D., Bousquet, O., Lal, T.: Learning with local and global consistency. In: Advances in Neural Information Processing Systems, Massachusetts, pp. 321–328 (2004)
8. Wang, F., Zhang, C.: Label propagation through linear neighborhoods. IEEE Transactions on Knowledge and Data Engineering 20(1), 55–67 (2008)
9. Cheng, H., Liu, Z., Yang, J.: Sparsity induced similarity measure for label propagation. In: IEEE International Conference on Computer Vision, pp. 317–324. IEEE Press, Kyoto (2009)
10. Yan, S., Wang, H.: Semi-supervised learning by sparse representation. In: SIAM International Conference on Data Mining, pp. 792–801. SIAM Press (2009)
11. Roweis, S., Saul, L.: Nonlinear dimensionality reduction by locally linear embedding. Science 290(5500), 2323–2326 (2000)
12. Donoho, D., Elad, M.: Maximal sparsity representation via ℓ1 minimization. Proceedings of the National Academy of Sciences of the United States of America 100(50), 2197–2202 (2003)
13. Wright, J., Yang, A., Ganesh, A.: Robust face recognition via sparse representation. IEEE Transaction on Pattern Analysis and Machine Intelligence 312(2), 210–227 (2009)
14. Wu, M., Scholkopf, B.: Transductive classification via local learning regularization. In: Proc. 11th Int. Conf. Artif. Intell. Statist., pp. 1529–1536. AAAI Press (2007)

# Multispectral Image Classification Using a New Bayesian Approach with Weighted Markov Random Fields

Shengxi Li, Ying Wang[⊠], Jie Li, and Xinbo Gao

School of Electronic Engineering, Xidian University, Xi'an 710071, China
yingwang@xidian.edu.cn

**Abstract.** This paper presents a novel nonparametric supervised spectral-spatial classification method for multispectral image. In multispectral images, if an unknown pixel shows similar digital number (DN) vectors as pixels in the training class, it will obtain higher posterior probability when assuming DN vectors of different classes follow a type of statistical distribution. The proposed method assumes the DN vectors follow a Gaussian mixture distribution in each class. Particularly, we use Bayesian nonparametric method to adaptively estimate the parameters in Gaussian mixture model. Then, we construct an anisotropic multilevel logistic spatial prior to capture the spatial contextual information provided by multispectral image. Finally, simulated annealing optimization algorithm is used to accomplish the maximum a posteriori classification. The proposed approach is compared with recently advanced multispectral image classification methods. The comparison results of classification suggested that the proposed approach outperformed other classifiers in overall accuracy and kappa coefficient.

**Keywords:** Bayesian nonparametric model · Gaussian mixture model · Markov random field · Multispectral image classification

## 1 Introduction

Land cover, which could provide valuable information for understanding the nature of hydrological, geographical, agricultural, ecological, and socioeconomic systems, is an underlying variable. It could impact and connect many aspects of human life with physical environments [1]-[2]. As the rapid development of spatial, spectral and temporal resolutions of remote sensing image over the past years, multispectral image classification has become one of the most common approaches to extract land cover information in remote sensing.

Focusing on multispectral image classification, the strategies proposed in literature generally are categorized as unsupervised and supervised schemes [3]-[5]. Unsupervised methods investigate data statistics by subdividing the image into clusters of pixels with similar characteristics, e.g., iterative self-organizing data analysis (ISODATA) and K-means classification. They do not require labeled information provided by user, while the procedure may lose correlation between the clusters it found and classes user desired. For handling this problem, supervised techniques are

© Springer-Verlag Berlin Heidelberg 2015
H. Zha et al. (Eds.): CCCV 2015, Part I, CCIS 546, pp. 168–178, 2015.
DOI: 10.1007/978-3-662-48558-3_17

characterized by finding explicit link between samples and classes. They have shown more promising accuracies in terms of image classification than unsupervised methods, e.g. the minimum distance classification (MinDC), the Mahalanobis distance classification (MDC), the maximum likelihood classification (MLC), the multinomial logistic regression (MLR) and support vector machine classification (SVM). With the development of statistical learning, the classification algorithms for multispectral image analysis in recently can also be divided into parametric and nonparametric schemes. The parametric method involves a fixed representation that does not grow structurally as more data are observed. Examples include MLC and ISODATA, which assume the digital number (DN) vectors of different classes follow the Gaussian distribution. In contrast, nonparametric method is based on representations that are allowed to grow structurally as more data are observed. In practice, the classification procedure often expects to introduce as few assumptions as possible, thus, the nonparametric approaches are often employed to "let the data speak" [6]. Recently, many spectral-spatial classification techniques have been proposed to impose the spatial information [7] for improving the result of spectral classification, such as mathematical morphological filters, composite kernels, graph kernels, partitional clustering and joint sparse representation. As a general statistical modeling method, Markov random fields (MRFs) have shown good performance in incorporating spatial information in remote sensing classifications [8]-[9].

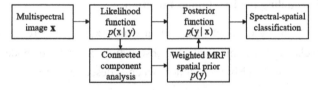

**Fig. 1.** Flowchart of proposed method.

In this paper, we proposed a novel nonparametric supervised spectral-spatial classification method. Firstly, considering the specificities and complexity of multispectral data and the fact that by using a sufficient number of Gaussians, almost all of the continuous density can be approximated to arbitrary accuracy [10], the Gaussian mixture distribution is constructed to describe the statistical properties of DN vectors in each class. Specially, the Bayesian nonparametric (BNP) method is used to adaptively estimate the parameters in Gaussian mixture model (GMM) and let the data determine the complexity of Gaussian mixture model by itself. A similar strategy has been designed in the field of brain MRI tissue classification [11]. Secondly and favorably, taking rich spatial information provided by multispectral image into consideration, an anisotropic multilevel logistic (MLL) spatial prior with region area information concerned is introduced to the maximum a posteriori (MAP) framework to obtain a more smooth and stable spectral-spatial classification result than what traditional isotropic multilevel logistic spatial prior gets. The flowchart of proposed method is presented in Fig. 1.

The remainder of this paper is organized as follows. Section 2 introduces the proposed nonparametric supervised spectral-spatial classification method in detail. Section 3 describes the data set we test on this paper and illustrates the performance of the proposed method in multispectral image classification. Conclusions are outlined in Section 4.

## 2     The Proposed Method

Similar to MLC method, we suggest that the DN vectors in multispectral image are regarded as random variable $x$, $x \in R^d$ where $d$ denotes the number of bands in multispectral image and $y$ denotes the corresponding class label. For an unknown pixel $x$ to be classified, according to the principle of maximum posterior probability, we employ Bayes' rules to arrange the unknown pixels into predefined classes.

$$p(y \mid x) = \frac{p(y)p(x \mid y)}{p(x)} \propto p(y)p(x \mid y) \tag{1}$$

where $p(x \mid y)$ is the likelihood function and $p(y)$ is the prior over the labels.

### 2.1     GMM Modeling for Likelihood Function

Given a remote sensing data set of a certain class $\{x_i\}_{i=1}^N$ , where $N$ denotes the number of pixels in the training set. An observation $x_i$ can be modeled as being generated from a Gaussian Mixture Model, which is described as:

$$\begin{aligned} c_i \mid \pi &\sim Multinomial(\cdot \mid \pi) \\ x_i \mid c_i = k &\sim Gaussian(\cdot \mid \theta_k) \end{aligned} \tag{2}$$

where $\pi = (\pi_1, \pi_2, \ldots, \pi_K)$ denotes mixing coefficients, $c_i$ denotes cluster label and $\theta_k$ stands for $(\mu_k, \Sigma_k)$ which are the mean vector and covariance matrix of each Gaussian component, respectively. Inspired by nonparametric statistics method, we assume the number of components in GMM is infinite, that is $K \to \infty$. Then BNP method is used to adaptively estimate the parameters in Gaussian mixture model.

Based on the infinite GMM (IGMM) assumption above, the parameters $\pi$ and $\theta_k$ are defined as following:

$$\begin{aligned} \pi \mid \alpha &\sim Stick(\alpha) \\ \theta_k &\sim H \end{aligned} \tag{3}$$

where $\alpha$ denotes concentration parameter in the Dirichlet distribution, $\pi \mid \alpha \sim Stick(\alpha)$ stands for:

$$\beta_k \sim Beta(1, \ \alpha)$$

$$\pi_k = \beta_k \prod_{l=1}^{k-1}(1-\beta_l), \ k \to \infty \tag{4}$$

and $\theta_k \sim H$ stands for:

$$\mu_k \sim Gaussian(\mu_0, \Sigma_k / \kappa_0)$$

$$\Sigma_k \sim InverseWishart_{v0}(\Lambda_0^{-1}) \tag{5}$$

We choose Gaussian distribution and Inverse Wishart distribution to describe the mean vector and covariance matrix in GMM [12] because they are conjugate priors for the Gaussian distribution, thus we can get a closed solution form for the posterior distribution for $C = \{c_i\}_{i=1}^N$ and $\Theta = \{\theta_k\}_{k=1}^K$ when $K \to \infty$.

Given an observation set $\{x_i\}_{i=1}^N$, we intend to infer the parameters $\{\pi, C, \Theta\}$ based on their posterior distribution. However, the posterior distribution cannot be computed analytically. The Gibbs sampler, a widely used Markov Chain Monte Carlo (MCMC) method, is imposed as an alternative way to sample their posterior probabilities and the obtained samples will approximate the posterior distribution precisely [13]. Under IGMM, the posterior distribution for the unknown parameters is defined as [14]:

$$p(C, \Theta, \pi, \alpha \mid x) \propto$$

$$p(x \mid C, \Theta)p(\Theta \mid H)\prod_{i=1}^N p(c_i \mid \pi)p(\pi \mid \alpha)p(\alpha) \tag{6}$$

Based on Eq. (3)-(5), we are able to integrate out $\pi$ and get the posterior distributions for $\Theta$ and $C$. The infinite Gaussian mixture model with Chinese restaurant process sampler we used is a Matlab implementation provided by Wood et al [13]. Then the likelihood function $p(x \mid y)$ in Bayes' formula of Eq. (1) has the following form:

$$p(x \mid y) = \sum_{k=1}^K \pi_k N(x \mid \theta_k) \tag{7}$$

## 2.2    Anisotropic MLL for Spatial Prior

For an unknown pixel $x_i$ to be classified, according to the principle of maximum likelihood (ML), which could calculate through Eq. (7), we can obtain $y_i'$, where denotes the corresponding spectral classification label. Given an input multispectral image, a spectral classification map will be generated, then we use connected component analysis (CCA) to obtain connected region area $R_i$ of each pixel, as shown in Fig. 2.

| 1 | 1 | 1 | 3 |
|---|---|---|---|
| 1 | 1 | 3 | 3 |
| 1 | 2 | 3 | 3 |
| 2 | 2 | 3 | 3 |

(a)

| 6 | 6 | 6 | 7 |
|---|---|---|---|
| 6 | 6 | 7 | 7 |
| 6 | 3 | 7 | 7 |
| 3 | 3 | 7 | 7 |

(b)

**Fig. 2.** (a) Spectral classification label of each pixel. (b) Corresponding region area information of each pixel.

In a multispectral image, two adjacent neighboring pixels have a high probability belong to the same class. MRFs exploit the continuity of neighboring labels to impose spatial contextual information in Bayesian schemes in terms of the maximum a posteriori rule. In this paper, we construct an anisotropic MLL spatial prior to capture the spatial contextual information to constraint the class labels $y$. This spatial prior is an extension of the traditional isotropic MLL prior and belongs to the family of MRF.

Through the Hammersly-Clifford theorem, the prior $p(y)$ over class label obeys the Gibbs distribution, which has following form:

$$p(y) = \frac{1}{Z} exp(-U(y)) \tag{8}$$

where $Z = \sum_y exp(-U(y))$ is a normalizing constant, $U(y) = \sum_{c \in C} V_c(y)$ is the energy function summing the clique potentials $V_c(y)$ over all possible cliques $C$. As we know, the commonly used isotropic MLL model defines $V_c(y)$ as

$$V(y_i, y_j) = \begin{cases} -\beta, & \text{if } y_i = y_j \\ \beta, & \text{otherwise} \end{cases} \tag{9}$$

In this paper, we take the region area information which captured by spectral classification into the isotropic MLL. Then a new clique potential $V^w(y_i, y_j)$ which reflect the interaction between regions is defined as:

$$V^w(y_i, y_j) = \begin{cases} -\beta \frac{|R_j|}{|R_i|}, & \text{if } y_i = y_j \\ \beta \frac{|R_j|}{|R_i|}, & \text{otherwise} \end{cases} \tag{10}$$

where $|R_i|$ denotes the area of a region $R_i$. The penalty term $|R_j|/|R_i|$ could reflect the relative size information between two adjacent regions. The function of new clique potential $V^w(y_i, y_j)$ can be described as a relative large region have more strong impact than those relative small region over the class label and one needs to provide more evidences for changing the label of a relative large region as that region may be a meaningful homogeneous region. Hence, we suppose the proposed aniso-tropic MLL spatial prior which named weighted MRF (WMRF) would lead to a more smooth and stable result compared with traditional isotropic MLL.

### 2.3    Computing the MAP Estimate via Simulated Annealing

Since it is difficult to maximize the joint probability of an MRF. The simulated an-nealing (SA) algorithm is used to compute the MAP estimate of final spectral-spatial classification map based on the spectral classification map [15] The SA algorithm for optimizing the global energy in the multispectral image can be summarized as an iteration of minimization of local energy function associated with randomly chosen pixels. The local energy function of a given pixel $x$ can described as:

$$U(x) \propto -\ln p(y \mid x) \propto -\ln p(x \mid y) - \ln p(y)$$
$$\propto -\ln p(x \mid y) + U(y) \tag{11}$$

where $-\ln p(x \mid y)$ is the spectral energy term obtained by Eq. (7), $U(y)$ is the spatial energy function computed over the local neighborhood via $V^w(y_i, y_j)$. In our work, an eight-neighborhood system is considered. The spectral spatial classification label is finally given by:

$$\hat{y} = \arg \min U(x) \tag{12}$$

## 3    Experiments

### 3.1    Data Sets

The multispectral image we used in this paper are acquired from SPOT6 satellite. It has four spectral bands that include blue band (0.455 to 0.525 $\mu$m ), green band (0.530 to 0.590 $\mu$m), red band (0.625 to 0.695 $\mu$m) and near infrared band (0.760 to 0.890 $\mu$m ). The spatial resolution is 2 m for each band. Two data sets are used to test the proposed classification algorithm and we also compare it with other advanced classification algorithms such as MinDC, MDC, MLC, MLR and SVM. These two data sets was acquired on September 30, 2012, covering Xidian University and Xia-nyang international airport in Xi'an, Shaanxi province. The image in University data set was $804 \times 690$ pixels and six classes of interests were considered: bare soil, build-ing, meadow, water, shadow and gravel. The image in Airport data set was $324 \times 426$ pixels and four classes of interests were considered: bare soil, building, meadow and airport. Fig. 3 and Fig. 4 present false color images and reference data about two data sets. Training sets are randomly selected from reference data set and the size of train-ing sets keep the ratio of 0.02 to test sets. Pixels from the training set are excluded from the test set in each case and vice versa.

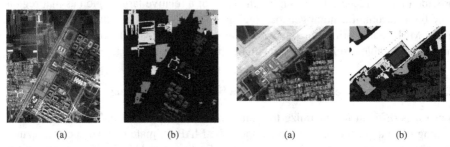

**Fig. 3.** Xidian University Area image. (a) Three band false color composite. (b) Reference data.

**Fig. 4.** Xianyang Airport Area image. (a) Three band false color composite. (b) Reference data.

## 3.2   Experimental Results

The infinite Gaussian mixture model with Chinese restaurant process sampler experimental results of two data sets are presented in Fig. 5 and Fig. 6. Fig. 5(a) reflects the trend of latent clusters number in the process of BNP mixture sampler sweeps. Fig. 5(b) presents the statistic frequency histogram of each class, which describes the latent clusters' quantity of data. We use the maximum frequency of occurrence to denote the number of latent cluster. Namely, the number of latent cluster of bare soil, building, meadow, water, shadow and gravel are 3, 3, 4, 2, 2 and 2 respectively in the first data set. The number of latent cluster of bare soil, building, meadow and airport are 2, 2, 3 and 2 in the second data set, respectively.

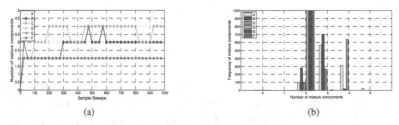

**Fig. 5.** BNP approach to sample the number of latent clusters. A. Bare soil; B. Building; C. Meadow; D. Water; E. Shadow; F. Gravel;

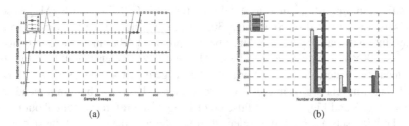

**Fig. 6.** BNP approach to sample the number of latent clusters. A. Bare soil; B. Building; C. Meadow; D. Airport;

The data's frequency distributions and different Gaussian mixture fitting functions of DN values for building and meadow belonged to first data set are presented in Fig. 7. The data's frequency distributions and different Gaussian mixture fitting functions of DN values for bare soil and airport belonged to the second data set are present in Fig. 8. According to the fitting results we can know the number of latent clusters estimated by BNP mixtures is consistent with the data's real frequency distributions, and meanwhile, the Gaussian mixture distribution can describe the data set's statistical property approximately.

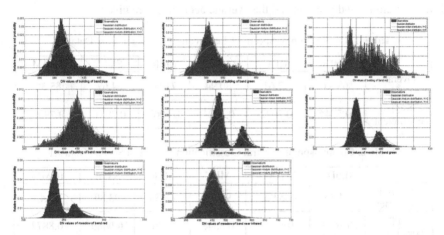

**Fig. 7.** Frequency distribution of DN values and its fitting likelihood functions by the Gaussian distribution, and Gaussian mixture distribution for bands blue, green, red and near infrared for building and meadow respectively.

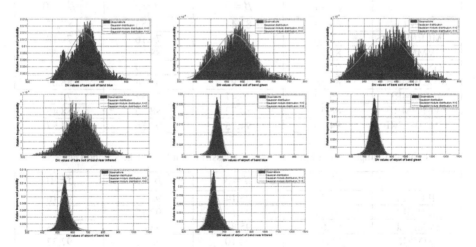

**Fig. 8.** Frequency distribution of DN values and its fitting likelihood functions by the Gaussian distribution, and Gaussian mixture distribution for bands blue, green, red and near infrared for bare soil and airport respectively.

The accuracy of proposed classification algorithm was assessed by the reference data using overall accuracies, and Kappa coefficient. The overall accuracies and the Kappa coefficients for MinDC, MDC, MLC, MLR, SVM and IGMM are presented in Table 1 and 2. Meanwhile, the overall accuracies for above spectral classification methods which imposing isotropic MLL and anisotropic MLL spatial prior named MLCMLL, MLRMLL, SVMMLL, IGMMMLL, MLCWMRF, MLRWMRF, SVMWMRF, IGMMWMRF are presented in Table 3 and 4. To obtain unbiased conclusions, the classification process was repeated 10 times with randomly selected different training and test sets and the average accuracies are given.

**Table 1.** Comparison of Spectral Classification Results in First Data set

|  | MinDC | MDC | MLC | MLR | SVM | IGMM |
|---|---|---|---|---|---|---|
| Overall Accuracy | 68.31 | 77.61 | 80.94 | 71.64 | 84.67 | **85.30** |
| Kappa coefficient | 0.5744 | 0.7022 | 0.7421 | 0.6067 | 0.7861 | **0.7996** |

**Table 2.** Comparison of Spectral Classification Results in Second Data set

|  | MinDC | MDC | MLC | MLR | SVM | IGMM |
|---|---|---|---|---|---|---|
| Overall Accuracy | 84.35 | 85.92 | 90.06 | 88.39 | **93.80** | 92.40 |
| Kappa coefficient | 0.7673 | 0.7952 | 0.8548 | 0.8267 | **0.9080** | 0.8877 |

**Table 3.** Comparison of Spectral-Spatial Classification Results in First Data set

|  | $\beta = 1$ | $\beta = 3$ | $\beta = 5$ | $\beta = 10$ |
|---|---|---|---|---|
| MLCMLL | 86.79 | 87.44 | 87.55 | 87.57 |
| MLRMLL | 73.88 | 74.11 | 74.16 | 74.18 |
| SVMMLL | 88.13 | 88.48 | 88.50 | 88.52 |
| IGMMMLL | 92.52 | 93.55 | 93.59 | 93.64 |
| MLCWMRF | 89.38 | 88.98 | 88.74 | 88.62 |
| MLRWMRF | 76.89 | 76.47 | 76.34 | 76.12 |
| SVMWMRF | 88.53 | 88.72 | 88.56 | 88.45 |
| IGMMWMRF | **94.83** | **94.75** | **94.58** | **94.57** |

**Table 4.** Comparison of Spectral-Spatial Classification Results in Second Data set

|  | $\beta = 1$ | $\beta = 3$ | $\beta = 5$ | $\beta = 10$ |
|---|---|---|---|---|
| MLCMLL | 94.27 | 95.14 | 95.13 | 95.16 |
| MLRMLL | 91.69 | 92.15 | 92.18 | 92.17 |
| SVMMLL | 95.67 | 95.87 | 95.87 | 95.88 |
| IGMMMLL | 96.42 | 97.10 | 97.21 | **97.37** |
| MLCWMRF | 97.30 | 97.21 | 97.17 | 97.05 |
| MLRWMRF | 92.68 | 92.50 | 92.65 | 92.64 |
| SVMWMRF | 95.79 | 95.89 | 95.92 | 95.82 |
| IGMMWMRF | **97.51** | **97.35** | **97.33** | **97.37** |

In general, IGMM and SVM could produce relatively better overall accuracy and Kappa coefficient comparison with MinDC, MDC, MLC and MLR according to the spectral classification results. The proposed IGMM spectral classification method produce relatively better results can be explained as achieved a better statistics fitting precision at the cost of higher model complexity. The proposed anisotropic MLL prior achieve better performance than traditional isotropic MLL prior according to the spectral-spatial classification results. It can be explained as big size region has relatively higher impact to adjacent neighboring pixels than those small size region, thus the proposed anisotropic MLL prior could get a more smooth and stable results. Particularly, the proposed nonparametric supervised spectral-spatial classification algorithm outperformed than other recently advanced spectral-spatial classification method. The thematic maps obtained from the two data sets can be seen in Fig. 9 and Fig. 10. The gray scale in Fig. 9(c) and Fig. 10(c) denotes the region area information of corresponding pixel (light represents very big area, dark represents very small area), which captured by spectral classification.

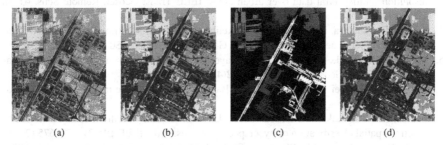

(a)                (b)                (c)                (d)

**Fig. 9.** Thematic maps obtained with the Xidian University data set: (a) IGMM method, (b) IGMMMLL method, (c) Area map, (d) IGMMWMRF method

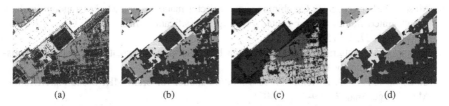

(a)                (b)                (c)                (d)

**Fig. 10.** Thematic maps obtained with the Xianyang International airport data set: (a) IGMM method, (b) IGMMMLL method, (c) Area map, (d) IGMMWMRF method.

## 4    Conclusion

This paper presents a new Bayesian approach with weighted Markov Random Fields for multispectral image classification. The proposed method shows competitive performance when compared with recent classification method, e.g. MinDC, MDC, MLC, MLR and SVM.

**Acknowledgments.** This research was supported partially by the National Natural Science Foundation of China (Grant Nos. 61125204, 61201294, 61201453 and 61432014), the Fundamental Research Funds for the Central Universities (Grant no. JB140225), and the Specialized Research Fund for the Doctoral Program of Higher Education of China (Grant nos. 20120203120009 and 20121401120015).

# References

1. Foody, G.M.: Status of land cover classification accuracy assessment. Remote Sens. Environ. **80**(1), 185–201 (2002)
2. Townsend, P.A., Helmers, D.P., Kingdon, C.C., McNeil, B.E., de Beurs, K.M., Eshleman, K.N.: Changes in the extent of surface mining and reclamation in the Central Appalachians detected using a 1976–2006 Landsat time series. Remote Sens. Environ. **113**(1), 62–72 (2009)
3. Shackelford, A.K., Davis, C.H.: A hierarchical fuzzy classification approach for high-resolution multispectral data over urban areas. IEEE Trans. Geosci. Remote Sens. **41**(9), 1920–1932 (2003)
4. Insanic, E., Siqueira, P.R.: A maximum likelihood approach to estimation of vector velocity in Doppler radar networks. IEEE Trans. Geosci. Remote Sens. **50**(2), 553–567 (2012)
5. Ruiz, P., Mateos, J., Camps-Valls, G.: Bayesian active remote sensing image classification. IEEE Trans. Geosci. Remote Sens. **52**(4), 2186–2196 (2014)
6. Gershman, S.J., Blei, D.M.: A tutorial on Bayesian nonparametric models. Journal of Mathematical Psychology **56**(1), 1–12 (2012)
7. Fauvel, M., Tarabalka, Y., Benediktsson, J.A., Chanussot, J., Tilton, J.C.: Advances in spectral–spatial classification of hyperspectral images. Proc. IEEE **101**(3), 652–675 (2013)
8. Li, J., Bioucas-Dias, J.M., Plaza, A.: Spectral–spatial hyperspectral image segmentation using subspace multinomial logistic regression and Markov random fields. IEEE Trans. Geosci. Remote Sens. **50**(3), 809–823 (2012)
9. Moser, G., Serpico, S.B.: Combining support vector machines and Markov random fields in an integrated framework for contextual image classification. IEEE Trans. Geosci. Remote Sens. **51**(5), 2734–2752 (2013)
10. Bishop, C.M.: Pattern Recognition and Machine Learning (Information Science and Statistics). Springer, New York (2007)
11. da Silva, A.R.F.: A Dirichlet process mixture model for brain MRI tissue classification. Med. Image Anal. **2**, 169–182 (2007)
12. Nguyen, N.T., Zheng, R., Han, Z.: On identifying primary user emulation attacks in cognitive radio systems using nonparametric bayesian classification. IEEE Transactions on Signal Processing **60**(3), 1432–1445 (2012)
13. Neal, R.M.: Markov chain sampling methods for dirichlet process mixture models. Journal of Computational and Graphical Statistics **9**(2), 249–265 (2000)
14. Wood, F., Goldwater, S., Black, M.J.: A nonparametric bayesian approach to spike sorting. In: 28th Annual International Conference of the IEEE Engineering in Medicine and Biology Society, pp. 1165–1168 (2006)
15. Geman, S., Geman, D.: Stochastic relaxation, Gibbs distributions, and the Bayesian restoration of images. IEEE Trans. Pattern Anal. Mach. Intell. **10**(6), 721–741 (1984)

# Effective Facial Expression Recognition
# via the Boosted Convolutional Neural Network

Zhenhai Liu, Hanzi Wang[(⊠)], Yan Yan, and Guanjun Guo

Fujian Key Laboratory of Sensing and Computing for Smart City,
School of Information Science and Engineering, Xiamen University, Fujian, China
cherler2011@gmail.com, {hanzi.wang,yanyan}@xmu.edu.cn,
ggj05@qq.com

**Abstract.** Facial Expression Recognition (FER) plays an important role in the
applications of human-centered computing. This paper presents a novel and effective FER via the Boosted Convolutional Neural Network (Boosted-CNN).
First, we use the Convolutional Neural Network to train a strong classifier to
classify different facial expressions. Based on the classification accuracy of
each expression, we use random sampling methods for imbalanced learning on
each expression to get better performance .The Extended Cohn-Kanade (CK+)
database and the JAFFE database are used to evaluate the performance of the
proposed Boosted-CNN method. Experimental results show that the proposed
method can achieve better classification rates compared with other state-of-art
methods.

**Keywords:** Facial Expression Recognition · Convolutional Neural
Network · Sampling methods · Imbalanced learning

## 1 Introduction

Facial expression contains crucial and important information about human appearance
and human activity. It plays an important role in the applications of human-centered
computing, such as human-machine interfaces, human emotion analysis, and medical
care. Facial expression recognition (FER) has attracted much attention during the past
few decades. Recent works have already achieved good performance on FER [1-5].
However, recognizing facial expression with high accuracy and reliability is still a
challenging problem due to the image variations caused by pose, illumination, age
and occlusion.

Existing methods generally address the FER problem by employing the hand-
crafted features [10, 2, 6, 8, 14] and constructing effective classifiers [1, 2, 6, 13]. The
feature-extraction stage and the classifier-construction stage are often performed sequentially and individually on these methods, and thus these methods always lack
feedback information from classifier-construction to feature-extraction. Therefore,
how to effectively use the feedback information still needs investigation.

Recently, the development of deep learning methods [13-29] and the outbreak
of big data have attracted growing attention from both industry and academia.

© Springer-Verlag Berlin Heidelberg 2015
H. Zha et al. (Eds.): CCCV 2015, Part I, CCIS 546, pp. 179–188, 2015.
DOI: 10.1007/978-3-662-48558-3_18

For example, large Convolutional Network models have demonstrated impressive classification performance on the ImageNet benchmark [15]. Ji et al. [16] proposed to use the the 3D Convolutional Neural Networks model for human action recognition and the method has achieved superior performance without relying on hand-crafted features. Several works [13, 22, 3] focus on the FER problem by using the deep learning to strengthen the discriminative capabilities of selected features.

When applied to the real-world facial expression recognition applications, the data in different classes could hardly keep balanced [23]. The unequal distribution across the classes in the real world exhibits naturally and commonly .To address this issue, some state-of-art sampling methods solutions are proposed, e.g. Random Oversampling [24, 25], SMOTE [27] and ADASYN [28].

Motivated by all of these issues discussed above, we propose a boosted-CNN method to address the FER problem. The method we propose has two main contributions given as follows.

1. Boosted-CNN learns discriminative features from raw images under the supervision of expression directly and it integrates feature extraction and classifier construction into one Boosted-CNN framework.
2. Boosted-CNN introduces boosting algorithms based on sampling methods to solve imbalance of different classes in facial expression recognition.

## 2    Related Works

In recent years, extensive methods have been proposed to solve the FER problem. The current FER methods can be categorized from two aspects: feature extraction and classifier construction.

For the feature extraction, most features are extracted from facial expression images based on the appearance-based and geometry-based information. For instance, Zhao et al. [10] used Volume Local Binary Patterns (VLBP) to recognize facial expressions. Kyperountas et al. [2] presented a method by using Salient Feature Vectors (SFVs) to analyze the facial expression image. An FER system based on supervised locally linear embedding (SLLE) has been proposed by Liang et al. [6]. Dahmane et al. [14] used the dynamic grid-based Histograms of Oriented Gradients (HOG) for emotion recognition. Lyons et al. [8] classified the facial expression by using the 2-D Gabor wavelet representation.

For the classifier construction, most existing methods construct classifiers to discriminate different expressions, such as Support Vector Machine (SVM) [1, 6], Linear Discriminant Analysis (LDA) [1, 2, 8], Principal Component Analysis (PCA), Discriminative K-SVD (D-KSVD) [5] and Graph-Preserving Sparse Nonnegative Matrix Factorization(GSNMF) [12].

Recently, there are some methods proposed for FER [3, 13, 22] based on the deep neutral networks. For example, Fasel [13] proposed to use the Convolutional Neutral Networks for FER. Meng et al. [22] proposed the AU-aware Deep Networks to address the FER problem. Ping et al. [3] presented the Boosted Deep Belief Network model (BDBN) to solve facial expression recognition problem.

# 3    The Proposed Boosted-CNN Method

## 3.1    Overview

The framework of our proposed Boosted-CNN method consists of three processes: a detection process, a CNN classifier process and a Boosting process, as shown in Fig. 1.

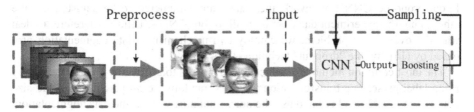

**Fig. 1.** The proposed Boosted-CNN method

At the first stage, we detect human faces in the image by using the traditional Viola-Jones face detection method [33]. The method has three key components. The first is the "Integral Image" which computes the Haar-like features very quickly. The second is the construction of an efficient classifier by using the AdaBoost learning algorithm [35] to select critical visual features from the set of potential features. The third is the combination of classifiers in a "cascade" way, which allows the classifier to discard background regions quickly and spends more computation on the promising face-like regions.

At the second stage, we take the detected face regions as the input for a CNN structure. CNN is a specific artificial network topology proposed by Yann and is also widely-used in the current object recognition task in [15]. The Convolutional architecture for fast feature embedding (CAAFE) [29] makes the implementation of CNN more convenient. With the advances in GPGPU programming, we can quick train deep CNN structure on millions of images.

At the final stage, we connect CNN with a boosted classifier which uses the random over-sampling technique. Boosting is an effective machine learning method which aims to create a highly accurate prediction classifier by combining many relatively weak classifiers.

In this paper, we propose an AdaBoost-like boosting algorithm based on the random over-sampling method for imbalanced learning to create a strong and robust classifier. The detail about this algorithm is described in Section 3.3.

The CNN model we use in this paper is based on the work of [15, 29]. The classification rate of each class is produced after training, and the boosted classifier takes the results as the input to adjust the class distribution balance. The Boosted-CNN repeats T times (T=10), to get a more accurate and reliable classifier.

Imbalanced learning often confronts the problems such as a complete lack of representation of certain important aspects of the minority class. The resulting classification rate of minority class may affect the mean classification rate of the whole task. However, the designed oversampling strategy tackles the problem of few data of the minority class without loss information of the dataset. In the training state, the CNN classifier selects more samples from the minority class. Therefore, the resulting classification rate of minority class are higher.

## 3.2    Reducing Over-Fitting

In our proposed CNN framework, there are many parameters to be adjusted. On the other hand, the experiment database is small for our CNN structure. Therefore, to deal with the over-fitting problem, we employ two mechanisms: data augmentation proposed by [15] and the "dropout" technique [20].

The most common method to reduce over-fitting is to artificially enlarge dataset by using label-preserving transformation. We first randomly crop patches with the size range from 32x32 to 24x24 and use the horizontal mirroring as the data augmentation. Then, we use the augmented data to train our CNN structure. At the test stage, the softmax layer of our network outputs an average classification prediction by extracting ten patches in total: the first 5 patches with the size 24x24 are cropped from top left, top right, center, bottom left, bottom right of the test image; the last 5 patches are the horizontal mirrors of the first 5 patches.

The dropout technique is proposed by Geoffrey et al. [20]. It sets zero to the output of each hidden neuron which does not contribute to both the forward propagation and back propagation with the probability. This technique can reduce the computational complexity during every iteration because "drop out" neurons do not participate in the next round computation.

## 3.3    Boosting Algorithm

In general, the database that exists unequal distributions between the classes can be considered as imbalanced. The common imbalance is referred to a between-class imbalance that the number of one class is severely bigger than the other classes, which exists in facial expression recognition [23]. In this work, we use random sampling methods to deal with the imbalanced learning. We modify the imbalanced data set by using a random oversampling mechanism to produce a balanced distribution. The random oversampling mechanism consists of selecting a set of randomly minority examples from the minority classes and adding them to the original set.

Specifically ,the random over-sampling scheme can be described as:

For a set of randomly selected examples in $S_t(k)$, we replicate $|E_t(k)|$ number of selected examples and add them to the set $S_t$. By this means, the number of examples in set $S_t$ is increased by the set $E_t$ and the distribution balance of the total training set S is adjusted accordingly. The boosting algorithm is described in Fig.2.

Given: $(x_1, y_1) \dots (x_m, y_m)$ where $x_i \in$ original set $S_1, y_i \in \{1,2, \dots n\}, m = |S_1|$.
Initialize: The threshold value $\varepsilon$, classe label $k = 1,2, \dots n$. The dataset $S_{t=1}(k)$.
The classification accuracy of class $k$ : $P_k^{t=0} = 0$.
The sample number of class $k$: $m_k^t = |S_t(k)|$.

For t=1,...T:
- Train a CNN classifier by using the given dataset $S_t$.
- Get the pre-trained CNN classifier $H_t: S_t \to \{1,2, \dots n\}$. Calculate each class classification accuracy :

$$P_k^t = \frac{\sum_{j=1}^{m_k^t} I(H_t(x_j)=y_j)}{m_k^t}, k = 1,2 \dots n. \; I(H(x) = y) \text{ is an indicator funtion.} \quad (1)$$

- Estimate the difference value of this accuracy and last accuracy:

$$J = \sum_k \left\| P_k^t - P_k^{t-1} \right\|_1. \quad (2)$$

if $J > \varepsilon$ continue. otherwise, break the loop.
- Normalize the accuracy $P^t$, form the set $\theta^t$ where $\rho_k^t \in \theta^t$ and $\sum_k \rho_k^t = 1$. Select the max value $\rho_K^t$ from $\theta^t$:

$$\rho_k^t = \frac{P_k^t}{\sum_k P_k^t}, k = 1, \dots, n. \; \theta^t = (\rho_1^t, \dots \rho_k^t, \dots, \rho_n^t). \quad (3)$$

$$K = \arg\rho_K^t = \arg\max_{1 \ll k \ll n} \theta_k^t. \quad (4)$$

- Update, for each class k=1,2,...n:
  o Calculate the selective number of randomly minority examples:

$$m_k^{t+1} = \lfloor m_k^t * (\rho_K^t/\rho_k^t) \rfloor. \quad (5)$$

$$|E_t(k)| = \left| m_k^{t+1} - m_k^t \right| \quad (6)$$

  o Produce dataset $E_t(k)$ using random over-sampling method in randomly minority dataset $S_t(k)$
  o Update dataset:

$$S_{t+1}(k) = S_t(k) + E_t(k) \quad (7)$$

**Fig. 2.** The boosting algorithm based on random over-sampling

## 4    Experimental Results

In this Section, we perform experiments on two facial expression databases to eva-luate the proposed Boosted-CNN algorithm, including the extended Cohn-Kanade (CK+) database [30] and JAFFE database [31], which have been widely used to test the performance of the FER methods.

## 4.1    Experiment on the CK+ Database

The CK+ database is created by Lucey et al. [30]. It contains 327 expressional image sequences with seven expressions: anger, contempt, disgust, fear, happiness, sadness and surprise. We choose three images from each image sequence for training by using the following method: from the last frame as the first frame, we pick out one image in every two frames, until it selects the three frames. One example is given in Fig. 3.

We also pick out the first frame from each image sequence to set up the "neutral" subset. Therefore, we get this database containing 8 subsets and about 1308 images.

**Fig. 3.** The selected frames from one image sequence

After the face detection [33] process, we take the 32x32 face regions as the input to CNN, and these face regions are randomly cropped to 24x24 by using data augmentation mentioned above.

Experiments on the CK+ database use   CNN structure as shown in Table 1: S1 structure. In this table, I(H,W) denotes the input layer, where H and W are the height and width of the input region. CR(O,K,S) means the convolutional layer, where O is the number of output feature maps; K is the size of kernel; S is the pixel of the stride for kernel. The max pooling layer is denoted by P(K,S), where K is the size of filter with a stride of S pixels. F(N) represents the full-connected layer and N represents the number of output neurons

Specifically, the S1 structure contains five learned layers: the first convolutional layer convolves the 24x24 regions with 16 different kernels of the size 3x3 (using a stride of 1 pixel) and outputs 16 feature maps. The second convolutional layer takes the max-pooled feature maps of the first convolutional layer as the input and convolves the feature maps with 512 kernels of the size 3x3 (using a stride of 1 pixel), and then outputs 32 feature maps. The third convolutional layer has 2048 kernels of the size 3x3 connected to the max-pooled feature maps from the second convolutional layers. The first full-connected layer has 1000 neurons connected to the output feature maps without pooling from the third convolutional layer. The final layer is the 8-softmax layer which predicts probabilities over the 8 class labels. The number of neurons in the learned layers on S1 is given by 7744, 2592, 256, 1000, 8.

**Table 1.** Summary of   CNN structure on CK+.

|    | Layer0 | Layer1 | Layer2 | Layer3 | Layer4 | Layer5 | Layer6 | Layer7 |
|----|--------|--------|--------|--------|--------|--------|--------|--------|
| S1 | I(24,24) | CR(16,3,1) | P(3,2) | CR(32,3,1) | P(3,2) | CR(64,3,1) | F(1000) | F(8) |

Based on the boosting algorithm we proposed above, we choose T=10 and $\epsilon$ = 0.001. In each loop, we make 100,000 iterations on the CNN structure. Table 2 shows the classification rates of 8 expressions between the basic CNN and Boosted-CNN.

**Table 2.** The classification rates of 8 expressions between Boosted-CNN and CNN.

|  | Neural | Anger | Contempt | Disgust | Fear | Happiness | Sadness | Surprise |
|---|---|---|---|---|---|---|---|---|
| Boosted-CNN | 1 | 0.988 | 0.993 | 0.993 | 0.998 | 0.997 | 0.947 | 0.997 |
| CNN | 0.997 | 0.87 | 0.923 | 0.979 | 0.992 | 0.994 | 0.85 | 0.991 |

Our CNN method and Boosted-CNN method obtain 95.5% and 99.1% average classification rates on CK+ database.    To be compared with our performance result, we choose some state-of-art methods evaluated on CK+ database and the original CK database [34].

The performance comparison can be seen from Fig. 4. The y-axis means the performance accuracy and the x-axis gives method names. CSPL[11]    achieved the classification rate of 89.89%  on CK database for 6-class under 10-Fold category which uses the common and specific information between expressions . Stewart et al [1] obtained 93.3% recognition on CK database for 6-class under Leave-one-subject-out (LOSO) category that [1] proposed method by   selecting a   subset of Gabor filters using AdaBoost followed by classification with Support Vector Machines (AdaGabor). BDBN[3] gets 96.7%   performance for 6-class   on CK+ database under 10-Fold category which   solved FER problem by using Boosted Deep Belief Network. Shan [4] presented the results that : the method Boosted-LBP based SVMs (Boosted-LBPSVM) gets 95.1% 6-class recognition on CK database and the method LBP based SVMs (LBPSVM) gets 92.6% 6-class recognition in leave-one-subject-out (LOSO) experiments.As shown in Fig. 5, the features learned from our CNN and Boosted-CNN contains more discriminative information for FER problem.

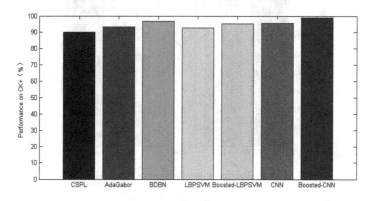

**Fig. 4.** Average classification rate on CK+

## 4.2    Experiments on JAFFE Database

The JAFFE database has 213 images posed some examples for each expression with 10 Japanese female expressers [31]. This database is so small that we design a different CNN structure for JAFFE. We also use the ReLUs activity function and "dropout" technique in the experiments. Compared with the structure used in the CK+, this CNN structure has less layers, less neurons and less parameters. S2 structure is the summary of the CNN structure which uses on the JAFFE database as shown in Table 3. The number of neurons in learned layers on S2 is given by: 5808, 972, 512, 8.

**Table 3.** Summary of CNN structure on JAFFE

|    | Layer0 | Layer1 | Layer2 | Layer3 | Layer4 | Layer5 | Layer6 |
|----|--------|--------|--------|--------|--------|--------|--------|
| S2 | I(24,24) | CR(12,3,1) | P(3,2) | CR(12,3,1) | P(3,2) | F(512) | F(8) |

We use parameters: T=10, $\varepsilon = 0.001$ on this experiment. In each loop we make 100000 iterations on the CNN structure. The average classification rates from the training CNN and Boosted-CNN are 93.5% and 95% on JAFFE under handout validation training/testing strategy.

We also choose some comparison methods evaluated on JAFFE. Boosted-LBP based on SVM (Boosted-LPBSVM) technique [4] obtains 81.0% performance of 10-fold strategy on JAFFE database. SLLE[6] gets 86.75% on JAFFE under Leave-one-subject-out (LOSO) strategy which uses feature extraction with supervised locally linear embedding (SLLE). BDBN[3] gets 91.8% on JAFFE under LOSO strategy. The comparison results are shown in Fig. 5, which demonstrates that the CNN and Boosted-CNN both outperform the other methods.

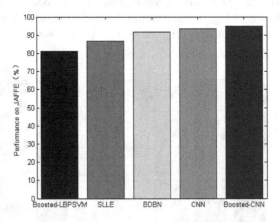

**Fig. 5.** Average classification rate on JAFFE

# 5    Conclusion and Future Work

This paper proposed a Boosting CNN method for FER problem. This method has applied the CNN structure to perform feature extraction and classifier construction training automatically and used the boosting algorithm to solve the imbalanced distribution of database.    As we can see on the experiment results above, it can achieve state-of-the-art FER performance on both the CK+ database and JAFFE database.

**Acknowledgements.** This work was supported by the National Natural Science Foundation of China under Grants 61472334, 61170179, and 61571379, and supported by the Fundamental Research Funds for the Central Universities under Grant 20720130720.

# References

1. Bartlett, M.S., Littlewort, G., Frank, M., Lainscsek, C., Fasel, I., Movellan, J.: Recognizing facial expression: machine learning and application to spontaneous behavior. In: IEEE Computer Society Conference on CVPR, vol. 2, pp. 568–573. IEEE (2005)
2. Kyperountas, M., Tefas, A., Pitas, I.: Salient feature and reliable classifier selection for facial expression classification. Pattern Recognition 43(3), 972–986 (2010)
3. Liu, P., Han, S., Meng, Z., Tong, Y.: Facial expression recognition via a boosted deep belief network. In: IEEE Conference on CVPR, pp. 1805–1812. IEEE (2014)
4. Shan, C., Gong, S., McOwan, P.W.: Facial expression recognition based on local binary patterns: A comprehensive study. Image and Vision Computing 27(6), 803–816 (2009)
5. Liu, W., Song, C., Wang, Y.: Facial expression recognition based on discriminative dictionary learning. In: ICPR, pp. 1839–1842. IEEE (2012)
6. Liang, D., Yang, J., Zheng, Z., Chang, Y.: A facial expression recognition system based on supervised locally linear embedding. Pattern Recognition Letters 26(15), 2374–2389 (2005)
7. Matsugu, M., Mori, K., Mitari, Y., Kaneda, Y.: Subject independent facial expression recognition with robust face detection using a convolutional neural network. Neural Networks 16(5), 555–559 (2003)
8. Lyons, M.J., Budynek, J., Plante, A., Akamatsu, S.: Classifying facial attributes using a 2-d gabor wavelet representation and discriminant analysis. In: Fourth IEEE International Conference on FG, 2000, pp. 202–207. IEEE (2000)
9. Donato, G., Bartlett, M.S., Hager, J.C., Ekman, P., Sejnowski, T.J.: Classifying facial actions. PAMI 21(10), 974–989 (1999)
10. Zhao, G., Pietikainen, M.: Dynamic texture recognition using local binary patterns with an application to facial expressions. PAMI 29(6), 915–928 (2007)
11. Zhong, L., Liu, Q., Yang, P., Liu, B., Huang, J., Metaxas, D.N.: Learning active facial patches for expression analysis. In: IEEE Conference on CVPR, pp. 2562–2569. IEEE (2012)
12. Zhi, R., Flierl, M., Ruan, Q., Kleijn, W.B.: Graph-preserving sparse nonnegative matrix factorization with application to facial expression recognition. Systems, Man, and Cybernetics, Part B: Cybernetics 41(1), 38–52 (2011)
13. Fasel, B.: Mutliscale Facial Expression Recognition using Convolutional Neural Networks. No. EPFL-REPORT-82837. IDIAP (2002)

14. Dahmane, M., Meunier, J.: Emotion recognition using dynamic grid-based HoG features. In: IEEE International Conference on FGW, pp. 884–888. IEEE (2011)
15. Ji, S., Xu, W., Yang, M., Yu, K.: 3D convolutional neural networks for human action recognition. PAMI 35(1), 221–231 (2013)
16. Bouvrie, J.: Notes on convolutional neural networks (2006)
17. Sun, Y., Wang, X., Tang, X.: Deep convolutional network cascade for facial point detection. In: IEEE Conference on CVPR, pp. 3476–3483. IEEE (2013)
18. Zeiler, M.D., Fergus, R.: Visualizing and understanding convolutional networks. In: Fleet, D., Pajdla, T., Schiele, B., Tuytelaars, T. (eds.) ECCV 2014, Part I. LNCS, vol. 8689, pp. 818–833. Springer, Heidelberg (2014)
19. Hinton, G.E., Srivastava, N., Krizhevsky, A., Sutskever, I., Salakhutdinov, R.R.: Improving neural networks by preventing co-adaptation of feature detectors. arXiv preprint arXiv:1207.0580 (2012)
20. Sutskever, I., Martens, J., Dahl, G., Hinton, G.: On the importance of initialization and momentum in deep learning. In: Proceedings of the 30th International Conference on Machine Learning, pp. 1139–1147 (2013)
21. Liu, M., Li, S., Shan, S., Chen, X.: Au-aware deep networks for facial expression recognition. In: 10th IEEE International Conference and Workshops on FG, pp. 1–6. IEEE (2013)
22. He, H., Garcia, E.A.: Learning from imbalanced data. Knowledge and Data Engineering 21(9), 1263–1284 (2009)
23. Holte, R.C., Acker, L., Porter, B.W.: Concept Learning and the Problem of Small Disjuncts. IJCAI 89, 813–818 (1989)
24. Mease, D., Wyner, A.J., Buja, A.: Boosted classification trees and class probability/quantile estimation. Journal of Machine Learning Research 8, 409–439 (2007)
25. Chawla, N.V., Bowyer, K.W., Hall, L.O., Kegelmeyer, W.P.: SMOTE: synthetic minority over-sampling technique. Journal of Artificial Intelligence Research 16(1), 321–357 (2002)
26. He, H., Bai, Y., Garcia, E.A., Li, S.: ADASYN: adaptive synthetic sampling approach for imbalanced learning. In: IEEE International Joint Conference on IJCNN, pp. 1322–1328. IEEE (2008)
27. Jia, Y., Shelhamer, E., Donahue, J., Karayev, S., Long, J., Girshick, R., Guadarrama, S., Darrell, T.: Caffe: convolutional architecture for fast feature embedding. In: Proceedings of the ACM International Conference on Multimedia, pp. 675–678. ACM (2014)
28. Lucey, P., Cohn, J. F., Kanade, T., Saragih, J., Ambadar, Z., Matthews, I.: The extended Cohn-Kanade dataset (CK+): a complete dataset for action unit and emotion-specified expression. In: IEEE Computer Society Conference on CVPRW, pp. 94–101. IEEE (2010)
29. Lyons, M.J., Akamatsu, S., Kamachi, M., Gyoba, J., Budynek, J.: The Japanese female facial expression (JAFFE) database (1998)
30. Buciu, I., Kotropoulos, C., Pitas, I.: ICA and Gabor representation for facial expression recognition. In: 2003 International Conference on ICIP, vol. 2, pp. II–855. IEEE (2003)
31. Viola, P., Jones, M.J.: Robust real-time face detection. International Journal of Computer Vision 57(2), 137–154 (2004)
32. Kanade, T., Cohn, J.F., Tian, Y.: Comprehensive database for facial expression analysis. In: Fourth IEEE International Conference on FG, pp. 46–53. IEEE (2000)
33. Freund, Y., Schapire, R.E.: A desicion-theoretic generalization of on-line learning and an application to boosting. In: Vitányi, P.M. (ed.) EuroCOLT 1995. LNCS, vol. 904, pp. 23–37. Springer, Heidelberg (1995)
34. Zhang, Z., Yan, Y., Wang, H.: Discriminative filter based regression learning for facial expression recognition. In: International Conference on Image Processing, pp. 1192–1196. IEEE (2013)

# Structured Sparse Coding for Classification via Reweighted $\ell_{2,1}$ Minimization

Yong Xu[1($\boxtimes$)], Yuping Sun[1,2], Yuhui Quan[2], and Yu Luo[1,2]

[1] South China University of Technology, Guangzhou 510006, China
yxu@scut.edu.cn, sun.yp@mail.scut.edu.cn, matluoy@nus.edu.sg
[2] National University of Singapore, Singapore 119076, Singapore
matquan@nus.edu.sg

**Abstract.** In recent years, sparse coding has been used in a wide range of applications including classification and recognition. Different from many other applications, the sparsity pattern of features in many classification tasks are structured and constrained in some feasible domain. In this paper, we proposed a re-weighted $\ell_{2,1}$ norm based structured sparse coding method to exploit such structures in the context of classification and recognition. In the proposed method, the dictionary is learned by imposing the class-specific structured sparsity on the sparse codes associated with each category, which can bring noticeable improvement on the discriminability of sparse codes. An alternating iterative algorithm is presented for the proposed sparse coding scheme. We evaluated our method by applying it to several image classification tasks. The experiments showed the improvement of the proposed structured sparse coding method over several existing discriminative sparse coding methods on tested data sets.

**Keywords:** Sparse coding · Reweighted $\ell_{2,1}$ minimization · Image classification

## 1 Introduction

In recent years, sparse model has been an important tool with a wide range of applications. Sparse modeling assumes that signals of interest can be succinctly expressed under some suitable system in a linear manner. The elements used for expressing signals are often referred as *atoms* and the collection of all such atoms is called a *dictionary* for sparse modeling. The computational method for sparse modeling is called *sparse coding*, which aims at finding a dictionary,

Yong Xu would like to thank the supports by National Nature Science Foundations of China (61273255 and 61070091), Engineering and Technology Research Center of Guangdong Province for Big Data Analysis and Processing ([2013]1589-1-11), Project of High Level Talents in Higher Institution of Guangdong Province (2013-2050205-47) and Guangdong Technological Innovation Project (2013KJCX0010). Yuping Sun would like to thank the support by China Scholarship Council Program. Yuhui Quan and Yu Luo would like to thank the partial support by Singapore MOE Research Grant R-146-000-178-112.

© Springer-Verlag Berlin Heidelberg 2015
H. Zha et al. (Eds.): CCCV 2015, Part I, CCIS 546, pp. 189–199, 2015.
DOI: 10.1007/978-3-662-48558-3_19

as well as the sparse coefficients, from input signals. This sparse scheme, which rigorously pursues the sparsity of the codes, works quite well in image processing and restoration. However, it is not enough to achieve high discriminability for classification and recognition tasks without exploiting extra structural information existing in signals.

While some recent approaches have attempted to pursue structured sparsity for classification either explicitly or implicitly, the disadvantages of these approaches are obvious. For example, the simultaneous low-rank and sparse constrains used in [35] are implemented with nuclear norm and $\ell_1$-norm, which would yield to bias solution as $\ell_1$-norm has heavier penalty on larger coefficients. Supervised sparse coding [34] do not explicitly impose structures on sparse codes, which often results in sub-optimal solutions. The explicit structured regularizations on sparse codes, including label consistency [11] and group Lasso [32], require the form of structure to be predefined, which is inflexible and is inaccurate when the size of dictionary is limited. This inspires us to develop an effective structured sparse coding method for classification. Motivated by the effectiveness of the reweighting scheme in compressed sensing [5], we develop a reweighted $\ell_{2,1}$ norm based method for structured sparse coding based classification, which is able to automatically discover the underlying structures of training data and obtain the sparsity patterns.

In this paper, a reweighted $\ell_{2,1}$ minimization model is constructed to exploit the class-specific joint structured sparsity patterns existing in labeled data. The weights are determined by the magnitude of sparse codes, which in turn forces the training samples to select active atoms that can span the subspace of the corresponding class and thus encourages adaptive structures on the sparse codes for classification. An alternating iterative algorithm is developed to solve the proposed model. Experimental results on face recognition, gender classification, and scene classification have demonstrated the excellent performance of our method in comparison with several existing representative dictionary learning methods.

The proposed structured sparse coding approach enjoys several advantages. Firstly, using reweighted $\ell_{2,1}$ regularization in the proposed method is able to reduce the bias on large coefficients, while the $\ell_{2,1}$ regularization based methods [21] cannot omit such a bias when dealing with classification tasks. Besides, the reweighting scheme updates the weights according to the magnitude of the sparse codes, which is more flexible compared to the standard weighting strategy proposed in [17,25]. Secondly, compared to the discriminative sparse coding methods [29,34] for classification, the proposed method is able to learn dictionaries by which distinct structured sparsity patterns can be enforced on the sparse codes of samples from different classes. Finally, our method could detect the subspace of data from each class spanned by atoms of the dictionary which helps to enhance the performance of classification.

## 2    Related Work

Group sparsity is a widely-used structured sparsity which assumes that atoms are selected by input signals in a group-wise manner instead of a singleton-wise one, see e.g. [9,12,13,28]. In the group sparsity setting, the coefficients are arranged into a predetermined set of groups, and the sparsity term penalizes the number of active groups. In the past years, various types of group sparsity have been exploited, e.g., overlapping groups [9], tree sparsity [13], and graph sparsity [2]. The group sparse coding has been used in several classification tasks, e.g., real time object recognition system [24], face recognition [10], and image classification [19,33]. Instead of considering correlation between dictionary atoms, many approaches proposed to seek for the collaborative structured sparsity by encoding the shared high-order information among related samples [4,21]. For example, in [21], a $\ell_{2,1}$-norm regularization is performed to select features across all related samples with collaborative structured sparsity, i.e., each feature either has small or large values for all data points at the same time. Recently there is a growing interest in exploiting block structured sparsity [6,7], i.e., sparse groups of features for all related samples are jointly encoded. Elhamifar et.al. [7] explicitly impose block structure on sparse codes for classification. Zhang et.al. [35] implicitly impose block structure on sparse codes by using simultaneous low-rank and sparse constraint.

In the classification case, a natural and simple way is to use sparse coefficients as features to train a classifier, see e.g. [15,29]. However the obtained sparse codes doesn't have enough discriminative power for classification. Thus many researches proposed to add additional discriminative constrains on the sparse codes during the sparse coding process, e.g. the class separation criterion (e.g. Fisher discrimination criterion [30,31]), prediction loss (e.g.logistic loss [18] and linear predictive errors [11,34]). Some approaches [22,31,36] partition a dictionary into multiple subdictionaries by associating each atom with certain class labels, and then impose discrimination to sparse codes of each subdictionary. Compared with our method, these approaches need to predefine the block structure of the dictionary.

## 3   Our Method

In this section, an effective dictionary learning model for structured sparse coding which induces structural sparsity on sparse codes with reweighted $\ell_{2,1}$-norm is proposed. Also an efficient alternating iterative algorithm is developed to solve the proposed model.

### 3.1   Problem Formulation

Let $\boldsymbol{Y} = [\boldsymbol{Y}_{[1]}, \boldsymbol{Y}_{[2]}, \ldots, \boldsymbol{Y}_{[K]}]$ denote a set of training samples from $K$ categories, where $\boldsymbol{Y}_{[k]}$ denotes the training samples from $k$-th category. One natural way to obtain class-specific structured sparsity patterns for samples from each category, is to construct a structured sparse coding model as follows,

$$\underset{\boldsymbol{D} \in \mathcal{X}, \boldsymbol{C}}{\operatorname{argmin}} \sum_{k=1}^{K} \frac{1}{2} \|\boldsymbol{Y}_{[k]} - \boldsymbol{D}\boldsymbol{C}_{[k]}\|_F^2 + \lambda \|\boldsymbol{C}_{[k]}\|_{2,0}, \tag{1}$$

where

$$\mathcal{X} = \{\boldsymbol{D} \in \mathbb{R}^{n \times m} : \|\boldsymbol{d}_j\|_2 = 1, 1 \leq j \leq m\}$$

denotes the feasible set of dictionary $\boldsymbol{D}$, which ensures that the atoms are appropriately normalized. And $\boldsymbol{C}_{[k]}$ is a sub-matrix of $\boldsymbol{C}$ collecting the sparse codes of signals from the $k$-th category (i.e. the sparse coefficients corresponding to $\boldsymbol{Y}_{[k]}$).

However, solving the $\ell_{2,0}$ norm related problem is a NP-hard problem. Thus we relax the model (1) to a weighted $\ell_{2,1}$ norm based structural sparse coding method as follows:

$$\underset{\boldsymbol{D} \in \mathcal{X}, \boldsymbol{C}}{\mathrm{argmin}} \sum_{k=1}^{K} \frac{1}{2} \|\boldsymbol{Y}_{[k]} - \boldsymbol{D}\boldsymbol{C}_{[k]}\|_F^2 + \lambda \|\boldsymbol{C}_{[k]}\|_{\boldsymbol{w}_k;2,1}, \tag{2}$$

where $\boldsymbol{w}_k$ is a weight vector for $k$-th category, $\lambda$ is a scalar controlling the weight of the structured sparsity prior, and $\|\cdot\|_{\boldsymbol{w};2,1}$ is the weighted $\ell_{2,1}$-norm defined as $\|\boldsymbol{X}\|_{\boldsymbol{w};2,1} = \sum_{i=1} w_i \|\boldsymbol{x}^i\|_2$. When all weights are set to have equal magnitude, the minimization (2) turns to be a standard $\ell_{2,1}$ minimization.

The choice of the weight matrix $\boldsymbol{W}$ is essential for classification, as the magnitude of each weight $W_{i,k}$ is able to decide how heavy penalty will be imposed on $i$-th row of $\boldsymbol{C}_{[k]}$ and thus has great influence on the quality of the resulting structural sparsity pattern. When the optimal dictionary is given, if most samples from the $k$-th category have significant responses to the $i$-th atom, the corresponding weight $W_{i,k}$ should be small, vice versa. However the optimal dictionary is unknown, thus a reweighted $\ell_{2,1}$ minimization is presented as follows,

$$\underset{\boldsymbol{D} \in \mathcal{X}, \boldsymbol{C}, \boldsymbol{W}}{\mathrm{argmin}} \sum_{k=1}^{K} \frac{1}{2} \|\boldsymbol{Y}_{[k]} - \boldsymbol{D}\boldsymbol{C}_{[k]}\|_F^2 + \lambda \|\boldsymbol{C}_{[k]}\|_{\boldsymbol{w}_k;2,1}, \tag{3}$$

where the reweighting scheme is employed to redefine the weights in each iteration of the learning process, as described in Sec. 3.2. The minimization (3) can be viewed as a relaxation of the $\ell_{2,0}$ minimization problem.

The reweighting scheme employed in our method provides a tool to explore the relationships between class-specific structured sparsity patterns and the weighed values, which is able to provide high discriminative information. To be more specific, when $\|\boldsymbol{c}_{[k]}^i\|_2$ is small, it implies that data from $k$-th category are not likely to fall into the subspace spanned by $i$-th atom. Setting $W_{i,k}$ large emphasizes the penalty on the corresponding sparse coefficients, which moves the $i$-th atom away from the favorite list of the samples from $k$-th category. On the other hand, when $\|\boldsymbol{c}_{[k]}^i\|_2$ is large, it implies that the data from the $k$-th category are likely to lie in the subspace spanned by $i$-th atom. Setting $W_{i,k}$ small would provide flexibility for the corresponding sparse coefficients, which improves the adaptivity of $i$-th atom to the underlying structures of data from the $k$-th category.

## 3.2   The Proposed Iterative Algorithm

It is nontrivial to solve the minimization (2). In this section an alternating iterative algorithm is proposed to separate the minimization into several simpler ones. The iteration stops until either of the following stopping criteria is satisfied: *(a)* the change of objective function is small enough; *(b)* the maximum iteration number has been reached. The learned dictionary and the obtained weight matrix are then used to code the test samples and the label prediction for each test sample is based on its corresponding class-specific representation residuals.

**Sparse Approximation.**   Given dictionary $D^{(t)}$ and the weight matrix $W^{(t)}$, the sparse coefficients $C = [C_{[1]}, \ldots, C_{[K]}]$ are calculated as follows:

$$
C^{(t+1)} = \underset{C}{\operatorname{argmin}} \sum_{k=1}^{K} \frac{1}{2} \| Y_{[k]} - DC_{[k]} \|_F^2 + \sum_{k=1}^{K} \lambda \| C_{[k]} \|_{w_k^{(t)};2,1}, \tag{4}
$$

which is separable and can be decomposed into $K$ independent subproblems:

$$
C_{[k]}^{(t+1)} = \underset{C}{\operatorname{argmin}} \| Y_{[k]} - DC \|_F^2 + \lambda \| C \|_{w_k^{(t)};2,1}, \quad \forall k. \tag{5}
$$

The reweighted $\ell_{2,1}$ minimization (5) is solved via the accelerated proximal gradient algorithm [23].

**Dictionary Update.**   Given the sparse codes $C^{(t+1)}$, the dictionary $D$ is updated as follows:

$$
D^{(t+1)} = \underset{D \in \mathcal{X}}{\operatorname{argmin}} \frac{1}{2} \| Y - DC^{(t+1)} \|_F^2, \tag{6}
$$

where $D^{(t+1)} = [d_1^{(t+1)}, \cdots, d_m^{(t+1)}]$ is updated atom by atom via the projected gradient descent [16]; see [3] for the details.

**Weight Refinement.**   Given the sparse codes $C^{(t+1)}$, based on the discussion in Sec. 3.1, we can calculate the weights as follows,

$$
W_{i,k} = \frac{1}{\| c_{[k]}^{i,(t+1)} \|_2 + \epsilon}, \quad \forall i, k, \tag{7}
$$

followed by a $\ell_1$ normalization on each weight vector corresponding to each category:

$$
w_k = \frac{\mu w_k}{\| w_k \|_1}, \quad \forall k, \tag{8}
$$

where $\mu$ is a constant implemented according to the dictionary size and $\epsilon$ is a sufficiently small positive parameter for stability.

### 3.3   Classification Process

Once the learning process is finished, for each category, we can construct a subset of atoms from the learned dictionary $D$ by measuring the joint sparse representations of related samples. Being associated with class-specific structured sparsity patterns, these subsets of atoms can be used for classifying test samples. For $k$-th category, the corresponding subset of atoms is defined as $D_{[k]} = \{d_i \mid \|c_{[k]}^i\|_2 > 0, 1 \leq i \leq m\}$. Then for each $k$, the sparse codes $c_{[k]}$ of a test signal $y$, is obtained by solving the following minimization:

$$c_{[k]} = \underset{c}{\operatorname{argmin}} \frac{1}{2}\|y - D_{[k]}c\|_2^2 + \alpha\|c\|_1, \tag{9}$$

where $\alpha$ is a parameter that balances the trade-off between sparsity and fidelity of the solution. The problem (9) is also solved by the accelerated proximal gradient algorithm [23]. Then $y$ is classified to be the class with the minimum prediction error:

$$\operatorname{identity}(y) = \underset{k}{\operatorname{argmin}} \frac{1}{2}\|y - D_{[k]}c_{[k]}\|_2^2 + \alpha\|c_{[k]}\|_1. \tag{10}$$

## 4   Experiment

The performance of the proposed method is demonstrated with several classification tasks, including face recognition, gender classification and scene classification. We compared our method with several state-of-the-art dictionary learning approaches, including Discriminative K-SVD (D-KSVD) [34], Label Consistent K-SVD (LC-KSVD) [11], Sparse Representation based Classifier (SRC) [27], Dictionary Learning with Structure Incoherence (DLSI) [22], dictionary learning with COmmonality and PARticularity (COPAR) [14], Joint Dictionary Learning (JDL) [36], Fisher Discrimination Dictionary Learning (FDDL) [31], Latent Dictionary Learning (LDL) [30]. Only the results available in the literature are reported.

To verify the effectiveness of the proposed reweighting scheme, a baseline method (denoted by Baseline) is implemented for comparison, which is based on the standard $\ell_{2,1}$ minimization. The training stage of the baseline method runs similarly to that of the proposed approach except all the weight are set to be the same constant. The classification stage of the baseline method is the same as which described in Section 3.3. The parameters of the baseline method are set to be the same as ours.

### 4.1   Implementation Details

**Parameter Setting.** There are five parameters in our approach, i.e., the dictionary size $m$, the regularization parameters $\lambda$ and $\alpha$, the reweighting parameters $\mu$ and $\epsilon$. In all the experiments, if no specific instructions mentioned, a five-fold cross validation scheme is used to find $\lambda$ and $\alpha$. To have a fair comparison, if no specific instructions mentioned, the dictionary sizes of all the compared methods mentioned above are set to be the same as [11,30]. Besides, the parameter $\mu$ is set equal to $m$ for simplicity and $\epsilon$ is set to be a small positive real number (for example $10^{-6}$).

**Initialization.** The initial dictionary $D^{(0)}$ is generated by sampling from training data. More precisely, we randomly select a certain number of samples from each category as the dictionary atoms. For the initialization of the weight matrix $W$, we set $W_{i,k}$ equal to 0.5 if the $i$-th initial atom is taken from the $k$-th category and 1 otherwise.

**Computational Time.** To demonstrate the scalability of our method, the proposed method is tested on two datasets of different sizes, the average training time and test time for Ext.YaleB of 504 dimension is 4s and 43s respectively, and for Scene-15 of dimension 3000 is 126s and 111s.

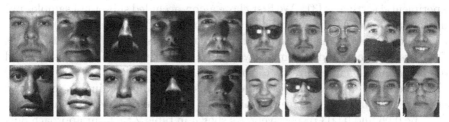

Samples of Ext. YaleB dataset                    Samples of AR face dataset

**Fig. 1.** Some sample images from dataset YaleB (left) and AR face (right)

## 4.2   Face Recognition

We demonstrate the effectiveness of our method in face recognition using the Extended YaleB dataset [8], which contains $2,414$ images of 38 human frontal faces under 64 illumination conditions and expressions. The original images were cropped to $192 \times 168$ pixels. As done in [34], each face image is projected into a 504-dimensional feature vector using a random matrix of zero-mean normal distribution. The dataset is randomly split into two halves. One half is used for training and the other half is used for testing. See Figure 1 for some examples.

The parameters used in this experiment are set as follows: $m = 570$, $\lambda = 0.01$ and $\alpha = 0.002$. We repeated the training and testing processes 10 times with different random splits of the training and testing samples to calculate the average recognition accuracies. The experimental results of all competing methods are summarized in Table 1. Note that the dictionary size of SRC is the same as the number of training samples, so we compare SRC with the same dictionary size as ours(denoted SRC*). It can be seen that our approach is competitive among all the compared methods. The proposed outperformed the baseline method and many state-of-the-art approaches except SRC. But note that the performance of the SRC method degrades dramatically when using dictionaries of the same size as ours.

**Table 1.** Recognition accuracies (%) of the compared methods on the Ext. YaleB dataset.

| KSVD [1] | SRC [27] | D-KSVD [34] | LC-KSVD [11] | LLC [26] | SRC* | Baseline | Our method |
|---|---|---|---|---|---|---|---|
| 93.10 | 97.20 | 94.10 | 95.00 | 90.70 | 80.50 | 84.63 | 94.52 |

## 4.3   Gender Classification

We conducted gender classification on the AR face database [20] with the same experimental setting as [31]. We first chose a non-occluded subset (14 samples per subject) from the AR face database, which consists of 50 males and 50 females, to conduct the experiments. Some sample images are shown in Figure 1. Images of the first 25 males and 25 females were used for testing. Each image is reduced to a 300-dimensional feature vector by PCA.

As there are only two classes and each class has enough training samples, we set the dictionary size relatively small ($m = 50$). The parameters $\lambda$ and $\alpha$ are set to be 0.06 and 0.003 respectively. As shown in table 2 that our approach outperformed all the tested methods excepted LDL [30]. Although the recognition accuracy of LDL is slightly better than ours, our approach use a dictionary with smaller size than LDL. Moreover, our method does not involve any discrimination term explicitly and thus has lower computational complexity than LDL.

**Table 2.** Classification accuracies (%) of the compared methods on the AR database.

| DLSI [22] | COPAR [14] | JDL [36] | FDDL [31] | LDL [30] | Baseline | Ours |
|---|---|---|---|---|---|---|
| 93.70 | 93.00 | 91.00 | 93.70 | 95.00 | 93.13 | 94.00 |

## 4.4   Scene Classification

Our method was applied to scene classification and evaluated on the Scene-15 dataset [15]. The Scene-15 dataset contains 15 scene categories, the number of images per category varies from 210 to 410, and the resolution of each image is about $250 \times 300$. See Figure 2 for the sample images per category from the dataset.

The 3000-dimensional SIFT-based spatial pyramid features [15] extracted from the images are used as the input of all the compared methods. Same as the standard experimental protocol used in [15], for each category 100 images are randomly picked up for training and the rest for testing. The parameters $m$, $\lambda$ and $\alpha$ are set to be 450, 0.05 and 0.003 respectively. Considering the randomness in the training and testing processes, we run all the experiments 10 times and report the average prediction accuracies. As shown in Table 3, our approach outperformed all the tested methods except FDDL [31], however the training and test time of FDDL is 20 times slower than ours.

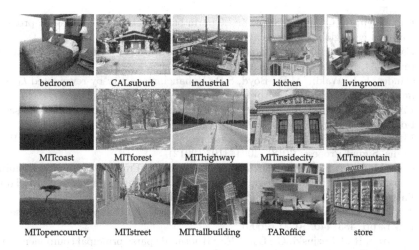

bedroom    CALsuburb    industrial    kitchen    livingroom

MITcoast    MITforest    MIThighway    MITinsidecity    MITmountain

MITopencountry    MITstreet    MITtallbuilding    PARoffice    store

**Fig. 2.** Example images from the Scene-15 dataset.

**Table 3.** Classification accuracies (%) on the Scene-15 dataset.

| LLC [26] | SRC [27] | KSVD [1] | D-KSVD [34] | LC-KSVD [11] | FDDL [31] | Baseline | Ours |
|----------|----------|----------|-------------|--------------|-----------|----------|------|
| 89.20    | 91.80    | 86.70    | 89.10       | 92.90        | 98.35     | 96.62    | 97.94 |

## 5  Summary

A novel dictionary learning approach for structured sparse coding is presented in this paper. Different from existing supervised dictionary learning methods, we proposed a reweighted $\ell_{2,1}$ minimization algorithm to exploit class-specific structured sparsity patterns for signals from each category, which brings benefits to dealing with multi-class classification problem. In the learning process, the dictionary is well adapted to the subspace of training data with a reweighting scheme, which strengthens its discriminability. An efficient alternating iterative scheme is developed to solve the proposed model. We applied our method to several classification tasks. The experimental results demonstrated the competitive performance of our method in comparison with some latest dictionary learning methods. In future, we would like to develop an effective algorithm to solve $\ell_{2,0}$ minimization problem together with the convergence analysis.

## References

1. Aharon, M., Elad, M., Bruckstein, A.: K-SVD: An algorithm for designing overcomplete dictionaries for sparse representation. IEEE Trans. Signal Process. **54**(11), 4311–4322 (2006)
2. Bach, F., Jenatton, R., Mairal, J., Obozinski, G., et al.: Structured sparsity through convex optimization. STAT SCI **27**(4), 450–468 (2012)

3. Bao, C., Ji, H., Quan, Y., Shen, Z.: L0 norm based dictionary learning by proximal methods with global convergence. In: CVPR, pp. 3858–3865. IEEE (2014)
4. Cai, X., Nie, F., Huang, H.: Exact top-k feature selection via $\ell_{2,0}$-norm constraint. In: IJCAI, pp. 1240–1246. AAAI Press (2013)
5. Candes, E.J., Wakin, M.B., Boyd, S.P.: Enhancing sparsity by reweighted $\ell_1$ minimization. J. Fourier Anal. Appl. **14**(5–6), 877–905 (2008)
6. Elhamifar, E., Vidal, R.: Robust classification using structured sparse representation. In: CVPR, pp. 1873–1879. IEEE (2011)
7. Elhamifar, E., Vidal, R.: Block-sparse recovery via convex optimization. IEEE Trans. Signal Process. **60**(8), 4094–4107 (2012)
8. Georghiades, A.S., Belhumeur, P.N., Kriegman, D.: From few to many: Illumination cone models for face recognition under variable lighting and pose. IEEE Trans. Pattern Anal. Mach. Intell. **23**(6), 643–660 (2001)
9. Jacob, L., Obozinski, G., Vert, J.-P.: Group lasso with overlap and graph lasso. In: ICML, pp. 433–440. ACM (2009)
10. Jenatton, R., Obozinski, G., Bach, F.: Structured sparse principal component analysis (2009). arXiv preprint arXiv:0909.1440
11. Jiang, Z., Lin, Z., Davis, L.: Label consistent K-SVD: Learning a discriminative dictionary for recognition. IEEE Trans. Pattern Anal. Mach. Intell. **35**(11), 2651–2664 (2013)
12. Kavukcuoglu, K., Ranzato, M., Fergus, R., LeCun, Y.: Learning invariant features through topographic filter maps. In: CVPR, pp. 1605–1612. IEEE (2009)
13. Kim, S., Xing, E.P.: Tree-guided group lasso for multi-task regression with structured sparsity. In: ICML, pp. 543–550 (2010)
14. Kong, S., Wang, D.: A dictionary learning approach for classification: separating the particularity and the commonality. In: Fitzgibbon, A., Lazebnik, S., Perona, P., Sato, Y., Schmid, C. (eds.) ECCV 2012, Part I. LNCS, vol. 7572, pp. 186–199. Springer, Heidelberg (2012)
15. Lazebnik, S., Schmid, C., Ponce, J.: Beyond bags of features: spatial pyramid matching for recognizing natural scene categories. In: CVPR, vol. 2, pp. 2169–2178. IEEE (2006)
16. Lin, C.-J.: Projected gradient methods for nonnegative matrix factorization. Neural computation **19**(10), 2756–2779 (2007)
17. Lu, C.-Y., Min, H., Gui, J., Zhu, L., Lei, Y.-K.: Face recognition via weighted sparse representation. Journal of Visual Communication and Image Representation **24**(2), 111–116 (2013)
18. Mairal, J., Bach, F., Ponce, J.: Task-driven dictionary learning. IEEE Trans. Pattern Anal. Mach. Intell. **34**(4), 791–804 (2012)
19. Majumdar, A., Ward, R.K.: Classification via group sparsity promoting regularization. In: ICASSP, pp. 861–864. IEEE (2009)
20. Martinez, A.M.: The AR face database. CVC Technical Report **24** (1998)
21. Nie, F., Huang, H., Cai, X., Ding, C.H.: Efficient and robust feature selection via joint l2,1-norms minimization. In: NIPS, pp. 1813–1821 (2010)
22. Ramirez, I., Sprechmann, P., Sapiro, G.: Classification and clustering via dictionary learning with structured incoherence and shared features. In: CVPR, pp. 3501–3508. IEEE (2010)
23. Shen, Z., Toh, K.-C., Yun, S.: An accelerated proximal gradient algorithm for frame-based image restoration via the balanced approach. SIAM J. Imaging Sci. **4**(2), 573–596 (2011)

24. Szlam, A., Gregor, K., LeCun, Y.: Fast approximations to structured sparse coding and applications to object classification. In: Fitzgibbon, A., Lazebnik, S., Perona, P., Sato, Y., Schmid, C. (eds.) ECCV 2012, Part V. LNCS, vol. 7576, pp. 200–213. Springer, Heidelberg (2012)
25. Tang, X., Feng, G., Cai, J.: Weighted group sparse representation for undersampled face recognition. Neurocomputing **145**, 402–415 (2014)
26. Wang, J., Yang, J., Yu, K., Lv, F., Huang, T., Gong, Y.: Locality-constrained linear coding for image classification. In: CVPR, pp. 3360–3367. IEEE (2010)
27. Wright, J., Yang, A.Y., Ganesh, A., Sastry, S.S., Ma, Y.: Robust face recognition via sparse representation. IEEE Trans. Pattern Anal. Mach. Intell. **31**(2), 210–227 (2009)
28. Xu, Y., Sun, Y., Quan, Y., Zheng, B.: Discriminative structured dictionary learning with hierarchical group sparsity. Comput. Vis. Image Underst. **136**, 59–68 (2015)
29. Yang, J., Yu, K., Gong, Y., Huang, T.: Linear spatial pyramid matching using sparse coding for image classification. In: CVPR, pp. 1794–1801. IEEE (2009)
30. Yang, M., Dai, D., Shen, L., Gool, L.V.: Latent dictionary learning for sparse representation based classification. In: CVPR, pp. 4138–4145. IEEE (2014)
31. Yang, M., Zhang, D., Feng, X.: Fisher discrimination dictionary learning for sparse representation. In: ICCV, pp. 543–550. IEEE (2011)
32. Yuan, M., Lin, Y.: Model selection and estimation in regression with grouped variables. J. R. Stat. Soc. Series B Stat. Methodol. **68**(1), 49–67 (2006)
33. Zelnik-Manor, L., Rosenblum, K., Eldar, Y.C.: Dictionary optimization for block-sparse representations. IEEE Trans. Signal Process. **60**(5), 2386–2395 (2012)
34. Zhang, Q., Li, B.: Discriminative K-SVD for dictionary learning in face recognition. In: CVPR, pp. 2691–2698. IEEE (2010)
35. Zhang, Y., Jiang, Z., Davis, L.S.: Learning structured low-rank representations for image classification. In: CVPR, pp. 676–683. IEEE (2013)
36. Zhou, N., Shen, Y., Peng, J., Fan, J.: Learning inter-related visual dictionary for object recognition. In: CVPR, pp. 3490–3497. IEEE (2012)

# Detail-Enhanced Cross-Modality Face Synthesis via Guided Image Filtering

Yunqi Dang, Feng Li, Zhaoxin Li, and Wangmeng Zuo[✉]

Computational Perception and Cognition Center, School of Computer Science and Technology,
Harbin Institute of Technology, Harbin 150001, China
dyqhitcs@126.com, {fengli_hit,cszli}@hotmail.com,
cswmzuo@gmail.com

**Abstract.** Face images in different modalities are often encountered in many applications, such as face image in photo and sketch style, visible light and near-infrared style. As an active yet challenging task, cross-modality face synthesis aims to transform face images between modalities. Many existing methods successfully recover global features for a given photo, however, fail to capture fine-scale details in the synthesis results. In this paper, we propose a two-step algorithm to tackle this problem. Firstly, KNN is used to select the $K$ most similar patches in training set for an input patch centered on each pixel. Then combination of patches is calculated for initial results. In the second step, guided image filtering is used on initial results with test photo as guidance. Fine-scale details can be transferred to the results via local linear transformation. Comparison experiments on public datasets demonstrated the proposed method is superior to the state-of-the-art method in simultaneously keeping global features and enhancing fine-scale details.

**Keywords:** Photo-sketch synthesis · Guided image filtering · KNN · Local linear transformation

## 1 Introduction

In many cases, we can obtain face image pairs of the same person in different modalities, such as face image in photo or sketch style, visible light (VIS) or near-infrared (NIR) style, etc. For example, since there are difficulties in obtaining photos of the criminal suspects, sketches of suspects are usually drawn by artists to hunt them. However, drawing face sketches is both time consuming and restricted by painting level of artists. Face images under NIR are on good condition and unaffected by visible lights in the environment. So, face recognition [1] using NIR images is contributive. Thus, automatic cross-modality face synthesis plays an important role in law enforcement. Besides, face sketch can also be applied to digital entertainment [2,3,4]. Studies on cross-modality face synthesis problem has been carried out for several years. And a number of algorithms had been proposed. Among these existing approaches, there are several representative ones. Linear subspace learning-based approaches [5,6,7] are based on the assumption that each output patch can be generated

© Springer-Verlag Berlin Heidelberg 2015
H. Zha et al. (Eds.): CCCV 2015, Part I, CCIS 546, pp. 200–209, 2015.
DOI: 10.1007/978-3-662-48558-3_20

by using a linear combination of the selected $K$ nearest neighbors. But the synthesis results tend to be over-smoothed and lose some details. Sparse representation-based method is also an important branch [8,9]. Image patches could be sparsely represented by an over-complete dictionary of atoms. Although it is effective to use sparse coding and dictionary learning to address this problem, it needs excessive time to learn the dictionary and mapping between dictionaries in different modalities.

In this paper, we propose a detail-enhanced approach for cross-modality face synthesis. Our method is composed of two steps. In the first step, we adopt KNN algorithm [10] to select the $K$ most similar patches in training dataset for input patch centered on each pixel of input photo. Then combination of the $K$ patches is calculated for generating the initial synthesis result. Second, we recover some fine-scale details of facial features on initial result by introducing guided image filtering [11]. Input test photo image is regarded as the guidance image, and initial synthesis result constructed by the KNN algorithm is input image. With the help of guidance image, we can keep global features while enhancing fine-scale details.

The remainder of this paper is organized as follows. In Section 2, we review the related work on cross-modality face synthesis, especially photo-sketch synthesis. Section 3 describes the proposed method, including the K-NN-based step and the guided image filtering-based step. Section 4 presents our experiments results. Finally, some conclusion remarks are presented in Section 5.

## 2    Related Work

In this section, we briefly review several work on recent cross-modality face synthesis. By far, most studies focused on face sketch synthesis, while NIR face synthesis received relatively less attention. The first kind of method is forward method. Tang et al. [5] presented a photo-to-sketch transformation method based on eigentransform by exploiting PCA. And their approach is based on the following assumption: the process of photo-to-sketch can be approximated as linear. However, this assumption is too strong because the mapping between photo and sketch may be nonlinear. Inspired by LLE (locally linear embedding), Liu et al.[12] proposed a nonlinear approach based on local linear preservation of geometry between photo and sketch and achieved better results.

Another kind of method is based on MRF [13], which characterizes the pixel-wise dependency and can generate smooth results. For example, Tang et al. [14] proposed a multi-scale MRF model for face photo-sketch synthesis and recognition. And they also applied face photo-sketch synthesis method to face recognition [15]. Zhou et al. [16] presented a weighted Markov random fields method to overcome the drawbacks that MRF-based method [14] cannot synthesize new sketch patches.

Besides, the sparse representation-based approaches also play an important role in accomplishing image reconstruction. A series of work for photo-sketch synthesis based on sparse representation have been proposed in [8], [17], and [18]. Yang et al. [17] proposed a two-step method based on sparse coding to address the problem of FSR (face super-resolution). Their model was then utilized by Chang et al. [8] for face photo-sketch synthesis. In [18], the multi-dictionary sparse representation model is used to generate details which is lack in the initial sketch by using LLE. While different from the above methods, Wang et al. [19] assumed that the two sparse representations are connected through a linear transformation rather than the same representations. The objective function was separated into three sub-problems: sparse coding for training samples, dictionary updating and linear transformation matrix updating.

For efficient implementation, Song et al. [20] proposed a real-time approach for face sketch synthesis, and the method can be extended to temporal domain. However, the experimental results also tend to lack of some detailed information.

# 3　　Cross-Modality Face Synthesis

In this section, we first present the KNN-based algorithm (baseline approach) and then propose an enhanced algorithm for face sketch synthesis. In [12], Liu et al. proposed a pseudo-sketch synthesis method based on the assumption that corresponding photo and sketch image patches are similar in geometrical structure. And in [20], Song et al. also utilized this model to their method. In order to address the problem of noisy sketch, they proposed a denoising approach called Spatial Sketch Denoising (SSD). However, the results are lack of some fine-scale details such as eyebrows, eyes, and nose. (see Fig. 1).

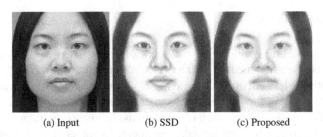

(a) Input　　　　　(b) SSD　　　　　(c) Proposed

**Fig. 1.** Cross-modality face synthesis results by using SSD method [20] and the proposed method. Comparing with our result, the result of SSD method lacks of some fine-scale details.

## 3.1　　K-NN-Based Algorithm

In the first step of the proposed method, KNN [12] is used for generating the initial sketch. The KNN-based method consists of two stages, namely KNN search and linear combination of the result patches. This method is selected as baseline.

First, the training face photo images and sketch images are both divided into patches for searching the $K$ most similar patches. Given a test face photo, we also divide it into patches. For an image patch centered at a pixel in test photo image, we collect $N$ patches around that patch from each training photo image. Then, its $K$ most similar patches can be searched from the corresponding $N$ sketch patches and the reconstruction coefficients of the linear mapping are calculated by using a conjugate gradient solver [21]. Second, a linear combination of the $K$ most similar sketch patches is used to generate the initial sketch image.

We denote the $\mathbf{T}_p$ as a patch centered at a pixel $p$ in the test photo and $\mathbf{S}_p$ as the estimated corresponding sketch patch. The linear combination of searched the $K$ most similar patches from training sketch patch is formulated as,

$$\mathbf{S}_p = \sum_{k=1}^{K} w_p^k \mathbf{I}_p^k, \tag{1}$$

where $\mathbf{I}_p^k$ is one of the $K$ most similar sketch image patches selected by using KNN search, and $w_p^k$ is the calculated coefficient. The KNN method is summarized in Algorithm-1.

---

**Algorithm-1.** KNN-based initial synthesis

**Input**: Training photo image $X$ and sketch image $Y$, test face photo
  $I$, patch size $s$, search radius $r$, number of candidates $K$
1. Divide $X$, $Y$ and $I$ into patches respectively
2. Search for the $K$ most similar patches
3. Calculate the linear coefficients $w_p^k$ in Eq. 1.
4. Get the initial sketch image $I'$ by Eq. 1.
**Output**: Initial sketch $I'$

---

### 3.2    Guided Image Filtering-Based Algorithm

The sketch image generated by using KNN-based synthesis is over-smoothed and lack of fine-scale details. To enhance more fine-scale details on the sketch images, in this section, we set sketch image generated by KNN-based synthesis as an initial sketch image, and introduce the guided image filtering to enhance the details based on the original gray-scale image as a guidance image.

**Guided Image Filtering.** Guided filtering proposed by He et al. [11] is an efficient image filtering method, whose output is based on local linear transform of guidance image. Guidance image can be the input image or another different image. With the help of guidance image, filtering output image can fully obtain details of the guidance image, meanwhile, keep overall characteristics of the input image. Guided image filtering is both effective and efficient in a flurry of applications, such as edge-aware smoothing, detail enhancement, etc.

Denote $I$ as the guidance image, $q$ as output. In [11], the filter output in pixel $i$ is represented by the following formula,

$$q_i = a_k I_i + b_k, \forall i \in \omega_k, \tag{2}$$

where $\omega_k$ is a window centered at the pixel $k$, and the $a_k$ and $b_k$ are the linear coefficients assumed to be constant in $\omega_k$. And a square window of radius $r$ is used. To calculate the linear coefficients $a_k$ and $b_k$, they define the mapping as the following,

$$q_i = p_i - n_i, \tag{3}$$

where $q_i$ is the output, $p_i$ is the input, and $n_i$ is noise. Therefore, a minimization function can be defined,

$$E(a_k, b_k) = \sum_{i \in \omega_k}((a_k I_i + b_k - p_i)^2 + \epsilon a_k^2), \tag{4}$$

where $\epsilon$ is the regularization parameter. The Equation (4) is the linear ridge regression model [22], and $a_k$ and $b_k$ can be calculated by,

$$a_k = \frac{\frac{1}{|\omega|}\sum_{i \in \omega_k} I_i p_i - \mu_k \overline{p_k}}{\sigma_k^2 + \epsilon}, \tag{5}$$

$$b_k = \overline{p_k} - a_k \mu_k, \tag{6}$$

where $\mu_k$ and $\sigma_k^2$ are the mean and variance of $I$ in the window $\omega_k$, $|\omega|$ is the number of pixels in $\omega_k$. For the reason that one pixel can be calculated repeatedly in all window which it is in, an average values of $q_i$ should be computed. So, the Equation (2) is reformulated as,

$$q_i = \frac{1}{|\omega|}\sum_{k|i \in \omega_k}(a_k I_i + b_k). \tag{7}$$

After computing $a_k$ and $b_k$ for all windows $w_k$, the linear function can be reformulated as,

$$q_i = \overline{a_i} I_i + \overline{b_i}, \tag{8}$$

where $\overline{a_i} = \frac{1}{|w|}\sum_{k \in w_i} a_k$ and $\overline{b_i} = \frac{1}{|w|}\sum_{k \in w_i} b_k$ are the average coefficients of all windows overlapping $i$.

---

**Algorithm-2.** Guided filter-based enhancement

**Input:** Initial sketch $I'$, test face photo $I$, window radius $r'$,
     regularization $\epsilon$

1. $mean_I = f_{mean}(I)$
   $mean_{I'} = f_{mean}(I')$
   $corr_I = f_{mean}(I.* I)$
   $corr_{II'} = f_{mean}(I.* I')$
2. $var_I = corr_I - mean_I.* mean_I$
   $cov_{II'} = corr_{II'} - mean_I.* mean_{I'}$
3. $a = cov_{II'}./(var_I + \epsilon)$
4. $b = mean_{I'} - a.* mean_I$
5. $mean_a = f_{mean}(a)$
   $mean_b = f_{mean}(b)$
6. $I'' = mean_a.* I + mean_b$

**Output:** Final sketch $I''$

---

**Enhancement with Guided Image Filtering.** To utilize its detail-enhancing capability, guided filtering is adopted to refine the output of KNN algorithm for the

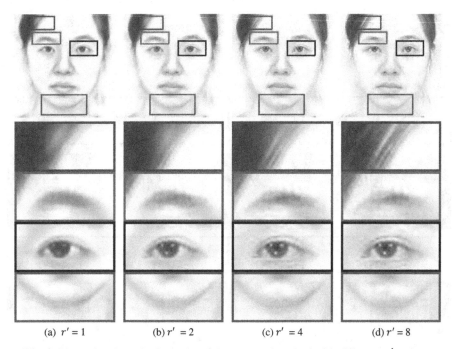

(a) $r' = 1$         (b) $r' = 2$         (c) $r' = 4$         (d) $r' = 8$

**Fig. 2.** Photo-sketch synthesis results of the proposed method with different $r'$ values.

synthesis of final face sketch image. More concretely, we at first obtain the initial sketch image estimate via KNN in Algorithm-1, then let $I$ denote the test face image as guidance image, we can utilize the Eq. (8) to filter the initial sketch. We summarize the proposed method in Algorithm-2, where $f_{mean}$ is a mean filter. The proposed approach involves two aspects: the KNN approach and the refinement algorithm using guided image filtering. It should be noted that our approach uses the test face photo as guidance for filtering, and the initial sketch generated by KNN as input of guided image filtering. While [20] selects generated initial sketch to guide the test face photo, this makes the results more similar with the face photo.

## 4    Experimental Results

In this section, we evaluate the proposed algorithms. The KNN algorithm [12] is set as the baseline. Firstly, different parameter settings are tested for evaluating our proposed approach. Then, we compare the results with the baseline algorithm, MRF method [14] and the SSD method [20] on the benchmark datasets. Further, we demonstrate that the proposed method can also be used in other applications such as VIS-NIR image synthesis, and the results are showed.

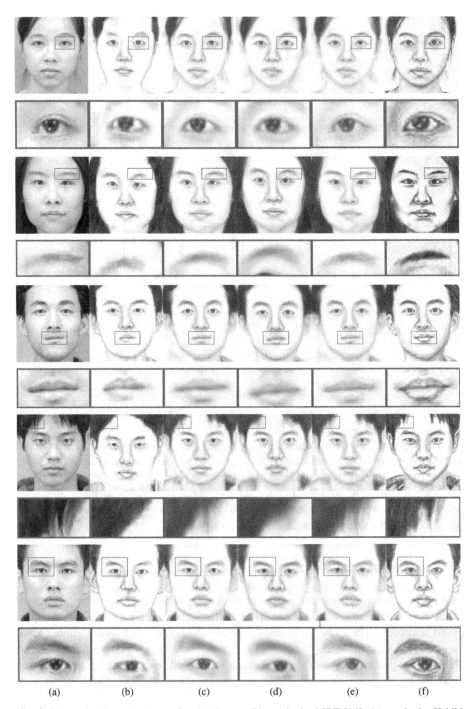

**Fig. 3.** Photo-sketch synthesis results. (a) photos; (b) results by MRF [14]; (c) results by K-NN search; (d) results by SSD [20]; (e) results by our method; (e) sketches drawn by artists.

## 4.1    Evaluation on the CUHK Benchmark Dataset

We evaluated our proposed algorithm on CUHK student dataset [14]. The dataset consists of 188 pairs of photo-sketch pair images, in which 88 pairs are used for training and the rest of images are used for testing. In our experiments, the search radius $r$ is set to be 8 pixels around each pixel. $K$, the number of candidate patches, is set to be 10 and the patch size $s$ is $5 \times 5$. The radius of window $r'$ is set to be 2, and the regularization parameter $\epsilon$ is set to 0.5 during processing of the guided image filtering. Our algorithm in experiments is coded in MATLAB and run on the computer with Intel(R) Xeon(R) CPU E3-1230 v3 @ 3.30GHz.

Fig. 2 shows synthesis results with different radius of window in guided image filtering. The larger the value of $r'$, the more details kept from the guidance image. However, if value of $r'$ is too big, synthesis results would be too similar with photo. In order to maintain sketch-style while retrieving some details, we adopt $r' = 2$ for guided image filtering in our following experiments. Fig. 3 shows the synthesis results and demonstrates that our method is better on enhancing fine-scale detail information compared with the KNN algorithms, MRF [14] and SSD method [20], e.g. hair, eyes, and other facial parts.

Further, we compared running time of the proposed method with the other two approaches. Among these methods, SSD is the most efficient method in generating sketches on good condition, which takes 4.97 seconds in average for synthesizing one sketch. The average runtime of MRF method is about 103.84 seconds. And for our method, the average running time is 57.46 seconds in KNN, and it is 0.007 seconds in the process of guided image filtering. Table 1 shows the comparison of three methods in runtime. It is worth noting that the algorithm of SSD is implemented with C++ and our program is unoptimized in MATLAB.

**Table 1.** Speed (*sec.*) comparison of three method

| Method | MRF | SSD | Proposed |
|--------|--------|------|----------|
| Time | 103.84 | 4.97 | 57.47 |

## 4.2    Visible-to-Near-Infrared Face Synthesis

Our model can also be used in other applications such as VIS-NIR face synthesis. The experiment was conducted on the CASIA NIR database [1] which contains 400 pairs of faces. 280 pairs are used for training and others are used for testing. Each pairs of faces has one face photo image and one corresponding NIR image. In this experiment, we set the search radius $r$ to 8 pixels around each pixel, the number of candidates $K$ is 10 and the patch size $s$ is $5 \times 5$ for baseline method. The radius of window $r'$ is set to be 5, and the regularization parameter $\epsilon$ is 0.5 for guided image filtering. Synthesis results are shown in Fig. 4. From the experimental results, we can see that our method can effectively address the problem of losing details and has much less artifacts than the baseline.

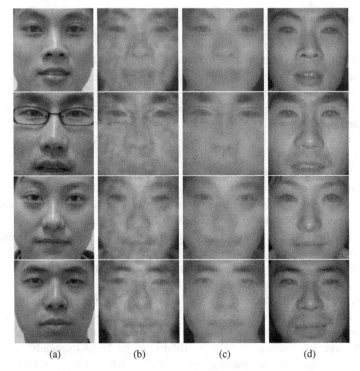

(a)          (b)          (c)          (d)

**Fig. 4.** VIS to NIR face synthesis results. (a) visible lights photos; (b) initial results using baseline method; (c)results by the proposed method; (d) ground truth.

## 5     Conclusions

In this paper, we propose a detail-enhanced cross-modality face synthesis approach. In order to solve the over-smoothed problem of face synthesis, we proposed a two-step algorithm which composes of a KNN-based method for initialization and the guided image filtering-based method for further refinement. In particular, guided image filtering-based method can enhance fine-scale details from initial synthesis results of KNN algorithm. Experimental results validate the superiority of our method comparing with the state-of-the-art on face sketch synthesis. Moreover, our proposed method can also be applied to VIS-NIR face synthesis.

## References

1. Li, S.Z., Chu, R., Liao, S., Zhang, L.: Illumination invariant face recognition using near-infrared images. IEEE Transactions on Pattern Analysis and Machine Intelligence **29**(4), 627–639 (2007)
2. Salisbury, M.P., Anderson, S.E., Barzel, R., Salesin, D.H.: Interactive pen-and-ink illustration. In: 21st annual conference on Computer graphics and interactive techniques, pp. 101–108. ACM, New York (1994)

3. Salisbury, M.P., Wong, M.T., Hughes, J.F., Salesin, D.H.: Orientable textures for image-based pen-and-ink illustration. In: 24th annual conference on Computer graphics and Interactive Techniques, pp. 401–406. ACM Press/Addison-Wesley Publishing Co, New York (1997)

4. Chen, H., Zheng, N.N., Liang, L., Li, Y., Xu, Y. Q., Shum, H.Y.: PicToon: a personalized image-based cartoon system. In: tenth ACM international conference on Multimedia, pp. 171–178. ACM, New York (2002)

5. Tang, X., Wang, X.: Face sketch recognition. IEEE Transactions on Circuits and Systems for Video Technology 14(1), 50–57 (2004)

6. Tang, X., Wang, X.: Face photo recognition using sketch. In: Proceedings of the 2002 International Conference on Image Processing, vol. 1, pp. I-257–I-260. IEEE (2002)

7. Tang, X., Wang, X.: Face sketch synthesis and recognition. In: Ninth IEEE International Conference on Computer Vision, pp. 687–694. IEEE (2003)

8. Chang, L., Zhou, M., Han, Y., Deng, X.: Face sketch synthesis via sparse representation. In: 20th International Conference on Pattern Recognition (ICPR), pp. 2146–2149. IEEE (2010)

9. Gao, X., Wang, N., Tao, D., Li, X.: Face sketch–photo synthesis and retrieval using sparse representation. IEEE Transactions on Circuits and Systems for Video Technology 22(8), 1213–1226 (2012)

10. Altman, N.S.: An introduction to kernel and nearest-neighbor nonparametric regression. The American Statistician 46(3), 175–185 (1992)

11. He, K., Sun, J., Tang, X.: Guided image filtering. IEEE Transactions on Pattern Analysis and Machine Intelligence 35(6), 1397–1409 (2013)

12. Liu, Q., Tang, X., Jin, H., Lu, H., Ma, S.: A nonlinear approach for face sketch synthesis and recognition. In: IEEE Computer Society Conference on Computer Vision and Pattern Recognition (CVPR), vol. 1, pp. 1005–1010. IEEE (2005)

13. Li, S.Z.: Markov random field modeling in image analysis. Springer, Berlin (2010)

14. Wang, X., Tang, X.: Face photo-sketch synthesis and recognition. IEEE Transactions on Pattern Analysis and Machine Intelligence 31(11), 1955–1967 (2009)

15. Wang, X., Tang, X.: Random sampling for subspace face recognition. International Journal of Computer Vision 70(1), 91–104 (2006)

16. Zhou, H., Kuang, Z., Wong, K.Y.: Markov weight fields for face sketch synthesis. In: IEEE Conference on Computer Vision and Pattern Recognition (CVPR), pp. 1091–1097. IEEE (2012)

17. Yang, J., Tang, H., Ma, Y., Huang, T.: Face hallucination via sparse coding. In: 15th IEEE International Conference on Image Processing (ICIP), pp. 1264–1267. IEEE (2008)

18. Wang, N., Gao, X., Tao, D., Li, X.: Face sketch-photo synthesis under multi-dictionary sparse representation framework. In: Sixth International Conference on Image and Graphics (ICIG), pp. 82–87. IEEE (2011)

19. Wang, S., Zhang, D., Liang, Y., Pan, Q.: Semi-coupled dictionary learning with applications to image super-resolution and photo-sketch synthesis. In: IEEE Conference on Computer Vision and Pattern Recognition (CVPR), pp. 2216–2223. IEEE (2012)

20. Song, Y., Bao, L., Yang, Q., Yang, M.-H.: Real-time exemplar-based face sketch synthesis. In: Fleet, D., Pajdla, T., Schiele, B., Tuytelaars, T. (eds.) ECCV 2014, Part VI. LNCS, vol. 8694, pp. 800–813. Springer, Heidelberg (2014)

21. Paige, C.C., Saunders, M.A.: LSQR: An algorithm for sparse linear equations and sparse least squares. ACM Transactions on Mathematical Software (TOMS) 8(1), 43–71 (1982)

22. Draper, N.R., Smith, H., Pownell, E.: Applied regression analysis. Wiley, New York (1966)

# Edge-Directed Single Image Super-Resolution via Cross-Resolution Sharpening Function Learning

Wei Han[1,2], Jun Chu[1,2]([✉]), Lingfeng Wang[3], and Chunhong Pan[3]

[1] Institute of Computer Vision, Nanchang Hangkong University, Nanchang, China
[2] Key Laboratory of Jiangxi Province for Image Processing
and Pattern Recongnition, Nanchang, China
chuj@nchu.edu.cn
[3] NLPR, Institute of Automation, Chinese Academy of Sciences, Beijing, China

**Abstract.** Edge-directed single image super-resolution methods have been paid more attentions due to their sharp edge preserving in the recovered high-resolution image. Their core is the high-resolution gradient estimation. In this paper, we propose a novel cross-resolution gradient sharpening function learning to obtain the high-resolution gradient. The main idea of **cross-resolution learning** is to learn a sharpening function from low-resolution, and use it in high-resolution. Specifically, a blurred low-resolution image is first constructed by performing bicubic down-sampling and up-sampling operations sequentially. The gradient sharpening function considered as a linear transform is learned from blurred low-resolution gradient to the input low-resolution image gradient. After that, the high-resolution gradient is estimated by applying the learned gradient sharpening function to the initial blurred gradient obtained from the bicubic up-sampled of the low-resolution image. Finally, edge-directed single image super-resolution reconstruction is performed to obtain the sharpened high-resolution image. Extensive experiments demonstrate the effectiveness of our method in comparison with the state-of-the-art approaches.

**Keywords:** Super-resolution · Gradient magnitude transformation · Linear transformation function

## 1 Introduction

Single image super-resolution is to estimate a high-resolution image from a given low-resolution image, and it can be used for various computer vision applications. The classical methods, such as interpolation based methods, often produce undesired artifacts in the high-resolution image, especially along the salient edges. To preserve local sharp edge structures in the recovered high-resolution image, in

J. Chu—This work was supported in part by the National Natural Science Foundation of China (Grant Nos. 61263046, 61403376 and 61175025).

H. Zha et al. (Eds.): CCCV 2015, Part I, CCIS 546, pp. 210–219, 2015.
DOI: 10.1007/978-3-662-48558-3_21

this paper, we propose a new cross-resolution sharpening method. In the following, we first briefly review the related work.

The single image super-resolution that related to our work can be mainly divided into two categories[1], i.e., learning based methods and reconstruction based methods (including edge-directed methods).

The learning based super-resolution methods [1–5] want to learn the corresponding relationship between low-resolution and high-resolution images from a training set. After that, they apply it to other low-resolution images for reconstructing the high-resolution images. These methods are based on offline training set, therefore, the training sample selection may affect the high-solution image reconstruction, and the computational cost of these methods may not be cheap. In [5], the correspondence between low-resolution and high-resolution patches is learned from the scale (resolution) space of the input image. The core idea is to use the cross-resolution similarity to reconstruct the high-resolution image. Motivated by this idea, in our method, the sharpening function is also learned by utilization of the cross-resolution similarity.

The reconstruction based super-resolution methods [6–17] recover the high-resolution image from low-resolution image by considering a reconstruction constraint. In [6–8], they consider the relationship between low-resolution and high-resolution image, and think that the down-sampling image of high-resolution should be close to the low-resolution image. However, it can take some undesired artifacts along salient edges. Compared with the above methods, in [9–16], their methods recover the high-resolution image from low-resolution image by enforcing gradient profile prior, and the enforced edge knowledge has the ability to produce sharp edges better. Especially in [10] and [12], their methods are the scaling sharpening and self-interpolation sharpening, and work well on points of edges. However, in [10], the corresponding point extraction may be prone to error, which further influences the final results. Following these methods, we also want to produce sharp edges in the recovered high-resolution image.

Motivated by Sun et al. [10] and Wang et al. [12], we propose a novel cross-resolution gradient sharpening function learning method to restore a high-resolution image. The main process is summarized in Fig. 1. Our main idea is to learn a sharpening function from low-resolution, and use it in high-resolution. The main contributions are highlighted as follows:

– Our cross-resolution gradient sharpening function learning method makes the transformation relationship, which is learnt from the low-resolution image, applied to super-resolution reconstruction directly. This method uses the similarity between different scales on the image itself (this self-similarity has been successfully applied to learning based methods for super-resolution). The advantage of the similarity is to avoid the offline training process, therefore, it can disaffiliate the dependence on an offline database.

---

[1] Note that, the interpolation based methods can also be regarded as single image super-resolution method. However, they are not very related to our work, thereby, we do not review them in detail in this paper.

– Our method, unlike the edge directed methods proposed by Sun, never needs to find the points on the edges and the corresponding relationship. First, we have advantages on running time, because we reduce the step of finding the edge points and their corresponding relationship. Second, our method can avoid the risk of error location of edge points in high-resolution image recovering.

The remainder of this paper is organized as follows. We introduce an edge-directed single-image super-resolution framework in Section 2. We indicate that the main difference from edge-directed super-resolution methods is in the estimation on the sharp gradient (or gradient magnitude). The cross-resolution gradient sharpening method is presented in Section 3. The implementation details of the proposed super-resolution algorithm are listed in Section 4. The experimental results are presented in Section 5. Finally, conclusion and future work are given in Section 6.

## 2    Edge-Directed Single-Image Super-Resolution

In edge-directed single image super-resolution framework, the high-resolution image $I_h$ is recovered from the input low-resolution image $I_l$ and the estimated high-resolution gradient $\widehat{\nabla I_h}$:

$$
\begin{aligned}
I_h^* &= \arg\min_{I_h} E(I_h|I_l, \widehat{\nabla I_h}) \\
&= \arg\min_{I_h} \|[I_h \otimes g]_{\downarrow(\beta)} - I_l\|_2^2 + \alpha \|\nabla I_h - \widehat{\nabla I_h}\|_2^2,
\end{aligned}
\tag{1}
$$

where $\otimes$ is the convolution operation with the blurry kernel $g$, $[\cdot]_{\downarrow(\beta)}$ is the down-sampling operation with factor $\beta$. The core behind the edge-directed single image super-resolution is the estimation of the high-resolution gradient $\widehat{\nabla I_h}$.

As presented in [12], the high-resolution gradient $\widehat{\nabla I_h}$ can be estimated uniformly by transforming the blurred gradient $\nabla I_h^u$, given by

$$
\widehat{\nabla I_h} = \text{Tran}(\nabla I_h^u),
\tag{2}
$$

where Tran(.) is a transformation function, and $I_h^u$ is the bicubic up-sampled high-resolution image. As discussed in [12], the transformation function proposed in [10] is the scaling function, which is offline learned from an image dataset.

The method of Sun et al. [10] is the scaling sharpening. They obtain a corresponding relationship between an up-sample image and a high-resolution image by offline training some samples, and use the corresponding relationship to reconstruct the high-resolution image. But this method requires to train in advance. Moreover, the corresponding point extraction may be prone to error, which can influence the final results.

In practical application, the gradient direction changes a little under the variation of scales. Hence, we only consider the gradient magnitudes, and Eqn. (2) is simplified as (please refer to [12] for details)

$$
\widehat{G_h} = \text{Tran}(G_h^u),
\tag{3}
$$

where $\widehat{G_h}$ and $G_h^u$ are the gradient magnitudes of $\widehat{\nabla I_h}$ and $\nabla I_h^u$, respectively. The finally sharpened gradient field $\widehat{\nabla I_h}$ is obtained by

$$\widehat{\nabla I_h} = \widehat{G_h} \cdot \theta_h^u . \tag{4}$$

where $\theta_h^u$ is the gradient direction of $\nabla I_h^u$. In the following, we only consider the sharpening process of the gradient magnitudes $G_h$.

# 3    Cross-Resolution Gradient Magnitude Sharpening

To estimate a sharp high-resolution image $I_h$, our objective is in conformity with Sun's. However, our method considers the corresponding relationship of all points in different scales on the high-resolution image $I_h$ and the low-resolution image $I_l$ rather than offline training some samples, and uses the corresponding relationship to reconstruct the high-resolution image. Specifically, we want to learn the linear transformation function $T_l$ on low-resolution, and then apply it on the high-resolution. We name it as cross-resolution sharpening function learning.

As shown in Fig. 1, we have the low-resolution gradient magnitude in Fig. 1(a), and want to reconstruct the high-resolution gradient magnitude in Fig. 1(e). The up-sampled gradient magnitude in Fig. 1(d) is used to estimate the high-resolution gradient magnitude in Fig. 1(e). In this process, we need to know the corresponding relationship $T_h$ between the up-sampled gradient magnitude and the high-resolution gradient magnitude. Therefore, how to estimate the $T_h$ is the key for high-resolution gradient magnitude reconstruction.

In our method, we first down-sample the low-resolution gradient magnitude $G_l$ (see Fig. 1(a)) to $G_{ll}$ (see Fig. 1(b)), and up-sample the gradient magnitude $G_{ll}$ to $G_l^u$ (see Fig. 1(c)). Here, we assume that the gradient magnitude transformation (the details about transformation will be described in the following subsection) from $G_l^u$ to $G_l$ is similar to the gradient magnitude transformation from $G_h^u$ to $\widehat{G_h}$. That is, the transformation $T_l$ is assumed to be similar to the transformation $T_h$.

Hence, we first calculate the linear transformation coefficient $T_l$ from the low-resolution gradient magnitude. Then, we obtain $T_h$ from $T_l$. Meanwhile, the high-resolution gradient is obtained by applying $T_h$ to the gradient magnitude shown in Fig. 1(d). In the following, we describe each step in detail.

## 3.1    Construction of $T_l$

The blurred low-resolution image is obtained by performing down-sampling and up-sampling operations sequentially, given by

$$I_l^u = [[I_l]_{\downarrow(\beta)}]_{\uparrow(\beta)}, \tag{5}$$

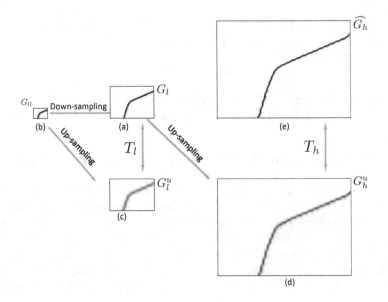

**Fig. 1.** Example of gradient magnitude sharpening with up-sampling scale factor of 3. (a) Input low-resolution gradient magnitude. (b) Bicubic down-sampled version of (a). (c) Bicubic up-sampled version of (b). (d) Bicubic up-sampled version of (a). (e) Output high-resolution one. $T_l$ and $T_h$ are the linear transformation functions.

and the gradient magnitude of a blurred low-resolution image $I_l^u$ is $G_l^u$. The low-resolution sharpening function is defined as a linear transformation function, given by

$$G_l = T_l \odot G_l^u \qquad (6)$$

where $G_l$ is the gradient magnitude of the input low-resolution image $I_l$, and $T_l$ is the low-resolution sharpening parameter with the same size of the input low-resolution image. The operation $\odot$ is the element-wise multiplication operation, satisfying that $(G_l)_{ij} = (T_l)_{ij}(G_l^u)_{ij}$, in which $()_{ij}$ is the $ij$-th element of the image. In this work, the parameter $T_l$ can be obtained by

$$T_l = G_l \oslash (G_l^u + \eta) \qquad (7)$$

where $\oslash$ is element-wise dividing operation, and $\eta = 10^{-4}$ is a small positive value to prevent dividing zero.

## 3.2 High-Resolution Gradient Construction

The purpose of $T_h$ is to make blurred high-resolution gradient sharp. Hence, it can be obtained from low-resolution sharpening function $T_l$. In this work, the high-resolution gradient sharpening function is constructed by up-sampling the low-resolution sharpening function $T_l$ directly, given by

$$T_h = [T_l]_{\uparrow(\beta)}. \qquad (8)$$

After $T_h$ is obtained, the high-resolution gradient magnitude $\widehat{G_h}$ is calculated by

$$\widehat{G_h} = T_h \odot G_h^u \qquad (9)$$

where $G_h^u$ is the gradient magnitudes of the up-sampled image $I_h^u$. Combining $\widehat{G_h}$ with the gradient direction $\theta_h^u$, we obtain the high-resolution gradient $\widehat{\nabla I_h}$ by Eqn. (4).

## 4    Implementation

The proposed super-resolution algorithm is listed as follow:

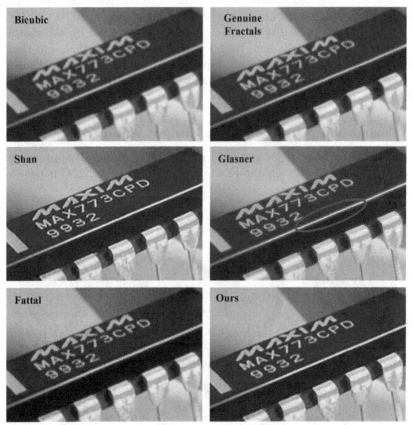

**Fig. 2.** Comparisons with the state-of-the-art approaches. All the results of high-resolution image experiments are obtained by the Bicubic, the commercial product Genuine Fractals, Shan [17], Glasner [5], Fattal [16] and ours.

**Step_1:** Initialing the high-resolution image $I_h^{init}$.

**Step_2:** Constructing the high-resolution gradient by four sub-steps.

    **2.1:** Calculating the low-resolution sharpening function $T_l$ by Eqn. (7).

    **2.2:** Calculating the high-resolution sharpening function $T_h$ by Eqn. (8).

    **2.3:** Calculating the high-resolution gradient magnitude $\widehat{G_h}$ by Eqn. (9).

    **2.4:** Calculating the high-resolution gradient $\widehat{\nabla I_h}$ by Eqn. (4).

**Step_3:** Obtaining the high-resolution gradient $I_h^\star$ by optimizing Eqn. (1).

It is worth noting that the initial high-resolution image $I_h^{init}$ and the optimization of Eqn. (1) are the same as the method of Wang [12].

## 5    Experiments and Analysis

In this section, we use extensive experiments to evaluate our method. First, we make comparisons of our method with several state-of-the-art methods. Then, representative methods from two categories, namely edge-directed reconstruction based and large-scale based, are evaluated to compare with ours. In our experiments, for each color image, we first transform it from RGB to YIQ. We only consider the Y (intensity) channel, which is up-sampled by our algorithm. The I and Q chromatic channels have low-frequency information, and they are interpolated by the bicubic method. Finally, we combine the three channels to form the high-resolution image. The visual comparisons are used to evaluate our method.

### 5.1    Comparisons with the State-of-the-Art Approaches

The visual comparisons of our method with four state-of-the-art approaches and one commercial product Genuine Fractals are shown in Fig. 2. Our results are

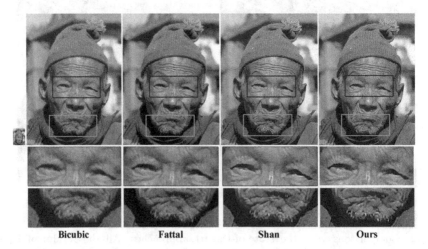

|  Bicubic  |  Fattal  |  Shan  |  Ours  |

**Fig. 3.** Comparison on Large-scale factor (X8). From left to right are the results of bicubic, Fattal [16], Shan [17] and ours. The second and third row are the local details for each method.

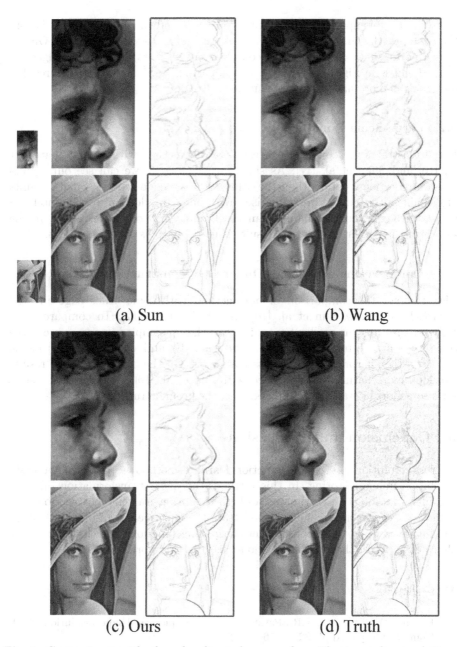

(a) Sun        (b) Wang

(c) Ours        (d) Truth

**Fig. 4.** Comparisons with the edge-directed approaches. The input low-resolution image are the small image in the left. The resluts of Sun [10] (a), Wang [12] (b), Ours (c) and the ground truth (d). We also present the gradient magnitude of the up-sampled images.

more sharp in comparison with Genuine Fractals and the bicubic interpolation. For example, the numbers and letters look very fuzzy, as shown in Fig. 2. On the edge aspects, the results of Glasner contain small artifacts along salient edges(see the red ellipse in Fig. 2). Moreover, in comparison to Shan and Fattal's results, our result is more natural, as we can see in Fig. 2.

### 5.2   Large-Scale Comparison

Fig. 3 illustrates the comparative results of our method with bicubic, Fattal et al. [16] and Shan et al. [17]. As shown in the Fig. 3, we can see our results contain more local details than the others. On the edge aspects, Shan's results are significantly blurred in comparison with ours. In addition, our method can generate sharper edges reliably than the Bicubic method, for example, in the aspect of the corner of eyes, our results is more sharp as shown in Fig. 3.

### 5.3   Comparisons with Edge-Directed Reconstruction Method

Fig. 4 shows the comparison of our method with some other edge-directed approaches, namely, Sun et al. [10] and Wang et al. [12]. To compare more fully, we also present gradient magnitude of the up-sampled images. we can see our results are better than those of Sun et al. [10] and Wang et al. [12] in the aspect of the sharpness along the salient edges. On the other hand, our results can look more natural, as compared with Sun et al. [10]. However, our results miss some local details, as compared with the ground truth.

## 6   Conclusion and Discussion

A cross-resolution sharpening function learning method is proposed for high-resolution image restoring. In this method, the linear transformation function on different resolution is estimated for high-resolution gradient construction. The extensive experimental results demonstrate the effectiveness of our method. In the future, we plan to propose other sharpening functions, which can preserve sharp edge better than the linear model used in this work.

## References

1. Freeman, W.T., Jones, T.R., Pasztor, E.C.: Example-based superresolution. IEEE Comput. Graph. Appl. **22**(2), 56–65 (2002)
2. Kim, K., Kwon, Y.: Example-based learning for singleimage SR and JPEG artifact removal, Max Planck'Insitut fur biologische Kybernetik, Tbingen, Germany Tech. Rep. 173 (2008)
3. Yang, J., Wright, J., Ma, Y., Huang, T.: Image super-resolution as sparse representation of raw image patches. In: Proc. IEEE Conf. Comput. Vision Pattern Recognit., pp. 1–8, June 2008

4. Chang, H., Yeung, D.-Y., Xiong, Y.: Super-resolution through neighbor embedding. In: Proc. IEEE Conf. Comput. Vision Pattern Recognit., June–July 2004, pp. 275–282 (2004)
5. Glasner, D., Bagon, S., Irani, M.: Super-resolution from a single image. In: International Conference on Computer Vision, pp. 349–356 (2009)
6. Irani, M., Peleg, S.: Motion analysis for image enhancement: Resolution, occlusion and transparency. J. Visual Commun. Image Representation 4(4), 324–335 (1993)
7. Baker, S., Kanade, T.: Limits on super-resolution and how to break them. IEEE Trans. Pattern Anal. Mach. Intell. 24(9), 1167–1183 (2002)
8. Lin, Z., Shum, H.-Y.: Fundamental limits of reconstruction-based superresolution algorithms under local translation. IEEE Trans. Pattern Anal. Mach. Intell. 26(1), 83–97 (2004)
9. Tai, Y.-W., Liu, S., Brown, M.S., Lin, S.: Super resolution using edge prior and single image detail synthesis. In: Proc. IEEE Conf. Comput. Vision Pattern Recognit., June 2010, pp. 2400–2407 (2010)
10. Sun, J., Xu, Z., Shum, H.-Y.: Image super-resolution using gradient profile prior. In: Proc. IEEE Conf. Comput. Vision Pattern Recognit., pp. 1–8 (2008)
11. Sun, J., Xu, Z., Shum, H.-Y.: Gradient profile prior and its applications in image super-resolution and enhancement. IEEE Trans. Image Process. 20(6), 1529–1542 (2011)
12. Wang, L.F., Xiang, S.M., Meng, G.F., Wu, H.Y., Pan, C.H.: Edge-Directed Single-Image Super-Resolution Via Adaptive Gradient Magnitude Self-Interpolation. IEEE Trans. Circuits and Systems for Video Technology 23(8), 1289–1299 (2013)
13. Fattal, R.: Image upsampling via imposed edge statistics. ACM Trans. Graph. 26(3), 95:1–95:8 (2007)
14. Dai, S., Han, M., Xu, W., Wu, Y., Gong, Y.: Soft edge smoothness prior for alpha channel super resolution. In: Proc. IEEE Conf. Comput. Vision Pattern Recognit., June 2007, pp. 1–8 (2007)
15. Morse, B.S., Schwartzwald, D.: Image magnification using level set reconstruction. In: Proc. IEEE Conf. Comput. Vision Pattern Recognit., December 2001, pp. 333–340 (2001)
16. Fattal, R.: Image upsampling via imposed edge statistics. ACM Transactions on Graphics 26(3), 95:1–95:8 (2007). (Proceedings of SIGGRAPH 2007)
17. Shan, Q., Li, Z., Jia, J., Tang, C.-K.: Fast image/video upsampling. ACM Transactions on Graphics 27(7), 153:1–153:7 (2008). (SIGGRAPH ASIA)

# Compressive Tracking Based on Particle Filter

Yun Gao, Hao Zhou, Guowu Yuan, and Xuejie Zhang[✉]

School of Information Science and Engineering, Yunnan University, Kunming, China
xjzhang@ynu.edu.cn

**Abstract.** Robust object tracking has been a challenging issue due to pose variation, illumination change, abrupt motion, background clutter, and etc.. Compressive sensing theory provided a new and effective way for real-time object tracking. In this paper, a compressive tracking method based on Particle Filter (PFCT) was proposed. The candidate objects were predicted based on Particle Filter. The sparse random Gaussian matrix was as the measurement matrix. The element number of a measurement vector was set as a special value, which was different for each video sequence. The proposed PFCT method ran in real-time and outperformed FCT on many challenging video sequences in terms of efficiency, accuracy and robustness.

**Keywords:** Object tracking · Compressive sensing · Measurement vector · Particle filter

## 1 Introduction

Robust visual object tracking has been one of the challenging tasks in the field of computer vision due to many factors such as pose variation, illumination change, abrupt motion, background clutter, and etc. For these challenging factors, the multi-feature fusion could improve the tracking stability [1]. However, more features led to the increase of computing complexity, not satisfying the requirement of the real-time tracking. Here the compressive sensing (CS) theory [2-3] stated that an original high-dimensional sparse or compressible signal can be reconstructed from a low-dimensional signal, whose dimension was far less than the number of Nyquist sampling. The CS theory came to fit in as a new and effective way for the stable and real-time tracking [1]. And the visual object tracking based on CS has received a lot of attentions [4-9]. In the field of computer vision, reference [4] first imported CS to the face recognition, where the face recognition was regarded as the classification based on the sparse vectors, and where it was shown that sparse representation was effective for face recognition. Then based on [4], reference [5] first imported the sparse representation to the field of visual object tracking. For a tracked or candidate object, the sparse representation based on the over-completed dictionary was achieved by solving the $l_1$ regularized least squares. Reference [6] reduced the feature dimension in [5] based on a sparse random Gaussian matrix of CS. Though the feature dimensions were reduced based on CS in these references, the complex sparse decomposition still affected the real-time of these tracking methods. Reference [7] decreased the dimension of Haar-like feature vectors based on a

© Springer-Verlag Berlin Heidelberg 2015
H. Zha et al. (Eds.): CCCV 2015, Part I, CCIS 546, pp. 220–229, 2015.
DOI: 10.1007/978-3-662-48558-3_22

sparse random Gaussian matrix. And the object was distinguished in the compressed domain based on a simple naive Bayes classifier, avoiding the complex sparse decomposition. The method not only enhanced the stability of the tracking, but ensured that the tracking was undertaken in real-time. Reference [8] further improved the tracking stability via an oversaturated sub-region classifier at the cost of victimizing the real-time of [7]. Reference [9] improved the real-time of [7] by a coarse-to-fine searching strategy. Reference [10] used a widely adopted particle filter framework [11] and a modified naive Bayes classifier for improving the tracking performance of [7]. These methods did show that it was an effective means for improving the real-time to distinguish the tracked object in the compressed domain. Nevertheless, it is still worth while studying the object tracking based on CS.

Three compressive tracking methods [7-9] reached the real-time tracking, however it was still time consuming for the strategy of searching candidates in a traversal style. References [7-10] used a similar measurement matrix with the fixed number of measurement elements, which was not always adapted to any video sequence. Reference [12] has shown that there is an adaptive measurement number for a different sequence. Inspired by [7-12], we proposed a compressive tracking based on Particle Filter (PFCT). In the proposed method, the candidate objects are predicted based on Particle Filter. The sparse random Gaussian matrix is as the measurement matrix. The element number of a measurement vector is set as a less value than that of [7-10]. The less value is different for each video sequence, which can result in a higher success rate. The rest of this paper is organized as follows. In Section 2, the related work about [9] is briefly introduced and the motivation of this paper is given. In Section 3, the proposed PFCT is indicated. Experiments in Section 4 show the performance of our proposed PFCT on challenging sequences, and Section 5 concludes this paper.

## 2    Fast Compressive Tracking

Reference [9] has given the method of Fast Compressive Tracking (FCT). In this section, we briefly introduce the tracking process of FCT and give the motivation of our proposed method.

FCT compressed a high-dimensional Haar-like feature vector to a low-dimensional measurement vector based on CS. The compressing process could be defined as the Formula (1).

$$v = Rx \tag{1}$$

where $x \in \mathbb{R}^{n \times 1}$ is a high-dimensional Haar-like feature vector of a given tracked or candidate region, $v \in \mathbb{R}^{m \times 1}$ is a corresponding low-dimensional measurement vector, and $R \in \mathbb{R}^{m \times n} (m \ll n)$ is a sparse random Gaussian matrix, which was defined as the Formula (2).

$$R(i, j) = r_{ij} = \sqrt{s} \times \begin{cases} 1 & \text{with probability } 1/2s \\ 0 & \text{with probability } 1-1/s \\ -1 & \text{with probability } 1/2s \end{cases} \tag{2}$$

where $s$ is the sparse degree of $R$, and $m$ is the element number of $v$. FCT sets $s = n/(a \log_{10}(n)) \approx n/4 \sim n/2.4$ with $n = 10^6 \sim 10^{10}$ and $a = 0.4$. The non-zero element number of every row vector for $R$ was 4 at most. $m$ was set as 100, assuming the original signals are 10-sparse.

The ith element $v_i$ of $v$ was the inner product about the ith row vector of $R$ and $x$. Assuming all elements of $v$ were independently distributed, $v$ could be modeled with a naive Bayes classifier as the Formula (3).

$$H(v) = \log\left(\frac{\prod_{i=1}^{m} p(v_i \mid y = 1)p(y = 1)}{\prod_{i=1}^{m} p(v_i \mid y = 0)p(y = 0)}\right) = \sum_{i=1}^{m} \log \frac{p(v_i \mid y = 1)}{p(v_i \mid y = 0)} \tag{3}$$

where $p(y = 1) = p(y = 0) = 0.5$, $y \in \{0,1\}$. FCT searched the candidates with a coarse-to-fine strategy. A candidate was the current tracking result, whose $H(v)$ was higher than $H(v)$ of other candidates. The conditional distributions $p(v_i \mid y = 1)$ and $p(v_i \mid y = 0)$ in $H(v)$ were assumed to be Gaussian distributed with four parameters $(\mu_i^1, \delta_i^1, \mu_i^0, \delta_i^0)$, as shown in Formula (4). $\mu_i^1$ and $\delta_i^1$ were updated by the Formula (5), so were $\mu_i^0$ and $\delta_i^0$ updated.

$$\begin{aligned} p(v_i \mid y = 1) &\sim N(\mu_i^1, \delta_i^1) \\ p(v_i \mid y = 0) &\sim N(\mu_i^0, \delta_i^0) \end{aligned} \tag{4}$$

$$\begin{aligned} \mu_i^1 &= \lambda \mu_i^1 + (1 - \lambda)\mu^1 \\ \delta_i^1 &= \sqrt{\lambda(\delta_i^1)^2 + (1 - \lambda)(\delta^1)^2 + \lambda(1 - \lambda)(\delta_i^1 - \delta^1)^2} \end{aligned} \tag{5}$$

where $\lambda > 0$ was the update rate, $\mu^1$ and $\delta^1$ were the Gaussian distribution parameters of $v_i$ as the Formula (6), and $q$ was the number of the positive samples.

$$\begin{aligned} \mu^1 &= \frac{1}{q}\sum_{k=0|y=1}^{q-1} v_i(k) \\ \delta^1 &= \sqrt{\sum_{k=0|y=1}^{q-1}(v_i(k) - \mu^1)^2} \end{aligned} \tag{6}$$

From the tracking processes of FCT, the coarse-to-fine strategy was a traversal style, which still resulted in the unnecessary computing about a large amount of candidates. FCT assumed that all original Haar-like feature vectors were 10-sparse, and then $m$ was set as 100. We experimented on the success rates with $m$ from 1 to 100 on a lot of video sequences, and six representative curves were shown in Fig. 1.

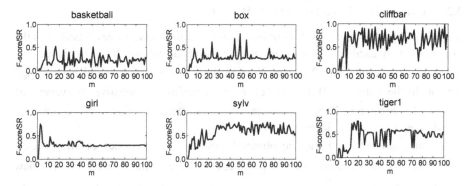

**Fig. 1.** Curves of $m$ and SR for FCT.

As shown in Fig. 1, $m = 10$ was not always corresponding to a higher success rate, and the success rate did not increase with the increase of $m$. Inspired by [7-12] and these experiment curves, we proposed a compressive tracking based on Particle Filter.

# 3    Proposed Method

The proposed method is a compressive tracking based on Particle Filter (PFCT), which is an extension of the FCT [9]. In our proposed method, the candidate objects are predicted based on Particle Filter. The sparse random Gaussian matrix is as the measurement matrix. The number of measurement elements is set as a special value for a high success rate. The specifically value is different for each tracked object.

## 3.1    The Element Number of Measurement Vector

The CS theory [13] indicated that the bound for $m$ was from Formula (7), which ensured that an original signal can be reconstructed.

$$m \geq cK \log(n / K) \tag{7}$$

where $n$ and $K$ are the dimension and the sparsity of an original signal, and $c$ is a very little constant depending on the original signal [13]. However, for a specifically feature vector, it is difficult to obtain its sparsity $K$ and its constant $c$ and to calculate an exact $m$. So the value of $m$ is obtained by an experimental observation style in PFCT. For the task of object tracking, it was expected that the value of $m$ can result in a high success rate. According to the phenomenon in Fig. 1, we set a value of $m$ in 1 to 100, which can result in a higher success rate than other values in 1 to 100. For a different tracked object, the value of $m$ is different.

## 3.2    Calculation Method of Particle Weights

Similar to [9], PFCT constructs an object classifier with a naive Bayes classifier in the Formula (3). A candidate is the current tracking result, whose $H(v)$ is higher than $H(v)$ of other candidates. The candidate as the tracking result should have a high weight. In the Formula (3), a value of $H(v)$ is positive or negative. However, the weight of a particle in Particle Filter cannot be negative. A value of $H(v)$ must be transformed to a reasonable particle weight.

A minimum $H_{p_{min}}(v)$ can be obtained from the $H(v)$ values of all particles, where $p_{min}$ is the serial number of a particle, calculated by the Formula (8). The new positive evaluation $\hat{H}_j(v)$ of the $j$th particle can be calculated by the Formula (9). The weight of the jth particle can be calculated by the Formula (10), where $\xi$ is a little positive constant for avoiding a very little particle weight.

$$p_{min} = \arg\min_{j\in[1,k]} H_j(v) \tag{8}$$

$$\hat{H}_j(v) = H_j(v) - H_{p_{min}}(v) \tag{9}$$

$$w_j = \hat{H}_j(v) + \xi \tag{10}$$

## 4    Experiments

The proposed method was evaluated in comparison with 4 state-of-the-art trackers on 10 publicly available challenging sequences. The Cliffbar, Dollar, Girl, Sylv, Tiger1 and Tiger2 sequences were provided in [14], the Basketball, Singer1 and Singer2 sequences were taken in [15], and the Box sequence was obtained in [16]. The 4 compared trackers were FCT [9], CT [8], ODFS [17] and TLD [18]. FCT, CT, ODFS and TLD used the source codes in MATLAB provided by the authors with default parameters. The proposed PFCT was implemented in MATLAB based on the FCT code, whose particle number was fixed as 100. For fair comparisons, the initial tracking positions and the ground truth positions of 10 sequences were publicly available, and the 5 trackers ran on the same hardware platform with Intel Quad-Core i5-3470 3.2GHz CPU and 4GB memory. The comparisons were performed from both quantitative evaluation and visual evaluation. The experimental results showed that PFCT ran faster and performed favorably against other 4 trackers on 10 challenging sequences in terms of efficiency, accuracy and robustness.

### 4.1    Quantitative Evaluation

In order to evaluate the overall performances of the 5 trackers, we performed the quantitative evaluations with 3 evaluation metrics: success rate (SR) [9], center location error

(CLE) [9] and average frame per second (FPS). An object in a sequence frame was successfully tracked if the score is not less than 0.5, $score = \dfrac{area(ROI_T \cap ROI_G)}{area(ROI_T \cup ROI_G)}$, where $ROI_T$ and $ROI_G$ were respectively the tracking bounding box and the ground truth bounding box. The CLE was the Euclidean distance between the central position of the tracking bounding box and the central position of the ground truth bounding box. The FPS was the frame number per second.

**Table 1.** m and SR (%). **Bold** fonts indicated the best performances.

| Sequence | PFCT | FCT | CT | ODFS | TLD |
|---|---|---|---|---|---|
| Basketball | **82.60** (100) | 27.21 | 25.83 | 76.66 | 0.97 |
| Box | **80.60** (20) | 25.86 | 38.36 | 37.50 | 68.10 |
| Cliffbar | **98.46** (18) | **98.46** | 87.69 | 93.85 | 41.54 |
| Dollar | **100.00** (23) | 98.46 | 92.31 | 80.00 | 40.00 |
| Girl | **75.00** (3) | 30.00 | 35.00 | 35.00 | 49.00 |
| Singer1 | **100.00** (7) | 29.71 | 92.00 | **100.00** | 32.86 |
| Singer2 | **69.86** (11) | 28.49 | 32.05 | 41.64 | 2.74 |
| Sylv | **99.25** (59) | 54.10 | 58.96 | 55.60 | 95.52 |
| Tiger1 | 42.86 (16) | 55.71 | **62.86** | 4.29 | 41.43 |
| Tiger2 | **75.00** (19) | 68.06 | 54.17 | 36.11 | 22.22 |
| average *m* | **35.47** | 100 | 50 | -- | -- |
| average SR | **84.12** | 37.04 | 47.94 | 63.61 | 29.99 |

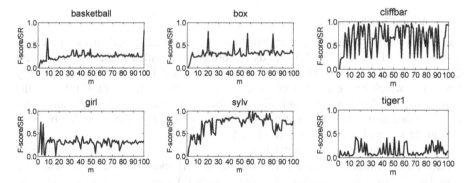

**Fig. 2.** Curves of *m* and SR for PFCT.

Table 1 showed the evaluation results in terms of *m* and SR. The *m* was the number of measurement elements for a compressive tracker. *m* was fixed as 100 for FCT, and *m* was fixed as 50 for CT. For PFCT, *m* was different for each sequence, which was noted in the bracket of the PFCT column and resulted in a high SR. Fig. 2 listed a part of the changing curves of SR with *m* for PFCT, where *m* is from 1 to 100. With the changes of *m*, the variation directions were similar to those in FCT.

The average $m$ of PFCT was 35.47. Except for the Tiger1 sequence, PFCT obtained a higher SR than other methods on 9 sequences. The average SR of PFCT was 84.12, higher than other methods.

**Table 2.** CLE (in pixels) amd average FPS. **Bold** fonts indicated the best performances.

| Sequence | PFCT | FCT | CT | ODFS | TLD |
|---|---|---|---|---|---|
| Basketball | 16.85 | 90.97 | 66.55 | **12.35** | 211.62 |
| Box | 22.53 | 107.38 | 31.83 | 133.93 | **10.35** |
| Cliffbar | 6.11 | 6.48 | 7.64 | 5.96 | **2.78** |
| Dollar | **16.46** | 16.76 | 19.85 | 17.35 | 67.40 |
| Girl | **25.99** | 40.90 | 37.48 | 37.67 | 28.82 |
| Singer1 | 23.81 | 22.59 | 23.15 | 15.16 | **14.18** |
| Singer2 | **33.52** | 49.90 | 86.84 | 53.53 | 199.64 |
| Sylv | **5.70** | 16.78 | 13.86 | 13.89 | 5.76 |
| Tiger1 | 30.10 | 22.51 | 22.00 | 78.07 | **4.36** |
| Tiger2 | 15.85 | 11.62 | 15.61 | 12.33 | **11.00** |
| average CLE | **14.99** | 27.50 | 25.57 | 30.84 | 23.66 |
| average FPS | **197.10** | 83.20 | 87.81 | 98.52 | 14.50 |

Table 2 showed the evaluation results about CLE and FPS. TLD on 5 sequences obtained a less CLE, because the CLE for TLD was calculated only based on the located frames, these located frames were a part of all frames, and the CLE for other 4 methods was calculated based on all frames. However, the average CLE of PFCT was less than those of other methods. The average FPS of PFCT was 197.10, far higher than those of other methods.

**4.2    Visual Evaluation**

For the Basketball sequence, the athletes underwent similar disturbances and abrupt motion. The ODFS and PFCT methods performed well with a higher SR and a less CLE. PFCT reduced the computing about a lot of candidates in many unnecessary directions, which brought a higher FPS, more than two times of FCT FPS. At the same time, the disturbances from other candidates in many unnecessary directions were avoided also, which brought that the SR of PFCT was higher than that of FCT, though the value of m is same to that of FCT.

The box in Box was in a clutter background, the object in Sylv underwent pose variation and illumination change, and the girl in Girl underwent occlusion and pose variation. For the three sequences, the TLD and PFCT methods performed well. The value of m in PFCT was less than that in FCT or CT, but a higher SR was obtained.

For the Cliffbar and Dollar sequences, the objects underwent clutter background. FCT, CT, ODFS and PFCT performed well. But the value of m for PFCT was less than FCT and CT, and PFCT obtained a comparative SR.

For the Singer1 and Singer2 sequences, the singers underwent illumination change. CT, ODFS and PFCT performed well on Singer1, and ODFS and PFCT obtained a SR to 100%. However, PFCT with m=7 achieved a far higher SR than FCT with m=100. Only PFCT performed well on Singer2 with a less m.

**Fig. 3.** Screenshots for some sample tracking results.

For the Tiger1 and Tiger2 sequences, the tiger toys underwent abrupt motion. FCT, CT and PFCT performed well. The SR of PFCT on Tiger2 was slightly higher than that of FCT or CT. The SR of PFCT on Tiger1 was slightly less than that of FCT or CT, however the value of m for PFCT was far less than that for FCT or CT. Some sample tracking results about these sequences were shown in Fig. 3.

# 5    Conclusions

In this paper, we proposed a compressive tracking based on Particle Filter (PFCT). The candidate objects were predicted based on Particle Filter, which calculated minority candidates and avoided the disturbances from other candidates in many unnecessary directions. The element number of a measurement vector was set as a special value among 1 to 100. The element number was different for each video sequence. The little disturbances and the special element number resulted in a high SR. The minority candidates and the small element number brought a high real-time. The experiments on challenging sequences showed that PFCT performed well in terms of SR, CLE and FPS.

**Acknowledgment.** The work is supported by National Natural Science Foundation of China (Grant No.: 61262067 and 61163024) and Application Foundation Project of Yunnan Province of China (Grant No.: 2011FB019).

# References

1. Li, X., Hu, W., Shen, C., et al.: A survey of appearance models in visual object tracking. ACM Transactions on Intelligent Systems and Technology (TIST) **4**(4), 58 (2013)
2. Candes, E.J., Tao, T.: Decoding by linear programming. IEEE Trans. Inform. Theory **51**(12), 4203–4215 (2005)
3. Candes, E.J., Tao, T.: Near-optimal signal recovery from random projections: Universal encoding strategies? IEEE Trans. Inform. Theory **52**(12), 5406–5425 (2006)
4. Wright, J., Yang, A.Y., Ganesh, A., et al.: Robust face recognition via sparse representation. IEEE Trans. Pattern Anal. Mach. Intell. **31**(2), 210–227 (2009)
5. Mei, X., Ling, H.: Robust visual tracking using $l1$ minimization. In: IEEE Conf. Computer Vision (ICCV), Kyoto, pp. 1436–1443 (2009)
6. Li, H.X., Shen, C.H., et al.: Real-time visual tracking using compressive sensing. In: IEEE Conf. Computer Vision and Pattern Recognition (CVPR), USA, pp. 1305–1312 (2011)
7. Zhang, K., Zhang, L., Yang, M.-H.: Real-time compressive tracking. In: Fitzgibbon, A., Lazebnik, S., Perona, P., Sato, Y., Schmid, C. (eds.) ECCV 2012, Part III. LNCS, vol. 7574, pp. 864–877. Springer, Heidelberg (2012)
8. Zhu, Q., Yan, J., Deng, D.: Compressive tracking via oversaturated sub-region classifiers. IET Comput. Vis. **7**(6), 448–455 (2013)
9. Zhang, K., Zhang, L., Yang, M.: Fast Compressive Tracking. IEEE Trans. Pattern Anal. Mach. Intell. **36**(10), 2002–2015 (2014)

10. Yao, X., Zhou, Y.: Real-time compressive tracking with a particle filter framework. In: Loo, C.K., Yap, K.S., Wong, K.W., Beng Jin, A.T., Huang, K. (eds.) ICONIP 2014, Part III. LNCS, vol. 8836, pp. 242–249. Springer, Heidelberg (2014)
11. Isard, M., Blake, A.: Condensation-conditional density propagation for visual tracking. International Journal of Computer Vision **29**(1), 5–28 (1998)
12. Gao, Y., Zhou, H., Zhang, X.: Enhanced fast compressive tracking based on adaptive measurement matrix. IET Computer Vision 2015. doi:10.1049/iet-cvi.2014.0431
13. Candès, E.J., Wakin, M.B.: An introduction to compressive sampling. IEEE Signal Process Magazine **25**(2), 21–30 (2008)
14. Babenko, B., Yang, M.H., Belongie, S.: Robust object tracking with online multiple instance learning. IEEE Trans. Pattern Anal. Mach. Intell. **33**(8), 1619–1632 (2011)
15. Kwon, J., Lee, K.M.: Visual tracking decomposition. In: IEEE Conf. Computer Vision and Pattern Recognition (CVPR), pp. 1269–1276 (2010)
16. Santner, J., Leistner, C., Saffari, A., et al.: Prost: parallel robust online simple tracking. In: IEEE Conf. Computer Vision and Pattern Recognition (CVPR), 2010, pp. 723–730 (2010)
17. Zhang, K., Zhang, L., Yang, M.: Real-Time Object Tracking Via Online Discriminative Feature Selection. IEEE Trans. Image Process. **22**(12), 4664–4677 (2013)
18. Kalal, Z., Matas, J., Mikolajczyk, K.: Pn learning: bootstrapping binary classifiers by structural constraints. In: IEEE Conf. Computer Vision and Pattern Recognition (CVPR), pp. 49–56 (2010)

# An Adaptive Threshold Algorithm
# for Moving Object Segmentation

Yumin Tian[✉], Dan Wang, Risan Lin, and Qichao Chen

School of Computer Science and Technology, Xidian University,
Xi'an 710071, Shannxi, China
ymtian@mail.xidian.edu.cn

**Abstract.** Connected region detection is usually used to obtain foreground regions from foreground image after moving object detection. In order to remove noise regions and retain true targets, a threshold that limits the circumference of foreground regions should be introduced. The method which uses the same threshold for all surveillance videos cannot handle scene changes. In this case, we propose an adaptive threshold algorithm for moving target segmentation. A strategy based on the combination of background modeling and Grabcut is presented to extract foreground objects and set an initial threshold. On the base of this, we can choose some foreground as samples and classify them by K-means clustering method. Finally, an appropriate threshold could be selected for moving object segmentation according to the classification result. Experimental results show that the proposed method has strong adaptability to various scenes and improves the accuracy oftarget segmentation.

**Keywords:** Moving object segmentation · Adaptive threshold · K-means clustering · Image segmentation

## 1    Introduction

In recent years, moving object detection [1-2] has been an important topic in the field of computer vision. As an essential step of intelligent surveillance technology, its results are crucial for subsequent advanced processing, such as object classification, tracking and activity analysis.

After the detection of moving targets we can obtain foreground images. In order to acquire the features of moving foreground objects further and facilitate subsequent tasks, it is necessary to separate motion areas from background. Since the results of detection is sensitive to sensors noise and background changes, pixels that belong to background are often falsely detected as foreground and, as a result, the performance of foreground object segmentation are heavily affected. To handle this problem, it is need to include a threshold to limit the circumference of foreground regions so that fake targets mixed with moving objects could be judged and rejected with the help of this threshold.

The performance of threshold algorithm determines the accuracy of object segmentation. A fixed threshold manually selected is usually not applicable to all video scenes, so it is worth to study the algorithm of adaptive threshold. In this paper, we

© Springer-Verlag Berlin Heidelberg 2015
H. Zha et al. (Eds.): CCCV 2015, Part I, CCIS 546, pp. 230–239, 2015.
DOI: 10.1007/978-3-662-48558-3_23

put forward an adaptive threshold algorithm to get motion areas apart, which mainly focus on three issues: how to select an initial threshold, how to classify foreground regions and how to adjust the threshold based on concrete situations. Among these problems, the selection of initial threshold is the foundation of other issues. It relates to the sample collection of K-means clustering method and therefore has a great effect on the quality of classification. To reasonably determine the initial threshold, a novel method based on Gaussian mixture model and Grabcut is applied to segment image, which ensures the integrity of targets and increases the accuracy of initial threshold. In addition, we use K-means to partition foreground areas and choose appropriate formulas in accordance with the actual situation to update threshold, resulting in a proper threshold and promotes the quality of moving object segmentation.

## 2    Object Segmentation Based on Fixed Threshold

After foreground detection, in order to acquire the characteristics of each foreground object, we usually adopt connected region detection algorithm [3] to separate foreground from background. If the results of targets detection are accurate enough, foreground segmentation will be liable to achieve desirable results. However, multiple factors interfering with the performance of objects detection exist in the real monitoring environment, such as leaf swing and camera shake. They contribute to the emergence of false alarms and make a serious impact on the accuracy of object segmentation [4]. In order to eliminate the possible influence of background or fake targets, it is need to distinguish between different foreground areas with a threshold. If the circumference of a region is less than the given threshold, it will be considered ineffective; otherwise it will be regard as an actual motion area. The easiest means of threshold value selection is to adopt a fixed threshold, i.e., manually set a same threshold for all videos on the basis of experimental experience. Figure 1 shows the object segmentation results of four test videos when the threshold is fixed at 100. The segmented objects are marked with green rectangles. For convenience, the videos are referred to as v1, v2, v3 and v4 respectively.

(a)    original frames

(b)    object segmentation results

**Fig. 1.** Foreground target segmentation results by using a fixed threshold

Since videos with differences in scene and resolution often lead to different objects detection results, their optimal thresholds of foreground segmentation are also significantly different. If we preset a unified and fixed threshold for all videos, the segmentation results will probably be unsatisfactory. As shown in figure 1, though the threshold is reasonable for v1, v2 suffers from the problem of error detection because its three regions generated by background objects are falsely segmented as objects. Meanwhile, several small targets in v3 and v4 are missed owing to the large threshold. Thus the method using fixed threshold fails to fit for different videos, and an adaptive threshold selection method should be chosen according to the specific situation.

# 3     Object Segmentation Algorithm Based on Adaptive Threshold

## 3.1     The Basic Steps of the Algorithm

The algorithm of adaptive threshold selection is mainly divided into three steps. Firstly, background modeling approach and Grabcut algorithm are combined to initialize the threshold. Secondly, some detected foreground areas are collected as samples based on the initial threshold and then they are classified by K-means clustering method. Finally, we choose a formula in accordance with the classification results and apply it to reasonably update the threshold. The threshold obtained by this algorithm can be used to separate true targets from background. Therefore we can acquire the features of moving targets and further to facilitate subsequent processing (e.g., object tracking and behavior recognition). The flow chart of this algorithm is shown in Figure 2. We define $m$ as the number of foreground regions whose contour lengths are larger than the initial threshold needed for K-means clustering, and $n$ is the current number of this type of foreground regions we segment from foreground images. The value of $m$ is generally selected to 200.

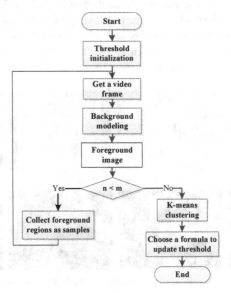

**Fig. 2.** Block diagram of the proposed algorithm

### 3.2    Threshold Initialization Based on Gaussian Mixture Model and Grabcut

In initial time period, the threshold should be given an initial value. As it will be used for target segmentation and the collection of training samples before K-means clustering, a proper initial threshold is of great importance to the classification results. In order to appropriately determine the initial threshold, we provide a new method combining Grabcut algorithm and Gaussian mixture background model to segment foreground regions in this paper. Grabcut [5-6] is an iterative Graphcut algorithm [7], and also an interactive image segmentation method with high accuracy, given part of background and foreground information, it can effectively extract objects from static images. The combination of background modeling approach and Grabcut method will help to efficiently and completely segment moving targets from foreground image, which solves the problem that background subtraction approach is prone to make objects incomplete. Setting the initial threshold based on intact foreground objects could increase the accuracy of target segmentation. The flowchart of the threshold initialization is shown in figure 3.

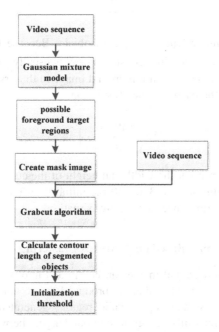

**Fig. 3.** Flow char of the threshold initialization algorithm

Firstly, the Gaussian mixture model put forward in [8] is utilized to preliminarily get all possible regions where motions have taken place from foreground images. Then median filtering and dilation operation of morphology are used for them to remove noise points and expand foreground areas. After that, the outer contours of these foreground regions could be found by applying connected region detection algorithm, according to which we can acquire the minimum enclosing rectangle for each region.

With all the operations above, we can get the information of mask image which is used for Grabcut initialization. When a pixel in the mask image is outside the rectangles we find, it will be marked as 0 on behalf of background, otherwise it will be marked as 3 representing pixels which probably belong to foreground. Finally, we use the mask image to initial Grabcut algorithm and segment each foreground region by Grabcut algorithm to get complete objects.

By using mask images containing part of background and foreground information for object segmentation we can get intact targets, which ensures the integrity of foreground objects. Furthermore, this algorithm is carried out only on foreground regions detected by Gaussian mixture model instead of the whole image, so that it can greatly reduce the number of sample points and cut down the time for target segmentation. In conclusion, our method can not only improve the segmentation accuracy, but also enhance the efficiency of the foreground object segmentation.

After extracting the first $N$ objects by the above approach, we initialize the threshold with reference to their lengths:

$$T = \frac{1}{2N} \sum_{i=1}^{N} C_i \tag{1}$$

Where $C_i$ is the contour length of the ith object. Because Grabcut algorithm is complicated in calculation and time consuming, $N$ is usually given a small value. If there are no targets segmented from foreground image in the first 100 frames, we will initial the threshold on the basis of video resolution:

$$T = 35 \times \left( \frac{W \cdot H}{320 \times 240} \right)^{\frac{1}{2}} \tag{2}$$

Where $W$ and $H$ represent the width and height of the current video respectively. For videos whose resolutions are 320x240 the initial threshold is set to 35, in other cases, it will be set with reference to the above situation.

## 3.3    Threshold Learning Based on K-Means Clustering

Connected regions in foreground image can be divided into two categories, one consists of invalid foreground regions that are produced due to noise and dynamic scene changes, and the other is made up of valid regions generated by moving objects. Usually, there are obvious differences in contour lengths between the two kinds of regions. This is due to the fact that the noise produced during object detection is generally small, while moving objects are relatively large. For this reason, we classify foreground regions by using the circumference of foreground regions as the classification feature, aiming to discard false regions and retain motion areas.

In the stage of classification method selection, owing to that we cannot know the types of foreground areas in advance, it is not appropriate to utilize methods which need to be informed of the categories of training samples before classification, such as SVM [9] and decision tree [10]. In view of this, we adopt K-means clustering method

[11-12] to describe foreground regions. It is performed on the premise that the value of K has been given, without needing to label the classes of samples, so K-means clustering method is suitable for this paper.

In the stage of sample collection, in order to avoid the monoculture of samples we collect the first $m$ targets whose lengths are above the initial threshold and a plurality of small foreground regions that are segmented during this period as training samples, and classify them into two groups by K-means clustering method. After the above processing, we can calculate the value of relevant variables for each subclass:

$$S_i = \sum_{j=1}^{L} o_j^i \tag{3}$$

$$\mu_i = \frac{1}{S_i} \sum_{j=1}^{L} o_j^i c_j \tag{4}$$

Where $S_i$ and $\mu_i$ stand for the number and average length of samples in the ith class respectively; $L$ is the total number of samples and $c_j$ represents the contour length of the jth sample. The ownership $o_j^i$ will be set to 1 if the jth sample belongs to the ith category, otherwise it will be set to 0.

### 3.4    Threshold Updating

After the clustering, subclasses are sorted to have descending average length (i.e. $\mu_1 \geq \mu_2$). We divide classification results into 4 situations and choose appropriate methods based on the specific situation to adjust the threshold. The update equations are:

$$T = \begin{cases} \mu_1 & \mu_1 < T_\mu \\ \mu_2 & \mu_2 > T_\mu \\ w_1 \cdot \mu_1 + w_2 \cdot \mu_2 & \mu_1 > 3T_\mu, \ S_1 < \dfrac{m}{4}, \mu_2 < T_\mu \\ \dfrac{1}{2}(\mu_1 + \mu_2) & else \end{cases} \tag{5}$$

Where $w_1 < w_2$ and $w_1 + w_2 = 1$. In our experiment, the values of $w_1$ and $w_2$ are adjusted to $w_1 = 0.2$ and $w_2 = 0.8$. $T_\mu$ is a decision threshold, which is set based on the variable from (2) and two times the value of it. If $\mu_1 < T_\mu$, i.e., the average lengths of both sub classes are less than $T_\mu$, it illustrates that the intruding objects are small or there are many noise points included in samples. To avoid the influence of background noise as far as possible, we take the larger value $\mu_1$ as a new threshold and K-means clustering algorithm will be used again to study the detection results. If $\mu_2 > T_\mu$, i.e., the average lengths of  both sub classes are more than $T_\mu$, it demonstrate that the foreground images detected by Gaussian mixture model are probably accurate and there are few invalid regions exist in the collected samples, so we only need to put the smaller value $\mu_2$ as the final threshold.

In addition, when $\mu_1 > T_\mu, \mu_2 < T_\mu$, there are often great differences between the two sub classes so that we can easily distinguish noise regions and motion areas. We regard the subclass with smaller sample mean as being composed of invalid foreground regions and the other one is perceived as consisting of valid moving targets. The threshold is updated to the mean value of $\mu_1$ and $\mu_2$. However, when targets are close to cameras or multiple objects stick together, it will lead to the generation of large foreground regions, if we take these regions into account during the process of clustering, it will result in a too large threshold and affect the reliability of target segmentation results. Considering that the subclass generated in this case usually have a large average length but a tiny number of samples, so when $\mu_1$ is large but $S_1$ is small (e.g., $\mu_1 > 3T_\mu$ and $S_1 < \frac{m}{4}$), we take a weighted sum of $\mu_1$ and $\mu_2$ as the threshold. After that, we can discriminate invalid areas and motion areas by the threshold and extract the static characteristics of foreground objects.

## 4    Experimental Results

In order to better understand the performance of the algorithm, we apply the proposed method on different videos having different scenes and resolutions.

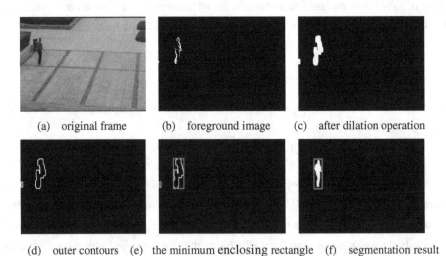

(a)    original frame        (b)    foreground image        (c)    after dilation operation

(d)    outer contours    (e)    the minimum enclosing rectangle    (f)    segmentation result

**Fig. 4.** Segmentation results of the method combining Grabcut and Gaussian mixture model

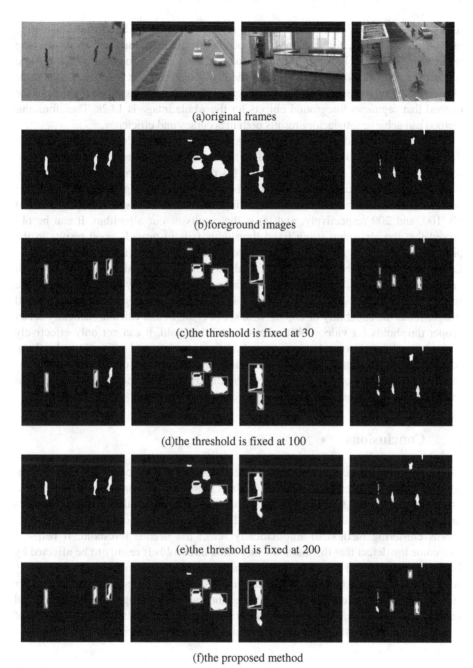

(a)original frames

(b)foreground images

(c)the threshold is fixed at 30

(d)the threshold is fixed at 100

(e)the threshold is fixed at 200

(f)the proposed method

**Fig. 5.** Comparison of the proposed algorithm to the method using fixed threshold

Figure 4 shows the experimental results of the threshold initialization algorithm which combines Grabcut algorithm and Gaussian mixture model for segmentation.

It can be seen clearly that the foreground regions detected by background modeling method are imperfect, for instance, their pixels are discontinuous and there are fake target and "holes" left behind in them. In contrast, the target segmented by our method is complete and real, which increase the initial threshold accuracy. Besides, for the same video frame, the processing time of the presented algorithm is 5.8s, while the time of the method that segments foreground objects for the whole image is 13.2s. Therefore, our method can achieve satisfactory results both in accuracy and efficiency.

We compare the adaptive threshold algorithm with the method that manually set the threshold to be 30, 100 and 200. The target segmentation results of test 4 video sequences are shown in Figure 5. Where (a) represents the original frames and (b) stands for the foreground images through morphological filtering processing. (c) ~ (e) are the segmentation results of the current frames when the threshold value is fixed at 30, 100, and 200 respectively, and (f) is the results of our algorithm. It can be observed that the algorithm using fixed thresholds fails to provide good results in the presence of different videos, since for a low threshold value, noise regions will be falsely detected as foreground objects, and for a high threshold value, part of small targets will be missed, resulting in a high false negative rate. By contrast, most of the time, the proposed method can perfectly segment moving targets from foreground image. It has the capability of coping with scene changes and can automatically select proper thresholds for videos. With the selected threshold, it can not only effectively remove invalid foreground regions resulted from background noise, but also keep segmented targets complete and avoid separating a target into several parts. It proves that the proposed algorithm can conquer the disadvantage of the method using fixed threshold and enhances the accuracy of the algorithm.

## 5    Conclusions

In this paper, we present a foreground object segmentation algorithm based on adaptive threshold. The method combining Grabcut algorithm and Gaussian mixture background model is used for target segmentation, which improves the integrity of targets and increases the accuracy of the initial threshold as well. Moreover, we apply K-means clustering method to automatically select the needed threshold. It helps to overcome the defect that the method using fixed thresholds is readily to be affected by background noise and the video resolution. In this way, this method can effectively segment moving targets from foreground images and thereby lays the foundation for subsequent tasks including target tracking and behavior recognition. Experimental results demonstrate that the proposed algorithm can obviously improve the quality of target segmentation, which proves the effectiveness of this algorithm.

# References

1. Ding, Y., Wenhui, L.: Robust moving object detection under complex background. Computer Science and Information Systems **7**(1), 201–210 (2010)
2. Chaohui, Z., Xiaohui, D., Shuoyu, X., et al.: An improved moving object detection algorithm based on frame difference and edge detection. In: Fourth International Conference on Image and Graphics, ICIG 2007, pp. 519–523. IEEE (2007)
3. Castleman, K.R.: Digital Image Processing. Prentice Hall &清华大学出版社 (1998)
4. Brutzer, S., Hoferlin, B., Heidemann, G.: Evaluation of background subtraction techniques for video surveillance. 2011 IEEE Conference on Computer Vision and Pattern Recognition (CVPR), pp. 1937–1944. IEEE (2011)
5. Rother, C., Blake, A., Kolmogorov, V.: Grabcut - interactive foreground extraction using iterated graph cuts. Proceedings of ACM SIGGRAPH **23**(3), 309–314 (2004)
6. Liu, Z., Shi, R., Shen, L., et al.: Unsupervised salient object segmentation based on kernel density estimation and two-phase graph cut. IEEE Transactions on Multimedia **14**(4), 1275–1289 (2012)
7. Zhang, L., Kong, H., Chin, C.T., et al.: Cytoplasm segmentation on cervical cell images using graph cut-based approach. Bio-Medical Materials and Engineering **24**(1), 1125–1131 (2014)
8. Zivkovic, Z.: Improved adaptive Gaussian mixture model for background subtraction. In: Proceedings of the 17th International Conference on Pattern Recognition, ICPR 2004, vol. 2, pp. 28–31. IEEE (2004)
9. Shalev-Shwartz, S., Singer, Y., Srebro, N., et al.: Pegasos: Primal estimated sub-gradient solver for svm. Mathematical Programming **127**(1), 3–30 (2011)
10. Pradhan, B.: A comparative study on the predictive ability of the decision tree, support vector machine and neuro-fuzzy models in landslide susceptibility mapping using GIS. Computers & Geosciences **51**, 350–365 (2013)
11. Lu, B., Wei, S.: One more efficient parallel initialization algorithm of K-means with mapreduce. In: Proceedings of the 4th International Conference on Computer Engineering and Networks, pp. 845–852. Springer International Publishing (2015)
12. He, K., Wen, F., Sun, J.: K-means hashing: an affinity-preserving quantization method for learning binary compact codes. In: 2013 IEEE Conference on Computer Vision and Pattern Recognition (CVPR), pp. 2938–2945. IEEE (2013)

# Interactive Registration and Segmentation for Multi-Atlas-Based Labeling of Brain MR Image

Qian Wang[1], Guorong Wu[2], Min-Jeong Kim[2], Lichi Zhang[1],
and Dinggang Shen[2](✉)

[1] Med-X Research Institute, School of Biomedical Engineering,
Shanghai Jiao Tong University, Shanghai, China
{wang.qian,lichizhang}@sjtu.edu.cn
[2] Department of Radiology and BRIC, University of North Carolina at Chapel Hill,
Chapel Hill, NC, USA
{grwu,minjeong_kim,dinggang_shen}@med.unc.edu

**Abstract.** In the conventional multi-atlas-based labeling methods, atlases are registered with each unlabeled image, which is then segmented by fusing the labels of all registered atlases. The registration is typically ignorant about the segmentation while the segmentation of each individual unlabeled image is independently considered, both of which potentially undermine the accuracy in labeling. In this work, we propose the interactive registration-segmentation scheme for multi-atlas-based labeling of brain MR images. First, we learn the distribution of all images (including atlases and unlabeled images) and register them to their common space in the groupwise manner. Then, we segment all unlabeled images simultaneously, by fusing the labels of the registered atlases in the common space as well as the tentative segmentation of the unlabeled images. Next, the (tentative) labeling feeds back to refine the registration, thus all images are more accurately aligned within the common space. The improved registration further boosts the accuracy to determine the segmentation of the unlabeled images. According to our experimental results, the iterative optimization to the interactive registration-segmentation scheme can improve the performances of the multi-atlas-based labeling significantly.

## 1 Introduction

It is needed by many studies that certain medical images should be labeled into different anatomical regions-of-interest (ROIs), in order to facilitate the following region-based analysis. Manual labeling, though probably accurate with well-trained experts, costs high especially for the large-scale population of images. On the contrary, automatic labeling method shows the advantage in reducing the needs of human interactions. Therefore, the technique is highly desirable in medical image analysis and has been intensively investigated recently.

To *label* (also known as to *segment* or to *parcellate*) brain MR images can be attained in many different ways. Among them, atlas-based segmentation provides

© Springer-Verlag Berlin Heidelberg 2015
H. Zha et al. (Eds.): CCCV 2015, Part I, CCIS 546, pp. 240–248, 2015.
DOI: 10.1007/978-3-662-48558-3_24

an efficient solution that yields comparable accuracy with respect to manual labeling. Specifically, after *registering* the atlas to an unlabeled image, the labeling information associated with the atlas then propagates to the unlabeled image and further *segments* it. If image registration is accurate, the well-established correspondences between the two images can guarantee that the propagated segmentation is highly reliable.

Instead of using a single atlas, the multi-atlas-based labeling strategy is more preferred in recent studies to alleviate the potential errors in registering a single atlas. To this end, the unlabeled image can be parcellated by fusing contributions from several registered atlases. For example, after all atlases are spatially normalized with the unlabeled image via registration, the majority voting scheme determines the to-be-estimated label at a specific voxel of the unlabeled image as the most frequent label from the same voxel locations of all registered atlases. In this way, the labeling accuracy is usually higher since the potential errors in registering certain atlases with the unlabeled image become less influential.

A typical scenario for multi-atlas-based labeling is to segment a population of images, in which only a few atlases are pre-labeled. Both *registration* and *segmentation*, the two major components in multi-atlas-based labeling, can thus be specially adapted for better performances. Though the labeling can propagate by registering atlases with each unlabeled image directly, more advanced registration schemes are beneficial for the sake of accurate labeling. In [12] , for instance, the population of images is embedded into a high-dimensional manifold where similar images are closely distributed. Higher labeling accuracy can be achieved, since the labeling is always propagated between similar images and the related registration is more reliable.

After (roughly) registering atlases with a certain unlabeled image, the segmentation of the unlabeled image can be determined in various ways [1,5,8,11]. Most methods in the literature apply the mono-directional label fusion by propagating the labeling from the atlases to the unlabeled image only. However, recent studies [8,4] show that the segmentation of an unlabeled image can also benefit from other unlabeled images. Specifically, a certain unlabeled image can finally be segmented from fusing both the labels of atlases and the tentative segmentation of other unlabeled images. In this way, not only the consistency across the segmentation of each unlabeled image and the atlases, but also the intrinsic consistency among all unlabeled images, are well preserved.

Though the multi-atlas-based labeling can split into *registration* followed by *segmentation*, the two components are usually independently considered. The interaction between them, which could improve the labeling accuracy, is mostly ignored. To this end, we propose a novel multi-atlas-based labeling method, which applies the *interactive registration-segmentation scheme* and thus significantly differs from other methods in the literature. The proposed method iteratively refines the registration of all images and then the segmentation of the unlabeled images. In particular, the groupwise registration [9,10,13] learns the distribution of the entire image population that consists of all atlases as well as unlabeled images, and deforms all images to a common space. We then segment the unlabeled images simultaneously in the common space, by fusing both the labeling of the registered atlases and the tentative segmentation of the unlabeled images. The (tentative) labeling of all images feeds back to further improve the registration accuracy in two folds: (1) the labeling helps better understand the distribution of the entire image population after all images are roughly aligned in the common space; (2) the labeling is regarded as additional image descriptors and can be used to guide the registration of all images directly. In this way, the segmentation contributes to register all images more accurately in the common space, which in turn leads to better estimation of the segmentation.

## 2    Method

We propose to solve the multi-atlas-based labeling problem via interactive registration and segmentation. Specifically, we register the image population, including atlases and unlabeled images, to a common space in the groupwise manner (Section 2.1). Then, the segmentation of each unlabeled image is derived from fusing not only the labeling of the registered atlases, but also the tentative segmentation of other unlabeled images (Section 2.2). Further, the tentative segmentation guides to register all images more accurately in the common space (Section 2.3). The proposed methodology will be summarized in Section 2.4.

### 2.1    Image Registration via Minimum Spanning Tree

We register all atlases and unlabeled images to their common space in the groupwise manner, by taking advantage of the distribution of the entire image population. In particular, all images are first embedded into a fully connected graph, where the nodes indicate individual images and the edge linking each pair of images records their in-between distance, i.e., the sum of square differences (SSD) of intensities. A minimum spanning tree (MST) is then extracted from the graph. The root of the tree is determined to represent the geometric median image in the population, from which the sum of distances to other images is the minimal. All images are connected with the root of the tree either directly or via other images/nodes. More detailed explanations on the construction of the MST can be found in [2,3,4]. Note that the node at the root of the tree, or the median image of the population, will act as the common space to which all images in the population are registered.

The learned MST helps register all images in the population to the root in a recursive manner. In particular, given each non-root image, its path that traverses along edges to the root of the tree can be easily identified. If the parent node of the image under consideration is the root, the direct registration (i.e., via diffeomorphic Demons [6]) will be computed immediately. Otherwise, the non-root image will utilize the deformation belonging to its parent node as an initialization and further refine to generate its own deformation towards the root. The recursive callbacks can eventually deform all images to the common space. Compared with the direct registration of two images that might be very different in anatomies, the MST provides robust initialization in estimating the deformation field.

Due to the essentially high-dimensional image data and the limited size of the image population, the estimation of the MST might be inaccurate. Here, we build the tree from an augmented population that consists of more simulated images. The simulated images are derived by perturbing the pre-determined median image in five steps [4]: (1) A set of images is directly registered with the median image; (2) All deformations are then inverted; (3) Principal component analysis (PCA) is applied to capture the variation within all inverted deformations; (4) By perturbing coefficients in the learned PCA model, a set of deformations can be simulated; (5) All simulated deformations are applied to warp the median image and generate a set of simulated images in the final. We follow the same setting in [4] to specify the number of the simulated images to be twice the size of the original image population. The augmented population, including atlases, unlabeled images, and simulated images, leads to the MST that better captures the distribution of the image population.

## 2.2  Segmentation via Label Fusion

After all images are registered to the common space, we are able to segment the unlabeled images given the atlases. We apply the local voting strategy for stochastic label fusion. Denoting the $m$-th ($m = 1, \cdots, M$) registered atlas as $I_m$ and $L_m$ as its label, the label for the $n$-th ($n = 1, \cdots, N$) unlabeled image $\mathcal{I}_n$ at $x$, or $\mathcal{L}_n(x)$, can be assigned with the label $l$ at the following likelihood

$$p(\mathcal{L}_n(x) = l) = \sum_{m=1}^{M} w(I_m, \mathcal{I}_n, x)\delta(L_m(x), l). \tag{1}$$

In the equation above, $\delta(L_m(x), l)$ returns 1 if and only if $L_m(x) = l$; otherwise 0. The weight $w(I_m, \mathcal{I}_n, x)$ indicates the contribution of $I_m$ to label $\mathcal{I}_n$ by $L_m$, and obviously relates to the similarity between $I_m$ and $\mathcal{I}_n$ at $x$. By using $d(I_m, \mathcal{I}_n, x)$ to denote the distance of the two respective intensity patches centered at $x$ of both $I_m$ and $\mathcal{I}_n$ (with the size $3 \times 3 \times 3$ in voxel), we define $w(I_m, \mathcal{I}_n, x) = \exp(-d^2(I_m, \mathcal{I}_n, x)/2\sigma^2)$ as $\sigma$ relates to the standard deviation of all patch-to-patch distances. The exact label of $\mathcal{L}_n(x)$ is determined as the value $l$ of the maximal likelihood in the final.

To segment a certain unlabeled image consistently with the entire population, the tentative labeling of other unlabeled images should also participate into the local voting. Therefore, the likelihood in labeling $\mathcal{I}_n(x)$ can be calculated by

$$p(\mathcal{L}_n(x) = l) := \sum_{m=1}^{M} w(I_m, \mathcal{I}_n, x)\delta(L_m(x), l) + \sum_{k=1}^{N} w(\mathcal{I}_k, \mathcal{I}_n, x)\delta(\mathcal{L}_k(x), l). \tag{2}$$

Stable solution to the above can be iteratively attained [4]. Eq.2 implies that the label $\mathcal{L}_n(x)$ complies with both the atlases and other unlabeled images. Also note that the simulated images, though participating into registration (Section 2.1), are not included in label fusion. All simulated images are instantiated by perturbing the median image, which would arbitrarily dominate the segmentation result with the simulated images included in label fusion.

### 2.3    Interactive Registration and Segmentation

Though the unlabeled images can be segmented in Section 2.2, the tentative segmentation is derived from the yet imperfect registration as in Section 2.1. On the contrary, the tentative segmentation is capable of feeding back for more accurate registration of all images in the common space, which can further improve the performance in segmentation. In our method, the registration benefits from the tentative segmentation in two folds:

1. The initial MST is estimated prior to the non-rigid registration. The high variation among all images, as well as the simple image distance measure (i.e., SSD of intensities), may lead to improperly estimated MST and thus limit the registration accuracy. On the other hand, after all images are roughly registered to the common space, the distribution of the entire image population is relatively compact and can be better learned by considering the consistency of the segmentation of all images. That is, the MST can be updated by considering the tentative segmentation.

2. The registration should also favor the consistency within the segmentation of individual images, which is only pursuit in the segmentation part of conventional methods though. In particular, we regard the tentative segmentation of images as additional image descriptors other than intensities. Besides to minimize the intensity inhomogeneity, the registration aims to directly eliminate the labeling inconsistency as well. In particular, we require the registration to align the boundaries of corresponding labels of individual images. The estimated deformation fields are then applied to register all images more accurately in the common space.

**Update MST.** To learn the MST for representing the image distribution, we propose to measure the image-to-image distance by the inconsistency between their segmentation, after all images are (roughly) registered to the common space. For any two (atlas or unlabeled) images $I_m$ and $I_n$, we calculate their overall Dice overlap ratio upon all labels

$$r(I_m, I_n) = (2 \sum_x \delta(L_m(x), L_n(x)))/(||I_m|| + ||I_n||), \tag{3}$$

where $|| \cdot ||$ computes the size of the labeled volume. The distance of the two images is then derived by $\exp(-r^2(I_m, I_n)/(2\beta^2))$, as $\beta$ is manually specified.

Given pairwise distances of all images, we are then able to build a new MST. Note that the root of the updated MST is still kept as the median image that is previously selected in the initial MST (Section 2.1). In this way, the common space in registration is fixed, though each non-root image will further refine its own deformation field. Moreover, the updated MST consists of only atlases and unlabeled images, while the simulated images are not incorporated. We argue that, after the initial registration in Section 2.1, the atlases and the unlabeled images distribute tightly in the nearby of the median image. Thus we do not need the simulated images to help update the tree.

**Update Registration.** We directly apply the (tentative) segmentation of all images to refine the deformation fields, in order to compensate for the inconsistency within the labeling. After deforming all images towards the median image, we first extract the boundaries of all labels for every warped image (i.e., by applying the Canny edge detector on the labeling map). The boundary voxels for a certain image then form a discrete pointset, which should be aligned with the label boundaries of other images. Next, we apply a Gaussian kernel to smooth the detected boundaries and convert the discrete boundary pointset into a continuous volume of Gaussian mixture [7] in the image space. Finally, the volumes of Gaussian mixtures for the labeling of a pair of images can be easily registered, i.e., via the diffeomorphic Demons [6]. The newly updated MST is also applied in the above, as the registration upon the label boundaries is performed in the recursive manner (c.f. in Section 2.1).

Note that all images further refine their registration to the common space after being warped following their previously estimated deformation fields. Therefore, we concatenate the previous deformation field of each image and its new deformation for refinement into a single field, which warps the image from its original space to the common space directly. To compensate for potential errors in the above, the concatenated deformation functions as an initialization, and is further adjusted by minimizing the intensity inhomogeneity between the specific image and the median image designating the common space. In particular, the registration adjustment is also achieved through the diffeomorphic Demons [6], yet with the high-resolution optimization only and very limited number of iterations. In this way, both the image intensity and the tentative segmentation contribute to update the registration.

## 2.4   Summary: The Interactive Registration-Segmentation Pipeline

We summarize the proposed method as follows:

1. Estimate the MST to organize all images in the population;
2. Register all images to the root of the tree and deform them to the common space;
3. Segment all unlabeled images in the common space via label fusion;
4. Go to Step 1 if not converged, continue otherwise;
5. Pull the segmentation result back to the space of each unlabeled image.

The solution above is in the iterative fashion. We impose a fixed number (i.e., 4) of iterations to be the convergence criterion, as the observed improvement upon the labeling accuracy becomes tiny after 4 iterations in our experiment. Then, after inverting the estimated deformations, the segmentation of each unlabeled image can be warped to the original image space in Step 5. The simple pullback of the segmentation might be contaminated by the errors in deforming the labels. Therefore, for each unlabeled image in Step 5, we register all atlases and other unlabeled images back to its original image space, and apply the label fusion (Section 2.2) for the final determination of the segmentation. The registration above can be efficiently solved, since the deformations between all images and the common space are known already. Moreover, note that our method is reduced to be MABMIS [4], if only a single iteration is allowed.

## 3    Experimental Results

We apply the proposed method to the NIREP dataset and compare with MABMIS [4] in order to demonstrate the importance of the interaction between registration and segmentation. The NIREP dataset consists of 16 images, each of which comes with 32 labeled ROIs. All images are resampled to the isotropic size of $256 \times 256 \times 256$ and properly pre-processed (including bias correction, skull-stripping, etc.).

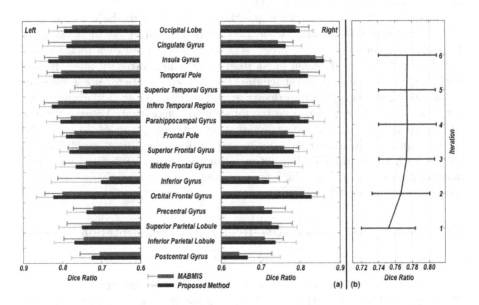

**Fig. 1.** (a) The average Dice ratios, as well as standard deviations, of 32 ROIs in the NIREP dataset yielded by MABMIS and the proposed method; (b) The iteration changes of the overall Dice ratio produced by our method.

We randomly partition all images into two equally sized subsets. By taking a certain subset of images as atlases in turn, we are able to label the other subset. The accuracy of the estimated segmentation is then evaluated against the ground truth (i.e., the manual segmentation). The average Dice ratios on all 32 labels, as well as the standard deviations, are plotted in Fig. 1(a). In particular, our method scores the overall Dice ratio at $77.45 \pm 3.39\%$ upon all labels, higher ($+2.14\%$) than $75.31 \pm 3.17\%$ of MABMIS. The results imply that the interactive registration-segmentation scheme lead to improved accuracy in multi-atlas-based labeling.

We also plot the iterative changes of the overall Dice ratio, as well as the standard deviations, in Fig. 1(b). Clearly the interaction between registration and segmentation boosts the labeling accuracy within limited number of iterations. By allowing 4 iterations in our experiment, it typically costs around 4 hours to label 8 images given another 8 atlases (single thread, Intel Core i5 CPU, 3.1GHz, 8G memory).

## 4   Discussion

In this work, we propose a novel multi-atlas-based labeling method for brain MR images, by utilizing the interactive registration-segmentation scheme. Different from most conventional methods, we allow the (tentative) segmentation of previously registered images to feed back, which results in better registration of all images and thus more accurate labeling as confirmed by the experimental result. Compared to [4], our method costs higher computation time in iterative optimization. However, significant improvement upon the speed performance is expected if introducing parallelization into our implementation. Moreover, large-scale study will also be conducted in the future to evaluate the performance of our method more comprehensively.

**Acknowledgments.** This work was supported in part by National Natural Science Foundation of China (NSFC) Grants (61473190, 61401271, 81471733).

## References

1. Coupé, P., Manjón, J.V., Fonov, V., Pruessner, J., Robles, M., Collins, D.L.: Patch-based segmentation using expert priors: Application to hippocampus and ventricle segmentation. NeuroImage **54**(2), 940–954 (2011)
2. Hamm, J., Ye, D.H., Verma, R., Davatzikos, C.: Gram: A framework for geodesic registration on anatomical manifolds. Medical Image Analysis **14**(5), 633–642 (2010)
3. Jia, H., Wu, G., Wang, Q., Kim, M., Shen, D.: iTree: Fast and accurate image registration based on the combinative and incremental tree. In: 2011 IEEE International Symposium on Biomedical Imaging: From Nano to Macro, pp. 1243–1246. IEEE (2011)
4. Jia, H., Yap, P.T., Shen, D.: Iterative multi-atlas-based multi-image segmentation with tree-based registration. Neuroimage **59**(1), 422–430 (2012)
5. Rousseau, F., Habas, P.A., Studholme, C.: A supervised patch-based approach for human brain labeling. IEEE Transactions on Medical Imaging **30**(10), 1852–1862 (2011)
6. Vercauteren, T., Pennec, X., Perchant, A., Ayache, N.: Diffeomorphic demons: Efficient non-parametric image registration. NeuroImage **45**(1), S61–S72 (2009)

7. Wang, F., Vemuri, B.C., Rangarajan, A., Eisenschenk, S.J.: Simultaneous nonrigid registration of multiple point sets and atlas construction. IEEE Transactions on Pattern Analysis and Machine Intelligence **30**(11), 2011–2022 (2008)
8. Wang, H., Suh, J.W., Das, S.R., Pluta, J.B., Craige, C., Yushkevich, P.A.: Multi-atlas segmentation with joint label fusion. IEEE Transactions on Pattern Analysis and Machine Intelligence **35**(3), 611–623 (2013)
9. Wang, Q., Chen, L., Yap, P.T., Wu, G., Shen, D.: Groupwise registration based on hierarchical image clustering and atlas synthesis. Human Brain Mapping **31**(8), 1128–1140 (2010)
10. Wang, Q., Wu, G., Yap, P.T., Shen, D.: Attribute vector guided groupwise registration. NeuroImage **50**(4), 1485–1496 (2010)
11. Warfield, S.K., Zou, K.H., Wells, W.M.: Simultaneous truth and performance level estimation (staple): an algorithm for the validation of image segmentation. IEEE Transactions on Medical Imaging **23**(7), 903–921 (2004)
12. Wolz, R., Aljabar, P., Hajnal, J.V., Hammers, A., Rueckert, D., Alzheimer's Disease Neuroimaging Initiative: Leap: learning embeddings for atlas propagation. NeuroImage **49**(2), 1316–1325 (2010)
13. Ying, S., Wu, G., Wang, Q., Shen, D.: Hierarchical unbiased graph shrinkage (hugs): A novel groupwise registration for large data set. NeuroImage **84**, 626–638 (2014)

# Negative-Supervised Cascaded Deep Learning for Traffic Sign Classification

Kaixuan Xie[1,2], Shiming Ge[2(✉)], Rui Yang[1,2], Xiang Lu[2], and Limin Sun[2]

[1] University of Chinese Academy of Sciences, Beijing, China
[2] Beijing Key Laboratory of IOT Information Security,
Institute of Information Engineering, Chinese Academy of Sciences, Beijing, China
{xiekaixuan,geshiming,yangrui,luxiang,sunlimin}@iie.ac.cn

**Abstract.** In this paper, we propose a novel deep learning framework for object classification called negative-supervised cascaded deep learning. There are two hierarchies in our cascaded method: the first one is a convolutional neural network trained on positive-only samples, which is used to select supervisory samples from a negative library. The second one is inherited from the trained first CNN. It is trained on positive and negative samples, which are selected from domain related database by utilizing negative-supervised mechanism. Experiments are applied this idea to traffic sign classification using two classic convolutional neural networks, LeNet-5 and AlexNet as baselines. Classification rates improved by 0.7% and 1.1% with LeNet-5 and AlexNet respectively, which demonstrates the efficiency and superiority of our proposed framework.

**Keywords:** Convolutional neural network · Deep learning · Negative-supervised · Object classification · Traffic sign classification

## 1 Introduction

Traffic signs play an important role in our daily life. They define a visual language providing useful information, which makes the driving safe and convenient. In intelligent transportation system (ITS), traffic sign recognition is a critical step for advance driver assistance system (ADAS) and autonomous intelligent vehicles[1]. Traffic sign recognition has two tasks: finding the locations and sizes of traffic signs in natural scene images (traffic sign detection) and classifying the detected traffic signs to their specific sub-classes (traffic sign classification)[2]. In this paper, we focus on traffic sign classification.

Due to the complex outdoor environment such as viewpoint variations, bad lighting conditions, motion-blur, occlusions, sun glare, physical damage, colors fading, clustered backgrounds, low resolution and so on, traffic signs are rotated, blurred, damaged and degenerated, which is shown in Fig. 4. Traffic sign recognition is more challenging in comparison with indoor object classification tasks, such as character and face recognition. The uncertainty and ambiguity of traffic signs do not stop the pace of research. To address traffic signs classification, many methods have been proposed according to existing survey literatures[3][4].

© Springer-Verlag Berlin Heidelberg 2015
H. Zha et al. (Eds.): CCCV 2015, Part I, CCIS 546, pp. 249–257, 2015.
DOI: 10.1007/978-3-662-48558-3_25

Traditional traffic sign classification has been approached with a number of popular machine learning methods, such as support vector machines[5], linear discriminant analysis[6], etc. These methods need to extract of features, such as Histogram of Gradients (HoG)[7], Local Binary Pattern (LBP)[8], Integral Channel Features[9] first. Recently, deep learning such as Convolutional Neural Networks (CNNs), was proposed for handling various classification tasks and has given state-of-the-art results in many vision tasks[10][11][12].

The existing deep learning based traffic sign classification methods[10][11][12] mainly learn a model to classify the detected sign to one specific class of traffic signs, and do not consider auxiliary information or extra knowledge such as background and attributes. It is argued that auxiliary information or extra knowledge could be used to augment model learning and improve classification performance. In [13], Kumar et al. presented two high-level visual features, attribute and smile, for face verification. In [14], in order to learn more discriminative representation for face classification task, Sun et. al. introduced verification signal to supervise deep learning face identification.

Motivated by [13][14], we propose a novel negative-supervised cascaded deep learning framework constructed by two hierarchies. The first deep learning module is trained with the positive samples (proposals belong to one class of objects) and then is used to select negative samples (proposals not belong to any class of objects) from domain related image database. The selected negative samples are combined with positive samples and then are trained with the second deep learning module to form final result. The major advantage of our method over those standard approaches is that we transfer knowledge from domain related data. We introduce the negative-supervised mechanism for traffic sign classification to verify the efficiency. Experimental results show that the proposed learning framework could improve classification performance without sacrificing computation performance in test stage.

The remainder of the paper is organized as follows. In Section 2, we review some closely related work and some relative knowledge. We propose negative-supervised cascaded deep convolution neural network framework in Section 3. Experiments are detailed in Section 4 and results are illustrated and analyzed in Section 5. At last we give conclusions in Section 6.

## 2   Related Work

Traffic sign classification is one of representatives of object classification and its purpose is to classify the specific sign to the corresponding class. Many machine learning methods are introduced to traffic sign classification, like k-d trees and random forests[15], SVM[5][16][17] and LDA[6]. These methods usually share the common process pipeline that consists of image pre-processing, feature extraction like HoG[7] or LBP[8]. And the processing time and classification accuracy of these methods are very dependent on the specifically designed features. By contrast, neural networks need less pre-processing and no independent feature extraction. In [10], Ciresan et. al. proposed a committee of CNNs and a

Multi-layer Perceptron (MLP) to perform traffic sign classification. In [11], they improved the method with multi-column deep neural network. Jin et al. [12] described an ensemble of CNNs and proposed a Hinge Loss Stochastic Gradient Descent (HLSGD) method to train CNNs. Most of traffic sign classification approaches modify their network architecture to improve their performance but they use only positive samples and ignore other information.

Traffic sign classification belongs to artificial intelligence. It can be regarded as a problem of knowledge mining, analysis and understanding, where transfer learning can truly be beneficial[18]. We are motivated by the transfer learning techniques[18][19]. Some knowledge is specific for individual domains or tasks and some knowledge may be common between different domains such that they may help improve performance for the target domain or task. We realize that various patches of scene images can be considered as common knowledge. We make them one specific negative class after scientific selection thus forming negative-supervised learning.

Taking all above into consideration, we proposed a negative-supervised cascaded deep learning framework. It consists of two cascaded deep convolutional neural networks (CNNs). We train the first CNN positive samples, and use it to select negative images from random patches as one component of training set in the second neural network. Experiments prove that negative-supervised mechanism improves the separability and recognition of the classifier.

## 3   Our Method

This section introduces our negative-supervised cascaded framework for classification via deep CNNs. Overall architecture of pipeline is illustrated in Fig. 1.

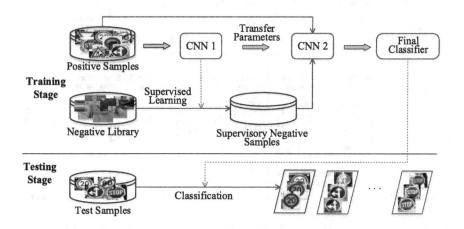

**Fig. 1.** Pipeline of Negative-supervised Cascaded Deep Learning

The first CNN is trained on positive samples. We use it to select discriminative negative samples from domain related negative sample library and train the second convolutional neural network on both positive and selected negative samples. The learned parameters of the first CNN are transferred to the second CNN for training.

In the following subsections, we first introduce two baseline CNNs [20][21], which are capable of achieving record-breaking results on a highly challenging data set using purely-positive learning. Then we detail our negative-supervised deep learning mechanism. Finally we construct a cascaded CNN to perform the task of traffic sign classification.

### 3.1 Deep Convolutional Neural Networks

CNNs are designed to recognize visual patterns directly from raw image pixels with minimal preprocessing. They can recognize patterns with variability and robustness. A CNN usually contains convolutional layers, pooling layers, fully-connected layers and finally a soft-max layer. We use the LeNet-5[20] and AlexNet[21] for our two baseline networks, which is shown in Fig.2.

LeNet-5 is originally designed for handwritten and machine-printed character recognition. It contains three convolutional layers and one fully-connected layer and ultimately a soft-max layer. Rectified Linear Units (ReLUs) $f(x) = max(0, x)$ is follow the convolutional layers and used to promote nonlinearity. Max-pooling layer is applied over neighboring neurons and used to lower in

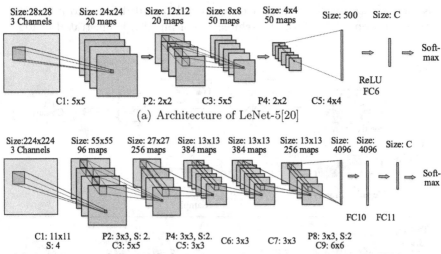

(a) Architecture of LeNet-5[20]

(b) Architecture of AlexNet[21]. Each convolutional layer follows a ReLU layer.

**Fig. 2.** Architecture of Deep CNN. C, P, FC are short for convolutional layer, max-pooling layer, fully-connected layer, respectively. S is short for stride and omitted if stride is 1.

dimension thus decreasing over-fitting. The fully-connected layers have 500 neurons each and followed by the soft-max layers and input images need to be scaled to 28 × 28 pixels.

The architecture of AlexNet is similar with LeNet-5 but much deeper. It contains five convolutional layers, two fully-connected layers and ultimately a soft-max layer. Additional response-normalization layers are applied across feature channels. The fully-connected layers have 4096 neurons each and followed by the soft-max layer. Similarly, the input images need to be scaled to 224 × 224 pixels to adapt to the neural network.

### 3.2  Negative-Supervised Learning

The goal of negative-supervised learning is to boost the discriminative ability of CNN by retraining another CNN with the supervisory negative samples. The supervisory negative samples refer to the samples that may have discriminative information in negative library. These supervisory negative samples provide additional information related to positive samples, thus making classification task more accurate.

We select them according to the confidence generated by the first CNN and extract the maximum confidence $MC$ of each positive sample after the soft-max layer. Knowing that the maximum confidence corresponds to the specific assigned category so we obtain the frequency of them. Then we put the same order of magnitude negative samples to the network and do the same procedure.

The probability density are illustrated as Fig.3. (a)(b) are the distributions of maximum confidence of positive and negative samples respectively. (c) is the standard deviation confidence of samples and it is shown that they have the same distribution. So we choose the supervisory samples based on maximum confidence. Maximum confidences are normalized between 0 and 1, most positive samples are convergent to a peak while negative samples are distributed scattered. It is obvious that the larger the maximum confidence is and the larger the standard deviation is, the more supervisory information the negative samples have. We select the supervisory negative samples that have $MC > T$, in which

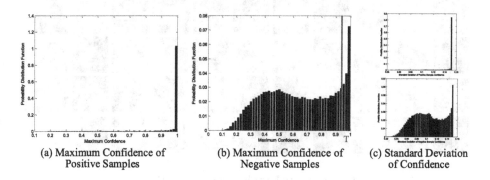

(a) Maximum Confidence of Positive Samples

(b) Maximum Confidence of Negative Samples

(c) Standard Deviation of Confidence

**Fig. 3.** Statistics of Standard Deviation of Confidence

$T$ is the threshold deduced from the confidence of validation set generated by the first CNN.

### 3.3 Traffic Sign Classification

In this subsection we describe the application of negative-supervised learning and realize it on traffic sign classification.

We use the traditional strategy to train the first CNN. we directly apply five convolutional layers and following two fully-connected layers and then fed to a soft-max layer corresponding to the number of positive classes defined as $C$. After the soft-max layer, we get $C$ values meaning the distinguish confidence. Then we apply the negative-supervised principle presented in Section 3.2 to select negative samples. Next we use both $C$ positive classes and additional $C+1$ class to train the following cascaded CNN.

## 4 Experiments

In this section, we introduce the positive training database and negative library. describe two baseline experimental results in comparison with our proposed method. The first experiment is trained on only positive samples. The second is trained on positive samples and randomly selected negative samples.

### 4.1 Database and Negative Library

The database, German Traffic Sign Recognition Benchmark(GTSRB)[22] shown in Fig.4 was created from approximately 10 hours of video that was recorded while driving on different road types in Germany during daytime. It is a large lifelike data set of more than 50,000 traffic sign images in 43 classes and contains images of more than 1700 traffic sign instances. The size of the traffic signs varies between 15×15 and 222×193 pixels [22].

**Fig. 4.** Partial Traffic Signs of GTSRB

The negative database is randomly selected from the SUN database[23], which is a comprehensive collection of annotated images covering a large variety of environmental scenes, places and the objects within. It has various outdoor scenes and using it as negative library can provide domain information for classification. We randomly cut patches from the SUN database and selected 100,000 patches that varies between 15 × 15 and 222 × 193 pixels, thus keeping correspondence with the positive database.

## 4.2   Training Convolutional Neural Networks

We apply the two baseline CNNs AlexNet and LeNet-5 for traffic sign classification on the benchmark GTSRB. The GTSRB data are split into two subsets. Set I is training data set, which contains 39209 training images in 43 classes. Set II is testing data set, which contains 12630 test images. Firstly, we use 43 classes positive samples in training set, directly apply five convolutional layers and following two fully-connected layers and then fed to a 43-way soft-max layer. Then we put nearly 300,000 negative samples to the network and get the confidence after soft-max layer. Next we make the threshold $T = 0.98$ and select negative samples whose maximum confidence more than $T$, thus we have approximately 40,000 positive samples and 100,000 negative samples plunged into the second CNN.

## 4.3   Experimental Results

This subsection give the classification rate of our proposed approach presented in Section 3 compared with positive-only samples training and additional randomly selected negative samples training. The only purpose of our experiments is to demonstrate that adding negative samples is useful to classification and if selecting negative samples scientifically can be more efficient. Our framework is compared with the basic CNNs and does not modify their architecture. For each basic CNN, we perform three schemes: positive samples only (Pos-only), positive and randomly selected negative samples (Neg-randomly), positive and negative-supervised negative samples (Neg-supervised).

**Table 1.** Classification Rate

| Training Network | Pos-only | Neg-randomly | Neg-supervised |
|---|---|---|---|
| LeNet-5 [20] | 87.2% | 87.5% | 87.9% |
| AlexNet [21] | 91.7% | 92.4% | 92.8% |

The classification rates are shown in Table.1. Firstly we simply use the two baselines LeNet-5 and AlexNet on only positive samples, the results are 87.2% and 91.7% respectively. Then we add negative samples generated randomly and the classification rate improve 0.3% and 0.7% each. Finally, we applied our negative-supervised mechanism to select negative samples and the rate reach

87.9% using LeNet-5 and 92.8% using AlexNet. These experiments show that useful information from domain related negative library can really help obtain related information and improve classification rate.

## 5  Conclusion and Discussion

This paper presented a negative-supervised cascaded deep convolutional neural network architecture. We proposed a negative sample selecting method to supervise CNN training. Experiments showed that only positive training set were not sufficient and can be improved by adding negative samples, especially specific selected negative samples. Negative-supervised mechanism can help utilize data more sufficient. And our framework can be utilized by all deep learning strategy and extended to other applications.

**Acknowledgments.** This work is supported in part by the National Natural Science Foundation of China (No.61402463), the Excellent Young Scientist Foundation of Institute of Information Engineering Chinese Academy of Sciences (No.1102008202), and the "Strategic Priority Research Program" of the Chinese Academy of Sciences (No.XDA06040101).

## References

1. Fleyeh, H., Dougherty, M.: Road and traffic sign detection and recognition. In: Proceedings of the 16th Mini-EURO Conference and 10th Meeting of EWGT, pp. 644–653 (2005)
2. Yang, Y., Luo, H., Xu, H., et al.: Towards real-time traffic sign detection and classification. In: 2014 IEEE 17th International Conference on Intelligent Transportation Systems (ITSC), pp. 87–92. IEEE, Qingdao (2014)
3. Fu, M.Y., Huang. Y.S.: A survey of traffic sign recognition. In: Proceedings of the 2010 International Conference on Wavelet Analysis and Pattern Recognition(ICWAPR), pp. 119–124. IEEE, Qingdao (2010)
4. Mogelmose, A., Trivedi, M.M., Moeslund, T.B.: Vision-based traffic sign detection and analysis for intelligent driver assistance systems: perspectives and survey. J IEEE Transactions on Intelligent Transportation Systems **13**, 1484–1497 (2012)
5. Maldonado-Bascn, S., Lafuente-Arroyo, S., Gil-Jimenez, P., et al.: Road-sign detection and recognition based on support vector machines. J. IEEE Transactions on Intelligent Transportation Systems **8**, 264–278 (2007)
6. Stallkamp, J., et al.: Man vs. computer: benchmarking machine learning algorithms for traffic sign recognition. Neural Networks **32**, 323–332 (2012)
7. Hasan, F., Janina, R.: Benchmark evaluation of HOG descriptors as features for classification of traffic signs. International Journal for Traffic and Transport Engineering **3**(4), 448–464 (2013)
8. Liu, C., Chang, F., Chen, Z.: Rapid multiclass traffic sign detection in high-resolution image. IEEE Transactions on Intelligent Transportation System **PP**(99), 1C–10 (2014)

9. Yang, Y., Luo, H., Xu, H., et al.: Towards real-time traffic sign detection and classification. In: IEEE 17th International Conference on Intelligent Transportation Systems (ITSC), pp. 87C–92 (2014)

10. Ciresan, D., Meier, U., Masci, J., et al.: A committee of neural networks for traffic sign classification. In: The 2011 International Joint Conference on Neural Networks (IJCNN), pp. 1918–1921. IEEE, California (2011)

11. Ciresan, D., Meier, U., Masci, J., et al.: Multi-column deep neural network for traffic sign classification. J. Neural Networks **32**, 333–338 (2012)

12. Jin, J., Fu, K., Zhang, C.: Traffic sign recognition with hinge loss trained convolutional neural networks. J. IEEE Intelligent Transportation Systems Society **15**(5), 1991–2000 (2014)

13. Kumar, N., Berg, A.C., Belhumeur, P.N., et al.: Describable visual attributes for face verification and image search. In: 2013 IEEE Transactions on Pattern Analysis and Machine Intelligence (PAMI), vol. 33(10), pp. 1962–1977. IEEE (2011)

14. Sun, Y., Chen, Y., Wang, X., et al.: Deep learning face representation by joint identification-verification. In: Advances in Neural Information Processing Systems (NIPS) (2014)

15. Zaklouta, F., Stanciulescu, B., Hamdoun, O.: Traffic sign classification using kd trees and random forests. In: The 2011 International Joint Conference on Neural Networks (IJCNN), pp. 2151–2155. IEEE, California (2011)

16. Greenhalgh, J., Mirmehdi, M.: Real-time detection and recognition of road traffic signs. J IEEE Transactions on Intelligent Transportation Systems **13**, 1498–1506 (2012)

17. Wang, G., Ren, G., Wu, Z., et al.: A hierarchical method for traffic sign classification with support vector machines. In: The 2013 International Joint Conference on Neural Networks (IJCNN), pp. 1–6. IEEE, Texas (2013)

18. Pan, S.J., Yang, Q.: A survey on transfer learning. J IEEE Transactions on Knowledge and Data Engineering **22**, 1345–1359 (2010)

19. Xu, C., Cetintas, S., Lee, K.C., et al.: Visual Sentiment Prediction with Deep Convolutional Neural Networks. J. arXiv preprint arXiv:1411.5731 (2014)

20. LeCun, Y., Bottou, L., Bengio, Y., et al.: Gradient-based learning applied to document recognition. J. Proceedings of the IEEE **86**, 2278–2324 (1998)

21. Krizhevsky, A., Sutskever, I., Hinton, G.E.: Imagenet classification with deep convolutional neural networks. In: Advances in Neural Information Processing Systems, pp. 1097–1105 (2012)

22. Stallkamp, J., Schlipsing, M., Salmen, J., et al.: The German traffic sign recognition benchmark: a multi-class classification competition. In: 2011 IEEE International Joint Conference on Neural Networks (IJCNN), pp. 1453–1460. IEEE, California (2011)

23. Xiao, J., Hays, J., Ehinger, K.A., et al.: Sun database: large-scale scene recognition from abbey to zoo. In: 2010 IEEE Conference on Computer Vision and Pattern Recognition (CVPR), pp. 3485–3492. IEEE, San Francisco (2010)

24. Sermanet, P., LeCun, Y.: Traffic sign recognition with multi-scale convolutional networks. In: 2011 IEEE International Joint Conference on Neural Networks (IJCNN), pp. 2809–2813. IEEE, California (2011)

# Saliency Detection Based on Non-uniform Quantification for RGB Channels and Weights for Lab Channels

Yahui Yuan[1], Aili Han[1(✉)], and Feilin Han[2]

[1] Department of Computer Science, Shandong University, Weihai 264209, China
hanal@sdu.edu.cn
[2] College of Computer Science and Technology, Zhejiang University, Hangzhou 310007, China

**Abstract.** We propose a non-uniform quantification method for RGB channels based on the different sensitivities of human eyes to the red, green and blue primary colors, which quantifies the R, G, B channels to different ranges, and then design a method of computing the weights for Lab channels and a method of computing the weighted color distance based on the different contributions of L,a,b channels to pixel saliency. Based on this, we present a saliency detection method using the non-uniform quantification method and the weighted color distance. First, we do the non-uniform quantification on an RGB image and convert the result into Lab space. And then, we compute the weights $w_L$, $w_a$, $w_b$ for L,a,b channels by means of histogram, and compute the weighted color distance of each pixel $I_k$ to all other pixels using the channel weights. Finally, the saliency of each pixel is computed using the weighted color distances. The proposed non-uniform quantification method, the weight computing method and the weighted color distance can be used in the early processing step for various applications based on color features. Experimental results show that our methods can improve the quality and efficiency for saliency detection to some extent.

**Keywords:** Saliency detection · Visual computing · Non-uniform quantification · Channel weight

## 1 Introduction

Human beings can understand complex scenes in real time because human visual process can choose a subset of perceptible information to reduce the complexity of scene analysis. The visual computing system should also have such function. How to select a valid subset of the given image is the key to improve the efficiency of visual computing system.

In order to select a valid subset of the given image, the existing saliency detection methods usually quantify the pixel values of RGB channels to the same range, which is called the uniform quantification method in this paper. In 1998, Itti et al. [1] proposed a visual attention system of combining multi-scale image features into a single saliency map, which reduces the input image to 640×480 pixels. In 2006, Harel et al. [2]

© Springer-Verlag Berlin Heidelberg 2015
H. Zha et al. (Eds.): CCCV 2015, Part I, CCIS 546, pp. 258–266, 2015.
DOI: 10.1007/978-3-662-48558-3_26

proposed a graph-based visual saliency model (GBVS), in which they first reduce the input image to 600×400 pixels, and then use the linear filters to get one or more feature maps that are down-sampled to 25×37 pixels. In 2007, Hou et al. [3] proposed a spectral residual approach for saliency detection, in which they first adjust the input image to 64×64 pixels by means of low pass filter and down-sample method, and then do the saliency detection on the 64×64 images. In 2011, Cheng et al. [4] proposed a global contrast based salient detection method, which includes two contrast methods, i.e., a histogram-based contrast (HC) method and a region contrast (RC) method. The HC method first uniformly quantifies each channel of the input image to 12 values, and then computes the contrast between a pixel and all the other pixels.

The above uniform quantification methods can reduce the number of image colors, which result in less computations, but they do not consider the sensitivity differences of human eyes to different colors. We propose a non-uniform quantification method based on the different sensitivities of human eyes to the red, green and blue primary colors. Different from the previous quantification methods, our method quantifies the R, G, B channels to different ranges, which will help for the performance improvement of saliency detection method.

## 2    Non-uniform Quantification for RGB Channels

For an RGB image, the values in R,G,B channels are in the range of 0 to 255, corresponding to $256^3 \approx 1.68*10^7$ kinds of colors. According to the visual attention theory [11,12], only when the difference between pixel values reaches a certain quantity, human eyes can perceive it. Therefore, the pixel values in R,G,B channels in an image can be separately quantified according to the different sensitivities of human eyes to different colors so as to reduce the amount of computations. The previous methods quantify the pixel values in R,G,B channels to the same range, which can reduce the total number of colors, but do not consider the sensitivity differences of human eyes to different colors. In this paper, we propose a non-uniform quantification method, which quantifies the values in R,G,B channels to different ranges based on the different sensitivities of human eyes to the red, green and blue primary colors.

### 2.1    Visual Sensitivity Tests on RGB Channels

In order to understand the sensitivities of human eyes to different colors, we did the sensitivity tests on a three-primary-colors image, in which we separately changed the pixel values in RGB channels step by step.

Experimentally, we observed that when the pixel value in R channel decreases to about 40, it is hard to distinguish the red region for human eyes; when the pixel value in G channel decreases to about 30, it is hard to distinguish the green region for human eyes; when the pixel value in B channel decreases to about 65, it is hard to distinguish the blue region for human eyes. The experimental results are shown in Fig.1. The experimental results show that the visual sensitivities of human eyes to the red, green and blue colors are different, and the sensitivity order is: green > red > blue.

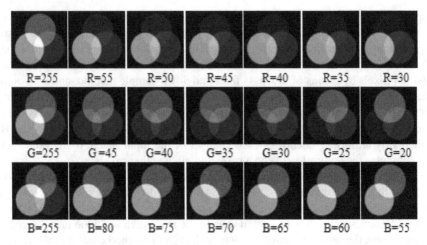

**Fig. 1.** The stepwise results of separately decreasing the pixel values in R,G,B channels in a three-primary-colors image.

From the visual sensitivity tests, we can know that the red in the black background is not salient when its pixel value is less than 40; the green is not salient when its pixel value is less than 30; the blue is not salient when its pixel value is less than 65.

## 2.2    Theory Basis of the Visual Sensitivity Order

The visible spectrum is shown in Fig.2(a), which are from [10]. The sensitivity of human eyes to a single color can be denoted by a luminosity function [10]. The luminosity functions under the light and dark environments are shown in Fig.2(b). From the luminosity function under the dark environment, we can know that human eyes are most sensitive to

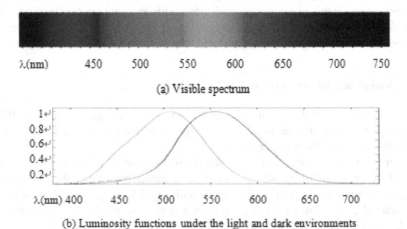

**Fig. 2.** Visible spectrum and luminosity functions [10].

the yellow-green color with 555nm wavelength, followed by green, red and blue. The closer the distance to both ends of the visible spectrum, the less sensitive the human eyes are. The experimental results in our visual sensitivity tests agree with this theory.

## 2.3    Non-uniform Quantification for RGB Channels

We design an algorithm of non-uniform quantification according to the experimental results in our visual sensitivity tests. Let $k_1$, $k_2$, $k_3$ denote the ranges of pixels values in RGB channels after non-uniform quantification, respectively. The total color number after non-uniform quantification is $k_1*k_2*k_3$, which is far less than that in the original RGB image. Therefore, the non-uniform quantification algorithm can reduce the amount of computations and improve the computational efficiency.

**Algorithm 1.** Non-uniform quantification
   Input: an RGB image $I$;
   Output: an RGB image $I'$ after non-uniform quantification
   (1) Quantify the pixel value in $R$ channel of image $I$ in step length of 40. The range of the pixel value in $R$ channel after non-uniform quantification is $k_1 = \lceil 256/40 \rceil$;
   (2) Quantify the pixel value in $G$ channel in step length of 30. The range of the pixel value in $G$ channel after non-uniform quantification is $k_2 = \lceil 256/30 \rceil$;
   (3) Quantify the pixel value in $B$ channel in step length of 65. The range of the pixel value in $B$ channel after non-uniform quantification is $k_3 = \lceil 256/65 \rceil$.

We applied the non-uniform quantification algorithm to a number of RGB images, three of them are shown in Fig.3. From the visual effects before and after the non-uniform quantification, we observed that after the non-uniform quantification, the difficulty of distinguishing the object and the background in an image does not increase. The non-uniform quantification algorithm can reduce the color number and so improve the computational efficiency.

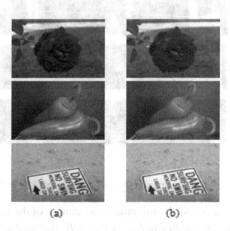

(a)                              (b)

**Fig. 3.** The visual effects before and after non-uniform quantification. (a) The original RGB images; (b) The images after non-uniform quantification.

From the non-uniform quantification algorithm, we know that $k_1 = \lceil 256/40 \rceil = 7$, $k_2 = \lceil 256/30 \rceil = 9$, $k_3 = \lceil 256/65 \rceil = 4$. Thus, the total color number after the non-uniform quantification is $k_1 * k_2 * k_3 = 252$. The total color number decreases from about $1.68 * 10^7$ to 252, which results in the significant improvement in the computational efficiency.

## 3    Computing the Weights for Lab Channels

The histograms of RGB channels in the images shown in Fig.4(a) are shown in Fig.4(b)~(d), and the histograms of Lab channels in the images shown in Fig.5(a) are shown in Fig.5(b)~(d). We observed that the differences between gray distributions in Lab color space are more obvious than that in RGB space. Therefore, in the following saliency detection algorithm, we compute the weights for Lab channels.

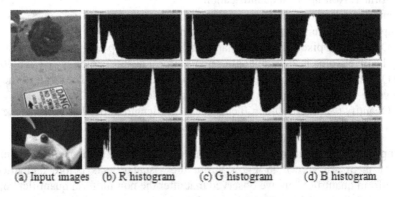

(a) Input images    (b) R histogram    (c) G histogram    (d) B histogram

**Fig. 4.** The input images and their histograms of R, G, B channels.

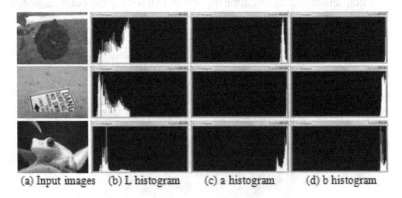

(a) Input images    (b) L histogram    (c) a histogram    (d) b histogram

**Fig. 5.** The input images and their histograms of L, a, b channels.

Let $miH_L$, $miH_a$, $miH_b$ denote the minimum coordinates of the bins with height greater than 5 in the L, a, b histograms, and $maH_L$, $maH_a$, $maH_b$ denote the maximum coordinates in the L, a, b histograms, respectively. We use the following formula to compute the weights $w_L$, $w_a$, $w_b$ for the L, a, b channels:

$$w_L = \frac{maH_L - miH_L}{\sum_{x \in L,a,b}(maH_x - miH_x)},$$

$$w_a = \frac{maH_a - miH_a}{\sum_{x \in L,a,b}(maH_x - miH_x)}, \tag{1}$$

$$w_b = \frac{maH_b - miH_b}{\sum_{x \in L,a,b}(maH_b - miH_b)}.$$

## 4    Saliency Detection Algorithm Based on Non-uniform Quantification and Channel Weights

The saliency of a pixel is defined as the color contrast of the pixel to all other pixels in the image in the HC method [4]. Our saliency definition is similar with that in the HC method, but we use the weighted color distance. By testing the visual sensitivity of human eyes to different colors, we know that different channels have different contributions to the saliency of pixels. Base on this observation, we give a weighted color distance $D_w(I_k, I_u)$ between pixels $I_k$ and $I_u$ in Lab color space:

$$D_w(I_k, I_u) = \frac{1}{w_L} \cdot \| v_{L_k} - v_{L_u} \| + \frac{1}{w_a} \cdot \| v_{a_k} - v_{a_u} \| + \frac{1}{w_b} \cdot \| v_{b_k} - v_{b_u} \| \tag{2}$$

For each pixel $I_k$, we compute its saliency $S(I_k)$ using the weighted distance $D_w(I_k, I_u)$:

$$S(I_k) = \sum_{\forall I_u \in I} D_w(I_k, I_u) \tag{3}$$

The saliency detection algorithm based on the proposed non-uniform quantification method for RGB channels and the weight computing method for Lab channels is given as follows.

**Algorithm 2.** Saliency detection algorithm

Input: an RGB image $I$;
Output: the saliency map of the input RGB image $I$
(1) Non-uniformly quantify each channel in the RGB image by Algorithm 1. The resulted image $I'$ contains less colors.
(2) Convert the resulted image $I'$ into Lab color space, and generate the histograms of L, a, b channels by means of histogram function.
(3) Compute the weights $w_L$, $w_a$, $w_b$ for Lab channels by means of formula (1).
(4) Compute the weighted color distances by means of formula (2).
(5) Compute the saliency value $S(I_k)$ of each pixel $I_k$ by means of formula (3) to get the saliency map of the given image.

Take the rose image shown in Fig.6(a) as an example. The image is first non-uniformly quantified into an image that contains less colors, as shown in Fig.6(b), which is then converted into Lab space to generate the histograms of L,a,b channels. From the histograms, we can get $minH_L$=14, $maxH_L$=99, $minH_a$=101, $maxH_a$=119, $minH_b$=117, $maxH_b$=119. The weights $w_L$, $w_a$, $w_b$ are computed by the following formula:

$$w_L =(99-14)/[(99-14)+(119-101)+ (119-117)]=83/(83+18+2) = 0.8058 ,$$
$$w_a =(119-101)/[ (99-14)+(119-101)+ (119-117)]=1/(83+18+2) =0.1748 , \qquad (4)$$
$$w_b =(119-117)/[ (99-14)+(119-101)+ (119-117)]=2/(83+18+2) = 0.0194 .$$

The final saliency map is shown in Fig.6(c). The experimental results of using different methods to the rose image are shown in the first line of Fig.7.

(a)                              (b)                              (c)

**Fig. 6.** Saliency detection based on non-uniform quantification and channel weights. (a) The original image; (b) The image after non-uniform quantification; (c) The saliency map.

## 5    Experimental Results and Analysis

We test our method on the MSRA-1000 [7] image dataset. In order to illustrate the effectiveness of our method, we compare the saliency maps obtained by our method with those obtained by the state-of-the-art saliency methods FT [7], HC [4], LC [8], RC [4] and SR [3], some of the experimental results are shown in Fig.7.

The experimental results show that, for the most images in the MSRA-1000 image dataset, the saliency maps obtained by our method are better than those by the LC and SR methods, and the overall results are not lower than those by the FT, HC and RC methods. For some images, the experimental results obtained by our method are more accurate. Take the rose image shown in Fig.6(a) as an example. The saliency maps obtained by FT, HC and RC methods include the rose region as well as the white horizontal region on the top side of the given image, and the white horizontal region is even more clearly than the rose region by using the FT and HC methods. The saliency map obtained by our method highlights the rose region better than the other methods, as shown in Fig.7.

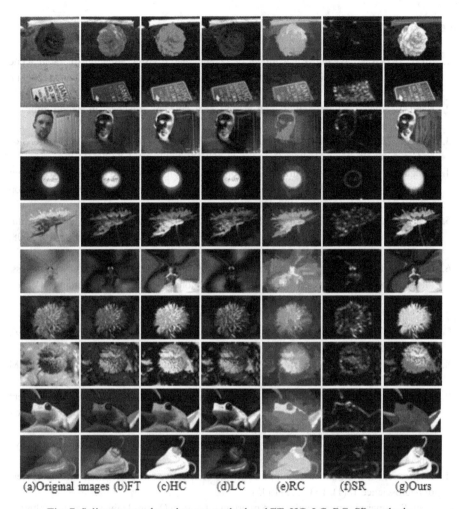

(a)Original images  (b)FT     (c)HC      (d)LC       (e)RC       (f)SR       (g)Ours

**Fig. 7.** Saliency maps by using our method and FT, HC, LC, RC, SR methods.

# 6    Conclusion

For the big data such as images or video, the usual method of decreasing the amount of computations is to down-sample the image. Another effective way is to decrease reasonably the range of pixel values in each channel. The existing methods do this usually by reducing the size of the image, while our method decreases the range of pixel values in each channel. Intuitively, the existing methods usually reduce the length and width of the image, which results in the loss of many image details, and our method reduce the range of pixel values in each channel, which does not lost the details of image but reduce the intensity of image details.

# References

1. Itti, L., Koch, C., Niebur, E.: A model of saliency-based visual attention for rapid scene analysis. IEEE Transactions on Pattern Analysis and Machine Intelligence **20**(11), 1254–1259 (1998)
2. Harel, J., Koch, C., Perona, P.: Graph-based visual saliency. Advances in Neural Information Processing Systems **19**, 545–552 (2006)
3. Hou, X., Zhang, L.: Saliency detection: a spectral residual approach. In: IEEE Conference on Computer Vision and Pattern Recognition (CVPR 2007), pp. 1-8 (2007)
4. Mingming, C., Guoxin, Z., Mitra, N.J., Xiaolei, H., Shimin, H.: Global contrast based salient region detection. In: 2011 IEEE Conference on Computer Vision and Pattern Recognition (CVPR 2011), vol. 42(7), pp. 409-416 (2011)
5. Achanta, R., Estrada, F.J., Wils, P., Süsstrunk, S.: Salient region detection and segmentation. In: Gasteratos, A., Vincze, M., Tsotsos, J.K. (eds.) ICVS 2008. LNCS, vol. 5008, pp. 66–75. Springer, Heidelberg (2008)
6. Peng, J., Haibin, L., Jingyi, Y., Jingliang, P.: Salient region detection by UFO: uniqueness, focusness and objectness. In: 2013 IEEE International Conference on Computer Vision (ICCV 2013), pp. 1976-1983 (2013)
7. Achanta, R., Hemami, S., Estrada, F., Süsstrunk, S.: Frequency-tuned salient region detection. In: IEEE Conference on Computer Vision and Pattern Recognition (CVPR 2009), pp. 1597-1604 (2009)
8. Yun, Z.: Visual attention detection in video sequences using spatiotemporal cues. ACM MM (2006)
9. Lu, S., Mahadevan, V., Vasconcelos, N.: Learning optimal seeds for diffusion-based salient object detection. In: 2014 IEEE Conference on Computer Vision and Pattern Recognition (CVPR 2014), pp. 2790-2797 (2014)
10. Wikipedia explanation of luminosity function. https://en.wikipedia.org/wiki/Luminosity_function
11. Desimone, R., Duncan, J.: Neural mechanisms of selective visual attention. Annual review of neuroscience **18**(1), 193–222 (1995)
12. Zeki, S.: Inner vision: an exploration of art and the brain.Oxford University Press (1999)

# Edge-Based Unsupervised Evaluation
# of Image Segmentation

Yihui Liang[1](✉), Han Huang[1], and Zhaoquan Cai[2]

[1] Software Engineering School, South China University of Technology,
Guangzhou, China
yihuiliangchn@gmail.com
[2] Research Department, Huizhou University, Huizhou, China

**Abstract.** This paper focuses on a fundamental problem in computer vision: how to evaluate the quality of image segmentation. Supervised evaluation methods provide a more accurate evaluation than the unsupervised methods, but these methods cannot work without manually-segmented reference segmentations. This shortcoming limits its applications. We present an edge-based evaluation method which works without the comparison with reference segmentations. Our method evaluates the quality of segmentation by three edge-based measures: the edge fitness, the intra-region edge error and the out-of-bound error. Experimental results show that our method provides a more accurate evaluation than those method based on the statistic of pixel values, and can be used in both segmentation evaluation and region evaluation. A significant linear correlation is shown between the evaluation scores of our method and two widely used supervised methods. The proposed methods show a high performance on the automatic choice of the best fitted parameters for region growing.

**Keywords:** Image segmentation · Objective evaluation · Unsupervised evaluation

## 1 Introduction

Segmenting a color image into multiple groups is a fundamental problem in the field of computer vision. While a volume of research has been devoted to this topic, relatively fewer work has been done on the segmentation evaluation. According to the classification made by Zhang et al.[1], segmentation evaluation methods can be divided into two categories: subjective evaluation and objective evaluation. This classification depends on whether human evaluators visually examine the segmentation result or not.

This work is supported by National Natural Science Foundation of China (61370102, 61170193, 61203310, 61370185), Guangdong Natural Science Foundation (2014A030306050, S2013010013432, S2012020011081, S2013010015940), the Ministry of Education - China Mobile Research Funds (MCM20130331), the Fundamental Research Funds for the Central Universities, SCUT (2014ZG0043,2015PT022) and The Pearl River Science & technology Star Project (2012J2200007).

© Springer-Verlag Berlin Heidelberg 2015
H. Zha et al. (Eds.): CCCV 2015, Part I, CCIS 546, pp. 267–276, 2015.
DOI: 10.1007/978-3-662-48558-3_27

Subjective evaluation methods quantify the quality of segmentation by the evaluators' subjective judgments. Consequently, the evaluation result is affected by evaluators' bias. In order to minimize the influence of subjective factors, involving a large group of evaluators is necessary for subjective evaluation[1]. Moreover, the group of evaluators must be background-varied, age-varied even gender-varied. The dependence of human examination makes subjective evaluation become a time-consuming method, and limits their application on real-time process.

Unlike the subjective evaluation, objective evaluation can work without the visual comparison by evaluators. Depending on whether the evaluation method compares segmentation result with the manually-segmented reference segmentation or not, objective evaluation methods can be further divided into two categories: supervised evaluation and unsupervised evaluation.

Supervised evaluation methods evaluate segmentation by comparing segmentation result with manually-segmented reference segmentation which is also known as ground-truth. Because of the direct comparison of segmentation results and reference segmentation, in most cases, these methods provides a more accurate measure than unsupervised methods. A variety of supervised methods have been proposed[2–4], and widely used to compare segmentation performance on a determined image set[5]. However, the time-consuming problem remain in supervised methods because of the dependence of reference images. In actuality, most applications of computer vision can not provide reference segmentation.

Unsupervised evaluation methods can work without any priori knowledge, these methods measure the quality of segmentation based on the segmentation criterions made by humans. The most attractive advantage of unsupervised evaluation is that reference segmentation is no necessary for these methods. The time-consuming problem no longer exists in supervised methods, moreover, these methods can apply on real-time system. A few unsupervised evaluation methods have been proposed. Early approaches aim at quantifying the difference and similarly of inter-region and intra-region in gray or color space. Entropy theory was introduced to unsupervised segmentation evaluation by Zhang et al.[6].

However, no evaluation method appears to be satisfactory in all cases[7]. In this paper, we propose a new unsupervised evaluation scheme. Unlike the existing methods which statistically analysis the pixel values in gray scale or color scale, our method analyses three measurements: the edge fitness, the intra-region edge error and the out-of-bound error, which will be described in detail in section 2.

## 2    Edge-Based Segmentation Evaluation

In this section, we first define symbols for the expression; secondly two representative unsupervised segmentation evaluation methods are introduced; in the third subsection, an edge-based segmentation evaluation method is proposed.

### 2.1    Symbols Definition

To unify the description, we make the following definitions:

- $S$ corresponds to a segmentation result,
- $N$ corresponds the number of pixels of the input image,
- $R$ corresponds to the set of regions $R = \{R_1, ..., R_{N_R}\}$ that forms $S$, and $N_R$ corresponds the number of regions
- $R_i$ corresponds the set of pixels in the $i$th region of $R$,
- $|R_i|$ corresponds the number of pixels within $R_i$,
- $f_v(p)$ corresponds the value of pixel $p$ with feature $v$.
- $D(v_1, v_2)$ corresponds the Euclidean distance between vector $v_1$ and $v_2$.
- $\mathcal{N}_k(p)$ corresponds the set of $k$ neighborhoods of pixel $p$, $k = \{4, 8, ...\}$,
- $u(t)$ corresponds a step function:

$$u(t) = \begin{cases} 1, & t > 0 \\ 0, & otherwise \end{cases} \qquad (1)$$

## 2.2 Related Work

Unsupervised evaluation methods quantify the quality of segmentation according to empirical goodness that defined by humans. In this subsection, two representative methods are introduced.

### Color-Based Segmentation Evaluation

Based on the visible color difference study, Chen et al. proposed a color-based unsupervised evaluation method[8]. The visible color difference evaluation function(VCD) is defined as:

$$E_{VCD}(S) = E_{\text{intra}}(S) + E_{\text{inter}}(S) \qquad (2)$$

where $E_{\text{intra}}(S)$ measures the intra-region visual color error, and $E_{\text{inter}}(S)$ measures the inter-region visual error.

The intra-region visual color error is defined as:

$$E_{\text{intra}}(S) = \sum_{R_i \in R} \sum_{p \in R_i} u\left(D\left(g(p), \hat{g}(i)\right) - t_1\right)/N \qquad (3)$$

where $g(p)$ and $\hat{g}(i)$ respectively denotes the value at pixel $p$ and the average color value of $i$th region in segmentation result in $L^*a^*b^*$ color space. $t_1$ denotes a threshold which is set to 6.

The inter-region visual error is defined as:

$$E_{\text{inter}}(S) = \frac{t_2}{N} \cdot \sum_{i=1}^{N_R} \sum_{j=1,2,...N_R \cap j \neq i} w_{i,j} \cdot u\left(t_1 - D\left(\hat{g}(i), \hat{g}(j)\right)\right) \qquad (4)$$

where $w_{i,j}$ is the length of the perimeter of the region $R_i$ common to the perimeter of the region $R_j$, and $t_2$ is a constant equal to 6.

The visible color difference evaluation utilizes $E_{intra}$ to penalize the color difference within regions, and $E_{inter}$ to penalize the similarity over regions.

**Entropy-Based Segmentation Evaluation**

Zhang el al. brought the information theory to segmentation evaluation and proposed a entropy-based evaluation method(EEM)[6]. The entropy is used as the basis to measure the uniformity of pixel characteristics within a segmentation region in EEM. The entropy-based evaluation function is defined as:

$$E_{EEM}(S) = H_r(S) + H_l(S) \tag{5}$$

where $H_r(S)$ measures the expected region entropy of segmentation, and $H_l(S)$ measures the layout entropy which is used to counteract the effect of over-segmentation and under-segmentation.

The definition of expected region entropy of segmentation can be written as:

$$H_r(S) = \sum_{i=1}^{N_R} \frac{|R_i|}{N} \cdot \left( -\sum_{m \in U_i} \frac{L_i(m)}{|R_i|} \cdot \lg \frac{L_i(m)}{|R_i|} \right) \tag{6}$$

where $U_i$ is the set of all possible gray values in the $i$th region, and $L_i(m)$ is the number of pixels in the $i$th region that have gray values equal to $m$.

The layout entropy is defined as:

$$H_l(S) = -\sum_{i=1}^{N_R} \frac{|R_i|}{N} \cdot \lg \frac{|R_i|}{N} \tag{7}$$

## 2.3   The Edge-Based Evaluation Criteria

Without any priori knowledge, most of evaluation criteria compute the statistics on the pixel values in gray scale or color scale. However, on one hand, the value of pixel is easy to affected by illumination and texture or other factors, especially in nature image, the accuracy of these method cannot guarantee; on the other hand, the statistics of pixel values can not provide a precise measurement for the applications like segmentation parameter optimization.

In our method, the edges of image which carries most information of image, are utilized as the basis for segmentation evaluation. We follow three rules to identify high-quality segmentation.

- Rule 1: region's outline should align with the edge of image. Edge is the discontinuous location of image, and good alignment with image edges guarantees the inter-region difference. Our method verifies whether the segmentation comply with this rule by the measure named edge fitness.

- Rule 2: fragmentary edges should not be contained in the region. This rule is inspired by the uniformity of pixels within each region. The region which overlaps edges may contains discontinuous pixels and should be punished. Our method verifies whether the segmentation comply with this rule by the measure named intra-region edge error.

- Rule 3: region should be confined by the edges. The pixels on the same side of the edge share the same characteristics, exceeding the edges violates the intra-region uniformity, which is a basic principle of image segmentation. Our method verifies whether the segmentation comply with this rule by the measure named out-of-edges error.

## 2.4 Edge-Based Evaluation Function

According to the above three rules, we define the edge-based evaluation function:

$$E_S(S) = \sum_{R_i \in S} \frac{|R_i|}{N} E(R_i) \tag{8}$$

where $E(R_i)$ is the evaluation of a region $R_i$ in segmentation $S$, defined as:

$$E(R_i) = [E_{r1}(R_i) - E_{r2}(R_i)] \cdot E_{r3}(R_i) \cdot E_A(R_i) \tag{9}$$

where $E_{r1}(R_i)$, $E_{r2}(R_i)$, $E_{r3}(R_i)$ is respectively measures the edge fitness, intra-region edge error and the out-of-edges error, and set up according to the above three rules. $E_A(R_i)$ is the expression of appearance evaluation.

In edge detection, false positive edges are inevitable. The false positives are caused by shadows, textures or other noises of image. Taking the false positives of edges into account, regions contains a small amount of edges is tolerable. Hence, the score of region in violation of rule 2 is set to additively decrease. When region is in violation of rule 3, the score is set to multiplicatively decrease.

The edge fitness of a region is defined as:

$$E_{r1}(R_i) = \frac{1}{|O(R_i)|} \cdot \sum_{p \in O(R_i)} f_B(h_B(p)) \tag{10}$$

where

- $B$ is the edge signal of input image obtained from a edge detector,
- $f_B(p)$ is the edge strength at the pixel $p$ in $B$,
- $O(R_i)$ denotes the set of pixels in the outline of region $R_i$,
- $|O(R_i)|$ denotes the number of pixels in $O(R_i)$,
- $h_B$ denotes the mapping from pixel $p$ to the nearest pixel $p'$ with nonzero value in the 12-neighborhoods of $p$ in edge signal $B$, and the definition of $h_B$ can be written as:

$$h_B : p \to p'$$
$$such \ that \ D(p, p') = \min_{\substack{f_B(p_0) > 0 \\ p_0 \in \mathcal{N}_{12}(p)}} D(p, p_0) \tag{11}$$

In Eq.10, the numerator specifies the sum of edge strength of those points which match region's outline, and the denominator is the perimeter of region. Region is encouraged to align with strong edges. Higher score is given to region whose outline aligns with a greater number of edges.

The Eq.12 mathematically gives the definition of intra-region edge error:

$$E_{r2}(R_i) = \frac{c}{|O(R_i)|} \cdot \sum_{p \in R_i} f_B(p) \tag{12}$$

In Eq.12, $c$ is a factor ranging from 0 to 1, associated with the noise sensitivity of edge detector, the numerator is the sum of the edge strength at each point within the region. And the denominator adjusts the scale to fit $E_{r1}(R)$. Lower score is given to the region which contains edges.

According to rule 3, region is confined by the edges. Here, we show how to punish the region which violates this rule. First, signal $C_B$ is obtained by "cutting" the region with the edges:

$$C_B(p) = \begin{cases} 1 & D(p, h_B(p)) > \tau, p \in R_i \\ 0 & otherwise \end{cases} \tag{13}$$

where $\tau$ is a parameter associated with the area of region which is defined as:

$$\tau = min\{2t \cdot \frac{|R_i|}{N}, t - 1\} \tag{14}$$

where $t$ is a constant and equal to 5.

In Eq.13, the values of points which near the edges are set to zero. therefore the region which exceeds edges is split into parts. Hence, we can determine whether the region exceeds by simply testing whether the region has been split instead. Let $N_c$ be the number of connected domain in $C_B$, $N_k$ be the number of pixels in the $k$th connected domain, the out-of-edge error can be written as:

$$E_{r3}(R) = \max_{k=1}^{N_c}(N_k) / \sum_{k=1}^{N_c} N_k \tag{15}$$

However, the finite accuracy of the edge may incorrectly decreases $E_{r3}$ followed by unnecessary punishment, which will be a fatal error when the region is small. To minimize this affect, the Eq.15 is modified as:

$$E_{r3}(R) = \left[ \max_{k=1}^{N_c}(N_k) / \sum_{k=1}^{N_c} N_k \right]^{\frac{1}{t-\tau}} \tag{16}$$

where $\tau$ and $t$ are given in Eq.14. In Eq.16, punishment on small regions is inhibited but big regions are still severely punished if they exceeds edges.

Next we discuss the fourth term $f_A(R)$ in the Eq.9. The expression of appearence evaluation can be written as :

$$E_A(R_i) = \frac{1}{\sqrt{2\pi}\sigma} e^{-\frac{(\frac{|R_i|}{N} - \mu)^2}{2\sigma^2}} \cdot \frac{|R_i|}{|O(R_i)|} \tag{17}$$

In Eq.17, the first term is a Gaussian probability density function which is employed to control the sizes of the regions, and $\mu, \sigma$ are constants. We set $\mu = 0.1$ and $\sigma = 0.35$ based on our experience. The second term, the ratio of region's area and perimeter suppresses the erroneous trend that regions increase the length of outline to fit edges.

Unlike color-based method or entropy-based method the quality of segmentation in our method is quantified completely according to the relationship between the edges and segments, even without knowing any pixel value of original image. By penalizing the regions that exceeds the edges and encouraging the fitness between the outline of region and the edges, the effects of under-segmentation or over-segmentation is counteracted in our method.

## 3 Experiments

We performed two sets of experiments to examine the performance of our edge-based method on the evaluation of segmentation and the evaluation of region.

### 3.1 Performance of Segmentation Evaluation

In this subsection, the correlation coefficients between the segmentation results' scores obtained from the unsupervised evaluation methods and the supervised evaluation methods, are reported.

In this experiment, segmentation results are obtained by a state-of-art segmentation algorithm named gPb-OWT-UCM [5] on Berkeley image dataset: BSDS500. The BSDS500 dataset consists of 200 training images and 200 test images. The above-mentioned measures are performed on the test images.

The scores of segmentation results are calculated by three unsupervised evaluation methods: our edge-based method, VCD[8] and EEM[6] and three supervised segmentation methods which compare the segmentation result with manually-segmented reference image: Segmentation Covering[2], Probabilistic Rand Index (PRI)[3] and Variation of Information (VI) [4]. These three supervised evaluation methods have since found wide acceptance for the task of the quantization of image segmentation performance[9–11].

Two edge detectors, including the classic Sobel edge detector and a recently proposed detector named mPb[12], are utilized as our methods' input in this experiment, and the factor $c$ in Eq.12 is respectively set to 0.3 and 1.

Table 1 presents the Pearson's linear correlation coefficients between the scores gotten from unsupervised and supervised evaluation methods. The segmentation is viewed better if VI is smaller or Covering and PRI are larger.

**Table 1.** The Correlation Analysis Result

| Supervised Methods / Unsupervised Methods | Covering | PRI | -VI |
|---|---|---|---|
| The proposed method based on mPb edge | 0.509 | 0.526 | 0.385 |
| The proposed method based on Sobel edge | 0.371 | 0.493 | 0.244 |
| VCD[8] | -0.447 | -0.325 | -0.381 |
| EEM[6] | -0.269 | 0.343 | -0.518 |

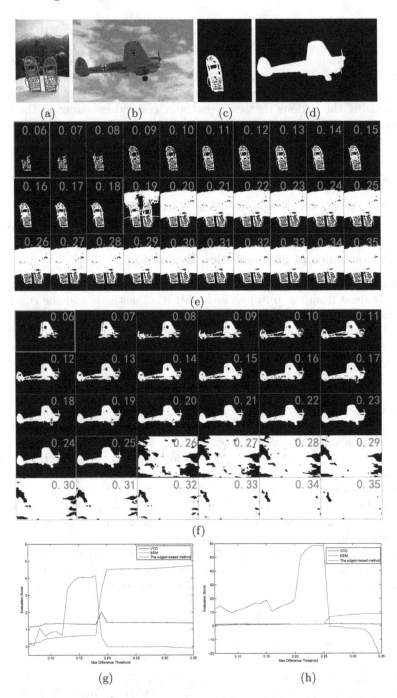

**Fig. 1.** The visual comparison of three best regions in the evaluation of three methods. (a)-(b): the test image from BSDS500 with a pre-given seed pixel(*). (c)-(d): ground-truth segmentation of the region where the pre-given pixel is. (e)-(f): the region growing result on (a)-(b) with different thresholds. In (e)-(f), the thresholds are marked at the upper right of each sub-image, the subimages with red, green, blue outer border is respectively the best regions in the evaluation of our method, EMM, VCD. (g)-(h): the scores of region growing results that are shown in (e)-(f) from three unsupervised segmentation methods.

For facilitate comparison, we take the opposite of VI in Table 1. Hance, the unsupervised method is positive correlated with the quality of segmentation if the correlation coefficients of it and the supervised methods are positive, or is negative correlated if the correlation coefficients are negative.

In Table 1, the positive correlation coefficients in the second and third row indicate that the proposed method is positive correlated with the quality of segmentation; the negative correlation coefficients in the fourth row indicate that the VCD is negative correlated with the quality of segmentation; the EMM is designed to be negative correlated with the quality of segmentation, but the correlation coefficient between EEM and PRI is positive, which indicates that the correlation between EEM and the quality of segmentation is not clear.

As it can be seen from Table 1, our method's correlation coefficients are higher than the VCD's. Therefore, the degree of correlation between our method and the supervised methods is higher than the VCD's. Statistically significant correlations are observed between our method and the Covering and PRI measures.

## 3.2 Region Evaluation Performance

In some computer vision application, such as defect detection of industrial products, peoples tend to be more concerned about the segmentation quality of only one region instead of the whole image. However, not all evaluation methods can evaluate a region.

To verify the performance of our method in region evaluation, region growing algorithm is run on a pre-given seed at different thresholds; regions obtained from the previous step are evaluated by our method, EMM, VCD; finally, the best regions are selected according to the evaluation scores. Fig.1 reports the visual comparison of the best regions of three unsupervised evaluation methods.

In Fig.1, the subimages (e) and (f) show that our edge-based evaluation is more accurate than EMM and VCD. Our method correctly selected the best region from 30 candidate regions, while the EMM and VCD not. In this case, the EMM prefer to a over-segmentation region and the VCD prefer to a under-segmentation region. As can be seen in Fig.1 (g),(h), the peaks of scores are appeared on the thresholds that produce visual-good regions in our method. Furthermore our method shown a significant difference of scores between the visual-good regions and visual-bad regions.

## 4 Conclusions

In this paper, we have presented a new edge-based unsupervised evaluation method of image segmentation. The main contributions of this paper are:

- the quality of segmentation is evaluated completely according to the relationship between the edges and segments in the proposed method. Therefore, it can apply on the evaluation of most types of image, as long as the edge detection result can be provided.

- the proposed method shows a stronger linear correlation with the supervised evaluation methods than the existed unsupervised evaluation methods.
- the proposed method can provide evaluation of both segmentation and region according to the application, and achieves a good performance on the parameter selection problem of region growing.

To produce an ideal edge-based evaluation of segmentation, suppression of the false positive edges should be considered. Therefore, our future work will utilize the texture feature to suppress the errors of evaluation caused by false positive edges.

# References

1. Zhang, H., Fritts, J.E., Goldman, S.A.: Image segmentation evaluation: a survey of unsupervised methods. Computer Vision and Image Understanding **110**(2), 260–280 (2008)
2. Malisiewicz, T., Efros, A.A.: Improving spatial support for objects via multiple segmentations (2007)
3. Unnikrishnan, R., Pantofaru, C., Hebert, M.: Toward objective evaluation of image segmentation algorithms. IEEE Transactions on Pattern Analysis and Machine Intelligence **29**(6), 929–944 (2007)
4. Meila, M.: Comparing clusterings: an axiomatic view. In: Proceedings of the 22nd International Conference on Machine Learning (ICML-05), pp. 577–584 (2005)
5. Arbelaez, P., Maire, M., Fowlkes, C., Malik, J.: Contour detection and hierarchical image segmentation. IEEE Transactions onPattern Analysis and Machine Intelligence **33**(5), 898–916 (2011)
6. Zhang, H., Fritts, J.E., Goldman, S.A.: An entropy-based objective evaluation method for image segmentation. In: Electronic Imaging 2004, pp. 38–49. International Society for Optics and Photonics (2003)
7. Chabrier, S., Emile, B., Rosenberger, C., Laurent, H.: Unsupervised performance evaluation of image segmentation. EURASIP Journal on Applied Signal Processing **2006**, 217–217 (2006)
8. Chen, H.C., Wang, S.J.: The use of visible color difference in the quantitative evaluation of color image segmentation. In: IEEE International Conference on Acoustics, Speech, and Signal Processing, Proceedings. (ICASSP 2004), vol. 3, pp. iii-593. IEEE (2004)
9. Carreira, J., Sminchisescu, C.: Cpmc: automatic object segmentation using constrained parametric min-cuts. IEEE Transactions on Pattern Analysis and Machine Intelligence **34**(7), 1312–1328 (2012)
10. Kim, T.H., Lee, K.M., Lee, S.U.: Learning full pairwise affinities for spectral segmentation. IEEE Transactions on Pattern Analysis and Machine Intelligence **35**(7), 1690–1703 (2013)
11. Donoser, M., Schmalstieg, D.: Discrete-continuous gradient orientation estimation for faster image segmentation. In: 2014 IEEE Conference on Computer Vision and Pattern Recognition (CVPR), pp. 3158–3165. IEEE (2014)
12. Maire, M., Arbeláez, P., Fowlkes, C., Malik, J.: Using contours to detect and localize junctions in natural images. In: IEEE Conference on Computer Vision and Pattern Recognition. CVPR 2008, pp. 1–8. IEEE (2008)

# An Adaptive Fuzzy Clustering Algorithm Based on Multi-threshold for Infrared Image Segmentation

Jin Liu$^{(\boxtimes)}$, Yanli Liu, and Qianqian Ge

School of Electronic Engineering, Xidian University, Xi'an 710071, China
jinliu@xidian.edu.cn, ylliu@stu.xidian.edu.cn,
geqianqina_ex@163.com

**Abstract.** To obtain the satisfied performance of infrared image segmentation in complex environments, an adaptive fuzzy clustering algorithm based on mul-ti-threshold (AFC_MT) is proposed. The methodology uses a coarse-fine concept to reduce the computational burden required for the fuzzy clustering and to improve the accuracy of segmentation that a single fuzzy clustering cannot reach. The coarse segmentation attempts to segment coarsely using the multi-thresholding technique. Firstly, the pseudo peaks in a multi-threshold algorithm are removed by introducing a control factor of peak areas and a control factor of peak widths to segment an image coarsely, then in order to find a finer segmentation result, the coarse segmentation result is clustered by an improved fuzzy clustering algorithm that introduces an adaptive function to get the most reasonable cluster number and that defines a logarithmic function as a measurement of distance. Experimental results show that AFC_MT behaves well in segmenting infrared images in complex environments.

**Keywords:** Adaptive fuzzy clustering · Infrared image segmentation · Multi-threshold segmentation · Pseudo-peak removal

## 1 Introduction

As the low-level processing technology of computer vision and image understanding and the key technology in automatic target recognition technology, image segmentation plays an important role in image analysis and pattern recognition. For example, an essential requirement of the recognition, tracking and accurate positioning of military targets is the precision and real-time segmentation of infrared images. Deciding how to separate an infrared target and complex background in an efficient and effective way has always been difficult in the field of the recognition, tracking and accurate positioning of military targets [1, 2]. Many efforts have been made on image segmentation, and accordingly a variety of segmentation algorithms are developed, such as a fast and robust level set method for image segmentation using fuzzy clustering and Lattice Boltzmann method [3], a nonlinear adaptive level set for image segmentation [4], and mean shift based FCM image segmentation algorithm [5]. However, these algorithms are specific for natural images, and there are fewer algorithms that can be applied to segmenting infrared images because of the less available information and lower

© Springer-Verlag Berlin Heidelberg 2015
H. Zha et al. (Eds.): CCCV 2015, Part I, CCIS 546, pp. 277–286, 2015.
DOI: 10.1007/978-3-662-48558-3_28

grayscale contrast of infrared images. Therefore it is still of the vital significance to study more general and effective infrared image segmentation algorithms.

A multi-threshold segmentation algorithm [6] becomes the most basic and widely used segmentation technique for its simple implementation, low computational cost, strong adaptability, stable performance and no requirement for prior knowledge. However, this method requires the gray histogram of an image for obvious peaks and valleys. When the grayscale difference between the objective and background of an image is small, there would be serious pseudo-peak interference. The study in [7] introduced a peak area, a peak width and a peak-to-valley ratio of a separate peak to remove a certain amount of pseudo peaks, which could achieve a good effect. But the three values are obtained by prior knowledge and experiment validation and cannot be adaptive, which is not conducive to real-time processing. As an unsupervised clustering segmentation algorithm, fuzzy c-means (FCM) algorithm is theoretically elegant and the most widely used based on the objective function [8]. However, it needs to set the number of clusters before clustering, which does not facilitate real-time processing. Moreover, the case that some object regions with low gray level are omitted or the background regions with similar grayscale as the objective regions are misclassified may occur for a separate use of an FCM algorithm. What's more, a good partition should satisfy two requirements: (a) divergence, i.e., the inter-cluster distances should be as big as possible; and (b) compactness, i.e., the intra-cluster distances should be as small as possible [11]. As a result, the value of the ratio of the compactness and the divergence can be the criterion of the clustering validity. According to this guideline, Xie and Beni [9, 10] take account of the inter-cluster distances and intra-cluster distances and define a validity function (XB index). By fully considering the relationship between inter-cluster distances and intra-cluster distances, Li and Yu [12] proposed a validity function that can adaptively select the best and the most reasonable number of clusters and have an ideal clustering effect, while the result is not ideal for infrared images in complex environments.

Inspired by these studies and the characteristics of infrared images, an adaptive fuzzy clustering algorithm based on multi-threshold (AFC_MT) is proposed. The idea of the proposed algorithm is stated as follows. First, a control factor of peak areas and a control factor of peak widths are introduced to remove the pseudo peaks that exist in a multi-threshold algorithm and the corresponding accurate valley positions act as the multiple thresholds to segment the image coarsely. Then an adaptive function is introduced in fuzzy clustering to adaptively determine the best cluster number and a logarithmic function is defined as the measurement of distance. Areas of small gray value difference are adaptively merged by the improved fuzzy clustering algorithm to achieve a fine segmentation.

## 2    Adaptive Fuzzy Clustering Algorithm Based on Multi-threshold for Infrared Image Segmentation

### 2.1    Multi-threshold Pseudo-Peak Removal

The multi-threshold segmentation method is based on the peak and valley characteristics of the grayscale histogram curve of an image to determine optimal thresholds to segment the image. This idea can be summarised as follows. The number of regions is determined by finding the main peak number in the grayscale histogram curve of an image, and the corresponding thresholds to divide each region are determined by the valleys between the major peaks. However, there is a serious pseudo-peak interference when it applies to infrared image segmentation in complex environments.

Motivated by the work in [7], we introduce a control factor of peak areas and a control factor of peak widths that calculate the minimum peak area and the minimum peak width, respectively, to remove a certain pseudo-peak interference and obtain more rational thresholds

$$MA = \Psi * IS \tag{1}$$

$$MW = \mu * IG \tag{2}$$

where $MA$ and $MW$ denote the minimum peak area and the minimum peak width, respectively, $\psi$ and $\mu$ the control factor of peak areas and control factor of peak widths (set as empirical values 0.001 and 0.15 in the experiments), respectively, and $IS$ and $IG$ the image size and the image grayscale, respectively. Valleys satisfying Eqs. (1) and (2) are the thresholds to coarsely segment the image. Since pixels of low-grayscale and high-grayscale that are few in number have a small effect on the segmentation result, but those of mid-grayscale have a great influence on the segmentation result, it is significant to remove the valleys in intermediate grayscale. The calculation for a peak width and a peak area is for two adjacent valleys, and therefore, the latter valley is determined by the previous one.

Different from the work in [7], where the peak area, the peak width and the peak-to-valley ratio of a separate peak are determined by priori knowledge and experimental verification, and the three values should be reset once the size or the grayscale of the image changed, which means the three values cannot be self-adapting when the image changes, our method can only set the two control factors even if the image changes. Moreover, the three values in [7] are set according to each image. However, our two control factors are set according to a majority of images.

## 2.2  Adaptive Fuzzy Clustering

Studies have shown that visual sensitivity to brightness difference varies with the background brightness nonlinearly [13]. A distance measurement based on the exponential function was proven to be more robust to noise and meet the vector distance criteria [14]. Moreover, the frequently-used visual model is the lowpass-logarithmic-highpass model of the visual system that can be used to explain most of the visual phenomenon [15]. Therefore, in order to simulate the visual perception characteristics better, an improved distance expression based on logarithmic function is applied to a fuzzy clustering algorithm. The similarity measure is defined as

$$d(g_i, v_j) = In(1 + \beta \| g_i - v_j \|) \tag{3}$$

where $\beta$ denotes a degree of freedom parameter for adjusting the curvature of a curve, $v_j$ the center of the $j$th cluster, and $g_i$ the pixel grayscale of the $i$th pixel.

A fuzzy clustering algorithm is an effective clustering analysis method, but it requires the number of clusters be set in advance, which makes the rationality of clustering result be validated. Thus, it is necessary for the number of clusters to be computed adaptively. As we already know that the geometric meaning of clustering is to classify the data and make the inter-difference as great as possible and the intra-difference as small as possible, and according to the point of view in information theory that entropy is the characterization of average information, consequently we introduce an adaptive function

$$L(c) = \frac{\sum_{j=1}^{c}(-\sum_{i=1}^{f}u_{ij}\ln(u_{ij}))d^2(v_j,X)\bigg/(c-1)}{-\sum_{j=1}^{c}\sum_{i=1}^{f}u_{ij}\ln(u_{ij})d^2(g_i,v_j)\bigg/(f-c)} \tag{4}$$

where $X = \sum_{j=1}^{c}\sum_{i=1}^{f}u_{ij}^m g_i \bigg/ f$ presents the center vector of all the pixels, $f$ and $c$ the

pixel grayscale and cluster number of an image, respectively, and $u_{ij}$ the membership degree of $i$th pixel belonging to the $j$th cluster. The numerator of adaptive function $L(c)$ denotes the sum of the entropy between classes and the denominator of $L(c)$ denotes the sum of the intra-entropy of all the clusters. As a result, the bigger $L(c)$ is, the more reliable the clustering result is. Hence, the clustering number $c$ is the best when $L(c)$ reaches its maximum value. We just need to compare two values of $L(c)$ in some local area since the solution point is the local minimum of the objective function in fuzzy clustering. As a consequence, the best number of clusters can be found by finding a point satisfies $L(c-1) > L(c-2)$ and $L(c-1) > L(c)$.

## 2.3     Algorithm

Now, we outline the AFC_MT algorithm based on the newly defined measurement of distance that can better simulate the human eye to perceive changes in brightness and the introduction of an adaptive function $L(c)$ that can adaptively compute the best number of clusters and a control factor of peak areas and a control factor of peak widths to calculate the minimum peak area and the minimum peak width, respectively, that can remove a certain pseudo peaks effectively.

The steps of implementation in our universal AFC_MT algorithm are stated as follows.

1. Calculate the possible thresholds using the traditional multi-threshold algorithm [6];
2. Remove the pseudo peaks based on the adaptively obtained minimum peak area and the minimum peak width shown in Eqs. (1) and (2) to obtain the accurate positions of valleys, and divide the image into $M$ regions according to the positions;

3. Morphological smooth the image obtained above;

4. Set the termination condition $\varepsilon > 0$, cluster number $c = 2$, the adaptive function $L(1) = 0$, the number of iterations $l = 0$, and the cluster center matrix $V^{(0)}$;

5. Calculate the partition matrix $U^{(l)}$ and the cluster center matrix $V^{(l+1)}$, i.e.,

$$u_{ij}^{(l)} = 1 \Big/ \sum_{j=1}^{c} (\frac{d(g_j, v_i)}{d(g_j, v_j)})^{2/(m-1)} \tag{5}$$

$$v_i^{(l+1)} = \sum_{j=1}^{f} (u_{ij})^m g_j \Big/ \sum_{j=1}^{f} (u_{ij})^m \tag{6}$$

6. Calculate the variation of partition matrix

$$\| V^{(l+1)} - V^{(l)} \| \tag{7}$$

If $\| V^{(l+1)} - V^{(l)} \| \le \varepsilon$, then go to step 7. Else let $l = l + 1$ and go to step 5.

7. Calculate $L(c)$. If $L(c-1) > L(c-2)$ and $L(c-1) > L(c)$ under the condition $c > 2$ and $c < M$, then stop the iteration to take the result when $c = c - 1$. Else go to step 5 with $c = c + 1$. If $c > M$, then take the result when $c = Arg\left\{\max_{2 \le c \le M} (L(c))\right\}$.

## 3    Experimental Results and Analysis

To validate the effectiveness of the proposed adaptive fuzzy clustering algorithm based on multi-threshold for infrared image segmentation, four comparative experiments on the method in [7] (MT), the FCM algorithm, the self-adapting FCM [12] (SFCM) and the AFC_MT algorithm are conducted to validate the effectiveness of the proposed method. Our experimental infrared images of size 320×240 are derived from the OTCBVS Benchmark Dataset [16]. For all experiments, the proposed method sets the degrees of freedom parameter $\beta$ to 0.1, and stopping threshold $\varepsilon$ for iteration to 0.00001. To compare FCM and AFC_MT better, we set the cluster number of FCM the same with that of AFC_MT which can be obtained adaptively. All the experiments are conducted on MATLAB R2012b installed in a computer with a 3.40GHz Intel Core i3 CPU and 4GB of RAM.

In infrared data 1, the background and objective are relatively simple, while the grayscale of objective area is close to that of the background, as shown in Fig. 1(a). Therefore, the FCM algorithm and the MT algorithm can separate the objective from background well with producing some misclassification and leakage points, as shown in Fig. 1(c) and (d). However, the SFCM algorithm cannot segment the objective well because of the low grayscale contrast, as shown in Fig. 1(e). The proposed algorithm filters out a certain pseudo peaks in the process of multi-threshold computation, and then adaptively selects the most reasonable number of clusters to obtain a more complete objective and a single background, as shown in Fig. 1(f).

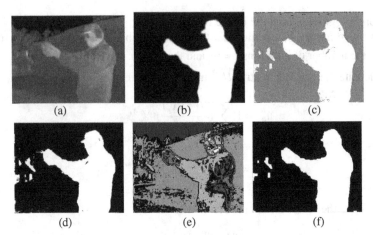

**Fig. 1.** Segmentation results on infrared data 1: (a) original image, (b) benchmark image, (c) MT segmentation with a peak area set to 100, a peak width to 50, and a peak-to-valley ratio to 10, (d) FCM segmentation with $c$ set to 2, (e) SFCM segmentation with adapting $c$ to 8, and (f) AFC_MT segmentation with adapting $c$ to 2.

In infrared data 2, the background is relatively complex, and its pixel grayscales are widely distributed. However, pixel grayscales of objective are not unique, and pixel grayscales of background overlap that of objective, as shown in Fig. 2(a). The objective of the segmentation result from the MT algorithm and the FCM algorithm is relatively integrated, but the pixel grayscales of background that are close to that of objective are misclassified, as shown in Fig. 2(c) and (d). However, the SFCM algorithm cannot segment the objective well, as shown in Fig. 2(e). The proposed algorithm can adaptively find the most reasonable cluster number and the segmentation result of AFC_MT is of more complete objective and single background, as shown in Fig. 2(f).

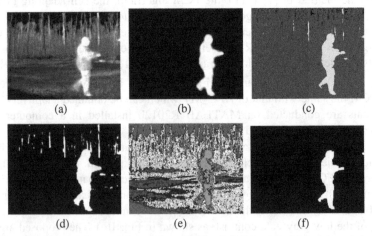

**Fig. 2.** Segmentation results on infrared data 1: (a) original image, (b) benchmark image, (c) MT segmentation with a peak area set to 100, a peak width to 50, and a peak-to-valley ratio to 1, (d) FCM segmentation with $c$ set to 2, (e) SFCM segmentation with adapting $c$ to 19, and (f) AFC_MT segmentation with adapting $c$ to 2.

In infrared data 3, the objective and background are relatively complex, and some pixels in background are similar to that in objective in grayscale, as shown in Fig. 3(a). The objective can be roughly segmented by the MT algorithm, but the parts that are of similar pixel grayscale cannot be distinguished from background, as shown in Fig. 3(c), and the objective in Fig. 3(d) segmented by the FCM algorithm is complete while the background is also classified as the objective. The objective cannot be separated from the background by the SFCM algorithm and the objective in Fig. 3(e) is separated into several parts. The segmentation result by the proposed algorithm consists of a more complete target and a single background, as shown in Fig. 3(f).

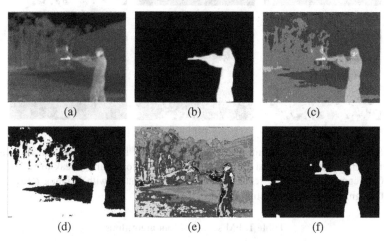

(a)                    (b)                    (c)

(d)                    (e)                    (f)

**Fig. 3.** Segmentation results on infrared data 1: (a) original image, (b) benchmark image, (c) MT segmentation with a peak area set to 300, a peak width to 40, and a peak-to-valley ratio to 1, (d) FCM segmentation with $C$ set to 2, (e) SFCM segmentation with adapting $C$ to 18, and (f) AFC_MT segmentation with adapting $C$ to 2.

In infrared data 4, the background is complex, and there is obvious interference, as shown in Fig. 4(a). It is difficult either for the MT algorithm or for the FCM algorithm to separate the objective from the background since the interference is obvious, as shown in Fig. 4(c) and (d). Moreover, the result of the SFCM is terrible misclassified, as shown in Fig. 4(e). The segmentation result by the proposed algorithm, as shown in Fig. 4(f), are of single background and more complete objective, which suffer no influence from the background that interferes a lot.

Two measures [3] [17], F-Measure (FM) and Localization error (LE), are utilized to compare the four methods. A higher score on FM means that a method is more accurate. Meanwhile, a small score on LE means that the localization error is small and the segmentation result is better. Scores in Tables 1 and 2 quantitatively show that the proposed method obtains competitive performance by comparing with the other three algorithms. In addition, comparisons in terms of running time of the four algorithms, represented by the average of running 100 times, are shown in Table 3. The running time of the proposed algorithm is reduced compared with the time-consuming FCM or the SFCM algorithm and meanwhile weighs against the MT algorithm, which means the coarse-fine concept reduces the computational burden required for the fuzzy clustering. All the experiments show that the proposed algorithm is a real-time and effective segmentation algorithm.

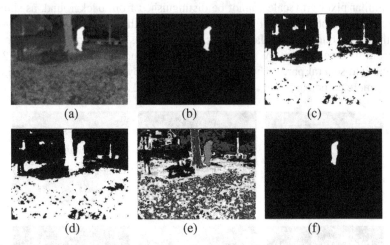

(a)                    (b)                    (c)

(d)                    (e)                    (f)

**Fig. 4.** Segmentation results on infrared data 1: (a) original image, (b) benchmark image, (c) MT segmentation with a peak area set to 100, a peak width to 50, and a peak-to-valley ratio to 5, (d) FCM segmentation with $c$ set to 2, (e) SFCM segmentation with adapting $c$ to15, and (f) AFC_MT segmentation with adapting $c$ to 2.

**Table 1.** FM scores of four algorithms

| Infrared data | MT | FCM | SFCM | AFC_MT |
|---|---|---|---|---|
| 1 | 0.9232 | 0.9493 | 0.3141 | 0.9554 |
| 2 | 0.8585 | 0.8029 | 0.1737 | 0.9034 |
| 3 | 0.3021 | 0.2887 | 0.0878 | 0.8475 |
| 4 | 0.0401 | 0.0443 | 0.0422 | 0.9520 |

**Table 2.** LE scores of four algorithms

| Infrared data | MT | FCM | SFCM | AFC_MT |
|---|---|---|---|---|
| 1 | 0.0352 | 0.0308 | 0.5727 | 0.0266 |
| 2 | 0.0202 | 0.0336 | 0.4506 | 0.0131 |
| 3 | 0.3925 | 0.4123 | 0.5378 | 0.0262 |
| 4 | 0.5834 | 0.5268 | 0.4855 | 0.0011 |

**Table 3.** Running time of four algorithms (Seconds)

| Infrared data | MT | FCM | SFCM | AFC_MT |
|---|---|---|---|---|
| 1 | 0.3562 | 0.5722 | 3.5472 | 0.2929 |
| 2 | 0.2995 | 0.6549 | 4.6334 | 0.3427 |
| 3 | 0.2937 | 0.6531 | 4.4177 | 0.3049 |
| 4 | 0.3053 | 0.6416 | 3.6259 | 0.3386 |

# 4    Conclusions

In this article, an adaptive fuzzy clustering algorithm based on multi-threshold (AFC_MT) for infrared image segmentation is proposed. It retains the characteristics of the multi-threshold algorithm in simple realization and fast speed, and can effectively remove pseudo-peak interference by introducing a control factor of peak areas and a control factor of peak widths in multi-threshold selection. In addition, the proposed algorithm can take full advantage of the fuzzy clustering algorithm in automatic classification without human intervention. The experimental results show that AFC_MT outperforms both of the MT, the FCM algorithm and the SFCM algorithm, and that it can achieve the desired effect on infrared image segmentation in a complex environment.

**Acknowledgments.** This research was supported in part by the National Natural Science Foundation of China (Grant No. 61101246) and the Fundamental Research Funds for the Central Universities (Grant No. JB150209).

# References

1. Gonzalez, R.C., Woods, R.E.: Digital Image Processing. Addison-Wesley, Massachusetts (1992)
2. Feng, D.Z., Wang, X., Liu, Y.H.: An edge detection method for infrared image based on grey relation analysis. In: 2nd IEEE International Symposium on System and Control in Aerospace and Astronautics, pp. 1-5. IEEE Press, Shenzhen (2008)
3. Balla-Arabé, S., Gao, X.B., Wang, B.: A fast and robust level set method for image segmentation using fuzzy clustering and lattice boltzmann method. IEEE Trans. on Cybernetics 43(3), 910–920 (2013)
4. Wang, B., Gao, X.B., Tao, D.C., Li, X.L.: A nonlinear adaptive level set for image segmentation. IEEE Trans. on Cybernetics 44(3), 418–428 (2014)
5. Cui, Z.H., Chen, S.S.G., Gao, L.Q.: Mean shift based FCM image segmentation algorithm. Journal of Control and Decision 29(6), 1130–1134 (2014)
6. Lim, Y.W., Lee, S.U.: On the color image segmentation algorithm based on the thresholding and the fuzzy c-means techniques. Pattern Recognition 23(9), 935–952 (1990)
7. Li, J.P., Fu, L.Q., Han, Y.: A method of object segmentation in complex environment. Journal of Projectiles, Rockets, Missiles and Guidance 30(4), 197–200 (2010)
8. Wang, S.H.: Research on methods for infrared image target segmentation. Xidian University, Xi'an (2013)
9. Pedrycz, W.: Knowledge-based Clustering: from Data to Information Granules. John Wiley & Sons (2005)
10. Xie, X.L., Beni, G.: A validity measure for fuzzy clustering. IEEE Trans on Pattern Analysis and Machine Intelligence 13(8), 841–847 (1991)
11. Li, Y., Yu F.S.: A new validity function for fuzzy clustering. In: 9th IEEE International Conference on Computational Intelligence and Natural Computing, pp. 462-465. IEEE Press, Wuhan (2009)

12. Witkin, A.P.: Scale-space filtering: a new approach to multi-scale description. In: IEEE International Conference on Acoustics, Speech, and Signal Processing, pp. 150-153. IEEE Press, California (1984)
13. Tan, H.B., Hou, Z.Q., Liu, R.: Region growing image segmentation based on human visual model. Journal of Image and Graphics 15(9), 1352–1356 (2010)
14. Wu, K.L., Yang, M.S.: Alternative c-means clustering algorithms. Pattern recognition 35(10), 2267–2278 (2002)
15. Xu, L.P.: Digital Image Processing. Science Press (2007)
16. The OTCBVS Benchmark Dataset, http://www.vcipl.okstate.edu/otcbvs/bench/
17. Chabrier, S., Laurent, H., Rosenberger, C., Zhang, Y.J.: Supervised evaluation of synthetic and real contour segmentation results, In: 14th Europen Signal Processing Conference, pp. 1143–1146, Florence (2006)

# Locally Linear Embedding Based Dynamic Texture Synthesis

Weigang Guo, Xinge You$^{(\boxtimes)}$, Ziqi Zhu, Yi Mou, and Dachuan Zheng

School of Electronics and Information Engineering,
Huazhong University of Science and Technology, Wuhan, China
youxg@mail.hust.edu.cn

**Abstract.** Dynamic textures are often modeled as a low-dimensional dynamic process. The process usually comprises an appearance model of dimension reduction, a Markovian dynamic model in latent space to synthesize consecutive new latent variables and a observation model to map new latent variables onto the observation space. Linear dynamic system(LDS) is effective in modeling simple dynamic scenes while is hard to capture the nonlinearities of video sequences, which often results in poor visual quality of the synthesized videos. In this paper,we propose a new framework for generating dynamic textures by using a new appearance model and a new observation model to preserves the non-linear correlation of video sequences. We use locally linear embedding(LLE) to create an manifold embedding of the input sequence, apply a Markovian dynamics to maintain the temporal coherence in the latent space and synthesize new manifold, and develop a novel neighbor embedding based method to reconstruct the new manifold into the image space to constitute new texture videos. Experiments show that our method is efficient in capturing complex appearance variation while maintaining the temporal coherence of the new synthesized texture videos.

**Keywords:** Dynamic texture synthesis · Dynamic system · Locally linear embedding

## 1 Introduction

Dimensionality reduction algorithms has been successfully applied to video analysis [1–4] for decades. A central difficulty in modeling time series data is in determining whether the model can capture the nonlinearities of the data without overfitting.

Sotto et al [5] models dynamic textures using a linear dynamic system(LDS), which was shown to be a promising technique for synthesis and analysis of dynamic textures. Texture video frames are unfolded into column vectors and constitute points set in the image space. The analysis consists in finding an appropriate space to describe the trajectory of the video frames and in modeling the trajectory basing on the dynamical system theory. The model allows for great power of editing and could create new images that were never a part of

© Springer-Verlag Berlin Heidelberg 2015
H. Zha et al. (Eds.): CCCV 2015, Part I, CCIS 546, pp. 287–295, 2015.
DOI: 10.1007/978-3-662-48558-3_29

the original sequence. However the visual quality of the output is usually not satisfactory because of the over-simplified linear model.

Yuan et al [6] extends this work by bringing in a feedback control to turn the system into a closed loop LDS. The feedback loop corrected the problem of signal decay, but the problem of blurry synthesized frames is still yet to be solved.

Che-Bin Liu [7] models dynamic textures using subspace mixtures, which propose to use Locally Linear coordination(LLC) [8] characterizing image manifolds and generates a much improved result.

Roberto [9] extends the SVD in basic LDS to a tensor decomposition technique(HOSVD) without unfolding the video frames into column vectors, which results in models requiring on average five times less coefficients, while still ensuring the same visual quality.

However, by using either [7] or [9], the visually quality of synthesized video sequences are still not satisfactory because of the over-simplified appearance models and observation models.

Ishan Awasthi [10] use nonlinear dimensionality reduction as the appearance model of the input texture video sequence, use a spline to move along the input manifold and learn the nonlinear mapping from the input to map the new manifold into the image space. This technique can create realistic new images, however they are often not visually consecutive when the input sequence comprises of relatively random and fast motion.

Here a similar but more formal alternative is suggested. Though we use the same appearance model, our dynamic model and observation model are totally different and more natural. Our work also chooses to use manifold based dimension reduction technique locally linear embedding (LLE) [11] to find the low-dimensional space. while instead of learning the nonlinear mapping from the input, we reconstruct the points from the low-dimensional manifold space to image space through neighbor embedding which was inspired by LLE itself.

LLE is a promising manifold learning method that has aroused a great deal of extension in machine learning and image processing. The algorithm is based on a geometric intuitions that points should preserve similar local geometry structure in both high- and low-dimensional space.

In LLE, the local properties of the data properties are constructed by writing the high-dimensional data points as a linear combination of their nearest neighbors. In the low-dimensional representation of the data, LLE attempts to retain the reconstruction weights in the linear combinations as good as possible. After the nonlinear embedding offers low-dimensional manifold representation of the texture video sequences, a Markovian dynamic model is used to maintain the temporal coherence of the low-dimensional series and create a similar manifold by driving the system with random noise. Then our approach is driven by a key question: how to map the new manifold back into the image space and constitute a new texture video. Our technique is inspired by LLE itself and still based on the assumption that data-points in the low- and high-dimensional space form manifolds with similar local geometry. Given a low-dimensional point of the new manifold, it can be reconstructed basing on a linear mapping that weights its neighbors from the original manifold. This local geometry is preserved in the high dimensional space, and since the corresponding high-dimensional representations of the neighbors are given from the original high-dimensional data points, the high-dimensional embedding of the point can be estimated.

Our main contribution is to propose a new framework for dynamic texture synthesis. And what's more, we develop a novel technique to estimate the high-dimensional representation of variables in the low-dimensional locally linear embedding space. Our framework is not available for other existing methods and is a new strategy for dynamic texture synthesis. The rest of this paper is organized as follows: section 2, section 3 and section 4 describe the appearance model, dynamic model and observation model of our framework for dynamic texture synthesis. The experiment results are presented in section 5. And finally we conclude the paper and present some future works in section 6.

## 2   Appearance Model

Suppose there are N points $Y = \{y_t\}_{t=1,...,N} \in R^D$ representing the input video frames which are unfolded into column vectors in a high-dimensional data. The $N$ points are assumed to lie on a nonlinear manifold of intrinsic dimension $d$ (typically $d \ll D$). Provided that sufficient data points are sampled from the manifold, each data point $y_i$ and its $k$ neighbors are expected to lie a locally linear patch of the manifold. The local geometry of each patch can be characterized by the reconstruction weights $W = \{w_{tj}\}_{t,j=1,...,N}$, with which a data point is reconstructed from its neighbors. The weights can be obtained by minimizing the following cost function.

$$\varepsilon(W) = \sum_{t=1}^{N} \left\| y_t - \sum_{j=1}^{N} w_{tj} y_{tj} \right\|^2 \tag{1}$$

$W$ is a sparse $N \times N$ matrix whose entries are set to 0, if $t$ and $j$ are not connected in the neighborhood graph, and equal to the corresponding reconstruction weight otherwise. The minimization is subjected to $\sum_{j=1}^{N} w_{tj} = 1$. The weights can be solved through constrained least squares, and they reflect the local geometries relating the data points to their neighbors. Then we need to compute the low-dimensional embedding representations of the data points so that they can best preserve the local geometry. Let the low-dimensional embedding coordinates be $X = \{x_t\}_{t=1,...,N} \subseteq R^d, d \ll D$. The objective can be obtained by minimizing the following cost function.

$$\varepsilon(X) = \sum_{i=1}^{N} \left\| x_t - \sum_{j=1}^{N} w_{tj} x_j \right\|^2 \tag{2}$$

The minimization is subject to $\frac{1}{N} \sum_{t=1}^{N} x_t = 0$ and $\frac{1}{N} \sum_{i=1}^{N} x_t x_t^T = \frac{1}{N} X^T X = I_d$, $I$ is the identity matrix. The low-dimensional embedding can be solved by computing the eigenvectors corresponding to the smallest $d$ nonzero eigenvalues of the inner product $(I - W)^T (I - W)$.

# 3    Dynamic Model

Similar to the Linear Dynamic System [5], automatic regression(AR) model is used as the dynamic model in our framework to generate the new state variables while maintaining the temporal coherence. The AR model is based on the assumption that each state variable in the time series depends on $m$ previous state variables, here, $m = 1$.

Given the latent variables $X = \{x_t\}_{t=1,\dots,N} \subseteq R^d$, $d \ll D$ obtained from the locally linear embedding(LLE), the sampling noise $v_t \sim N(0, Q)$ can drive the system matrix A to generate $L$ new state variables $X^* = \{x_t^*\}_{t=1,\dots,L} \subseteq R^d$ according to (3). $L$ is usually two times larger than $N$.

$$x_t = Ax_{t-1} + v_t, v_t \sim N(0, Q) \tag{3}$$

System matrix $A$ can be estimated based on the least squares approximation in (4).

$$A = X_{2:N} Pinv(X_{1:N-1}) \tag{4}$$

Also the noise variance $Q$ can be obtained by (5).

$$Q = \frac{1}{T-1} \sum_{t=1}^{N-1} x_t^{'} (x_t^{'})^T \tag{5}$$
$$x_t^{'} = x_{t+1} - Ax_t$$

# 4    Observation Model

Once the new state vectors $X^*$ are generated, a novel technique is proposed to reconstruct the new state variables from the low dimensional embedding space into the high dimensional image output space. As in LLE, local geometry is characterized by how a variable corresponding a texture frame can be reconstructed by its neighbors and this property should be preserved in the low-dimensional space. The property is symmetric, and the reconstruction weights between a variable and its neighbor in the low-dimensional space should also be preserved in the high-dimensional space.

For each newly synthesized variable $x_t^*$ in the low-dimension space, like in LLE, we first need to find its $K_O$ nearest neighbors $X_t = \{x_{tj}\}_{j=1,\dots,K_O}$ in X and compute the reconstruction weights of neighbors by minimizing the reconstruction error.

$$\varepsilon(W) = \|x_t^* - \sum_{j=1}^{K_O} w_{tj} x_j\|^2 \tag{6}$$

The solution to the constrained least squares problem can be find in [12].

$$G_t = (x_t^* \Gamma^T - X_n)^T (x_t^* \Gamma^T - X_n)$$
$$W_t = \frac{G_t^{-1} \Gamma}{\Gamma^T G_t^{-1} \Gamma} \tag{7}$$

$G_t$ is local gram matrix regarding $x_t^*$, $\Gamma = [1, \ldots, 1]^T$ is the vector of ones with $K_O$ entries, $X_n$ is a $d \times K$ matrix whose columns are the $K_O$ nearest neighbors of $x_t^*$.

Then the optimum high-dimensional representation of $x_t^*$ can be achieved by the linear combination of the corresponding high-dimensional neighbor $Y_t = \{y_{tj}\}_{j=1,\ldots,K_O}$ in $Y$ basing on the reconstruction weights $W_t$.

$$y_t^* = \sum_{j=1}^{K_O} w_{tj} y_{tj} \tag{8}$$

The complete framework of our algorithm is summarized as Algorithm 1.

---

**Algorithm 1.** Locally Linear Embedding based Dynamic Texture Synthesis

---

**Input:** texture video sequence $Y$;
1: FOR each frame $\{y_t\}_{i=1,\ldots,N}$ in the input texture video sequence $Y$;
2: Unfold it into column vector and find the set of $K_A$ nearest neighbors $y_{tj}$ through KNN in $Y$;
3: Compute the reconstruction weights of the neighbors that minimize the reconstruction error: $\varepsilon(W) = \|y_t - \sum_{j=1}^{K_A} w_{tj} y_{tj}\|^2$;
4: END;
5: Compute the low-dimensional embedding state variables $X = \{x_t\}_{t=1,\ldots,N}$ in the $d-$dimensional space so that they can best preserve the local geometry by minimizing the cost function defined in (2): $\varepsilon(X) = \sum_{t=1}^{N} \|x_t - \sum_{t=1}^{N} w_{tj} x_{tj}\|^2$ ;
6: Generate $L$ new state variables $X^* = \{x_t\}_{t=1,\ldots,L}$ according to (3);
7: FOR each newly synthesized variable $x_t^*$;
8: Find the set of $K_O$ nearest neighbors $\{x_{tj}\}_{j=1,\ldots,K_O}$ through KNN in $X$ and their corresponding high-dimensional representation $Y_t = \{y_{tj}\}_{j=1,\ldots,K_o}$;
9: Compute the reconstruction weights $W$ of neighbors by minimizing the reconstruction error in 6: $\varepsilon(W) = \|x_t^* - \sum_{j=1}^{K_O} w_{tj} x_j\|^2$;
10: Construct the high-dimensional representation of $x_t^*$ basing on the reconstruction weights $W_t$: $y_t^* = \sum_{j=1}^{K_O} w_{tj} y_{tj}$;
11: END;
**Output:** longer texture video $Y^* = \{y_t^*\}_{t=1,\ldots,L}$;

---

## 5   Experiments

We have synthesized many dynamic textures using out proposed method. The inputs texture sequences used in our experiments are from[1] and DynTex

**Fig. 1.** The images on the top row are from the original wave sequence. The second row is synthesized by the basic LDS. The bottom row is synthesized by our method.

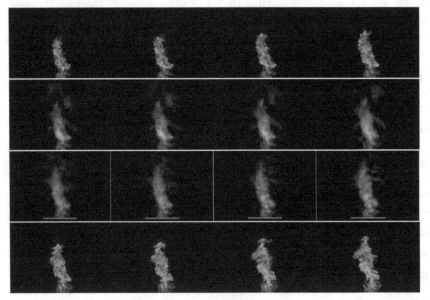

**Fig. 2.** The images on the top row are from the original flame sequence. The second row is synthesized by the basic LDS. The third row is synthesized by HOSVD. The bottom row is synthesized by our method.

---

[1] http://www.cc.gatech.edu/cpl/projects/graphcuttextures/

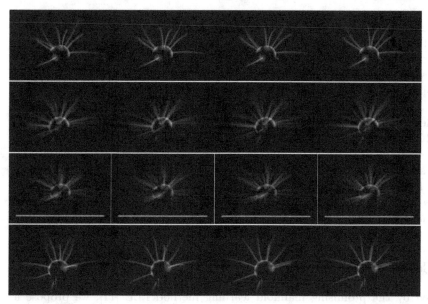

**Fig. 3.** The images on the top row are from the original sparkle sequence. The second row is synthesized by the basic LDS. The third row is synthesized by HOSVD. The bottom row is synthesized by our method.

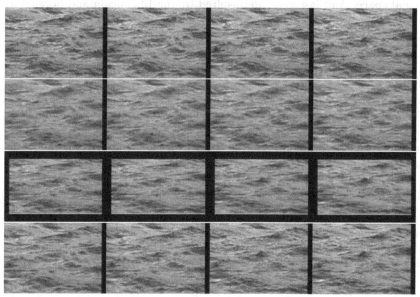

**Fig. 4.** The images on the top row are from the original river sequence. The second row is synthesized by the basic LDS. The third row is synthesized by HOSVD. The bottom row is synthesized by our method.

Database [13]. Most inputs videos have resolutions of 150 by 100 and lengths of 60 to 150 frames while the lengths of the outputs sequences were two times or greater than the original sequences. In our experiments, we set the low dimension $d$ varying from 10 to 20. The neighborhood size $K$ is between 10 and 20 in the appearance model and is between 2 and 10 in the observation model.

Fig.1, Fig.2, Fig.3 and Fig.4 shows the synthesis results for four sequences, each depicting different dynamics, by basic LDS, HOSVD [9], and our method. The HOSVD based synthesis results are downloaded from[2]. As can been seen, the basic LDS method yields blurred images and a decreasing quality as the synthesized sequence becomes longer. The HOSVD generates improved results while the visual quality is still not satisfactory. And our method can synthesize images most similar to the original frames, and like the basic LDS, the temporal coherence of the synthesized videos is also well guaranteed. What's more, the whole synthesis process is simple and in real-time.

## 6    Conclusions

Inspired by the promising manifold learning method LLE [11], we propose a new framework for dynamic texture synthesis. We use the LLE to capture the low-dimensional embedding of the input texture sequences. Automatic regression(AR) model is then adopted to model the texture dynamics in the low-dimensional space. And lastly we are inspired by the LLE again and develop a new technique to reconstruct the high-dimensional embedding of the newly synthesized latent variables. Both the appearance model and the observation model in our framework are nonlinear and the experiment results demonstrate that our framework can generate longer and higher-quality dynamic textures than relevant works.

Some future work will be pursued to make the proposed method more applicable. Though our proposed observation model can ensure higher visual quality of the synthesized images, the temporal coherence can be hardly maintained as the synthesized sequence becomes longer. That is because the dynamic model in our framework is too simple to capture complex temporal variation in the low-dimensional space. In the future, some other dynamic models may be created or applied in this framework to achieve more stable synthesis process.

**Acknowledgement.** This work is supported partially by the National Natural Science Foundation (NSFC) of China (Grant no. 61272203), the Ph.D. Programs Foundation of Ministry of Education of China (Grant no. 20110142110060).

## References

1. Soatto, S., Doretto, G., Wu, Y.N.: Dynamic textures. In: 2001 Proceedings of the Eighth IEEE International Conference on Computer Vision, ICCV 2001, vol. 2, pp. 439–446. IEEE (2001)

---

[2] http://lcav.epfl.ch/reproducible_research/CostantiniIP07_1

2. Wang, J., Hertzmann, A., Blei, D.M.: Gaussian process dynamical models. In: Advances in Neural Information Processing Systems, pp. 1441–1448 (2005)
3. Rahimi, A., Darrell, T., Recht, B.: Learning appearance manifolds from video. In: 2005 IEEE Computer Society Conference on Computer Vision and Pattern Recognition, CVPR 2005, vol. 1, pp. 868–875. IEEE (2005)
4. Lin, R.-S., Liu, C.-B., Yang, M.-H., Ahuja, N., Levinson, S.E.: Learning nonlinear manifolds from time series. In: Leonardis, A., Bischof, H., Pinz, A. (eds.) ECCV 2006. LNCS, vol. 3952, pp. 245–256. Springer, Heidelberg (2006)
5. Doretto, G., Chiuso, A., Wu, Y.N., Soatto, S.: Dynamic textures. International Journal of Computer Vision 51(2), 91–109 (2003)
6. Yuan, L., Wen, F., Liu, C., Shum, H.-Y.: Synthesizing dynamic texture with closed-loop linear dynamic system. In: Pajdla, T., Matas, J. (George) (eds.) ECCV 2004. LNCS, vol. 3022, pp. 603–616. Springer, Heidelberg (2004)
7. Liu, C.B., Lin, R., Ahuja, N.: Modeling dynamic textures using subspace mixtures. In: 2005 IEEE International Conference on Multimedia and Expo, ICME 2005, pp. 1378–1381. IEEE (2005)
8. Teh, Y.W., Roweis, S.T.: Automatic alignment of local representations. In: Advances in Neural Information Processing Systems, pp. 841–848 (2002)
9. Costantini, R., Sbaiz, L., Susstrunk, S.: Higher order svd analysis for dynamic texture synthesis. IEEE Transactions on Image Processing 17(1), 42–52 (2008)
10. Awasthi, I., Elgammal, A.: Learning nonlinear manifolds of dynamic textures. In: Advances in Computer Graphics and Computer Vision, pp. 395–405. Springer (2007)
11. Roweis, S.T., Saul, L.K.: Nonlinear dimensionality reduction by locally linear embedding. Science 290(5500), 2323–2326 (2000)
12. Chang, H., Yeung, D.Y., Xiong, Y.: Super-resolution through neighbor embedding. In: 2004 Proceedings of the 2004 IEEE Computer Society Conference on Computer Vision and Pattern Recognition, CVPR 2004, vol. 1, pp. I-I. IEEE (2004)
13. Péteri, R., Fazekas, S., Huiskes, M.J.: Dyntex: A comprehensive database of dynamic textures. Pattern Recognition Letters 31(12), 1627–1632 (2010)

# A Deep Joint Learning Approach
# for Age Invariant Face Verification

Ya Li[1,2], Guangrun Wang[2], Liang Lin[2(✉)], and Huiyou Chang[2]

[1] Guangzhou University, Guangzhou 510006, China
[2] Sun Yat-sen University, Guangzhou 510006, China
liya@gzhu.edu.cn, wanggrun@mail2.sysu.edu.cn,
linliang@ieee.org, isschy@mail.sysu.edu.cn

**Abstract.** Age-related research has become an attractive topic in recent years due to its wide range of application scenarios. In spite of the great advancement in face related works in recent years, face recognition across ages is still a challenging problem. In this paper, we propose a new deep Convolutional Neural Network (CNN) model for age-invariant face verification, which can learn features, distance metrics and threshold simultaneously. We also introduce two tricks to overcome insufficient memory capacity issue and to reduce computational cost. Experimental results show our method outperforms other state-of-the-art methods on MORPH-II database, which improves the rank-1 recognition rate from the current best performance 92.80% to 93.6%.

**Keywords:** Face verification · Age invariant · Face recognition · Deep CNN · Joint learning

## 1 Introduction

Age-related research has become an attractive topic in recent years due to its wide range of application scenarios. Age information is useful in many applications, such as age-specific human-computer interaction, security surveillance monitoring, age-based face images retrieval, automatic face simulation and intelligent advertisement system etc..

In spite of the great advancement in face related works in recent years, face recognition across ages is still a challenging problem. In paper [1], face verification achieved near-human performance on Labeled Faces in the Wild (LFW) dataset using high-dimensional Local Binary Pattern feature (HD-LBP). The work in paper [2,3] even achieved exceed-human ability on face verification using deep learning method. To our best knowledge, there is no such good result on age invariant recognition.

The challenges on age invariant recognition include large intra-subject variations and great inter-subject similarity. As well known, human face appearance will change greatly with the aging process. The changes are different in the different age period as shown in Fig.1(a). From birth to adulthood, the greatest change is the craniofacial growth, that is shape change; and from adulthood to

© Springer-Verlag Berlin Heidelberg 2015
H. Zha et al. (Eds.): CCCV 2015, Part I, CCIS 546, pp. 296–305, 2015.
DOI: 10.1007/978-3-662-48558-3_30

old age, the most perceptible change becomes skin aging, that is texture change [4]. These changes of same person are the intra-subject variations. Meanwhile, different persons on same age period maybe look like same, that is the inter-subject similarity as shown in Fig.1(b). Therefore, enlarging the inter-subject

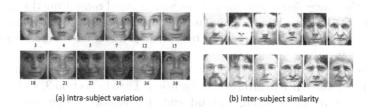

(a) Intra-subject variation                    (b) Inter-subject similarity

**Fig. 1.** Example images showing intra-subject variations and the inter-subject similarity. (a) Shows face appearance changes with the aging process. Images come from the FG-NET database [10]. (b)Shows different persons on same age period maybe look like same.

differences while reducing the intra-subject variations is a crucial goal in age invariant recognition as well as face recognition. Many approaches are realized based on this goal in the traditional face recognition such as Linear Discriminant Analysis (LDA) [5], Bayesian face [6,7] and metric learning [8]. However, these models are limited by their linear nature. Of course, many recent studies have made improvements to address these limits. For example, in order to measure similarity between images traditional metric learning methods require a fixed distance threshold. Li et al. [9] proposed to learn a decision function for face matching problem that could be looked as a joint model of a distance metric and a threshold locally adapted rule. But this model is limited by its shallow structures.

In this work, we train a deep convolutional network to learn features, distance metric and threshold function simultaneously. We aim at not only preserving similarity of the same person across ages while discriminating the different individuals, but also learning implicit adaptive thresholds at the same time. Generally it requires positive semi-definite for the Mahalanobis metric, so directly optimizing the metric matrix is computational intensive. Inspired by [9], we learn Mahalanobis metric and distance thresholds jointly, and further factorize the matrix into a fully-connected layer on the top of our deep architecture. In this way, the distance metric and distance thresholds is seamlessly integrated with the image feature represented by the other layers of neural networks. The joint optimization can be then efficiently achieved via the standard backward propagation. Therefore, by means of the nonlinear learning of deep neural networks, we improve the previous models and achieve the state-of-the-art result in age invariant verification.

There are two tricks to overcome insufficient memory capacity issue and to reduce computational cost. Considering the capacity of memory, we scale up our approach to the large amount of training data by using a batch-process strategy.

In each round of training, we randomly select a relatively small number of images, and use them to organize the training pairs. By taking the training pairs as the inputs, we update the model parameters by the stochastic gradient descent (SGD) algorithm and use backpropagation algorithm to compute gradient. In order to reduce the computational cost, we calculate the gradients on the images instead of the proceeded image pairs. Thus we can avoid computing the gradients repeatedly, because one image can be included into more than one training pairs. So the computational cost is reduced by only depending on the number of the selected images.

The reminder of this paper is organized as follows. In the next section, we first review related works in age invariant recognition. Then in Section 3, we introduce our deep joint metric learning method and the network framework. And we present our experiment in Section 4. Finally, Section 5 gives some conclusions.

## 2    Related Work

In the literature, most age-related works focus on age estimation before [10–18], including exact age estimation and age group estimation. Lanitis et al. [10] first present an exact age estimation method using the statistical face model which established according to the aging function. Geng et al. [11] propose an algorithm named AGES to learn aging pattern subspace which can reconstruct the face image missing in the training samples. Fu et al. [12] involve the manifold ways for age estimation and compared experiment results by several manifold methods. Guo et al. [13] propose using biological inspired features (BIF) and principal component analysis (PCA) dimension reduction for facial image description, and they use support vector machine (SVM) classification method for age estimation. In paper [15], Guo et al. focus on cross-data age estimation and introduce a "correlation" item to measure two different populations' correlation and project two different aging patterns into a common space. More recently, Geng et al. [16] extend their label distribution learning algorithms [14] and propose two adaptive label distribution learning algorithms IIS-ALDL and BFGS-ALDL which can learn the parameters of label distribution adaptively. Li et al. [17] propose a novel hierarchical feature composition and selection model used in facial age estimation. To the best of our knowledge, until now there is only one paper in literature using deep model for age estimation. In [18], Yan et al. use deep Convolutional Neural Network (CNN) to extract facial features and SVM classifier to estimate age groups.

Recent years, more and more works focus on age invariant recognition. In paper [19], Park et al. propose a 3D facial aging model and simulation method for age-invariant face recognition. This is a generative approach, which try to compensate the 3D facial images of lacked age before recognition. Ling et al. [20] combine gradient orientation pyramid (GOP) with SVM for face verification. For an image pair they used the cosine distances between each one's multi scale gradient orientation as the feature vector, and then they use SVM for classification. In [21], Li et al. propose a new method to used in age invariant recognition, which is a variation of random subspace LDA. What's more, they represent each face using two patch-based local feature descriptors SIFT and LBP, so their method is named multi-feature discriminant analysis (MFDA). Based on the observation: different person usually share common characteristics and the same person contain intrinsic features which are relatively invariant across ages, Gong et al. [22] express a facial image using age component, identity component and a noise term. And they adopt Expectation Maximization (EM) algorithm to estimate this generative model parameters. More recently, Chen et al. [23] suppose that if two young persons look alike, it is likely that they also look similar when they are old. And they propose a data-driven approach called cross-age reference coding (CARC) for age invariant recognition.

## 3   Deep Joint Metric Learning Framework

we train a deep convolutional network to learn features, distance metrics and threshold simultaneously. In this section, we first introduce the classical metric learning method and the optimization objective of our model. Then we present our deep model. Finally, we show how to use our method for age invariant face recognition.

### 3.1   Optimization Objective

Following the early work of Xing et al. [24], for pairwise images $(x, y)$, most distance metrics learning approaches learn a Mahalanobis-like distance: $d(x, y) = (x - y)^t M(x - y)$, where $M$ is a positive semi-definite (PSD) matrix. Suppose category labels of pairwise images are $c(x)$ and $c(y)$. $x$, $y$ are in the same class or are similar, if $c(x) = c(y)$. A simple way is minimum the distance between samples in the same class.

If metric learning is used in matching problem, it requires a threshold to decide whether $x$ and $y$ are matched. We formulate it as following:

$$(x - y)^t M(x - y) \leq d, \quad M \succeq 0. \tag{1}$$

However, it is inappropriate for a fixed threshold $d$. Because maybe the distance of intra-subject is lager than the distance of inter-subject. Li et al. [9] propose to learn threshold adaptively, $d$ is a function related with $(x, y)$ instead of a constant, so inequation (1) becomes to $(x - y)^T M(x - y) \leq d(x, y)$. Thus, the decision function $f(x, y)$ can be written as:

$$f(x, y) = d(x, y) - (x - y)^t M(x - y) \begin{cases} \geq 0 & \text{if } c(x) = c(y) \\ < 0 & \text{otherwise} \end{cases}. \tag{2}$$

Since the metric $M$ itself is quadratic, we assume $d(x, y)$ as a simple quadratic form, i.e.,

$$d(x, y) = \frac{1}{2} x^t \widetilde{A} x + \frac{1}{2} y^t \widetilde{A} y + x^t \widetilde{B} y + c^t(x + y) + b. \tag{3}$$

Substitute Eq.(3) in Eq.(2), we get:

$$f(x,y) = \frac{1}{2}x^t(\widetilde{A} - 2M)x + \frac{1}{2}y^t(\widetilde{A} - 2M)y + x^t(\widetilde{B} + 2M)y + c^t(x+y) + b$$

$$= \frac{1}{2}x^t Ax + \frac{1}{2}y^t Ay + x^t By + c^t(x+y) + b, \tag{4}$$

where $A = (\widetilde{A} - 2M)$ and $B = (\widetilde{B} + 2M)$. Suppose $A$ is PSD and $B$ is negative semi-definite (NSD), $A$ and $B$ can be factorized as $L_A^T L_A$ and $L_B^T L_B$. Eq.(4) can be further written as:

$$f(x,y) = \frac{1}{2}x^t L_A^T L_A x + \frac{1}{2}y^t L_A^T L_A y - x^t L_B^T L_B y + c^t(x+y) + b$$

$$= \frac{1}{2}(L_A x)^t(L_A x) + \frac{1}{2}(L_A y)^t(L_A y) - (L_B x)^t(L_B y) + c^t x + c^t y + b \tag{5}$$

Through above transformation, face recognition is cast into computing the decision function (5). For an age instance $z$ of person $P$, we wish to learn a reidentification model to successfully identify another age instance $z'$ of the same person. This can be achieved by learning metrics $L_A$, $L_B$ and vector $c$, subject to the value of $f(z, z')$ as large as possible for same person while as small as possible for different person. Given a training set $Z = \{(z_i, y_i)\}_{i=1}^N$, where $y_i$ is the class label, i.e. person ID, N is the total person number, we define a pairwise set $\Omega = \{\Omega_k = (z_i, z_j)\}$. Taking pairwise set $\Omega$ as input, we can maximize the sum of $l(\Omega_k) \times f(\Omega_k)$, where $l(\Omega_k)$ is the label of image pair $\Omega_k$, if $z_i$ and $z_j$ come from the same person, $l(\Omega_k) = -1$, otherwise, $l(\Omega_k) = 1$. So our objective is maximize the sum of $l(\Omega_k) \times f(\Omega_k)$. Further more, we ignore the pairs that $f(\Omega_k) > 1$, here the choice of the constant 1 is arbitrary but not important, and changing it to any other positive constant $c$ results only in the matrices being replaced by $c$ times. We denote $(L_A, L_B, c)^T$ as $W$, our hinge-loss like objective function is:

$$H(W) = \sum_{\Omega} \max\{0, l(\Omega_k) \times f(\Omega_k) + 1\} \quad k = 1, 2...N^2 \tag{6}$$

## 3.2   Deep Architecture

$L_A$, $L_B$ and $c$ discussed in previous section can be looked as the weight of the fully-connected layer in deep CNN. Using one CNN network we realize the feature extracting, metric and threshold learning simultaneously. The parameters of the three components can be obtained by using network propagation algorithms.

As the publicly available datasets with person age information are relatively small, we use a relatively small network for our model. Fig. 2 shows the overall network architecture, which contains 7 layers. The first layer is a convolutional layer including 32 kernels of size $5 \times 5 \times 3$ with a stride of 2 pixels. The second layer is a max-pooling layer. The third layer is also a convolutional layer taking the max-pooling output as input and filters it with 32 kernels of size $5 \times 5 \times 16$ with a stride of 1 pixel. The fourth layer is a max-pooling layer followed by three

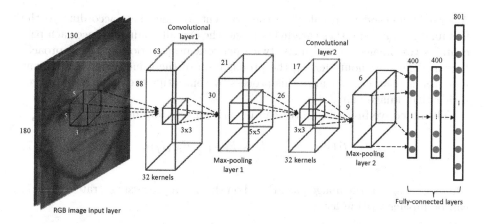

**Fig. 2.** Architecture of our model. The first and the third layers are convolutional layers, the second and the fourth are max-pooling layers. The last three layers are fully-connected layers.

fully-connected layers including two 400 dimension fully-connected layers and one 801 dimension fully-connected layer. We use rectified linear units (ReLU) for neurons in the convolutional layers. In fact, we can look feature extraction stage extracts 400 dimensional features by stacking two convolution-pooling layers and a fully-connected layer. The second fully-connected layer takes the role of projecting features to a common space. And the metric and threshold learning stage is realized by the third fully-connected layer with 801 dimension outputs, which learns the matrices $L_A$, $L_B$ and vector $c$ simultaneously.

### 3.3   Learning Algorithm

**Batch Process.** We apply batch learning strategy to optimize the parameters, due to the limited memory. For $N$ training images, the pairs number is $O(N^2)$. Even for a moderate dataset, it is impossible to load all image pairs into memory to train the network. How to choose pairs used in batch process? A simple way is to generate pairs randomly. However, this method makes the negative pairs are far more than positive pairs, because the person number be approximately double the pairs number and the likelihood of two pairs sharing the same person is very small.

To solve this problem we propose pairs generation rule as follows. In each iteration, we select a fixed number of persons(classes), and generate image pairs only using these persons. In order to ensure the training samples without loss of generality, we randomly select samples according to one ratio of positive and negative samples.

**Parameter Optimization.** As well know, the key step of CNN is updating the model parameters by the stochastic gradient descent (SGD) algorithm.

A straight method is to calculate the gradient for each pair according to the loss function and sum these gradients to get the overall gradient. Since each pair contains two images, it will incur twice network propagation in this approach. It is inefficient without sharing the propagation of the same image in different pairs. In fact, we can optimize this process by computing the gradient of images rather than image pairs.

The objective function Eq.(6) can be written as following form:

$$H(W) = \sum_{i,j \in m} loss(F_W(I_i), F_W(I_j)), \qquad (7)$$

where $< I_i, I_j >$ is the image pair. Based on the batch processing strategy, Eq.(7) can be further written as:

$$H(W) = H(F_W(I_1), F_W(I_2), ..., F_W(I_m)), \qquad (8)$$

where $\{I_i\}$ represents the set of all the distinct images in the pairs, and $m$ denotes the number of the distinct images. Compute the desired partial derivatives, which are given as:

$$\frac{\partial H}{\partial W^l} = \sum_{i=1}^{m} \frac{\partial H}{\partial X_i^l} \cdot \frac{\partial X_i^l}{\partial W^l}, \qquad (9)$$

$$\frac{\partial H}{\partial X_i^l} = \frac{\partial H}{\partial X_i^{l+1}} \cdot \frac{\partial X_i^{l+1}}{\partial X_i^l}, \qquad (10)$$

where $W$ represents the network parameters, $X_i^l$ represents the feature maps of the image $I_i$ at the $l^{th}$ layer. The right item of Eq.(9) is the sum of $\frac{\partial H}{\partial X_i^l} \cdot \frac{\partial X_i^l}{\partial W^l}$, it is denoted as $\frac{\partial H}{\partial W^l}(I_i')$ shortly.

The Eq.(9) shows that the overall gradient is the sum of the image-based gradient. The Eq.(10) shows that the partial derivative of each image respect to the feature maps can be calculated recursively. So the gradients of network parameters can be obtained by back propagation algorithm. Algorithm 1 shows the detail.

## 4     Experiment

The experiment is carried on MORPH-II database [25]. MORPH-II contains more than 55,000 face images of more than 13,000 individuals and ages range from 16 to 77. The average number of images per individual is 4. The individuals come from different races, among them Africans' images accounted for about 77%, the European images about 19%, and the remaining includes Hispanic, Asian and other races. The training data consists of 20000 face images from 10000 subjects, with each subject having two images with the largest age gap. The test data is composed of a gallery set and a probe set from the remaining 3000 subjects. The gallery set is composed of the youngest face images of

---

**Algorithm 1.** Deep joint learning algorithm

---

**Input:**
  Training set $X = \{(x_i, l_i)\}$, initialized parameters $W$, learning rate $\alpha(t)$, $t \leftarrow 0$
**Output:**
  Network parameters $W$
1: **while** $t < T$ **do**
2:   $t \leftarrow t + 1$
3:   Sample training persons randomly from X
4:   Sample pairwise training set $\Omega_k$ from $\{< I_i, I_j >\}$
5:   **for all** $\{I_i\}$ **do**
6:     Calculate the whole network's output $F(I_i)$ and each layer's feature maps $X_i$ by forward propagation
7:   **end for**
8:   **for all** $\{I_i\}$ **do**
9:     $\frac{\partial H}{\partial F_W(I_i)} = 0$
10:     **for all** image pair $\Omega_k$ i.e. $< I_p, I_q >$ **do**
11:       **if** $f(\Omega_k) > 1$ **then**
12:         **if** $I_i = I_p$ **then**
13:           $\frac{\partial H}{\partial F_W(I_i)} + = \frac{\partial H}{\partial F_W(I_p)}$
14:         **else if** $I_i = I_q$ **then**
15:           $\frac{\partial H}{\partial F_W(I_i)} + = \frac{\partial H}{\partial F_W(I_q)}$
16:         **end if**
17:       **end if**
18:     **end for**
19:     Calculate $\frac{\partial H}{\partial W}(I_i')$ using back propagation (Eq.(9) and Eq.(10))
20:     Sum the partial derivative $\Delta W = \Delta W + \frac{\partial H}{\partial W}(I_i')$
21:   **end for**
22:   $W^t = W^{t-1} - \alpha_t \Delta W$
23: **end while**

---

**Table 1.** Rank-1 identification rates on the MORPH database. Our method achieves the highest recognition rate compared to other state-of-the-art methods

| Method | Recognition rate |
|---|---|
| Park et al. [19] | 79.8% |
| MFDA [21] | 83.9% |
| HFA [22] | 91.1% |
| CARC [23] | 92.8% |
| Ours | **93.6%** |

each subject. The probe set is composed of the oldest face images of each subject. This experimental setting is same with [23] and [22].

We compare our deep CNN model against several state-of-the-art methods for age invariant face recognition on MORPH-II, including CARC [23], HFA [22],

Probe images

Rank-1 results

Ground- truth

**Fig. 3.** Some examples of rank-1 failed retrievals. The first row are the probe images, the second row is the rank-1 result of our method, and the third row is the ground-truth, i.e. correct matched image in the gallery.

MFDA [21] and method proposed in paper [19]. The comparative results are reported in Table 1. It is encouraging to see that our approach significantly outperforms the current best-performance method CARC by improving the rank-1 identification rate from 92.80% to 93.60%. To our best knowledge, this is the best identification rank-1 result on MORPH-II. For top-10 and top-20, our model achieves 98.8% and 99.34% respectively. Finally, we show some examples of rank-1 failed retrievals in Fig. 3. In spite of the rank-1 retrievals are incorrect in these cases, we can find that the probe images are looked be more similar to the incorrect rank-1 matched images than the true images.

## 5    Conclusion

In this paper, we propose a new deep CNN model for age-invariant face recognition, which can learn features, distance metrics and threshold simultaneously. Experimental results show our method outperforms other state-of-the-art methods on MORPH-II database. We also introduce two tricks to overcome insufficient memory capacity issue and to reduce computational cost. In the future, we want to investigate other facial attributes recognition, like expression, gender, ethnicity and head pose etc..

**Acknowledgments.** This research is supported by the National High Technology Research and Development Program of China (No.2013AA013801), the Science and Technology Planning Project of Guangdong Province(No. 2013B010406005) and the Guangdong Natural Science Foundation (No. S2013040012570). The authors would like to thank the reviewers for their comments and suggestions.

## References

1. Chen, D., Cao, X., Wen, F., Sun, J.: Blessing of dimensionality: high-dimensional feature and its efficient compression for face verification. In: CVPR (2013)
2. Lu, C., Tang, X.: Surpassing human-level face verification performance on LFW with GaussianFace. ArXiv e-prints (2014)

3. Sun, Y., Chen, Y., Wang, X., Tang, X.: Deep learning face representation by joint identification-verification. In: NIPS (2014)
4. Fu, Y., Guo, G., Huang, T.S.: Age synthesis and estimation via faces: A survey. TPAMI 32(11), 1955–1976 (2010)
5. Belhumeur, P.N., Hespanha, J.P., Kriegman, D.J.: Eigenfaces vs. Fisherfaces: Recognition using class specific linear projection. TPAMI 19(7), 711–720 (1997)
6. Moghaddam, B., Jebara, T., Pentland, A.: Bayesian face recognition. Pattern Recognition 33, 1771–1782 (2000)
7. Chen, D., Cao, X., Wang, L., Wen, F., Sun, J.: Bayesian face revisited: a joint formulation. In: Fitzgibbon, A., Lazebnik, S., Perona, P., Sato, Y., Schmid, C. (eds.) ECCV 2012, Part III. LNCS, vol. 7574, pp. 566–579. Springer, Heidelberg (2012)
8. Guillaumin, M., Verbeek, J., Schmid, C.: Is that you? Metric learning approaches for face identification. In: ICCV (2009)
9. Li, Z., Chang, S., Liang, F., Huang, T.S., Cao, L., Smith, J.R.: Learning locally-adaptive decision functions for person verification. In: CVPR (2013)
10. Lanitis, A., Taylor, C.J., Cootes, T.: Toward automatic simulation of aging effects on face images. TPAMI 24(4), 442–455 (2002)
11. Geng, X., Zhou, Z.H., Smith-Miles, K.: Automatic age estimation based on facial aging patterns. TPAMI 29(12), 2234–2240 (2007)
12. Fu, Y., Huang, T.S.: Human age estimation with regression on discriminative aging manifold. TMM 10(4), 578–584 (2008)
13. Guo, G., Mu, G., Fu, Y., Huang, T.: Human age estimation using bio-inspired features. In: CVPR (2009)
14. Geng, X., Yin, C., Zhou, Z.H.: Facial age estimation by learning from label distributions. TPAMI 35(10), 2401–2412 (2013)
15. Guo, G., Zhang, C.: A study on cross-population age estimation. In: CVPR (2014)
16. Geng, X., Wang, Q., Xia, Y.: Facial age estimation by adaptive label distribution learning. In: ICPR (2014)
17. Li, Y., Peng, Z., Liang, D., Chang, H. and Cai, Z.: Facial age estimation by using stacked feature composition and selection. The Visual Computer, 1–12 (2015)
18. Yan, C., Lang, C., Wang, T., Du, X., Zhang, C.: Age estimation based on convolutional neural network. In: Ooi, W.T., Snoek, C.G.M., Tan, H.K., Ho, C.-K., Huet, B., Ngo, C.-W. (eds.) PCM 2014. LNCS, vol. 8879, pp. 211–220. Springer, Heidelberg (2014)
19. Park, U., Tong, Y., Jain, A.K.: Age-invariant face recognition. TPAMI 32(5), 947–954 (2010)
20. Ling, H., Soatto, S., Ramanathan, N., Jacobs, D.W.: Face verification across age progression using discriminative methods. TIFS 5(1), 82–91 (2010)
21. Li, Z., Park, U., Jain, A.K.: A discriminative model for age invariant face recognition. TIFS 6(3-2), 1028–1037 (2011)
22. Gong, D., Li, Z., Lin, D., Liu, J., Tang, X.: Hidden factor analysis for age invariant face recognition. In: ICCV (2013)
23. Chen, B.-C., Chen, C.-S., Hsu, W.H.: Cross-age reference coding for age-invariant face recognition and retrieval. In: Fleet, D., Pajdla, T., Schiele, B., Tuytelaars, T. (eds.) ECCV 2014, Part VI. LNCS, vol. 8694, pp. 768–783. Springer, Heidelberg (2014)
24. Xing, E.P., Jordan, M.I., Russell, S., Ng, A.Y.: Distance metric learning with application to clustering with side-information. In: NIPS (2002)
25. Ricanek, K., Tesafaye, T.: Morph: a longitudinal image database of normal adult age-progression. In: FG (2006)

# A New Similarity Measure
# for Non-local Means Denoising

Bin Cai[1,2], Wei Liu[1], Zhong Zheng[1], and Zeng-Fu Wang[1,2(✉)]

[1] Institute of Intelligent Machines, Chinese Academy of Sciences, Hefei 230031, Anhui, China
zfwang@ustc.edu.cn
[2] School of Information Science and Technology,
University of Science and Technology of China, Hefei 230027, Anhui, China

**Abstract.** Non-local means (NLM) denoising algorithm is a good similarity measure based denoising algorithm for images with repetitive textures. However, NLM cannot handle the large rotation. In this paper, we propose a rotation-invariant and noise-resistant similarity measure based on improved LBP operator, and use it to search for similar image patches. In addition, in order to speed up the algorithm, an automatic selection strategy of similar patches is proposed. Consequently, the self-similarity can be used to obtain more similar patches for denoising. Experiment results demonstrate that the proposed method achieved higher peak signal-to-noise ratio (PSNR) and more visual pleasing results than some state-of-art methods.

**Keywords:** Rotation-invariant · Similarity measure · NLM · PSNR

## 1 Introduction

The goal of image denoising methods is to recover the original image from a noisy measurement. Several methods have been proposed to remove the noise and recover the true image. Most of them can be divided into two parts, spatial filtering algorithm and transform domain filtering algorithm. The former mainly includes the mean filtering, median filtering, wiener filtering and non-local means (NLM) filtering, etc [1-3]. The latter mainly includes wavelet threshold filtering [4-6], and filtering method based on dictionary learning [7-9], etc. The NLM [3] algorithm extends the local calculation model to non-local and it has been proved to have better performance than other classic denoising algorithm. This denoising filter searches similar patches and uses them in a weighted average, which the weights depend on the amount of similarity. So, the similarity measurement between patches is the most important part in NLM denoising algorithm.

In order to obtain better filtering performance, many researchers have conducted the thorough research on the basis of NLM [10-15]. By sparse 3D transform-domain collaborative filtering, the BM3D algorithm obtains very good filtering effect. For the research on the speed of operation, researchers mainly use the pre-selection method [16-17]. Although these methods in a certain extent, improve the filtering performance, there are still some shortcomings. Most improved filtering algorithms cannot handle rotation or mirroring.

© Springer-Verlag Berlin Heidelberg 2015
H. Zha et al. (Eds.): CCCV 2015, Part I, CCIS 546, pp. 306–316, 2015.
DOI: 10.1007/978-3-662-48558-3_31

Local binary pattern (LBP) operator was proposed by Ojala et al. [18]. Although it can capture the very local structure of the texture, the original LBP codes are sensitive to noise and image rotation. Therefore, we propose an improved LBP operator, and put forward an improved method for searching for similar image patches on the basis of the improved LBP operator. The improved similarity measure methods are as follows. Given a pixel $i$, $N(i)$ denotes a square neighborhood of fixed size and centered at pixel $i$, $N(j)$ centered at pixel $j$ is the neighborhood of patch $N(i)$. We obtain $N'(i)$, $N'(j)$ by rotating $N(i)$ and $N(j)$ which based on the improved LBP operator of pixel $i$ and $j$. Then the distance between $N'(i)$ and $N'(j)$ is defined as the similarity measurement of pixel $i$ and $j$. And in order to obtain the most suitable similar patches and speed up the algorithm, we propose an automatic selection method. As the improved similarity measure can better reflect the similarity between image patches, the proposed algorithm can remove noise more effectively while preserving the image details.

## 2    NLM Algorithm

Given a noisy image $g = \{g(i) \mid i \in \Omega\}$, where $\Omega$ represents the image area, the filtered image $\hat{f}$ at the point $i$ is then computed by

$$\hat{f}(i) = \frac{\sum_{j \in I} w(i, j) g(j)}{\sum_{j \in I} w(i, j)} \tag{1}$$

$$w(i, j) = \exp(-\frac{d(i, j)}{h^2}) \tag{2}$$

$$d(i, j) = \| N(i) - N(j) \|_{2,a}^2 \tag{3}$$

Where $a$ is the standard deviation of the Gauss function, $d(i, j)$ is the distance between patches, $I$ is the neighborhood pixel of pixel $i$. And the family of weights $w(i, j)$ depend on the similarity between the pixels $i$ and $j$.

The NLM algorithm not only compares the difference between the gray values of the pixels, but also considers the redundancy in the image structure. However, it is not invariant under any transformation such as rotations or mirroring. So, it did not make full use of the self similarity of the image information.

## 3    Improved NLM Algorithm

In this section we propose an improved block matching algorithm which is invariant under rotation and mirroring. First, An improved LBP operator will be introduced. Then we will show how it works for our improved block matching algorithm. Finally, we will analysis how our proposed improved NLM algorithm works.

## 3.1    Improved LBP Operator

The original LBP[18] is a gray-scale texture operator. Given a central pixel $g_c$, a pattern number is computed by comparing its value with those of its neighborhoods:

$$LBP_{R,P} = \sum_{p=0}^{P-1} s(g_p - g_c)2^p \qquad (4)$$

Where $s(x) = \begin{cases} 1, x \geq 0 \\ 0, x < 0 \end{cases}$, $g_p$ is the neighbor of $g_c$. $P$ is the sample number of $g_p$, $R$ is the radius of the neighborhood. As the original LBP operator can capture the very local structure of texture, it is widely used texture classification, face recognition and so on. So, this ability just can be applied to NLM algorithm. As the original LBP operator is sensitive to noise and rotation, we propose an improved LBP operator $ILBP_{R,P}^{ri}$ :

$$ILBP_{R,P}^{ri} = \min\{ROR(LBPM_{R,P}, k), k = 0, \cdots, P-1\} \qquad (5)$$

$$LBPM_{R,P} = \sum_{p=0}^{P-1} s(\overline{g_p} - \overline{g_c})2^p \qquad (6)$$

Where $\overline{g_c}$ is the means of $g_c$ and its 8-connected. $\overline{g_p}$ is the means of $g_p$ and its 4-connected (see in Fig. 1). Due to this strategy, the $LBPM_{R,P}$ is robust to noise , it can also keep the difference between the neighborhood points even the radius is small( $R = 1$ ). $ROR(\bullet, k)$ [18]performs a circular k-step bit-wise right shift on $LBPM_{R,P}$, so, the $ILBP_{R,P}^{ri}$ is rotation-invariant.

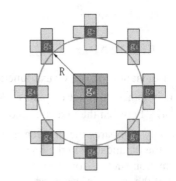

**Fig. 1.** The $(R, P)$ neighborhood type used to    $LBPM_{R,P}$ operator:    central pixel and its $P = 8$ neighbors on circle of radius $R$ .

## 3.2    Rotation-Invariant and Noise-Resistant Similarity Measurement

There are many similar structures in natural images. In order to determine the similarity between two pixels, the standard block matching method of NLM usually compares the gray value between the corresponding position of each patch. However, there are not only the original block translation results, more is rotated by the original block. If we use the standard block matching method, many similar patch has not been able to find, and this will diminish the contributions of these similar structure to suppress noise.

Based on the above analysis, we propose an improved similarity measure method. The new one can make better use of the redundant information, thus we can obtain a better filtering effect. Here are the details.

Suppose the size of $N(i)$ and $N(j)$ is $(2R+1)\times(2R+1)$. We can obtain $ILBP_{R,P}^{ri}$ of pixel $i$ and $j$ with radius R, neighborhood sample points $P = 8$ using Eq. (5), Eq.(6). We can also obtain the circular step $k_i$ bit-wise right shift from $LBPM_{R,P}$ to $ILBP_{R,P}^{ri}$ of pixel $i$, and the circular step $k_j$ bit-wise right shift from $LBPM_{R,P}$ to $ILBP_{R,P}^{ri}$ of pixel $j$. So, the rotated patch $N'(i)$ from $N(i)$ is then computed by

$$N(i) = \{ \boldsymbol{x}_{r,8r}, r = 0,\cdots, R \}$$
$$= \{ [ \boldsymbol{x}_{r,8r,0}, \cdots, \boldsymbol{x}_{r,8r,k_i-1}, \boldsymbol{x}_{r,8r,k_i}, \cdots, \boldsymbol{x}_{r,8r,8r-1} ]^T \} \quad (7)$$

$$N'(i) = \{ \boldsymbol{x}'_{r,8r}, r = 0,\cdots, R \}$$
$$= \{ [ \boldsymbol{x}_{r,8r,k_i}, \cdots, \boldsymbol{x}_{r,8r,8r-1}, \boldsymbol{x}_{r,8r,0}, \cdots, \boldsymbol{x}_{r,8r,k_i-1} ]^T \} \quad (8)$$

Where $\boldsymbol{x}_{r,8r}$ are the neighbors of pixel $i$ on radius $r$, and $\boldsymbol{x}'_{r,8r}$ is the result by a circular $k_i$ step bit-wise right shift from $\boldsymbol{x}_{r,8r}$ (see in Fig. 2). We can also obtain $N'(j)$ rotated from $N(j)$ using the same strategy.

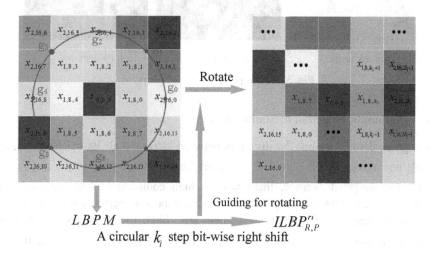

Fig. 2. Illustration of patch rotation

Let $d_1$ be the distance between $N'(i)$ and $N'(j)$. So, the similarity of the pixel $i$ and $j$ can be measured by distance $d_1$.

$$d_1 = \| N'(i) - N'(j) \|^2_{2,a} \tag{9}$$

Fig. 3 shows the advantage in finding similar pixels using our new similarity measure method. We can see, for a given sample point (red box), our improved similarity measure method can still accurately find more similar pixels even in the noise environment.

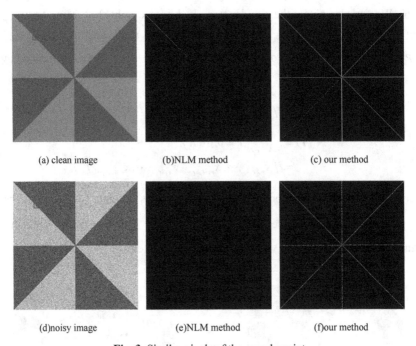

(a) clean image          (b)NLM method          (c) our method

(d)noisy image          (e)NLM method          (f)our method

**Fig. 3.** Similar pixels of the sample point

## 3.3     Automatic Selection of Similar Sets

For a given pixel $i$, we put the distances between $N(i)$ and all its neighbor patches $N(j)$ into vector $\mathbf{v} = (d_{i,j} \mid j = 1, \cdots, n)$ using Eq. (9). If we take all the distance in $\mathbf{v}$ for the weighted average, there will be high complexity. And the dissimilar patches for the weighted average will reduce the denoising performance. So we propose an automatic selection of the similar sets. First, the distances $d_{i,j}$ in $\mathbf{v}$ are sorted in non-descending order, denoted as $\hat{\mathbf{v}} = (d_{i,j}(k) \mid k = 1, \cdots, n)$, $k$ is the sequence number of $d_{i,j}$ in $\hat{\mathbf{v}}$. Second, we divide $\hat{\mathbf{v}}$ into $L$ segments (in experiment $L = 10$), and get the mean value of each segment into vector $\bar{\mathbf{v}}$.

$$\overline{\mathbf{v}} = (\overline{d}_l \mid \overline{d}_l = \frac{1}{L_1} \sum_{k=(l-1)\cdot L_1 +1}^{l\cdot L_1} d_{i,j}(k), l = 1,\cdots, L) \tag{10}$$

where $L_1 = \frac{n}{L}$, and $n$ is the number of pixels in the neighborhood of $i$. Third, we find the maximum gradient of $\overline{d}_l$ in vector $\overline{\mathbf{v}}$ as follows:

$$grad_M = \max(g_l \mid g_l = \overline{d}_{l+1} - \overline{d}_l, l = 1,\cdots, L-1) \tag{11}$$

Where $M$ denotes the position of the maximum gradient. So, the similar sets $P$ can be computed as follows:

$$P = \{N(j) \mid d_{i,j}(k), k = 1,\cdots, M\cdot L_1\} \tag{12}$$

### 3.4    Modification of the Filter

We want to modify the NLM algorithm using our improved similarity measure instead of the standard patch matching method. By replacing $d$ in Eq. (2) by $d_l$ in Eq.(9), our improved NLM algorithm is rotationally invariant. And we get the similar patches in Eq. (12) for the weighted average.

Besides, in order to reduce the influence of noise on the similarity calculation, we use the denoised image which is filtered by the original NLM algorithm with smaller parameters as the guiding image for the similarity calculation.

## 4    Experiments and Discussion

The implementations of our improved NLM algorithm produce competitive results. In our experiments, we add Gaussian white noise of different variance .The test images are show in Fig. 4. Table 1 compares the PSNR [19] and the MSSIM [20] of our improved NLM algorithm, NLM [3], PNLM [14], DDID [21], BM3D [13] and SHIFTABLE-BF [22] for the test images. In all the experimentation we have fixed a search window of $21\times21$ pixels and a similarity square neighborhood $N(i)$ of $5\times5$ pixels, and the filtering parameter $h = 10\sigma$ [3].

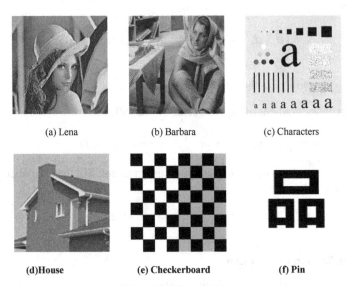

(a) Lena              (b) Barbara              (c) Characters

(d)House              (e) Checkerboard              (f) Pin

**Fig. 4.** Test image.

As can be seen from Tab.1, compared with the original NLM, our proposed method in comparison with PSNR and MSSIM were significantly improved. And in most cases our proposed method are superior to the selected state of the art method. This shows that, our proposed method can effectively suppress noise and preserve image edge structure information. When the noise standard deviation is large ( $\delta = 50, 70$ ), our proposed method is almost the highest in PSNR and MSSIM compared to NLM, PNLM, SHIFTABLE-BF, DDID, BM3D. For the Checkerboard image with the noise standard deviation $\delta = 70$, the PSNR improvements of our proposed method over BM3D is +4dB. This shows that in case of serious noise pollution, our proposed method has better filtering ability. Especially for the Checkerboard image with the noise standard deviation $\delta = 70$, the MSSIM improvements of our proposed method over the others is +0.1. This shows that in case of serious noise pollution, the proposed algorithm is superior to other methods in the ability to preserve the original structure of the image.

We can see in Fig. 5, 6, the edge of the image filtered by NLM and SHIFTABLE-BF is blurry and lack contrast. And noises still exist in the image filtered by PNLM. The denoising effect of the image filtered by BM3D and DDID is good, but a lot of artificial texture is unnecessarily added. However, the image filtered by our proposed method has better visual effect, and the ringing effect is significantly less than the other methods, the image contrast is higher, homogeneous region is more smooth, besides, the edge and the detail information are preserved better and more clearly. This is mainly because in contrast to the original method, our improved NLM algorithm considers the rotation of the patch, therefore one can find more suitable regions for the weighted average and yield improved results.

**Table 1.** Performance comparison of different denoising methods (PSNR/MSSIM)

| $\sigma$ | | NLM | PNLM | SHIFTAB LE-BF | DDID | BM3D | Ours |
|---|---|---|---|---|---|---|---|
| Lena | 30 | 24.36/ 0.7266 | 26.92/ 0.7937 | 24.93/ 0.6948 | 28.00/ 0.8391 | **28.02/ 0.8392** | 27.4/ 0.8229 |
| | 50 | 21.46/ 0.6124 | 24.24/ 0.6682 | 22.84/ 0.5546 | 25.05/ 0.7476 | 25.03/ 0.7394 | **25.15/ 0.7576** |
| | 70 | 19.94/ 0.5361 | 22.26/ 0.5429 | 20.77/ 0.4422 | 23.80/ 0.6875 | 23.61/ 0.6784 | **23.89/ 0.7066** |
| Barbara | 30 | 23.57/ 0.6625 | 26.04/ 0.7684 | 24.41/ 0.6837 | **27.26/ 0.8288** | 27.12/ 0.8112 | 26.46/ 0.7838 |
| | 50 | 20.80/ 0.5407 | 23.48/ 0.6425 | 22.59/ 0.5766 | 24.39/ **0.7190** | **24.51/** 0.7088 | 24.49/ 0.7103. |
| | 70 | 19.25/ 0.4609 | 21.48/ 0.5307 | 20.59/ 0.4722 | 21.98/ 0.6084 | 23.06/ 0.6401 | **23.12/ 0.6496** |
| Character | 30 | 25.65/ 0.8278 | 26.20/ 0.8521 | 25.87/ 0.7231 | **27.35/ 0.8760** | 27.27/ 0.8674 | 26.60/ 0.8693 |
| | 50 | 20.25/ 0.7285 | 23.62/ 0.7770 | 21.03/ 0.5688 | 24.06/ 0.7838 | 23.37/ 0.7644 | **24.48/ 0.8140** |
| | 70 | 17.27/ 0.6201 | 21.39/ 0.6647 | 18.13/ 0.3840 | 22.14/ 0.7220 | 21.66/ 0.7174 | **22.75/ 0.7797** |
| House | 30 | 27.92/ 0.7919 | 30.44/ 0.7925 | 27.71/ 0.6389 | 31.79/ 0.8398 | **32.07/ 0.8469** | 31.65/ 0.8411 |
| | 50 | 24.67/ 0.7271 | 27.06/ 0.6637 | 24.32/ 0.4599 | 29.24/ 0.7936 | 29.46/ 0.7995 | **29.58/ 0.8129** |
| | 70 | 22.92/ 0.6723 | 24.73/ 0.5438 | 21.73/ 0.3449 | 27.36/ 0.7521 | 27.75/ 0.7618 | **28.06/ 0.7874** |
| Checker-board | 30 | 32.15/ 0.9460 | 31.68/ 0.8730 | 31.77/ 0.7923 | 34.66/ 0.9015 | 36.46/ 0.9577 | **39.46/ 0.9738** |
| | 50 | 25.81/ 0.8808 | 27.49/ 0.8207 | 26.54/ 0.6210 | 29.73/ 0.8482 | 28.87/ 0.8581 | **32.86/ 0.9542** |
| | 70 | 20.67/ 0.7391 | 24.11/ 0.7260 | 21.33/ 0.4572 | 25.73/ 0.7966 | 25.97/ 0.8316 | **29.97/ 0.9365** |
| Pin | 30 | 35.93/ 0.9606 | 33.69/ 0.9133 | 34.78/ 0.8457 | 39.03/ 0.9591 | **40.77/** 0.9724 | 40.54/ **0.9801** |
| | 50 | 30.53/ 0.9401 | 30.51/ 0.8846 | 30.25/ 0.7682 | 34.63/ 0.9327 | 32.44/ 0.9243 | **36.13/ 0.9645** |
| | 70 | 23.81/ 0.8771 | 27.50/ 0.7697 | 25.44/ 0.7046 | 31.36/ 0.9046 | 29.77/ 0.8997 | **32.58/ 0.9501** |

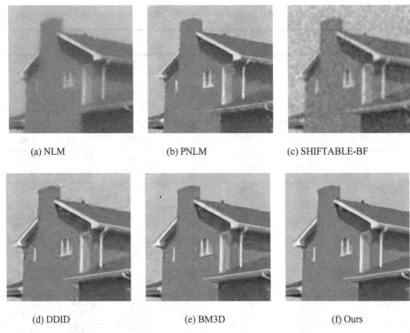

Fig. 5. Comparison of filtering results of House ( $\sigma = 50$ )

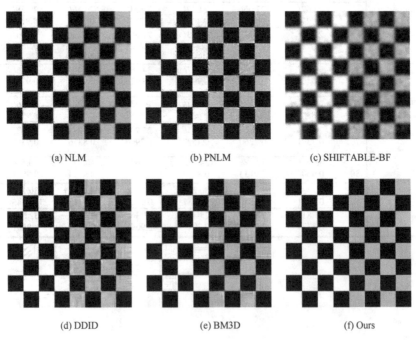

Fig. 6. Comparison of filtering results of Checkerboard ( $\sigma = 50$ )

# 5 Conclusion

We have proposed a rotation-invariant and noise-resistant similarity measure that will be used for our improved non-local means algorithm. Before calculating the distance between two patches, the patches are rotated to the same dominant orientation based on the guidance of the improved LBP operator. Moreover, we propose an automatic selection of the similar patches for the weighted average, it helps us get the most suitable similar patches and accelerate the proposed method. Thanks to the similarity measure scheme, our proposed method achieves competitive results with some state-of-the-art methods.

# References

1. Huang, H., Lee, T.: Data adaptive median filters for signal and image denoising using a generalized SURE criterion. IEEE Signal Processing Letters 13(9), 561–564 (2006)
2. Yuan, S., Tan, Y.: Impulse noise removal by a global noise detector and adaptive median filter. Signal Processing. 86(8), 2123–2128 (2006)
3. Buades, A., Coll, B., Morel, J.: A non-local algorithm for image denoising. In: IEEE Computer Society Conference on Computer Vision and Pattern Recognition, vol. 2, pp. 60-65. San Diego (2005)
4. Sender, L., Selesnick, I.: Bivariate shrinkage functions for wavelet-based denoising exploiting interscale dependency. IEEE Transactions on Signal Processing 20(11), 2744–2756 (2002)
5. Portilla, J., Strela, V., Wainwright, M.: Image denoising using scale mixtures of Gaussians in the wavelet domain. IEEE Transactions on Image Processing 12(11), 1338–1351 (2003)
6. Yin, M., Liu, W., Zhao, X.: Image denoising using trivariate prior model in nonsubsampled dual-tree complex contourlet transform domain and non-local means filter in spatial domain. Optik - International Journal for Light and Electron Optics 124(24), 6896–6904 (2013)
7. Michael, E.: Image denoising via sparse and redundant representations over learned dictionaries. IEEE Transactions on Image Processing 15(12), 3736–3745 (2006)
8. Chen, G., Xiong, C., Corso, J.: Dictionary transfer for image denoising via domain adaptation. In: Proceedings of IEEE International Conference on Image Processing, pp. 1189-1192 (2012)
9. Sun, D., Gao, Q., Lu, Y.: A novel image denoising algorithm using linear Bayesian MAP estimation based on sparse representation. Signal Processing 100, 132–145 (2014)
10. Tasdizen, T.: Principal neighborhood dictionaries for nonlocal means image denoising. IEEE Transactions on Image Processing 18(12), 2649–2660 (2009)
11. Grewenig, S., Zimmer, S., Weickert, J.: Rotationally invariant similarity measures for non-local image denoising. Journal of Visual Communication and Image Representation 22(2), 117–130 (2011)
12. Deledalle, C., Denis, L., Tupin, F.: Iterative weighted maximum likelihood denoising with probabilistic patch-based weights. IEEE Transactions on Image Processing 18(12), 2661–2672 (2009)
13. Dabov, K., Foi, A., Katkovnik, V.: Image denoising by sparse 3D transform-domain collaborative filtering. IEEE Transactions on Image Processing 16(8), 2080–2095 (2007)

14. Yue, W., Brian, T., Premkumar, N., Joseph, P.: Probabilistic Non-Local Means. IEEE Signal Processing Letters **20**(8), 763–766 (2013)
15. Deledalle, C., Duval, V., Salmon, J.: Non-Local Methods with Shape-Adaptive Patches (NLM-SAP). Journal of Mathematical Imaging and Vision **43**(2), 103–120 (2012)
16. Mahmoudi, M., Sapiro, G.: Fast image and video denoising via nonlocal means of similar neighborhoods. IEEE Signal Processing Letters **12**(12), 839–842 (2005)
17. Coupé, P., Yger, P., Prima, S.: An optimized blockwise nonlocal means denoising filter for 3-D magnetic images. IEEE Transactions on Medical Imaging **27**(4), 425–441 (2008)
18. Ojala, T., Pietikainen, M., Maenpaa, T.: Multiresolution gray-scale and rotation invariant texture classification with local binary patterns. IEEE Transactions on Pattern Analysis and Machine Intelligence **24**(7), 971–987 (2002)
19. Zhou, W., Bovik, A., Sheikh, H., Simoncelli, E.: Image quality assessment: from error visibility to structural similarity. IEEE Transactions on Image Processing. **13**(4), 600–612 (2004)
20. Alessandroa, F., Vladimir, K., Karen, E.: Pointwise shape adaptive DCT for high quality denoising and deblocking of grayscale and color images. IEEE Transactions on Image Processing. **16**(5), 1395–1411 (2007)
21. Knaus, C., Zwicker, M.: Dual-domain image denoising. In: IEEE International Conference on Image Processing, pp. 440-444 (2013)
22. Chaudhury, K.N.: Acceleration of the shiftable O(1) algorithm for bilateral filtering and non-local means. IEEE Transactions on Image Proc. **22**(4), 1291–1300 (2013)

# Mixture Models for Object Detection

Xiaoqin Kuang, Nong Sang[✉], Feifei Chen, Changxin Gao, and Runmin Wang

Science and Technology on Multi-spectral Information Processing Laboratory,
School of Automation, Huazhong University of Science and Technology, Wuhan, China
{kxqkuang,nsang,ffchen,cgao,runminwang}@hust.edu.cn

**Abstract.** In this paper, we propose an approach based on mixture of multiple components and mid-level part models for object detection in natural scenes. It is difficult to represent an object category with a monolithic model as the intra-variance in the category. To solve this, we use multi-component models and part models to describe the global variation and local deformation respectively. We obtain multi-components by clustering to form visual similar object group and training discriminant model for each one. The mid-level part models are learned automatically. We apply max-pooling to generate the feature vector using all part models and then train the SVM classifier based on these feature vectors. When detecting in image, we first achieve object candidates using multi-component models, and then the performance is refined by using part models and SVM classifier. Experiments on standard benchmarks demonstrate this coarse-to-fine detection system performs competitively.

**Keywords:** Object detection · Mixture model · Multiple components · Mid-level parts · Max-pooling

## 1 Introduction

Object detection in natural scenes has been an important topic in computer vision for decades. However, it is still a challenge as the object varies greatly within each category. The variation comes not only from the illuminations, viewpoint, deformation, structure, but also the intra-variation of the object subcategory. Thus local deformation and global variation should be considered seriously.

Local variation is represented by local features. There are many researches have been focus on these issues. Hough transform based method [1, 2, 3, 4, 5, 6] has been applied popularly in the field. They vote with elements as boundaries, contours or patches which are collected with low-level features by point or edge detecting, line matching. They are not distinctive to the given object class. The Implicit Shape Model [1] generates codebooks by clustering patches which is found around interest point. Plenty discovered patches contain less semantic information with little structure information.

Mid-level semantic concepts corresponding to attributes and parts to promote the object detection have become more and more popular in recent years. These mid-level semantic concepts are commonly obtained by manually annotation or clustering on low-level features. Paper [7] proposes a convenient method to label parts in which

© Springer-Verlag Berlin Heidelberg 2015
H. Zha et al. (Eds.): CCCV 2015, Part I, CCIS 546, pp. 317–324, 2015.
DOI: 10.1007/978-3-662-48558-3_32

parts are discovered with partial correspondence by annotating important matching points between instances of a category, which still need human participate in. Annotation work is time-consuming and hard to do when facing more new categories. Discovering mid-level semantic parts automatically is important and challenging.

Inspired by the works of discovering parts automatically [8, 9, 10], we obtain parts by learning discriminative detectors with training images. We follow the idea [8] to generate a small group patches for training part detectors, which is generalizing and consistent in semantic as well. Selecting a subset of discriminative part detectors in the training procedure is an important issue.

The trained part detectors represent local identity and robust to some structure deformation, while the global appearance also affords key information to the object detection. In order to solve the intra-variation in object, multiple components are proposed. Exemplar-SVM [12] trained separate HOG [11] detector for each positive exemplar. But training with single exemplar would not be expected generalize enough. The method of multi-component models in [13] picks 'seed' object and aligned the rest object to the seed as the component. It needs keypoint and mask annotation when aligning. Felzenszwalb and Girshick etc. [14] propose a detection system of mixtures of multi-scale deformable part models allowing for small deformation and multiple postures. But the numbers of components and parts are predefined and not referring to the data.

We follow their work of mixture models, but our multi-components and part models are discovered during training. In detection, the candidate windows are generated with multi-component models, and then part detectors are used to refine the performance. Each candidate is evaluated by the part models with feature vector using max-pooling technique. The overview of the proposed approach is shown in Fig. 1. Our approach shows competitive performance on the open dataset.

The rest of the paper is structured as follows. In Sec. 2 and Sec. 3 we describe the details of generating multi-components and discovering object parts. The experiments and analysis are presented in Sec. 4. Finally Sec. 5 concludes this paper.

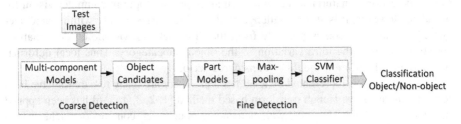

**Fig. 1.** Overview of our detection system with mixture models.

## 2    Multiple Components Generation

The challenge for object detection is the intra-variations induced by posture, viewpoint, subcategories, etc. The monolithic model is not enough to represent the object category of intra-variations. A natural strategy is to use multiple models to detect the category. One way is to use models predefined by hand such as the different view or posture, but this is not convenient to choose artificially. The other way is to find models automatically.

We cluster using whitened HOG features. Whitened HOG features are considered to be better for clustering and classification [15], since the whitening removes the correlations and leaves the discriminative gradients. Firstly, we compute the covariance matrix $\Sigma$ and mean feature $\mu_0$ on HOG features with all background samples. Then we cluster the positive objects using whitened features which are transformed from the HOG feature $x$ to $\hat{x} = \Sigma^{-1/2}(x - \mu_0)$.

We set a fixed number $k$ in advance to the object cluster number according to the data complexity. If the data samples within the category have great variation in posture, structure, illumination, etc., we set $k$ a large number. Conversely, we set $k$ a small number when dada samples are simple and have not much variation. Components work as a guide to the coarse detection, so clustering is enough to generate generalizing and representative model which separate the variation among the category to different groups and forms similar visual groups. After clustering, we train LDA model to each of them since it has the similar performance with SVM but accelerates the computation [15]. The LDA model is a linear classifier over $x$ with weights given by $\omega = \Sigma^{-1}(x_{mean} - \mu_0)$ , and $x_{mean}$ is the mean feature of the cluster. The covariance matrix $\Sigma$ and mean feature $\mu_0$ are both computed in advance with all background.

Finally, we measure the redundancy between a pair of components by their cosine similarity $\langle \omega_i / \|\omega_i\| , \omega_j / \|\omega_j\| \rangle$, redundant components are removed.

## 3    Discovering Mid-level Part Models

Candidate windows are generated to describe the global appearance of object, and then are sent to the part detectors for further measurement. In this section, we describe the procedure of discovering the mid-level parts. The flow is illustrated in Fig. 2.

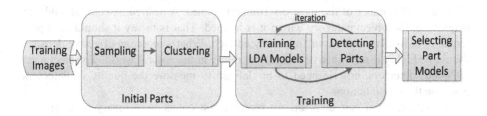

**Fig. 2.** Procedure of discovering of mid-level part models

### 3.1    Clustering

Given a set of training data, our goal is to learn a compact collection of part detectors for the category. Every training image is equally containing distinctive parts, so we sample densely to get all possible sub-windows and collect hundreds of thousands of parts. Let $\mathcal{D}$ be object images, $N$ be background images. Patches are represented by augmented HOG descriptors [14] with the same dimensions.

Clustering is applied to generate 'seed' for training the initial detectors. We run $k$-means to cluster patches. As mentioned in [8], the number of clusters is set quite high since they do not trust $k$-means to generalize well, so we set $k$ quite high ($k = S/5$, where $S$ is the number of patches sampled for clustering) similar to them to ensure the consistency of each cluster. Clusters with less than 4 patches are regarded as poor seeds and removed. We cluster the training samples with $k$-means using whitened HOG features same as the components generation.

## 3.2   Training

Naturally, clusters are probably rough and impure due to this unsupervised clustering. So the training scheme is followed which aims at collecting patches purer and more consistent.

We apply LDA to train detector for each cluster. In order to improve the consistency, we use the cross-validation to refine detectors. We divide $\mathcal{D}$ into two equal, non-overlapping subsets ($\mathcal{D}_1$, $\mathcal{D}_2$) as train-set and validation-set. Given the initial clusters obtained from train-set $\mathcal{D}_1$, we train the discriminative classifier for each of them, using patches in $N$ as negative samples.

We run the trained detectors in validation-set $\mathcal{D}_2$ to discover the corresponding patches, and then new clusters are formed by the top $m$ scores of detections. We set $m = 6$ to keep the purity of each cluster.

After this training and detection, we switch the role of $\mathcal{D}_1$ and $\mathcal{D}_2$ and repeat the process until convergence. During the iteration, the detections with small number of patches are eliminated since they occur rarely to characterize the appearance of object.

## 3.3   Part Selecting

The training procedure has produced numerous candidate detectors; the next task is to select a small number of the most discriminative ones. A desired detector should fire majority of the object category where it is learned. That is to say it should be representative to its class and occur frequently enough. What's more, an effective detector should be highly discriminative that it fires rarely in the natural world. To select a set of 'good' detectors, criteria need to be defined to measure the quality of detectors based on these two notions.

Concretely, for a part detector, we represent an object by a binary tuple $(s_i; y_i)$ where $s_i$ is the highest detection score of patches within object $i$ ($s_i = \max_j \omega^T x(i)_j$, in which $x(\cdot)_j$ indicate one patch in the object region); $y_i$ is the class label of this object. We set a high threshold $\tau$ and consider the patch with score $s_i > \tau$ as a firing; thus the representativeness in positive samples is computed as

$$r = \frac{\sum_i 1(s_i > \tau) \cdot s_i}{|\mathcal{D}|}$$

where $1(\cdot)$ is the indicator function which equals 1 only if the corresponding logical expression is established and 0 otherwise, and $|\mathcal{D}|$ is the number of positive samples.

Following the conception in [8] we evaluate the discriminativeness of detectors as the ratio of number of firings on $\mathcal{D}$ to number of firings on $\mathcal{D} \cup \mathcal{N}$. We write it as

$$d = \frac{\sum_i 1(s_i > \tau) \cdot 1(y_i = y_0)}{\sum_i 1(s_i > \tau) \cdot 1(y_i = y_0) + \sum_i 1(s_i > \tau) \cdot 1(y_i = y_1)}$$

where $y_0$ is the label of the object category from which the detector is learnt, and $y_1$ is the label of non-object.

All detectors are ranked using a linear combination of the above two scores. Then the detectors with top scoring are retained. Fig. 3 gives some examples of selected part with high scores. Patches are densely sampled so redundancy exists among parts. Thus the final step is to remove redundant part detectors. We measure the redundancy between a pair of detectors by their cosine similarity, detectors that have similarity larger than 0.5 from the last ranking to first are removed.

**Fig. 3.** Some selected part detectors with top scores.

## 4    Experiments

**Object Detection:** Component models are applied to capture the entire object, so they are defined by coarse template which has lower resolution than part models. We expand the components by flipping the models to discover the mirrored object in images. Part detectors are used to generate the image-level descriptor for the detection candidates. The image vector is formed by summarizing the part scores of selected detectors using max-pooling. We use a 2-level spatial pyramid ($1 \times 1, 2 \times 2$ grids) to pooling; we stack the maximum detection score of each detector of each cell in the pyramid. Finally encodings of all the detectors are concatenated to form the feature vector of image representation. We train a linear-SVM using these obtained feature vector of object and background. Then each candidate is evaluated by the classifier. We follow up traditional object detection methods to search in images in a sliding-window manner with multiple components. The obtained candidates will be measured by part models. We generate feature vector for each candidate by max-pooling and then classify it as object or non-object by the learned SVM classifier.

**Dataset:** The UIUC Cars single-scale test set contains 170 images with 200 side views of cars of approximately the same scale. The multi-scale test set contains 108 images with 139 cars at multiple scales. The images are low contrast with some cars partially occluded and multiple objects would occur. The training set contains 550 training cars of size 100×40 and 500 negative training examples of the same size.

**Implementation Details:** As the training objects have the same scale of $100 \times 40$, we describe object with $13 \times 5$ cells by augmented HOG features of dimensionality $d = 31$. The object descriptor has 2015 dimensions after concatenating all cells. The part models have twice resolution of the component models, each HOG cell is $4 \times 4$ pixels. We obtain patches by sampling densely with $7 \times 7$ cells and the patch descriptor has 1519 dimensions. The sliding-window search for multiple scale test set detection is in multiple scale. We set number of levels in an octave $\lambda = 10$ as the scale in the feature pyramid. Fine sampling of scale space is important for high detection performance.

**Results:** We adhered to the experimental evaluation criteria based on bounding-box overlap as previous works. The detections are considered be true as its overlap area with the ground truth less than 0.5.

Using the multi-component models, we obtained recall at 99.5% and precision at 72.6% with for the UIUC-Single; and recall at 99.3% and precision at 50.2% for the UIUC- Multi. The recall is high but there existing a lot of false positive in the results.

We use the 154 learned part detectors to remove the false object and refine the performance. Finally, with the mixture models, we get the recall at 99.5%, precision at 99.5% and recall-precision EER at 99.5% for the single-scale test set; recall at 99.3%, precision at 96.5% and recall-precision EER at 99.3% for the multi-scale test set. Table 1 presents the results at recall-precision equal error rate compared to other methods.

**Table 1.** Performance of different methods on the two UIUC datasets at recall-precision equal error rate (EER)

| Methods | ISM. No MDL | ISM +MDL | Hough Forest | HF Weaker supervision | Our approach |
|---|---|---|---|---|---|
| UIUC-Single | 91% | 97.5% | 98.5% | 94.4% | 99.5% |
| UIUC-Multi | - | 95% | 98.6% | - | 99.3% |

In order to analyze the impact of the part models numbers, we select a set of different number of detectors with percentage from 10% to 100% (the detector number varies from 15 to 154). The performance changes are illustrated in Fig. 4 and Fig. 5. Despite some fluctuates existing, we can see that the mixture system still performs quite well compared to entire object models only.

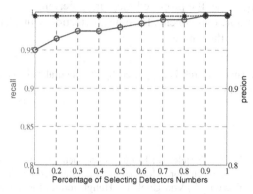

**Fig. 4.** Performance changes as the detectors numbers changes of UIUC-Single set

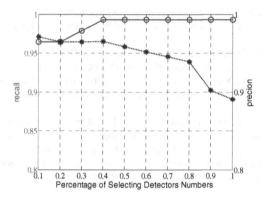

**Fig. 5.** Performance changes as the detectors numbers changes of UIUC-Multi set

For the UIUC-Single set, the recall gradually promotes when the detectors amount increasing, while the precision stays stable. For the UIUC-Multi set, the recall gradually promotes and tends stable at last, but the precision fluctuates and descends gradually when the amount increasing.

For a certain small amount of part detectors, the number increasing will promote the performance. However, for a certain great amount of part detectors, the detection performance will have some decrease as the number increasing. This is because the quality of detectors are sorted by measurement in descending order and the bottom ones have poor representativeness and descriminativeness which usually refer to unimportant part or the background. This further shows that part models can represent the object appearance well as if selecting a group of fine models.

## 5    Conclusion

We have presented a method of object detection. This mixture models of multi-components and part models can represent the global appearance of object, and also adapt to the intra-variation of the category. The key problem of generating distinctive semantic parts is solved by the proposed measure criterion. We showed the ability of part models and multiple components for object detection. Our method achieves competitive performance on the dataset.

**Acknowledgements.** This research is supported by the Natural Science Foundation of China No.61401170 and No.61433007).

# References

1. Leibe, B., Leonardis, A., Schiele, B.: Robust object detection with interleaved categorization and segmentation. International Journal of Computer Vision **77**(1–3), 259–289 (2008)
2. Gall, J., Yao, A., Razavi, N., Van Gool, L.: Hough forests for object detection, tracking, and action recognitions. IEEE Transactions on Pattern Analysis and Machine Intelligence. **33**(11), 2188–2202 (2011)
3. Maji, S., Malik, J.: Object detection using a max-margin hough transform. In: 2009 IEEE Conference on Computer Vision and Pattern Recognition (CVPR), pp. 1038–1045. Miami, FL (2009)
4. Kontschieder, P., Riemenschneider, H., Donoser, M., Bischof, H.: Discriminative learning of contour fragments for object detection. In: BMVC, pp. 1–12 (2011)
5. Razavi, N., Gall, J., Van Gool, L.: Scalable multi-class object detection. In: 2011 IEEE Conference on Computer Vision and Pattern Recognition (CVPR), pp. 1505–1512. IEEE (2011)
6. Razavi, N., Gall, J., Kohli, P., van Gool, L.: Latent hough transform for object detection. In: Fitzgibbon, A., Lazebnik, S., Perona, P., Sato, Y., Schmid, C. (eds.) ECCV 2012, Part III. LNCS, vol. 7574, pp. 312–325. Springer, Heidelberg (2012)
7. Maji, S., Shakhnarovich, G.: Part discovery from partial correspondence. In: 2013 IEEE Conference on Computer Vision and Pattern Recognition (CVPR), pp. 931–938. Portland, OR (2013)
8. Singh, S., Gupta, A., Efros, A.A.: Unsupervised discovery of mid-level discriminative patches. In: European Conference on Computer Vision, pp. 73–86 (2012)
9. Juneja, M., Vedaldi, A., Jawahar, C.V., Zisserman, A.: Blocks that shout: distinctive parts for scene classification. In: 2013 IEEE Conference on Computer Vision and Pattern Recognition (CVPR), pp. 923–930. Portland, OR (2013)
10. Endres, I., Shih, K.J., Jiaa, J., Hoiem, D.: Learning collections of part models for object recognition. In: 2013 IEEE Conference on Computer Vision and Pattern Recognition (CVPR), pp. 939–946. Portland, OR (2013)
11. Dalal, N., Triggs, B.: Histograms of oriented gradients for human detection, In: 2005 IEEE Computer Society Conference on Computer Vision and Pattern Recognition, CVPR 2005, vol. 1, pp. 886–893. San Diego, CA, USA (2005)
12. Malisiewicz, T., Gupta, A., Efros, A.A.: Ensemble of exemplar-SVMs for object detection and beyond, In: 2011 IEEE International Conference on Computer Vision (ICCV), pp. 89–96. Barcelona (2011)
13. Gu, C., Arbeláez, P., Lin, Y., Yu, K., Malik, J.: Multi-component models for object detection. In: Fitzgibbon, A., Lazebnik, S., Perona, P., Sato, Y., Schmid, C. (eds.) ECCV 2012, Part IV. LNCS, vol. 7575, pp. 445–458. Springer, Heidelberg (2012)
14. Felzenszwalb, P.F., Girshick, R.B., McAllester, D., Ramanan, D.: Object Detection with Discriminatively Trained Part-Based Models. IEEE Transactions on Pattern Analysis and Machine Intelligence **29**(9), 1627–1645 (2010)
15. Hariharan, B., Malik, J., Ramanan, D.: Discriminative decorrelation for clustering and classification. In: European Conference on Computer Vision, pp. 459–472 (2012)

# An Image Forensic Technique Based on 2D Lighting Estimation Using Spherical Harmonic Frames

Wenyong Zhao$^{(\boxtimes)}$ and Hong Liu

Engineering Lab on Intelligent Perception for Internet of Things (ELIP),
Shenzhen Graduate School, Peking University, Beijing, China
`zhaowenyong@pkusz.edu.cn`, `hongliu@pku.edu.cn`

**Abstract.** In this paper, a novel approach for exposing digital image tampering based on the theory of spherical harmonic frames is presented. We describe a robust technique for exposing digital forgeries that we utilize the information along a 2D occluding contour and estimate the lighting feature using spherical harmonic frames. Spherical harmonic frames are generated by the rotation along the symmetry axes of a symmetry group. The lighting-based digital forensic technique using spherical harmonic frames inherits the robust property of frames and improve the statistical results compared with spherical harmonic bases. Experimental results performed using spherical harmonic frames prove the robust measurements and discriminability of the complex lighting environments from synthetic data and real data. The application of identifying the tampered images reveals the improvement of our method.

**Keywords:** Spherical harmonic frames · Digital forensic technique · Lighting

## 1 Introduction

A major effort of the research community has been devoted to the digital forensic technique of exposing image tampering[1–5]. As the recent advances in computational photography, computer vision, and computer graphic, the development of friendly and easy-to-use manipulation tools has made the community into a crisis of confidence, which is caused by pervasive use of digital fakes in legal certification, the media, advertising, entertainment industry, national security, and more. In this new environment, the demand for efficient forensic tools that can accurately and trustfully expose the digital fakes is emerging.

This work is supported by Postdoctoral Science Foundation of China No. 2013M540822, National Natural Science Foundation of China(NSFC, No. 61340046, 60875050, 60675025), National High Technology Research and Development Program of China(863 Program, No. 2006AA04Z247), Scientific and Technical Innovation Commission of Shenzhen Municipality (No. JCYJ20120614152234873, CXC201104210010A, JCYJ20130331144631730, JCYJ20130331144716089).

© Springer-Verlag Berlin Heidelberg 2015
H. Zha et al. (Eds.): CCCV 2015, Part I, CCIS 546, pp. 325–334, 2015.
DOI: 10.1007/978-3-662-48558-3_33

In the area of image forensic, researchers have successfully developed a variety of image authentication tools according to different situations. When utilizing multiple images to generate a tampered image, since the image targets are captured under different lighting conditions, it is difficult to keep lighting consistency between different targets. Using lighting inconsistency between the different targets of one image to identify image authenticity is one technology of image forensics. In previous work, Johnson and Farid [6] use lighting information extracted from 2D occluding contour to identify the authenticity of the image. In order to extract 3D lighting information in a single image, and they take advantage of the spot position of the human eye to estimate the direction of light [7]. Johnson, Farid [8], Stork [9] and Kee [10], utilize spherical harmonic lighting model to estimate complex lighting environment. However, due to the degradation effects of noise contamination and data incompletion on obtained 2D information, the lighting-based forensic tool using spherical harmonics model can not distinguish illumination characteristics robustly.

Actually, the lighting-based forensic tool using spherical harmonic basis to identify tampered images will be trapped in the imprecise 2D-information extraction from a single image. Lighting measurements and discrimination using basis functions may be affected by many factors in real scenes, such as the difference of tested objects, the limitation of the available data and the error of recovered 2D information. In this paper, to conquer these noise contamination and data incompletion of 2D information, we present a robust diffuse lighting model using spherical harmonic frames in 2D space. In the novel 2D lighting model, we improve the detective ability of the lighting-based forensic tool compared with spherical harmonic basis. To the best of our knowledge, our method is the first that proposes a diffuse lighting model using spherical harmonic frames to be applied in 2D space and presents a robust forensic tool which can resist the noise contamination and data incompletion caused by the capture of 2D information.

The rest of this paper is organized as follows. We briefly introduce related works on the irradiance expressions for a convex Lambertian object in real 3D complex lighting environments in Sect.2. In Sect.3, we analyze lighting estimation using the 2D achievable data. In Sect.4, experiments which are performed using synthetic and real data reveal the comparisons between bases and frames lighting models. The forensic applications are also presented using different lighting models. In the end, the conclusion is given.

## 2   Lighting Model Using Bases and Frames

The irradiance for a convex Lambertian object can be expressed in terms of spherical harmonic bases and spherical harmonic frames. Next, we will describe the lighting model in terms of these two expansions.

In terms of spherical harmonic bases $Y_{l,k}$ with order $l$ and degree $k$, the irradiance of a convex diffuse object can be described as

$$E(\boldsymbol{n}) = \sum_{l=0}^{2} \sum_{-l \leq k \leq l} \left(\frac{4\pi}{2l+1}\right)^{1/2} A_l L_{l,k} Y_{l,k} \tag{1}$$

The corresponding image intensity is

$$I(\boldsymbol{n}) = \sum_{l=0}^{2} \sum_{-l \le k \le l} \rho \left( \frac{4\pi}{2l+1} \right)^{1/2} A_l L_{l,k} Y_{l,k} \tag{2}$$

where $\boldsymbol{n}$ is the normal vector of 3D object, $\rho$ is the surface albedo, $A_l$ is the coefficient of transfer function in order $l$, the product $\rho \left( \frac{4\pi}{2l+1} \right)^{1/2} A_l$ is always treated as a constant to compute the nine lighting coefficients $L_{l,k}$ in the least square method.

In the work [11], the authors derive a similar formation of lighting model in terms of spherical harmonic frames. The irradiance in terms of spherical harmonic frames is expressed as

$$E(\boldsymbol{n}) = \sum_{l=0}^{2} \sum_{t=0}^{n(l)-1} \left( \frac{4\pi}{2l+1} \right)^{1/2} A_l L_{l,t} Y_{l,t}^d \tag{3}$$

The corresponding image intensity is

$$I(\boldsymbol{n}) = \sum_{l=0}^{2} \sum_{t=0}^{n(l)-1} \rho \left( \frac{4\pi}{2l+1} \right)^{1/2} A_l L_{l,t} Y_{l,t}^d \tag{4}$$

where $n(l)$ is the number of frame elements in subspace $H_l$. The number of elements of frames is determined by the redundancy of frames which is integer $n$ multiples of spherical harmonics. Compared with the lighting expression in spherical harmonics which are only described by 9 coefficients, the redundant information provided by spherical harmonic frames can describe not only along the original perpendicular axes, but also along the the symmetry axes of a subgroup of $SO(3)$. An element of spherical harmonic frame is generated by the rotation of spherical harmonics,

$$Y_{l,m}^s = \sum_{m=d(s),|k| \le l} M_{m,k}^s Y_{l,k}(\theta, \phi) \tag{5}$$

where $M$ (denoted as a Wigner-D matrix $D^l$) indexed by $s$ is the $s$-th rotation representation for subspaces $H_l$. It represents a $(2l+1) \times (2l+1)$ rotation matrix between a symmetry axis of a symmetry group and original $z$-axis.

## 3   Lighting Estimation

At present, it is still a tough problem to recover 3D geometry from a single image. For an object in a single image, there is no known 3D geometry information to be provided for the solution of equations (2) and (4). However, the occlusion contour of an object remains the 2D geometric information, which simplifies the estimation of lighting field from a single image. Under the orthogonal projection, the surface normal along the occluding contour of an object is $\boldsymbol{n}_{z=0} = (x, y, 0)$.

The character of its lighting field can be described by five coefficients of spherical harmonics, since there is no geometric information about $z$-component of the surface normal. In the lighting model described by spherical harmonic frames, the redundant lighting coefficients which are more than five basis coefficients provide a robust character from the 2D geometric information. The property of frame offers a robustness against noise and incomplete data [11].

In terms of spherical harmonic frames, the image intensity of one geometric point along 2D contour can be expressed as

$$I(\boldsymbol{n}_{z=0}) = \sum_{l=0}^{2} \sum_{t=0}^{n(l)-1} \rho \left(\frac{4\pi}{2l+1}\right)^{1/2} A_l L_{l,t} Y_{l,t}^d(\boldsymbol{n}_{z=0}) \tag{6}$$

Correspondingly, in terms of spherical harmonic bases, the image intensity is

$$I(\boldsymbol{n}_{z=0}) = \sum_{l=0}^{2} \sum_{-l \le k \le l} \rho \left(\frac{4\pi}{2l+1}\right)^{1/2} A_l L_{l,k} Y_{l,k}(\boldsymbol{n}_{z=0}) \tag{7}$$

In Eq. (6) and (7), the lighting coefficients of a diffuse object with a constant albedo $\rho$ can be solved using the least square procedure.

## 3.1    2D Information Extraction

In order to analyze the lighting characteristics of a diffuse object in one image, we should get information from 2D occluding contour of the object, including the normal vector and the intensity. The related process of information extraction along the 2D contour is illustrated in Fig. 1.

For the image information extracting along the 2D contour, the article [12] has pointed out that simply using the intensity close to the border is often sufficient. Then, the 2D contour intensity can be extracted from the pixels in the opposite direction to the surface normal. The $z$-component of normal vector along the 2D contour is zero due to the orthogonal projection. Then, the $x$, $y$ components of normal vector can be obtained by fitting curve of the contour. Thus, the intensity of the 2D contour can be determined by the following formula,

$$I(\boldsymbol{n}_{z=0}) = I(\boldsymbol{p} + \alpha \boldsymbol{n}_{z=0}) \tag{8}$$

where $\alpha > 0$ is an offset value along the normal $\boldsymbol{n}_{z=0}$ at the boundary point $\boldsymbol{p}$.

## 4    Experiments

The proposed approach using spherical harmonic frames has been evaluated for the robust performance using two sets of images. One is Lambertian spheres rendered by the ten light probes [11] and the other set is the real natural images which are photogrphed by ourselves or collected from Flickr website, etc. Results of both show advantages in the measurement of image consistency

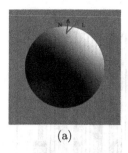
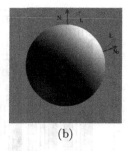

(a)                                    (b)

**Fig. 1.** (a) 3D information extraction from a sphere (b) 2D information extraction along the boundary of a sphere. $L$ denotes the light direction, $N$ denotes the surface normal; $N_1$ and $N_2$ are the normal vectors along the occluding contour.

and discrimination using spherical harmonic frames compared with orthogonal spherical harmonic bases. We also present the identification results of two tampered images. The lighting coefficients are only computed in the green channel of all test images.

## 4.1 Synthetic Data

In a single image, we need to use the 2D information along the occluding contours to estimate lighting coefficients. The available information of geometry and intensity is always restricted in a limited range. Many factors may affect the final results of estimation, such as the shape differences of objects, the limitation of the available data, the error of the derived 2D information and the effects of highlights and cast shadows. Considering the above factors, we simulate the disturbed data of surface normals and intensities.

First, we divide the tests into two groups: a unit circle and a unit semicircle. The data of circle and semicircle are tested to show the sensitivity of the estimation to surface normal extent. Second, considering the differences of the available data from different objects, we randomly sample in the semicircle group. That is to say, the starting point of the semicircle is randomly selected on the $z = 0$ circle of unit sphere. Third, to simulate the error of the recovered signal and the effects of highlights and cast shadows, we add Gaussian noise to the surface normal or intensity of the 2D information.

We construct two classes of spherical harmonic frames to estimate lighting from 2D occluding boundaries, total spherical harmonic frames and partial spherical harmonic frames [11]. For comparison, we also present the results of orthogonal spherical harmonic basis functions. Six frames are constructed: **T**, **ICO** (two total frames are generated by tetrahedron and icosahedron, respectively), **Tii**, **ICOii** (two partial frames are generated by tetrahedron and icosahedron, respectively), and two other frames through cyclic group **C3**, **C5**.

The lighting environments are characterized by the coefficients of spherical harmonic basis functions, **C3** frame, **C5** frame, **T** frame, **ICO** frame, **Tii** frame and **ICOii** frame, correspondingly. These coefficients are computed using the

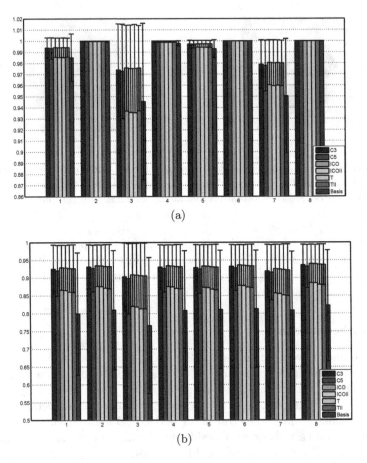

**Fig. 2.** (a) diagram of consistency of different samples in the identical lighting environments; (b) diagram of inconsistency of different samples in the different lighting environments. The grouped bars (1, 3, 5, 7) and (2, 4, 6, 8) exhibit statistical results of lighting correlation of unit semicircle data and unit circle data, respectively. The grouped bars (1, 2), (3, 4), (5, 6) and (7, 8) display the results of contaminated noise, 15% normal plus 15% intensity, 15% normal plus 30% intensity, 15% normal, and 30% normal, respectively. The color bars represent the means of statistical measurement computed by frames and basis; the error bars represent the standard deviations correspondingly. Each color bar and error bar reveal the statistical result from all 100 groups noise data of one class.

least square procedure. For analyzing the consistency of the identical lighting environment, statistical results of the lighting consistency from synthetic data are considered. A correlation indicates the consistent degree of different samples in an identical lighting environment. Fig. 2(a) illustrates the correlation of different samples in the identical lighting environment. Fig. 2(b) illustrates the inconsistent measurement of different lighting. Lower mean and greater standard

**Fig. 3.** Twenty-seven natural images with a light dark cover to show the analyzed boundaries.

derivation indicate that the consistency measurement is less robust. The robustness of the lighting estimation characterized by different approaches is evaluated by the corresponding mean value and standard derivation. When only small noise of the surface normal is added, the consistency measurements of frames and basis have approximate results. When both normal and intensity noise are added, the correlation of identical lighting measured by frames exhibits more robustness than basis, particularly in the semicircle group. Moreover, the lighting consistency in the semicircle group reduces more rapidly. As the noise-resistant property, the variation of frame coefficients is less than the variation of basis coefficients. Thus, the consistency of lighting characterized by frame coefficients is superior to the result characterized by basis coefficients. Moreover, as shown in (b), the inconsistency of lighting characterized by frame coefficients is suppressed in a limited extent.

### 4.2 Real Images

To test the noise-resistant property of our lighting model, we select 27 natural images of multiple objects in natural lighting environments from Flickr, USC-SIPI database and the others photographed by ourselves. To ensure the forensic application in the real complex situation, various objects in images including people, plants, animals and sculptures are considered. The 2D occluding contours in one image are captured using the painting tool of Adobe Photoshop by painting along the boundaries of objects, which are shown in Fig. 3.

**Table 1.** The statistical results estimated using spherical harmonic frames

|      | T | Tii | ICO | ICOii | Basis |
|------|--------|--------|--------|--------|--------|
| mean | 0.9105 | 0.9112 | 0.9064 | 0.9041 | 0.9048 |
| var  | 0.0628 | 0.0621 | 0.0677 | 0.0717 | 0.0664 |

There are 12 pairs of objects from the same scene and 351 pairs of objects from different scenes in all tested images. The lighting coefficients of objects are computed using spherical harmonic basis lighting model and spherical harmonic frames lighting model, respectively. For the pairs in the identical scene, the mean and derivation of lighting correlation computed using spherical harmonic basis lighting model are 0.9048 and 0.0664, respectively. For comparison, the mean and derivation of lighting correlation computed in spherical harmonic frames lighting model (**T, ICO, Tii, ICOii**) are listed in Table 1. The listed results of real images confirm to the ones of synthetic data, the correlation evaluated by spherical harmonic frames can keep better similarity measurements as the redundancy of frames. As the product moment correlation which represents the lighting similarity is sensitive to extreme magnitudes [13], the absolute values of frame coefficients will be decreased with the increase of the redundancy. The higher redundancy of frames will reduce the evaluation of the similarity. The redundancy of frames will be considered properly to keep the advantage of consistency measurements.

### 4.3 Tampered Images

Two tampered images are generated using the Adobe Photoshop, shown in Fig. 4. The operated images are from Fig. 3. The rendered sphere of a tested object which reflects the lighting information of one environment is shown correspondingly [14]. The consistency and inconsistency of lighting coefficients estimated from the objects in the tampered images are listed in Table 2 and Table 3. The similarity measurements are given using spherical harmonic basis, spherical harmonic frames **T, Tii, ICO** and **ICOii**. The consistency of objects in the identical environment (2VS3) reveals that the lighting similarity measurements using spherical harmonic frames have a better evaluation than spherical harmonic basis. In addition, the inconsistency of objects in the different environments (1VS2, 1VS3) measured by the correlation reveals that the dissimilarity evaluated by spherical harmonic frames can be suppressed effectively, compared with spherical harmonic basis. Thus, for the forensic application in the real scenes, the lighting model based on spherical harmonic frames can possess a robust measurement and discrimination compared with spherical harmonic basis, which can provide an assistance in identifying the tampered images.

| (a) Tampered image 1 | (b) Tampered image 2 |
|---|---|

**Fig. 4.** Two tampered images. The rendered spheres which reflect the lighting environments are shown correspondingly.

**Table 2.** The consistency of tampered image 1

|      | Basis  | T      | Tii    | ICO    | ICOii  |
|------|--------|--------|--------|--------|--------|
| 1VS2 | 0.3627 | 0.3330 | 0.2790 | 0.3068 | 0.3100 |
| 1VS3 | -.1544 | -.0794 | -.1296 | -.1224 | -.1145 |
| 2VS3 | 0.8458 | 0.8941 | 0.8970 | 0.8881 | 0.8891 |

**Table 3.** The consistency of tampered image 2

|      | Basis  | T      | Tii    | ICO    | ICOii  |
|------|--------|--------|--------|--------|--------|
| 1VS2 | 0.4660 | 0.4716 | 0.5160 | 0.4869 | 0.4332 |
| 1VS3 | 0.3514 | 0.3751 | 0.4281 | 0.3922 | 0.3341 |
| 2VS3 | 0.9675 | 0.9789 | 0.9815 | 0.9770 | 0.9784 |

## 5    Conclusion

In this paper, we propose a novel robust lighting model using spherical harmonic frames to characterize the lighting of diffuse objects in different complex environments. The available 2D information is trapped in the limit and noise of occluding contours. The redundancy of frames provides a robust property to estimate the 2D lighting information. The related statistical results in experiments demonstrate the robust measurements and discrimination using the lighting model in terms of spherical harmonic frames in 2D space. Further more, we improve the forensic technology through spherical harmonic frames lighting model compared with spherical harmonic bases lighting model, which is shown in the tampered cases.

**Acknowledgments.** The authors wish to thank the anonymous reviewers for their insightful comments.

# References

1. Farid, H.: A Survey of Image Forgery Detection. IEEE Signal Processing Magazine **26**, 16–25 (2009)
2. Fridrich, J.: Digital Image Forensics. IEEE Signal Processing Magazine **26**, 26–37 (2009)
3. Swaminathan, A., Wu, M., Liu, K.J.R.: Component Forensics: Theory, methodologies, and applications. IEEE Signal Processing Magazine **26**, 38–48 (2009)
4. Ng, T.T., Chang, S.F.: Identifying and Prefiltering Images: Distinguishing between natural photography and photorealistic computer graphics. IEEE Signal Processing Magazine **26**, 49–58 (2009)
5. Rocha, A., Scheirer, W., Boult, T.E., Goldenstein, S.: Vision of the unseen: Current trends and challenges in digital image and video forensics. ACM Computing Surveys (CSUR) **43**, 26:1–26:42 (2011)
6. Johnson, M.K., Farid, H.: Exposing digital forgeries by detecting inconsistencies in lighting. In: Proceedings of the 7th Workshop on Multimedia and Security, pp. 1–10. ACM (2005)
7. Johnson, M.K., Farid, H.: Exposing digital forgeries through specular highlights on the eye. In: 9th International Workshop on Information Hiding, pp. 311–325 (2007)
8. Johnson, M.K., Farid, H.: Exposing Digital Forgeries in Complex Lighting Environments. IEEE Transactions on Information Forensics and Security **2**, 450–461 (2007)
9. Stork, D.G., Johnson, M.K.: Lighting analysis of diffusely illuminated tableaus in realist paintings: an application to detecting 'compositing' in the portraits of Garth Herrick. In: Electronic Imaging: Media Forensics and Security, pp. 72540L1-8. SPIE (2009)
10. Farid, H., Kee, E.: Exposing digital forgeries from 3-D lighting environments. In: IEEE International Workshop on Information Forensics and Security (2010)
11. Zhao, W.Y., Chen, S.L., Zheng, Y., Chen, S.L., Peng, S.L.: Lighting Estimation of a Convex Lambertian Object Using Redundant Spherical Harmonic Frames. Journal of Computer Science and Technology **28**, 454–467 (2013)
12. Nillius, P., Eklundh, J.O.: Automatic estimation of the projected light source direction. In: Proceedings of the 2001 IEEE Computer Society Conference on Computer Vision and Pattern Recognition, pp. 1076–1083. IEEE (2001)
13. Brunelli, R., Messelodi, S.: Robust estimation of correlation with applications to computer vision. Pattern Recognition, 833–841 (1995)
14. Ramamoorthi, R., Hanrahan, P.: An efficient representation for irradiance environment maps. In: Proceeding SIGGRAPH 2001 Proceedings of the 28th Annual Conference on Computer Graphics and Interactive Techniques, pp. 497–500. ACM (2001)

# Class Relatedness Oriented Discriminative Dictionary Learning

Pengju Liu, Hongzhi Zhang, Kai Zhang, Changchun Luo,
and Wangmeng Zuo[✉]

Center of Computational Perception and Cognition,
School of Computer Science and Technology,
Harbin Institute of Technology, Harbin 150001, China
cswmzuo@gmail.com

**Abstract.** Discriminative dictionary learning (DDL) has recently attracted intensive attention due to its representative and discriminative power in various classification tasks. However, most of the existing DDL methods fall into two extreme cases, i.e., they either learn a global dictionary for all classes or train a class-specific dictionary, leading to less discriminative dictionary as the former do not consider correspondence between dictionary atoms and class labels while the latter ignore dictionary relatedness between different classes. To tackle this issue, in this paper we propose a well-principled DDL method which adaptively builds the relationship between dictionary and class labels. To be specific, we separatively impose a joint sparsity constraint on the coding vectors of each class to learn the class correspondence and relatedness for the dictionary. Experimental results on object classification and face recognition demonstrate that our proposed method can outperform many state-of-the-art DDL methods with more powerful and discriminative dictionary.

**Keywords:** Dictionary learning · Joint sparsity · $\ell_{1,\infty}$-norm · Support vector machine · Class relatedness

## 1 Introduction

Discriminative dictionary learning (DDL), with the goal of learning a dictionary to linearly represent the training data while enforcing the coding vectors or/and reconstruction error to be discriminative, has been successfully applied in pattern recognition applications such as image classification [1,2] and face recognition [3]. The success of DDL lies in that there usually exists a compact dictionary which can be learned from the available training data for more effective and efficient classification.

Different from unsupervised dictionary learning methods which only require the dictionary to faithfully represent training data, the DDL methods concentrate on discriminative classification capability of the dictionary as its goal is to assign correct class labels to test data. To enrich such capability, how to design relationship between dictionary atoms and class labels plays a vital role in dictionary training stage. Based on relationship between dictionary atoms and class

© Springer-Verlag Berlin Heidelberg 2015
H. Zha et al. (Eds.): CCCV 2015, Part I, CCIS 546, pp. 335–343, 2015.
DOI: 10.1007/978-3-662-48558-3_34

labels, existing DDL methods can be divided into two main categories: one is global dictionary learning methods which associate each dictionary atom to all classes, the other is class-specific dictionary learning methods which assign each dictionary atom to only a single class. For global dictionary learning methods, the coding vectors are generally explored for classification and are usually jointly optimized with a classifier. Mairal et al. [4] proposed a DDL method by training a classifier of coding vectors for digging recognition and texture classification. Zhang and Li [5] proposed a joint learning algorithm base on KSVD for face recognition. Pham et al. [6] proposed to jointly train the dictionary and classifier for face recognition and object categorization. Cai et al. [7] introduced linear support vector machines (SVM) to jointly optimize the dictionary and classifier and thus making the coding vectors and dictionary more adaptive and flexible. Even though a global dictionary with small size can be powerful enough to represent training data and thereby the testing phase is very efficient, all the above methods fail to consider correspondence between dictionary atoms and class labels.

In the class-specific DDL methods, each dictionary atom is assigned to a single class and the dictionary atoms associated with different classes are encouraged to be as independent as possible. Ramirez et al. [1] proposed a structured dictionary learning scheme by promoting the discriminative ability between different class-specific sub-dictionaries. Castrodad and Sapiro [8] learned a set of class-specific sub-dictionaries with non-negative penalty on both dictionary atoms and coding vectors. Yang et al. [3] proposed a DDL framework which employs Fisher discrimination criterion to learn a class-specific dictionary. Since each dictionary atom has a single label, the reconstruction error with respect to each class could be used for classification. However, those methods ignored the dictionary relatedness across different classes, e.g., one dictionary atom can be helpful for the reconstruction of samples from different classes. Consequently, when there are numerous classes, the size of dictionary would be very large which will increase the memory and computational complexity for real applications.

As a matter of fact, the two DDL categories build relationship between dictionary atoms and class labels in two extreme manners. In order to make a trade-off to adaptively build the relationship, we propose a well-principled DDL scheme in which a joint sparsity constraint is separatively imposed on the coding vectors of each class by applying $\ell_{1,\infty}$-norm regularizer to the coding vectors of each class. Since the $\ell_{1,\infty}$-norm is a matrix norm that encourages entire rows of the matrix to be zeros, the resultant row sparsity of coding vectors of a specific class would build relationship between the specific class and the whole dictionary. Therefore, some samples can be sparsely represented by the dictionary atoms from the same and different classes. To make the coding vectors more discriminative, as in [7] we also add a discrimination term to the objective function which is formulated as sum of the weighted Euclidean distances between all pairs of coding vectors. What is more, a multi-class linear SVM classifier is incorporated into the DDL scheme to learn a dictionary in training phase and classify input samples in the testing phase.

The remainder of this paper is organized as follows. In Section 2, we briefly introduce the DDL scheme. In Section 3, we present the proposed DDL model and corresponding optimization procedure. To verify the efficiency of the proposed DDL method on classification problems, some experiments are conducted and the results are analyzed in Section 4. Finally, we conclude the paper in Section 5.

## 2    A Brief Review of the DDL Models

Suppose that $\mathbf{X} = [\mathbf{X}_1, \mathbf{X}_2, ..., \mathbf{X}_C]$ is a set of training samples with $C$ classes, where $\mathbf{X}_c$ is the subset containing $n_c$ samples from the $c$-th class. Correspondingly, let $\mathbf{A} = [\mathbf{A}_1, \mathbf{A}_2, ..., \mathbf{A}_C]$ be the coding matrix of $\mathbf{X}$ over the dictionary. A general DDL model can be described as follows

$$\langle \mathbf{D}, \mathbf{A} \rangle = \arg \min_{\mathbf{D}, \mathbf{A}} \mathcal{R}(\mathbf{X}, \mathbf{D}, \mathbf{A}) + \lambda_1 \|\mathbf{A}\| + \lambda_2 \mathcal{L}(\mathbf{A}), \tag{1}$$

where $\mathbf{D} = [\mathbf{d}_1, \mathbf{d}_2, ..., \mathbf{d}_K]$ is the dictionary, $\lambda_1$ and $\lambda_2$ are the trade-off parameters, $\mathcal{R}(\mathbf{X}, \mathbf{D}, \mathbf{A})$ is the reconstruction error term, $\|\mathbf{A}\|$ denotes a certain norm for $\mathbf{A}$, and $\mathcal{L}(\mathbf{A})$ denotes the discrimination term for $\mathbf{A}$.

In general, $\|\mathbf{A}\|$ is set to be $\|\mathbf{A}\|_1$ to ensure sparsity of the coding vectors since it tends to produce better classification results [9]. However, $\ell_1$-norm sparse coding suffers from high computation burden. To tackle this problem, some researchers attempt to use $\ell_2$-norm regularizer and their results can be very competitive with well-designed classification rule or classifier.

## 3    Main Results

Instead of learning a global dictionary without class specific property or a class-specific dictionary without class relatedness property, we propose to adaptively learn the relationship between dictionary atoms and class labels. In our proposed method, we simply assume a training sample can be sparsely represented by the dictionary atoms from the same and different classes. Under this assumption, we take advantage of $\ell_{1,\infty}$-norm which penalizes the sum of maximum absolute values of each row for a matrix. To be specific, the $\ell_{1,\infty}$-norm encourages entire rows of a matrix to be zeros and can be utilized for a joint sparse regularization. Thus, we replace $\|\mathbf{A}\|$ by $\sum_{c=1}^{C} \|\mathbf{A}_c\|_{1,\infty}$, where $\|\mathbf{A}_c\|_{1,\infty}$ forces that $\mathbf{X}_c$ should be jointly and sparsely represented by the dictionary and thus regularize the dictionary to have class relatedness property.

For the discrimination term, to enlarge similarity of coding vectors from same class and dissimilarity of coding vectors from different classes, we adopt sum of weighted Euclidean distances between all pairs of coding vectors to indicate the discrimination capability,

$$\mathcal{L}(\mathbf{A}) = \sum_{i,j} w_{ij} \|\mathbf{a}_i - \mathbf{a}_j\|_2^2, \tag{2}$$

where $\mathbf{a}_i$ and $\mathbf{a}_j$ denote the coding vectors of $i$-th and $j$-th sample, respectively, and $w_{ij}$ is the associated weight which plays a key role in the discrimination term. It has been pointed out that with the symmetry, consistency and balance constraints on the weights, a multi-class linear SVM can be fused into the discrimination term. According to [7], Eq. (2) can be further rewritten as

$$\mathcal{L}(\mathbf{A}) = 2 \sum_{c=1}^{C} \mathcal{L}(\mathbf{A}, \mathbf{y}^c, \mathbf{u}_c, b_c), \qquad (3)$$

where $\mathbf{y}^c = [y_1^c, y_2^c, \ldots, y_n^c]$, $n$ is the number of training samples, $y_i^c = 1$ if $y_i = c$ and otherwise $y_i^c = -1$, $\mathbf{u}_c$ is the normal to the $c$-th classs hyperplane of SVM, $b_c$ is the corresponding bias. To be specific, $\mathcal{L}(\mathbf{A}, \mathbf{y}^c, \mathbf{u}_c, b_c) = \|\mathbf{u}_c\|_2^2 + \theta \ell(\mathbf{A}, \mathbf{y}^c, \mathbf{u}_c, b_c)$, where $\ell(\mathbf{A}, \mathbf{y}^c, \mathbf{u}_c, b_c)$ is the hinge loss function and $\theta$ is a predefined constant. For the reconstruction error term, we formulate it as $\mathcal{R}(\mathbf{X}, \mathbf{D}, \mathbf{A}) = \|\mathbf{X} - \mathbf{DA}\|_F^2$. Note that $\|\mathbf{X} - \mathbf{DA}\|_F^2 = \sum_{c=1}^{C} \|\mathbf{X}_c - \mathbf{DA}_c\|_F^2$. As a result, our model can be formulated as follows

$$\min_{\mathbf{D},\mathbf{A},\mathbf{U},\mathbf{b}} \sum_{c=1}^{C} \|\mathbf{X}_c - \mathbf{DA}_c\|_F^2 + \lambda_1 \sum_{c=1}^{C} \|\mathbf{A}_c\|_{1,\infty} + 2\lambda_2 \sum_{c=1}^{C} \mathcal{L}(\mathbf{A}, \mathbf{y}^c, \mathbf{u}_c, b_c), \qquad (4)$$

where $\mathbf{U}$ and $\mathbf{b}$ are a collection of $\mathbf{u}_c$ and $b_c$, $c = 1, 2, \ldots, C$, respectively.

### 3.1   Model Training

Eq. (4) is a joint optimization problem and can be solved in an alternative minimization scheme [7]. Thus, we alternatively optimize the objective function with respect to $\mathbf{D}$, $\mathbf{A}$ and $\langle \mathbf{U}, \mathbf{b} \rangle$ as follows.

By fixing $\mathbf{D}$ and $\langle \mathbf{U}, \mathbf{b} \rangle$, we can separately calculate $\mathbf{A}_c$ by solving the following problem:

$$\langle \mathbf{A}_c \rangle = \arg\min_{\mathbf{A}_c} \|\mathbf{X}_c - \mathbf{DA}_c\|_F^2 + \lambda_1 \|\mathbf{A}_c\|_{1,\infty} + 2\lambda_2 \sum_{c=1}^{C} \mathcal{L}(\mathbf{A}_c, \mathbf{y}^c). \qquad (5)$$

To efficiently solve Eq. (5), we introduce an auxiliary variable $\mathbf{A}_c'$, resulting in an equivalent problem as follows

$$\langle \mathbf{A}_c, \mathbf{A}_c' \rangle = \arg\min_{\mathbf{A}_c, \mathbf{A}_c'} \|\mathbf{X}_c - \mathbf{DA}_c\|_F^2 + \lambda_1 \|\mathbf{A}_c'\|_{1,\infty} + 2\lambda_2 \sum_{c=1}^{C} \mathcal{L}(\mathbf{A}_c, \mathbf{y}^c) + \frac{\mu}{2} \|\mathbf{A}_c - \mathbf{A}_c'\|_F^2, \qquad (6)$$

where $\mu$ is a positive penalty parameter. We then use the augmented Lagrangian method to alternatively optimize $\mathbf{A}_c$ and $\mathbf{A}_c'$ until convergence as follow. ($i$) When $\mathbf{A}_c'$ is fixed, let $\mathbf{a}_i^c$ denotes the coding vector of $i$-th sample from $c$-th class and $\mathbf{a}_i'^c$ is the corresponding auxiliary variable, we can optimize $\mathbf{A}_c$ in columns,

$$\langle \mathbf{a}_i^c \rangle = \arg\min_{\mathbf{a}_i^c} \|\mathbf{x}_i^c - \mathbf{Da}_i^c\|_2^2 + 2\lambda_2 \theta \sum_{c=1}^{C} \ell(\mathbf{a}_i^c, y_i^c) + \frac{\mu}{2} \|\mathbf{a}_i^c - \mathbf{a}_i'^c\|_2^2, \qquad (7)$$

---

**Algorithm 1** Algorithm of the proposed DDL model.

---

**Input:** $\mathbf{D}_{init}, \mathbf{A}_{init}, \mathbf{A}'_{init}, \mathbf{U}_{init}, \mathbf{b}_{init}, \lambda_1, \lambda_2, \theta, \mu$.
**Output:** $\mathbf{D}, \mathbf{U}, \mathbf{b}$

1: **while** not converged **do**
2:    **for** $c = 1$ to $C$ **do**
3:       **while** not converged **do**
4:          **for** $i = 1$ to $n_c$ **do**
5:             $\mathbf{a}_i^c \leftarrow \arg\min_{\mathbf{a}_i^c} \|\mathbf{x}_i^c - \mathbf{D}\mathbf{a}_i^c\|^2 + 2\lambda_2\theta\sum_{c=1}^C \ell(\mathbf{a}_i^c, y_i^c) + \frac{\mu}{2}\|\mathbf{a}_i^c - \mathbf{a}_i'^c\|_2^2$
6:          **end for**
7:          $\mathbf{A}'_c \leftarrow \arg\min_{\mathbf{A}'_c} \lambda_1\|\mathbf{A}'_\mathbf{c}\|_{1,\infty} + \frac{\mu}{2}\|\mathbf{A}'_c - \mathbf{A}_c\|_F^2$
8:       **end while**
9:    **end for**
10:   $\mathbf{D} \leftarrow \arg\min_{\mathbf{D}} \|\mathbf{X} - \mathbf{D}\mathbf{A}\|_F^2 \quad s.t. \quad \|\mathbf{d}_k\|^2 \leq 1, \quad k = 1, 2, \ldots, K.$
11:   **for** $c = 1$ to $C$ **do**
12:     $\mathbf{u}_c, b_c \leftarrow$ by multi-class linear SVM
13:   **end for**
14: **end while**

---

According to [7], $\mathbf{a}_i^c$ has a closed-form solution. ($ii$) When $\mathbf{A}_c$ is fixed, we get the following problem which can be solved by the projected gradient method [10],

$$\langle \mathbf{A}'_c \rangle = \arg\min_{\mathbf{A}'_c} \lambda_1\|\mathbf{A}'_\mathbf{c}\|_{1,\infty} + \frac{\mu}{2}\|\mathbf{A}'_c - \mathbf{A}_c\|_F^2. \tag{8}$$

By fixing $\mathbf{A}$ and $\langle \mathbf{U}, \mathbf{b} \rangle$, the optimization problem with respect to $\mathbf{D}$ is as follows

$$\langle \mathbf{D} \rangle = \arg\min_{\mathbf{D}} \|\mathbf{X} - \mathbf{D}\mathbf{A}\|_F^2 \quad s.t. \quad \|\mathbf{d}_k\|_2^2 \leq 1, \quad k = 1, 2, \ldots, K, \tag{9}$$

where the constraint is to avoid the scaling issue of the atoms. This problem can be solved effectively by the Lagrange dual method [11].

By fixing $\mathbf{D}$ and $\mathbf{A}$, we can update $\langle \mathbf{U}, \mathbf{b} \rangle$ by solving the following problem

$$\langle \mathbf{U}, \mathbf{b} \rangle = \arg\min_{\mathbf{U}, \mathbf{b}} \sum_{c=1}^C \mathcal{L}(\mathbf{A}_\mathbf{c}, \mathbf{y}^c, \mathbf{u}_c, b_c). \tag{10}$$

Eq. (10) is actually a multi-class linear SVM problem and can be solved by the SVM solver in [12]. Algorithm 1 summarizes the optimization procedure.

## 3.2 Model Testing

Once the dictionary $\mathbf{D}$ and the classifier parameters $\langle \mathbf{U}, \mathbf{b} \rangle$ are learned, we perform classification as follows: for a test sample $\mathbf{x}$, we first calculate the sparse coding vector. As $\ell_{1,\infty}$-norm is a matrix norm and thus cannot tackle with a single vector, we instead use $\ell_1$-norm regularization to get the coding vector, resulting in the following tractable problem [13,14]

$$\langle \mathbf{a} \rangle = \arg\min_{\mathbf{a}} \|\mathbf{x} - \mathbf{D}\mathbf{a}\|_2^2 + \lambda_1\|\mathbf{a}\|_1. \tag{11}$$

We then apply learned SVM classifier to identify the test sample as follows

$$Label(\mathbf{x}) = \arg\max_c \mathbf{u}_c^T \mathbf{a} + b_c. \tag{12}$$

## 4 Experiments

To verify effectiveness of the proposed DDL model, extensive experiments on Caltech-101 object database [15], AR [16] and Extended Yale B [17] face database are carried out and performance of the proposed model are compared with the base-line sparse representation based classification (SRC) [18] method and state-of-the-art DDL methods including DKSVD [5], LC-KSVD [19], dictionary learning with structure incoherence (DLSI) [1], Fisher discrimination dictionary learning (FDDL) [3] and SVGDL [7]. All the experiments are carried out in Matlab (R2014a) environment running on a modern computer with Intel(R) Xeon(R) CPU 3.30 GHz and 32 GB memory. Note that we fix $\theta = 0.2$ and set $\mu = \lambda_1$ in all the experiments.

### 4.1 Object Classification

Caltech-101 object database contains 9,144 images from 102 object classes (101 common object classes and a background class). For each class, its number varies from 31 to 800. Following [7], we randomly select 5, 10, 15, 20, 25 and 30 images per object for training and the rest are used for testing. The number of dictionary atoms is set to be 510 in all the cases. We set $\lambda_1 = 5$ and $\lambda_2 = 0.1$. As shown in Table 1, SRC achieves the worst accuracy which is possibly attributed to lack of discriminative dictionary learning. With a class-specific dictionary, FDDL outperforms K-SVD and LCKSVD, however, when the training number is high (say 25, 30) per class, there is no significant gain over K-SVD and LCSVD. By learning a discriminative dictionary under the guidance of SVM, SVGDL has a better classification accuracy than LCKSVD and FDDL. However, our proposed DDL method outperforms SVGDL which indicates that the adaptive class relatedness learning can lead to more discriminative dictionary.

**Table 1.** The classification accuracy results on Caltech-101 database.

| Training number | 5 | 10 | 15 | 20 | 25 | 30 |
|---|---|---|---|---|---|---|
| SRC | 0.488 | 0.601 | 0.649 | 0.677 | 0.692 | 0.707 |
| K-SVD | 0.498 | 0.598 | 0.652 | 0.687 | 0.710 | 0.732 |
| DKSVD | 0.496 | 0.595 | 0.651 | 0.686 | 0.711 | 0.730 |
| LCKSVD | 0.540 | 0.631 | 0.677 | 0.705 | 0.723 | 0.736 |
| FDDL | 0.536 | 0.636 | 0.668 | 0.698 | 0.717 | 0.731 |
| SVGDL | 0.553 | 0.643 | 0.696 | 0.723 | 0.751 | 0.767 |
| **Proposed** | **0.576** | **0.668** | **0.709** | **0.750** | **0.770** | **0.788** |

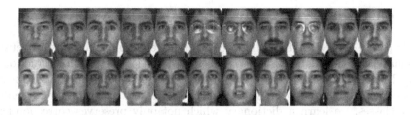

**Fig. 1.** Resized face images in the AR database.

## 4.2 Face Recognition

We also apply our algorithm to face recognition (FR) on two widely used databases: AR and Extended Yale B. The features are reduced to 300 dimensions by PCA for all FR experiments. Note that here we also make comparisons with the SVM method.

(1) The AR database consists of over 4,000 face images from 126 individuals. As in [18], we use a set containing 1,400 face images from 50 female and 50 male subjects. For each subject, there are 7 images for training and 7 images for testing. The face images are resized to 60×43 as shown in Fig. 1. Here the number of dictionary atoms is set to be 500. In this experiment, we set $\lambda_1 = 0.02$ and $\lambda_2 = 0.00005$. The experimental results of different methods are listed in Table 2. To the best of our knowledge, the recognition accuracy of 0.951 achieved by the proposed DDL method is the best result ever reported on this database with the same training and testing samples.

**Table 2.** The recognition accuracy results on AR database.

| Methods | SRC | SVM | DKSVD | LC-KSVD | DLSI | FDDL | SVGDL | **Proposed** |
|---|---|---|---|---|---|---|---|---|
| Accuracy | 0.888 | 0.871 | 0.854 | 0.897 | 0.898 | 0.920 | 0.946 | **0.951** |

(2) The Extended Yale B database consists of 2,414 face images from 38 persons. All the images are cropped into the size of 54×48. We randomly select 20 images of each person for training and the rest are used for testing. In this experiment, the number of the dictionary atoms is 380, $\lambda_1 = 0.1$ and $\lambda_2 = 0.0005$. As one can see from Table 3, our proposed DDL method achieves the best recognition accuracy.

**Table 3.** The recognition accuracy results on Extended Yale B database.

| Methods | SRC | SVM | DKSVD | LC-KSVD | DLSI | FDDL | SVGDL | **Proposed** |
|---|---|---|---|---|---|---|---|---|
| Accuracy | 0.900 | 0.888 | 0.753 | 0.906 | 0.890 | 0.919 | 0.961 | **0.971** |

## 5   Conclusions

In this paper, a novel DDL method which adaptively builds relationship between dictionary and class labels is presented. Instead of learning a global dictionary which lacks of correspondence between the dictionary atoms and class labels or a class-specific dictionary which misses the dictionary relatedness between different classes, we learn a dictionary which not only preserves correspondence between the dictionary atoms and class labels but also remains class relatedness between different classes, leading to a more powerful and discriminative dictionary. Experimental results on object classification and face recognition demonstrate superiority of our proposed method over many state-of-the-art DDL methods. Thus, we argue that our proposed method can provide a new insight to current dictionary learning based pattern recognition methods.

## References

1. Ramirez, I., Sprechmann, P., Sapiro, G.: Classification and clustering via dictionary learning with structured incoherence and shared features. In: 23rd IEEE Conference on Computer Vision and Pattern Recognition, pp. 3501–3508 (2010)
2. Tošić, I., Frossard, P.: Dictionary Learning, What is the right representation for my signal? IEEE Signal Proc. Mag. **28**, 27–38 (2011)
3. Yang, M., Zhang, D., Feng, X.: Fisher discrimination dictionary learning for sparse representation. In: IEEE International Conference on Computer Vision, pp. 543–550 (2011)
4. Mairal, J., Bach, F., Ponce, J.: Task-driven dictionary learning. IEEE Trans. Pattern Anal. Mach. Intell. **34**, 791–804 (2012)
5. Zhang, Q., Li, B.: Discriminative K-SVD for dictionary learning in face recognition. In: 23rd IEEE Conference on Computer Vision and Pattern Recognition, pp. 3501–3508 (2010)
6. Pham, D., Svetha, V.: Joint learning and dictionary construction for pattern recognition. In: 26th IEEE Conference on Computer Vision and Pattern Recognition (2008)
7. Cai, S., Zuo, W., Zhang, L., Feng, X., Wang, P.: Support vector guided dictionary learning. In: Fleet, D., Pajdla, T., Schiele, B., Tuytelaars, T. (eds.) ECCV 2014, Part IV. LNCS, vol. 8692, pp. 624–639. Springer, Heidelberg (2014)
8. Castrodad, A., Sapiro, G.: Sparse modeling of human actions from motion imagery. Int. J. Comput. Vis. **100**, 1–15 (2012)
9. Gao, S., Tsang, I.W.H., Chia, L.T.: Laplacian sparse coding, hypergraph laplacian sparse coding, and applications. IEEE Transactions on Pattern Analysis and Machine Intelligence **35**(1), 92–104 (2013)
10. Quattoni, A., Carreras, X., Collins, M., Darrell, T.: An efficient projection for $\ell_{1,\infty}$ regularization. In: The 26th Annual International Conference on Machine Learning, vol. 382 (2009)
11. Lee, H., Battle, A.: Efficient sparse coding algorithms. In: 20th Annual Conference on Neural Information Processing Systems, pp. 801–808 (2007)
12. Yang, J., Yu, K., Gong, Y., Huang, T.: Linear spatial pyramid matching using sparse coding for image classification. In: IEEE Conference on Computer Vision and Pattern Recognition, pp. 1794–1801 (2009)

13. Yang, A.Y., Sastry, S.S., Ganesh, A., Ma, Y.: Fast $\ell$1-minimization algorithms and an application in robust face recognition: a review. In: IEEE International Conference on Image Processing, pp. 1849–1852 (2010)
14. Zuo, W., Meng, D., Zhang, L., Feng, X., Zhang, D.: A generalized iterated shrinkage algorithm for non-convex sparse coding. In: Proceedings of the IEEE International Conference on Computer Vision, pp. 217–224 (2013)
15. Fei-Fei, L., Fergus, R., Perona, P.: Learning generative visual models from few training examples: an incremental bayesian approach tested on 101 object categories. In: Proceedings of the 2004 IEEE Computer Society Conference on Computer Vision and Pattern Recognition, pp. 178–186 (2004)
16. Martinez, A., Benavente, R.: The AR face database. CVC Technical report (1998)
17. Lee, K.C., Ho, J., Kriegman, D.: Acquiring linear subspaces for face recognition under variable lighting. IEEE Transactions on Pattern Analysis and Machine Intelligence **27**, 684–698 (2005)
18. Wright, J., Yang, A.Y., Ganesh, A., Sastry, S.S., Ma, Y.: Robust face recognition via sparse representation. IEEE Transactions on Pattern Analysis and Machine Intelligence **31**, 210–227 (2009)
19. Jiang, Z., Lin, Z., Davis, L.: Label consistent K-SVD: learning a discriminative dictionary for recognition. IEEE Transactions on Pattern Analysis and Machine Intelligence **35**, 2651–2664 (2013)

# Building an Effective Template Dictionary
# for Robust Offline Video Tracking

Fei Liu, Xiaoqin Zhang$^{(\boxtimes)}$, Mingyu Fan, Di Wang,
Hongxing Jiang, and Xiuzi Ye

College of Mathematics and Information Science,
Wenzhou University, Wenzhou, China
`zhangxiaoqinnan@gmail.com`

**Abstract.** Sparse representation is one of most influential framework for visual tracking. However, how to build an effective template dictionary for tracking is less investigated. In this paper, we propose a template dictionary construction method which is effective for offline video tracking. The template dictionary is constructed including several non-polluted templates, and their offsprings. These templates are selectively updated to absorb the appearance variations and prevent the model from drifting. Furthermore, our tracking algorithm is conducted in a bi-directional way, and the optimization process employed in our work is efficiently solved by two-stage sparse representation, which can greatly improve the tracking performance. Experimental results demonstrate that the proposed template dictionary is robust for offline video tracking.

**Keywords:** Visual tracking · Sparse representation · Offline video · Dictionary learning

## 1 Introduction

Visual tracking, as a fundamental task in many visual systems, is to infer moving objects' states, e.g. location, scale, or velocity, from the observations in a video. According to the different video sources, the tracking tasks can be roughly classified into the following two cases: *online* tracking and *offline* tracking. Online visual tracking estimates the target state forward in time with no observations in the future. While for offline tracking, all video frames are available in advance. Offline tracking has received significant attention due to its crucial value in many multimedia applications, such video annotation, video retrieval, event analysis, object based video compression, etc.

Generally speaking, for any tracking algorithms, handling appearance variations of an object is a fundamental and challenging task. Consequently, how to effectively represent such appearance variations plays a critical role in visual tracking. An image patch model [1], which takes the set of pixels in the object region as the representation of the object, is a direct way to model the object, but it loses the discriminative information that is contained in the pixel values. Color histogram [2] provides global statistical information about the pixel

H. Zha et al. (Eds.): CCCV 2015, Part I, CCIS 546, pp. 344–354, 2015.
DOI: 10.1007/978-3-662-48558-3_35

values in object region. The color histogram is robust to noise, but it has two major problems: (a) the histogram is very sensitive to illumination changes; (b) the relative positions of the pixels in the image are ignored. In [3], curves or splines are used to represent the apparent boundary of the object. Due to the simplistic representation, which is confined to the apparent boundary, the algorithm is sensitive to image noise, leading to tracking failures in cluttered backgrounds. To model the multi-modal distribution of the appearance, a set of MOG (Mixture of Gaussians) based appearance models [4–8] has been proposed. Usually, 3-5 components are employed in their appearance models, which are not enough to accommodate the variations of the object appearance. Another category of appearance models is based on subspace learning. For example, in [9], a view-based eigenbasis representation of the object is learned off-line. However, it is very difficult to collect training samples that cover all possible viewing conditions. Later, some researchers update the object subspace in the tracking process to capture the changes in appearance. The pioneering work on applying the incremental subspace learning to tracking is by Lim *et al.* [10], where they extend the SKL (Sequential Karhunen-Loeve) [11] algorithm to effectively learn the variations of both appearance and illumination. Zhang *et al.* [12] proposed a graph embedding-based learning algorithm for object tracking, which can simultaneously learn the subspace of the target and the local discriminative structure of the target against the background.

Recently, sparse representation with $l_1$-norm constraint has received more and more attentions because of its compact representation and robustness to image noise and outliers. It has been widely applied in visual tracking [13–18]. Although the application of sparse representation in visual tracking has achieved great success, they have less investigated with respect to the following aspect: how to build an effective template dictionary for visual tracking. For sparse representation, it needs an overcomplete template dictionary, and thus a new sample can be approximated by a linear combination of these templates with coefficients as sparse as possible. For online tracking, it is impossible to build an overcomplete template dictionary in advance. Thus, a dictionary with a few templates are initialized at the beginning and is adaptively updated [13] in the tracking process. However, this strategy greatly limits the tracking performance for the following two reasons: (1) the dictionary is far from the overcomplete; (2) the tracking errors are gradually introduced into the dictionary during the updating process, leading to the drifting problem. By contrast, building an overcomplete template dictionary is possible for offline tracking since all video frames are available. Now the question is how to construct an effective template dictionary with a relative small cost?

Traditionally, there are some work addressing the template dictionary construction problem in signal processing field [19–22]. Aharon et al. [19] propose a alternative optimization method for dictionary learning which alternates between sparse coding of the examples based on the current dictionary and a process of updating the dictionary atoms to better fit the data. Yaghoobi et al. [20] extends the dictionary learning problem by introducing different constraints and it is solved by a majorization method. Skretting and Engan [22] propose a recursive least squares learning algorithm, which can be used for learning overcomplete dictionaries for sparse signal representation. However, in the video stream applications, we can not label so much sample data before training or learning.

Based on by the forgoing discussions, we propose a template dictionary construction method which is effective for offline video tracking. The main features of our method are summarized as follows:

• Several non-polluted templates and their offsprings extracted in some key frames are incorporated into the sparse representation based optimization process seamlessly to overcome the drifting problem. All templates are carefully and selectively updated based on their weights, aiming at effectively capturing the variational appearance changes.

• The tracker is conducted in a bi-directional way, and optimization is efficiently solved by two-stage sparse representation which alleviates the great computational load suffered by the sparse coding problem when the dictionary is large.

The remainder of this paper is structured as follows. Section 2 gives a brief introduction of the sparse representation framework in the tracking context. The detail of the proposed tracking algorithm is introduced in Section 3. The experiments are reported in the Section 4, and some conclusions are made in Section 5.

## 2   Sparse Representation for Visual Tracking

In the tracking context, the manifold of the object in a period time is assumed to lie in a linear subspace. This is reasonable because the variations of the appearance mode are usually reflected on a special low-dimensional subspace. It means that any new sample of the same object can be approximately spanned by a set of templates.

Given a set of rectified image templates $\mathbf{V} = [\mathbf{v_1}, \mathbf{v_2}, \cdots, \mathbf{v_n}] \in \mathbb{R}^{d \times n}$, a new rectified image candidate $\mathbf{m} \in \mathbb{R}^d$ can be approximated by a linear combination of these templates.

$$\mathbf{m} \approx \mathbf{Va} = a_1\mathbf{v_1} + a_2\mathbf{v_2} + \cdots + a_n\mathbf{v_n} \tag{1}$$

where $\mathbf{a} = (a_1, a_2, \cdots, a_n)^T$ is the coefficient vector. When the size $n$ of the template set is big enough, $\mathbf{a} = [0, \cdots, 0, \beta, \cdots, 0, \cdots, 0]^T$ is a sparse vector, forming the sparse representation of $\mathbf{m}$ on the image templates $\mathbf{V}$.

In real tracking applications, the image candidate $\mathbf{m}$ is inevitable corrupted by the sensor noise or partially occluded. In this case, the above linear model (1) is modified as

$$\mathbf{m} = \mathbf{Va} + \mathbf{e} = a_1\mathbf{v_1} + a_2\mathbf{v_2} + \cdots + a_n\mathbf{v_n} + \mathbf{e} \tag{2}$$

where $\mathbf{e}$ is a error vector. The nonzero entries of $\mathbf{e}$ correspond to pixels in $\mathbf{m}$ which are corrupted or occluded. However, the locations of the corrupted pixels differ for different image candidates and are not known. Meanwhile the errors may have arbitrary magnitudes.

A good solution is to form the errors in a sparse representation way. Here, the templates for the error part are defined as $\mathbf{I} = [\mathbf{i_1}, \mathbf{i_2}, \cdots, \mathbf{i_d}]$. Each trivial template $\mathbf{i_k}$ is a vector with only one nonzero entry in the position $k$, which explicitly codes the pixels being corrupted by noise or occluded. Then the error vector $\mathbf{e}$ is sparely represented with combination of these trivial templates:

$$\mathbf{e} = \mathbf{Ie} = e_1\mathbf{i_1} + e_2\mathbf{i_2} + \cdots + e_n\mathbf{i_d} \tag{3}$$

where $e_k$ is the coefficient of the $k$th trivial template. By reformulating Equation (2) into a matrix form, it becomes

$$\mathbf{m} = [\mathbf{V} \ \ \mathbf{I}]\begin{bmatrix} \mathbf{a} \\ \mathbf{e} \end{bmatrix} = \mathbf{Dp} \tag{4}$$

The coefficient vector $\mathbf{p}$ is recovered after solving the following $\ell_1$-norm minimization problem:

$$\hat{\mathbf{p}} = \arg\min\|\mathbf{p}\|_1 \quad \text{subject to} \quad \mathbf{Dp} = \mathbf{m} \tag{5}$$

The above optimization problem can be solved by linear programming. After obtaining the sparse coefficients $\hat{\mathbf{p}}$, the input image $\mathbf{m}$ can be represented in a sparse way.

# 3 Proposed Tracking System

To give a clear view, the flowchart of the proposed tracking algorithm is shown in Fig. 1. There are four major components in the tracking system: (1) the construction of the template dictionary; (2) the two-stage sparse optimization; (3) the bi-tracking process; (4) the selective updating of the template dictionary. Each component is described in detail in the following sections.

## 3.1 Template Dictionary Construction

In [13,18], the template dictionary is constructed from a dense sampling around the object which is manually labled in the first frame. This dictionary is far from overcomplete and thus limits the tracking performance. As stated in Section 1, it is possible to build a relative large template dictionary for offline tracking since all video frames are available. However, even for offline tracking, the issue of how to build an effective template dictionary is less investigated.

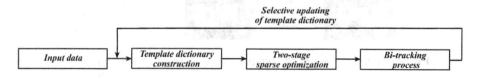

**Fig. 1.** The flow chart of the proposed tracking algorithm

Inspired by the key-frame based tracking algorithms [23–25], we propose a key-frame based algorithm to construct a large and effective template dictionary. To collect more representative templates, we first manually select a set of key frames and initialize the object region within these frames (see the top row of Fig. 2). Then the object regions are normalized to a predefined size to form a set of representative and non-polluted templates. Fortunately, for the offline video based multimedia applications, such as video annotation and retrieval, they are tolerable to make such labeling. However, only using the labeled templates is not enough for robust offline tracking for the following reasons: 1) the misalignment between dictionary templates and image candidates will degenerate the tracking performance; 2) the labeled templates are not enough to absorb the variations of the object appearance.

To overcome these limitations, we propose a template dictionary consists of three kinds of template: (1) a set of fixed templates which are pure and non-polluted; (2) a set of variational templates which capture the the variations of the object appearance; (3) a set of travail templates for handling noise and occlusion. The travail templates are defined as in Section 2. The other two kinds of template are defined as follows.

**Non-polluted Templates.** As shown in the top row of Fig. 2, the object region to be tracked is manually labeled in $k$ key frames which are specified by the user. According to the position of the region in the $i$th frame, a set of new image regions are generated by perturbing the object regions with 0-2 pixels. The dense sampling around the object region can alleviate the misalignment problem. Then, these image regions are rectified to form a non-polluted template set $D_n^i = [d_{n,1}^i, d_{n,2}^i \cdots, d_{n,j}^i]$, where $d_{n,j}^i$ is the $j$th non-polluted template extracted from the $i$th frame. Therefore, the non-polluted template set for all the $k$ key frames are represented as $D_n = [D_n^1, D_n^2, \cdots, D_n^k]$.

**Variational Templates.** As shown in the bottom row of Fig. 2, for each subsequence between two key frames, the variational templates are initialized by randomly linear combination of the non-polluted templates derived from the two key frames, aiming at effectively capturing the changes in the object appearance.

**Fig. 2.** An illustration of the template dictionary construction process

In more detail, let us take the subsequence between the first key frame and the second key frame as an example. Let $D_v = [d_{v,1}, d_{v,2}, \cdots, d_{v,j}]$ denote the variational template set. Each template in the variational template set is obtained as follows.

$$d_{v,j} = \alpha d_{n,l}^1 + (1 - \alpha) d_{n,m}^2$$

where $\alpha \in (0, 1)$ is a uniformly distributed random number, and $d_{n,l}^1, d_{n,m}^2$ are non-polluted templates which are randomly selected in the first frame and the second frame. Together with the selective updating strategy (see Section 3.4), these templates can effectively capture the variations of the object appearance.

As a result, the whole template dictionary can be represented by $\mathcal{D} = [D_n, D_v, D_t]$, where $D_t$ is the template dictionary of the trivial templates.

## 3.2  Two-Stage Sparse Optimization

As stated in Section 3.1, the constructed template dictionary is large, so the corresponding $l_1$-norm constraint optimization problem in Eq. (5) is time consuming. To overcome this problem, we propose an efficient two-stage sparse representation based algorithm for solving the optimization problem.

Before introducing the optimization process, let us first recall the symbols used in the previous sections. When star tracking, the template dictionary is composed of the non-polluted templates $D_n = [D_n^1, D_n^2, \cdots, D_n^k]$, the variational templates $D_v$, and the trivial templates $D_t$. For the tracking task on the subsequence between the first key frame and the second key frame, the non-polluted templates $D_n^1$ and $D_n^2$ are used to prevent the model drifting problem. The variational templates $D_v$, which are built by linear combination of the non-polluted templates $D_n^1$ and $D_n^2$, are used to capture the variations of object appearance. For the rest of the non-polluted templates $D_n' = [D_n^3, \cdots, D_n^k]$, we select them as follow.

---

**Algorithm 1.** Stage I: selection of the non-polluted templates

---

**Input**: non-polluted templates matrix $D_n' = [D_n^3, \cdots, D_n^k]$, and an image candidate $y$.

1. Calculate the distance between $y$ and each template $d_i$ in $D_n'$, and then obtain a nearest subset $I$ in $D_n'$ based on the distances: $D_n'' = \{D_n | d_i \in D_n' \text{ and } i \in I\}$.

2. Solve the non-negative least squares problem:

$$\beta^* = \arg\min_{\beta} ||D_n'' \beta - y||_2, \text{ s.t. } \beta \geq 0$$

3. Select the non-polluted templates from $D_n''$ as follow.

$$D_n^s = \{D_n'' | d_i \in D_n'' \text{ and } \beta_i^* \geq 0\}$$

**Output**: the selected non-polluted templates $D_n^s$;

---

In this way, a large number of templates in $D_n'$ can be filtered out, and thus greatly improve the optimization efficiency. Fortunately, the selection mechanism is reasonable in tracking process. By stacking all the above templates into the final dictionary $\mathbf{D} = [D_n^1, D_n^2, D_n^s, D_v, D_t]$, the optimization problem in Stage II is conducted as in Eq. (5).

### 3.3  Bi-tracking Process

To utilize the context information in the nearest frames, the tracking process is not conducted in the sequential order on time axis.

Let us take the subsequence between the first key frame and the second key frame as an example. For example, started from the key frame 1, tracking is firstly conducted on the frame with number 1, and then the tracker is transferred to the frame with number 2; afterwards, the tracker goes back to the frame with number 3 and moves to the frame with number 4. This process is continued until all the frames in the subsequence are tracked twice. For each frame, we have two different tracking results, and we choose the frame where the two tracking results have the minimal difference as the intersection of bi-tracking process, so as to obtain the tracking results of the whole subsequences.

### 3.4  Template Updating

In most tracking applications, the tracker must simultaneously deal with the changes of both the target and the environment. So it is necessary to design a adaption scheme for the appearance model. However, over updating of the model may gradually introduce the noise of background into the target model, causing the model drift away finally. Thus, a proper updating scheme is of significant importance for the tracking system.

In this work, several kinds of templates are used. We adopt different updating scheme for different kind of templates as follows:

- The non-polluted templates are manually labeled before start tracking. For each subsequence, the non-polluted templates are selected according to the algorithm in Section 3.2.
- The variational templates are generated by linear combination of the non-polluted templates within the corresponding subsequence, and are updated based on the template weight as in [13].

## 4    Experimental Results

To validate the claimed contribution of our work, we first conduct two comparison experiments involving different dictionaries and different tracking processes. Then, the comparison experiments with several state-of- the-art tracking algorithms are carried out to show the effectiveness of the proposed tracking system. All the experiments are conducted with Matlab on a platform with Pentium IV 3.2GHz CPU and 1G memory.

### 4.1 Different Dictionaries

In this part, we compare our work with the traditional $L_1$ tracker [13]. The bi-tracking process and the hard constraint of the label key frames are not activated to make a fair comparison.

As shown in Fig. 3, $L_1$ tracker quickly fail to track the object when the object undergoes large changes in pose and illumination. While our method with a more complete dictionary can successfully track the object through the whole sequences. The reason are two-fold: (1) the dictionary used in $L_1$ tracker is far from over-complete, and thus when the appearance changes can not be represented by the given dictionary, leading to tracking failure; (2) the updating strategy employed in L1 tracker introduces tracking errors to the dictionary, which cause the template to drift away from the object. The non-polluted templates selected from the key frames in our method can effectively prevent the drifting problem.

### 4.2 Different Tracking Processes

To show the effectiveness of the bi-tracking process, we test our method on two challenge sequences by using bi-tracking process and normal tracking process respectively.

Fig. 4 shows some key frames of the tracking results of the testing sequences. We can see that the normal tracking process can not capture the abrupt motion

(a) football (key frames: 73,145,217,290,362)

(b) shaking (Key frames: 55,109,246,302,365)

**Fig. 3.** Tracking performance of different dictionaries (red: our method, green: L1 tracker).

(a) basketball (key frames: 75,145,290,335,480)

(b) skate (key frames: 72,79,198,263,323)

**Fig. 4.** Tracking performance of different tracking processes (red: bi-tracking process, blue: normal tracking process).

**Fig. 5.** Tracking performance of different tracking algorithms (red: our method, green: MIL, magenta: SSOB). (key frames: 82, 164, 319 ,412, 527)

of the object although many non-polluted templates from the key frames are constructed. In contrast, the bi-tracking process can handle this problem well. The reason is the motion is constrained from both tracking directions, and thus improve the tracking robustness.

### 4.3  Comparison with Other Tracking Algorithms

To make the experiments more convincing, we conduct a comparison experiment between our algorithm and two state-of- the-art discriminative tracking algorithms, which are referred as Semi-Supervised On-line Boosting (SSOB) [26], Multiple Instance Learning (MIL) [27][1].

As shown in Fig. 5, we can see that MIL fails to track the object at frame 80 and can not recover the track in the remaining part of the sequence. The reason is that the Harr feature is not discriminative enough when the appearance of the object changes. The SSOB tracker loses track of the object at frame 409. The proposed method has a better tracking performance over MIL and SSOB.

## 5  Conclusion

This paper has proposed an effective template dictionary construction method. In the dictionary, we adopt a set of templates including several non-polluted templates, their offsprings, a stable template and other variational templates. These templates are selectively updated to absorb the appearance variations and prevent the model from drifting. Moreover, the tracker can be conducted in a bi-directional way. Several comparison experiment results demonstrate the effectiveness of the proposed tracking algorithm.

**Acknowledgement.** This work is supported by NSFC (Grant Nos. 61472285, 6141101224, 61473212, 61203241 and 61305035), Zhejiang Provincial Natural Science Foundation (Grants Nos. LY12F03016, LY15F030011 and LQ13F030009), Project of science and technology plans of Zhejiang Province (Grants Nos. 2014C31062, 2015C31168), the Education Department Foundation of Zhejiang Province (No. Y201016645).

---

[1] The source codes are downloaded from the authors' webpage.

# References

1. Hager, G., Belhumeur, P.: Efficient region tracking with parametric models of geometry and illumination. IEEE Transactions on Pattern Analysis and Machine Intelligence **20**(10), 1025–1039 (1998)
2. Comaniciu, D., Ramesh, V., Meer, P.: Kernel-based object tracking. IEEE Transactions on Pattern Analysis and Machine Intelligence **25**(50), 234–240 (2003)
3. Isard, M., Blake, A.: Condensation: conditional density propagation for visual tracking. International Journal of Computer Vision **29**(1), 5–28 (1998)
4. Jepson, A., Fleet, D., El-Maraghi, T.: Robust online appearance models for visual tracking. IEEE Transactions on Pattern Analysis and Machine Intelligence **25**(10), 1296–1311 (2003)
5. Zhou, S., Chellappa, R., Moghaddam, B.: Visual Tracking and Recongnition Using Appear- ance-adaptive Models in Particles Filters. IEEE Transactions on Image Processing **13**(11), 1491–1506 (2004)
6. Wang, H., Suter, D., Schindler, K., Shen, C.: Adaptive Object Tracking Based on an Effective Appearance Filter. IEEE Transactions on Pattern Analysis and Machine Intelligence **29**(9), 1661–1667 (2007)
7. Zhang, X., Hu, W., Bao, H., Maybank, S.: Robust Head Tracking Based on Multiple Cues Fusion in the Kernel-Bayesian Framework. IEEE Transactions on Circuits and Systems for Video Technology **23**(7), 1197–1208 (2013)
8. Zhang, X., Hu, W., Xie, N., Bao, H., Maybank, S.: A Robust Tracking System for Low Frame Rate Video. International Journal of Computer Vision **112**(2), 1–26 (2015)
9. Black, M., Jepson, A.: EigenTracking: Robust Matching and Tracking of Articulated Objects Using a View-Based Representation. International Journal of Computer Vision **26**(1), 63–84 (2004)
10. Lim, J., Ross, D., Lin, R., Yang, M.: Incremental learning for visual tracking. In: Advances in Neural Information Processing Systems, pp. 793–800 (2004)
11. Levy, A., Lindenbaum, M.: Sequential Karhunen-Loeve Basis Extraction and its Application to Images. IEEE Transactions on Image Processing **9**(8), 1371–1374 (2000)
12. Zhang, X., Hu, W., Chen, S., Maybank, S.: Graph-Embedding-Based Learning for Robust Object Tracking. IEEE Transactions on Industrial Electronics **61**(2), 1072–1084 (2014)
13. Mei, X., Ling, H.: Robust visual tracking using $L_1$ minimization. In: Proceedings of International Conference on Computer Vision, pp. 1–8 (2009)
14. Liu, B., Yang, V., Huang, J., Meer, P., Gong, L., Kulikowski, C.: Robust and fast collaborative tracking with two stage sparse optimization. In: Proceedings of European Conference on Computer Vision, pp. 624–637 (2010)
15. Li, H., Shen, C., Shi, Q.: Real-time visual tracking using compressive sensing. In: Proceedings of International Conference on Computer Vision and Pattern Recognition, vol. 42, pp. 1305–1312 (2011)
16. Zhang, X., Li, W., Hu, W., Ling, H., Maybank, S.: Block covariance based tracker with a subtle template dictionary. Pattern Recognition **46**(7), 1750–1761 (2013)
17. Jia, X., Lu, H., Yang, M.: Visual tracking via adaptive structural local sparse appearance model. In: Proceedings of IEEE Conference on Computer Vision and Pattern Recognition, pp. 1822–1829 (2012)
18. Zhang, T., Ghanem, B., Liu, S., Ahuja, N.: Robust visual tracking via multi-task sparse learning. In: Proceedings of IEEE Conference on Computer Vision and Pattern Recognition, pp. 2042–2049 (2012)

19. Aharon, M., Elad, M., Bruckstein, A.: K-SVD: An Algorithm for Designing Over-complete Dictionaries for Sparse Representation. IEEE Transactions on Signal Processing **54**(11), 4311–4322 (2006)
20. Yaghoobi, M., Blumensath, T., Davies, M.E.: Dictionary learning for sparse approximations with the majorization method. IEEE Transactions on Signal Processing **57**(6), 2178–2191 (2009)
21. Mairal, J., Bach, F., Ponce, J., Sapiro, G.: Online dictionary learning for sparse coding. In: Proceedings of International Conference on Machine Learning, pp. 689–696 (2009)
22. Skretting, K., Engan, K.: Recursive least squares dictionary learning algorithm. IEEE Transactions on Signal Processing **58**(4), 2121–2130 (2010)
23. Agarwala, A., Hertzmann, A., Salesin, D., Seitz, S.: Keyframe-based tracking for rotoscoping and animation. ACM Transactions on Graphics **24**(3), 584–591 (2005)
24. Wei, Y., Sun, J., Tang, X., Shum, H.: Interactive offline tracking for color objects. In: Proceedings of International Conference on Computer Vision (2007)
25. Wei, X., Chai, J.: Interactive tracking of 2D generic objects with spacetime optimization. In: Proceedings of European Conference on Computer Vision, pp. 657–670 (2008)
26. Grabner, H., Grabner, M., Bischof, H.: Semi-supervised on-line boosting for robust tracking. In: Proceedings of European Conference on Computer Vision, pp. 234–247 (2008)
27. Babenko, B., Yang, M., Belongie, S.: Robust Object Tracking with Online Multiple Instance Learning. IEEE Transactions on Pattern Analysis and Machine Intelligence **33**(8), 1619–1632 (2011)

# Learning Blur Invariant Face Descriptors
# for Face Verification Under Realistic Environment

Zhan-Xiang Feng[1], Yang Yuan[1], and Jian-Huang Lai[1,2(✉)]

[1] School of Information Science and Technology, Sun-Yat-Sen University, Guangzhou, China
fengzhx@mail2.sysu.edu.cn, 493170451@qq.com
[2] Guangdong Key Laboratory of Information Security Technology,
Sun-Yat-Sen University, Guangzhou, China
stsljh@mail.sysu.edu.cn

**Abstract.** Face verification technology has been widely used in realist applications such as surveillance, access control and passport authentication. It remains one of the most active research topics in computer vision and pattern recognition. Recently, more research efforts for face verification have focused on uncontrolled environment while current face verification techniques have been proven to be robust and efficient for controlled environment. In this paper, we focus to study on the issue of blur and low resolution (LR), which is common in video surveillance and real application. We propose a descriptor which uses the Fisher Kernel framework to encode the multi-scale absolute phase difference feature of the local image. Then we combine the feature with multiple metric learning approach to achieve a blur robust descriptor that is compact and discriminant. Experiment on blurred ferret dataset and realistic face dataset validates the efficiency of the proposed approach.

**Keywords:** Face verification · Blur invariant · Fisher kernel · Metric learning

## 1 Introduction

As one of the most active research topics in computer vision and biometric, face verification technology has achieved great progress in last decades and performs well in the controlled environment. However, in realistic application under uncontrolled environment, face verification technique faces many challenges, among them blur and LR is one of the most challenging and common problem. On one hand, owing to the long distance and low image quality, face images that appear in video surveillance are often blurred and LR. On the other hand, in some cases, restricted by the storage size of memory chips, we can only obtain low quality images. As blurred and LR face images lost image details and discriminative information, existing face verification approaches degrades significantly when dealing with blurred and LR face images.

Methods to cope with blur and LR can be categorized in three types, namely Super Resolution(SR), coupled mappings and blur invariant descriptor. SR based approaches first infer the HR image from LR image and then use the recovered image for recognition. Wang et al. [12] uses PCA to represent input LR face image from the

© Springer-Verlag Berlin Heidelberg 2015
H. Zha et al. (Eds.): CCCV 2015, Part I, CCIS 546, pp. 355–365, 2015.
DOI: 10.1007/978-3-662-48558-3_36

subspace constructed by training LR images and then infer HR face image using the same parameters. Coupled mappings approach is proposed by Li et al. [13], which aims to map the LR and HR image from different resolution to a common subspace. Zhou et al.[14] further improved the method by introducing LDA into coupled mappings to improve discriminant ability. Blur invariant descriptor based approach aims to design a descriptor that is blur invariant. Ojansivu et al. [3]proposed Local Phase Quantization(LPQ) descriptor for texture classification, proving that local phase of face images is blur invariant, Ahonen et al. [2] applied LPQ to face recognition.

In recent years, fisher kernel framework has attracted increasing attention. It is introduced by Jaakkola et al. [4] and used by Perronnin et al. [5] for image classification. Fisher kernel framework combines the generative model and discriminative model. It first computes a generative model such as GMM model using training samples, then encodes the derivative of parameters on log-likelihood function of the generative model using sum-pooling to form a novel descriptor. Fisher kernel framework has proved the efficiency in many fields such as Speaker verification[6], audio classification[7] and image classification[8].

After the extraction of facial descriptor, metric learning is often used to improve the discriminant ability and reduce the dimension of the final feature. Cui et al. [9] proposed a multiple metric learning method to integrate the face region descriptors of all blocks from an image and consider the correlation between different image blocks.

Since SR methods aims to enhance image rather than recognize blur and LR image, a discriminant and robust blur invariant descriptor is preferred for blur and LR face recognition. Although LPQ is proven to be blur invariant, it lacks discriminant ability because histogram is usually computed to get a global feature of the face when using LPQ. To improve the generalization ability of LPQ, we describe the phase difference feature in a local and dense manner and then utilize fisher kernel framework to get a novel blur invariant face descriptor. To further reduce the gap between gallery and test faces, we combine the descriptor with improved multiple metric learning approach to achieve a blur robust descriptor that is compact and discriminant.

The contribution of the paper is summarized as follows:

1) We utilize multi-scale phase feature in a local dense manner and generate a novel blur robust face descriptor using fisher kernel framework.

2) We prove that PMML method cannot guarantee convergence during learning and propose a method to solve the problem by using Stein's loss function and updating the parameter individually for each block.

3) We build a novel realistic face database which consists of blurred certificate photos and realistic photos with varying illumination and pose. Experiment on blurred Feret database and realistic face database prove the effect of our proposal.

The rest of the paper is organized as follows. Section 2 presents details of our Proposal. Section 3 shows results of our experiment. Section 4 concludes the paper.

## 2     Blur Invariant Face Descriptor via Multiple Metric Learning

### 2.1     Proposed Framework

The framework is shown in fig.1. For each input image, we first detect the face region and extract feature points using stasm[10] for face alignment. After alignment we will partition the face image into $m \times n$ blocks and then for each block we will extract multi-scale absolute phase difference features. During training, we gather features from each block together to train a GMM model using EM algorithm and then encode the fisher kernel feature by sum-pooling the derivative of parameters of the model for each input descriptor. Then we will use fisher kernel features to learn a metric matrix for each block to increase discriminability and compensate face misalignment by multiple metric learning. During testing, we extract multi-scale absolute phase difference features and then encode the features by the model learned. Finally, we compute the similarity of two input images by averaging the projection distance of each block using the multiple projection matrixes.

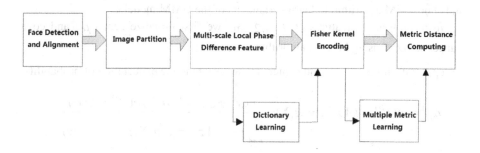

**Fig. 1.** Proposed Framework

### 2.2     Multi-scale Absolute Phase Difference Feature

Although LPQ is a blur invariant descriptor, it only considers the relative size between the phase of the center pixel and its surrounding pixels, thus lots of useful information is discarded. To improve performance of LPQ, we compute the multi-scale absolute local phase difference between the center pixel and the surrounding pixels.

Given pixel $x_c$, with 8 surrounding pixels $x_k, k = 1 \ldots 8$ and phase $\angle F(u, x_c)$ and $\angle F(u, x_t), t = 1 \ldots 8$ at frequency $u$, we have:

$$d_p(u) = [\angle F(u, x_1) - \angle F(u, x_c), \ldots, \angle F(u, x_8) - \angle F(u, x_c)]^T \tag{1}$$

We compute the phase difference vector at 4 frequencies and concatenate them:

$$d_p = [d_p(u_1)^T d_p(u_2)^T d_p(u_3)^T d_p(u_4)^T]^T \tag{2}$$

where $u_1 = [a, 0]^T$, $u_2 = [0, \alpha]^T$, $u_3 = [\alpha, \alpha]^T$, $u_3 = [\alpha, -\alpha]^T$, $a = \dfrac{1}{M}$ and $M$ is the size of the convolution window. By adding the spatial coordinate, we get the single scale absolute frequency phase difference descriptor :

$$d_{final} = [d_p^T \quad \frac{x}{w} - \frac{1}{2} \quad \frac{y}{h} - \frac{1}{2}]^T \tag{3}$$

where $x$, $y$ denotes the position of the feature, $w$ and $h$ represents width and height of input image. Multi-scale absolute frequency phase difference descriptor can be obtained by changing $M$ and concatenating the corresponding features.

## 2.3    Fisher Kernel Encoding

After feature extraction, we utilize fisher kernel framework to further improve discriminant ability of the proposed feature. We adopt GMM model as generative model and choose EM algorithm to learn parameters of the GMM model :

Given $m$ training features $x^{(i)}, i = 1, 2 \ldots m$, we first initialize center $\mu_k$ and covariance matrix $\Sigma_k$ using kmeans algorithm.

E step: for each sample $i$ and center $k$, we compute the expectation of probability

$$\alpha_k^{(i)} = p(z^{(i)} = k \mid x^{(i)}; w, \mu, \Sigma) = \frac{p(x^{(i)} \mid z^{(i)} = k, \mu, \Sigma) p(z^{(i)} = k; w)}{\sum\limits_{l=1}^{K} p(x^{(i)} \mid z^{(i)} = l, \mu, \Sigma) p(z^{(i)} = l; w)} \tag{4}$$

M step: update the parameters iteratively:

$$w_k = \frac{1}{m} \sum_{i=1}^{m} \alpha_k^{(i)}, \mu_k = \frac{\sum\limits_{i=1}^{m} \alpha_k^{(i)} x^{(i)}}{\sum\limits_{i=1}^{m} \alpha_k^{(i)}}, \Sigma_k = \frac{\sum\limits_{i=1}^{m} \alpha_k^{(i)} (x^{(i)} - \mu_k)(x^{(i)} - \mu_k)^T}{\sum\limits_{i=1}^{m} \alpha_k^{(i)}} \tag{5}$$

When iteration converges, we will get the GMM generative model dictionary of fisher kernel. Then we can get the derivative of the center and covariance matrix by:

$$g_{\mu,i}^{X} = \frac{1}{T\sqrt{w_i}} \sum_{t=1}^{T} \gamma_t(i)(\frac{x_t - \mu_i}{\sigma_i}) \tag{6}$$

$$g_{\sigma,i}^{X} = \frac{1}{T\sqrt{2w_i}} \sum_{t=1}^{T} \gamma_t(i)[\frac{(x_t - \mu_i)^2}{\sigma_i^2} - 1] \tag{7}$$

$$\gamma_t(i) = \frac{w_i p(x_t \mid \mu_i, \Sigma_i)}{\sum_{j=1}^{K} w_j p(x_t \mid \mu_j, \Sigma_j)} \tag{8}$$

Then we will normalize the feature using $L2$ norm by computing $g_\lambda^X = \frac{g_\lambda^X}{\parallel g_\lambda^X \parallel^2}$,
followed by power normalization method proposed by Florent et al.[8] to get the blur invariant descriptor: $g_\lambda^X = sign(g_\lambda^X) \mid g_\lambda^X \mid^\alpha$, as we partition the face image into $m \times n$
blocks, the final feature can be concatenated as $g_{\lambda,B}^X = \{g_{\lambda,b}^X, b=1,...,B, B=m*n\}$.

## 2.4 Multiple Metric Learning

To further fit the feature to face verification and improve generalization ability, we need to learn a metric that maximizes the feature margins of different persons. Cui et al. [9] proposed PMML method to learn a projection matrix for each block and consider correlation between different image blocks. However, we found that the iteration of the PMML learning algorithm may be divergent especially when dealing with many training samples. The divergence of iteration is caused by hinge loss function and the overall learning rate $\alpha$ shared by all blocks. Now we prove that hinge loss function and overall learning rate may lead to divergence:

To ensure the convergence, the following condition should be satisfied:

$$tr(\mu G_k^T zz^T G_k) = \mu z^T G_k G_k^T z = \mu dW_k(z_i^K, z_j^K) = \mu p_k > -1 \tag{9}$$

where $z = z_i^K - z_j^K$ and $p_k = dW_k(z_i^K, z_j^K)$, assume that $K = 1$, then $\alpha$ is:

$$\frac{p_k}{1 - \alpha p_k} - (\xi_{ij}^t - \frac{n}{2\gamma}\alpha) = 0 \tag{10}$$

$$\mu p_k = \frac{\alpha p_k}{1 - \alpha p_k} = -\frac{n}{2\gamma}\alpha^2 + \xi_{ij}^t\alpha \tag{11}$$

Since $-\frac{n}{2\gamma}$ is determined by sample size $n$ and $\gamma$, we cannot guarantee that
$\mu p_k > -1$ and thus the convergence of the iteration cannot be guaranteed.

To overcome this problem, we adopted LogDet Divergence(Stein's loss) [15] as regularization constraint since LogDet Divergence is scale invariant and convex. Besides, it is proven that using LogDet Divergence for iteration will keep the matrix positive definite. As different face part varies quite a lot , we use different $\alpha_k$ and introduce a slack variable $\xi_k$ for the matrix of each block $W_k$ to update the parameter when $\delta_{ij}dW_k(z_i^k, z_j^k) < (\xi_{ij})_k$. Optimization function of our proposal is:

$$\min_{W_1,...W_K} \frac{1}{K}\sum_{k=1}^{K} D_{ld}(W_k,W_0) + \frac{\gamma}{n}\sum_{i,j}\ell(\xi_{ij},\delta_{ij}\rho-\tau)$$

$$s.t. \quad \frac{\delta_{ij}}{K}\sum_{k=1}^{K} dW_k(z_i^k,z_j^k) \le \xi_{ij} \; and \; \delta_{ij}dW_k(z_i^k,z_j^k) < (\xi_{ij})_k \tag{12}$$

$$where \; \ell(\xi,\xi_0) = \begin{cases} 0 & \frac{\delta_{ij}}{K}\sum_{k=1}^{K} dW_k^t(z_i^k,z_j^k) > \delta_{ij}\rho-\pi \\ D_{ld}(diag(\xi),diag(\xi_0)) & otherwise \end{cases} \tag{13}$$

$$D_{ld}(X,Y) = tr(XY^{-1}) - \log\det(XY^{-1}) - n, \; dW_k(z_i^k,z_j^k) = (z_i^k - z_j^k)^T W_k(z_i^k - z_j^k) \tag{14}$$

The algorithm of the method is shown below, Cholesky method is proposed by Dhillon et al.[16].After we get the projection matrices, we can compute the distance between two input face images by:

$$\rho = mean\{\frac{\delta_{ij}}{K}\sum_{k=1}^{K}(z_i^k - z_j^k)^T W_k(z_i^k - z_j^k), i,j \in G\} \tag{15}$$

---

**Input**: training pairs $\{(z_i^k,z_j^k),\delta_{ij}\}$ and $\rho,\tau,\rho_k,\tau_k,\gamma,G_0$, $G_0 \in R^{n\times r}$

**Initialize** t=1, $G_k^1 = G_0$, $\eta_{ij}^k = 0$, $(\xi_{ij}^k)^1 = \delta_{ij}\rho_k - \tau_k$, $B_k = I_r$, $k=1,...,K$

0: **Repeat** :

1: Pick a pair of samples $(z_i^k,z_j^k)$, compute distance $p_k^t$ for $k=1,...,K$

2: **if** $\frac{\delta_{ij}}{K}\sum_{k=1}^{K} p_k^t > \delta_{ij}\rho - \tau$

3:   **for** $k=1,...,K$ , repeat

4:     **if** $p_k^t > \delta_{ij}\rho_k - \tau_k$

5:     $\alpha_k = \min(\eta_{ij}^k, \frac{\delta_{ij}\gamma}{\gamma+1}(\frac{1}{p_k^t} - \frac{1}{(\xi_{ij}^k)^t}))$

6:     $\eta_{ij}^k = \eta_{ij}^k - \alpha_k$

7:     $\beta = \delta_{ij}\alpha_k / (1 - \delta_{ij}\alpha_k p_k^t)$

8 :     $\omega = (B_k^t)^T G_0^T(z_i^k - z_j^k)$

9:     update $B_k$ by CholUpdateMult$(\beta,\omega,B_k)$

10:     $(\xi_{ij}^k)^{t+1} = \gamma(\xi_{ij}^k)^t / (\gamma + \delta_{ij}\alpha_k(\xi_{ij}^k)^t)$

11:     $t = t+1$

15: **Go back to Step 1 Until convergence**

16: **return** $\{W_k, for \; k=0,...,K\}$, $G_k = G_0 B_k$, $W_k = G_k G_k^T$

where $p_k^t = (z_i^k - z_j^k)^T W_k^t(z_i^k - z_j^k) = (z_i^k - z_j^k)^T G_0 B_k^t(B_k^t)^T G_0^T(z_i^k - z_j^k)$ , $G_0$ is the PCA projection matrix of the training samples

## 3    Experiment

This section shows the experimental result of our proposed approach compared to LBP [1] and LPQ over the blurred ferret dataset [11] and the realistic face dataset. From the experiments we verify the efficiency of our proposal. In default, we extract 3 scale features with win size of M=3,5 and 7, partition the face image into 5*5 blocks, set the number of Gaussian kernels to 32 and set verification threshold to 0.6.

### 3.1    Blurred FERET Face Dataset

Feret dataset is a classical dataset. The training set contains 1002 images from 429 persons. We use the gallery dataset as training set, which contains 1196 gallery face images and use the fafb dataset as prob set by blurring the face images with Gaussian blurriness of $\sigma = \{0,1,2,3,4\}$, examples of blurred face images could be seen in fig.2.

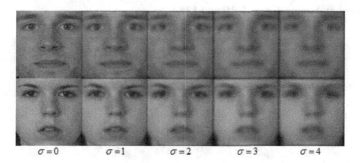

$\sigma=0$     $\sigma=1$     $\sigma=2$     $\sigma=3$     $\sigma=4$

**Fig. 2.** Examples of blurred feret dataset

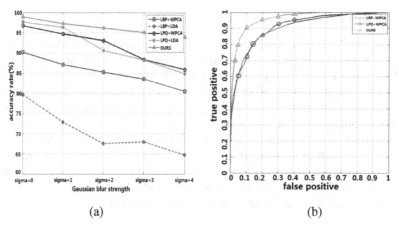

(a)            (b)

**Fig. 3.** (a) Accuracy rate compared to LBP and LPQ over blurred Feret. (b) ROC curve compared to LBP and LPQ over realistic face dataset

We compared our approach with LBP and LPQ, the results are plotted on fig.3. From fig.3a, we can find that the proposal outperforms LBP and LPQ over all blurrness. Besides, as blurriness of face image changes, the accuracy of the proposal remains satisfactory. When $\sigma = 0$ the accuracy of the proposal when recognizing clear images is 98.91% and when $\sigma = 4$ the accuracy is 93.89%,declines only 5%, which is much better than LBP and LPQ, with decline of accuracy of more than 10%.

### 3.2     Realistic Face Dataset

We have also tested the proposed approach in realistic environment, the realistic face dataset contains 3000 persons, the gallery face images are stored in second chinese generation id card, which are of low resolution and blurred. The prob face images are taken under real environment with changes of illumination and pose. We choose 1500 image pairs for training and rest for testing. ROC curve compared with LBP and LPQ is in fig 3b. From the result we can see that the proposal performs well in realistic environment and outperforms LBP and LPQ.

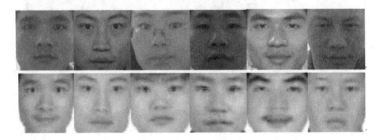

**Fig. 4.** Examples of realistic face dataset

### 3.3     Parameter Analysis

As can be seen in Fig.5a, recognition accuracy increases when number of blocks increases.  However, computation time also increases with the increase of block number. To balance both accuracy and computational efficiency, we choose to partition the input face image into 5x5 blocks. Fig.5b shows the relationship between accuracy and number of gaussian kernels. Similarly, we set gaussian center number 32 to balance both accuracy and computational efficiency.

Relationship between accuracy and scale of feature can be seen in table 1. As we can see, the performance of the proposal will increase if we choose to increase the scale of features. Effect of our Multiple Metric Learning is shown in Fig.6. After metric learning, margin between different person is enlarged and distance between the same person is smaller than distance between different person.

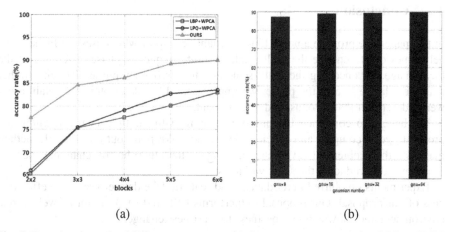

(a)                                              (b)

**Fig. 5.** Experiment result of different parameters. (a) Accuracy rate compared to LBP and LPQ with different block number. (b) Accuracy rate with different number of GMM centers

**Table 1.** Relation between Accuracy Rate and feature scale

| Win size | Accuracy (%) |
|----------|--------------|
| $win = 3$ | 84.26% |
| $win = 3, 5$ | 86.65% |
| $win = 3, 5, 7$ | 90.03% |

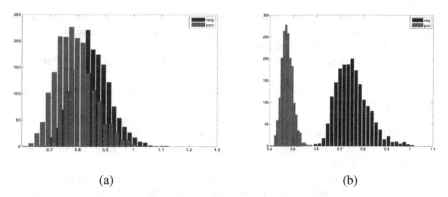

(a)                                              (b)

**Fig. 6.** (a) Data distribution before metric learning. (b) Data distribution after metric learning

### 3.4    Computational Efficiency

Our system is implemented using Matlab R2012b on a Intel(R) Core(TM) i7-4790 CPU @ 3.60GHZ. Time for computing the feature of an input image with size of 128x128 is 0.217 second, which we believe to be fast enough for single image matching but faster computation speed may be needed for tasks like video face matching.

# 4     Conclusion

In this paper, we propose a novel blur invariant descriptor which uses the Fisher Kernel framework to encode the multi-scale absolute frequency phase difference of the local image. By encoding the multi-scale absolute frequency phase difference rather than the relative size of the phase, we improve the LPQ descriptor and obtain a powerful descriptor that is robust and discriminant.

We have also combined the proposed feature with multiple metric learning approach to get a compact and efficient description. We point out that PMML method may face the problem of divergence and revise the algorithm by changing the loss function and introducing the slack variables.

Experiments on blurred Feret dataset and realistic face dataset verify the effectiveness of our proposal. Our proposal outperforms LBP and LPQ, performs well in real environment and shows good robustness to blurriness change.

**Acknowledgments.** This project was supported by National Science & Technology Pillar Program (No. 2012BAK16B06) and GuangZhou Program (2014J4100114,   2014Y2-00165).

# References

1. Ahonen, T., et al.: Face description with local binary patterns: Application to facerecognition. IEEE Transactions on Pattern Analysis and Machine Intelligence (2006)
2. Ahonen, T., et al.: Recognition of blurred faces using local phase quantization. In: ICPR (2008)
3. Ojansivu, V., Heikkilä, J.: Blur insensitive texture classification using local phase quantization. In: Elmoataz, A., Lezoray, O., Nouboud, F., Mammass, D. (eds.) ICISP 2008. LNCS, vol. 5099, pp. 236–243. Springer, Heidelberg (2008)
4. Jaakkola, T, Haussler, D.: Exploiting generative models in discriminative classifiers. NIPS (1999)
5. Perronnin, F, Dance, C.: Fisher kernels on visual vocabularies for image categorization. In: CVPR (2007)
6. Wan, V., Renals, S.: Speaker verification using sequence discriminant support vector machines. IEEE Transactions on Speech and Audio Processing 13(2), 203–210 (2005)
7. Moreno, P.J., Rifkin, R.: Using the fisher kernel method for web audio classification. In: ICASSP 2000 (2000)
8. Perronnin, F., Sánchez, J., Mensink, T.: Improving the fisher kernel for large-scale image classification. In: Daniilidis, K., Maragos, P., Paragios, N. (eds.) ECCV 2010, Part IV. LNCS, vol. 6314, pp. 143–156. Springer, Heidelberg (2010)
9. Cui, Z., et al.: Fusing robust face region descriptors via multiple metric learning for face recognition in the wild. In: CVPR 2013 (2013)
10. Milborrow, S., Nicolls, F.: Locating facial features with an extended active shape model. In: Forsyth, D., Torr, P., Zisserman, A. (eds.) ECCV 2008, Part IV. LNCS, vol. 5305, pp. 504–513. Springer, Heidelberg (2008)
11. Phillips, P.J., et al.: The FERET evaluation methodology for face recognition algorithms. IEEE Transactions on Pattern Analysis and Machine Intelligence (2000)

12. Wang, X., Tang, X.: Hallucinating face by eigen transformation. IEEE Transactions on Systems, Man, and Cybernetics, Part C: Applications and Reviews (2005)
13. Li, B., et al.: Low-resolution face recognition via coupled locality preserving mappings. Signal Processing Letters, IEEE **17**(1), 20–23 (2010)
14. Zhou, C., et al.: Low -resolution face recognition via simultaneous discriminant analysis. IJCB (2011)
15. Davis, J.V., et al.: Information-theoretic metric learning. In: Proceedings of the 24th International Conference on Machine Learning. ACM (2007)
16. Dhillon, I.S., Tropp, J.A.: Matrix nearness problems with Bregman divergences. SIAM Journal on Matrix Analysis and Applications **29**(4), 1120–1146 (2007)

# Modified Numerical Scheme for Perona-Malik Model in Image Restoration

Zhiyi Ruan, Youjian Shen$^{(\boxtimes)}$, and Fengling Liu

College of Mathematics and Statistics, Hainan Normal University,
No. 99 Longkun South Road, Haikou 571158, China
{fafurzy,flliu116}@163.com, yjshen678@qq.com

**Abstract.** This paper proposes a difference scheme based on nonlinear diffusion Perona-Malik model for numerical calculation in image restoration. Our scheme can adapt to determine the tangent directions to the isophote lines based on two mutually orthogonal directional derivatives, which results that diffusion is along the edges as much as possible. One of typical edge stopping functions for Perona-Malik model is modified in order to improve robust calculation and satisfy the compatibility, stability and convergence for our numerical scheme. Computer experimental results indicate that the algorithm corresponding to our numerical scheme is very efficient for noise removal in regardless whether the noise is serious or not.

**Keywords:** Image restoration · Difference scheme · Numerical calculation · Perona-Malik model · Nonlinear diffusion

## 1 Introduction

Historically, image restoration is not only one of the oldest concerns but also one of the most important and fundamental tasks [1]. Removing the noise while preserving image edges is difficult but much desired. Nowadays, for this aim there emerge three main directions: stochastic modeling, wavelets and partial differential equation (PDE) approaches [2][3].

For PDE-based methods, Perona-Malik (P-M) model (ref. [4]) is considered to be the most classic equation so that it has attracted much attention in recent decades; see [5], [6] and [7], etc. However, P-M model is pathological [5][8]. In other words, robust calculation of diffusion coefficient is a severe challenge for the model when the noise of the initial image is sharp oscillation. A classical method to overcome this disadvantage is the smooth version of P-M model proposed by Catté et al. in [5]. As two-dimensional Gaussian kernel $G_\sigma$ is introduced into edge stopping function, their model can smooth the flat and edge regions adaptively. However, it's difficult to choose proper scale parameter $\sigma$. In order to further improve the cases depending seriously on the gradient values of an image, Guo et al. proposed an adaptive P-M model by variable exponent term $|\nabla u|^{\alpha(|\nabla G_\sigma * u|^2)}$ (Edge indicator function must satisfy $0 \leq \alpha(\cdot) \leq 2$.) replacing

© Springer-Verlag Berlin Heidelberg 2015
H. Zha et al. (Eds.): CCCV 2015, Part I, CCIS 546, pp. 366–375, 2015.
DOI: 10.1007/978-3-662-48558-3_37

$|\nabla u|^2$ for edge stopping function in [7]. When the model is applied to image processing, experimental results show that it can achieve higher quality images for peak signal to noise ratio (PSNR) and image edge has been preserved better. A similar model was mentioned by Maiseli et al. [9] with different edge indicator function from [7].

This paper improves robust calculation of P-M model by modifying one of typical edge stopping functions. Meanwhile, we present a new numerical scheme for P-M model. P-M model is recalled in Sect. 2.1 and our scheme is deduced from the aspect of numerical analysis in Sect. 2.2. According to the product of two mutually orthogonal directional derivatives is negative or not, we give two distinct second-order mixed partial derivatives. The form of our difference equation makes diffusion along the edges (the isophote lines) as much as possible. Thus, our scheme neither has very strong isotropic smoothing properties like heat equation nor restores images only depending on the difference of gray level value among different pixels. After proving the compatibility, stability and convergence of the difference equation (Sect. 2.3), Sect. 3 makes use of Lena image and Cameraman image added Gaussian noise for different variances to test the capability of our new scheme in image restoration. Compared with those models proposed by [4], [5] and [7], experimental results show that our algorithm has significant advantages. Conclusion is in Sect. 4.

## 2 Nonlinear Diffusion in Image Restoration

In image processing, the oldest and most investigated equation is probably the parabolic linear heat equation [10][11]. Although it has successful applications, there exists a drawback that it is too smoothing so that edges will be lost, i.e., image becomes severely blurred after being processed. Many researchers have tried to find more effective models or algorithms for removing the noise while preserving the edge as much as possible [1].

### 2.1 Perona-Malik Model

In [4], Perona and Malik proposed anisotropic diffusion equation as follows

$$u_t = div(c(|\nabla u|^2)\nabla u), \ u(x,y,0) = u_0(x,y), \tag{1}$$

which is called P-M model, where $u_0$ is initial image and edge stopping function $c(\cdot)$ is strictly monotonically decreasing function satisfying $c(0) = 1$, $c(s) \geq 0$ and $c(s) \rightarrow 0$ as $s \rightarrow +\infty$. In addition, denoting respectively by $div$ and $\nabla$ the divergence operator and the gradient operator (i.e., $\nabla u = (u_x, u_y)$ and $|\nabla u|^2 = u_x^2 + u_y^2$) with respect to the space variables $(x, y)$.

After researching experiment, there are two edge stopping functions adopted widely, i.e., $c(s) = (1 + s/K)^{-1}$ and $c(s) = exp(-s/K)$, where $K$ is a positive constant. For the former, we will investigate further the function $c(s) = (1 + s/K)^{-1/3}$ in improving robust calculation of P-M model.

On the one hand, in flat areas P-M model acts as the heat equation which is isotropic smoothing since $c$ approximates to a constant as the value of the gradient is almost equal to zero. On the other hand, its regularization near the region's boundaries is weaken even stopped such that the edge are preserved.

According to the definition of divergence operator, (1) can be written as the form of second-order partial derivatives in spatial directions, i.e.,

$$\frac{\partial u}{\partial t} = c_{11}(\nabla u) \cdot u_{xx} + 2c_{12}(\nabla u) \cdot u_{xy} + c_{22}(\nabla u) \cdot u_{yy}, \tag{2}$$

where diffusion coefficients satisfy

$$\begin{cases} c_{11}(\nabla u) = 2u_x^2 c'(|\nabla u|^2) + c(|\nabla u|^2), \\ c_{12}(\nabla u) = 2u_x u_y c'(|\nabla u|^2), \\ c_{22}(\nabla u) = 2u_y^2 c'(|\nabla u|^2) + c(|\nabla u|^2). \end{cases}$$

To facilitate the writing, in the back content $c_{11}(\nabla u)$, $c_{12}(\nabla u)$, and $c_{22}(\nabla u)$ is abbreviated as $c_{11}$, $c_{12}$, and $c_{22}$, respectively.

## 2.2   Modified Numerical Scheme

As a matter of fact, a stable 4-nearest-neighbors discretization of Laplacian operator given by [4] for P-M model is weaken even almost stopped when the value of $|\nabla u|$ is tremendous. In such a case, the edge are protected, but noise on the edge is still retained. On the one hand, if the noise of the initial image $u_0$ is sharp oscillations, P-M model will face a severe challenge which is how to calculate robustly the diffusion coefficients $c$ from the outset. On the other hand, it's difficult to identify the true boundary or "boundary" caused by noise. Unfortunately, P-M model with the 4-nearest-neighbors discretization of Laplacian operator can't exhibit theoretically expected effect in practical applications.

Finite difference method is utilized for the discretization of partial derivatives since digital image has a natural regular grid. In this Section, we will transform P-M model into an explicit difference scheme for the numerical calculation. In terms of (2), the differential quotients with respect to the spatial variables $(x, y)$ are approximated by center difference quotients and the differential quotient with respect to the temporal variable $t$ is approximated by forward difference quotient in this paper.

Introduce the time step size $\Delta t$ and the spatial step sizes $\Delta x$, $\Delta y$ into difference equation, i.e., $t = n \cdot \Delta t$, $x = i \cdot \Delta x$ and $y = j \cdot \Delta y$. It follows that

$$\left(\frac{\partial u}{\partial t}\right)^n = \frac{u^{n+1} - u^n}{\Delta t}, \left(\frac{\partial u}{\partial x}\right)_{i,j} = \frac{u_{i+1,j} - u_{i-1,j}}{2\Delta x}, \left(\frac{\partial u}{\partial y}\right)_{i,j} = \frac{u_{i,j+1} - u_{i,j-1}}{2\Delta y},$$

$$\left(\frac{\partial^2 u}{\partial x^2}\right)_{i,j} = \frac{u_{i+1,j} - 2u_{i,j} + u_{i-1,j}}{(\Delta x)^2}, \left(\frac{\partial^2 u}{\partial y^2}\right)_{i,j} = \frac{u_{i,j+1} - 2u_{i,j} + u_{i,j-1}}{(\Delta y)^2}.$$

$$\tag{3}$$

It is necessary to point out that the difference quotient of second-order mixed partial derivative used commonly (e.g., given in [12]):

$$\left(\frac{\partial^2 u}{\partial x \partial y}\right)_{i,j} = \frac{u_{i+1,j+1} - u_{i+1,j-1} - u_{i-1,j+1} + u_{i-1,j-1}}{4\Delta x \Delta y}$$

couldn't make sure of the stability and convergence of the corresponding difference scheme in iterative procedure. Considering the coefficients of $u_{i+1,j+1}$, $u_{i+1,j-1}$, $u_{i-1,j+1}$ and $u_{i-1,j-1}$ in the difference quotient mentioned as above, half are negative and half are positive. Furthermore, the righthand coefficients of (2) rely strictly upon two mutually orthogonal directional derivatives in numerically. Therefore, this difference equation doesn't satisfy the maximum principle.

Without loss of generality, we set $k = \Delta t$ and $h = \Delta x = \Delta y$. As $h \to 0$, let's consider Taylor Expansions of four terms $u_{i+1,j+1}$, $u_{i+1,j-1}$, $u_{i-1,j+1}$ and $u_{i-1,j-1}$ at point $(i,j)$, i.e.,

$$u_{i+1,j+1} = \left[1 + h\left(\frac{\partial}{\partial x} + \frac{\partial}{\partial y}\right) + \frac{h^2}{2}\left(\frac{\partial}{\partial x} + \frac{\partial}{\partial y}\right)^2 + \frac{h^3}{6}\left(\frac{\partial}{\partial x} + \frac{\partial}{\partial y}\right)^3\right] u_{i,j}, \quad (4)$$

$$u_{i+1,j-1} = \left[1 + h\left(\frac{\partial}{\partial x} - \frac{\partial}{\partial y}\right) + \frac{h^2}{2}\left(\frac{\partial}{\partial x} - \frac{\partial}{\partial y}\right)^2 + \frac{h^3}{6}\left(\frac{\partial}{\partial x} - \frac{\partial}{\partial y}\right)^3\right] u_{i,j}, \quad (5)$$

$$u_{i-1,j+1} = \left[1 - h\left(\frac{\partial}{\partial x} - \frac{\partial}{\partial y}\right) + \frac{h^2}{2}\left(\frac{\partial}{\partial x} - \frac{\partial}{\partial y}\right)^2 - \frac{h^3}{6}\left(\frac{\partial}{\partial x} - \frac{\partial}{\partial y}\right)^3\right] u_{i,j}, \quad (6)$$

$$u_{i-1,j-1} = \left[1 - h\left(\frac{\partial}{\partial x} + \frac{\partial}{\partial y}\right) + \frac{h^2}{2}\left(\frac{\partial}{\partial x} + \frac{\partial}{\partial y}\right)^2 - \frac{h^3}{6}\left(\frac{\partial}{\partial x} + \frac{\partial}{\partial y}\right)^3\right] u_{i,j}, \quad (7)$$

where all of remainders are $\mathcal{O}(h^4)$. To eliminate first-order partial derivatives, let (5) add (6) and (4) add (7). Therefore, we deduce the following two equations with respect to second-order mixed partial derivative:

$$2\left(\frac{\partial^2 u}{\partial x \partial y}\right)_{i,j} = \frac{2u_{i,j} - u_{i+1,j-1} - u_{i-1,j+1}}{h^2} + \left(\frac{\partial^2 u}{\partial x^2} + \frac{\partial^2 u}{\partial y^2}\right)_{i,j} + \mathcal{O}(h^2), \quad (8)$$

$$2\left(\frac{\partial^2 u}{\partial x \partial y}\right)_{i,j} = \frac{u_{i+1,j+1} + u_{i-1,j-1} - 2u_{i,j}}{h^2} - \left(\frac{\partial^2 u}{\partial x^2} + \frac{\partial^2 u}{\partial y^2}\right)_{i,j} + \mathcal{O}(h^2). \quad (9)$$

For the discrete approximation of $u_{xy}$ in (2), we choose to apply (8) if coefficient $c_{12}$ is negative, and (9) if $c_{12}$ is nonnegative. Our choices can fundamentally avoid the divergent and unstable result caused from the case mentioned as above for the difference form given by [12]. In addition, it's possible to result in appearing negative coefficients for other terms (for example, $u_{i,j}$, $u_{i+1,j}$ and $u_{i,j-1}$, etc). However, we only require some appropriate constraints for this.

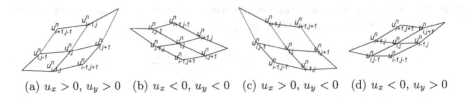

(a) $u_x > 0$, $u_y > 0$   (b) $u_x < 0$, $u_y < 0$   (c) $u_x > 0$, $u_y < 0$   (d) $u_x < 0$, $u_y > 0$

**Fig. 1.** Illustration of Difference Equation (10)

In such choices, we obtain the following Difference Equation of P-M model by (3), (8) and (9):

$$
u_{i,j}^{n+1} = \begin{cases} C_1 u_{i,j}^n + C_2 u_{i+1,j}^n + C_2 u_{i-1,j}^n + C_3 u_{i,j+1}^n \\ \quad + C_3 u_{i,j-1}^n + C_4 u_{i+1,j-1}^n + C_4 u_{i-1,j+1}^n, & \text{if } c_{12} < 0 \\ C_1 u_{i,j}^n + C_2 u_{i+1,j}^n + C_2 u_{i-1,j}^n + C_3 u_{i,j+1}^n \\ \quad + C_3 u_{i,j-1}^n + C_4 u_{i+1,j+1}^n + C_4 u_{i-1,j-1}^n, & \text{if } c_{12} \geq 0 \end{cases}
\tag{10}
$$

where

$$
\begin{cases} C_1 = 1 - 2rc_{11} - 2rc_{22} + 2r|c_{12}|, \\ C_2 = r(c_{11} - |c_{12}|), \\ C_3 = r(c_{22} - |c_{12}|), \\ C_4 = r|c_{12}|, \end{cases}
$$

where $r = k/h^2$. There is no doubt that ideal initial values are original degraded noisy images. As shown in Fig. 1, it's not hard to see that the diffusion form is related closely with the tangent directions to the isophote lines in image.

## 2.3   Compatibility, Stability and Convergence

**Theorem 1.** *Difference Equation (10) is compatible with (2).*

*Proof.* Firstly, we prove the theorem in the case $c_{12} < 0$. We obtain local truncation error of (10) as follows

$$
T_{i,j}^n = \left[ \frac{u_{i,j}^{n+1} - u_{i,j}^n}{k} - |c_{12}| \frac{u_{i+1,j-1}^n + u_{i-1,j+1}^n - 2u_{i,j}^n}{h^2} \right.
$$
$$
\left. - (c_{11} - |c_{12}|) \frac{u_{i+1,j}^n + u_{i-1,j}^n - 2u_{i,j}^n}{h^2} - (c_{22} - |c_{12}|) \frac{u_{i,j+1}^n + u_{i,j-1}^n - 2u_{i,j}^n}{h^2} \right]
$$
$$
- \left[ \frac{\partial u}{\partial t} - \left( c_{11} \frac{\partial^2 u}{\partial x^2} + 2c_{12} \frac{\partial^2 u}{\partial x \partial y} + c_{22} \frac{\partial^2 u}{\partial y^2} \right) \right]_{i,j}^n .
$$

As $k \to 0$ and $h \to 0$, we have Taylor Expansions of the righthand terms $u_{i,j}^{n+1}$, $u_{i+1,j}^n$ and $u_{i-1,j+1}^n$, etc. in (10) at point $(i, j, n)$. Then, it is easy to deduce that $T_{i,j}^n = \mathcal{O}(k + h^2) \to 0$.

For the case $c_{12} \geq 0$, the same result can be obtained similarly. Consequently, we conclude that (10) is compatible with (2).                                                    □

**Theorem 2.** For $c(s) = (1 + s/K)^{-p}$ $(0 < p \le 1/3)$, Difference Equation (10) is stable if $r \le 1/4$.

*Proof.* It's apparent from (10) that the sum of the righthand coefficients $C_i$ ($i = 1, \cdots, 4$) is equal to 1. Firstly, we will prove that every coefficient is nonnegative, i.e.,

$$\begin{cases} 1 - 4r\left[(u_x^2 + u_y^2 + |u_xu_y|)c'(|\nabla u|^2) + c(|\nabla u|^2)\right] \ge 0, \\ r\left[2(max\{u_x^2, u_y^2\} + |u_xu_y|)c'(|\nabla u|^2) + c(|\nabla u|^2)\right] \ge 0, \\ -2r|u_xu_y|c'(|\nabla u|^2) \ge 0. \end{cases} \tag{11}$$

In fact, according to the monotonicity of edge stopping function $c(\cdot)$, the last inequality of (11) is naturally true because both the time and spatial step size are positive constants. Next, let's prove the second inequality of (11). It is straightforward to show that

$$2(max\{u_x^2, u_y^2\} + |u_xu_y|) \le 2(u_x^2 + u_y^2) + (u_x^2 + u_y^2) = 3|\nabla u|^2.$$

By differentiating the function $c(s) = (1 + s/K)^{-p}$ with respect to $s$, we can get

$$c'(s) = -\frac{p/K}{(1 + s/K)^{p+1}} = -\frac{p/K}{1 + s/K}c(s).$$

For $p \le 1/3$, we can deduce

$$2(max\{u_x^2, u_y^2\} + |u_xu_y|)c'(|\nabla u|^2) + c(|\nabla u|^2) \ge 0.$$

Similarly, in terms of the first inequality, we can easily obtain

$$0 \le (u_x^2 + u_y^2 + |u_xu_y|)c'(|\nabla u|^2) + c(|\nabla u|^2) \le 1.$$

So the first inequality of (11) is true if $r \le 1/4$.

Denoting by $u_{max}^0$ and $u_{min}^0$ the maximum and minimum of initial values respectively. In fact, we can obtain

$$u_{min}^0 \le u_{i,j}^n \le u_{max}^0$$

for every $(i, j, n)$ by means of the maximum principle. More generally, for each positive integer $n$ there exists a positive constant $P$ such that

$$\|u^n\| \le P\|u^0\|,$$

where the norm $\|u\| = \left[\sum_{i,j}(u_{i,j})^2\right]^{\frac{1}{2}}$. Combined this with Theorem 1, the conclusion is proved. $\square$

Therefore, all values always remain boundedness in the whole iterative procedure. In fact, as has been proved in Theorem 2, the gray level value of all pixels will tend to some constant with increasing of iteration count. In general, it is a common drawback for the explicit difference scheme. Thus, we need to control the number of iterations to avoid blurring the image.

Since (10) is linear, we obtain the following theorem (ref. [13]):

**Theorem 3.** Under Theorem 1, stability of Difference Equation (10) is a necessary and sufficient condition that it be convergent.

## 3    Numerical Comparison

In this Section, we will compare the denoising effect of the algorithm for our numerical scheme with the algorithms for P-M model [4], Catté-Lions-Morel-Coll (C-L-M-C) model [5] and Guo-Sun-Zhang-Wu (G-S-Z-W) model [7] which are programmed by 4-nearest-neighbors discretization of Laplacian operator. These denoising algorithms are tested on standard Lena image (see Fig. 2(a)), Cameraman image (see Fig. 2(b)) and the versions added Gaussian noise for different variances. Gray level value of each pixel is an integer from 0 to 255.

(a) Lena     (b) Cameraman

**Fig. 2.** The standard images ($512 \times 512$ pixels)

PSNR which is applied to evaluate the quality of the restored images in this paper is defined as

$$PSNR = 10 \times \log \left( \frac{255^2}{MSE} \right),$$

where $MSE$ (mean square error) is defined as

$$MSE = \frac{\sum_{j=1}^{N} \sum_{i=1}^{M} \left[ u_{i,j} - (u_0)_{i,j} \right]^2}{M \times N},$$

where $M$ and $N$ represent respectively the number of image pixels in rows and columns. All algorithms are run in Matlab R2008a on a Pentium(R) Dual-Core CPU T4300 @ 2.10GHz processor. In addition, the iterative stopping criterion of all algorithms is set to acquire the maximal PSNR.

First noisy observation is generated by adding the Gaussian white noise for mean $\mu = 0$ and standard deviation $\sigma = 25$ into Lena image ($PSNR = 22.6017$, see Fig. 3(a)). All parameters used in these denoising algorithms are shown in the title of Fig. 3 ($r = 0.1$, $c_1(s) = (1 + s)^{-1/3}$ and $c_2(s) = (1 + s/32)^{-1}$). The denoising effect is shown in Fig. 3(b)-3(f). PSNR and iteration count are seen in Table 1.

As can be seen from Table 1, PSNR and iteration count of the algorithm corresponding to our scheme is essentially flat with the algorithms for C-L-M-C model and G-S-Z-W model. For the 4-nearest-neighbors discretization of P-M model, $c_2(s)$ performs worse than $c_1(s)$ and becomes the worst by lowest PSNR and largest iteration count. Judging from this, the function $c(s) = (1 + s/K)^{-1/3}$

(a)        (b)        (c)        (d)        (e)        (f)

**Fig. 3.** Lena image. (a) Noise image corrupted by Gaussian noise for $\sigma = 25$; (b) Our algorithm with $c_1(s)$; (c) P-M model with $c_1(s)$; (d) P-M model with $c_2(s)$; (e) C-L-M-C model with $c_2(s)$, $\sigma = 0.5$ for Gaussian kernel; (f) G-S-Z-W model with $c_2(s)$, $\sigma = 0.5$ for Gaussian kernel and $k = 0.5$ for variable exponent coefficient.

**Table 1.** PSNR (dB) and iteration count (steps) for Fig. 3

|  | (b) | (c) | (d) | (e) | (f) |
|---|---|---|---|---|---|
| PSNR | 33.7858 | 33.4970 | 31.7632 | 33.6233 | 33.6192 |
| Iteration count | 84 | 69 | 192 | 94 | 90 |

(a)        (b)        (c)        (d)        (e)        (f)

**Fig. 4.** Lena image. (a) Noise image corrupted by Gaussian noise for $\sigma = 100$; (b) Our algorithm with $c_1(s)$; (c) P-M model with $c_1(s)$; (d) P-M model with $c_2(s)$; (e) C-L-M-C model with $c_2(s)$, $\sigma = 1.5$ for Gaussian kernel; (f) G-S-Z-W model with $c_2(s)$, $\sigma = 1.5$ for Gaussian kernel and $k = 1$ for variable exponent coefficient.

**Table 2.** PSNR (dB) and iteration count (steps) for Fig. 4

|  | (b) | (c) | (d) | (e) | (f) |
|---|---|---|---|---|---|
| PSNR | 25.1603 | 23.8122 | 22.9253 | 23.9372 | 23.9288 |
| Iteration count | 288 | 208 | 1331 | 192 | 188 |

is more beneficial for calculating robustly of P-M model than typical function $c(s) = (1 + s/K)^{-1}$.

Second noisy observation is generated by adding the Gaussian white noise for mean $\mu = 0$ and standard deviation $\sigma = 100$ into Lena image ($PSNR = 12.5610$, see Fig. 4(a)). All parameters used in these denoising algorithms are shown in the title of Fig. 4 ($r = 0.1$, $c_1(s) = (1 + s)^{-1/3}$ and $c_2(s) = (1 + s/32)^{-1}$). The denoising effect is shown in Fig. 4(b)-4(f). PSNR and iteration count are seen in Table 2.

Last noisy observation is generated by adding the Gaussian white noise for mean $\mu = 0$ and standard deviation $\sigma = 100$ into Cameraman image ($PSNR =$

13.1543, see Fig. 5(a)). All parameters used in these denoising algorithms are shown in the title of Fig. 5 ($r = 0.2$, $c_1(s) = (1+s)^{-1/3}$ and $c_2(s) = (1+s/16)^{-1}$). The denoising effect is shown in Fig. 5(b)-5(f). PSNR and iteration count are seen in Table 3.

(a)          (b)          (c)          (d)          (e)          (f)

**Fig. 5.** Cameraman image. (a) Noise image corrupted by Gaussian noise for $\sigma = 100$; (b) Our algorithm with $c_1(s)$; (c) P-M model with $c_1(s)$; (d) P-M model with $c_2(s)$; (e) C-L-M-C model with $c_2(s)$, $\sigma = 1.5$ for Gaussian kernel; (f) G-S-Z-W model with $c_2(s)$, $\sigma = 1.5$ for Gaussian kernel and $k = 1$ for variable exponent coefficient.

**Table 3.** PSNR (dB) and iteration count (steps) for Fig. 5

|                 | (b)     | (c)     | (d)     | (e)     | (f)     |
|-----------------|---------|---------|---------|---------|---------|
| PSNR            | 23.1283 | 21.9037 | 21.2401 | 22.1715 | 22.1549 |
| Iteration count | 141     | 104     | 1292    | 147     | 144     |

Obviously, ours performs best in these denoising algorithms according to the comparison data seen in Table 2 and 3 in spite of being added more noise. And the experimental results have almost no difference among the algorithms for P-M model with $c_1(s)$, C-L-M-C model and G-S-Z-W model with $c_2(s)$. The denoising effect of P-M model with $c_2(s)$ is still the worst. This indicates again that $c(s) = (1 + s/K)^{-1/3}$ is indeed conducive to improve robust calculation of P-M model.

## 4    Conclusion

This paper proposes a modified numerical scheme based on nonlinear diffusion P-M model in image restoration. Our new scheme not only has isotropic smoothing properties acting as heat equation, but can calculate the diffusion intensity relying on the gradient value of gray image like P-M model. Furthermore, it also can determine adaptively the diffusion directions according to the gray level value of pixels in images. Judging from experimental results, our algorithm is more effective in achieving the purpose of diffusing along the edges than the algorithms for P-M model etc. which are programmed by 4-nearest-neighbors discretization of Laplacian operator. Meanwhile, in terms of calculating robustly, the function $c(s) = (1 + s/K)^{-1/3}$ is more suitable to be adopted for P-M model.

**Acknowledgments.** The authors would like to thank the National Natural Science Foundation of China (Grant No. 11461018) and the Postgraduate Innovative Research Project of Hainan Province in China (Grant No. Hys2014-55).

# References

1. Aubert, G., Kornprobst, P.: Mathematical Problems in Image Processing: Partial Differential Equations and the Calculus of Variations. Applied Mathematical Sciences. Springer, New York (2002)
2. Chan, T.F., Shen, J.: Image Processing and Analysis: Variational, PDE, Wavelet, and Stochastic Methods. SIAM, Philadelphia (2005)
3. Aubert, G., Kornprobst, P.: Mathematics of Image Processing. Encyclopedia of Mathematical Physics **3**, 1–9 (2006)
4. Perona, P., Malik, J.: Scale-space and Edge Detection using Anisotropic Diffusion. IEEE Transactions on Pattern Analysis and Machine Intelligence **12**(7), 629–639 (1990)
5. Catté, F., Lions, P.L., Morel, J.M., et al.: Image Selective Smoothing and Edge Detection by Nonlinear Diffusion. SIAM Journal of Numerical Analysis **29**, 182–193 (1992)
6. Colombo, M., Gobbino, M.: Slow Time Behavior of the Semidiscrete Perona-Malik Scheme in One Dimension. SIAM Journal of Mathematical Analysis **43**(6), 2564–2600 (2011)
7. Guo, Z., Sun, J., Zhang, D., et al.: Adaptive Perona-Malik Model Based on the Variable Exponent for Image Denoising. IEEE Transactions on Image Processing **21**(3), 958–967 (2012)
8. Kichenassamy, S.: The Perona-Malik paradox. SIAM Journal of Applied Mathematics **57**(5), 1328–1342 (1997)
9. Maiseli, B., Elisha, O., Mei, J., et al.: Edge Preservation Image Enlargement and Enhancement Method Based on the Adaptive Perona-Malik Non-linear Diffusion Model. IET Image Processing **8**(12), 753–760 (2014)
10. Koenderink, J.J.: The Structure of Images. Biological Cybernetics **50**, 363–370 (1984)
11. ter Bart, M.: Haar Romeny: Geometry-driven Diffusion in Computer Vision. Computational Imaging and Vision. Kluwer Academic Publishers, Dordrecht (1994)
12. Xiao, Z., Xu, Z., Zhang, F., et al.: ESPI Filtering Method Based on Anisotropic coherence Diffusion and Perona-Malik Diffusion. Chinese Optics Letters **11**, 101101-1–101101-4 (2013)
13. Lax, P.D., Richtmyer, R.D.: Survey of the Stability of Linear Finite Difference Equations. Connumcarrons on Pure and Applied Mathematics **ix**, 267–293 (1956)

# Abnormal Event Detection Based on Multi-scale Markov Random Field

Lei Qin[1]([✉]), Yituo Ye[2], Li Su[2], and Qingming Huang[2]

[1] Key Lab of Intelligent Information Processing of Chinese Academy
of Sciences (CAS), Institute of Computing Technology, CAS, Beijing 100190, China
qinlei@ict.ac.cn
[2] School of Computer and Control Engineering,
University of Chinese Academy of Sciences, Beijing 100190, China

**Abstract.** In this paper, we present a novel unsupervised method for abnormal behavior detection, which considers both local and global contextual information. For the local contextual representation, we firstly divide video frames into local regions, then extract low-level feature such as histogram of orientated optical flow (HOF) and sequential feature which is composed of K temporal adjacent frames for each region. The global contextual feature encodes the statistical characteristics of those local features like orientation entropy and magnitude variance. An online clustering algorithm is introduced to generate dictionaries for the local and global features respectively. Then, for any new incoming feature, a maximum posterior estimation of the degree of normality is computed by multi-scale Markov Random Field (mMRF) based on the learned model. The proposed method is evaluated on hours of real world surveillance videos. Experimental results validate the effectiveness of the method, and the detection performance is promising.

**Keywords:** Computer vision · Anomaly detection · Multi-scale markov random field

## 1 Introduction

Detecting abnormal behaviors in videos is one of the most promising fields in computer vision. It is receiving increasing attention due to its wide range of practical applications such as smart surveillance, suggesting frames of interest that should be analyzed by an expert, and summarizing the interesting content.

However, there are still several problems in anomaly detection especially for the scene consisting of complex correlated activities performed by multiple people. Firstly, unusual activities seldom occur and the large intraclass diversity of unusual and usual activities makes them even harder to be predefined. The main paradigm for abnormality detection in videos recently is to extract features and to learn a model on normal samples from the video. So that anomaly is detected as the one fitting the model badly. Various methods may differ in the feature they used and the model they built. Secondly, the visual context for scene

© Springer-Verlag Berlin Heidelberg 2015
H. Zha et al. (Eds.): CCCV 2015, Part I, CCIS 546, pp. 376–386, 2015.
DOI: 10.1007/978-3-662-48558-3_38

tends to change over time, which makes the incrementally updated process even more necessary.

Based on these problems, several methods have been proposed. Specifically,[2], [4], [11] determine abnormality based on the trajectory for each object. However, trajectory is too dependent on the tracking algorithm and may be unreliable in crowd scenes. [1] proposes a simple approach that measures typical optical flow speed and direction for each local grid to determine anomaly. Yet this method discards the relationship among local regions which may contain the contextual information. Approaches using Bayesian topic model [7], [13] evaluate the abnormality based on the interaction of local activities, but they only run in batch mode. Mehran et al. [9] present a new way to formulate the abnormal crowd behavior by adopting the social force model, and then use Latent Dirichlet Allocation (LDA) to detect abnormality. In [12], they define a chaotic invariant to describe the event. [6] utilizes a space-time Markov random field model for abnormality detection and the events that could not be described by the model is regarded as anomaly. [14] provides a framework using sparse coding method which builds a dictionary for spatial-temporal cuboid dynamically and anomaly is detected as the one with a large value of the proposed objective function.

Methods[9] can be viewed as "global", for they attempt to find the global abnormal event (GAE) in a video clip. Methods [1], [14], [6], in contrast, focus on the local abnormal event (LAE). However, few methods can be applied both in global and local scale as the situations are often different. Additionally, most methods directly utilize the low level feature such as optical flow, but these features may be not stable enough and may discard some useful contextual information. So how to take contextual information into consideration is important for the abnormal event detection.

In this work, we introduce a novel unsupervised method based on contextual information and mMRF. In the feature part, both local and global features are utilized, which are corresponding to the different scales of the mMRF. For the local scale, we divide each frame of the video into a grid of local regions. HOF is used to encode the low level information, and sequence composed of K adjacent frames is also extracted for the local feature representation. Sequence characters the temporal relationship of the low level features for each local region and it may bring more contextual information. The global feature corresponds to the global scale in mMRF, and it is used to describe the situation for the whole frame with utilizing features such as orientation entropy,magnitude variance. In the model part, mMRF is employed. It can describe the spatial relationship between the local features. Different from the space-time markov random field model proposed by [6], structure of mMRF is hierarchical and it combined different scale of features. It can deal with both GAE and LAE.

The contributions of our methods are mainly two folds: first, contextual information is introduced to describe the action more precisely, take loitering activity in the subway station dataset [1] as an example, a person would stay a few frames in the video and this may be well described by the sequential information.

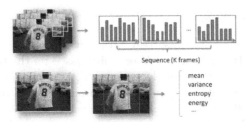

**Fig. 1.** Both local and global feature, the upper row show the sequential information used in this paper, and the bottom one show the global feature which is the statistical information of all the local feature.

Second, mMRF extends MRF to multiple scale, it combines the features in different scales so that mMRF can cope with both LAE and GAE.

## 2   Activity Representation

In this section, local feature, global feature and the corresponding similarity function are presented in section 2.1. Then model acquisition and maintenance using online clustering algorithm is illustrated in section 2.2.

### 2.1   Features and the Corresponding Similarity

**Local Feature.** First, each frame is divided into $M$ by $N$ local regions. The number of local regions depends on how finely we want to capture the motion details. For every local region, two kinds of information are utilized, the low level information (HOF) and the sequential information.

As Fig.1 shows, a sequence is defined as $K$ temporal adjacent frames for every local region, which can be represented by $K$ histograms. Sequence takes the temporal relationship between the HOF features into consideration and it may bring more contextual information. Over all, we combine HOF and sequential information to describe the local activity in this paper.

**Similarity of the Local Feature.** For the low level information such as HOF, we directly use the common chi-square distance to measure their similarity, and we denote $sim_f(f_1, f_2)$ for the similarity of these features, where $f_1$ and $f_2$ denote the low level feature. As for the sequential information proposed above, the similarity of sequences should obey several requirements. 1) The similarity should take alignment into consideration. For sequences of the same action may be segmented in different ways but their similarity should be high. 2) The similarity should be able to measure sequences with different length.

We utilize the edit distance [10] mainly used in natural language processing to measure the similarity between sequences. On the whole, edit distance measures the number of operations required to transform a string into another. The basic operations include replacement, delete and insert. For example, edit distance of string '1234' and '123' is 1 with a delete or insert operation, and distance of string '1234' and '1235' is also 1 with a replace operation. Meanwhile, edit distance of two strings sharing a similar structure would be small. Edit distance of string '1234' with '4123' is 2, with a delete and insert operation, however the traditional distance of them is 4, for every two elements at the same position are different. So it can contribute to the alignment. As described above, requirement 1) and 2) would be satisfied by the edit distance. We denote $sim_s(s_1, s_2)$ as the similarity of sequences. $s_1$ and $s_2$ just represent two sequences.

It should be noted that elements of the sequence are histograms. Chi-square distance and a threshold $\theta$ is used to determine whether they are equal in this paper, given by

$$equal(H_1, H_2) = \begin{cases} 1, \chi^2(H_1, H_2) < \theta \\ 0, otherwise \end{cases} \tag{1}$$

Based on this function, edit distance [10] can be introduced to measure the similarity between the two sequences and it is computed using a dynamic programming algorithm.

**Global Feature.** Global feature should represent the condition of the whole frame, and we use statistical value of the local regions to characterize it, for example, the mean moving orientation, the disorder of the orientation and so on. In this paper, orientation entropy, magnitude entropy, orientation variance, magnitude variance [5] and Kinetic Energy [15] are utilized. By using these global features, we can have a general idea about what happened in each frame, and this may be hard for local feature alone. For the distance for global feature, we just use the Euclidean distance to measure their similarity and $sim_g(g_1, g_2)$ is used to denote the similarity, where $g_1$ and $g_2$ denote the global feature.

### 2.2   Model Acquisition and Maintenance

For the first M frames, with the local feature as sequence and the global feature, an online clustering algorithm is introduced to construct the model. In this paper, basic leader-follower clustering algorithm [3] is utilized. The main procedure is as follows: given a new sample $x$, find its nearest clustering center $w_j$ and the corresponding distance $d$. If $d$ is smaller than a threshold $\sigma$ , the clustering center should be modulated, otherwise a new clustering center should be added. Dictionaries of the local feature and global feature are stored in the model, and they would be updated by the new coming features.

## 3   Abnormality Detection Based on Multi-scale MRF

### 3.1   Structure of Multi-scale MRF

In this paper, we just use two scales for the mMRF, global and local scale. As the Fig. 2 shows, the global scale is for the full frame, and we divide frames into a grid of small regions ($M$ by $N$) for local scale. Each local region denotes a local node and the whole frame represents the global node. The blue nodes mean the

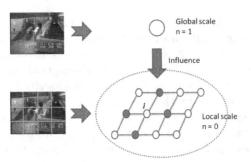

**Fig. 2.** Structure of the mMRF.

neighbors of node $i$ in the local scale. The global node may affect all the local nodes, which may act as some kind of prior knowledge. Then for node $i$, its state may be determined by its similarity with the model, its neighbors in local scale and the global node in the global scale. We combine the different scale by the energy function. Based on the centers and the corresponding frequencies for the features, we can get the node evidence and the pairwise evidence. Ultimately, inference on the graph will yield the maximum a posteriori (MAP) labeling that specifies which nodes are normal or abnormal.

### 3.2    Energy Function of the Multi-scale Markov Random Field

The energy function in the mMRF model is following:

$$E(X) = \sum_i \gamma_i E_i(X) \tag{2}$$

where $i$ denotes different scales and $\gamma_i$ is the weight for each scale. As for this paper, $E(X) = \gamma E_{local}(X) + (1 - \gamma)E_{global}(X)$, where $E_{local}(X)$ denotes the local scale energy function and $E_{global}$ denotes the global scale energy function. $\gamma$ is used to weight the two scales.

For the local scale, the energy consists of two parts: node evidence and pairwise evidence and it can be represented as:

$$E_{local}(X) = \sum_i h(x_i) + \alpha \sum_{i,j \in neighbour} s(x_i, x_j) \tag{3}$$

where $h(x_i)$ is the node evidence and $s(x_i, x_j)$ is the pair-wise evidence. The value $\alpha$ is a constant to weight the pair-wise evidence, and $x_i$ denotes the label telling whether node $i$ is normal or abnormal. ( $x_i = 0$ signifies node $i$ is normal and $x_i = 1$ signifies node $i$ is abnormal).

The node evidence function measures the similarity between the event and the model. It can be divided into two terms: the similarity for the HOF feature $h_f(x_i)$ and the similarity for the sequential feature $h_s(x_i)$ . Simply speaking, for node $i$, if the HOF feature and sequential feature are very similar with the clustering center always occurring before, $h_f(x_i = 0)$ and $h_s(x_i = 0)$ will become higher.

Complementarily, $h_f(x_i = 1) = 1 - h_f(x_i = 0)$, $h_s(x_i = 1) = 1 - h_s(x_i = 0)$. We compute both $h_f(x_i = 0)$ and $h_s(x_i = 0)$ based on the model:

$$\begin{cases} h_f(x_i = 0) = \sum_j \sum_k fref_k \times sim_f(f_{i,j}, mf_k) \\ h_s(x_i = 0) = \sum_j fref_j \times sim_s(s_i, ms_j) \end{cases} \tag{4}$$

where $fref_k$ and $fref_j$ denote the frequency of HOF clustering center $mf_k$ and sequence feature clustering center $mf_j$, it is defined as the possibility of the occurrence of the feature cluster, which is computed as the number of the samples of each clustering center divided by the total samples. $f_{i,j}$ denotes the $j$th HOF for observation, $s_i$ denotes the sequential information, $sim_f(\cdot)$ is the similarity for HOF and $sim_s(\cdot)$ denotes the sequence similarity proposed in section 2. Both $h_f(x_i = 0)$ and $h_s(x_i = 0)$ are computed as the sum of the product of the clusters frequency and the similarity of the feature and the clustering center. Abnormal events seldom happen, and their similarities with most clustering centers are small. When abnormal event happened, $h_f(x_i = 0)$ and $h_s(x_i = 0)$ may have a small value then $h_f(x_i = 1)$ and $h_s(x_i = 1)$ will be high. We combine $h_f(x_i)$ and $h_s(x_i)$ for the node evidence, and $h(x_i = 0) = (1 - \tau)h_f(x_i = 0) + \tau h_s(x_i = 0)$ , where $\tau$ is a weighting constant set with $0 < \tau < 1$.

The pair-wise evidence function measures the similarity between the neighboring nodes. When $x_i = 0$, $x_j = 0$, $s(x_i = 0, x_j = 0) = sim_s(s_i, s_j)$, and $s(x_i = 1, x_j = 1)$ is also defined as $sim_s(s_i, s_j)$. Otherwise, $ss(x_i, x_j) = 1 - s(x_i = 0, x_j = 0)$. For the global scale, the energy is set as $E_{global}(X) = \sum_j \sum_k freg_k \times sim_g(g_j, mg_k)$ , where $g$ denotes the coming global feature, $freg_k$ denotes the frequency of global feature clustering center $mg_k$. The same as the local energy function, when the event is abnormal, $E_{global}(X = 1)$ should have a large value and $E_{global}(X = 0)$ would be high in normal condition.

Given the parameters for every node and link of the mMRF, we carry out MAP inference to maximize the energy function. Loopy belief propagation with max-sum message passing is used, which provides the MAP labeling whether each node is normal or not.

## 4    Experimental Results

In this section, we show the empirical performance of the proposed abnormal event detection algorithm on several published datasets. Section 4.1 introduces global abnormal event detection based on the UMN dataset[1]. Experiments on local abnormal event detection are introduced in section 4.2, which is based on the subway station dataset provided by Adam et al.[1]. The cross validation strategy is used to select parameters.

---

[1] Unusual crowd activity dataset of the University of Minnesota. (http://mha.cs.umn.edu/movies/crowdactivityall.avi).

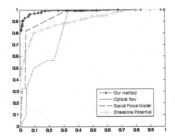

**Fig. 3.** The ROCs for frame level GAE detection in the UMN dataset.

**Table 1.** Comparison of the accuracy by our approach and other methods.

| Method | AUC |
|---|---|
| Social Force [9] | 0.96 |
| Optical flow | 0.84 |
| Streakline Potential [8] | 0.90 |
| Ours( mMRF ) | 0.973 |
| Ours (HOF alone ) | 0.624 |

### 4.1   Global Abnormal Event Detection

**Datasets.** We use the UMN dataset to verify the effectiveness of our method on the GAE. The UMN dataset consists of 11 clips of the crowded escape events in 3 different scenes including both indoor and outdoor scenes.

**Experimental Results.** For every clip, we use the first 400 frames for training and rest for testing (We use the first 250 frames for training in clip 3, for abnormal has already happened when it comes to the 400th frame). The local region size is $16 \times 16$ for each one, and we just use HOF to represent the local feature. Because the abnormal in UMN is GAE, the parameter $\gamma$ should be set low to add weight of the global feature. In this experiment, $\gamma$ is set to be 0.2, and the other parameter are set as $\alpha = 0.6$, $\tau = 0.5$. We use different threshold $\theta$ for the online clustering algorithm to get the ROC curve as showed in Fig.3, and value in the curve is set to be the mean of all the 11 clips. We compare the results using mMRF which combined all the features and the method only using local feature alone.

From the ROC curve shown in Fig.3 and Table 1, we can see that the method using mMRF perform better, the mean AUC of methods using mMRF is 0.973 and it outperforms 0.624 using local feature. The reason mainly due to the contribution of the global feature. People are just wandering in normal condition. When abnormal happened, they escaping all round or just in one direction. Only from a fixed local region, it may be hard to determine whether abnormal happens, but combined with the global feature such as kinetic energy, the detection

**Table 2.** Comparison of the accuracy using HOF information alone and other sequence similarity. Numbers in the first row denotes count for each abnormal activity in the ground truth.

|  | LT | NP | WD | II | Misc | Total | False alarm |
|---|---|---|---|---|---|---|---|
| Ground truth | 14 | 13 | 26 | 4 | 9 | 66 | - |
| Ours(HOF) | 8 | 7 | 24 | 2 | 2 | 43 | 23 |
| Ours(HOF + chi-square distance) | 13 | 8 | 23 | 4 | 8 | 56 | 15 |
| Ours(HOF + edit distance) | 14 | 8 | 24 | 4 | 8 | 58 | 5 |
| Jaechual Kim[6] | 13 | 8 | 24 | 4 | 8 | 57 | 6 |
| Bin Zhao[14] | 14 | 9 | 25 | 4 | 8 | 60 | 5 |

(a) LT          (b) WD          (c) II          (d) MISC          (e) NP

**Fig. 4.** Examples of the detected unusual event in the subway entrance surveillance video by our algorithm. LT: loitering; WD: wrong direction; NP: no payment; MISC: misc; II: irregular interactions between people.

may be much easier. Moreover, we also provide the quantitative comparisons to the state-of-the-art methods, the AUC of the method using mMRF range from 0.951 to 0.985, and it is comparable with the method in [9] for 0.96 and the method [8] for 0.90.

### 4.2  Subway Station Dataset

The dataset used for LAE are two video sequences taken from a fixed surveillance camera at a subway station, one monitoring the exit gate and the other monitoring the entrance gate. In both cases, there are one to ten people appearing in the scene at the same time. The frame size is $512 \times 384$, and the length of videos are 96 and 43 minutes correspondingly.

For both videos, we divide every frame into $64 \times 48$ local regions and extracts HOF and sequential feature from each region. Sequence length in this paper is set as 10. Global feature described in section 2 is also used. On the whole, two kinds of experiments are carried out. First, we verify the effectiveness of the sequential information we proposed. As a comparison, anomaly detection which utilizes the HOF alone is also conducted. Then we do experiments to verify the good performance of our sequence similarity. Sequence similarity in this paper is based on the edit distance, and chi-square distance is used for comparison.

**The Entrance Gate.** For the entrance gate, we use the first 12 minutes for training and rest for testing. The local region size is $8 \times 8$ for each one, and the length of the sequence is set to be 10. The parameter $\gamma$ was set 0.8 so that the weight of the local feature is high. And we set $\alpha = 0.6$, $\tau = 0.5$, $\theta = 1.4$ correspondingly. Because of the stationary camera, we conducted background

**Table 3.** Comparison of the accuracy using HOF information alone and other sequence similarity. Numbers in the first row denotes count for each abnormal activity in the ground truth

|  | LT | WD | Misc | Total | False alarm |
|---|---|---|---|---|---|
| Ground truth | 3 | 9 | 7 | 19 | - |
| Ours(HOF) | 2 | 9 | 2 | 13 | 14 |
| Ours(HOF + chi-square distance) | 3 | 8 | 7 | 19 | 9 |
| Ours(HOF + edit distance) | 3 | 9 | 7 | 19 | 3 |
| Jaechual Kim[6] | 3 | 9 | 7 | 19 | 3 |
| Bin Zhao[14] | 3 | 9 | 7 | 19 | 2 |

(a) LT          (b) WD          (c) MISC

**Fig. 5.** Examples of the detected unusual event in the subway entrance surveillance video. LT: loitering; WD: wrong direction; MISC: misc; MISS: miss; FA: false alarm.

subtraction first and extracted features from the foreground. The results of the experiment are as Table 2. Fig.4(a) - (e) show the examples for abnormal activities LT, WD, II, Misc and NP correspondingly.

The second row and the fourth row of Table 2 show the comparison of the anomaly detection with and without using the sequential information. Both of them provide similar results in the abnormalities such as "wrong direction". For the feature HOF is quite useful in describing the motion direction information. However, the method which does not utilize the sequence performs poorly in the abnormalities such as "Misc" which is often caused when a person abruptly stops walking or runs fast. The reason may be that HOF alone discards the temporal information between the low level features. Besides, false alarm rate for this method is high because optical flow information is not stable and is sensitive to the optical flow parameters and illumination changes. The third row and the fourth row compare with the results using chi-square distance and edit distance. As analyzed before, chi-square distance does not take alignment into consideration and it may bring a relatively high false alarm rate. We also compare our results with the method used in [6] and [14] in the fifth and the sixth row, and we can see that the results are comparable. It should be noted that, the method in [6] and [14] is specially designed for the local abnormal event detection and it may be not suitable for the global abnormal event detection.

**The Exit Gate.** For the exit gate, we use the first 8 minutes for training and rest for testing. The other parameters are set the same as the entrance gate. The results can be seen in Table 3. Fig.5(a) - (c) are detected by our methods, which corresponds to the LT, WD and Misc.

Same as the entrance gate, the second row and the fourth row of Table 3 show the comparison of the anomaly detection with and without using the sequential information. And the third row and the fourth row compare with the results using chi-square distance and edit distance. The results are consistent with the Table 2 and these results may verify the effectiveness of our methods.

## 5 Conclusion

In this paper, we propose a novel unsupervised framework based on contextual information and multi-scale markov random field for abnormal behavior detection. Both local and global features are utilized, and each corresponds to different scales of the multi-scale markov random field. With combing these features in mMRF, both GAE and LAE can be detected, and the experimental results verify the effectiveness of the proposed method.

**Acknowledgments.** This work was supported in part by National Basic Research Program of China(973 Program): 2012CB316400, in part by National Natural Science Foundation of China: 61332016, 61133003, 61390510, 61472389.

## References

1. Adam, A., Rivlin, E., Shimshoni, I., Reinitz, D.: Robust real-time unusual event detection using multiple fixed-location monitors. IEEE Transactions on Pattern Analysis and Machine Intelligence **30**(3), 555–560 (2008)
2. Basharat, A., Gritai, A., Shah, M.: Learning object motion patterns for anomaly detection and improved object detection. In: IEEE Conference on Computer Vision and Pattern Recognition, pp. 1–8. IEEE (2008)
3. Duda, R.O., Hart, P.E., Stork, D.G.: Pattern classification and scene analysis (1995)
4. Hu, W., Xiao, X., Fu, Z., Xie, D., Tan, T., Maybank, S.: A system for learning statistical motion patterns. IEEE Transactions on Pattern Analysis and Machine Intelligence **28**(9), 1450–1464 (2006)
5. Ihaddadene, N., Djeraba, C.: Real-time crowd motion analysis. In: 19th International Conference on Pattern Recognition, pp. 1–4. IEEE (2008)
6. Kim, J., Grauman, K.: Observe locally, infer globally: a space-time mrf for detecting abnormal activities with incremental updates. In: IEEE Conference on Computer Vision and Pattern Recognition, pp. 2921–2928. IEEE (2009)
7. Li, J., Gong, S., Xiang, T.: Global behaviour inference using probabilistic latent semantic analysis. In: The British Machine Vision Conference (2008)
8. Mehran, R., Moore, B.E., Shah, M.: A streakline representation of flow in crowded scenes. In: Daniilidis, K., Maragos, P., Paragios, N. (eds.) ECCV 2010, Part III. LNCS, vol. 6313, pp. 439–452. Springer, Heidelberg (2010)
9. Mehran, R., Oyama, A., Shah, M.: Abnormal crowd behavior detection using social force model. In: IEEE Conference on Computer Vision and Pattern Recognition, pp. 935–942. IEEE (2009)
10. Navarro, G.: A guided tour to approximate string matching. ACM computing surveys (CSUR) **33**(1), 31–88 (2001)

11. Stauffer, C., Grimson, W.E.L.: Learning patterns of activity using real-time tracking. IEEE Transactions on Pattern Analysis and Machine Intelligence **22**(8), 747–757 (2000)
12. Wu, S., Moore, B.E., Shah, M.: Chaotic invariants of lagrangian particle trajectories for anomaly detection in crowded scenes. In: IEEE Conference on Computer Vision and Pattern Recognition, pp. 2054–2060. IEEE (2010)
13. Xiang, T., Gong, S.: Incremental and adaptive abnormal behaviour detection. Computer Vision and Image Understanding **111**(1), 59–73 (2008)
14. Zhao, B., Fei-Fei, L., Xing, E.P.: Online detection of unusual events in videos via dynamic sparse coding. In: IEEE Conference on Computer Vision and Pattern Recognition, pp. 3313–3320. IEEE (2011)
15. Zhong, Z., Ye, W., Wang, S., Yang, M., Xu, Y.: Crowd energy and feature analysis. In: IEEE International Conference on Integration Technology, pp. 144–150. IEEE (2007)

# Light-Weight Spatial Distribution Embedding of Adjacent Features for Image Search

Yan Zhang[1,2], Yao Zhao[1,2], Shikui Wei[3(✉)], and Zhenfeng Zhu[1,2]

[1] Institute of Information Science, Beijing Jiaotong University, Beijing 100044, China
[2] Beijing Key Laboratory of Advanced Information Science and Network Technology,
Beijing 100044, China
[3] Hubei Key Laboratory of Intelligent Vision Based Monitoring for Hydroelectric Engineering,
China Three Gorges University, Yichang 443002, Hubei, China
shkwei@bjtu.edu.cn

**Abstract.** Binary code embedding methods can effectively compensate the quantization error of bag-of-words (BoW) model and remarkably improve the image search performance. However, the existing embedding schemes commonly generate binary code by projecting local feature from original feature space into a compact binary space. The spatial relationship between the local feature and its neighbors are ignored. In this paper, we proposed two light-weight binary code embedding schemes, named content similarity embedding (CSE) and scale similarity embedding (SSE), to better balance the image search performance and resource cost. Specially, the spatial distribution information for any local feature and its nearest neighbors are encoded into only several bits, which are used to verify the asserted matches of local features. The experimental results show that the proposed image search scheme achieves a better balance between image search performance and resource usage (i.e., time cost and memory usage).

**Keywords:** Image search · Product quantization · Embedding · Bow

## 1  Introduction

Content-based image search is the core technique for many real-world visual applications, such as frame fusion based video copy detection [1], logo detection [2], visual content recognition [3]. However, image search remains a challenge due to the deviation of semantic understanding between human and computer, and the appearance variations in scale, orientation, illuminations, etc. [4]. In consideration of the robustness and effectiveness of local visual features, the image searching frameworks based on local features are commonly employed in both research and industrial areas. Local features like SIFT [5], SURF [6], etc., are originally proposed for image matching, which are generally invariant to image scale and rotation, and are shown to provide robust matching across a substantial range of affine distortion. Nevertheless, original matching schemes between

© Springer-Verlag Berlin Heidelberg 2015
H. Zha et al. (Eds.): CCCV 2015, Part I, CCIS 546, pp. 387–397, 2015.
DOI: 10.1007/978-3-662-48558-3_39

two images are generally based on the similarity measurement of local feature sets, which requires large cost in both computation and storage.

To facilitate the image search with large scale image datasets, pioneering scheme, named Bag-of-Words (BoWs) model [7], is proposed for significantly simplifying the matching process. The key idea of BoW is to quantize each local feature into one or several so-called visual words, and represent each image as a collection of orderless visual words. After mapping local features into visual words, lots of excellent techniques in text retrieval area can be directly employed, which makes it possible to represent, index, and retrieve images like text documents. Although the BoW model shows impressive performance in both image search accuracy and time cost, it suffers greatly from visual word ambiguity and quantization error, i.e., representing a high dimensional descriptor with a visual word results in large information loss. It is possible for BoW model to quantize totally different local features into the same visual word when the visual dictionary is small. This will unavoidably cause false matches and decrease image search accuracy. A straightforward solution to this problem is to build a large scale visual dictionary [8]. However, it is not easy for the traditional methods like k-mean clustering to build a large scale visual dictionary due to their high computing cost. In addition, the performance improvement will trend smoothing when dictionary size is large enough. Another solution is to build a compact binary code for each local feature [4]. In this way, each local feature is associated with one visual word and one binary code. Since the binary code can greatly filter out false matches, the image search accuracy is remarkably improved. More significantly, the searching time cost is greatly reduced. However, this kind of embedding method separately build a binary code for each local feature, yet the spatial relationships among local features are not taken into account. Therefore, these methods severely limit the discriminative power of binary codes. To address this issue, multiple visual phrase (MVP) [9] is proposed in recent years. Instead of visual word, a multiple visual phrase is used to represent each local feature by exploring the spatial distribution of local features. In fact, the existing MVP scheme will result in large computing cost and memory usage since the MVP of each local feature is associated with several adjacent local features and their correlation information.

In this paper, our key goal is to design a light-weight image search framework, which can achieves a better balance between search performance and resource cost. This framework consists two key components, i.e., large-scale visual dictionary construction and light-weight binary code embedding. To constructing a large-scale visual dictionary, the optimal product quantization (OPQ) [10] is employed. Since a large-scale visual dictionary is built by Cartesian product of a set of small sub-dictionaries, the visual word assignment is extremely efficient and the memory usage for storing the dictionary is much less than traditional ones. To fully explore the spatial information among local features but reduce computational cost and memory usage, we propose two light-weight binary code embedding schemes, named content similarity embedding(CSE) and scale similarity embedding(SSE). Since spatial clues among local features are encoded into only several bits, the memory usage is much less than the existing schemes. The experimental results show the proposed image search schemes achieve a better balance between image search performance and resource usage (i.e., time cost and memory usage).

## 2    Related Work

Local descriptors like SIFT provide robust matching across a substantial range of affine distortion. But matching local descriptors is time-consuming because each image may contain thousands of high-dimensional descriptors. An efficient solution is to quantize local descriptors into visual words [7]. However, due to the quantization error, many false matches occur when matching two images, which unavoidably decrease the image search accuracy. To improve the discriminative power of BoW model, one solution is to build a compact binary code for each local feature [4]. Although embedding methods can filter out false matches, it has been illustrated that single visual word cannot preserve the spatial information in images, which has been proven important for visual matching.

To introduce spatial information into BoW model, lots of works are conducted to combine multiple visual words with spatial information. For example, descriptive visual phrase (DVP) is generated in [12] by selecting two nearby visual words. Generally, considering visual words in groups rather than single visual word captures stronger discriminative power. However, in the existing visual phrase methods, two visual phrases are matched only if they have the same number of visual words, which reduces the match flexibility. In [13], Geometry preserving Visual Phrase(GVP) is proposed to encode the spatial information of local features, including both co-occurrences and the local and long-range spatial layouts of visual words. With little increase in memory usage and computational time, the improvement of search accuracy is witnessed. However, GVP only captures the translation invariance. Although its extension to scale and rotation invariance can be achieved by increasing dimension of the offset space, more memory usage and time cost will be needed. Spatial coding [14] is proposed to efficiently check spatial consistency globally. It uses spatial maps to record the spatial relationship of all matched feature pairs. Nevertheless, spatial coding is very sensitive to rotation due to the intrinsic limitation of the spatial map. Zhang etc. in [9] proposed a multi-order visual phrase (MVP) which contains two complementary clues: center visual word quantized from the local descriptor and the visual and spatial clues of multiple nearby local features. This method shows an impressive performance improvement in image search accuracy. However, it needs large memory to store the MVP information and more computational time in online searching phase. In [15], a novel geometric relation which computes a binary signature leveraging existence and nonexistence of interest points in the neighborhood area was proposed. But it only consider the adjacent area instead of adjacent features which will results in a lot of mismatch.

To address abovementioned issues, we design a light-weight image search framework and propose two simple but effective binary embedding schemes. By encoding spatial distribution information among local features into several bits, the proposed image search framework can better balance the image search accuracy and resource cost.

# 3    The Proposed Approach

In this section, the proposed light-weight image search scheme is discussed in details. The overall framework includes four key components, i.e., large-scale visual dictionary construction, light-weight binary code embedding, image database indexing, and similarity querying. In this paper, we focus on the first two tasks. To give a complete discussion about image search scheme, the implementation details about indexing and querying are also presented in this section.

## 3.1    Large-Scale Visual Dictionary Construction

Our final goal is to reduce the time complexity and memory usage while remaining comparable image search accuracy. To this end, we firstly need to generate a large-scale visual dictionary for reducing quantization error. In fact, most of existing methods generate visual dictionary by clustering a large training set of local features in their original feature space. In this way, it will lead to an intractable computation cost when training a large-scale visual dictionary. More importantly, the memory usage for storing the dictionary itself is not trivial. To avoid these issues, we employ partitioned k-means clustering (or Product Quantization) to build a large-scale visual dictionary. For further reducing the quantization error, an optimal step is used to improve the product quantization method. Here, a short review about product quantization is presented as follows:

### Product Quantization

Product quantization is an extremely efficient vector quantization approach, which can compactly encode high dimensional vectors for fast approximate nearest neighbor (ANN) search. Product quantization involves two key steps: (1) decomposing the $D$-dimensional vector space into $S$ subspaces; (2) computing a sub-dictionary for each subspace.

For the original $D$-dimensional representation space of local features $X^D$, it is first divided into $S$ subspaces with dimensions $D/S$. In each subspace $X^m$, $s \in \{1,2, \cdots S\}$, a small sub-dictionary $D^m$ is built. The objective function of product quantization is as follows:

$$\min\nolimits_{D^1,D^2,......D^S} \sum\nolimits_X ||x - d(i(x))||^2 \tag{1}$$

$$d \in D = D^1 \times D^2 \times ...... \times D^S$$

Here, $x = [x^1, x^2, ......, x^S]$ is any training sample, the function $i(\cdot)$ is called an *encoder*, and function $d(\cdot)$ is called a *decoder*, $d(i(x))$ is the visual word of $x$. $D = D^1 \times D^2 \times ...... \times D^S$ is the final visual dictionary constructed by Cartesian product of $M$ sub-dictionaries $\{D^1, D^2, \cdots D^S\}$ .

**Optimized Product Quantization**

To further reduce the quantization error, T. Ge etc. in [10] introduce an iterative optimization step into product quantization. Specially, an orthonormal matrix $R$ is introduced into the space decomposition process. For each iteration, the $D$-dimensional vector space is first transformed by $R$ before decomposing it into $S$ subspaces. Therefore, the visual dictionary constructing process can be split into two iterative steps. First, an orthogonal matrix $R$ is initialized and fixed, and sub-dictionaries $\{D^s\}_{s=1}^S$ are calculated by following the objective function (1). Then, the currently generated sub-dictionaries $\{D^s\}_{s=1}^S$ are fixed, and the orthogonal matrix $R$ is optimized. The optimized product quantization can be formulated as follows:

$$min_R \sum_X \left\| RX - c(i(X)) \right\|^2 \qquad (2)$$

where $X$ is the set of training samples, and $c(i(X))$ is the visual word of $X$.

For the product quantization scheme, the problem of building a large-scale visual dictionary is transferred into build a series of small visual sub-dictionaries. Since the memory usage for storing these visual sub-dictionaries is trivial, the memory usage is less than traditional ones. In our work, the value of $S$ is set to 2, and the value of $k$ is set to 1000. Therefore, we finally get a large-scale dictionary with 1M visual words.

## 3.2    Light-Weight Binary Code Embedding

Although a large-scale visual dictionary can remarkably alleviate the problem of quantization error, additional binary code can still improve the image search accuracy furthermore. Therefore, this paper focuses mainly on the design of binary code embedding schemes. Two light-weight binary code embedding schemes, named content similarity embedding and scale similarity embedding, are proposed. The proposed scheme can be treated as light-weight MVP. For the original MVP scheme, both the nearest neighbors of current local features and their spatial relationship are recorded when indexing images, which will result in a big indexing structure. Instead, the proposed schemes encode the spatial relationship into light-weight binary codes. In this way, the memory usage will be greatly reduced. In addition, the proposed method is also different from traditional embedding schemes. For the existing embedding schemes like Hamming embedding, the binary codes are generated by projecting local features from the original representation space into a binary space. Generally, the generated code is treated as a compact version of original local feature. In contrast, the proposed schemes only encode spatial distribution information surrounding the local feature. The implementation details are discussed as follows:

### Content Similarity Embedding (CSE)

The content similarity embedding is based on an underlying assumption that the spatial distribution with the nearest $N$ neighbors in content is similar for two matched local features. Therefore, we can verify the asserted matches of local features by comparing their spatial clues with the nearest $N$ neighbors in content similarity.

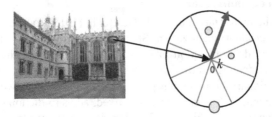

**Fig. 1.** Illustration of CSE scheme, where red line indicates the dominant orientation of $k$

To encode the spatial clue for any local feature k in image, we first find out the nearest N local features surrounding k as shown in Fig.1. Yellow dots indicates the neighborhood interest points with different scales. Then, the region containing the nearest N neighbors are divided into 8 equal portions $\{P^i, i = 1 \ldots \ldots 8\}$ started from the dominant orientation of current local feature. Finally, a binary code $b_k = (b_k^1, \cdots, b_k^i, \cdots, b_k^8)$ is generated by encoding occurrence of neighbors in each portion in counterclockwise, which is formulated as follows:

$$b_k^i = \begin{cases} 1, & if\ one\ of\ N\ neighbors\ falls\ into\ P^i \\ 0, & othewise \end{cases} \qquad (3)$$

In Fig.1, the binary code for local feature $k$ is $b_k = 10001010$.

### Scale Similarity Embedding (SSE)

For the content similarity embedding, the nearest $N$ neighbors are selected by computing the content similarity of local features. To capture the scale invariance surrounding each local feature, we propose a scale similarity embedding scheme. The key assumption is that the spatial distribution with the nearest $N$ neighbors in scale is similar for two matched local features.

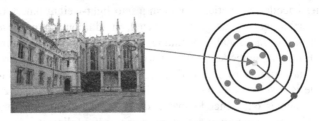

**Fig. 2.** Illustration of SSE scheme. Red dot is the $M^{th}$ nearest neighbor in content similarity, and blue dots indicate 4 nearest neighbors in scale similarity.

Similarly, for any local feature $k$ in image, we first select $M$ nearest neighbors in content for it. As shown in Fig. 2, we select $M$ nearest neighbors, which include both green and blue points. Then, 4 local features (blue points in Fig.2) whose scales are closest to the scale of k are selected from the $M$ nearest neighbors. According to the distance between $k$ and its $M^{th}$ neighbor, we make a circular region as $k$'s neighborhood region, which is partitioned into a set of patches $\{P^i, i = 1, \cdots, 4\}$. By encoding occurrence of scale-similar neighbors in patches, we can generate a compact binary code, which is formulated as follows:

$$b_k^i = \begin{cases} 1, \text{if any nerghbor keypoint exiet in } P^i \\ 0, \qquad\qquad\qquad\qquad\text{othewise} \end{cases} \qquad (3)$$

In Fig.2, the binary code for local feature $k$ is $b_k = 1011$.

## 3.3    Indexing and Retrieval

### Indexing

To speed up the image searching process, we also build an inverted table for the image database against the pre-trained dictionary **D**. For each local feature in database image, it is first quantized into the nearest visual word $w_k$, and then an item is inserted into the list associated with the visual word $w_k$. As shown in Fig.3, both ID of image and spatial embedding code (SEC) are contained in the item.

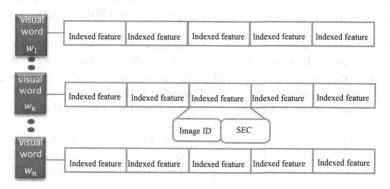

**Fig. 3.** Illustration of the inverted indexing structure with spatial embedding codes

### Retrieval

Given a query image $Q$, we also quantize the local features extracted $Q$ into visual words against the pre-trained dictionary $D$, and generate the corresponding binary codes of these local features. For each visual word in $Q$, the corresponding lists in inverted table are returned. By a voting procedure, we can get a similarity score for each potentially matched image. In particular, we use match order computed by spatial verification to measure the importance of matched local features to image similarity ,i.e., high order matches between query $Q$ and a database image $D$ are more important for image similarity. The image similarity can be formulated as follows:

$$score(Q,D) = \frac{\sum_{w_q=w_d} idf(w_q) \times (1+\alpha)^{order(b_q,b_d)}}{norm(D)} \quad (4)$$

where, $w_q$ and $w_d$ denote the visual words in query image Q and database image D, respectively; $b_q$ and $b_d$ are corresponding special binary codes associated with $w_q$ and $w_d$; $idf(w_q)$ is the inverse document frequency of visual word $w_q$, and $norm(D)$ is L2-norm of term frequency vector of database image D. $order(b_q,b_d)$ is the order between $b_q$ and $b_d$, which is defined as follows:

$$order(b_q,b_d) = L - hd(b_q,b_d) \quad (5)$$

where, $L$ is the length of the binary code, $L$ is set to 8 and 4 in CSE and SSE, respectively, $hd$ represents the Hamming distance of $b_q$ and $b_d$.

# 4    Experiments

## 4.1    Datasets

We test the proposed methods on two commonly used datasets: UKbench dataset [16] and Oxford5K dataset [17]. All experiments are conducted under the same configuration conditions on a PC with a 2-core 3.2Ghz processor and 8GB memory.

**UKbench.** UKbench dataset, contains 2,550 objects, each of which has 4 images under 4 different viewpoints for object search. So the total number of images in this dataset is 10200. In this experiment, all of the 10200 images are used as database images and queries either. And we measured the retrieval performance by the top-four candidates, which means how many similar images are returned at the first four images, called N-S score.

**Oxford5K.** For landmark search, we use the Oxford5K dataset, which contains 5,062 annotated landmark images. The collection has 11 different landmark categories and 5 queries for each category. The performance is measured by mean Average Precision (MAP).

## 4.2    Evaluation on Image Search Performance

In our experiments, the popular SIFT descriptor is employed as local feature. We decompose the 128-dimensional SIFT vector space into 2 subspaces, and then train 2 sub-dictionaries with 1000 visual sub-words in two subspaces. Therefore, we obtain the final large-scale visual dictionary with 1M visual words.

**Effect of Key Parameters**
For the content similarity embedding (CSE) method, we need extract the nearest $N$ neighbors for each local feature as spatial clues. Likewise, for scale similarity embedding

(SSE) method, the radius $r_k$ is the distance between the current local feature $k$ and its $M^{th}$ nearest neighbor. Therefore, the selection of $N$ and $M$ will affect the experimental results. In addition, the selection of $\alpha$ in Eq.4 will affect both CSE and SSE schemes. To evaluate the effect of different parameters, we carry out some experiments on UKbench dataset by employing different value combinations of $N$, $M$ and $\alpha$. The experimental results are illustrated in Fig.4. Clearly, for both CSE and SSE schemes, the number of nearest neighbors have remarkable effect on image search accuracy. When the number of $N$ and $M$ increase from zero to a certain value, the search accuracy trend to the best. However, this conclusion is reasonable. When the value $N$ and $M$ is too small, the nearest neighbors cannot provide enough spatial clues. At other extreme, when the value $N$ and $M$ is too large, the reliability of spatial clues will lose. Therefore, both extreme cases will lead to bad performance. Similar conclusion can be obtained for the parameter $\alpha$, yet the reason is different. As indicated in Eq.4, larger $\alpha$ puts larger weight to spatial verification. There is also two extreme cases. When $\alpha$ is too small, the effect of spatial verification is trivial on image similarity calculation. On the contrary, if $\alpha$ is too large, spatial codes will dominate the image similarity calculation. Both extreme cases will result in bad performance.

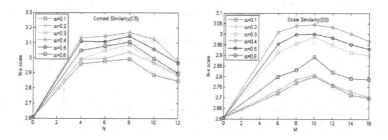

**Fig. 4.** The influence of $N$, $M$ and $\alpha$ on Ukbench dataset

In the following experiments, the values of $N$, $M$ and $\alpha$ are fixed to 8, 10 and 0.4 respectively.

**Evaluation of Image Search Performance**

Our final goal is to design a light-weight image search framework so as to better balance the search performance and resource cost. In this section, the proposed methods are compared with existing schemes under the same conditions. The experimental results are demonstrated in Table.1 and Table.2. Clearly, introducing embedding codes into the original OPQ BoW model remarkably improves the image search performance in terms of effectiveness. For the different BoW+ Embedding schemes, the proposed OPQ+CSE scheme achieves the best search accuracy on Ukbench dataset and comparable accuracy on Oxford5K dataset. For the time cost and memory usage in querying phrase, the proposed schemes, i.e., OPQ+CSE, OPQ+SSE, OPQ+CSE+SSE, outperform the OPQ+MVP scheme. That's because that MVP needs 64 bits to preserve the spatial and visual clues for each local features [9], meanwhile the proposed schemes only need at most 12bits (CSE+SSE). And to verify the neighbor keypoints of two MVPs, at most conduct $4 \times 4 = 16$ times of verification, at the same time we only need to calculate the hamming distance for one time. It means that the proposed methods indeed better balance the image search accuracy and resource cost. Notice that the image search accuracy have a remarkable degeneration when CSE and SSE are combined. The possible reason is that a long binary code possibly leads to large order in Eq.5. Therefore, spatial codes will dominate the image similarity calculation which result in bad image performance.

**Table 1.** Retrieval performance on Ukbench for 10200 query images

|                   | OPQ    | OPQ+MVP | OPQ+CSE | OPQ+SSE | OPQ+CSE+SSE |
|-------------------|--------|---------|---------|---------|-------------|
| Performance(N-S)  | 2.6050 | 3.1463  | 3.1657  | 3.0443  | 3.0749      |
| Index time(s)     | 1056.5 | 3081.8  | 3453.1  | 1964.4  | 4151.8      |
| Search time(s)    | 0.1432 | 0.7612  | 0.2369  | 0.2123  | 0.3068      |
| Index storage(MB) | 28.5   | 217.0   | 53      | 42.8    | 61.6        |

**Table 2.** Retrieval performance on Oxford5K for 55 query images

|                   | OPQ    | OPQ+MVP | OPQ+CSE | OPQ+SSE | OPQ+CSE+SSE |
|-------------------|--------|---------|---------|---------|-------------|
| Performance(MAP)  | 0.2475 | 0.5172  | 0.4921  | 0.4683  | 0.4027      |
| Index time(s)     | 901.1  | 4986.7  | 4625.6  | 2821.4  | 6555.7      |
| Search time(s)    | 0.2279 | 1.6751  | 0.7650  | 0.7434  | 0.8139      |
| Index storage(MB) | 33     | 306.0   | 55.9    | 50.2    | 61.6        |

## 5    Conclusion

In this paper, we design a light-weight image search framework to better balance the image search performance and resource cost. Instead of extracting a compact binary code from local feature itself, the proposed binary code embedding schemes only encode the spatial distribution information of nearest neighbors surrounding the current local feature. Besides content similarity, the scale similarity is also employed to select neighbors. Since spatial distributions among local features are encoded into only several bits, both the memory usage and time cost are much less than existing schemes. The experimental results show the proposed image search scheme achieves a better balance between image search performance and resource usage (i.e., time cost and memory usage).

**Acknowledgements.** This work was supported in part by National Basic Research Program of China (No.2012CB316400), National Natural Science Foundation of China (No.61202241, No.61210006), Program for Changjiang Scholars and Innovative Research Team in University (No.IRT201206), Fundamental Research Funds for the Central Universities (No.2015JBM028), and Joint Fund of Ministry of Education of China and China Mobile (No.MCM20130421).

# References

1. Wei, S.K., Zhao, Y., Zhu, C., Xu, C.S., Zhu, Z.F.: Frame Fusion for Video Copy Detection. IEEE Transactions on Circuits and Systems for Video Technology **21**(1), January 2011
2. Yan, W.Q., Wang, J., Kankanhalli, M.S.: Automatic Video Logo Detection and Removal. Multimedia Systems **10**(5), 379–391 (2005)
3. Belongie, S., Malik, J., Puzicha, J.: Shape Matching and Object Recognition Using Shape Contexts. IEEE Trans. Pattern Anal. Mach. Intell. **24**(4), 509–522 (2002)
4. Wei, S.K., Xu, D., Li, X., Zhao, Y.: Joint Optimization Toward Effective and Efficient Image Search. IEEE Transactions on Cybernetics **43**(6), December 2013
5. Lowe, D.G.: Distinctive Image Features from Scale Invariant Keypoints. Int. J. Comput. Vis. **60**(2), 91–110 (2004)
6. Bay, H., Tuytelaars, T., Gool, L.V.: Speeded-up Robust Features (SURF). Comput. Vis. Image Underst. **110**(3), 346–359 (2008)
7. Sivic, J., Zisserman, A.: Video Google: a text retrieval approach to object matching in videos. In: Proc. IEEE Int. Conf. Comput. Vision, vol. 2, pp. 1470–1477 (2003)
8. Jegou, H., Douze, M., Schmid, C.: Product Quantization for Nearest Neighbor Search. IEEE Trans. Pattern Anal. Mach. Intell. **33**(1), 117–128 (2011)
9. Zhang, S.L., Tian, Q., Huang, Q.M., Gao, W., Rui, Y.: Multi-order visual phrase for scalable image search. In: ICIMCS 2013, August 17–19, 2013
10. Ge, T.Z., He, K.M., Ke, Q.F., Sun, J.: Optimized Product Quantization. IEEE Transactions on Pattern Analysis and Machine Intelligence (TPAMI) (2014)
11. Jegou, H., Douze, M., Schmid, C.: Hamming embedding and weak geometric consistency for large scale image search. In: Forsyth, D., Torr, P., Zisserman, A. (eds.) ECCV 2008, Part I. LNCS, vol. 5302, pp. 304–317. Springer, Heidelberg (2008)
12. Zhang, S., Tian, Q., Hua, G., Huang, Q., Li, S.: Descriptive visual words and visual phrases for image applications. In: ACM Multimedia, pp. 75–84 (2009)
13. Zhang, Y., Jia, Z., Chen, T.: Image retrieval with geometry-preserving visual phrases. In: Proc. IEEE Conf. Compute. Vis. Pattern Recognit., pp. 809–816 (2011)
14. Zhou, W., Lu, Y., Li, H., Song, Y., Tian, Q.: Spatial coding for large scale partial-duplicate web image search. In: Proceedings of the ACM International Conference on Multimedia, pp. 511–520 (2010)
15. Ozkan, S., Esen, E., Akar, G.B.: Visual group binary signature for video copy detection. In: International Conference on Pattern Recognition (ICPR), August 2014
16. Nistér, D., Stewénius, H.: Scalable recognition with a vocabulary tree. In: CVPR (2006)
17. Philbin, J., Chum, O., Isard, M., Sivic, J., Zisserman, A.: Object retrieval with large vocabularies and fast spatial matching. In: Proceedings of the IEEE Conference on Computer Vision and Pattern Recognition (2007)

# Cross-Level: A Practical Strategy for Convolutional Neural Networks Based Image Classification

Yu Liu[1], Baocai Yin[1], Jun Yu[1], and Zeng-Fu Wang[1,2(✉)]

[1] Department of Automation, University of Science and Technology of China,
Hefei 230026, China
{liuyu1,yinbc}@mail.ustc.edu.cn, {harryjun,zfwang}@ustc.edu.cn
[2] Institute of Intelligent Machines, Chinese Academy of Sciences, Hefei 230031, China

**Abstract.** Convolutional neural networks (CNNs) have exhibited great potential in the field of image classification in the past few years. In this paper, we present a novel strategy named cross-level to improve the existing CNNs' architecture in which different levels of feature representation in a network are merely connected in series. The basic idea of cross-level is to establish a convolutional layer between two nonadjacent levels, aiming to learn more sufficient feature representations. The proposed cross-level strategy can be naturally combined into a CNN without any change on its original architecture, which makes this strategy very practical and convenient. Three popular CNNs for image classification are employed to illustrate its implementation in detail. Experimental results on the dataset adopted by the ImageNet Large-Scale Visual Recognition Challenge (ILSVRC) verify the effectiveness of the proposed cross-level strategy on image classification. Furthermore, a new CNN with cross-level architecture is introduced in this paper to demonstrate the value of the proposed strategy in the future CNN design.

**Keywords:** Convolutional Neural Networks (CNNs) · Image classification · Network architecture · Feature representation · Deep learning

## 1 Introduction

As an important issue in the field of computer vision, image classification has achieved great progress in the past decade, which is primarily driven by the ever-increasing demand of image retrieval technique on the internet. Many worldwide competitions on image classification have been carried out, such as the Pattern Analysis, Statistical Modelling and Computational Learning, Visual Object Classes (PASCAL VOC) Challenge from 2005 to 2012 and ImageNet Large-Scale Visual Recognition Challenge (ILSVRC) since 2010. It is notable that the performance of visual object recognition has obtained a dramatic improvement since convolutional neural networks (CNNs) [1,2] were first introduced into image classification by Krizhevsky et al. [3] in 2012. In the last three years, a variety of

© Springer-Verlag Berlin Heidelberg 2015
H. Zha et al. (Eds.): CCCV 2015, Part I, CCIS 546, pp. 398–406, 2015.
DOI: 10.1007/978-3-662-48558-3_40

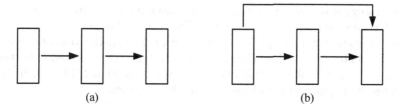

**Fig. 1.** Comparison of (a) Conventional structure of CNN and (b) the improved structure with cross-level strategy. Note that a block denotes a level of representation and an arrow denotes some operational layers between two levels.

CNN-based classification approaches have been presented [4–7], and the latest reported method [8] can even surpass the human-level performance.

Historically, convolutional network was first applied to visual object recognition by LeCun et al. [1], in which the problem of handwritten digit recognition was well tackled by a network containing two convolutional layers and two fully-connected layers. However, this method did not obtain enough attentions in generalized visual recognition for a long time, until the rise of deep learning theory [9,10] as well as the huge improvement on the computation capacity of hardware. Staring with the AlexNet [3], many representative CNN architectures such as Network in Network (NIN) [5] and GoogLeNet [7] have been proposed in the literature. As a typical category of deep neural networks, CNNs are designed for hierarchical data/feature representation mechanism from lower level to higher level, in which each level consists of a certain number of feature maps. The feature maps in a certain level are obtained from the maps in its previous level through several operations such as linear convolution, non-linear activation and spatial pooling. In this article, to make the following descriptions clearer, we use the term *layer* to specially denote a certain operation between two adjacent levels of feature maps, and the term *level* to indicate the data representation stage which is characterized by a set of feature maps. The existing CNNs share similar architectures, namely, alternate convolutional layers for feature extraction and spatial pooling layers like max-pooling for dimension reduction. Different levels of representation in a network are merely connected in series. In other words, each layer only locates between two adjacent levels, and there is no layer or direct connection between two nonadjacent levels. Fig. 1(a) shows the core structure of existing CNNs. However, the connection mechanism of visual neurons is generally believed to be very complex from the perspective of visual neuroscience [11,12].

In this paper, we mainly argue that the existing serial connection approach can be improved by adding direct connections between two nonadjacent levels. Specifically, a convolutional layer is established between two nonadjacent levels to realize this idea. This strategy is logically named cross-level, and it can be naturally combined into a CNN without any change on its original architecture. The illustration of cross-level strategy is shown in Fig. 1(b). The primary motivation of this strategy is to learn more sufficient feature representations to pursue a better performance on image classification. The rest of this paper is organized as follows. In Section 2, three popular CNNs for image classification are reviewed. The implementation details of the cross-level strategy are presented in Section 3. The experimental results for validation are given in Section 4. Finally, Section 5 concludes the paper and puts forward some future work.

## 2    Related Work

In this section, we briefly review three representative deep convolutional neural networks presented for image classification in the last three years, which are the AlexNet [3], Network-in-Network (NIN) [5] and GoogLeNet [7].

The AlexNet [3] proposed in 2012 can be viewed as a milestone in the field of image classification. It is the first time that CNN was employed for generalized image classification. The classification method based on AlexNet is the winner of ILSVRC 2012 with a significant breakthrough with respect to the previous approaches. The AlexNet reported in [3] contains five convolutional layers and three fully-connected layers, and each of these layers is followed by a point-wise non-linear activation layer called Rectified linear units (ReLUs). In this work, the non-linear activation is also viewed as a layer for the consistency of layer definition in Section 1. There is a local response normalization (LRN) layer that follows the first as well as the second convolutional layer (Actually, it is after the ReLU layer. Since a convolution layer in a CNN is usually followed by a non-linear layer like ReLU, the non-linear layer will not be explicitly mentioned later). There are three max-pooling layers in AlexNet. The first two follow the two LRN layers, respectively. The last max-pooling layer follows the fifth convolutional layer. The core structure of AlexNet locates between the second and third max-pooling layers, which contains three convolutional layers each with $3 \times 3$ convolution kernel. Four levels of feature maps of spatial size $13 \times 13$ are connected by these three convolutional layers. The authors reported in [3] that the removal of any of these layers leads to a loss of about 2% in terms of top-1 performance. The core structure of AlexNet is shown in Fig. 2(a).

Lin et al. [5] proposed NIN to obtain a better representation of local patches by adding a multi-layer perceptron after a convolution layer. In their method, they use a three-layer perceptron, and it is essentially equivalent to add two $1 \times 1$ convolutional layers after a $3 \times 3$ or $5 \times 5$ convolutional layer. Thus, the core structure or unit of NIN has three convolutional layers in series, as shown in Fig. 2(b). The network applied in [5] has four such units and there is a max-pooling layer between every two units. Furthermore, after the last three-layer convolution unit, instead of employing traditional fully-connected layers, the authors generate one feature map for each class and use the global average pooling scheme to obtain the resulting vector, which can reduce the number of parameters to a great extent and prevent overfitting for neural networks.

GoogLeNet, a 22-layer deep convolutional network proposed by Szegedy et al. [7], is the winner of ILSVRC 2014 classification competition. Since

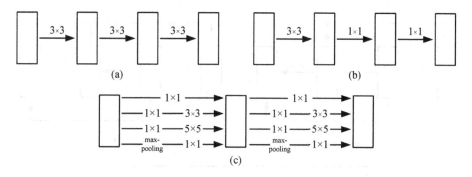

**Fig. 2.** Core structures of three CNNs. (a)AlexNet, (b)NIN, and (c)GoogLeNet.

increasing the depth of a network directly needs a sharp increase use of computational resources and tends to cause severe overfitting, the GoogLeNet is designed to make a balance between the network size and computational budget. The core structure adopted in GoogLeNet is called Inception. Fig. 2(c) shows two serial Inceptions. In each Inception, the feature maps in the output level are obtained from four branches, namely, a $1 \times 1$ convolution layer, a $3 \times 3$ convolution layer with a $1 \times 1$ layer for parameter reduction, a $5 \times 5$ convolution layer with a $1 \times 1$ layer for parameter reduction, and a max-pooling layer followed by a $1 \times 1$ layer to limit the number of output feature maps for parameter reduction in the next level. It is worthwhile to note that the intermediate feature maps generated in the last three branches do not construct a level of representation since those three $1 \times 1$ layers are essentially designed for parameter reduction. Therefore, there are only three levels of representation in Fig. 2(c). In GoogLeNet, there are totally nine Inceptions which are separated into three parts. The first part and last part both have two Inceptions just like the illustration given in Fig. 2(c). The middle part has five Inceptions in series. Moreover, there is no max-pooling layer within each of the three parts, so all the feature maps within each part have the same spatial size. In GoogLeNet, there exists a max-pooling layer between every two parts for dimension reduction of feature maps.

## 3    Cross-Level

In this section, we mainly describe the implementation details of the cross-level strategy via the above three convolutional networks, namely, the AlexNet [3], Network-in-Network (NIN) [5] and GoogLeNet [7]. Fig. 3 shows the improved structure of each network after applying the cross-level strategy. The basic idea of cross-level is to establish a convolutional layer between two nonadjacent levels. Naturally, the added convolution layer can be called cross layer. Thus, the feature maps in the output level come from two aspects: the layers in the original structure and the cross layer. In our approach, considering the cost of computational resource, the size of convolution kernel in each cross layer is fixed to $1 \times 1$,

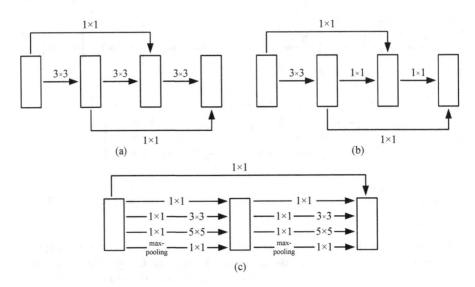

**Fig. 3.** The improved structure of three networks after applying the cross-level strategy.(a)AlexNet, (b)NIN, and (c)GoogLeNet.

and the number of feature maps generated by a cross layer is universally set as half number of the original maps in that level.

As shown in Fig. 3(a), for the AlexNet, two 1 × 1 convolutional layers are established from the first and second levels to the third and fourth levels, respectively. Notice that the core structure shown in Fig. 2(a) appears only once in the AlexNet, all the other parts of the network are not changed. The situation of NIN is similar to that of AlexNet, as shown in Fig. 3(b). The only difference is there are several core structures/units (see Fig. 2(b)) in the NIN architecture. For each unit except the first and last one, two 1 × 1 convolutional layers are added on the original structure. Thus, when there are four units [5], only four 1 × 1 layers are created on the second and third units, while the other parts in NIN remain unchanged. Finally, Fig. 3(c) shows the modified structure of GoogLeNet with cross-level strategy, which connects the input level of the former Inception and the output level of the latter one with a 1 × 1 convolutional layer. As mentioned before, the GoogLeNet also contains a structure of five consecutive Inceptions. The cross-level strategy deals with this situation just using the same approach in AlexNet (see Fig. 3(a)) and NIN (see Fig. 3(b)). Accordingly, there are totally six 1 × 1 convolutional layers added on the original GoogLeNet after applying the cross-level strategy.

From the above three examples, we can see that the cross-level strategy can be easily applied to an existing CNN without changing it original architecture, and the depth of the network also remains the same. The only requirement is that all the feature maps within the two cross-connected levels must have the same spatial size. That is to say, there must be no inside spatial pooling layers with stride larger than one.

It is worthwhile to notice that some existing CNN architectures have partly applied the cross-level strategy in some specific applications. Fan et al. [13] introduced a CNN with multiple paths for human tracking. In their method, the network between the first convolutional and the output layer is split into two branches, namely, global branch and local branch. The global branch is the same as traditional CNN architecture, which consists of several convolutional layers and pooling layers. The purpose of global branch is to enlarge the receptive field to address global structures. The local branch only has a convolutional layer, which aims to extract more details about local structures. Sermanet and LeCun [14] employed a similar multi-scale CNN architecture for traffic sign recognition. In [15], Sun et al. proposed a face verification method based on CNN, in which the last hidden layer is connected with both the third and fourth convolutional layers. The main purpose of this design is to avoid the loss of useful information, since the fourth layer contains too few neurons. The networks used in the publications referred above are generally known as multi-scale CNNs. Although these CNNs have bypassing connections, there exist clear difference between them and the CNNs applying the proposed cross-level strategy. In the above multi-scale CNNs, bypassing connections only connected with the output layer. Moreover, the main motivation using multi-scale CNNs is for specific object recognition such as human and face, in which features with different scales are all required in the output layer. However, the target of the proposed cross-level strategy is generalized object classification [3,5,7], and the basic motivation of this strategy is to extract more features with different scales at each feature representation level, not just the output one. Thus, the design of CNNs using the cross-level strategy is more flexible.

## 4   Experiments

The AlexNet [3], Network-in-Network (NIN) [5] and GoogLeNet [7] are first employed to verify the effectiveness of the proposed cross-level strategy for image classification. In this work, we use the dataset adopted by ILSVRC, which is a subset of ImageNet. It contains 1000 categories and each category has about 1300 images. Totally, there are about 1.28 million training images and 50000 validation images. The experimental setup is exactly similar to the approach reported in [3]. All the images are first down-sampled to a fixed spatial resolution of $256 \times 256$ and the mean intensity over the training set from each pixel is subtracted. All the models are learned using stochastic gradient decent algorithm. All the experiments are conducted on Caffe [16], which is a popular deep learning framework created by Jia et al. The implementation files of all the above three networks are available on Caffes website [17], and the parameters in our experiments are set as default values. The cross-level strategy is applied to these three networks by modifying the corresponding network definition files. For simplicity, the modified versions of these three networks are named AlexNet-Cross, NIN-Cross and GoogLeNet-Cross, respectively. For a fair comparison, all the parameters with respect to model training remain the same with the original networks.

The top-1 and top-5 accuracy rates are tested for each learned CNN model using the validation image sets. For each test image, only the central patch of appropriate size is extracted for prediction, i.e., single-view prediction is applied. It is worthwhile to note that we do not apply some widely used strategies such as multi-view prediction and model fusion [3] to pursue a high accuracy rate, which are always required in ILSVRC competition. The main purpose here is to make a pure comparison between a network and its improved version with cross-level strategy. Thus, we just test the accuracy rate based on single model as well as single view in this paper. Table 1 lists the top-1 and top-5 accuracy rates of six learned CNN models. For all of these three networks, it can be seen from Table 1 that the cross-level strategy results in a rise of about 1% in terms of both top-1 and top-5 accuracy rates. In particular, the performance improvement of GoogLeNet is the most significant. From our perspective, this is mainly because the proportion of levels which are influenced by the cross-level strategy in GoogLeNet is the highest among these three networks.

**Table 1.** The top-1 and top-5 accuracy rates of six learned CNN models.

| Model | Top-1 | Top-5 |
|---|---|---|
| AlexNet | 56.48% | 79.56% |
| AlexNet-Cross | 57.37% | 80.52% |
| NIN | 59.42% | 81.60% |
| NIN-Cross | 60.56% | 82.61% |
| GoogLeNet | 68.93% | 88.90% |
| GoogLeNet-Cross | 70.28% | 90.08% |

In addition to the existing networks, the cross-level strategy can be also used for the design of new networks. To verify this point, as well as to further demonstrate the effectiveness of the cross-level strategy from the other point of view, we design a new CNN architecture by referring to GoogLeNet. Specifically, we just remove two branches in the Inception of GoogLeNet, while all the other structures remain the same, mainly including the depth of network and the number of feature maps each branch generates. We apply the cross-level strategy to this new network just as the way to GoogLeNet. The core structure of the designed network is shown in Fig. 4, in which only the $1 \times 1$ and $3 \times 3$ branches are preserved. The same training and testing approaches are used to this network. The top-1 and top-5 accuracy rates obtained are 68.74% and 88.78%, respectively. We can see from Table 1 that the performance of this new network is very close to that of GoogLeNet, but the number of feature maps as well as training parameters is significantly decreased.

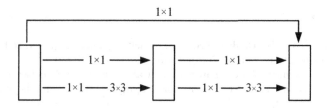

**Fig. 4.** The core structure of the new designed network.

## 5   Conclusion

***Contribution-*** This paper presents a novel strategy called cross-level for CNN-based image classification. The basic idea is to establish a convolutional layer between two nonadjacent levels in the network, which aims to learn more sufficient feature representations for a better classification performance. Experimental results on three popular convolutional networks demonstrate the effectiveness of the proposed cross-level strategy. We also exhibit the potential of the cross-level strategy used for the design of new networks.

***Limitation-*** There still exist some limitations in this work. First, the number of feature maps generated by a cross layer is normally set as half number of the original maps in that level in our method. The impact of this proportional factor on the classification performance is not fully studied, which is mainly due to the reason that CNN model training is very time-consuming. Second, only one single model for each network is learned and only the central patch in each test image is extracted for prediction. Thus, this work has not been completed and we have not obtained an ultimate result on classification accuracy.

***Future Work-*** Considering the above limitations, we will conduct more experiments to further study the impact of the above proportional factor. Furthermore, we will design some new networks using the cross-level strategy and attempt to obtain a competitive result via the approaches like model fusion as well as multi-view prediction.

**Acknowledgments.** This work was supported by the National Natural Science Foundation of China (No. 61472393 and No. 61303150), the National Science and Technology Major Project of the Ministry of Science and Technology of China (No. 2012GB102007), and the Anhui Province Initiative Funds on Intelligent Speech Technology and Industrialization (No. 13Z02008). The authors greatly acknowledge the support of IFLYTEK CO.,LTD.

# References

1. LeCun, Y., Boser, B., Denker, J.S., et al.: Backpropagation applied to handwritten zip code recognition. Neural Computation **1**, 541–551 (1989)
2. LeCun, Y., Kavukcuoglu K., Farabet C., et al.: Convolutional networks and applications in vision. In: IEEE International Symposium on Circuits and Systems, pp. 254–256 (2010)
3. Krizhevsky, A., Sutskever, I., Hinton, G.E.: ImageNet classification with deep convoluntional neural networks. Advances in Neural Information Processing Systems **25**, 1106–1114 (2012)
4. Zeiler, M.D., Fergus, R.: Visualizing and understanding convolutional networks. In: Fleet, D., Pajdla, T., Schiele, B., Tuytelaars, T. (eds.) ECCV 2014, Part I. LNCS, vol. 8689, pp. 818–833. Springer, Heidelberg (2014)
5. Lin, M., Chen Q., Yan, S.: Network in network (2013). arXiv: 1312.4400 [cs.NE]
6. He, K., Zhang, X., Ren, S., et al.: Spatial Pyramid Pooling in Deep Convolutional Networks for Visual Recognition (2014). arXiv: 1406.4729 [cs.CV]
7. Szegedy, C., Liu, W., Jia Y., et al.: Going deeper with convolutions (2014). arXiv: 1409.4842 [cs.CV]
8. He, K., Zhang, X., Ren, S., et al.: Delving deep into rectifiers: Surpassing human-Level performance on imageNet classification (2015). arXiv: 1502.01852 [cs.CV]
9. Hinton, G.E., Salakhutdinov, R.R.: Reducing the dimensionality of data with neural networks. Science **313**, 504–507 (2006)
10. Bengio, Y., Courville, A., Vincent, P.: Representation learning: A review and new perspectives. IEEE Transactions on Pattern Analysis and Machine Intelligence **35**, 1798–1828 (2013)
11. Desimone, R., Duncan, J.: Neural mechanisms of selective visual attention. Annual review of neuroscience **18**, 193–222 (1995)
12. Spirkovska, L., Reid, M.B.: Robust position, scale, and rotation invariant object recognition using higher-order neural networks. Pattern Recognition **25**, 975–985 (1992)
13. Fan, J., Xu, W., Wu, Y., et al.: Human tracking using convolutional neural networks. IEEE Transactions on Neural Networks **21**, 1610–1623 (2010)
14. Sermanet, P., LeCun, Y.: Traffic sign recognition with multi-scale convolutional networks. In: International Joint Conference on Neural Networks, pp. 2809–2813 (2011)
15. Sun, Y., Wang, X., Tang, X.: Deep learning face representation from predicting 10,000 classes. In: IEEE International Conference on Computer Vision and Pattern Recognition (CVPR), pp. 1891–1898 (2014)
16. Jia, Y., Shelhamer, E., Donahue, J., et al.: Caffe: Convolutional architecture for fast feature embedding. In: ACM International Conference on Multimedia, pp. 675–678 (2014)
17. Caffe website. http://caffe.berkeleyvision.org/

# Superpixel-Based Global Contrast Driven Saliency Detection in Low Contrast Images

Nan Mu[1] and Xin Xu[1,2(✉)]

[1] School of Computer Science and Technology,
Wuhan University of Science and Technology, Wuhan 430081, China
xuxin0336@163.com
[2] Hubei Province Key Laboratory of Intelligent Information Processing and Real-time
Industrial System, Wuhan University of Science and Technology, Wuhan 430081, China

**Abstract.** Due to the low signal to noise ratio, saliency detection in low contrast images has been a great challenge in computer vision. In this paper we propose a novel approach to detect salient object based on the computation of global saliencies in superpixel image blocks. This method tackles the image through a simple contrast measure, which first computes the global difference of two superpixels to obtain the resulting saliency map. Then, the map is refined by introducing the inter-superpixel similarity approach. The proposed model perfectly extracts the salient object in low contrast visibility conditions, which has been tested on three public datasets, as well as a nighttime image dataset. Experimental results demonstrate that the proposed method outperforms existing state-of-the-art saliency detection models.

**Keywords:** Superpixel segmentation · Low contrast · Salient object detection · Global saliency

## 1 Introduction

Visual saliency refers to a selection mechanism, the task of which is to extract the most important information for further processing. The research of saliency detection in natural images has proven to be useful for computer vision applications. With the development of various saliency models, it has witnessed tremendous advances in visual saliency detection in recent years. Most of these models focus on the contrast difference between salient objects and background region. Since the contrast between image elements (pixel, superpixel, or region) can be analogously used to compare the saliency of these elements, the natural images can be converted to saliency maps.

These models can work well in images with high contrast between foreground and background. But for detecting salient object in a relatively low contrast scene, they may face difficulties. Fig. 1 illustrates the saliency detection results using two state-of-the-art methods [1, 2]. The three testing images have low contrast between the visual salient objects and the background. In [1], Achanta *et al.* estimated the saliency by computing the difference between a pixel and the mean of the whole image in

© Springer-Verlag Berlin Heidelberg 2015
H. Zha et al. (Eds.): CCCV 2015, Part I, CCIS 546, pp. 407–417, 2015.
DOI: 10.1007/978-3-662-48558-3_41

LAB color space. However, for the low contrast images, this approach fails to separate the salient object from the background, as in Fig. 1(b). In [2], Goferman *et al.* combined the local feature and global feature of the image patches to compute image saliency. This method can highlight the edges of the salient objects but miss the interior information, as in Fig. 1(c).

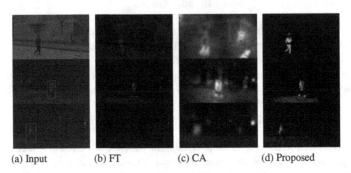

(a) Input          (b) FT          (c) CA          (d) Proposed

**Fig. 1.** Examples of saliency detection results. (a) Input low contrast images with manually labeled rectangle. (b-c) Saliency maps obtained by two state-of-the-art methods [1, 2]. (d) Saliency maps obtained by the proposed method.

Generally speaking, most existing saliency detection approaches can be broadly classified into three main categories, in which the local contrast, global contrast, and the local-global contrast are considered, respectively.

*1) The local contrast based saliency methods*, which compute the distinctiveness of the image region in a local scope. The most popular method in this category is the saliency model proposed by Itti *et al.* [3], which computed the three local contrasts (luminance, color and direction) in different scales. Bruce and Tsotsos [4] utilized the information maximization approach to perform the local saliency computation. Han *et al.* [5] calculated the image saliency based on the sparse coding theory related to the local complexity.

*2) The global contrast based saliency methods*, which compute the distinctiveness of the image region over the entire image. Zhang *et al.* [6] measured the bottom-up saliency by extracting two features (difference of Gaussians and ICA-derived) of the entire image. Rosin [7] created the saliency map by utilizing the edge detection, distance transform, and thresholding approaches.

*3) The local-global contrast based saliency methods*, which consider both the local and global components, and then integrate them. Cheng *et al.* [8] proposed a global contrast model based on the region segmentation and refined the results by adopting a region based local contrast approach. Borji and Itti [9] proposed a saliency detection framework by measuring the local and global patch rarities and fusing them in a final map.

These contrast based methods have been successfully applied for proto-object detection. However, they perform poorly on low contrast images. It is a challenging task to acquire the effective features in low contrast images, and so far, only a handful of researches mention about the low contrast saliency detection. Wang *et al.* [10]

introduced a Salient Contrast Change (SCC) feature for object detection and tracking in low contrast videos. Han *et al.* [11] combined the multi-feature contrast weighted inhibition model and the fuzzy connection facilitation model to implement the contour detection in night vision images. Although these researches analyzed the influencing factors of night scene and put forward the effective measures to tackle with the night videos, there is still difficulty in extracting the salient objects accurately with low computational complexity.

To solve these problems, this paper presents a global contrast method based on local difference of each superpixel block, which can extract the salient object from low contrast images efficiently. The overview of the proposed method is shown in Fig.2. Unlike existing approaches, the proposed method does not require any training pre-processing, thus the computation is more efficient. This research utilizes the superpixel as the basic element, and operates on the simplified image by measuring the contrast difference between every two superpixel blocks in LAB color space. The proposed saliency model has a more preferable performance than the existing models for the saliency detection in low contrast images. The method has been tested on the MSRA dataset created by Liu *et al.* [12], the SED dataset created by Alpert *et al.* [13], the CSSD dataset created by Yan *et al.* [14], and the nighttime image dataset created by this project to corroborate its performance.

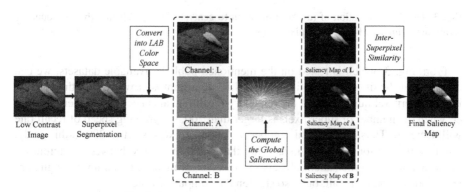

**Fig. 2.** An overview of the proposed framework.

The rest of this paper is organized as follows. Section 2 describes the proposed salient object detection method. Section 3 presents the experimental comparison result of the proposed method with other existing saliency models. Finally, the conclusions are drawn in section 4.

## 2    Proposed Algorithm

The details of the proposed superpixel-based global contrast driven salient object detection algorithm are presented in this section.

## 2.1  Superpixel Segmentation

To simplify the operations, this study utilizes the superpixel segmentation method to partition the original image into a number of superpixels. We adopt the *simple linear iterative clustering* (SLIC) algorithm [15] to perform this process. The SLIC algorithm has an excellently perceptual characteristic, and the computational speed is very fast. In this work, we choose the optimal number (denoted as $n$) of the superpixels by analyzing the relation with the processing time and the boundary recall rate. Fig. 3 (a) and (b) plot the dependency of time taken and boundary recall rate on the number of superpixels, respectively.

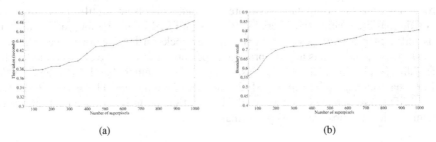

(a)                                                      (b)

**Fig. 3.** The linear variation of (a) the time taken to generate superpixels and (b) the boundary recall rate influenced by the superpixel number.

From Fig. 3, which is tested on the mentioned publicly available datasets, we can observe that the time consumption of the SLIC algorithm is growing with the increasing of superpixel numbers, and the boundary recall rate also becomes higher. However, when the number of superpixels is larger than 200, the growing speed of recall rate will decrease. Thus, the optimal number $n$ of superpixels is set to 200 in this study, this is sufficient for our work in learning the global difference between different regions and detecting the salient objects in low contrast images. It can not only guarantee a good boundary recall, but also shorten the computing time.

## 2.2  Global Contrast Approach

The original image is first converted into the CIELab space and decomposed into the respective L, A and B components. For each component, the superpixels are denoted as $SP_L(i)$, $SP_A(i)$, and $SP_B(i)$, respectively ($i = 1, \cdots, n$). The corresponding saliency value of each superpixel in every component is denoted as $SV_L(i)$, $SV_A(i)$, and $SV_B(i)$, respectively. We define the saliency value of superpixel $SP_L(i)$ by measuring the difference between each pixel value inside it (denoted as $SP_L(i; x, y)$) and the mean values of all other superpixels (denoted as $\overline{SP_L}(j)$, $j = 1, \cdots, n$), which is computed as:

$$SV_L(i) = \sum_{j=1}^{n} w(i, j) \cdot \left| SP_L(i; x, y) - \overline{SP_L}(j) \right|. \tag{1}$$

The weight $w(i, j)$ between superpixel $SP_L(i)$ and $SP_L(j)$ is obtained by computing the pixel number (denoted as $Num(j)$) in superpixel area $SP_L(j)$, and the Euclidean distance between the spatial center of $SP_L(i)$ and $SP_L(j)$, which are denoted as $c(i)$ and $c(j)$, respectively. The specific calculation is shown as follows:

$$w(i, j) = \frac{Num(j)}{|c(i) - c(j)|}. \tag{2}$$

The above algorithm is then executed in A and B components to compute the saliency value $SV_A(i)$ and $SV_B(i)$ of each superpixel. The saliency map (denoted as $S_{Map}$) is obtained by fusing the saliency map of L, A and B components via:

$$S_{Map} = \sqrt{SV_L \cdot SV_L + SV_A \cdot SV_A + SV_B \cdot SV_B}. \tag{3}$$

The resulting saliency map $S_{Map}$ is normalized in the interval [0, 1], and the normalized feature map is calculated by:

$$S_{Map} = \frac{S_{Map} - \min(S_{Map})}{\max(S_{map}) - \min(S_{Map})}. \tag{4}$$

To further enhance the performance, the generated saliency map is smoothed by a median filter, which can better highlight the edges of the salient objects.

## 2.3   Internal Similarity Measure

We also introduce the inter-superpixel similarity measure [16] to refine the resulting saliency map. Each superpixel is assigned to a superpixel-level histogram $H_k(i)$, which is calculated based on the color quantization table with $m$ entries. The histogram is normalized to have $\sum_{k=1}^{m} H_k(i) = 1$. The inter-superpixel similarity between two superpixel $SP(i)$ and $SP(j)$ is obtained by:

$$S(i, j) = \frac{S_{color}(i, j)}{|c(i) - c(j)|}. \tag{5}$$

The color similarity $S_{color}(i, j)$ is computed as the sum of intersection between each histogram:

$$S_{color}(i, j) = \sum_{k=1}^{m} \min\{H_k(i), H_k(j)\}. \tag{6}$$

The final saliency value for each superpixel is recalculated by exploiting the inter-superpixel similarity measure, so that the superpixels with higher similarity will have more similar values.

$$S'_{Map}(i) = \frac{\sum_{j=1}^{n} S(i, j) \cdot S_{Map}(j)}{\sum_{j=1}^{n} S(i, j)}. \tag{7}$$

The performance evaluation of the saliency maps obtained by the proposed method is described in the next section.

## 3    Experimental Results

A number of experiments were conducted to validate the performance of the proposed method on four datasets: (1) the MSRA dataset [12], in which the principle salient objects are labeled by different human subjects, (2) the SED dataset [13], which provides the ground truth, segmented by three human subjects. (3) the CSSD dataset [14], which is more challenging, including complex scenes, and (4) the nighttime image dataset created by the proposed research, which contains plenty of low contrast images in the evening, the resolution of these various images is $1280 \times 720 \times 24b$.

We compared our saliency model with eight existing state-of-the-art saliency models including *frequency-tuned* (FT) method [1], *context-aware* (CA) method [2], *saliency using natural statistics* (SUN) method [6], *non-parametric* (NP) method [17], *image signature* (IS) method [18], *patch distinction* (PD) method [19], *graph-based manifold ranking* (GBMR) method [20], and *saliency optimization* (SO) method [21].

In order to evaluate the performance of the proposed saliency model, we have introduced the *receiver operating characteristic* (ROC) graph to test the accuracy of generated saliency maps. The ROC graph is a two-dimensional graph which contains the *True Positive Rate* (TPR) and the *False Positive Rate* (FPR). The ROC curve is generated by plotting the obtained TPRs and FPRs, the ROC performance comparison of the eight methods and the proposed method is shown in Fig. 4, which are tested on the MSRA, SED, CSSD and the nighttime image dataset, respectively.

It can be seen from Fig. 4 that the proposed method has a better performance than other eight state-of-the-art saliency methods in MSRA, SED, CSSD, and nighttime image dataset, the overall performance will decline in the nighttime images which have a relatively low contrast. The *area under the curve* (AUC) is calculated to give an intuitive comparison. The AUC can indicate how well the generated saliency map predicts the human interesting area. Table 1 shows the AUC value of the various saliency models on the four datasets. It can be observed that the proposed model has state-of-the-art performance on the mentioned four datasets.

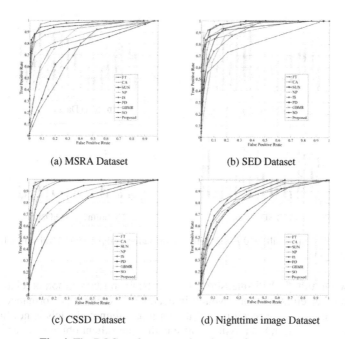

(a) MSRA Dataset                    (b) SED Dataset

(c) CSSD Dataset                    (d) Nighttime image Dataset

**Fig. 4.** The ROC performance plots for the four datasets.

**Table 1.** The AUC performance of saliency maps from various saliency models on four datasets.

| Datasets | Saliency models | | | | | | | | |
|---|---|---|---|---|---|---|---|---|---|
| | *FT* | *CA* | *SUN* | *NP* | *IS* | *PD* | *GBMR* | *SO* | *Proposed* |
| *MSRA* | 0.7515 | 0.9149 | 0.7188 | 0.8458 | 0.7396 | 0.9287 | 0.8722 | 0.9317 | 0.9551 |
| *SED* | 0.7326 | 0.9135 | 0.8806 | 0.8643 | 0.8356 | 0.9428 | 0.8469 | 0.9051 | 0.9458 |
| *CSSD* | 0.7382 | 0.9408 | 0.7280 | 0.9317 | 0.9365 | 0.9507 | 0.8039 | 0.8693 | 0.9518 |
| *Nighttime image* | 0.6978 | 0.7283 | 0.7533 | 0.8305 | 0.8506 | 0.8281 | 0.7991 | 0.8685 | 0.8767 |

For an objective comparison to quantitatively evaluate the performance for detecting the salient object, we introduce the precision, recall criteria, which calculated by comparing the binarized saliency map and the ground-truth mask. To further evaluate the accuracy of obtained binary mask of the saliency map, the F-*measure* is given by:

$$F_{measure} = \frac{(1+\beta^2)Precision \times Recall}{\beta^2 \times Precision + Recall}.$$

(8)

The proposed method uses $\beta^2 = 0.5$ to weigh the precision and recall. The comparison of precision, recall, and F-measure of these various methods are shown as:

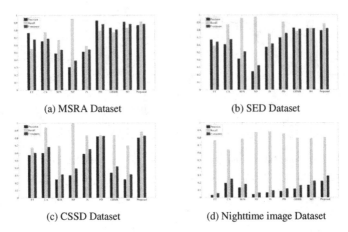

(a) MSRA Dataset                    (b) SED Dataset

(c) CSSD Dataset                    (d) Nighttime image Dataset

**Fig. 5.** The Precision, recall, and F-measure performance comparison of various saliency models on four datasets.

As shown in Fig. 5, the F-measure value of the proposed method is relatively higher than the other eight methods, which indicates an excellent performance to predict the human eye gaze. The recall rate of the various saliency models is not high on the nighttime image dataset, the possible cause is that the salient objects in our dataset are too small, which results in a low F-measure performance.

The run-time performance is also considered to evaluate the efficiency of various algorithms. The experiment is measured on Intel 2.9GHZ CPU machine with 4GB RAM. All approaches use Matlab implementations. It can be observed from Table 2 that the run-time of IS method is time-saving, but can only generate the low resolution saliency maps. The computational complexity of the proposed method is slightly higher than the superpixel-based method GBMR, whereas our method can get more accurate estimations.

**Table 2.** The computational run-time (in second) of various saliency models on four datasets.

| Datasets | Saliency models | | | | | | | | |
|---|---|---|---|---|---|---|---|---|---|
| | FT | CA | SUN | NP | IS | PD | GBMR | SO | Proposed |
| MSRA | 0.29 | 96.19 | 3.07 | 10.36 | 0.15 | 23.38 | 3.37 | 1.19 | 5.20 |
| SED | 0.22 | 33.56 | 1.57 | 2.00 | 0.15 | 5.20 | 0.85 | 1.03 | 2.30 |
| CSSD | 0.28 | 81.58 | 2.07 | 2.13 | 0.14 | 7.64 | 0.87 | 1.11 | 3.24 |
| Nighttime image | 1.62 | 98.79 | 25.00 | 47.85 | 0.24 | 151.39 | 8.72 | 17.12 | 38.43 |

The subjective comparison is shown in Fig. 6 and Fig. 7. From Fig. 6, the saliency maps obtained by the GBMR, SO and the proposed method have a uniform salient region, and the saliency objects are more similar with the ground-truth binary masks. The saliency maps of NP can't clearly distinguish the salient region from their surroundings. The CA and PD method have good detection effects, but the salient objects they detect are not uniform, and their time consumption is very high. The other approaches can not correctly detect the real salient objects under the condition of complicated background. From Fig. 7, it is evident that our model can better detect the salient objects in low contrast images, and is more effective than the others.

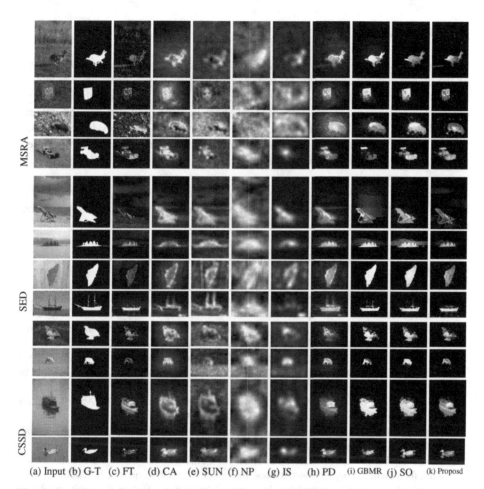

**Fig. 6.** Qualitative comparisons on MSRA, SED, and CSSD datasets. (a) testing low contrast images, (b) ground-truth binary masks, (c-j) saliency maps obtained by various state-of-the-art saliency models (k) saliency maps obtained by the proposed method.

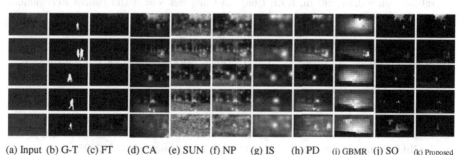

(a) Input (b) G-T  (c) FT     (d) CA     (e) SUN (f) NP      (g) IS      (h) PD    (i) GBMR (j) SO    (k) Proposed

**Fig. 7.** Qualitative comparison on nighttime image dataset.

## 4    Conclusions

In this paper, we have proposed an effective superpixel-based saliency model based on the global contrast and the inter-superpixel similarity. Experiments have been carried out on the public available MSRA, SED, CSSD dataset and our nighttime image dataset for salient object detection. Results show that the proposed method outperforms the eight state-of-the-art saliency models. Most of the existing saliency computational methods fail to perform well on low contrast images, while the proposed approach has excellent performance on this task.

**Acknowledgments.** This work was supported by the Natural Science Foundation of Hubei Provincial of China (2014CFB247) and the National Natural Science Foundation of China (No. 61440016).

## References

1. Achanta, R., Hemami, S., Estrada, F., Susstrunk, S.: Frequency-tuned salient region detection. In: IEEE Conf. on Computer Vision and Pattern Recognition, pp. 1597–1604 (2009)
2. Goferman, S., Zelnik-Manor, L., Tal, A.: Context-aware saliency detection. IEEE Trans. on Pattern Analysis and Machine Intelligence 34(10), 1915–1926 (2012)
3. Itti, L., Koch, C., Niebur, E.: A model of saliency-based visual attention for rapid scene analysis. IEEE Trans. Pattern Analysis and Machine Intelligence 20(11), 1254–1259 (1998)
4. Bruce, N.D.B., Tsotsos, J.K.: Saliency, attention, and visual search: An information theoretic approach. Journal of Vision 9(3), art. no. 5 (2009)
5. Han, B., Zhu, H., Ding, Y.: Bottom-up saliency based on weighted sparse coding residual. In: Proceedings of the ACM Int. Conf. on Multimedia, pp. 1117–1120 (2011)
6. Zhang, L., Tong, M.H., Marks, T.K., Shan, H., Cottrell, G.W.: SUN: A Bayesian framework for saliency using natural statistics. Journal of Vision 8(7), art. no. 32 (2008)
7. Rosin, P.L.: A simple method for detecting salient regions. Pattern Recognition 42(11), 2363–2371 (2009)
8. Cheng, M.-M., Zhang, G.-X., Mitra, N.J., Huang, X., Hu, S.-M.: Global contrast based salient region detection. In: IEEE Conf. on Computer Vision and Pattern Recognition, pp. 409–416 (2011)
9. Borji, A., Itti, L.: Exploiting local and global patch rarities for saliency detection. In: IEEE Conf. on Computer Vision and Pattern Recognition, pp. 478–485 (2011)
10. Wang, L., Huang, K., Huang, Y., Tan, T.: Object detection and tracking for night surveillance based on salient contrast analysis. In: IEEE Int. Conf. on Image Processing, pp. 1113–1116 (2009)
11. Han, J., Yue, J., Zhang, Y., Bai, L.-F.: Salient contour extraction from complex natural scene in night vision image. Infrared Physics & Technology 63, 165–177 (2014)
12. Liu, T., Sun, J., Zheng, N.-N., Tang, X., Shum, H.-Y.: Learning to detect a salient object. In: IEEE Conf. on Computer Vision and Pattern Recognition, pp. 1–8 (2007)
13. Alpert, S., Galun, M., Basri, R., Brandt, A.: Image segmentation by probabilistic bottom-up aggregation and cue integration. In: IEEE Conf. on Computer Vision and Pattern Recognition, pp. 1–8 (2007)

14. Yan, Q., Xu, L., Shi, J., Jia, J.: Hierarchical saliency detection. In: IEEE Conf. on Computer Vision and Pattern Recognition, pp. 1155–1162 (2013)
15. Achanta, R., Shaji, A., Smith, K., Lucchi, A., Fua, P., Susstrunk, S.: SLIC superpixels compared to state-of-the-art superpixel methods. IEEE Trans. on Pattern Analysis and Machine Intelligence 34(11), 2274–2282 (2012)
16. Liu, Z., Meur, L., Luo, S.: Superpixel-based saliency detection. In: International Workshop on Image Analysis for Multimedia Interactive Services, pp. 1–4 (2013)
17. Murray, N., Vanrell, M., Otazu, X., Parraga, C.A.: Saliency estimation using a non-parametric low-level vision model. In: IEEE Conf. on Computer Vision and Pattern Recognition, pp. 433–440 (2011)
18. Hou, X., Harel, J., Koch, C.: Image Signature: Highlighting sparse salient regions. IEEE Trans. on Pattern Analysis and Machine Intelligence 34(1), 194–201 (2012)
19. Margolin, R., Zelnik-Manor, L., Tal, A.: What makes a patch distinct? IEEE Conf. on Computer Vision and Pattern Recognition, pp. 1139–1146 (2013)
20. Yang, C., Zhang, L., Lu, H., Ruan, X., Yang, M.-H.: Saliency detection via graph-based manifold ranking. In: IEEE Conf. on Computer Vision and Pattern Recognition, pp. 3166–3137 (2013)
21. Zhu, W., Liang, S., Wei, Y., Sun, J.: Saliency optimization from robust background detection. In: IEEE Conf. on Computer Vision and Pattern Recognition, pp. 2814–2821 (2014)

# Decoupled Marginal Distribution of Gradient Magnitude and Laplacian of Gaussian for Texture Classification

Wufeng Xue[1], Xuanqin Mou[1]([✉]), and Lei Zhang[2]

[1] Xi'an Jiaotong University, Xi'an, China
xqmou@mail.xjtu.edu.cn
[2] Hong Kong Polytechnic University, Hong Kong, China

**Abstract.** We propose a novel descriptor for classification of texture images based on two isotropic low level features: the gradient magnitude (GM) and the Laplacian of Gaussian (LOG). The local descriptor is devised as the concatenation of the marginal distributions and a decoupled marginal distributions of the two features in local patch. The isotropic low level features and the computation of the two distributions ensure the rotation invariance and its robustness. To make the descriptors contrast invariant, within each image and across difference images of the same class, L2-normalization and Weber normalization are implied to the two features. After examined on three benchmark datasets, the proposed descriptor is showed to be more effective than other filter bank based features. Besides, the proposed descriptor can achieve very good performance even with small patch.

**Keywords:** Gradient Magnitude · Laplacian of Gaussian · Decoupled marginal distributions · Texture classification

## 1 Introduction

Due to the wide applications in object recognition, remote sensing, image retrieval, industrial inspection, medical image analysis, etc., texture classification has been a long lasting hot topic for decades. Generally, two procedures make a texture classification system: the feature representation and the classifier. For the classifier, the most employed ones are k-NN and SVM with $\chi^2$ kernel used. Therefore the classification problem reduces to a feature design problem. Following the paradigm of the Bag of Words (BOW), describing a texture image can be accomplished by: local structure description, texton dictionary learning and global histogram computation over the texton dictionary [1]. The global histogram computation acts as a joint distribution of the local descriptors over a partition of a high dimensional descriptor space and is fed into the classifier as the input feature. Local structure of texture images can be captured by the response of filter bank [1–4] or some pre-defined local patterns obtained by thresholding operation [5–8]. Texton dictionary can then be learned using unsupervised clustering method for the filter-bank based descriptor or be pre-defined

© Springer-Verlag Berlin Heidelberg 2015
H. Zha et al. (Eds.): CCCV 2015, Part I, CCIS 546, pp. 418–428, 2015.
DOI: 10.1007/978-3-662-48558-3_42

for the later ones. In this work, we only focus on the filter bank based descriptors. As for the filter banks, Gaussian derivatives, particularly, the gradient magnitude (GM) and the Laplacian of Gaussian (LOG) are employed in this work and explored in the context of texture classification.

As low level features, Gaussian derivatives have been used in many areas such as object recognition [9,10], human detection [11], image quality assessment [12,13], as well as texture classification [14,15]. Other filters like Gabor filters [16,17], Steerable filters [18] and wavelets [19] have also been used for texture classification in early times. However, in these methods the filter responses are directly used to represent the local structures. The mutual interaction among these filters and the correlation between neighboring responses are ignored. In this paper, we propose a novel descriptor, which we refer to as GL_Mars in the following paper, based on the local statistics of the GM and LOG features: the marginal distribution and the decoupled marginal distribution.

## 1.1 Related Work

Representation based on filter banks with the BOW paradigm provides one of the predominant solutions for texture classification. The VZ-classifier proposed in [14] investigated four filter banks in texture classification, out of which three consisted of Gaussians, LOG, and Gaussian derivatives. Among them, the MR8 set was demonstrated to perform better than others and will be used as a competitor in our experiments. In this VZ-MR8 method, the local structure of texture image was represented by the multi-response to the filter bank. The correlation between response coefficients in the neighboring area should have been considered. Besides, the employed filters have large support and may cause fine detail loss in the response domain.

Although much efforts have been devoted into devising filter bank based local descriptors for texture images and good classification performances have been achieved by some of them, the necessity of the filter banks is challenged by Varma and Zisserman [20,21]. They argued that textures can be better classified using the joint distribution of the intensity values over very compact neighborhood. When the image patch is represented in a MRF manner, even better performance can be obtained. In this VZ-patch method, we can say that the texture images are filtered by only one filter, which is the Kronecker delta function. Due to its patch based manner, the feature dimension will increase squarely as patch size increase.

Instead of using the Gaussian derivatives directly, Crosier and Griffin [15] proposed to represent local texture structures by the largest component of seven basic image features (BIF), which were computed based on Gaussian derivatives up to the second order. These Gaussian derivatives corporately defined seven components of local structure. A texture image can be described by the histograms over these components, resulting to a vector of $(7-1)^4$ dimension. Excellent performance was achieved by this method.

Besides these predefined filter banks, Liu et. al. [22,23] proposed the random projection to encode local texture structure. Taking advantage of the sparse nature of texture images and the related theories in compressed sensing that sparse signal can be nearly-perfect reconstructed by a small number of random projections of the signal, the random features facilitate well the classification of texture images. This method achieved excellent performance while reduces dramatically the feature dimension.

## 1.2 Contributions

The contributions of this paper lie in three folds.

Firstly, we propose a novel descriptor called GL_Mars for texture classification: the marginal distribution and a proposed decoupled marginal distribution of the GM and LOG vectors. The mutual interaction between the GM and LOG is decoupled in this descriptor and state-of-the-art performance for texture classification is achieved.

Secondly, we propose to compute the local statistics contrary to using the response itself directly. We find the local statistics gives more rotation invariance and keep the dimension of the descriptor low, which will favor the partition of the descriptor space. Besides, only a few quantization levels could give high performance, which makes the descriptor a low dimension vector.

Thirdly, we investigate the effects of four different normalization procedures.

The paper is organized as follows. Section 2 gives the motivation and the computation of the proposed texture descriptors. Section 3 gives the classification results on three benchmark texture dataset and investigate the role of the local statistic computation and the normalization procedure. Conclusions are given in Section 4.

# 2    Texture Classification Based on GM and LOG

## 2.1    Marginal Distributions of GM and LOG

Most image information is conveyed by the contrast or discontinuity of the intensity values. Inspired by the work in [20], which predicted the image quality with the statistics of normalized GM and LOG features, and discriminated well the distorted images with different level of degradation, we propose a novel descriptor for the task of texture classification. We argue that the local statistics is more effective than the response of filter bank and proposed to describe the local texture structure with the marginal distribution and a newly proposed decoupled marginal distribution.

### Marginal Distribution.
Denote by $I$ a texture image. Its GM map and LOG map can be computed as:

$$G = \sqrt{[I * h_x]^2 + [I * h_y]^2}, \tag{1}$$

$$L = I * h_{LOG}, \tag{2}$$

where "$*$" is the linear convolution operator and $h_d, d \in x, y$, is the Gaussian partial derivative filter applied along the horizontal ($x$) or vertical ($y$) direction, and $h_{LOG}$ is the Laplacian of Gaussian function. The square operation is implemented in point-wise manner. The only parameter of these three filters is the scale parameter $\sigma$. To make the range of the output same, they are $L_1$-normalized before the convolution operation. Both the resulted GM and LOG features are rotation invariant, which is required by texture classification.

The marginal distribution of the GM for natural images follows a Weibull distribution [13] while the LOG follows a Laplacian distribution. Difference in image content only gives rise to the change of shape parameter. Texture image is usually constituted by repetition of some basic luminance patterns and is probably sparser in the high-dimensional space than natural image. Thus the global statistics may be not sufficient to tell the difference between different classes. To develop a texture classification method, we use the local statistics of GM and LOG vectors to capture the texture structures. We firstly use the marginal distributions of the GM and LOG response for a local patch as the local texture descriptor. After quantizing $G$ into $M$ levels $g_1, g_2, ..., g_M$ and $L$ into $N$ levels $l_1, l_2, ..., l_N$, the first part of the descriptor can be formulated as:

$$h_{\sigma,1} = [p(G_\sigma = g_m)_m, p(L_\sigma = l_n)_n], \tag{3}$$

where $p(\cdot)$ computes the marginal distribution of the GM and LOG vector in a local patch, and $m = 1, ... M, n = 1, ... N$. The subscript indicates the scale parameter the gaussian derivative filters.

### Decoupled Marginal Distribution
The marginal distribution only captures the first order statistics of the GM and LOG features and the mutual interaction between the two is ignored. Actually, the GM feature and the LOG feature are closely related. To obtain a statistics that can take into account this interaction, a decoupled marginal distribution is introduced as the second part of the descriptor:

$$q(G = g_m) = \frac{1}{N} \sum_{n=1}^{N} p(G = g_m | L = l_n), \tag{4}$$

$$q(L = l_n) = \frac{1}{M} \sum_{m=1}^{M} p(L = l_n | G = g_m). \tag{5}$$

When LOG has a uniform marginal distributions, that is $p(L = l_n) = \frac{1}{N}$ , then from Eq. 4, we can get

$$q(G = g_m) = \sum_{n=1}^{N} p(G = g_m | L = l_n) p(L = l_n)$$
$$= \sum_{n=1}^{N} p(G = g_m, L = l_n) = p'(G = g_m) \tag{6}$$

We use $p'$ since it's not a real marginal distribution. Similar result can be derived for Eq. 5. From this point, $q$ can be viewed as the marginal distribution of GM/LOG when LOG/GM has a uniform distribution. By this way, the effect of one feature to the marginal probability of the other one can be removed. Therefore we call it decoupled marginal distribution. Then, the second part of the descriptor can be formulated as:

$$h_{\sigma,2} = [q(G_\sigma = g_m)_m, q(L_\sigma = l_n)_n].$$ (7)

## 2.2  Normalization of GM and LOG

Before the computation of $h_{\sigma,1}$ and $h_{\sigma,2}$, the two features GM and LOG are normalized within each patch. We investigate the effect of four difference normalization methods to the classification accuracy. Let $G(x)$ and $L(x)$ be the GM and LOG vectors in a local patch centered at location $\mathbf{x}$, then they can be normalized by:

- $L_2$-normalization

$$G_{L2}(x) = \frac{G(x)}{\|G(x)\|_2}, L_{L2}(x) = \frac{L(x)}{\|L(x)\|_2}$$ (8)

- Weber-normalization [21]

$$G_{WB}(x) = G(x) \times \frac{\log\left(1 + \|G(x)\|_2/0.03\right)}{\|G(x)\|_2)},$$
$$L_{WB}(x) = L(x) \times \frac{\log\left(1 + \|L(x)\|_2/0.03\right)}{\|L(x)\|_2)}.$$ (9)

- Sum-$L_2$ normalization

$$G_{SL2}(x) = \frac{2G(x)}{\|G(x)\|_2 + \|L(x)\|_2}, L_{SL2}(x) = \frac{2L(x)}{\|G(x)\|_2 + \|L(x)\|_2}.$$ (10)

- Sum-Weber normalization

$$G_{SWB}(x) = G(x) \times \frac{\log\left(1 + \sqrt{\|G(x)\|_2^2 + \|L(x)\|_2^2}/0.03\right)}{\sqrt{\|G(x)\|_2^2 + \|L(x)\|_2^2}},$$
$$L_{SWB}(x) = L(x) \times \frac{\log\left(1 + \sqrt{\|G(x)\|_2^2 + \|L(x)\|_2^2}/0.03\right)}{\sqrt{\|G(x)\|_2^2 + \|L(x)\|_2^2}}.$$ (11)

The first two normalization have been used in [4,21]. These normalization can well remove the contrast difference of patches across the whole images while keep the local structure within that patch. In the Sum-$L_2$ and Sum-Weber normalization, we consider the summation of the $L_2$-norm of the two features due to the fact that it represents the energy of the texture structure in that patch. We will investigate the effects of these normalization procedure to the classification accuracy in Section 3.

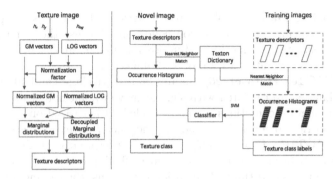

**Fig. 1.** The flowchart of the proposed method for texture classification.

### 2.3   Texture Image Representation and Classification

The whole flowchart of the proposed method is shown in Figure 1. In the left shows the computation of the proposed local descriptors. In the right shows the training procedure and the test procedure. Follow the framework of BOW, a texture image is represented by a normalized occurrence frequency of the local descriptors over a pre-computed set of cluster centers i.e. texton dictionary. For the descriptor of local texture structure, we use the concatenation of the marginal distribution and the decoupled marginal distribution: $H_\sigma = [h_{\sigma,1}, h_{\sigma,2}]$. For the texton dictionary, we use the spectrum K-Means [24] to generate the cluster centers. In the occurrence computation, the $\chi^2$ distance is used to find the nearest texton in the dictionary. To make the descriptor robust to scale variation, we compute the descriptor over 4 scales. The resulted multi-scale descriptor is of $4 \times (2M + 2N)$ dimension.

With the representation of the texture image available, the Support vector machine (SVM) is used to train the classifier on the training data and then test the performance on the test data. Two kernel functions are employed in SVM: the Gaussian Radial Basis Function (RBF) kernel and the $\chi^2$ kernel:

$$K(H_i, H_j) = exp(-\gamma \|H_i - H_j\|^2) \tag{12}$$

$$K(H_i, H_j) = exp(-\frac{\gamma}{2} \sum_k \frac{[H_i(k) - H_j(k)]^2}{H_i(k) + H_j(k)}). \tag{13}$$

For simplicity, we use the *kernel +normalization* to denote the different settings in the following paper. For example, *RBF+Weber* means Weber normalization is employed in the descriptors and RBF kernel is used in the SVM.

## 3   Classification Results and Analysis

### 3.1   Texture Datasets and Experiments Settings

Three challenging texture datasets are selected for the evaluation of the proposed descriptors in texture classification.

**The CUReT Dataset** [25] contains images of 61 materials imaged under 205 different viewing and illumination conditions. We use the same subset of images that has been previously used in other works: 92 images of are included for each materials, result in a total of 5612 images.

**The UIUCTex Dataset** [26] contains 25 texture classes and 40 images per class. The images are captured with significant viewpoint and scale variations, and the illumination conditions are uncontrolled. Other variations include non-planarity, non-rigid deformations, and inhomogeneity of texture patterns.

**The KTH-TIPS Dataset** [27] contains 10 texture classes. For each class, the images are captured in a combination of 9 different scales spanning two octaves, three poses and three illumination conditions, thus giving a total of 81 image per class.

For these datasets, we randomly select half of the images in each class as the training set and the rest as the test set. The train-test procedure is repeated 1000 times and the mean classification accuracy is used as the final performance. To learn the texton dictionary, one quarter of the images in each class is used to generate samples as the input of the K-Means algorithm. In this work, SVM is implemented by LibSVM library [28].

In all the following experiments, the quantization levels $M$ and $N$ are both set to 6 for the GM and LOG features. Without specific description, the block size will be set to 13. The four scale parameters are set to [0.5, 1.0, 3.0, 5.0]. The cluster size $K$ is set to 20 in each texture class for all the three datasets.

As in this work we only focus on the filter-bank based methods, the competitors used in our experiment only include some classic or recent methods of this category, as introduced in the related work. Besides, the results of the influential work LBP method is also used for comparison.

## 3.2  Effect of the Normalization and Patch Size

We first investigate the effects of the four normalization methods and the patch size to the classification performance. The patch size for the local statistics computation is varied from $5 \times 5$ to $21 \times 21$. The results are illustrated in Figure 2.

On CUReT, the Sum-Weber normalization delivers the best performance with both the RBF kernel and the $\chi^2$ kernel. Besides, the Sum-$L_2$ normalization always performs better than $L_2$ normalization. These evidence the benefit of the summation normalization of the GM and LOG vectors. On KTH-TIPS, the $L_2$-normalization gives the best results with both of the two kernel. Except for the $L_2$-normalization with RBF kernel, the advantage of the summation normalization can be observed for the rest settings when the patch size is not too large. On UIUCTex, the Weber normalization shows clear superiority against the other three ones. Besides, the sum-normalization Sum-Weber and Sum-$L_2$ lost to the separate normalization $L_2$-norm and Weber-norm, respectively.

As for the patch size, we can draw from the curves in Figure 3.2 that when the local patch is larger than $13 \times 13$, the classification accuracy won't necessarily increase with the patch size. In addition, we conduct a comparison of the performance of GL_Mars using $\chi^2 + Sum\text{-}Weber$ settings, VZ-MR8 and VZ-patch

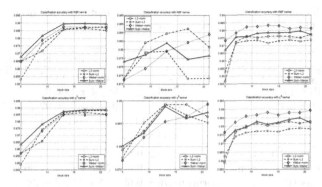

**Fig. 2.** The effect of the normalization method on the performance of texture classification for the three datasets. Up row: results with RBF kernel; Bottom row: results with $\chi^2$ kernel. Left:CUReT; Middle: KTH-TIPS; Right: UIUCTex.

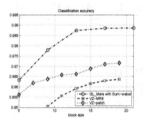

**Fig. 3.** Performance comparison of GL_Mars using Sum-Weber normalization, VZ-patch and VZ-MR8 as the patch size varies. The data source of VZ-MR8 and VZ-patch is from [21].

**Fig. 4.** The effect of the number of training images on UIUCTeX. The results of VZ-patch and VZ-MR8 are from [21], the results of LBP are computed by us.

for different patch size on CUReT. Note that VZ-patch can obtain well accuracy even with very compact support. The results are show in Figure 3.2. The results for the two competitors are from [21]. We can observe a clear and consistent superiority of GL_Mars over VZ-patch and VZ-MR8. Even with patch size of $5 \times 5$, GL_Mars can still achieve an accuracy of $96.33 \pm 1.10\%$.

### 3.3 Performance Comparison on the Three Datasets

Firstly, we show in Table.1 the performance comparison of GL_Mars with other competitors. The used competitors include multiple resolution $LBP^{riu2}$ [5], VZ-MR8 [14], VZ-patch [21], BIF [15], and RP [23].

From this table, we can draw that the proposed GL_Mars with different settings all perform better or approximately the same with the state-of-the-art method. The results that are better than the best of the five competitors are highlighted in bold font. For CUReT and KTH-TIPS, GL_Mars can performs better than BIF and RP with multiple settings. For UIUCTex, only with

**Table 1.** Performance comparison of the proposed method with other state-of-art methods.(%) (The results for LBP is computed by us.)

| | CUReT | UIUCTex | KTH-TIPS |
|---|---|---|---|
| $LBP^{riu2}_{1,8+3,16+5,24}$ [5] | 95.72 | $94.03 \pm 1.13$ | $97.11 \pm 1.81$ |
| VZ-MR8 [14] | 97.43 | $92.94 \pm 1.06$ | 94.8 |
| VZ-patch [21] | 97.17 | $97.83 \pm 0.66$ | $92.4 \pm 2.1$ |
| BIF [15] | $98.6 \pm 0.1$ | $98.8 \pm 0.1$ | $98.5 \pm 0.1$ |
| RP [23] | $98.43 \pm 0.22$ | \ | \ |
| GL_Mars (RBF+$L_2$-norm) | $98.58 \pm 0.54$ | $97.61 \pm 0.67$ | $98.38 \pm 1.12$ |
| GL_Mars (RBF+Sum-$L_2$) | $98.61 \pm 0.66$ | $97.17 \pm 0.80$ | $97.96 \pm 1.22$ |
| GL_Mars (RBF+Weber-norm) | $98.76 \pm 0.69$ | $98.33 \pm 0.62$ | $97.96 \pm 1.19$ |
| GL_Mars (RBF+Sum-Weber) | $98.95 \pm 0.57$ | $97.85 \pm 0.66$ | $98.15 \pm 1.56$ |
| GL_Mars ($\chi^2$+$L_2$-norm) | $98.53 \pm 0.65$ | $98.04 \pm 0.61$ | $98.92 \pm 1.26$ |
| GL_Mars ($\chi^2$+Sum-$L_2$) | $98.65 \pm 0.58$ | $97.72 \pm 0.70$ | $98.93 \pm 1.06$ |
| GL_Mars ($\chi^2$+Weber-norm) | $98.50 \pm 0.78$ | $98.81 \pm 0.51$ | $98.54 \pm 1.13$ |
| GL_Mars ($\chi^2$+Sum-Weber) | $98.74 \pm 0.88$ | $98.13 \pm 0.63$ | $98.87 \pm 1.11$ |

$\chi^2 + Weber$-$norm$, GL_Mars performs a little better than BIF. When the patch size for the local statistic computation is varied from $5 \times 5$ to $21 \times 21$, the best classification accuracy of GL_Mars are $98.84 \pm 0.61, 98.94 \pm 0.49, 98.88 \pm 0.10$ for CUReT, UIUCTex and KTH-TIPS, respectively.

We also examine the robustness of the proposed method with respect to the number of training images on UIUCTeX dataset. The number of the training images increases from 5 to 20 and the classification accuracy of GL_Mars with $\chi^2 + Weber$-$norm$ is computed. For comparison, the corresponding results of VZ-patch and VZ-MR8 are taken from [21]. Figure 3.2 shows the results. GL_Mars demonstrates great advantage over VZ-MR8 and LBP, keeping a $1 \sim 2$ percent improvement over VZ-patch, for all the settings of the number of training images.

## 4   Conclusions

In this work, we proposed a novel texture descriptor GL_Mars for texture classification. The descriptor consists of the marginal distribution and a new decoupled marginal distribution. When being examined on three benchmark texture datasets, GL_Mars delivers better performance than the referred filter bank based methods and the multiple resolution LBP. In the meantime, GL_Mars possesses the following advantages: very good performance with small patch; constant dimension of the descriptors; more robust results to the number of training images. Besides, as for the four normalization methods, the superiority of the summation normalization can be observed on two datasets.

# References

1. Leung, T., Malik, J.: Representing and recognizing the visual appearance of materials using three-dimensional textons. IJCV **43**(1), 29–44 (2001)
2. Schmid, C.: Constructing models for content-based image retrieval. In: CVPR 2001, vol. 2, pp. II–39. IEEE (2001)
3. Varma, M., Zisserman, A.: Unifying statistical texture classification frameworks. Image and Vision Computing **22**(14), 1175–1183 (2004)
4. Varma, M.: Statistical Approaches to texture classification. PhD thesis (2004)
5. Ojala, T., Pietikäinen, M., Mäenpää, T.: Multiresolution gray-scale and rotation invariant texture classification with local binary patterns. IEEE TPAMI **24**(7), 971–987 (2002)
6. Fathi, A., Naghsh-Nilchi, A.R.: Noise tolerant local binary pattern operator for efficient texture analysis. Pattern Recognition Letters **33**(9), 1093–1100 (2012)
7. Guo, Z., Zhang, L., Zhang, D.: Rotation invariant texture classification using lbp variance (lbpv) with global matching. Pattern Recognition **43**(3), 706–719 (2010)
8. Liu, L., Zhao, L., Long, Y., Kuang, G., Fieguth, P.: Extended local binary patterns for texture classification. Image and Vision Computing **30**(2), 86–99 (2012)
9. Cheng, M.-M., Zhang, Z., Lin, W.-Y., Torr, P.: Bing: binarized normed gradients for objectness estimation at 300fps. In: CVPR 2014, pp. 3286–3293. IEEE (2014)
10. Lowe, D.G.: Distinctive image features from scale-invariant keypoints. IJCV **60**(2), 91–110 (2004)
11. Dalal, N., Triggs, B.: Histograms of oriented gradients for human detection. In: CVPR 2005, vol. 1, pp. 886–893. IEEE (2005)
12. Xue, W., Mou, X., Zhang, L., Bovik, A.C., Feng, X.: Blind image quality assessment using joint statistics of gradient magnitude and laplacian features. IEEE TIP **23**(11), 4850–4862 (2014)
13. Liu, A., Lin, W., Narwaria, M.: Image quality assessment based on gradient similarity. IEEE TIP **21**(4), 1500–1512 (2012)
14. Varma, M., Zisserman, A.: A statistical approach to texture classification from single images. IJCV **62**(1–2), 61–81 (2005)
15. Crosier, M., Griffin, L.D.: Texture classification with a dictionary of basic image features. In: CVPR 2008, pp. 1–7. IEEE (2008)
16. Bovik, A.C., Clark, M., Geisler, W.S.: Multichannel texture analysis using localized spatial filters. IEEE TPAMI **12**(1), 55–73 (1990)
17. Manjunath, B.S., Ma, W.-Y.: Texture features for browsing and retrieval of image data. IEEE TPAMI **18**(8), 837–842 (1996)
18. Heeger, D.J., Bergen, J.R.: Pyramid-based texture analysis/synthesis. In: Annual conference on Computer Graphics and Interactive Techniques, pp. 229–238. ACM (1995)
19. Chang, T., Kuo, C.C.J.: Texture analysis and classification with tree-structured wavelet transform. IEEE TIP **2**(4), 429–441 (1993)
20. Varma, M., Zisserman, A.: Texture classification: are filter banks necessary? In: CVPR 2003, vol. 2, pp. II–691. IEEE (2003)
21. Varma, M., Zisserman, A.: A statistical approach to material classification using image patch exemplars. IEEE TPAMI **31**(11), 2032–2047 (2009)
22. Liu, L., Fieguth, P., Kuang, G.: Compressed sensing for robust texture classification. In: Kimmel, R., Klette, R., Sugimoto, A. (eds.) ACCV 2010, Part I. LNCS, vol. 6492, pp. 383–396. Springer, Heidelberg (2011)

23. Liu, L., Fieguth, P.W.: Texture classification from random features. IEEE TPAMI **34**(3), 574–586 (2012)
24. Chen, X., Cai, D.: Large scale spectral clustering with landmark-based representation. In: AAAI (2011)
25. Cula, O.G., Dana, K.J.: Compact representation of bidirectional texture functions. In: CVPR 2001, vol. 1, pp. I–1041. IEEE (2001)
26. Lazebnik, S., Schmid, C., Ponce, J.: A sparse texture representation using local affine regions. IEEE TPAMI **27**(8), 1265–1278 (2005)
27. Hayman, E., Caputo, B., Fritz, M., Eklundh, J.-O.: On the significance of real-world conditions for material classification. In: Pajdla, T., Matas, J.G. (eds.) ECCV 2004. LNCS, vol. 3024, pp. 253–266. Springer, Heidelberg (2004)
28. Chang, C.-C., Lin, C.-J.: Libsvm: A library for support vector machines. ACM TIST **2**(3), 27 (2011)

# MR Image Segmentation Using Active Contour Model Incorporated with Sobel Edge Detection

Honggang Zhang[✉], Yunhong Wang, Qingjie Liu, and Di Huang

Intelligent Recognition and Image Processing Lab,
School of Computer Science and Engineering, Beihang University, Beijing 100191, China
{hgzhang,yhwang,liuqingjie,dhuang}@buaa.edu.cn

**Abstract.** This paper proposes a segmentation method which combines Active contour model with Sobel edge detection. The introduction of distance regularized formulation eliminates the need for reinitialization when we minimize the energy function by using the level set method. We test our method on MR image and compare it with several methods in the literature. The results achieved are better than the ones of existing techniques, showing the effectiveness of the proposed method.

**Keywords:** Image segmentation · Active contour model · Edge detection operator · Level set method

## 1 Introduction

Image segmentation has been widely used in medical analysis such as identifying tumors or soft tissue injuries from medical illustration [1], [2]. Active contour model is an excellent method and has been applied to image segmentation [3], [4], [11]. The general idea is to first initialize a curve around the object and then makes the curve move toward the object's interior morphology under the control of an energy function and finally stop at the boundary of the target area. Compare with classical image segmentation methods, active contour model has two advantages. Firstly, active contour model can be easily derived by energy minimization framework [5], [6]. Secondly, active contour model is able to achieve the sub-pixel accuracy of object boundaries [7]. It can be divided into two types: parametric active contour model and geometric active contour model. Parametric active contour was introduced by Kass et. al [8]. The energy function is minimized to attract the contour toward the edges, in which first derivative and second derivative were used to control the smoothness of the active contour, and therefore their method belongs to parametric active contour. However, the main disadvantage of the parametric active contour models is that the relation between the parametrization of the contour and geometry of the objects is not obvious.

To overcome the drawback of the parametric active contour model, geometric active contour model was proposed, which can be further categorized into edge-based models and region-based models. Edge-based models use edge information to attract

© Springer-Verlag Berlin Heidelberg 2015
H. Zha et al. (Eds.): CCCV 2015, Part I, CCIS 546, pp. 429–437, 2015.
DOI: 10.1007/978-3-662-48558-3_43

the active contour move toward the object boundaries. But it still remains a challenge to find a proper trade-off between noise smoothing and edge information preservation, especially in the real condition. While, most MR image is noisy, if the isotropic smoothing such as Gaussian is strong, the edge would be smooth too. Region-based models used a certain region descriptor to guide the motion of the active contour, and therefore it could detect contours without edges. However, the region-based models are limited by intensity homogeneity. In fact, intensity inhomogeneity often occurs in MR images. Tsai et al. [9] proposed region-based model which regards image segmentation as a problem of finding a best approximation of the original image by a piecewise smooth function. The model has certain ability to solve intensity inhomogeneity. Michailovich et al. [10] proposed an active contour model using the Bhattacharyya difference between the intensity distributions inside and ouside a con-tour, and to some extent, solved the limitation of intensity homogeneity.

In this paper, the region-based active contour model and Sobel edge detection are combined. The proposed method is evaluated on some MR images, and the experimental results show that it is effective for such an issue.

The remainder of the paper is organized as follows. Section 2 introduces the Sobel operator based edge detection, and Section 3 presents how the region based active contour model is combined with the Sobel operator. We describe the solution of the energy function using the distance regularized level set method in Section 4. Experimental results are shown and analyzed in Section 5. Section 6 concludes the paper.

## 2     An Edge Detection Model Based on Sobel Operator

In digital images, the edge is a collection of pixels whose gray values have great changes. Therefore, it is the most basic feature of the image. Edge extraction is one of the most important and fundamental techniques in image processing and many related domains.

Sobel edge detection is a gradient based edge detection method. It has two advantages. Firstly, it is based on convolving the image with a small filter, and thus relatively inexpensive in terms of computation. Secondly, it actually uses an average factor to smooth the random noise of the image.

The operator contains two 3-dimensional matrices: one for horizontal changes, and anotherfor vertical ones. The two 3*3 kernels convolved with the original image are used to calculate the approximation of the horizontal and vertical differences. If we define $I$ as the original image, Gx and Gy are two images which contain the longitudinal and transverse edge detection result. Then Gx and Gy are obtained as follows:

$$G_y = \begin{bmatrix} -1 & -2 & -1 \\ 0 & 0 & 0 \\ +1 & +2 & +1 \end{bmatrix} * I \ and \ G_x = \begin{bmatrix} -1 & 0 & +1 \\ -2 & 0 & +2 \\ -1 & 0 & +1 \end{bmatrix} * I \tag{1}$$

where '*' is the convolution operator. At each point of the image, the gradient of $I$(x, y) is defined as $f$, and denotes the change of $f$. The resulting gradient approximations are combined to give the gradient magnitude:

$$mag(\nabla f) = \sqrt{G_x{}^2 + G_y{}^2} \qquad (2)$$

For faster computation, (2) is approximated as:

$$mag(\nabla f) \approx |G_x| + |G_y| \qquad (3)$$

This expression still preserves the relative changes in intensity. According to the value of $mag(\nabla f)$, we can determine whether there is an edge passing through the point (x, y).

# 3    Region-Based Active Contour Model Combines with Sobel Operater

Let $\Omega \in R^2$ be the image domain, and $I : \Omega \rightarrow R$ be a given gray level image. Mumford and Shah [12] solved the image segmentation problem by minimizing a function. By this way, they found a contour C which segments the image. The energy function is defined as follows:

$$F^{MS}(u, C) = \int_\Omega (u - I)^2 dx + \mu \int_{\Omega \backslash C} |\nabla u|^2 dx + v|C| \qquad (4)$$

Where $v|C|$ is the Euclidean length, or more generally, the length of the contour C. The role of the first two terms is smooth image and ensures an image $u$ that approximates the original image $I$. The minimized problem is called the minimal partition problem. In practice, the function is difficult to minimize mathematically.

Chan and Vense proposed an active contour model which is a particular case of the minimal partition problem [13]. It is a simplified version of Mumford–Shah model. The C-V model introduced the energy function by:

$$F(C, c_1, c_2) = \mu \cdot length(C) + v \cdot area(insideC)$$

$$+ \alpha_1 \int_{inside(C)} |I - c_1|^2 dxdy + \alpha_2 \int_{outside(C)} |I - c_2|^2 dxdy \qquad (5)$$

where $c_1$ and $c_2$ are two constants that approximate the image intensity in inside(C) and outside(C). The inside(C) and outside(C) represent the areas inside and outside the contour C. They also added some regularizing terms, e.g. the length of $C$ and the area inside $C$, and $\mu$, $v$, $\alpha_1$, $\alpha_2$ are fixed parameters.

In the (5), the two regularizing terms are not only difficult to calculate accurately, but have no relation with image of the geometric structure of the image as well. Therefore, we embed Sobel operater into the energy function to highlight gradient cues.

| $Z_1$ | $Z_2$ | $Z_3$ |
|------|------|------|
| $Z_4$ | $Z_5$ | $Z_6$ |
| $Z_7$ | $Z_8$ | $Z_9$ |

(a)

| -1 | -2 | -1 |
|----|-----|----|
| 0 | 0.5 | 0 |
| 1 | 2 | 1 |

(b)

| -1 | 0 | 1 |
|----|-----|---|
| -2 | 0.5 | 2 |
| -1 | 0 | 1 |

(c)

**Fig. 1.** (a) 3x3 region of an image. (b) 0° Sobel kernel. (c) 90° Sobel kernel

We replace the center of one kernel from 0 to m, and the one of another kernel is thus 1-m. To simplify this case, we set m at 0.5 in our study. The two 3x3 templates are shown as Fig. 1 (b) and (c). Every point in the image uses these two kernels for convolution. Then, (1) becomes:

$$G_{x_{plus}} = (Z_7 + 2 \times Z_8 + Z_9) - (Z_1 + 2 \times Z_2 + Z_3) + 0.5 \times Z_5$$

$$G_{y_{plus}} = (Z_3 + 2 \times Z_6 + Z_9) - (Z_1 + 2 \times Z_4 + Z_7) + 0.5 \times Z_5 \qquad (6)$$

We define $I_{plus}$ as:

$$I_{plus} = G_{x_{plus}} + G_{y_{plus}} \qquad (7)$$

By this way, we embed the Sobel operater to the center pixel. Then, we replaced $I$ with $I_{plus}$, and the energy function (5) can be written as:

$$F_{plus}(C, c_1, c_2) = \alpha_1 \int_{inside(C)} |I_{plus} - c_1|^2 dxdy + \alpha_2 \int_{outside(C)} |I_{plus} - c_2|^2 dxdy \quad (8)$$

The minimal function problem can be formulated and solved using the level set method. In this paper, we introduce the distance regularization energy [14], which is presented in the next section.

## 4    The Distance Regularized Level Set Formulation of the Function

In level set methods [15], an evolving curve $C$ is represented by the zero level set of a Lipschitz function $\Phi$. So, $C = \{(x, y) \in \Omega : \Phi(x, y) = 0\}$, which is called a level set function, and we choose $\varphi$ to be positive inside $C$ and negative outside $C$. Let $H$ be the Heaviside function, therefore, the new energy still denoted by $F_{plus}(\Phi, c_1, c_2)$, becomes:

$$F_{plus}(\Phi, c_1, c_2) = \alpha_1 \int_{\Phi \geq 0} |I_{plus} - c_1|^2 dxdy + \alpha_2 \int_{\Phi < 0} |I_{plus} - c_2|^2 dxdy \qquad (9)$$

The Heavised function $H$ is approximated by a smooth function $H_\epsilon$ which is defined by

$$H_\epsilon(x) = \frac{1}{2}\left[1 + \frac{2}{\pi}arctan\left(\frac{x}{\epsilon}\right)\right] \qquad (10)$$

The derivative of $H_\epsilon$ is

$$\sigma_\epsilon(x) = \frac{d}{dx}H_\epsilon(x) = \frac{1}{\pi}\frac{\epsilon}{\epsilon^2 + x^2} \qquad (11)$$

The two terms of $F_{plus}$ can be rewritten in the following way:

$$\int_{\Phi \geq 0}\left|I_{plus} - c_1\right|^2 dxdy = \int_\Omega \left|I_{plus} - c_1\right|^2 H(\Phi)dxdy$$

$$\int_{\Phi < 0}\left|I_{plus} - c_2\right|^2 dxdy = \int_\Omega \left|I_{plus} - c_2\right|^2(1 - H(\Phi))dxdy \qquad (12)$$

Then (10) can be written as:

$$F_{plus}(\Phi, c_1, c_2) = \alpha_1 \int_\Omega \left|I_{plus} - c_1\right|^2 H(\Phi)dxdy$$

$$+ \alpha_2 \int_\Omega \left|I_{plus} - c_2\right|^2(1 - H(\Phi))dxdy \qquad (13)$$

In order to keep the regularity of the level set function, we should preserve the stability of level set evolution. Therefore, we introduce a distance regularization term in the level set formulation. As proposed in [16], we define the level set regularization term as:

$$P(\Phi) = \int \frac{1}{2}(\nabla \varphi(x) - 1)^2 dx \qquad (14)$$

Then, we minimize the energy function:

$$F(\Phi, c_1, c_2) = F_{plus}(\Phi, c_1, c_2) + \mu P(\Phi) \qquad (15)$$

The function (16) can be minimized by the Euler-Lagrange equation:    (paramterizing the descent direction by an artificial time):

$$\frac{\partial \Phi}{\partial t} = \mu div\left[\nabla\Phi\left(1 - \frac{1}{\nabla\Phi}\right)\right] + \sigma_\epsilon(\Phi)\left[\alpha_2(I_{plus} - c_2)^2 - \alpha_1(I_{plus} - c_1)^2\right] \qquad (16)$$

where $\mu, \alpha_1, \alpha_2$ are fixed parameters. In the end, we introduce $\tau$, and then we reach the result:

$$\Phi_{k+1} = \Phi_k + \tau \frac{\partial \Phi_k}{\partial t} \qquad (17)$$

## 5    Experimental Result

The proposed method is validated on MR images. Both the traditional region-based model and the active contour model incorporated with Sobel edge detection are used to segment MR images for comparison. We also compare our method with the

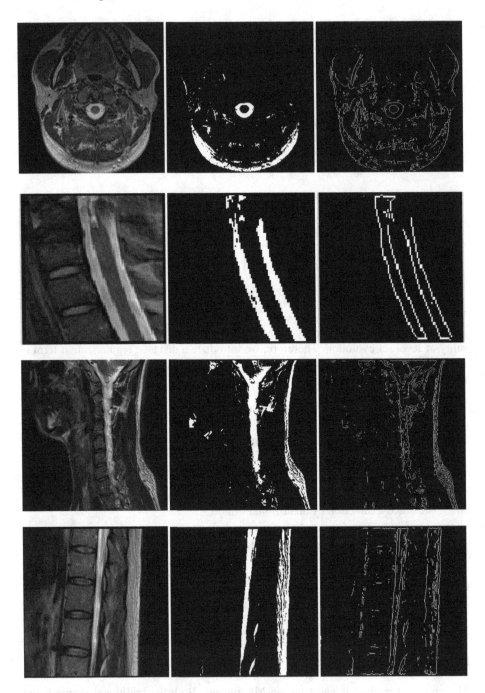

**Fig. 2.** Error of thresholding and Sobel edge detection for MR image. Column 1: Original images. Column 2: Thresholding results. Column 3: Result of Sobel edge detection.

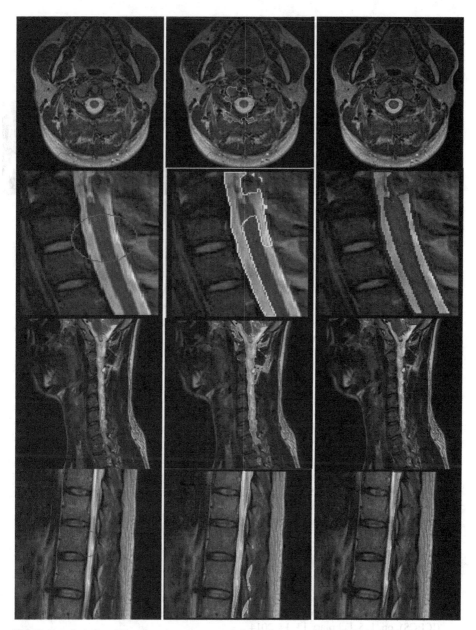

**Fig. 3.** Results of traditional active contour model and our method. Column 1: Initial contour and original image. Column 2: traditional active contour model method. Column 3: the proposed method.

thresh-old method and the edge detection method. It turns out that the proposed active con-tour model that is combined with Sobel edge detection achieves better results than the other two methods. The results are shown in Fig.2 to Fig.4. The MR image in

Fig. 2 is segmented with simple thresholding and Sobel edge detection, and the result are not enough. The second and third columns in Fig. 3 show the results with the same initial contours. The Fig. 4 shows the contour evolution process from the initial contour to the final contour using our method.

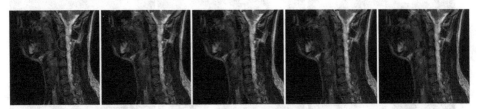

**Fig. 4.** Results of our method for MR images. The contour evolution process from the initial contour to the final contour    is displayed.

The region-based active contour model combined with Sobel edge detection is able to segment the target from the image, but traditional active contour model fails. Because of the simple thresholding, edge detection and traditional active contour model could only use single information of the image while the active contour model with Sobel operater combines the region-base model with edge information other than single information. At the same time, it also inherits the advantage of Sobel operator which could smooth the random noise of image.

## 6    Conclusion

In this paper, we present a region-based active contour model combined with the Sobel edge detection operator. The proposed method is able to provide better quality of MR image segmentation. With distance regularized level set formulation, the pro-cess of segmentation can maintain the stability of level set evolution. As the experi-mental results demonstrate, our method works better than some well-known methods of MR image segmentation.

## Refeerences

1. Prakash, R.M., Kumari, R.S.S.: Nonsubsampled contourlet transform based expectation maximization method with adaptive mean shift for automatic segmentation of MR brain images. In: 2014 International Conference on Electronics and Communication Systems (ICECS), pp. 1–5, February 13–14, 2014
2. Rodtook, A., Makhanov, S.S.: Multi-feature gradient vector flow snakes for adaptive segmentation of the ultrasound images of breast cancer. Journal of Visual Communication and Image Representation **24**(6), 1414–1430 (2013)
3. Malladi, R., Sethian, J.A., Vemuri, B.C.: Shape modeling with front propagation: a level set approach. IEEE Trans. Pattern Anal. Mach. Intell. **17**(2), 158–175 (1995)

4. Li, C., Xu, C., Gui, C., Fox, M.D.: Level set evolution without re-initialization: a new variational formulation. In: Proc. IEEE Conf. Computer Vision and Pattern Recognition, vol. 1, pp. 430–436 (2005)

5. Chen, Y., Tagare, H., Thiruvenkadam, S., Huang, F., Wilson, D., Gopinath, K., Briggs, R., Geiser, E.: Using prior shapes in geometric active contours in a variational framework. Int. J. Comput. Vis. **50**, 315–328 (2002)

6. Leventon, M., Grimson, W., Faugeras, O.: Statistical shape influence in geodesic active contours. In: Proc. IEEE Conf. Computer Vision and Pattern Recognition, vol. I, pp. 316–323 (2000)

7. Caselles, V., Kimmel, R., Sapiro, G.: Geodesic active contours. Int. J. Comput. Vis. **22**, 61–79 (1997)

8. Kass, M., Witkin, A., Terzopoulos, D.: Snakes: active contour models. Int. J. Comput. Vis. **1**, 321–331 (1987)

9. Tsai, A., Yezzi, A., Willsky, A.S.: Curve evolution implementation of the Mumford-Shah functional for image segmentation, denoising, interpolation, and magnification. IEEE Trans. Image Process. **10**(8), 1169–1186 (2001)

10. Michailovich, O., Rathi, Y., Tannenbaum, A.: Image segmentation using active contours driven by the bhattacharyya gradient flow. IEEE Trans. Image Process. **16**(11), 2787–2801 (2007)

11. He, N., Zhang, P., Lu, K.: A geometric active contours model for multiple objects segmentation. In: Huang, D.-S., Wunsch II, D.C., Levine, D.S., Jo, K.-H. (eds.) ICIC 2008. LNCS, vol. 5226, pp. 1141–1148. Springer, Heidelberg (2008)

12. Mumford, D., Shah, J.: Optimal approximations by piecewise smooth functions and associated variational problems. Commun. Pure Appl. Math. **42**, 577–685 (1989)

13. Chan, T., Vese, L.: Active contours without edges. IEEE Trans. Image Process. **10**(2), 266–277 (2001)

14. Li, C., Kao, C.-Y., Gore, J.C., Ding, Z.: Minimization of Region-Scalable Fitting Energy for Image Segmentation. IEEE Transactions on Image Processing **17**(10), 1940–1949 (2008)

15. Zhao, H.-K., Osher, S., Merriman, B., Kang, M.: Implicit and nonparametric shape reconstruction from unorganized data using a variational level set method. Computer Vision and Image Understanding **80**(3), 295–314 (2000)

16. Li, C., Xu, C., Gui, C., Fox, M.D.: Level set evolution without re-initialization: a new variational formulation. In: IEEE Computer Society Conference on Computer Vision and Pattern Recognition, vol. 1, pp. 430–436, June 20-25, 2005

# Spatial-Temporal Feature Fusion for Human Fall Detection

Xin Ma[✉], Haibo Wang, Bingxia Xue, and Yibin Li

School of Control Science and Engineering, Shandong University, Jinan 250061, China
{maxin,liyb}@sdu.edu.cn, hbwang1427@gmail.com

**Abstract.** When suddenly falling to the ground, elderly people can get seriously injured. This paper presents a vision-based fall detection approach by using a low-cost depth camera. The approach is based on a novel combination of three feature types: curvature scale space (CSS), morphological, and temporal features. CSS and morphological features capture different properties of human silhouette during the falling procedure. All the two collected feature vectors are clustered to generate occurrence histogram as fall representations. Meanwhile, the trajectory of a skeleton point that depicts the temporal property of fall action is used as a complimentary representation. For each individual feature, ELM classifier is trained separately for fall prediction. Finally, their prediction scores are fused together to decide whether fall happens or not. For evaluating the approach, we built a depth dataset by capturing 6 daily actions (falling, bending, sitting, squatting, walking, and lying) from 20 subjects. Extensive experiments show that the proposed approach achieves an average 85.89% fall detection accuracy, which apparently outperforms using each feature type individually.

**Keywords:** Fall detection · Spatial-temporal feature · ELM

## 1 Introduction

When falling to the ground, elderly people need to be rescued as promptly as possible. Automatic fall detection becomes an emerging technique. Although wearable sensor has been used for fall detection [1], wearing a sensor will cause inconvenience to one's daily life. An unobtrusive technique is more favourable, but it needs to mount many ambient devices, such as vibration, sound sensor, infrared motion detector and pressure sensor, on room walls [2], which raises the cost of the solution, and may bring side effect to the human's health.

This work was supported in part by the National High Technology Research and Development Program of China under Grant No. 2015AA042307, Shandong Province Science and Technology Development Foundation under Grant No. 2014GGE27572, Shandong Province Independent Innovation and Achievement Transformation Special Fund under Grant No. 2014ZZCX04302, the Fundamental Research Funds of Shandong University under Grant No. 2015JC027, 2015JC051.

© Springer-Verlag Berlin Heidelberg 2015
H. Zha et al. (Eds.): CCCV 2015, Part I, CCIS 546, pp. 438–447, 2015.
DOI: 10.1007/978-3-662-48558-3_44

Camera is the more convenient unobtrusive sensor for human fall detection [3]. Moreover, camera can not only capture human activities but also record contextual information, which may be significant for fall detection.

Shape analysis in 3D space is more robust to viewpoint and partial occlusion as compared to 2D shape features. With a reconstructed human volume, tracking the trajectory of the centroid and orientation of 3D human volume can detect falls [4]. Although fall detection becomes easier with 3D model, reconstructing the model is computationally demanding, and calibrating multiple cameras is still challenging [5]. Recently, Microsoft releases Kinect as a low-cost tool for 3D depth acquisition. Kinect is robust to the variation of visible lights, thus being able to work day and night. Moreover, the identity of the detected subject is well masked in the depth map of Kinect. Many depth-based applications have emerged, such as 3D skeleton analysis [6], 3D head detection [7] and 3D gait recognition [8].

In this paper, we present a new fall detection approach by using the depth map of Kinect. Unlike previous purely shape-based [9] or motion-based [10] approaches, the proposed approach bases off a combination of three spatial and temporal features: Curvature Scale Space (CSS) features [11], morphological and temporal features. Since the three types of features are different in terms of the number of features at each video frame, one Extreme Learning Machine (ELM) [12] classifier is separately trained for each feature. Only in the final decision, the prediction scores of the three classifiers are fused to predict whether fall happens or not.

The rest of the paper is organized as follows. Section 2 presents the proposed fall detection approach. Section 3 describes experimental results. Section 4 closes the paper with concluding remarks.

## 2   The Proposed Approach

Fig. 1 shows pipeline of the proposed fall detection approach. Three types of features (CSS, morphological and temporal) are extracted from each frame of the input depth videos. A bag-of-words model is then built for the CSS and morphological features, respectively. By mapping the collected feature vectors of a video clip to the words book, the histogram of occurrence counts is used to represent the video clip. Meanwhile, temporal features are directly vectorized as the third representation of a video clip (normalized to be 50-frames). An individual classifier is trained separately for each feature type, whose prediction score is combined to decide whether fall happens or not.

### 2.1   Preprocessing

Given input videos the first step is to segment human body from background by using the adaptive Gaussian Mixture Model (GMM) [13]. Following it, silhouette is extracted by using a simple edge detector [14].

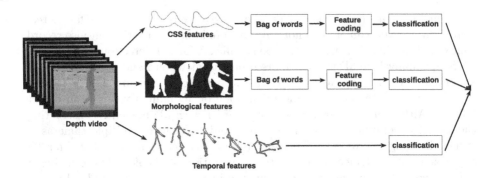

**Fig. 1.** Pipeline of the proposed fall detection approach. CSS, morphological and temporal features are extracted from input depth videos depicting various daily actions. A bag-of-words model is then built for the CSS and morphological features, respectively. The histogram of occurrence counts of the bagged words is used to encode each action. Meanwhile, temporal features are directly vectorized as the third action representation (normalized to be 50-frames). An individual classifier is trained separately for each feature type, whose prediction score is finally combined to decide whether fall happens or not.

The number of pixels on different silhouette is different, ranging from 10 to 50. To unify the pixel number for better CSS extraction, we uniformly sample 24 points on each extracted silhouette to form a compact silhouette. Then we process the compact silhouettes by normalizing their lengths to [0, 1] and smoothing them over time by averaging over the previous and the next four frames.

## 2.2   Spatial-Temporal Features

**Curvature Scale Space (CSS).** Curvature Scale Space (CSS) feature [11,15] is robust to translation, rotation, scaling and local deformation. Given a closed shape curve $\Gamma(x, y)$ with $(x, y)$ at Cartesian coordinates, we re-parameterize $\Gamma(x, y)$ in terms of its arc length $u$: $\Gamma(u) = (x(u), y(u))$. The curvature $\kappa$ of each $\Gamma_\sigma$ is $\kappa(u, \sigma)$. The CSS image of $\Gamma$ is defined at $\kappa(u, \sigma) = 0$, called the zero-crossing $(ZP)$ point. There are two types of $ZP$: $ZP_+$ - the start point of a concavity arc where $\kappa(u, \sigma)$ changes from negative to positive, and $ZP_-$ - the start point of a convexity arc where $\kappa(u, \sigma)$ changes from positive to negative. On a closed curve, $ZP_+$ and $ZP_-$ always appear as a pair. The arc between a pair of $ZP_+$ and $ZP_-$ is either concave $(ZP_+, ZP_-)$ or convex $(ZP_-, ZP_+)$. Since it is extracted from the curvatures at multiple scales, $ZP$ is invariant to rotation, translation and uniform scaling. To make it further robust against local deformation, we resample the CSS features by curve interpolation. During the curve evolution, we keep increasing $\sigma$ until $\Gamma_\sigma$ shrinks to a circle-like shape, in which all $ZP$s disappear. On a CSS image, the $(u, \sigma)$ coordinates of all $ZP$s form a set of continuous curves. The $(u, \sigma)$ coordinates of the maxima point of each curve constitute our CSS feature vector.

**Table 1.** 15 morphological features used in the paper.

| Name | Interpretation |
|---|---|
| Area | the actual number of pixels in the foreground region |
| Perimeter | the distance between each adjoining pair of pixels around the border of the region |
| EquivDiameter | the diameter of a circle with the same area as the region |
| MajorAxisLength | the length (in pixels) of the major axis of the ellipse that has the same normalized second central moments as the region |
| MinorAxisLength | the length (in pixels) of the minor axis of the ellipse that has the same normalized second central moments as the region |
| Eccentricity | the eccentricity of the ellipse that has the same second-moments as the region |
| Extent | the ratio of pixels in the region to pixels in the total bounding box |
| Solidity | the proportion of the pixels in the convex hull and also in the region |
| ConvexArea | the number of pixels in the convex hull of the region |
| smoothness | a measure of contour smoothness |
| compactness | a ratio of perimeter to the region area |
| Hausdorff Dimension | the number that represents the generalized fractal dimension of a 2D matrix |
| average radial ratio | the ratio of the radial distance of the contour over the radial distance of the minimally inscribing sphere |
| area overlap ratio | the area of the object over the area of the minimally inscribing circle |
| Stddis | the standard deviation of the distance of contour points normalized by the maximum distance |

**Morphological Features.** By filling the extracted shape silhouette, we obtain a foreground human region whose properties might uniquely characterize the depicted action. Thus we measure the region properties by computing its various morphological values. To this end we first detect the bounding rectangle of the region, and then normalize the bounded rectangle to the same $60 \times 80$ size. On the normalized patch, 15 morphological values are measured as detailed in Table 1. The values capture various regional properties such as area, perimeter, eccentricity, extent, smoothness, compactness and etc.

**Temporal Features.** Along with the depth map, the Kinect SDK can provide the 3D coordinates of 20 skeleton points. For each action the trajectories of the skeleton points can be very different. Thus, it is necessary to apply the trajectory of these skeleton points for fall detection. Unfortunately, when a person falls to the ground, the Kinect SDK fails to detect most of the skeleton points except the shoulder center. Therefore, we only consider the trajectory information of the shoulder center (shown in Fig. 2). Let $V$ denote the 3D coordinates of the shoulder center at time $t$

$$V = (x_t, y_t, z_t). \tag{1}$$

To reduce the influence of coordinate center, we calculate the relative coordinates as our temporal feature

$$F_t = \{x_t - x_{t-1}, y_t - y_{t-1}, z_t - z_{t-1} | t = 2, 3, ..., T\} \tag{2}$$

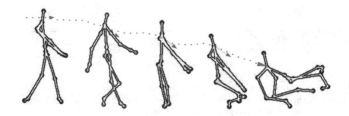

**Fig. 2.** Illustrating the temporal features. Kinect SDK could track the 3-D trajectory of upto 20 skeleton points. Among the points, the shoulder center is the only one that can be correctly tracked when a person falls to the ground. Thus, only the relative coordinates of the shoulder center is considered for fall detection. In particular, 50 frames are sampled from each sequence for the feature extraction, forming a vector of $3 \times 50 = 150$ dimensions.

where $T$ is the sequence length. Throughout the paper, $T$ is fixed at 50, indicating that we sample 50 frames from each sequence. Therefore, the temporal feature is a vector of $3 \times 50 = 150$ dimensions.

### 2.3  Feature Encoding

Both the CSS and the morphological features do not show obvious temporal consistency. Therefore, we neglect their temporal order, and use the Bag-of-Words (BoW) model [16] to generate distribution-based action representations. Since the numbers of CSS and morphological features can be different on each frame, an individual BoW model is separately built for each feature type.

In the first stage of BoW modeling, $K$-means clustering is applied over all feature vectors to generate a codebook. Each cluster center is a codeword, as a representative of similar feature vectors. Then by mapping the collected vectors of a video clip to the codebook, we have a histogram of occurrence counts of the words, which is the BoW representation of video action. Since both the CSS and the morphological features are in low-dimensional space (summarized in Table 2), building the BoW models is relatively fast.

The value of $K$ is critical in the $K$-means clustering. We experimented with several values, and empirically found that fixing $K = 100$ is good enough for both the CSS and morphological features.

**Table 2.** Summary of the three feature types.

| Features | CSS | Morphological | Temporal |
|---|---|---|---|
| Original Dimension | 2 | 15 | 3 |
| # of Clustering Centers | 100 | 100 | N/A |
| # of Action representation | 100 | 100 | $3 \times 50 = 150$ |

## 2.4    Classification and Fusion

Extreme learning machine (ELM) [12] is a single-hidden-layer feed-forward neural network. Given samples $\{\mathbf{x}_j\}$ and their labels $\{\mathbf{t}_j\}$, ELM is modeled by

$$\sum_{i=1}^{L} \beta_i \cdot g(\omega_i \cdot \mathbf{x}_j + \mathbf{b}_i) = \mathbf{y}_j, j = 1, \cdots N, \tag{3}$$

where $g(x)$ is an activation function, $L$ indicates the number of hidden neurons, and $\omega_i$, $\mathbf{b}_i$ and $\beta_i$ are input weights, biases and output weights of the $i$th hidden neuron, respectively.

Rewriting Eq. 3 in matrix form leads to

$$\mathbf{H}\beta = \mathbf{Y}, \tag{4}$$

where $\mathbf{Y} = [\mathbf{y}_1^T, \cdots, \mathbf{y}_N^T]^T$, and $\mathbf{H}$ is the hidden layer output matrix,

$$\mathbf{H} = \begin{bmatrix} g(\omega_1\mathbf{x}_1 + \mathbf{b}_1) & \cdots & g(\omega_L\mathbf{x}_1 + \mathbf{b}_L) \\ \vdots & \cdots & \vdots \\ g(\omega_1\mathbf{x}_N + \mathbf{b}_1) & \cdots & g(\omega_L\mathbf{x}_N + \mathbf{b}_L) \end{bmatrix}_{N \times L}. \tag{5}$$

The $i$th column of $\mathbf{H}$ is the output of the $i$th hidden neuron with respect to the inputs $\mathbf{x}_1, \cdots, \mathbf{x}_N$. At training stage, by randomly initializing $\{\omega_i\}$ and $\{\mathbf{b}_i\}$, $\beta$ can be efficiently optimized via least squares.

An individual ELM classifier is separately trained for each feature representation. Let $\mathbf{Y}_c$, $\mathbf{Y}_m$ and $\mathbf{Y}_t$ denote the labels predicted with the CSS, morphological and temporal features, respectively. The final predicted labels $\mathbf{Y}$ are designed as the weighted combination of $\mathbf{Y}_c$, $\mathbf{Y}_m$ and $\mathbf{Y}_t$

$$\mathbf{Y} = w_c\mathbf{Y}_c + w_m\mathbf{Y}_m + w_t\mathbf{Y}_t, \tag{6}$$

where $w_c$, $w_m$ and $w_t$ stand for feature significance. Through watching experimental results, we find that morphological features yield better fall detection accuracy than the CSS and temporal features. Therefore, we empirically set $w_c = 0.2$, $w_m = 0.5$ and $w_t = 0.3$.

## 3    Experimental Results

### 3.1    Dataset

SDUFall dataset [1] consists of 6 daily actions captured from 20 subjects: falling, bending, squatting, sitting, lying, and walking. Each subject repeats the same action 10 times, with each time one or more of the following conditions changed: carrying or not carrying something, light turning on or off, random walking-in direction and random viewpoint to the Kinect camera. The camera was installed $1.5m$ high for the action capturing. A total of $6 \times 20 \times 10 = 1200$ video clips are collected. Video frame is at size of $320 \times 240$, saved at $30fps$ in the AVI format. The baseline sequence length is about 8 seconds.

---

[1] http://www.sucro.org/homepage/wanghaibo/SDUFall.html

## 3.2  Settings

The CSS feature extraction was implemented in C++ while all the other modules were implemented in MATLAB. All the experiments were conducted with MATLAB 7.10 (R2010a) on a PC with Intel (R) Core (TM) i3-2120 CPU and 2.00 GB RAM. 5-folder cross validation on a per subject basis was repeated many times until every 5 subjects have been used as the test set.

The proposed approach is compared with using CSS [9], morphological and temporal feature individually. 100 cluster centers are applied for both the CSS and morphological clustering. The number of neurons in ELM is fixed at 80.

## 3.3  Results

Fig. 3 shows the confusion matrices of using (a) CSS features, (b) morphological features, (c) temporal features, and (d) the proposed approach that fuses the

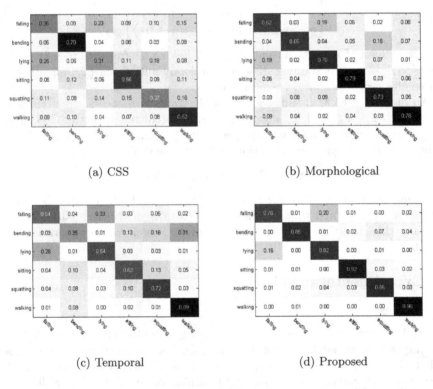

(a) CSS                                    (b) Morphological

(c) Temporal                               (d) Proposed

**Fig. 3.** Classification confusion matrices of using (a) CSS features, (b) morphological features, (c) temporal features, and (d) the proposed approach that fuses the three features. Among the three features, morphological feature is most discriminative. Fusing the three features greatly reduces the misclassification rates as compared to using each feature individually. It is also shown that falling and lying are likely to be mutually misclassified, indicating that their dissimilarities are only subtle.

**Fig. 4.** Action samples that are most likely to be correctly classified (left, green-rectangle enclosed) and mis-classified (right, red-rectangle enclosed). The arrow under each sequence indicates the sequence order. Note that in order to increase the variation of our dataset, each subject repeats the same action by walking in from different directions.

**Table 3.** Classification accuracy (+ standard deviation) in distinguishing fall from non-fall actions.

| Method | Fall vs Non-Fall Accuracy |
|---|---|
| CSS | 62.07 ± 4.50% |
| Morphological | 76.96 ± 6.11% |
| Temporal | 72.76 ± 4.89% |
| Proposed | 85.89 ± 5.02% |

three features. Among the three features, morphological feature has the lowest misclassification rates since it calculates different statistics of the shape. Fusing the three features further reduces the misclassification rates ad the merits of the three feature types are combined. It is thus proven that the three features are mutually beneficial. It is also shown in the figure that falling and lying are likely to be mutually misclassified, indicating that their dissimilarities are subtle. Fig. 4 shows action samples that are likely to be correctly classified and misclassified. The misclassified falling action is largely attributed to the inaccurate track of the skeleton trajectory.

By treating the other five activities (sitting, walking, squatting, lying, and bending) as a single nonfall class, we are able to calculate the fall-versus-nonfall classification accuracy based off the results of Fig. 3. Table 3 shows the calculated accuracy. Fusing the three features in the proposed approach significantly outperforms using each feature individually.

## 4 Conclusions

In this paper, we presented a new vision-based fall detection approach that uses only a low-cost Kinect camera. The approach is based off the fusion of three independent features. The CSS and morphological features capture different properties of human silhouette. But since the two features have no explicit temporal consistency, we cluster all collected feature vectors to generate occurrence histogram as the representation of an action. Meanwhile, we integrate the trajectory of a skeleton point that captures the temporal property of an action as a complimentary feature.

Extensive evaluation shows that the proposed approach achieves an average 85.89% accuracy in distinguishing fall from five other daily activities (walking, lying, sitting, squatting, and bending). However, it should be pointed that the proposed approach increases the computation complexity compared to the methods with only one kind of feature. In the future, we will optimize the weights for fusing the three prediction results which is set empirically. Moreover, we will capture more subtle daily activities such as eating, calling, laughing and carrying objects. Meanwhile, we will also integrate our dataset to other publicly available RGBD dataset for more general and precise fall detection.

## References

1. Shany, T., Redmond, S., Narayanan, M., Lovell, N.: Sensors-based wearable systems for monitoring of human movement and falls. IEEE Sensors Journal 12(3), 658–670 (2012)
2. Doukas, C., Maglogiannis, I.: Emergency fall incidents detection in assisted living environments utilizing motion, sound, and visual perceptual components. IEEE Transactions on Information Technology in Biomedicine 15(2), 277–289 (2011)
3. Popoola, O., Wang, K.: Video-based abnormal human behavior recognition-a review. IEEE Transactions on Systems, Man, and Cybernetics, Part C: Applications and Reviews 42(6), 865–878 (2012)
4. Yu, M., Naqvi, S., Rhuma, A., Chambers, J.: One class boundary method classifiers for application in a video-based fall detection system. IET Computer Vision 6(2), 90–100 (2012)
5. Auvinet, E., Multon, F., Saint-Arnaud, A., Rousseau, J., Meunier, J.: Fall detection with multiple cameras: An occlusion-resistant method based on 3-d silhouette vertical distribution. IEEE Transactions on Information Technology in Biomedicine 15(2), 290–300 (2011)
6. Planinc, R., Kampel, M.: Introducing the use of depth data for fall detection. Personal and Ubiquitous Computing 17(6), 1063–1072 (2013)
7. Nghiem, A.T., Auvinet, E., Meunier, J.: Head detection using kinect camera and its application to fall detection. In: Proceedings of the 11th International Conference on Information Science, Signal Processing and their Applications, pp. 164–169 (2012)

8. Parra-Dominguez, G., Taati, B., Mihailidis, A.: 3D human motion analysis to detect abnormal events on stairs. In: Proceedings of the Second International Conference on 3D Imaging, Modeling, Processing, Visualization and Transmission, pp. 97–103 (2012)
9. Ma, X., Wang, H., Xue, B., Zhou, M., Ji, B., Li, Y.: Depth-based human fall detection via shape features and improved extreme learning machine. IEEE Journal of Biomedical and Health Informatics **18**(6), 1915–1922 (2014)
10. Mirmahboub, B., Samavi, S., Karimi, N., Shirani, S.: Automatic monocular system for human fall detection based on variations in silhouette area. IEEE Transactions on Biomedical Engineering **60**(2), 427–436 (2013)
11. Mokhtarian, F.: Silhouette-based isolated object recognition through curvature scale space. IEEE Transactions on Pattern Analysis and Machine Intelligence **17**(5), 539–544 (1995)
12. Huang, G.-B., Zhu, Q.-Y., Siew, C.-K.: Extreme learning machine: a new learning scheme of feedforward neural networks. In: Proceedings of IEEE International Joint Conference on Neural Networks, vol. 2, pp. 985–990 (2004)
13. Stauffer, C., Grimson, W.E.L.: Adaptive background mixture models for real-time tracking. In: Proceedings of IEEE Computer Society Conference on Computer Vision and Pattern Recognition, vol. 2 (1999)
14. Ding, L., Goshtasby, A.: On the canny edge detector. Pattern Recognition **34**(3), 721–725 (2001)
15. Mokhtarian, F., Mackworth, A.K.: A theory of multiscale, curvature-based shape representation for planar curves. IEEE Transactions on Pattern Analysis and Machine Intelligence **14**(8), 789–805 (1992)
16. Fei-Fei, L., Perona, P.: A bayesian hierarchical model for learning natural scene categories. In: Proceedings of IEEE Computer Society Conference on Computer Vision and Pattern Recognition, vol. 2, pp. 524–531 (2005)

# Color Image Segmentation Combining Rough Depth Information

Wen Su[1,2], Jing Qian[1,2], Zhiming Pi[1], and Zeng-Fu Wang[1,2(✉)]

[1] University of Science and Technology of China, Hefei, Anhui, China
zfwang@ustc.edu.cn
[2] Institute of Intelligent Machines, Chinese Academy of Sciences, Hefei, Anhui, China

**Abstract.** A novel color image segmentation method is presented in this paper. Firstly a *Luv* color histogram based method is used to estimate the color bandwidth, then a mean shift algorithm with adaptive color bandwidth is employed to pre-segment the input image. Next, a boundary detection algorithm based machine learning is used to calculate the probability boundary of objects from both depth and color information. Then, a correction procedure is performed by mapping the depth boundary onto the color image. Finally, Graph cut is used to segment color image based on Gaussian Mixture Model which is built with the above pre-segmentation and correction results. The experimental results show that the segmentation algorithm is an effective one. It can effectively segment an image into some semantic objects.

**Keywords:** Image segmentation · Depth map · Adaptive mean shift · Gaussian mixture model · Graph cut

## 1 Introduction

The use of depth information has been the subject of a number of vision-related tasks such as image segmentation and retrieval. For the task of image segmentation, depth information has obvious advantages as compared with color information. Firstly it is invariant to lighting and/or texture variation; secondly it is invariant to camera pose and perspective change. Therefore using depth can potentially enable successful segmentation independent of illumination or view, significantly expanding the range of operation conditions. In this background, the color image segmentation combining depth information has received much attention.

Recently, many efforts have been made. Crabb et al. employed depth map to extract foreground objects in real time[1]. In their segmentation the color image is only used to support a small fraction (1%-2%) of the pixels which are not solved by the depth threshold. Another interesting use of depth is implemented in [2]. Several channels of the depth camera are used and combined with the color channel to assist background subtraction. A new indoor scene dataset, completing with accurate depth maps and dense label coverage, is introduced in

© Springer-Verlag Berlin Heidelberg 2015
H. Zha et al. (Eds.): CCCV 2015, Part I, CCIS 546, pp. 448–457, 2015.
DOI: 10.1007/978-3-662-48558-3_45

[3] by Nathan Silberman et al. Their model which is evaluated on this dataset is inclined to solve the indoor image segmentation. Meir Johnathan Dahan et al. present a technique [4] which is the most relevant work with ours. However, their results depend on the color image segmentation method greatly.

In this paper we segment image with an improved mean shift algorithm with adaptive color bandwidth. Then we strengthen segmentation results combining color and depth effectively. This algorithm can weaken the illumination changes and object shadow effects on image segmentation. In particular, it can reduce errors of segmentation in the neighboring semantic objects segmentation which have the same color.

The rest of this paper is organized as follows. Section 2 discusses our algorithm. Section 3 gives the experiments and discussions. Finally, we conclude the paper and give remarks in Section 4.

## 2   Algorithm

### 2.1   Preprocess

Before segmenting combining the information from depth map, several problems must be solved. Firstly the depth data spatial resolution does not always match the photometric resolution. Secondly in many cases the depth image is imperfect and contains numerous artifacts. As a result, we preprocess the depth map with the cross-bilateral filter [5] and the joint bilateral filter [7] before combining it in the color image segmentation.

### 2.2   Adaptive Mean Shift Image Segmentation

Since the spatial resolution of color images is often higher compared with the depth map, the color image can provide more accurate information such as the outline of the semantic objects, color, texture and structure. Therefore, the image segmentation algorithm should be a color based one. We select the Mean Shift algorithm [8–11] for the purpose of image segmentation.

Let $C_i : (L_i, u_i, v_i)$ and $C_j : (L_j, u_j, v_j)$ be two points of the CIE LUV [12] color space respectively, then the Euclidean distance of the two points (that is, the two colors) is given by

$$disc_{ij} = \sqrt{(L_i - L_j)^2 + (u_i - u_j)^2 + (v_i - v_j)^2} \tag{1}$$

It is well known that the bandwidth parameters are important parameters that determine the step length and direction in an iterative process of Mean Shift algorithm, and therefore affect the final result of segmentation. The existing methods of bandwidth parameter determination can be found in [13]. In this paper we develop an adaptive bandwidth parameter determination algorithm. The details are as below.

In our application, the dimension of feature space for image segmentation is equal to five: two for spatial dimension, and three for color dimension. For simplicity, the corresponding bandwidth Matrix can be expressed by

$$H = diag(h_x, h_y, h_l, h_u, h_v)$$

where $h_s = h_x = h_y$ is spatial bandwidth, and $h_c = h_l = h_u = h_v$ is color bandwidth. The two spatial bandwidths mainly affect the computation speed of the algorithm, while the three color bandwidths heavily affect the segmentation result. Due to the fact above, we only consider the problem of color bandwidth selection when the two spatial bandwidths are given.

We have found that different images have different optimal color bandwidth. In our adaptive color bandwidth determination algorithm, the color bandwidth $h_c$ can be obtained by the steps as below:

(1) Calculate LUV values of all pixels in image, and obtain the normalized LUV repre-sentation of image shown in Fig.1.
(2) Divide the color cube into $N_l * N_u * N_v$ equal parts (as shown in Fig.1, each of them is a rectangular solid and corresponds to a LUV color cluster or mode), count the number of pixels falling in each rectangular solid, and then create the 3D color histogram of the image according to the statistics. Here $N_l$, $N_u$, and $N_v$ are segment numbers along l-axis, u-axis, and v-axis of color space $Luv$ respectively.
(3) Find all local peaks as follows: check each rectangular solid mentioned above, if the number of pixels falling in a rectangular solid is bigger than the number of pixels falling in other rectangular solid surrounding it and meanwhile is bigger than the threshold set by system, then consider the rectangular solid to be a local peak (the black points in Fig.2, note and the number of pixels falling in the rectangular solid is called the value of the local peak) and save the corresponding information of location and number of pixels respectively. As a result, the local peaks detected are ranked in descending order.
(4) Compare the values of each local peaks with m threshold values $Th_i$, $i = 1, 2, m$ set by system, and count the number $p_i$, $i = 1, 2, m$ of local peaks, whose values are larger than the corresponding threshold values $Th_i$, $i = 1, 2, m$. These local peaks are called effective peaks. It is obvious that the bigger the threshold value $Th_i$ is, the less the number $p_i$ is. The colors corresponding to the above effective peaks consist of the main color clusters of image.
(5) Determine the color bandwidth $h_c$ as below.

$$h_c = w * disC_{top} + (1 - w) * disC_{val} \qquad (2)$$

where, $disC_{top}$ is the mean Euclidean distance between arbitrary two local peaks within the range of $k$ bigger local peaks that is given by

$$disC_{top} = \frac{1}{N_{top}} \sum_{i<j}^{k} (n_i + n_j) disC_{ij}, \; N_{top} = k \sum_{i=1}^{k} n_i$$

Here, $disC_{ij}$ is defined by (1), and $n_i$ is the value of the $i_{th}$ biggest peak. Similarly, $disC_{val}$ is the mean Euclidean distance of all effective peaks to their center:

$$disC_{val} = \frac{1}{m}\sum_{i=1}^{m} w_{vi}\left(\frac{1}{p_i}\sum_{j=1}^{p_i} disC_{ic}\right), w_{vi} = \frac{p_i}{\sum_{i=1}^{m} p_i}, \sum_{i=1}^{m} w_{vi} = 1$$

where, $disC_{ic}$ is the Euclidean distance of an effective peak corresponding to threshold values $Th_i$ to the center of all effective peaks.

Besides, $w$ is a weight defined by

$$w = \frac{\sum_{i=1}^{k} n_i}{\sum_{i=1}^{m} p_i}$$

Finally, in our experiments, the parameter $k$ is set to be 8.

It can be seen from (2) that the color bandwidth $h_c$ is selected to be dependent upon the values of $disC_{top}$ and $disC_{val}$, and the weight of $w$ in our system.

After selection of color bandwidth $h_c$, we should select a proper kernel function for the iterative process of Mean Shift algorithm. In our system, we use the Gauss kernel function [14] for the purpose.

In this way, we can obtain adaptive color bandwidth based segmentation result. Fig.4 (c) shows the segmentation result to an example image by improved Mean Shift algorithm of ours based on adaptive color bandwidth determination.

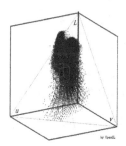

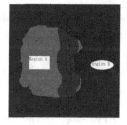

**Fig. 2.** Probability boundary calculation and dilation

**Fig. 1.** Adaptive Bandwidth

## 2.3   Probability Boundary with Depth Discontinuities

Adaptive Mean Shift image segmentation algorithm as well as general image segmentation method depend on the color information greatly. Therefore, if the color of semantic object is similar while depth is discontinuities (occlusion) or the depth is continuous while objects have different colors, the accuracy of segmentation algorithm is reduced. Depth information give us insight into solving this problem. In general, the boundary with depth discontinuous correspond to the boundary of two semantic objects. We need to find reliable boundary with depth discontinuities, According to the boundary we correct segmentation results coming from adaptive Mean Shift image segmentation algorithm.

We apply a robust probability boundary with depth discontinuities algorithm combining depth map and color image. The algorithm is based on the probability boundary detection algorithm [6]. The main steps include: a) Applying of probability boundary detection algorithm to calculate the depth map and color image probability boundary (Fig.3 (c)(d)), here the probability boundary map refers to a map which each pixel in is a probability of being part of edge.). b) Two probability map are fused so as to correcting the probability boundary map of depth map based on the probability boundary map of color image to obtain a more reliable probability boundary map of depth. c) The thresholds are set on the probability boundary map of depth to extract reliable depth jump boundary. d) Obtain the binarization result of probability boundary of depth map.

---

**A probability boundary algorithm combining depth map and color image**

---

a) calculating the probability boundaries map of color image $P_{color}(x)$ and the probability boundaries map of depth map $P_{depth}(x)$;

b) fusing the two map $P(x) = P_{color}(x) * P_{depth}(x)$;

c) extracting a more reliable probability boundaries:

$$E_{anchor}(x) = \begin{cases} 1, & p(x) > Th \\ 0, & p(x) \leq Th \end{cases}$$

where $Th$ is the threshold;

d) binarized probability boundaries map of depth:

$$E_{depth}(x) = \begin{cases} 1, & p_{depth}(x) > Th \\ 0, & p_{depth}(x) \leq Th \end{cases}$$

$$E(x) = \begin{cases} 1, & E_{anchor}(x) \bigcup \{E_{depth}(x) \xrightarrow{\text{connect to}} E_{anchor}(x)\} \\ 0, & \text{other} \end{cases}$$

---

Experimental results show that our algorithm performed better than the algorithm which depends on the depth information exclusively. Because we obtain the probability boundary of depth with the introduction of color, texture, and other information.

## 2.4   Graph Cut Based on GMM Modeling

Mean Shift algorithm separate different objects into patches according to the color information. However, if a patch has similar color while depth is discontinuous, then the patch is not belong to same object. Or, if there are two patches

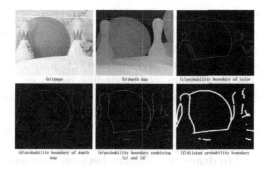

**Fig. 3.** Adjacency pattern analysis

whose color is different while depth is continuous, then the two patches should belong to the same object. The former should appear depth discontinuity probability boundary in a patch, while the latter should not appear depth discontinuity probability boundary at the location of the two patch adjacenting in the depth map. As a result, we can correct segmentation depending on depth discontinuities probability boundary.

We map reliable depth discontinuities probability boundary to the color image segmentation. Because of the factors such as noises and the error that acquisition equipment cause, depth discontinuous probability boundary may not be coincide with the boundary of segmented regions. We apply depth boundary dilation operation on the probability boundary, and dilate the boundary with $\delta$ pixels(we take $\delta$ as 3 in the experiment), as shown in Fig.3 (f).

After mapping, different labels is set to both sides of the dilated probability boundary. For the segmented regions which has intersection over the both sides of dilated depth discontinuous probability boundary, the region area which calculated from the difference set is counted, and the other region area which is neighbor to both sides is counted as well. We label the regions through comparing the size of two area. The difference set between the segmented regions and the dilated depth discontinuous probability boundary has three adjacency patterns with the dilated depth discontinuous probability boundary. One is that it is neighbor to one side of dilated depth discontinuous probability boundary only. Then we label the segmented region with the neighboring boundary. Another one is that it has an intersection over both sides of the dilated depth discontinuous probability boundary while the intersection on the same side is discontent (such as B). As shown in Fig.2. Then we count the area of the neighboring regions on the two sides separately and label the region with the bigger area label. The last one is that the difference set is a single connected region. We can not judge the label so that we do not set the label temporarily.

After getting the corrected segmentation which we call as seed labels, as shown in Fig.4 (d), we have translate the segmentation problem to labeling the region which we cannot judge above.It has many possibilities because there are lots of seed labels in the image already. In order to solve the problem, a graph cut optimization based on Gaussian Mixture Model (GMM) is implemented, similar to [4]. We have a relatively reliable initial solution to the following graph cut optimization. The seed labels defines $| L |$ layers in the depth. These layers are built from objects, parts of objects, and some objects joined together. Mapping the seed labels to the depth map, corresponding depth regions are obtained. Each region is considered to be the seed for a label l in the segmentation. Hence, $| L |$ is the number of labels used in the graph-cut procedure. For each of the $| L |$ segments, a GMM, similar to [14], is fit. We use two Gaussians for each modality: two for the color image $pc^l(\bullet)$ and two for the depth image $pd^l(\bullet)$. These models are used to define the distance between elements in the definition of the energy function of the graph-cut segmentation. We use the regular construction of the graph G: every pixel in the image is a node v in the graph, and we use 4-connectivity for the edges e which are called n-links. Every node v is also connected with edges, which are called t-links, to the terminal nodes $t_l$.

After the calculation of a minimum cut on the graph, we are left with a labeling assignment for unlabeled pixels, which leads directly to a minimization of the energy function defined (3). The energy function is consisted of two terms. The first one is data term, which is refers to the t-links. The second one is smooth term, which is refers to the n-links.

$$E(X) = \sum_p E_d(x_p) + \sum_{p,q} E_s(x_p, x_q) \tag{3}$$

The two types of energy terms fit the two types of edges in the graph: the smoothness term as the n-link and the data-term as the t-link. We assign the weights of the two types of links as (4) and (5).

$$E_d(x_p) = max(\alpha \cdot L_p^{cl}, L_p^{dl}) \tag{4}$$

$$E_s(x_p, x_q) = (max(\beta \cdot \mu \parallel I_p - I_q \parallel, \varphi \parallel D_p - D_q \parallel))^{-1}) \tag{5}$$

In the data term, $\alpha$ is the weight which is used to adjust the ratio between the color information and depth information. $L_p^{cl}$ and $L_p^{dl}$ are defined as (6) and (7). $pc^l(\bullet)$ and $pd^l(\bullet)$ are the GMM models for each l, for color and depth, respectively. $I_p$ and $D_p$ are the color and depth values at pixel p, respectively. We merge the color and depth channels by using the maximum of their distance to the respective model. This way fitting each pixel gives lower energy for a good match. The actual weights on the t-links are calculated using the negative data term.

$$L_p^{cl} = -ln(pc^l(I_p)) \tag{6}$$

$$L_p^{dl} = -ln(pd^l(D_p)) \tag{7}$$

In the smooth term, we also combine the color information and the depth information. The n-links is refers to the similarity between the two connected node in the graph. We calculate the similarity from the color image and depth map separately and set the weights as the higher one. In this term, the $\beta$ is the weight either. $\mu \parallel I_p - I_q \parallel$ and $\varphi \parallel D_p - D_q \parallel$ are expectation operators over the whole color and depth map image, respectively.

By running the minimum cut algorithm [15] [16] [17], each pixels of color image are assigned a label to determine which segmentation the pixel belongs to. Finally we get the optimal segmentation of the color image.

## 3   Experiments

We used the images with four different scenes to make the experiments of segmentation. The experimental results as shown in Fig.4 indicate that the algorithm presented in this paper has a good performance. The results are influenced by the lighting or texture variation more slightly. We can effectively segment objects from an image, especially in the case of two objects of the same color are mutual supported. This paper uses three segmentation evaluation: PR [18], VI [19] as well as GCE [20]. PR refers to the proportion of consistent pixels between tested segmented image and the ground truth (The Probabilistic Rand Index). The Variation of Information (VI) metric defines the distance between two segmentations as the average conditional entropy of one segmentation given the other, and thus roughly measures the amount of randomness in one segmentation which cannot be explained by the other. The Global Consistency Error (GCE) measures the extent to which one segmentation can be viewed as a refinement of the other. Segmentations which are related in this manner are considered to be consistent, since they could represent the same natural image segmented at different scales. The experiments indicates that our algorithm has improvement on most of three indicators as shown in Tab.1.

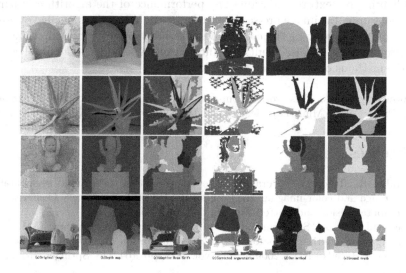

**Fig. 4.** Experiments results

**Table 1.** Three kinds of evaluation indexes

PR

|  | A | B | C | D | mean |
|---|---|---|---|---|---|
| Mean Shift | 0.6448 | **0.7303** | 0.7955 | 0.6401 | 0.7027 |
| Graph cut | 0.7965 | 0.5686 | 0.6744 | 0.6397 | 0.6631 |
| Adaptive Mean Shift | **0.8899** | 0.4641 | **0.9190** | 0.7060 | 0.7448 |
| Our Method | 0.8118 | 0.6618 | 0.8611 | **0.8080** | **0.7857** |

VI

|  | A | B | C | D | mean |
|---|---|---|---|---|---|
| Mean Shift | 1.8496 | **1.3086** | 2.0168 | 1.8248 | 1.7500 |
| Graph cut | 1.6316 | 2.0625 | 2.4687 | 1.9013 | 2.0160 |
| Adaptive Mean Shift | 1.5194 | 4.2297 | 1.6564 | 2.3827 | 2.4471 |
| Our Method | **1.3175** | 1.7850 | **1.2917** | **1.1823** | **1.3941** |

GCE

|  | A | B | C | D | mean |
|---|---|---|---|---|---|
| Mean Shift | 0.1222 | 0.1882 | 0.2656 | 0.3786 | 0.2387 |
| Graph cut | 0.2085 | 0.3094 | 0.3931 | 0.4006 | 0.3279 |
| Adaptive Mean Shift | 0.2592 | **0.1101** | **0.0668** | 0.0619 | **0.1245** |
| Our Method | **0.1089** | 0.2784 | 0.1802 | **0.0562** | 0.1560 |

## 4 Conclusion

This paper presents a novel segmentation algorithm combining both color image and depth map. The experimental results show that the segmentation algorithm is an effective one. It can effectively implement segmentation with less influence from lighting or texture variation. The performance of the algorithm is partly dependent upon the image pre-segmentation result. When the scene have a great change on the lighting or the color and depth are similar in the same time, the algorithm may give a false result. The future work is to address the problem and find the methods of overcoming the difficulties.

**Acknowledgments.** This work is Supported by National Science and Technology Major Project of the Ministry of Science and Technology of China (No.2012GB102007).

## References

1. Crabb, R., Tracey, C., Puranik, A., et al.: Real-time foreground segmentation via range and color imaging. In: Proc. of IEEE Computer Society Conference on Computer Vision and Pattern Recognition, pp. 1–5 (2008)
2. Leens, J., Piérard, S., Barnich, O., Van Droogenbroeck, M., Wagner, J.-M.: Combining color, depth, and motion for video segmentation. In: Fritz, M., Schiele, B., Piater, J.H. (eds.) ICVS 2009. LNCS, vol. 5815, pp. 104–113. Springer, Heidelberg (2009)
3. Silberman, N., Fergus, R.: Indoor scene segmentation using a structured light sensor. In: proc. of IEEE International Conference on Computer Vision, pp. 601–608 (2011)

 4. Dahan, M.J., Chen, N., Shamir, A., et al.: Combining color and depth for enhanced image segmentation and retargeting. The Visual Computer **28**(12), 1181–1193 (2012)
 5. Paris, S., Durand, F.: A fast approximation of the bilateral filter using a signal processing approach. In: Leonardis, A., Bischof, H., Pinz, A. (eds.) ECCV 2006. LNCS, vol. 3954, pp. 568–580. Springer, Heidelberg (2006)
 6. Martin, D.R., Fowlkes, C.C., Malik, J.: Learning to detect natural image boundaries using local brightness, color, and texture cues. IEEE Transactions on Pattern Analysis and Machine Intelligence **26**(5), 530–549 (2004)
 7. Riemens, A.K., Gangwal, O.P., Barenbrug, B., et al.: Multistep joint bilateral depth upsampling. In: International Society for Optics and Photonics, pp. 72570M–72570M-12 (2009)
 8. Fukunaga, K., Hostetler, L.: The estimation of the gradient of a density function, with applications in pattern recognition. IEEE Transactions on Information Theory **21**(1), 32–40 (1975)
 9. Cheng, Y.: Mean shift, mode seeking, and clustering. IEEE Transactions on Pattern Analysis and Machine Intelligence **17**(8), 790–799 (1995)
10. Comaniciu, D., Meer, P.: Mean shift analysis and applications. In: Proc. of IEEE International Conference on Computer Vision, vol. 2, pp. 1197–1203 (1999)
11. Georgescu, B., Shimshoni, I., Meer, P.: Mean shift based clustering in high dimensions: a texture classification example. In: Proc. of IEEE International Conference on Computer Vision, pp. 456–463 (2003)
12. Cheng, H.D., Jiang, X.H., Sun, Y., et al.: Color image segmentation: advances and prospects. Pattern Recognition **34**(12), 2259–2281 (2011)
13. Comaniciu, D., Ramesh, V., Meer, P.: The variable bandwidth mean shift and data-driven scale selection. In: Proc. of IEEE International Conference on Computer Vision, vol. 1, pp. 438–445 (2001)
14. Rother, C., Kolmogorov, V., Blake, A.: Grabcut: Interactive foreground extraction using iterated graph cuts. ACM Transactions on Graphics (TOG) **23**(3), 309–314 (2004)
15. Zabih, R.D., Veksler, O., Boykov, Y.: System and method for fast approximate energy minimization via graph cuts. U.S. Patent No. 6,744,923 (2004)
16. Kolmogorov, V., Zabin, R.: What energy functions can be minimized via graph cuts? IEEE Transactions on Pattern Analysis and Machine Intelligence **26**(2), 147–159 (2004)
17. Boykov, Y., Kolmogorov, V.: An experimental comparison of min-cut/max-flow algorithms for energy minimization in vision. IEEE Transactions on Pattern Analysis and Machine Intelligence **26**(9), 1124–1137 (2004)
18. Pantofaru, C., Hebert, M.: A Comparison of Image Segmentation Algorithms technical report. Robotics Inst., Carnegie Mellon Univ. (2005)
19. Meila, M.: Comparing clusterings: an axiomatic view. In: Proc. of International Conference on Machine Learning, pp. 577–584 (2005)
20. Martin, D., Fowlkes, C., Tal, D., et al.: A database of human segmented natural images and its application to evaluating segmentation algorithms and measuring ecological statistics. In: Proc. of IEEE International Conference on Computer Vision, vol. 2, pp. 416–423 (2001)

# Author Index

Printed in the United States
By Bookmasters